D1598407

KARL MARX
FREDERICK ENGELS

COLLECTED WORKS
VOLUME
32

KARL MARX
FREDERICK ENGELS

COLLECTED
WORKS

INTERNATIONAL PUBLISHERS

NEW YORK

KARL MARX
FREDERICK ENGELS

Volume
32

KARL MARX: 1861-63

INTERNATIONAL PUBLISHERS

NEW YORK

This volume has been prepared jointly by Lawrence & Wishart Ltd., London, International Publishers Co. Inc., New York, and Progress Publishers, Moscow, in collaboration with the Institute of Marxism-Leninism, Moscow.

Editorial commissions:
GREAT BRITAIN: Eric Hobsbawm, John Hoffman, Nicholas Jacobs, Monty Johnstone, Martin Milligan, Jeff Skelley, Ernst Wangermann.
USA: Louis Diskin, Philip S. Foner, James E. Jackson, Leonard B. Levenson, Victor Perlo, Betty Smith, Dirk J. Struik.
USSR: for Progress Publishers—A. K. Avelichev, N. P. Karmanova, Yu. V. Semyonov, M. K. Shcheglova; for the Institute of Marxism-Leninism— P. N. Fedoseyev, L. I. Golman, N. Yu. Kolpinsky, A. I. Malysh, M. P. Mchedlov, V. N. Pospelova, G. L. Smirnov.

Library of Congress Cataloging in Publication Data

Marx, Karl, 1818-1883.
    Karl Marx, Frederick Engels: collected works.

    1. Socialism—Collected works. 2. Economics— Collected works. I. Engels, Friedrich. 1820-1895. Works. English. 1975. II. Title.
HX 39. 5. A 16 1975   335.4   73-84671
ISBN 0-7178-0532-8 (v. 32).

Printed in the Union of Soviet Socialist Republics

Contents

KARL MARX

ECONOMIC WORKS

1861-1863

ECONOMIC MANUSCRIPT OF 1861-63

(Continuation)

A Contribution to the Critique
of Political Economy

NOTES AND INDEXES

ILLUSTRATIONS

Preface

Volume 32 of the *Collected Works* of Marx and Engels contains the continuation of Marx's economic manuscript of 1861-1863, its central part—"Theories of Surplus Value" (notebooks XII-XV, pp. 636-944 of the manuscript), the beginning of the manuscript being published in volumes 30 and 31 of the present edition.

Marx proceeds here with his historico-critical analysis of the views held by bourgeois political economists—Ricardo and Malthus; he traces the disintegration of the Ricardian school and considers the views of socialist Ricardians. In the closing part of the volume, "Revenue and Its Sources", Marx analyses, among other things, the essence of vulgar political economy.

The whole manuscript is printed here in accordance with its new publication in the languages of the original in *Marx-Engels Gesamtausgabe* (*MEGA*), Zweite Abteilung, Bd. 3, Berlin, 1976-82.

Obvious slips of the pen in Marx's text have been corrected by the Editors without comment. The proper and geographical names and other words abbreviated by the author are given in full. Defects in the manuscript are indicated in footnotes, places where the text is damaged or illegible are marked by dots. Where possible, editorial reconstructions are given in square brackets.

Foreign words and phrases are given as used by Marx, with the translation supplied in footnotes where necessary. English phrases, expressions and individual words occurring in the original are set in small caps. Longer passages and quotations in English are given in asterisks. Some of the words are now somewhat archaic or have undergone changes in usage. For example, the term "nigger", which has acquired generally—and especially in the USA—a more profane and unacceptable status than it had in Europe during the

19th century. The passages from English economists quoted by Marx in French are given according to the English editions used by the author. In all cases the form of quoting used by Marx is respected. The language in which Marx quotes is indicated unless it is German.

The text of and notes to Volume 32 were prepared by Yelena Vashchenko. The volume was edited by Larisa Miskievich (Institute of Marxism-Leninism of the CC CPSU). The name index was compiled by Vardan Azatian; the index of quoted and mentioned literature and the index of periodicals by Yelena Vashchenko (Institute of Marxism-Leninism of the CC CPSU).

The translations included in Volume 32 are based on the three-volume edition of Marx's *Theories of Surplus Value,* published by Progress Publishers, Moscow. They were made by Emile Burns, Renate Simpson and Jack Cohen and edited by Salo Ryazanskaya and Richard Dixon. These translations have been editorially checked with the new *MEGA* edition by Svetlana Gerasimenko, Natalia Karmanova, Mzia Pitskhelauri and Alla Varavitskaya. The volume was prepared for the press by Svetlana Gerasimenko, Mzia Pitskhelauri and Alla Varavitskaya (Progress Publishers).

Scientific editor for this volume was Vitaly Vygodsky (Institute of Marxism-Leninism of the CC CPSU).

KARL MARX

ECONOMIC WORKS

1861-1863

ECONOMIC MANUSCRIPT
OF 1861-63
(Continuation)

A CONTRIBUTION TO THE CRITIQUE
OF POLITICAL ECONOMY

[I) THE PRODUCTION PROCESS OF CAPITAL]

[5) THEORIES OF SURPLUS VALUE][1]

XII

    5) *Theories of Surplus Value*[2]
      h) Ricardo
        *Table, with elucidation, of differential rent (Observations on
        the influence of the* CHANGE *in value of means of subsistence
        and raw material—therefore also in the value of machin-
        ery—on the organic composition of capital)*
        Ricardo's theory of rent
        Adam Smith's theory of rent
        Ricardo's theory of surplus value
        Ricardo's theory of profit[3]

XIII

    5) *Theories of Surplus Value, etc.*
      h) Ricardo
      Ricardo's theory of profit
      Ricardo's theory of accumulation. Critique of this (de-
      velopment of crises from the basic form of capital)
      Ricardo's MISCELLANEA. *Conclusion of Ricardo (John
      Barton)*
      i) Malthus

XIV

    5) *Theories of Surplus Value*
      i) Malthus
      k) Disintegration of the Ricardian school (Torrens, James
        Mill, Prévost, polemical writings, McCulloch,
        Wakefield, Stirling, John Stuart Mill)
      l) Adversaries of the economists
      m) Ramsay. (Bray as adversary of the economists)

n) *Cherbuliez*
o) *Richard Jones.* (End of this Part 5)
  Episode: REVENUE AND ITS SOURCES

XV

5) *Theories of Surplus Value*
   l) *Proletarian opposition on the basis of Ricardo*
   (*Compound interest*; fall in the rate of profit based on
   this.) So-called amassment as a mere phenomenon of
   circulation. (Stocks, etc.—circulation reservoirs)
   2) *Ravenstone.* Conclusion
   3 and 4) Hodgskin
   (Interest-bearing capital. Existing wealth in relation to
   the movement of production.)
   (Interest-bearing capital and commercial capital in
   relation to industrial capital. Older forms. Derivative
   forms.) (Development of interest-bearing capital on the
   basis of capitalist production.) (*Usury.* Luther, etc.)
   Vulgar political economy[4]

[XII-636 (CONTINUATION)] RICARDO'S THEORY OF SURPLUS VALUE

(Just to add a further comment to what has already been said: Ricardo knows no other difference between VALUE and NATURAL PRICE than that the latter is the MONETARY EXPRESSION of the VALUE, and that it can therefore change because of a CHANGE in value of the PRECIOUS METALS, without VALUE itself changing. This CHANGE, however, only affects the evaluation or the EXPRESSION of VALUE IN MONEY. Thus, he says, for instance:

* "It" (foreign trade) "can only be regulated by altering the *natural price*, not the *natural value*, at which commodities can be produced in those countries, and that is effected by altering the distribution of the precious metals" * (l.c., [p.] 409).) [5]

Nowhere does Ricardo consider *surplus value* separately and independently from its particular forms—profit (interest) and rent. His observations on the organic composition of capital, which is of such decisive importance, are therefore confined to those differences in the organic composition which he took over from Adam Smith (actually from the Physiocrats), namely, those arising from the process of circulation (fixed and circulating capital). Nowhere does he touch on or perceive the differences in the organic composition within the actual process of production. Hence his confusion of *value* with *cost price*,[6] his wrong theory of rent, his erroneous laws relating to the causes of the rise and fall in the rate of profit, etc.

Profit and surplus value are only identical when the capital advanced is identical with the capital laid out directly in wages. (Rent is not taken into account here since the surplus value is, in the first place, entirely appropriated by the capitalist, [irrespective of] what portion he has subsequently to hand over to his CO-PARTNERS. Furthermore, Ricardo himself presents rent as an item which is separated, detached from profit.) In his observations on profit and wages, Ricardo also abstracts from the constant part of capital, which is not laid out in wages. He treats the matter as though the entire capital were laid out directly in wages. *To this extent,* therefore, he considers *surplus value* and *not profit,* hence it is possible to speak of his theory of surplus value. On the other hand, however, he thinks that he is dealing with profit as such, and in fact views which are based on the assumption of profit and not of surplus value, constantly creep in. Where he correctly sets forth the laws of surplus value, he distorts them by immediately expressing them as laws of profit. On the other hand, he seeks to present the laws of profit directly, without the intermediate links, as laws of surplus value.

When we speak of his theory of surplus value, we are, therefore, speaking of his theory of profit, in so far as he confuses the latter with surplus value, i.e. in so far as he only considers profit in relation to variable capital, the part of capital laid out in wages. We shall later deal with what he says of profit as distinct from surplus value.[a]

It is so much in the nature of the subject-matter that surplus value can only be considered in relation to the variable capital, capital laid out directly in wages—and without an understanding of surplus value no theory of profit is possible—that Ricardo treats the entire capital as variable capital and *abstracts* from constant capital, although he occasionally mentions it in the form of ADVANCES.

[XII-637] (In Chapter XXVI, "On Gross and Net Revenue") Ricardo speaks of:

*"trades where *profits* are in *proportion to the capital,* and not in proportion to the *quantity of labour* employed"* (l.c., p. 418).

What does his whole doctrine of AVERAGE PROFIT (on which his theory of rent depends) mean, but that PROFITS "ARE IN PROPORTION TO THE CAPITAL, AND NOT IN PROPORTION TO THE QUANTITY OF LABOUR EMPLOYED"? If they were "IN PROPORTION TO THE QUANTITY OF LABOUR EMPLOYED", then equal capitals would yield very *unequal* profits, since their profit would be equal to the surplus value created in their own TRADE; the surplus value however depends not on the size of the capital as a whole, but on the size of the variable capital, which = THE QUANTITY OF LABOUR EMPLOYED. What then is the meaning of attributing to a specific use of capital, to *specific TRADES,* by way of exception, THAT IN

---

[a] See this volume, pp. 59-64, 67-68.—*Ed.*

THEM PROFITS ARE PROPORTIONATE TO THE AMOUNT OF CAPITAL and not to THE QUANTITY OF LABOUR EMPLOYED? With a given rate of surplus value, the AMOUNT of surplus value for a particular capital must always depend, not on the absolute size of the capital, but on the QUANTITY OF LABOUR EMPLOYED. On the other hand, if the AVERAGE RATE OF PROFIT is given, the AMOUNT OF PROFIT must always depend on the AMOUNT OF CAPITAL EMPLOYED and not on the QUANTITY OF LABOUR EMPLOYED. Ricardo expressly mentions such TRADES as

* "carrying trade, the distant foreign trade, and trades where expensive machinery is required" * (l.c., [p.] 418).

That is to say, he speaks of TRADES which employ relatively large amounts of constant, and little variable capital. At the same time, they are TRADES in which, compared with others, the TOTAL AMOUNT of the capital advanced is large, or which can only be carried on with *large capitals*. If the RATE of profit is given, the AMOUNT OF PROFITS depends altogether on the *size* of the capitals advanced. This, however, by no means distinguishes the TRADES in which large capitals and much constant capital are employed (the two always go together) from those in which small capitals are employed, but is merely an application of the theory that equal capitals yield equal profits, a larger capital therefore yields more profit than a smaller capital. This has nothing to do with the "QUANTITY OF LABOUR EMPLOYED". But whether the rate of profit in general is great or small, depends indeed on the TOTAL QUANTITY OF LABOUR EMPLOYED BY THE CAPITAL OF THE WHOLE CLASS OF CAPITALISTS, and on THE PROPORTIONAL QUANTITY OF *UNPAID* LABOUR EMPLOYED; AND, LASTLY, on THE PROPORTION BETWEEN THE CAPITAL EMPLOYED IN LABOUR, AND THE CAPITAL MERELY REPRODUCED AS A CONDITION OF PRODUCTION.

Ricardo himself argues against Adam Smith's view,

that a higher rate of profit in * foreign trade ("that the great profits, which are sometimes made by particular merchants in foreign trade") "will elevate the general rate of profits in the country" * (l.c., CH. VII, "On Foreign Trade", [p.] 132).

He says:

* "They contend, that the equality of profits will be brought about by the general rise of profits; and I am of opinion, that the profits of the favoured trade will speedily submit to the general level" * ([pp.] 132-33).

We shall see later,[a] how far his view is correct THAT EXCEPTIONAL PROFITS (when they are not caused by the rise in market price above the value) do not raise the GENERAL RATE OF PROFIT *in spite of the equalisation* [of profits], and also how far his view is correct that

---

[a] See this volume, pp. 71-72.— *Ed.*

FOREIGN TRADE and the expansion of the market can *not* raise the rate of profit. But granted that he is right, and, on the whole granted the "EQUALITY OF PROFITS", how can he distinguish between TRADES "WHERE PROFITS ARE IN *PROPORTION TO THE CAPITAL*" and OTHERS WHERE THEY ARE "IN PROPORTION TO THE QUANTITY OF LABOUR EMPLOYED"?

In the same CH. XXVI, "On Gross and Net Revenue", Ricardo says:

* "I admit, that from the nature of rent, a given capital employed in agriculture, on any but the land last cultivated, puts in motion a greater quantity of labour than an equal capital employed in manufactures and trade"* (l.c., [p.] 419).

The whole statement is nonsense. In the first place, according to Ricardo, A GREATER QUANTITY OF LABOUR is EMPLOYED on the LAND LAST CULTIVATED than on all the other land. That is why, according to him, rent arises on the other land. How, therefore, is a given capital to set in motion a greater quantity of labour than in MANUFACTURES AND TRADE, on all other land *except* the LAND LAST CULTIVATED? That the product of the better land has a *market value* that is *higher* than the *individual* value, which is determined by the QUANTITY OF LABOUR EMPLOYED BY THE CAPITAL THAT CULTIVATES it, is surely not the same thing as that THIS CAPITAL "PUTS IN MOTION A GREATER QUANTITY OF LABOUR THAN AN EQUAL CAPITAL EMPLOYED IN MANUFACTURES AND TRADE"? But it would have been correct, had Ricardo said that, apart from differences in the fertility of the land, altogether rent arises because agricultural capital sets in motion a greater quantity of labour in proportion to the constant part of the capital, than does the average capital in NON-AGRICULTURAL INDUSTRY.

[XII-638] Ricardo overlooks the fact that, *with a given surplus value*, various factors may raise or lower and in general influence the profit. Because he identifies surplus value with profit, he quite consistently seeks to demonstrate that the rise and fall in the rate of profit is caused only by circumstances that make the rate of surplus value rise or fall. Apart from the circumstances which, when the amount of surplus value is given, influence the *rate of profit*, although not the AMOUNT OF PROFIT, he furthermore overlooks the fact that the rate of profit depends on the AMOUNT of surplus value, and by no means on the *rate of surplus value*. When the rate of surplus value, i.e. of SURPLUS labour, is given, the AMOUNT of surplus value depends on the organic composition of the capital, that is to say, on the number of workers which a capital OF GIVEN VALUE, for instance £100, employs. It depends on the rate of surplus value if the organic composition of the capital is given. It is thus determined by two factors: the number of workers simultaneously employed and the rate of surplus labour. If the capital increases, then the AMOUNT OF SURPLUS VALUE also increases whatever its organic composition, provided it remains unchanged. But this in no way alters the fact that for a CAPITAL OF GIVEN VALUE, for example 100, it remains the same. If in this case it is 10, then it is 100 for [£]1,000, but this does not alter the proportion.

(*Ricardo*:

* "There cannot be *two rates of profit in the same employment,* and therefore when the value of the produce is in different proportions to capital, it is the rent which will differ, and not the profit" * (CH. XII, "Land-Tax", [pp.] 212-13).

This only applies to the normal rate of profit "IN THE SAME EMPLOYMENT". Otherwise it is in direct contradiction to the statements quoted earlier on [a] (CH. II, "On Rent", [pp.] 60, 61):

* "The exchangeable value of all commodities, whether they be manufactured, or the produce of the mines, or the produce of land, is always regulated, not by the less quantity of labour that will suffice for their production under circumstances highly favorable, and exclusively enjoyed by those who have peculiar facilities of production; but by the greater quantity of labour necessarily bestowed on their production by those who have no such facilities; by those who continue to produce them under the most unfavorable circumstances; meaning—by *the most unfavorable circumstances, the most unfavorable under which the quantity of produce required, renders it necessary to carry on the production.*" *)

In CH. XII, "Land-Tax", Ricardo incidentally makes the following remark directed against Say; it shows that the Englishman is always very conscious of the economic distinctions whereas the Continental constantly forgets them:

* "M. Say supposes, 'A landlord by his *assiduity, economy and skill,* to increase his annual revenue by 5,000 francs'[b]; but a landlord has no means of employing his assiduity, economy and skill on his land, unless he farms it himself; and then it is in quality of capitalist and farmer that he makes the improvement, and not in quality of landlord. It is not conceivable that he could so augment the produce of his farm by any *peculiar* skill" * //the "SKILL" therefore is *plus ou moins*[c] empty talk// * "on his part, without first increasing the quantity of capital employed upon it" * (l.c., [p.] 209).

In *CH. XIII,* "Taxes on Gold" (important for Ricardo's theory of money), Ricardo makes some additional reflections or further definitions relating to MARKET PRICE and NATURAL PRICE. They amount to this, how long the equalisation of the two prices takes depends on whether the particular TRADE permits a rapid or slow increase or reduction of SUPPLY, which in turn is equivalent to a *rapid or slow*

---

[a] See present edition, Vol. 31, pp. 428, 526-27.— *Ed.*
[b] J.-B. Say, *Traité d'économie politique...,* 2nd ed., Vol. 2, Paris, 1814, pp. 353-54.— *Ed.*
[c] More or less.— *Ed.*

TRANSFER OR WITHDRAWAL of capital TO OR FROM THE TRADE IN QUESTION. Ricardo has been criticised by many writers (Sismondi, etc.) because, in his observations on rent, he disregards the difficulties that the WITHDRAWAL OF CAPITAL presents for the farmer who employs a great deal of fixed capital, etc. (The history of England from 1815 to 1830 provides *strong proof* for this.) Although this objection is quite correct, it does *not in any way* affect the theory, it leaves it *quite untouched*, because in this case it is invariably only a question of the *plus ou moins* rapid or slow operation of the economic law. But as regards the *reverse* objection, which refers to the APPLICATION OF NEW CAPITAL TO NEW SOILS, the situation is quite different. Ricardo assumes that this can take place *without the intervention* of the LANDLORD, that in this case capital is operating in a field of action [XII-639], in which it does not meet with any resistance. But this is *fundamentally wrong*. In order to prove this assumption, that this is indeed so, where capitalist production and landed property are developed, Ricardo always presupposes cases in which landed property does *not* exist, either in fact or in law, and where capitalist production too is *not yet* developed, at least not on the land.

The statements just referred to are the following:

*"The rise in the price of commodities, in consequence of taxation or of difficulty of production, will in all cases ultimately ensue; but the *duration of the interval*, before the market price will conform to the natural price, *must depend on the nature of the commodity*, and on *the facility with which it can be reduced in quantity*. If the quantity of the commodity taxed could not be diminished, if the capital of the farmer or [of] the hatter for instance, could not be withdrawn to other employments, it would be of no consequence that their profits were reduced below the general level by means of a tax; unless the demand for their commodities should increase, they would never be able to elevate the market price of corn and of hats up to their increased natural price. Their threats to leave their employments, and remove their capitals to more favoured trades, would be treated as an idle menace which could not be carried into effect; and consequently the price would not be raised by diminished production. *Commodities*, however, of all descriptions can *be reduced in quantity*, and *capital can be removed from trades which are less profitable to those which are more so, but with different degrees of rapidity*. In proportion as the supply of a particular commodity can be more easily reduced, without inconvenience to the producer, the price of it will more quickly rise after the difficulty of its production has been increased by taxation, or by any other means" ([pp.] 214-15). "The agreement of the market and natural prices of all commodities, depends at all times on the facility with which the supply can be increased or diminished. In the case of gold, houses, and labour, as well as many other things, this effect cannot, under some circumstances, be speedily produced. But it is different with those commodities which are consumed and reproduced from year to year, such as hats, shoes, corn, and cloth; they may be reduced, if necessary, and the interval cannot be long before the supply is contracted in proportion to the increased charge of producing them"* (l.c., [pp.] 220-21).

In the same Ch. XIII, "Taxes on Gold", Ricardo speaks of

*"*rent being* not *a creation, but merely a transfer of wealth*"* (l.c., [p.] 221).

* Is profit *a creation* of wealth, or is it not rather a *transfer* of the surplus labour, from the workman to the capitalist? As to *wages* too, they are, in fact, not a *creation* of wealth. But they are not a transfer. They are the appropriation of part of the produce of labour to those who produced it.*

In the same chapter Ricardo says:

*"A *tax on raw produce* from the surface of the earth, will ... fall on the *consumer*, and will in no way affect rent; unless, by diminishing the funds for the maintenance of labour, it lowers wages, reduces the population, and diminishes the demand for corn"* ([p.] 221).

Whether Ricardo is right when he says that "A TAX ON RAW PRODUCE FROM THE SURFACE OF THE EARTH" falls neither on the LANDLORD nor on the farmer but on the CONSUMER, does not concern us here. I maintain, however, that, if he is right, such a tax may *raise the rent*, whereas he thinks that it does not affect it, unless, by increasing the price of the means of subsistence, etc., it diminishes capital, etc., population and the demand for corn. For Ricardo imagines that an increase in the price of RAW PRODUCE only affects the *rate of profit* in so far as it raises the price of the *means of subsistence* of the worker. And it is true that an increase in the price of RAW PRODUCE can only in this way affect the *rate of surplus value* and consequently *surplus value* itself, *thereby* affecting the rate of profit. But assuming a given *surplus value*, an increase in the price of the "RAW PRODUCE FROM THE SURFACE OF THE EARTH" would *raise* the value of constant capital in proportion to the variable, would increase the ratio of constant capital to variable and *therefore* reduce the *rate of profit*, thus raising the *rent*. Ricardo starts out from the viewpoint [XII-640] that in so far as the rise or fall in the price of the *raw produce* does not affect wages, it does not affect profit; for, he argues //except in one passage to which we shall return at a later stage[a]// that the rate of profit remains the same, whether the value of the capital advanced falls or rises. If the value of the capital advanced grows, then the value of the product grows and also the part of the product which forms the surplus product, [i.e.] profit. The reverse happens when the value of the capital advanced falls. This is only correct, if the values of variable and constant capital change in the *same proportion*, whether the change is caused by a rise in the price of raw materials or by taxes, etc. In

---

[a] See this volume, pp. 63-64, 67.— *Ed.*

this case the rate remains unaffected, because [no] CHANGE HAS TAKEN PLACE IN THE ORGANIC COMPOSITION OF THE CAPITAL. And even then it must be *assumed*—as is the case with TEMPORARY CHANGES—that wages remain the same, whether the price of RAW PRODUCE rises or falls (in other words [wages] remain the same, that is, their value remains unchanged irrespective of any rise or fall in the use value of the wages).

The following possibilities exist:

First the two major differences:

A) A CHANGE *in the mode of production* brings about a change in the *proportion* between the amounts of constant and variable capital employed. In this case the rate of surplus value remains the same provided wages remain constant (in terms of value). But the surplus value itself is affected if a different number of workers is employed by the same capital, i.e. if there is an alteration in the variable capital. If the CHANGE in the mode of production results in a relative fall in constant capital, the surplus value grows and thus the rate of profit. The reverse case produces the opposite result.

It is here assumed throughout that the value *pro tanto,* per *100* for example, of constant and variable capital remains *the same.*

In this case the CHANGE in the mode of production cannot affect constant and variable capital equally; that is, for instance, constant and variable capital—without a change in value—cannot increase or diminish to the same extent, for the fall or rise is here always the result of a change in the productivity of labour. A CHANGE in the mode of production has not the same but a *different* effect [on constant and variable capital]; and this has nothing to do with whether a large or small amount of capital has to be employed with a given ORGANIC COMPOSITION *of capital.*

B) *The mode of production remains the same.* There is a CHANGE *in the ratio of constant to variable capital,* while their relative volume remains the same (so that each of them forms the same ALIQUOT PART of the total capital as before). This change in their ratio is caused by a *change in the value* of the commodities which enter into constant or variable capital.⁹

The following possibilities exist here:

The value of the constant capital remains the same while that of the variable capital rises or falls. This would always affect the surplus value, and thereby the rate of profit. The value of the variable capital remains the same while that of the constant rises or falls. Then the rate of profit would fall in the first case and rise in the second. If both fall simultaneously, but in different proportions, then the one has always risen or fallen as compared with the other.

The value of the constant and of the variable capital is *equally* affected, whether both rise or both fall. If both rise, then the rate of profit falls, not because the constant capital rises but because the variable capital *rises* and accordingly the surplus value falls (for only the value [of the variable capital] rises, although it sets in motion the same number of workers as before, or perhaps even a smaller number). If both fall, then the rate of profit rises, not because constant capital falls, but because the variable falls (in terms of value) and therefore the surplus value increases.

C) Change in the mode of production and change in the value of the elements that form constant or variable capital. Here one CHANGE may neutralise the other, for example, when the amount of constant capital grows while its value falls or remains the same (i.e. it falls *pro tanto*, per 100) or when its amount falls but its value rises in the same proportion or remains the same (i.e. it rises *pro tanto*). In this case there would be no change at all in the organic composition. The rate of profit would remain unchanged. But it can never happen—except in the case of agricultural capital—that the amount of the constant capital falls as compared with the variable capital, while its value *rises.*

This type of nullification cannot possibly apply to variable capital (while the real wage remains unchanged).

Except for this one case, it is therefore only possible for the value and amount of the constant capital to fall or rise simultaneously in relation to the variable capital, its value therefore rises or falls absolutely as compared with the variable capital. This CASE has already been considered. Or they may fall or rise simultaneously [XII-641] but in unequal proportion. On the assumption made, this possibility always reduces itself to the case in which the value of the constant capital rises or falls relatively to the variable.

This also includes the other case. For if the amount of the constant capital rises, then the amount of the variable capital falls relatively, and vice versa. Similarly with the value.

It is clear that what has been regarded here as a *variation* within the *organic composition* of one capital, can apply equally to the difference in the *organic composition* between *different capitals,* capitals in DIFFERENT TRADES.

Firstly: Instead of a variation in the organic composition of *one* capital—a difference in the *organic composition of different* capitals.

Secondly: Alteration in the organic composition through a *change in value* in the two parts of one capital, similarly a difference in the *value* of the *raw materials* and *machinery employed* by different capitals. This does not apply to variable capital, since equal wages in the DIFFERENT TRADES are assumed. The difference in the VALUE OF DIFFERENT DAYS OF LABOUR IN DIFFERENT TRADES has nothing to do with it. If the labour of a goldsmith is dearer than that of a LABOURER, then the surplus time of the goldsmith is proportionately dearer than that of the PEASANT.

(See *p. 632.*[a]) On HOUSE RENT *Adam Smith* says:

* "Whatever part of the whole rent of a house is *over and above* what is *sufficient* for affording this reasonable *profit*" (to the builder) "naturally goes to the ground rent; and where the owner of the ground, and the owner of the building, are two different persons, it is in most cases completely paid to the former. In country houses, at a distance from any great town, where there is a plentiful choice of ground, the ground rent is scarcely any thing, or no more than what the space upon which the house stands, would pay employed in agriculture"* (BOOK V, CH. II).[7]

In the case of the GROUND RENT OF HOUSES, SITUATION constitutes just as decisive a factor for the differential rent, as FERTILITY (and SITUATION) in the case of AGRICULTURAL RENT.

Adam Smith shares with the Physiocrats, not only the partiality for AGRICULTURE and the LANDLORD, but also the view that they are particularly suitable OBJECTS OF TAXATION. He says:

* "Both ground rents, and the ordinary rent of land, are a species of revenue, which the owner in many cases enjoys, without any care or attention of his own. Though a part of this revenue should be taken from him, in order to defray the expenses of the State, no discouragement will thereby be given to any sort of industry. The annual produce of the land and labour of the society, the real wealth and revenue of the great body of the people, might be the same after such a tax as before. Ground rents, and the ordinary rent of land are, therefore, perhaps, the species of revenue, which can best bear to have a peculiar tax imposed upon them"* (BOOK V, CH. II).

The considerations which Ricardo (p. 230)[b] advances are very philistine.

In CH. XV, "Taxes on Profits", Ricardo says:

* "Taxes on those commodities, which are generally denominated luxuries, fall on those only who make use of them.... But taxes on necessaries do not affect the consumers of necessaries, in proportion to that quantity that may be consumed by them, but often in a much higher proportion."* For example, *a tax on corn. "It alters the rate of profits of stock. Whatever raises the wages of labour, lowers the

---

[a] See present edition, Vol. 31, p. 572.—*Ed.*

[b] D. Ricardo, *On the Principles of Political Economy, and Taxation*, 3rd ed., London, 1821.—*Ed.*

profits of stock; therefore every tax on any commodity consumed by the labourer, has a tendency to lower the rate of profits"* ([p.] 231).

TAXES ON CONSUMERS are at the same time TAXES ON PRODUCERS, in so far as the object TAXED enters not only into individual consumption but also into industrial consumption, or only into the latter. This does not, however, apply only to the NECESSARIES CONSUMED BY WORKMEN. It applies to all materials INDUSTRIALLY CONSUMED BY THE CAPITALIST. Every tax of this kind reduces the rate of profit, because it raises the value of the constant capital in relation to the variable. For example, a tax imposed on flax or wool. [XII-642] The flax rises in price. The flax spinner can therefore no longer purchase the same quantity of flax with a capital of 100. Since the mode of production has remained the same, he needs the same number of workers to spin the same quantity of flax. But the flax has a greater value than before, in relation to the capital laid out in wages. The rate of profit therefore falls. It does not help him at all that the price of LINEN YARN rises. The absolute level of this price is in fact immaterial to him. What matters is only the excess of this price over the price of the ADVANCES. If he wanted to raise [the price of] the total product, not only by [the amount necessary to cover the increase in] the price of the flax, but to such an extent that the same quantity of yarn would yield him the same profit as before, then the demand—which is already falling as a result of the rising price of the raw material of the yarn—would fall still further because of the artificial rise which is due to the higher profit. Although, ON AN AVERAGE the rate of profit is given, it is not possible in such cases to raise the price in this way.

In regard to case C, [p.] 640, it should also be noted:

It would be possible for the wages to rise but for constant capital to fall *in terms of value*, not in *physical terms*. If the rise and fall were proportional on both sides, the rate of profit could remain unchanged. For instance, if the constant capital were £60, wages 40 and the rate of surplus value 50%, then the product would be 120. The rate of profit would be 20%. If the constant capital fell to 40, although its volume [in physical terms] remained unchanged, and wages rose to 60, while the surplus value fell from 50% to $33^1/_3$%, then the product would be 120 and the rate of profit 20. This is wrong. According to the assumption, the total value of the quantity of labour employed=£60. Hence, if the wage rose to 60, surplus value and therefore the rate of profit would be 0. But if it did not rise to such an extent, then any rise in the wage would bring about a fall in the surplus value. If wages rose to 50, then the surplus value=£10, if [they rose] to £45, then [the surplus value would be] 15, etc. Under all circumstances, therefore, the surplus value and the rate of profit would fall to the same degree. For we are measuring the unchanged total capital here. While the magnitude of the capital (the total capital) remains the same the rate of profit must always rise and fall, not with the rate of surplus value but with the ABSOLUTE AMOUNT OF SURPLUS VALUE. But if, in the above example, the flax fell so low that the amount which the same number of workers were spinning could be bought for £40, then we would have the following:

Constant capital	Variable capital	Surplus value	Value of the product	Capital advanced	Rate of profit
£40	50	10	100	90	$11^1/_9\%$

The rate of profit would have fallen below 20%.
But supposing:

Constant capital	Variable capital	Surplus value	Value of the product	Capital advanced	Rate of profit
30	50	10	90	80	$12^1/_2\%$

Supposing:

Constant capital	Variable capital	Surplus value	Value of the product	Capital advanced	Rate of profit
20	50	10	80	70	$.14^2/_7\%$

According to the assumption, the fall in the value of the constant capital never completely counterbalances the rise in the value of the variable capital. On the assumption made, it can never entirely cancel it out, since for the rate of profit to be 20, [£]10 would have to be $^1/_5$ of the total capital advanced. But in the case in which the variable capital=50, this would only be possible when the constant capital=0. Assume, on the other hand, that variable capital rose only to 45; in this case the surplus value would be 15. And, say, the constant capital fell to 30, in this case

Constant capital	Variable capital	Surplus value	Value of the product	Capital advanced	Rate of profit
30	45	15	90	75	20%

In this case the two movements cancel each other out entirely. [XII-643] Assume further:

Constant capital	Variable capital	Surplus value	Value of the product	Capital advanced	Rate of profit
20	45	15	80	65	$23^1/_{13}\%$

Even with the fall in the surplus value,[a] therefore, the rate of profit could *rise* in this case, because of the proportionately

_____

[a] In comparison with the initial case $60c+40v+20s$. — *Ed.*

greater fall in the value of the constant capital. More workers could be employed with the same capital of 100, despite the rise in wages and the fall in the rate of surplus value. Despite the fall in the rate of surplus value, the amount of surplus value, and hence the profit, would increase, because the number of workers had increased. For the above ratio of $20c+45v$ gives us the following proportions with a capital outlay of 100:

Constant capital	Variable capital	Surplus value	Value of the product	Capital advanced	Rate of profit
$30^{10}/_{13}$	$69^3/_{13}$	$23^1/_{13}$	$123^1/_{13}$	100	$23^1/_{13}\%$

The relation between the rate of surplus value and the number of workers becomes very important here. Ricardo never considers it.

[In] Cʜ. XV, "Taxes on Profits", Ricardo says:

* "In a former part of this work, we discussed the effects of the division of capital into *fixed and circulating,* or rather into *durable and perishable capital,* on the prices of commodities. We shewed that two manufacturers might employ precisely the same amount of capital, and might derive from it precisely the same amount of profits, but that they would sell their commodities for very different sums of money, according as the capitals they employed were rapidly, or slowly, consumed and reproduced. The one might sell his goods for £4,000, the other for £10,000, and they might both employ £10,000 of capital, and obtain 20% profit, or £2,000. The capital of one might consist, for example, of £2,000 circulating capital, to be reproduced, and £8,000 fixed, in buildings and machinery; the capital of the other, on the contrary, might consist of £8,000 of circulating, and of only 2,000 fixed capital in machinery, and buildings. Now, if each of these persons were to be taxed ten per cent on his income, or £200, the one, to make his business yield him the *general rate of profit,* must raise his goods from £10,000 to £10,200; the other would also be obliged to raise the price of his goods from £4,000 to £4,200. Before the tax, the goods sold by one of these manufacturers were $2^1/_2$ times more valuable than the goods of the other; after the tax they will be 2.42 times more valuable: the one kind will have risen two per cent; the other five per cent: consequently a tax upon income, whilst money continued unaltered in value, would alter the relative prices *and* value of commodities" * ([pp.] 234-35).

The error lies in this final "ᴀɴᴅ" — "ᴘʀɪᴄᴇꜱ ᴀɴᴅ ᴠᴀʟᴜᴇ". This ᴄʜᴀɴɢᴇ ᴏꜰ ᴘʀɪᴄᴇꜱ would only show — just as in the case of capital containing different proportions of fixed and circulating capital — that the establishment of the ɢᴇɴᴇʀᴀʟ ʀᴀᴛᴇ ᴏꜰ ᴘʀᴏꜰɪᴛ requires that the prices or cost prices which are determined and regulated by that general rate of profit [are] very different from the *values* of the commodities. And this most important aspect of the question does not exist for Ricardo at all.

In the same ᴄʜᴀᴘᴛᴇʀ he says:

* "If a country were not taxed, and money should fall in value, its abundance in every market" * //here [he expresses] the absurd notion that *a fall in the value of

money ought to be accompanied by its abundance in every market// [XII-644] "would produce similar effects in each. If meat rose 20 per cent, bread, beer, shoes, labour, and *every commodity,* would also rise 20 per cent; it is necessary they should do so, to secure to each trade the same rate of profits. But this is no longer true when any of these commodities is taxed; if, in that case they should all rise in proportion to the fall in the value of money, *profits would be rendered unequal;* in the case of the commodities taxed, *profits would be raised above the general level,* and capital *would be removed from one employment to another, till an equilibrium of profits was restored,* which could only be, after *the relative prices were altered"* * ([pp. 236-]37).

And so the EQUILIBRIUM OF PROFITS is altogether brought about by [alterations in] the RELATIVE VALUES; the REAL VALUES OF the COMMODITIES ARE ALTERED, AND SO ADAPTED THAT THEY CORRESPOND, NOT TO THEIR REAL VALUE, BUT TO THE AVERAGE PROFIT they yield.

In Ch. XVII: "Taxes on Other Commodities than Raw Produce", Ricardo says:

* "Mr. Buchanan considers corn and raw produce as at a monopoly price, because they yield a rent: all commodities which yield a rent, he supposes, must be at a monopoly price; and thence he infers, that all taxes on raw produce would fall on the landlord, and not on the consumer.

" 'The *price of corn,*' he says, 'which always affords a rent, *being in no respect influenced by the expenses of its production,* those *expenses must be paid out of the rent; and when they* rise or fall, therefore, the consequence is not a higher or lower price, but a higher or lower rent. In this view, all taxes on farm servants, horses, or the implements of agriculture, are in reality land taxes; the burden falling on the farmer during the currency of his lease, and on the landlord, when the lease comes to be renewed. In like manner all those improved implements of husbandry which save expense to the farmer, such as machines for threshing and reaping, whatever gives him easier access to the market, such as good roads, canals and bridges, though they lessen the original cost of corn, *do not lessen its market price.* Whatever is saved by those improvements, therefore, belongs to the landlord as part of his rent.' ª

"It is evident" * (says Ricardo) * "that if we yield to Mr. Buchanan the basis on which his argument is built, namely, that the price of corn always yields a rent, all the consequences which he contends for would follow of course" * ([pp.] 292-93).

THIS IS BY NO MEANS EVIDENT. What Buchanan bases his argument on is not THAT ALL CORN YIELDS A RENT, but THAT ALL CORN WHICH YIELDS A RENT IS SOLD AT A *MONOPOLY PRICE,* and that MONOPOLY PRICE—in the sense in which Adam Smith explains it and it has the same meaning with Ricardo—is "THE VERY HIGHEST PRICE AT WHICH THE CONSUMERS ARE WILLING TO PURCHASE THE COMMODITY".[8]

But this is wrong. CORN WHICH YIELDS A RENT (apart from differential rent) is not SOLD AT A MONOPOLY PRICE in Buchanan's sense. It is sold at a monopoly price, only in so far as it is sold above its *cost price, i.e. at its value.* Its price is determined by the QUANTITY OF LABOUR REALISED

ª D. Buchanan, *Observations on the Subjects Treated of in Dr. Smith's Inquiry into the Nature and Causes of the Wealth of Nations,* Edinburgh, 1814, pp. 37-38.— *Ed.*

IN IT, not by the EXPENSES OF ITS PRODUCTION, and the rent is the excess of the VALUE over the cost price, it is therefore determined by the latter. The smaller is the cost ·price relatively to the VALUE, the greater will be [the rent], and the greater the cost price in relation to the VALUE, the smaller [the rent]. All IMPROVEMENTS lower the value of the corn because [they reduce] the quantity of labour required for its production. Whether they reduce the rent, depends on various circumstances. If the corn becomes cheaper, and if wages are thereby reduced, then the rate of surplus value rises. Furthermore, the FARMER'S EXPENSES in seeds, fodder, etc., would fall. And therewith the rate of profit in all other, NON-AGRICULTURAL TRADES would rise, hence *also* in agriculture. The relative amounts of IMMEDIATE and ACCUMULATED LABOUR would remain unchanged in the NON-AGRICULTURAL TRADES; the number of workers (in relation to constant capital) would remain the same, but the value of the variable capital would fall, the surplus value [XII-645] would therefore rise, and also the rate of profit. *Consequently* [they would] also [rise] in AGRICULTURAL TRADE. Rent falls here because the rate of profit rises. *Corn becomes cheaper, but its cost price rises. Hence the difference between its value and its cost price falls.*

According to our assumption the ratio for the average NON-AGRICULTURAL CAPITAL$=80c+20v$, the rate of surplus value$=50\%$, hence surplus value$=10$ and the rate of profit$=10\%$. The value of the product of the average capital of 100 therefore$=110$.

If one assumes, that as a result of the lowering of the price of grain, wages fell by $^1/_4$, then *the same number of workers* employed on a constant capital of £80, that is on the same amount of raw material and machinery, would now cost only 15. And the same amount of commodities would be worth $80c+15v+15s$, since, according to the assumption, the quantity of labour which they perform$=£30$. Thus the value of the same amount of commodities$=110$, as before. But the capital advanced would now amount only to 95 and 15 on $95=15^{15}/_{19}\%$. If, however, the same amount of capital were laid out, that is 100, then the ratio would be: $84^4/_{19}c+15^{15}/_{19}v$. The profit, however, would be $15^{15}/_{19}$. And the value of the product would amount to £$115^{15}/_{19}$. According to the assumption, however, the AGRICULTURAL capital$=60c+40v$ and the value of its product$=120$. Rent$=10$, while the cost price$=110$. Now the rent$=$only $4^4/_{19}$. For $115^{15}/_{19}+4^4/_{19}=£120$.

We see here that the average capital of 100 produces commodities at a cost price of $115^{15}/_{19}$ instead of the previous 110. Has this caused the average price of the commodity to rise? Its value has remained the same, since the same amount of labour is required to transform the same amount of raw material and machinery into product. But the same capital of 100 sets in motion more labour, and while previously it transformed 80, now it transforms $84^4/_{19}$ constant capital into product. A greater proportion of this labour is, however, now unpaid. Hence there is an increase in profit and in the *total value* of the commodities produced by £100. The value of the individual commodity has remained the same, but more commodities *at the same value* are being produced with a capital of 100. What is however the position of the cost price in the individual TRADES?

Let us assume that the NON-AGRICULTURAL CAPITAL consisted of the following capitals:

		Product	Difference between value and cost price
1) $80c+20v$	In order	$=110$ (*value*$=110$)	$=0$
2) $60c+40v$	to sell at	$=110$ (value$=120$)	$=-10$
3) $85c+15v$	the same	$=110$ (value$=107^1/_2$)	$=+2^1/_2$
4) $95c+ 5v$	cost prices	$=110$ (value$=102^1/_2$)	$=+7^1/_2$

Thus the average
capital$=80c+20v$

For 2) the difference$=-10$, for 3)+4)$=+10$. For the whole capital of $400=0-10+10=0$. If the product of the capital of 400 is sold at 440, then the commodities produced by it are sold at *their value*. This yields [a profit of] 10%. But [in case] 2), the commodities are sold at £10 below their value, [in case] 3) at $2^1/_2$ above their value and [in case] 4) at $7^1/_2$ above their value. Only [in case] 1) are they sold at their value if they are sold at their cost price, i.e., 100 capital+10 profit.

[XII-646] But what would be the situation as a result of the fall in wages by $^1/_4$?

For capital 1). Instead of $80c+20v$, [the outlay is] now $84^4/_{19}c + 15^{15}/_{19}v$, *profit* $15^{15}/_{19}$, *value of the product* $115^{15}/_{19}$.

For capital 2). Now only 30 laid out in wages, since $^1/_4$ of $40=10$ and $40-10=30$. The product$=60c+30v$ and the surplus value$=30$. (For the *value of the labour applied*$=£60$.) On a capital of 90 [the wages]$=33^1/_3$%. For [a capital of] 100 the ratio is: $66^2/_3c + 33^1/_3v$ *and the value*$= 133^1/_3$. The rate of profit$=33^1/_3$.

For capital 3). Now only $11^1/_4$ [laid out] in wages, for $^1/_4$ of $15=3^3/_4$ and $15-3^3/_4=11^1/_4$. The product would be $85c+11^1/_4v$ and the surplus value equal to $11^1/_4$. (Value of the labour

Page 645 of Notebook XII of the Economic Manuscript
of 1861-1863

applied=$22^2/_4$.) On a capital of $96^1/_4$. But this [the wages]=$11^{53}/_{77}\%$. For 100 the *ratio* is $88^{24}/_{77}c + 11^{53}/_{77}v$. The rate of profit=$11^{53}/_{77}$ and [the value of the] product=$111^{53}/_{77}$.

For capital 4). Now only $3^3/_4$ laid out in wages, for $^1/_4$ of $5=1^1/_4$ and $5-1^1/_4=3^3/_4$. The product $95c+3^3/_4v$ and the surplus value equal to $3^3/_4$ (for the value of the total labour=$7^2/_4$). On a capital of $98^3/_4$. This [the wages]=$3^{63}/_{79}\%$. For 100 the ratio is: $96^{16}/_{79}c + 3^{63}/_{79}v$. The rate of profit=$3^{63}/_{79}$. The value [of the product]=$103^{63}/_{79}$.

We would therefore have the following:

	Rate of profit		Product	Difference between cost price and value
1) $84^4/_{19}c + 15^{15}/_{19}v$	$15^{15}/_{19}$	In order	=116 (value=$115^{15}/_{19}$)	$=+\ ^4/_{19}$
2) $66^2/_3c + 33^1/_3v$	$33^1/_3$	to sell at	=116 (value=$133^1/_3$)	$=-17^1/_3$
3) $88^{24}/_{77}c + 11^{53}/_{77}v$	$11^{53}/_{77}$	the same	=116 (value=$111^{53}/_{77}$)	$=+\ 4^{24}/_{77}$
4) $96^{16}/_{79}c + 3^{63}/_{79}v$	$3^{63}/_{79}$	cost prices	=116 (value=$103^{63}/_{79}$)	$=+12^{16}/_{79}$

Total: 400   64 (to the nearest whole number)

This makes 16%. More exactly, a little more than £$16^1/_7$.[9] The calculation is not quite correct because we have disregarded, not taken into account a fraction of the average profit; this makes the negative difference in 2) appear a little too large and [the positive] in 1), 3), 4) a little too small. But it can be seen that otherwise the positive and negative differences would cancel out; further, it can be seen that on the one hand the sale of 2) *below* its value and of 3) and particularly of 4) *above* their value would increase considerably. True, the addition to or reduction of the price would not be so great for the individual product as might appear here, since in all 4 categories more labour is employed and hence more constant capital (raw materials and machinery) is transformed into product. The increase or reduction in price would thus be spread over a larger volume of commodities. Nevertheless it would still be considerable. It is thus evident that a fall in wages would cause a rise in the cost prices of 1), 3), 4), in fact a very considerable rise in the cost price of 4). It is the same law as that developed by Ricardo in relation to the difference between circulating and fixed capital,[10] but he did not by any means prove, nor could he have proved, that this is reconcilable with the law of value and that the value of the products remains the same for the total capital.

[XII-647] The calculation and the adjustment becomes much

more complicated if we take into account those differences in the organic composition of the capital which arise from the circulation process. For in our calculation, above, we assumed that the whole of the *constant capital* which has been advanced, enters into the product, i.e. that it contains only the wear and tear of the fixed capital, for one year, for example (since we have to calculate the profit for the year). The values of the total product would otherwise be very different, whereas here they only change with the variable capital. Secondly, with a constant rate of surplus value but varying periods of circulation, there would be greater differences in the *amount of surplus value created*, relatively to the capital advanced. Leaving out of account any differences in variable capital, the amounts of the surplus values would be proportionate to the amounts of the values created by the same capitals. The rate of profit would be even lower where a relatively large part of the constant capital consisted of fixed capital and considerably higher, where a relatively large part of the capital consisted of circulating capital. It would be highest where the variable capital was relatively large as compared with the constant capital and where the fixed portion of the latter was at the same time relatively small. If the ratio of circulating to fixed capital in the constant capital were *the same* in the different capitals, then the only determining factor would be the difference between variable and constant capital. If the ratio of variable to constant capital were the same, then it would be the difference between fixed and circulating capital, that is, only the difference within the constant capital itself.

As we have seen above, the FARMER'S rate of profit would rise, in any case, if, as a result of the lower price of corn, the general rate of profit of the NON-AGRICULTURAL CAPITAL increased. The question is whether his rate of profit would rise directly, and this appears to depend on the nature of the IMPROVEMENTS. If the IMPROVEMENTS were of such a kind that the capital laid out in wages decreased considerably compared with that laid out in machinery, etc., then his rate of profit need not necessarily rise directly. If, for example, it was such that he required $^1/_4$ less workers, then instead of his original outlay of £40 in wages, he would now pay only 30. Thus his capital would be $60c + 30v$, or on 100 it would be $66^2/_3c + 33^1/_3v$. And since the labour costing 40 [provides a surplus value of] 20, the labour costing 30 provides 15. And $16^2/_3$ [surplus value is derived] from the labour costing $33^1/_3$. Thus the organic composition [of the agricultural capital] would grow closer to the NON-AGRICULTURAL CAPITAL. And in the above case, with a simultaneous decrease in wages by $^1/_4$, it would even come within the range of that of the non-agricultural capital.[11] In this case, rent (absolute rent) would disappear.

Following upon the above-quoted passage on Buchanan, Ricardo says:

* "I hope I have made it sufficiently clear, that until a country is cultivated in every part, and up to the highest degree, there is always *a portion of capital employed on the land* which yields no rent, *and*" (!) "that it is this portion of capital, the result of which, as in manufactures, is divided between profits and wages that *regulates the price of corn.* The price of corn, then, which does not afford a rent, being influenced by the expenses of its production, those expenses cannot be paid out of rent. The consequence therefore of those expenses increasing, is a higher price, and not a lower rent" * (l.c., [p.] 293).

Since absolute rent is equal to the excess of the value of the AGRICULTURAL product over its price of production, it is clear that all factors which reduce the *total quantity* of labour required in the production OF CORN, etc., reduce the rent, because they reduce the value, hence the excess of the value over the price of production. In so far as the price of production consists of EXPENSES, its fall is identical and goes hand in hand with the fall in value. But in so far as the price of production (or the EXPENSES)=THE CAPITAL ADVANCED+the AVERAGE PROFIT, the very reverse is the case. The market value of the product falls, but that part of it, which=the price of production, rises, if the general rate of profit rises as a result of the fall in the market value of corn. The rent, therefore, falls, because the EXPENSES in this sense rise—and this is how Ricardo takes expenses elsewhere, when he speaks of COST OF PRODUCTION. Improvements in agriculture, which bring about an increase in constant capital as compared with variable, would reduce rent considerably, even if the total quantity of labour employed fell only slightly, or so slightly that it did not influence wages (surplus value, directly) at all. Suppose, as a result of such improvements, the composition of the capital altered from $60c+40v$ to $66^2/_3c+33^1/_3v$ (this might occur, for example, as a result of rising wages, caused by emigration, war, discovery of new markets, PROSPERITY IN THE NON-AGRICULTURAL INDUSTRY, [or it could occur as a result of the] competition of foreign corn, the farmer might feel impelled to find means of employing more constant capital and less variable; the same circumstances could continue to operate after the introduction of the improvement and wages therefore might not fall despite the improvement). [XII-648] Then the value of the AGRICULTURAL PRODUCT would be reduced from 120 to $116^2/_3$, that is by $3^1/_3$. The rate of profit would continue to be 10%.

The rent would fall from 10 to $6^2/_3$ and, moreover, this reduction would have taken place without any reduction whatsoever in wages.

The absolute rent may rise because the general rate of profit falls, owing to new advances in industry. The rate of profit may fall due to a rise in rent, because of an increase in the value of AGRICULTURAL PRODUCE which is accompanied by an increase in the difference between its value and its cost price. (At the same time, the rate of profit falls because wages rise.)

The absolute rent can fall, because the value of AGRICULTURAL PRODUCE falls and the general rate of profit rises. It can fall, because the value of the AGRICULTURAL PRODUCE falls as a result of a fundamental change in the ORGANIC COMPOSITION OF CAPITAL, without the rate of profit rising. It can disappear completely, as soon as the *value of the AGRICULTURAL PRODUCE* becomes=the *cost price*, in other words when the AGRICULTURAL CAPITAL has the same composition as the NON-AGRICULTURAL AVERAGE CAPITAL.

Ricardo's proposition would only be correct if expressed like this: When the value of AGRICULTURAL PRODUCE=its cost price, then there is no absolute rent. But he is wrong because he says: There is no ABSOLUTE RENT *because* value and cost price are altogether identical, both in industry and in agriculture. On the contrary, agriculture would belong to an exceptional class of industry, if its value and cost price were identical.

Even when admitting that there may be no portion of LAND which does not pay a rent, Ricardo believes that by referring to the fact that at least some portion of the capital EMPLOYED on the LAND pays no rent he substantially improves his case. The one FACT is as irrelevant to the theory as the other. The real question is this: Do the products of these lands or of this capital regulate the market value? Or must they not rather sell their products *below* their value, because their ADDITIONAL SUPPLY is only saleable *at,* not *above,* this market value which is regulated without them. So far as the portion of capital is concerned, the matter is simple, because for the FARMER who invests an ADDITIONAL *amount of capital* LANDED PROPERTY *does not exist* and as a capitalist he is only concerned with the cost price; if he possesses the ADDITIONAL capital, it is more advantageous for him to invest it on his FARM, even *below* the AVERAGE PROFIT, than to *lend it out* and to receive only interest and no profit. So far as the land is concerned, those portions of land which do not pay a rent form component parts of estates that pay rent and are not separable from the estates with which they are let; they cannot however be let in isolation from the rest to a

CAPITALIST FARMER (but perhaps to a COTTIER or to a SMALL CAPITALIST). In relation to these bits of land, the FARMER is again not confronted by "LANDED PROPERTY". Alternatively, the PROPRIETOR must cultivate the land himself. The FARMER cannot pay a rent for it and the LANDLORD does not let it *for nothing,* unless he wants to have his land made arable in this fashion without incurring any expense.

The situation would be different in a country in which the COMPOSITION of the AGRICULTURAL CAPITAL = the AVERAGE COMPOSITION of the NON-AGRICULTURAL CAPITAL, which presupposes a high level of development in agriculture or a low level of development in industry. In this case the value of the AGRICULTURAL PRODUCE = its cost price. Only differential rent could be paid then. The land which yields no differential rent but *only* an AGRICULTURAL RENT, could then pay no rent. For if the farmer sells the agricultural produce at its value, it only covers its cost price. *He* therefore pays no rent. The PROPRIETOR must then cultivate the land himself, or the so-called *fermage*[a] collected by him is a part of his tenant's profit or even of his wages. That this might be the case in one country does not mean that the opposite might not happen in another country. Where, however, industry—and therefore capitalist production— is at a low level of development, there are no CAPITALIST FARMERS, whose existence would presuppose capitalist production on the land. Thus, quite different circumstances have to be considered here, from those involved in the economic organisation in which landed property as an economic category exists only in the form of rent.

In the same CH. XVII, Ricardo says:

* "Raw produce is not at a monopoly price, because the market price of barley and wheat is as much regulated by their *cost of production,* as the market price of cloth and linen. The only difference is this, that *one portion of the capital* employed in agriculture regulates the price of corn, namely, that portion which pays no rent; whereas, in the *production of manufactured commodities, every portion of capital is employed with the same results;* and as *no portion pays rent, every portion is equally a regulator of price"* * (l.c., pp. 290-91).

This assertion, THAT EVERY PORTION OF CAPITAL IS EMPLOYED WITH THE SAME RESULTS and that none pays RENT (which is, however, called SURPLUS PROFIT here) is not only wrong, but has been refuted by Ricardo himself [XII-650] [12] as we have seen previously.[b]

We now come to the presentation of Ricardo's theory of surplus value.

---

a Rent.— *Ed.*
b See present edition, Vol. 31, pp. 428, 526-27 and also this volume, p. 13.— *Ed.*

1) Quantity of Labour and Value of Labour

Ricardo opens Cʜ. *I*, "On Value", with the following heading of
Sᴇᴄᴛ. *I*:

* "The value of a commodity, or the quantity of any other commodity for which
it will exchange, depends on the *relative quantity of labour* which is necessary for its
production, and not on the greater or less compensation which is paid for *that
labour*." *

In the style which runs through the whole of his enquiry,
Ricardo begins his book here by stating that the determination of
the value of commodities by labour time is *not* incompatible with
wages, in other words with the varying compensation paid for that
labour time or that quantity of labour. From the very outset, he
turns against Adam Smith's confusion between the determination
of the value of commodities by the ᴘʀᴏᴘᴏʀᴛɪᴏɴᴀʟ ǫᴜᴀɴᴛɪᴛʏ ᴏꜰ ʟᴀʙᴏᴜʀ
ʀᴇǫᴜɪʀᴇᴅ ꜰᴏʀ ᴛʜᴇɪʀ ᴘʀᴏᴅᴜᴄᴛɪᴏɴ ᴀɴᴅ ᴛʜᴇ *ᴠᴀʟᴜᴇ ᴏꜰ ʟᴀʙᴏᴜʀ* (or the compensation paid for ʟᴀʙᴏᴜʀ).

It is clear that the proportional quantity of labour contained in
two commodities A and B, is absolutely unaffected by whether the
workers who produce A and B receive much or little of the
product of their labour. The value of A and B is determined by
the *quantity of labour* which their production costs, and not by the
costs of labour to the ᴏᴡɴᴇʀꜱ of A and B. Quantity of labour and
value of labour are two different things. The quantity of labour
which is contained in A and B respectively, has nothing to do with
how much of the *labour* contained in A and B the owners of A
and B have *paid* or even *performed themselves*. A and B are
exchanged not in proportion to the *paid* labour contained in
them, but in proportion to the total quantity of labour they
contain, paid and unpaid.

* "Adam Smith, who so accurately defined the original source of exchangeable
value and who was bound in consistency to maintain, that all things became more
or less valuable in proportion as more or less labour was bestowed on their
production, has himself erected another standard measure of value, and speaks of
things being more or less valuable, in proportion as they will *exchange for more or less
of this standard measure*... as if *these were two equivalent expressions,* and as if because a
man's labour had become doubly efficient, and he could therefore produce twice
the quantity of a commodity, he would necessarily receive twice the former quantity
in exchange for it" * (that is for his * labour). "If this indeed were true, *if the reward
of the labourer were always in proportion to what he produced, the quantity of labour*
[bestowed on a commodity, and the quantity of labour] *which that commodity would
purchase, would be equal,* and either might accurately measure the variations of other
things: *but they are not equal*" * ([p.] 5).

Adam Smith nowhere asserts ᴛʜᴀᴛ "ᴛʜᴇꜱᴇ ᴡᴇʀᴇ ᴛᴡᴏ ᴇǫᴜɪᴠᴀʟᴇɴᴛ
ᴇxᴘʀᴇꜱꜱɪᴏɴꜱ". On the contrary, he says: Because in capitalist

production, the wage of the worker is *no* longer equal to his product, therefore, the quantity of labour which a commodity costs and the quantity of commodities that the worker can purchase with this labour are two different things—*for this very reason* the relative quantity of labour contained in commodities ceases to determine their value, which is now determined rather by the VALUE OF LABOUR, by the quantity of labour that I can purchase, or command with a given amount of commodities. Thus the VALUE OF LABOUR, instead of the RELATIVE QUANTITY OF LABOUR becomes the measure of value. Ricardo's reply to Adam Smith is correct—that the *relative quantity of labour* which is contained in two commodities is in no way affected by how much of this quantity of labour falls to the workers themselves and by the way this labour is remunerated; if the RELATIVE QUANTITY OF LABOUR was the measure of value of commodities *before* the supervention of wages (wages that differ from the value of the products themselves), there is therefore no reason at all, why it should not continue to be so *after* wages have come into being. He argues correctly, that Adam Smith could use both expressions so long as they were EQUIVALENT, but that this is no reason for using the wrong expression instead of the right one when they have ceased to be EQUIVALENT.

But Ricardo has by no means thereby solved the problem which is the real cause of Adam Smith's contradiction. VALUE OF LABOUR and QUANTITY OF LABOUR remain "EQUIVALENT EXPRESSIONS", so long as it is a question of *objectified labour*! [XII-651] They cease to be equivalents as soon as *objectified labour* is exchanged for *living labour*.

Two *commodities* exchange in proportion to the *labour objectified in them*. Equal quantities of objectified labour are exchanged for one another. Labour time is their STANDARD MEASURE, but precisely for this reason they are "MORE OR LESS VALUABLE, IN PROPORTION AS THEY WILL EXCHANGE FOR MORE OR LESS OF THIS STANDARD MEASURE". If the commodity A contains one working day, then it will exchange against any quantity of commodities which likewise contains one working day and it is "MORE OR LESS VALUABLE" in proportion as it exchanges for more or less objectified labour in other commodities, since this exchange relationship expresses, is identical with, the relative quantity of labour which it itself contains.

Now wage labour, however, is a *commodity*. It is even the basis on which the production of *products* as *commodities* takes place. The *law of value* is not applicable to it. Capitalist production therefore is not governed at all by this law. Therein lies a contradiction. This is the first of Adam Smith's problems. The second—which we shall find further amplified by Malthus[a]—lies in the fact that the *utilisation* of a commodity (as capital) is proportional not to the amount of labour it contains, but to the extent to which it commands the *labour of others,* gives power over *more* labour of others than it itself contains. This is IN FACT a second latent reason for asserting that since the beginning of capitalist production, the value of commodities is determined not by the labour they contain but by the living labour which they command, in other words, by the *value of labour.*

Ricardo simply answers that this is how matters are in capitalist production. Not only does he fail to solve the problem; he does not even realise its existence in Adam Smith's work. In conformity with the whole arrangement of his investigation, Ricardo is satisfied with demonstrating that the changing value of labour—in short, wages—does not *invalidate* the determination of the value of the *commodities,* which are distinct from labour itself, by the relative quantity of labour contained in them. "*THEY ARE NOT EQUAL*", that is "THE QUANTITY OF LABOUR BESTOWED ON A COMMODITY, AND THE QUANTITY OF LABOUR WHICH THAT COMMODITY WOULD PURCHASE". He contents himself with stating this fact. But how does the commodity labour differ from other commodities? One is *living labour* and the other *objectified* labour. They are, therefore, only two different forms of labour. Since the difference is only a matter of form, why should a law apply to one and not to the other? Ricardo does not answer—he does not even raise this question.

Nor does it help when he says:

* "Is not the value of labour ... variable; being not only affected, as all other things" * (should read *commodities) "are, by the proportion between the supply and demand, which uniformly varies with every change in the condition of the community, but also by the varying price of food and other necessaries, on which the *wages of labour* are expended?" * ([p.] 7).

That the PRICE OF LABOUR, like that of other commodities, changes with DEMAND and SUPPLY proves nothing in regard to the *VALUE OF LABOUR,* according to Ricardo, just as this change of price with SUPPLY and DEMAND proves nothing in regard to the VALUE OF OTHER COMMODITIES. But that the "WAGES OF LABOUR"—which is only another expression for the VALUE OF LABOUR—are affected by "THE VARYING PRICE OF FOOD AND OTHER NECESSARIES, ON WHICH THE WAGES OF LABOUR ARE EXPENDED", shows just as little why the VALUE OF LABOUR is (or appears to be) determined differently from the VALUE of other COMMODITIES. For

---

[a] See this volume, pp. 210-11.—*Ed.*

these too are affected by the VARYING PRICE OF OTHER COMMODITIES WHICH ENTER INTO THEIR PRODUCTION, AGAINST WHICH THEY ARE EXCHANGED. And after all, the EXPENDITURE OF THE WAGES OF LABOUR UPON FOOD AND NECESSARIES means nothing other than the EXCHANGE of the VALUE OF LABOUR AGAINST FOOD AND NECESSARIES. The question is just why LABOUR and the *commodities against which it is exchanged,* do not exchange according to the law of value, according to the relative quantities of labour.

Posed in this way, and *presupposing* the *law of value,* the question is intrinsically insoluble, because LABOUR as such is counterposed to *commodity,* a definite quantity of immediate labour as such is counterposed to a definite quantity of objectified labour.

This weakness in Ricardo's discourse, as we shall see later,[a] has contributed to the disintegration of his school, and led to the proposition of absurd hypotheses.

[XII-652] *Wakefield* is right when he says:

* "Treating *labour* as a *commodity,* and *capital,* the produce of labour, as another, then, if the *value of these two commodities were regulated by equal quantities of labour,* a given amount of labour would, under all circumstances, exchange for that quantity of capital which had been produced by the same amount of labour; *antecedent labour* [...] *would always exchange for the same amount of present labour* [...] But the value of labour, in relation to other commodities, in so far, at least, as wages depend upon share, is determined, *not by equal quantities of labour,* but by the proportion between supply and demand" * (E. G. Wakefield, Note on p. [230], 231 of Vol. I of his edition of Adam Smith's *Wealth of Nations,* London, 1835.[13])

This is also one of Bailey's hobby-horses; to be looked up later.[b] Also *Say,* who is very pleased to find that here, all of a sudden, SUPPLY AND DEMAND are said to be the decisive factors.[c]

2) Value of Labour Capacity. VALUE OF LABOUR

In order to determine surplus value, Ricardo, like the Physiocrats, Adam Smith, etc., must first determine the *value of labour capacity* or, as he puts it—following Adam Smith and his predecessors—THE VALUE OF LABOUR.

Re 1. Another point to be noted here: CH. I, SECT. 3, bears the following heading:

* "Not only *the labour applied immediately* to commodities affects their value, but the *labour also* which *is bestowed* on the implements, tools, and buildings, with which such labour is assisted" * [Ricardo, *On the Principles of Political Economy...,* 3rd ed., London, 1821, p. 16].

---

a See this volume, pp. 258 et seq.— *Ed.*
b Ibid., pp. 334-39.— *Ed.*
c Cf. ibid., p. 36.— *Ed.*

Thus the value of a commodity is equally determined by the quantity of *objectified* (*past*) labour and by the quantity of *living* (*immediate*) labour required for its production. In other words: the quantities of labour are in no way affected by the *formal difference* of whether the labour is objectified or living, past or present (immediate). If this difference is of no significance in the determination of the value of commodities, why does it assume such decisive importance when past labour (capital) is exchanged against living labour? Why should it, in this case, invalidate the law of value, since the difference *in itself,* as shown in the case of commodities, has no effect on the determination of value? Ricardo does not answer this question, he does not even raise it.

How then is the *value* or NATURAL PRICE of labour determined? According to *Ricardo,* the NATURAL PRICE is in fact nothing but the MONETARY EXPRESSION OF VALUE.

* "*Labour,* like all other things which are purchased and sold, and which may be increased or diminished [in quantity]" * (i.e. like all other commodities) * "has its natural and its market price. *The natural price of labour* is that price which is necessary to enable the labourers, one with another, to subsist and perpetuate their race, without either increase or diminution." * (Should read: *with that rate of increase required by the average progress of production.) "The power of the labourer to support himself, and the family which may be necessary to keep up the number of labourers, ... depends on *the price of the food, necessaries, and conveniences, required for the support of the labourer and his family.* With a rise in the price of food and necessaries, the natural price of labour will rise; with the fall in their price, the natural price of labour will fall" ([p.] 86).

"It is not to be understood that the natural price of labour, estimated even in food and necessaries, is absolutely fixed and constant. It varies at different times in the same country, and very materially differs in different countries. It essentially depends on the habits and customs of the people" * ([p.] 91).

The VALUE OF LABOUR is therefore determined by the *means of subsistence* which, in a given society, are traditionally *necessary* for the maintenance and reproduction of the labourers.

But why? By what law is the VALUE OF LABOUR determined in this way?

Ricardo has in fact no answer, other than that the law OF SUPPLY AND DEMAND reduced the average price of labour to the means of subsistence that are necessary (physically or socially necessary in a given society) for the maintenance of the labourer. [XII-653] He determines *value* here, in one of the basic propositions of the whole system, by *demand and supply*—as Say notes with malicious pleasure. (See Constancio's translation.[14])

Instead of *labour,* Ricardo should have discussed labour *capacity.* But had he done so, *capital* would also have been revealed as the material conditions of labour, confronting the labourer as power that had acquired an independent existence. And capital would at once have been revealed as a *definite social relationship*. Ricardo thus only distinguishes capital as "ACCUMULATED LABOUR" from "IMMEDIATE LABOUR". And it is something purely physical, only an element in the *labour process*, from which the relation between the worker and capital, WAGES AND PROFITS, could never be developed.

* "*Capital* is that part of the wealth of a country which is employed in production, and consists of food, clothing, tools, raw materials, machinery, etc., necessary to give effect to labour" ([p.] 89). "*Less capital*, which is the same thing as *less labour*" ([p.] 73). "Labour and *capital*, that is, *accumulated labour*" * (l.c., p. 499).

The jump which Ricardo makes here is correctly sensed by *Bailey*:

* "Mr. Ricardo, ingeniously enough, avoids a difficulty, which, on a first view, threatens to encumber his doctrine, that value depends on the quantity of labour employed in production. If this principle is rigidly adhered to, it follows, that the *value of labour* depends *on the quantity of labour employed in producing it*—which is evidently absurd. By a dexterous turn, therefore, Mr. Ricardo makes the value of labour depend on the quantity of labour required to produce wages, or, to give him the benefit of his own language, he maintains, that *the value of labour is to be estimated* by the quantity of labour required to produce wages; by which he means, the quantity of labour required to produce the money or commodities given to the labourer. This is similar to saying, that the value of cloth is to be estimated, not by the quantity of labour bestowed upon its production, but by the quantity of labour bestowed on the production of silver, for which the cloth is exchanged" * (*A Critical Dissertation on the Nature, Measures, and Causes of Value etc.*, London, 1825, [pp.] 50-51).

Literally the objection raised here is correct. Ricardo distinguishes between NOMINAL and REAL WAGES. NOMINAL WAGES are wages expressed in money, MONEY WAGES.

"NOMINAL WAGES" are "THE NUMBER OF POUNDS THAT MAY BE ANNUALLY PAID TO THE LABOURER", but REAL WAGES are "THE NUMBER OF DAY'S WORK,[a] NECESSARY TO OBTAIN THOSE POUNDS" (Ricardo, l.c. [p.] 152).

As WAGES=the NECESSARIES for the LABOURER, and the value of these WAGES (the REAL WAGES)=the value of these NECESSARIES, it is obvious that the value of these NECESSARIES=the REAL WAGES,=the labour which they can command. If the value of the NECESSARIES changes, then the value of the REAL WAGES changes. Assume that the NECESSARIES of the labourer consist only of corn, and that the quantity of means of subsistence which he requires is 1 qr of corn per month. Then the value of his wages=the value of 1 qr of corn; if the value of the qr

---

a In the manuscript these words are followed by the German equivalent in brackets.— *Ed.*

of corn rises or falls, then the value of the month's labour rises or falls. But however much the value of the qr of corn rises or falls (however much or little labour the qr of corn contains), it is always=to the value of one month's labour. And here we have the *hidden reason* for Adam Smith's assertion, that as soon as capital, and consequently wage labour, intervenes, the value of the product is not regulated by the QUANTITY OF LABOUR BESTOWED UPON it, BUT by THE QUANTITY OF LABOUR IT CAN COMMAND. The value of corn (AND OF OTHER NECESSARIES) determined by labour time, changes; but, so long as the NATURAL PRICE OF LABOUR is paid, the quantity of labour that the qr of corn can command remains the same. Labour has, therefore, a *permanent relative value as compared with corn.* That is why for Smith too, the VALUE OF LABOUR and the VALUE OF CORN (FOR *FOOD.* See Deacon *Hume*[15]) [are] STANDARD MEASURES OF VALUE, BECAUSE A CERTAIN QUANTITY OF CORN SO LONG AS THE NATURAL PRICE OF LABOUR IS PAID, COMMANDS A CERTAIN QUANTITY OF LABOUR, WHATEVER THE QUANTITY OF LABOUR BESTOWED UPON ONE QR OF CORN. The same quantity of labour always commands the same *use value,* or rather the same use value always commands *the same quantity of labour.* Even Ricardo determines the VALUE OF LABOUR, ITS NATURAL PRICE, in this way. Ricardo says: The qr of CORN may have very different values, although it always commands—or is commanded by—the same [XII-654] quantity of labour. Yes, says Adam Smith: However much the value of the qr of corn, determined by labour time, may change, the worker must always pay (sacrifice) the same quantity of labour in order to buy it. The value of corn therefore alters, but the value of labour does not, since 1 month's labour =1 qr of corn. The value of corn too changes only in so far as we are considering the labour required for its production. If, on the other hand, we examine the quantity of labour against which it exchanges, which it sets into motion, its value does not change. And that is precisely why the QUANTITY OF LABOUR, AGAINST WHICH A QR OF CORN IS EXCHANGED, [is] THE *STANDARD MEASURE OF VALUE.* But the values of the other commodities have the same relation to labour as they have to corn. A given quantity of corn commands * a given quantity of labour. A given quantity of every other commodity commands a certain quantity of corn. Hence every other commodity—or rather the value of every other commodity—is expressed by the quantity of labour it commands, since it is expressed by the quantity of corn it commands, and the latter is expressed by the quantity of labour it commands.*

But how is the value of other commodities in relation to corn (NECESSARIES) determined? By the QUANTITY OF LABOUR THEY COMMAND. And how is the QUANTITY OF LABOUR THEY COMMAND determined? By the

QUANTITY OF CORN THAT LABOUR COMMANDS. Here Adam Smith is inevitably caught up in a *cercle vicieux*.[a] (Although, BY THE BY, he *never* uses this MEASURE OF VALUE when making an actual analysis.) Moreover here he confuses—as Ricardo also often does—labour, the *intrinsic* measure of value, with *money, the external measure,* which presupposes that value is already determined; although he and Ricardo have declared that labour is

"THE FOUNDATION OF THE VALUE OF COMMODITIES" while "THE COMPARATIVE QUANTITY OF LABOUR WHICH IS NECESSARY TO THEIR PRODUCTION" is "THE RULE WHICH DETERMINES THE RESPECTIVE QUANTITIES OF GOODS WHICH SHALL BE GIVEN IN EXCHANGE FOR EACH OTHER" (Ricardo, l.c., p. 80).

Adam Smith errs when he concludes from the fact that a definite quantity of labour is EXCHANGEABLE for a definite quantity of use value, that this *definite quantity of labour* is the measure of value and that it always has *the same value,* whereas the same quantity of use value can represent very different exchange values. But Ricardo errs twice over; firstly because he does not understand the problem which causes Adam Smith's errors; secondly because disregarding the law of value of commodities and taking refuge in the LAW OF SUPPLY AND DEMAND, he himself determines the *value of labour,* not by the quantity of labour BESTOWED UPON THE FORCE OF LABOUR, BUT UPON THE WAGES ALLOTTED TO THE LABOURER. Thus IN FACT he says: The value of labour is determined by the value of the money which is paid for it! And what determines this? What determines the amount of money that is paid for it? The quantity of use value that a given amount of labour commands or the quantity of labour that a definite quantity of use value commands. And thereby he falls *literally* into the very inconsistency which he himself condemned in Smith.

This, as we have seen, also prevents him from grasping the specific distinction between *commodity* and *capital,* between the exchange of commodity for commodity and the exchange of capital for commodity—in accordance with the law of exchange of commodities.

The above example was this: 1 qr of corn=1 month's labour, say 30 working days. (A working day of 12 hours.) In this case the value of 1 qr corn < 30 working days. IF 1 qr corn were the product of 30 working days, the value of the labour=its product. There would be no surplus value, and therefore no profit. No capital. In actual fact, therefore, if 1 qr corn represents the wages for 30 working days, the value of 1 qr corn always < 30 working days.

---

[a] Vicious circle.— *Ed.*

The surplus value depends on how much less it is. For example, 1 qr corn=25 working days. Then the surplus value=5 working days=$\frac{1}{6}$ of the total labour time. If 1 qr (8 BUSHELS)=25 working days, then 30 working days=1 qr 1 $\frac{3}{5}$ BUSHELS. The *value* of the 30 working days (i.e. the wage) is therefore always smaller than the value of the product which contains the labour of 30 working days. The value of the corn is thus determined not by the [XII-655] labour which it commands, for which it exchanges, but by the labour which is contained in it. On the other hand, the *value of the 30 days' labour* is always determined by 1 qr corn, whatever this may be.

3) Surplus Value

Apart from the confusion between LABOUR and labour capacity, Ricardo defines the AVERAGE WAGES or the VALUE OF LABOUR correctly. For he says that it is determined neither by the money nor by the means of subsistence which the labourer receives, but by the *labour time which it costs to produce them*, that is, by the *quantity of labour objectified* in the means of subsistence of the labourer. This he calls the REAL WAGES. (See later.[a])

This definition, moreover, necessarily follows from his theory. Since the VALUE OF LABOUR is determined by the *value of the necessary means of subsistence* on which this VALUE IS TO BE EXPENDED, and the VALUE OF NECESSARIES, LIKE THAT OF ALL OTHER COMMODITIES, IS DETERMINED BY THE QUANTITY OF LABOUR BESTOWED UPON THEM, it naturally follows THAT THE VALUE OF LABOUR=THE VALUE OF NECESSARIES= THE QUANTITY OF LABOUR BESTOWED UPON THESE NECESSARIES.

However correct this formula is (apart from the direct opposition of LABOUR and CAPITAL), it is, nevertheless, inadequate. Although in replacement of his WAGES the individual labourer does not directly *produce—or reproduce*, taking into account the continuity of this process—products on which he lives //he may produce products which do not enter into his consumption at all, and even if he produces NECESSARIES, he may, due to the division of labour, only produce A SINGLE PART OF the NECESSARIES, for instance CORN—and GIVES IT ONLY ONE FORM (e.g. in that OF CORN, NOT OF BREAD)//, but he *produces* commodities to the *value* of his means of subsistence, that is, he produces the *value* of his means of subsistence. This means, therefore, if we consider his daily average consumption, that the labour time which is contained in his daily NECESSARIES, forms one

---

part of h i s *working day*. He works one part of the day in order to reproduce the *value* of his NECESSARIES; the commodities which he produces in this part of the working day have the same value, or represent a *quantity* of labour time equal to that contained in his daily NECESSARIES. *It depends on the value of these* NECESSARIES (in other words on the social productivity of labour and not on the productivity of the individual branch of production in which he works) *how great a part of his working day* is devoted to the reproduction or production of the *value,* i.e. the equivalent, of his means of subsistence. Ricardo of course assumes that the labour time contained in the daily NECESSARIES=the labour time which the labourer must work daily in order to reproduce the value of these NECESSARIES. But by not *directly* showing that one *part* of the labourer's *working day* is assigned to the reproduction of the value of his own labour capacity, he introduces a difficulty and obscures the clear understanding of the relationship. A twofold confusion arises from this. The *origin of surplus value* does not become clear and consequently Ricardo is reproached by his successors for having failed to grasp and expound the nature of surplus value. That is part of the reason for their scholastic attempts at explaining it. But because thus the origin and nature of surplus value is not clearly comprehended, the surplus labour+the necessary labour, in short, the *total working day,* is regarded as a fixed magnitude, the differences in the amount of surplus value are overlooked, and the productivity of capital, the *compulsion to perform surplus labour*—on the one hand [capital's enforcement of] absolute [surplus value], and on the other its innate urge to shorten the necessary labour time—are not recognised, and therefore the *historical* justification for capital is not set forth. Adam Smith, however, had already stated the correct formula. Important as it was, to resolve VALUE into LABOUR, it was equally important to resolve SURPLUS VALUE into SURPLUS LABOUR, and to do so in explicit terms.

Ricardo starts out from the actual fact of capitalist production. The value of labour < the value of the product which it creates. The value of the product therefore > the value of the labour which produces it, or the value of the WAGES. The excess of the value of the product *over* the value of the WAGES=the surplus value. (Ricardo wrongly uses the word *profit,* but, as we noted earlier, he identifies profit with surplus value here and is really speaking of the latter.) For him it is a fact, that the value of the product > the value of the WAGES. How this fact arises, remains unclear. The total working day *is* greater than that part of the working day which is required for the production of the WAGES. Why? That does not emerge. The *magnitude of the total working day* is therefore wrongly assumed to be *fixed*, and directly entails wrong conclusions. The increase or decrease in surplus value can therefore be explained *only* from the growing or diminishing productivity of social labour which produces the NECESSARIES. That is to say, only relative surplus value is understood.

[XII-656] It is obvious that if the labourer needed his whole day to produce his own means of subsistence (i.e. commodities equal to the value of his own means of subsistence), there could be no surplus value, and therefore no capitalist production and no wage labour. This can only exist when the productivity of social labour is sufficiently developed to make possible some sort of excess of the total working day over the labour time required for the reproduction of the WAGES—i.e. *surplus labour*, whatever its magnitude. But it is equally obvious, that with a given labour time ([a given] length of the working day) the productivity of labour may be very different, on the other hand, with a given productivity of labour, the labour time, the length of the working day, may be very different. Furthermore, it is clear that though the existence of *surplus labour* presupposes that the productivity of labour has reached a certain level, the mere *possibility* of this surplus labour (i.e. the existence of that necessary minimum productivity of labour), does not in itself make it a *reality*. For this to occur, the labourer must first be *compelled* to work beyond the limits [of necessary labour], and this compulsion is exerted by capital. This is missing in Ricardo's work, and therefore also the whole struggle over the regulation of the normal working day.

At a low stage of development of the social productive power of labour, that is to say, where the surplus labour is relatively small, the class of those who live on the labour of others will generally be small in relation to the number of labourers. It can considerably grow (proportionately) in the measure in which productivity and therefore relative surplus value develop.

It is moreover UNDERSTOOD that the *value of labour* varies greatly in the same country at different periods and in different countries during the same period. The temperate zones are however the home of capitalist production. The *social* productive power of labour may be very undeveloped; yet this may be compensated precisely in the production of the NECESSARIES, on the one hand, by the fertility of the natural agents, such as the land; on the other hand, by the limited requirements of the population, due to climate, etc.—this is, for instance, the case in India. Where conditions are primitive, the minimum wage may be very small (quantitatively in use values) because the social needs are not yet developed though it may cost much labour. But even if an average amount of labour were required to produce this minimum wage, the surplus value created, although it would be high in proportion to the wage (to the necessary labour time), would, even with a high rate of surplus value, be just as meagre (proportionately)—when expressed in terms of use values—as the wage itself.

Let the necessary labour time=10, the surplus labour=2, and the total working day=12 hours. If the necessary labour time=12, the surplus labour=$2^2/_5$ and the total working day=$14^2/_5$ hours, then the values produced would be very different. In the first case [they]=12 hours, in the second=$14^2/_5$ hours. Similarly, the absolute magnitude of the surplus value: In the former case [it]=2 hours, in the latter=$2^2/_5$. And yet the *rate of surplus value* or of *surplus labour* would be the same, because $2:10=2^2/_5:12$. If, in the second case, the variable capital which is laid out were greater, then so also would be the surplus value or surplus labour appropriated by it. If in the latter case, the surplus labour were to rise by $^5/_5$ hours instead of by $^2/_5$ hours, so that it=3 hours and the total working day=15 hours, then, although the *necessary labour time* or the minimum wage had increased, the *rate of surplus value* would have risen, for $2:10=^1/_5$; but $3:12=^1/_4$. Both could occur if, as a result of the corn, etc., becoming dearer, the minimum wage had increased from 10 to 12 hours. Even in this case, therefore, not only might the rate of surplus value remain the same, but the AMOUNT and RATE of surplus value might grow. But let us suppose that the necessary wage=10 hours, as previously, the surplus labour=2 hours and all other conditions remained the same (that is, leaving out of account here any lowering in the production costs of constant capital). Now let the labourer work $2^2/_5$ hours longer, and appropriate 2 hours, while the $^2/_5$ forms surplus labour. In this case wages and surplus value would increase in equal proportion, the former, however, representing more than the necessary wage or the necessary labour time.

If one takes a *given* magnitude and divides it into two parts, it is clear that one part can only increase in so far as the other decreases, and vice versa. But this is by no means the case with growing magnitudes (fluxions [16]). And the working day represents such a growing magnitude (as long as no normal working day has been won). With such magnitudes, both parts can grow, either to an equal or unequal extent. An increase in one is not brought about by a decrease in the other and vice versa. This is moreover the only case in which wages and surplus value, in terms of *exchange value*, can both *increase* and possibly even in *equal proportions*. That they can increase in terms of use value is self-evident; this can increase [XII-657] even if, for example, the value of LABOUR decreases. From 1797 to 1815, when the price of corn and [also] the nominal wage rose considerably in England, the daily hours of labour increased greatly in the principal industries, which were then in a phase of ruthless expansion; and I believe that this arrested the fall in the rate of profit, because it arrested the fall in the rate of surplus value. In this case, however, whatever the circumstances, the normal working day is lengthened and the normal span of life of the labourer, hence the normal duration of his labour capacity, is correspondingly shortened. This applies where a constant lengthening [of the working day] occurs. If it is only temporary, in order to compensate for a temporary rise in wages, it may (except in the case of children and women) have no other result than to prevent a fall in the rate of profit in those enterprises where the nature of the work makes a prolongation of labour time possible. (This is least possible in agriculture.)

Ricardo did not consider this at all since he investigated neither the origin of surplus value nor absolute surplus value and therefore regarded the working day as a given magnitude. For this case, therefore, *his law*—that surplus value and wages (he erroneously says profit and wages) in terms of exchange value can rise or fall only in *inverse* proportion— *is incorrect.*

Firstly let us assume that the necessary labour time and the surplus labour remain constant. That is 10+2; the working day=12 hours, surplus value=2 hours; the rate of surplus value=$^1/_5$.

The necessary labour time remains the same; surplus labour increases from 2 to 4 hours. Hence 10+4=a working day of 14 hours; surplus value=4 hours; rate of surplus value=4:10=$^4/_{10}=^2/_5$.

In both cases the necessary labour time is the same; but the surplus value in the one case is twice as great as in the other and the working day in the second case is $^1/_6$ longer than in the first. Furthermore, although the wage is the same, the values produced, corresponding to the quantities of labour, would be very different; in the first case [it]=12 hours, in the second=12+$^{12}/_6$=14. It is therefore wrong to say that, presupposing that the *wage remains the same* (in terms of value, of necessary labour time), the surplus value contained in two commodities is proportionate to the quantities of labour contained in them. This is only correct where the *normal working day* is the same.

Let us further assume that as a result of the rise in the productive power of labour, the necessary wage (although it remains CONSTANT in terms of EXPENDED use values) falls from 10 to 9 hours and similarly that the surplus labour time falls from 2 to $1\,^4/_5$ hours $(^9/_5)$. In this case $10:9=2:1\,^4/_5$. Thus the surplus labour time would fall in the same proportion as the necessary labour time. The rate of surplus value would be the same in both cases, for $2=^{10}/_5$ and $1\,^4/_5=^9/_5$. $1\,^4/_5:9=2:10$. The quantity of use values that could be bought with the surplus value, would—according to the assumption—also remain the same. (But this would apply only to those use values which are NECESSARIES.) The working day would decrease from 12 to $10\,^4/_5$. The amount of value produced in the second case would be smaller than that produced in the first. And despite these unequal quantities of labour, the rate of surplus value would be the same in both cases.

In discussing surplus value we have distinguished between surplus value and the rate of surplus value. Considered in relation to one working day, the surplus value=the absolute number of hours which it represents, 2, 3, etc. The rate=the proportion of this number of hours to the number of hours which makes up the necessary labour time. This distinction is very important, because it indicates the varying length of the working day. If the surplus value=2, then [the rate]=$^1/_5$, if the necessary labour time=10; and $^1/_6$, if the necessary labour time=12. In the first case the working day=12 hours and in the second=14. In the first case the rate of surplus value is greater, while at the same time the labourer works a smaller number of hours per day. In the second case the rate of surplus value is smaller, the value of the labour capacity is greater, while at the same time the labourer works a greater number of hours per day. This shows that, with a constant surplus value (but a working day of unequal length), the rate of surplus value may be different. The earlier case, 10:2 and $9:1\,^4/_5$, shows how with a constant rate of surplus value (but a working day of unequal length), the surplus value itself may be different (in one case 2[hours] and in the other $1\,^4/_5$).

I have shown previously (CH. II), that if the length of the working day and also the necessary labour time, and therefore the rate of surplus value are given, the amount of surplus value depends on the *number* of workers simultaneously employed by the same capital.[a] This was a tautological statement. For if

---

1 working day gives me 2 surplus hours, then 12 working days give me 24 surplus hours or 2 surplus days. The statement, however, becomes very important in connection with the determination of profit, which is equal to the proportion of surplus value to the capital advanced, thus depending on the absolute amount of surplus value. It becomes important because capitals of equal size but different organic composition employ unequal numbers of labourers; they must thus produce unequal amounts of surplus value, and therefore unequal profits. With a falling rate of surplus value, the profit may rise and with a rising rate of surplus value, the profit may fall; or the profit may remain unchanged, if a rise or fall in the rate of surplus value is compensated by a counter movement affecting the number of workers employed. Here we see immediately, how extremely wrong it is [XII-658] to identify the laws relating to the rise and fall of surplus value with the laws relating to the rise and fall of profit. If one merely considers the simple law of surplus value, then it seems a tautology to say that with a given rate of surplus value (and a given length of the working day), the ABSOLUTE AMOUNT of surplus value depends on the amount of capital employed. For an increase in this amount of capital and an increase in the number of labourers simultaneously employed are, on the assumption made, identical, or merely [different] expressions of the same fact. But when one turns to an examination of profit, where the amount of the total capital employed and the number of workers employed vary greatly for capitals of equal size, then the importance of the law becomes clear.

Ricardo starts by considering *commodities* of a given value, that is to say, commodities which represent a *given* quantity of labour. And from this starting-point, absolute and relative surplus value appear to be always identical. (This at any rate explains the one-sidedness of his mode of procedure and corresponds with his whole method of investigation: to start with the *value* of the commodities as determined by the definite labour time they contain, and then to examine to what extent this is affected by wages, profits, etc.) This appearance is nevertheless false, since it is not a question of commodities here, but of capitalist production, of commodities as products of capital. Assume that a capital employs a certain number of workers, for example 20, and that wages=£20. To simplify matters let us assume that the fixed capital=0, i.e. we leave it out of account. Further, assume that these 20 workers spin £80 of cotton into yarn, if they work 12 hours per day. If 1 lb. of cotton costs 1 s. then 20 lbs cost £1 and

£80=1,600 lbs. If 20 workers spin 1,600 lbs in 12 hours, then [they spin] $^{1,600}/_{12}$ lbs=133 $^1/_3$ lbs in 1 hour. Thus, if the necessary labour time=10 hours, then the surplus labour time=2 [hours] and this=266 $^2/_3$ lbs yarn. The value of the 1,600 lbs would=£104. For if 10 hours of work=£20, then 1 hour of work=£2 and 2 hours of work=£4, hence 12=24. (80+24=£104.) But if each of the workers worked 4 hours of surplus labour, then their product=£8 (I mean the surplus value which they create—their product IN FACT=£28 [17]). The total product=£121 $^1/_3$.[18] And this £121 $^1/_3$=1,866 $^2/_3$ lbs of yarn. As before, since the conditions of production remained the same, 1 lb. of yarn would have the same value; it would contain the same amount of labour time. Moreover, according to the assumption, the necessary wages— their value, the labour time they contained—would have remained CONSTANT.

Whether these 1,866 $^2/_3$ lbs of yarn were being produced under the first set of conditions or under the second, i.e. with 2 or with 4 hours surplus labour, they would have the same value in both cases. The value therefore of the additional 266 $^2/_3$ lbs of cotton that are spun, is £13 6 $^2/_3$s. This, added to the £80 for the 1,600 lbs, amounts to £93 6 $^2/_3$s. and in both cases 4 working hours more for 20 men=£8. Altogether £28 for the labour, that is £121 6 $^2/_3$s. The wages are, in both cases, the same. The lb. of yarn costs in both cases 1 $^3/_{10}$s. Since the value of the lb. of cotton=1s., what remained for the newly added labour in 1 lb. of yarn would in both cases amount to $^3/_{10}$s.=3 $^3/_5$d. (or $^{18}/_5$d.). Nevertheless, under the conditions assumed, the relation between value and surplus value in each lb. of yarn would be very different. In the first case, since the necessary labour=£20 and the surplus labour=£4, or since the former=10 hours and the latter=2 hours, the ratio of surplus labour to necessary labour=2:10=$^2/_{10}$=$^1/_5$. (Similarly £4:£20=$^4/_{20}$=$^1/_5$.) The 3 $^3/_5$d. in a lb. of yarn would in this case contain $^1/_5$ unpaid labour=$^{18}/_{25}$d. or $^{72}/_{25}$f.=2 $^{22}/_{25}$f. In the second case, on the other hand, the necessary labour=£20 (10 working hours), the surplus labour=£8 (4 working hours). The ratio of surplus labour to necessary labour= =8:20=$^8/_{20}$=$^4/_{10}$=$^2/_5$. Thus the 3 $^3/_5$d. in a lb. of yarn would contain $^2/_5$ unpaid labour, i.e. 5 $^{19}/_{25}$f. or 1d. 1 $^{19}/_{25}$f. [XII-659] Although the yarn has the same value in both cases and although the same wages are paid in both cases, the surplus value in a 1lb. of yarn is in one case twice as large as in the other. The ratio of value of labour to surplus value is of course the same in the individual commodity, that is, in a portion of the product, as in the whole product. In the one case, the capital advanced=£93 $6^2/_3$s. for cotton, and how much for wages? The wages for 1,600 lbs=£20 here, hence for the additional $266^2/_3$ lbs=£$3^1/_3$. This makes £$23^1/_3$. And the total capital outlay is £93 $6^2/_3$s.+£$23^1/_3$=£116 $13^1/_3$s. The product=£121 $6^2/_3$s. (The additional outlay in [variable] capital, of £$3^1/_3$, only yields $13^1/_3$s. surplus value. £20:£4=£$3^1/_3$:£$^2/_3$=$13^1/_3$s. (£$^1/_5$=4s.)

In the other case, however, the capital outlay would amount to only £93 $6^2/_3$[s.]+£20=[£]113 $6^2/_3$[s.] and £4 would have to be added to the £4 surplus value. The same number of lbs of yarn are produced in both cases and both have the same value, that is to say, they represent equal total quantities of labour, but these equal total quantities of labour are set in motion by capitals of unequal size, although the wages are the same; but the working days are of unequal length and, *therefore*, unequal quantities of unpaid labour are produced. Taking the individual lb. of yarn, the wages paid for it, or the amounts of *paid* labour a pound contains, are different. The same wages are spread over a larger volume of commodities here, not because labour is more productive in the one case than in the other, but because the total amount of unpaid surplus labour which is set into motion in the one case is greater than in the other. With the *same* quantity of *paid* labour, therefore, more lbs of yarn are produced in the one case than in the other, although in both cases the same quantities of yarn are produced, representing the same quantity of total labour (paid and unpaid). If, on the other hand, the productivity of labour had increased in the second case, then the value of the lb. of yarn would at all events have fallen (whatever the ratio of surplus value to variable capital).

In such a case, therefore, it would be wrong to say that— because the *value* of the lb. of yarn=1s. $3^3/_5$d., the value of the labour which is added is also fixed and=$3^3/_5$d., and the wages, i.e. the *necessary labour time*, remain, according to the assumption, *unchanged*—the surplus value [must] be the same and the 2 capitals under otherwise equal conditions would have produced the yarn with equal profits. This would be correct if we were concerned with 1 lb. of yarn, but we are in fact concerned here with a capital which has produced $1,866^2/_3$ lbs yarn. And in order to know the amount of profit (actually of surplus value) on one lb., we must know the length of the working day, or the quantity of unpaid labour (when the productivity is given) that the capital sets in motion. But this information cannot be gathered by looking at the individual commodity.

Thus Ricardo deals only with what I have called the *relative surplus value*. From the outset he assumes, as Adam Smith and his predecessors seem to have done as well, that the *length of the working day is given*. (At most, Adam Smith mentions differences in the length of the working day in *different* branches of labour, which are levelled out or compensated by the relatively greater intensity of labour, difficulty, unpleasantness, etc.) On the basis of this postulate Ricardo, on the whole, explains relative surplus value correctly. Before we give the principal points of his theory, we shall cite a few more passages to illustrate Ricardo's point of view.

* "The labour of a million of men in manufactures, will allways produce the *same value*, but will not always produce the same riches" * (l.c., [p.] 320).

This means that the product of their daily labour will always be the product of 1 million working days containing *the same* labour time; this is wrong, or is only true where *the same* normal working day—taking into account the DIFFERENT DIFFICULTIES etc. OF DIFFERENT BRANCHES OF LABOUR—has been generally established.

Even then, however, the statement is wrong in the general form in which it is expressed here. If the normal working day is 12 hours, and the annual product of one man is, in terms of money, £50 and the value of money remains unchanged, then, in this case, the product of 1 million men would always=£50 million per year. If the necessary labour=6 hours, then the capital laid out for these million men=£25,000,000 per annum. The surplus value also=£25 million. The product would always be 50 million, whether the workers received 25 or 30 or 40 million. But in the first case the surplus value=25 million, in the second=20 million and in the third=10 million. If the capital advanced consisted only of *variable* capital, i.e. only of the capital which is laid out in the *wages* of these 1 million men, then Ricardo would be right. He is, therefore, only right in the *one* case, where the total capital=the variable capital; a presupposition which pervades all his, and Adam Smith's, [XII-660] observations regarding the capital of society as a whole, but in capitalist production this precondition does not exist in a single TRADE, much less in the production of society as a whole.

That *part of the constant capital* which enters into the labour process without entering into the valorisation process, does not enter into the product (into the *value of the product*), and, therefore, important as it is in the determination of the general rate of profit, it does not concern us here, where we are considering the *value* of the *annual product*. But matters are quite different with that part of constant capital which enters into the annual product. We have seen that a portion of this part of constant capital, or what appears as constant capital in one sphere of production, appears as a direct product of labour within another sphere of production, during *the same* production period of one year; a large part of the capital laid out annually, which *appears* to be constant capital from the standpoint of the individual capitalist or the particular sphere of production, therefore, resolves itself into *variable* capital from the standpoint of society or of the capitalist class. This part is thus included in the 50 million, in that part of the 50 million which forms variable capital or is laid out in wages. But the position is different with that *part of the constant capital* which is used up in order to replace the constant capital consumed in industry and agriculture—with the consumed part of the constant capital employed *in* those branches of production which produce constant capital, raw material in its primary form, fixed capital and *matières instrumentales.*[a] The value of this part reappears, it is reproduced in the product. In what proportion [it] enters into the value of the whole product depends entirely on its actual magnitude—provided the productivity of labour does not change; but however the productivity may change, the value of this part will always have a *definite* magnitude. (On the average, apart from certain exceptions in agriculture, the amount of the product, i.e. the *wealth*—which Ricardo distinguishes from the VALUE—produced by 1 million men will, indeed, also depend on the magnitude of this constant capital which is antecedent to production.) This part of the value of the product would not exist without the new labour of 1 million men during the year. On the other hand, the labour of 1 million men would not yield the same amount of product without this constant capital which exists independently of their year's labour. It enters into the labour process as a condition of production but not a single additional hour is worked in order to reproduce this part in terms of its value. As value it is, therefore, not the result of the year's labour, although its value would not have been reproduced *without* this year's labour. If the part of the constant capital which enters into the product were 25 million, then the value of the product of the 1 million men would be 75 million; if this part [of the constant capital] were 10 million, then [the value of the product] would only be 60 million, etc. And since the ratio of constant capital to variable capital increases in the course of capitalist development,

---

[a] Instrumental materials.— *Ed.*

the value of the annual product of 1 million men will tend to rise continuously, in proportion to the growth of the past labour which plays a part in their annual production. This alone shows that Ricardo was unable to understand either the essence of accumulation or the nature of profit. With the growth in the proportion of constant to variable capital, grows also the productivity of labour, the productive forces brought into being, with which social labour operates. As a result of this increasing productivity of labour, however, a part of the existing constant capital is continuously depreciated in value, for its value depends not on the labour time that it cost originally, but on the labour time with which it can be reproduced, and this is continuously diminishing as the productivity of labour grows. Although, therefore, the value of the constant capital does not increase in proportion to its amount, it increases nevertheless, because its amount increases even more rapidly than its value falls. But we shall return later to Ricardo's views on accumulation.[a] It is evident, however, that if the length of the working day is given, the value of the annual product of the labour of 1 million [men] will differ greatly according to the different amount of constant capital that enters into the product; and that, despite the growing productivity of labour, it will be greater where the constant capital forms a large part of the total capital, than under social conditions where it forms a relatively small part of the total capital. With the advance in the productivity of social labour, accompanied as it is by the growth of constant capital, a relatively ever increasing part of the annual product of labour will, therefore, fall to the share of capital as such, and thus property in the form of capital (apart from REVENUE) will be constantly increasing and proportionately that part of value which the individual worker and even the working class creates, will be steadily decreasing, [XII-661] compared with the product of their past labour that confronts them as capital. The alienation and the antagonism between labour capacity and the objective conditions of labour which have become independent in the form of capital, thereby grow continuously. (Not taking into account the variable capital, i.e. that part of the product of the annual labour which is required for the reproduction of the working class; even these means of subsistence, however, confront them as capital.)

Ricardo's view, that the working day *is given, limited, a fixed magnitude,* is also expressed by him elsewhere, for instance:

---

[a] See this volume, pp. 103 et seq.— *Ed.*

* "They" (the wages of labour and the profits of stock) *are* "*together* always *of the same value*" * (l.c., p. 499 (CH. XXXII, "Mr. Malthus' Opinions on Rent")),

in other words this only means that the (daily) labour time whose product is *divided* between the WAGES OF LABOUR and the PROFITS OF STOCK, is always *the same,* is *constant.*

* "Wages and profits together will be of *the same value*" * (l.c., [p.] 491, note).

I hardly need to repeat here that in these passages one should always read SURPLUS VALUE instead of PROFIT.

* "Wages and profits taken together will continue *always* of the same value" * (pp. 490[-91]).

* "Wages are to be estimated by their *real value,* viz., by the *quantity of labour and capital employed in producing them,* and not by their *nominal value* either in coats, hats, money, or corn" * (l.c., CH. I, "On Value", [p.] 50).

The value of the means of subsistence which the worker obtains (buys with his WAGES), corn, clothes, etc., is determined by the total labour time required for their production, the quantity of immediate labour as well as the quantity of objectified labour NECESSARY FOR THEIR PRODUCTION. But Ricardo confuses the issue because he does not state it plainly, he does not say: * "their [the wages'] *real value,* viz., that quantity of the working day required to reproduce the value of their [the workers'] own necessaries, the equivalent of the necessaries paid to them, or exchanged for their labour".* REAL WAGES have to be determined by the AVERAGE TIME which the worker must work each day in order to produce or reproduce his own WAGES.

* "The labourer is only paid a really high price for his labour, when his wages will purchase the produce of a great deal of labour" * (l.c., [p.] 322, [note]).

4) Relative Surplus Value

This is IN FACT the only form of surplus value which Ricardo analyses under the name of *profit.*

The quantity of labour required for the production of a commodity, and contained in it, determines its value, which is thus a *given* factor, a *definite amount.* This amount is divided between wage labourer and capitalist. (Ricardo, like Adam Smith, does not take constant capital into account here.) It is obvious that the share of one can only rise or fall in proportion to the fall or rise of the share of the other. Since the value of the commodities is due to the labour of the workers, labour is under all circumstances the prerequisite of value, but there can be no labour unless the worker lives and maintains himself, i.e. receives the necessary wages (the minimum wages, wages = the value of labour capacity). Wages and surplus value—these two categories into which the value of the commodity or the product itself is divided—are therefore not only in inverse proportion to each other, but the *prius,* the determinant factor is the movement of wages. Their rise or fall causes the opposite movement on the part of profit (surplus value). Wages do not rise or fall because profit (surplus value) falls or rises, but on the contrary, surplus value (profit) falls or rises because wages rise or fall. The *surplus product* (one should really say *surplus value*) which remains after the working class has received its share of its own annual production forms the substance on which the capitalist class lives.

Since the value of the commodities is determined by the quantity of labour contained in them, and since wages and surplus value (profit) are only *shares,* proportions in which two classes of producers divide the value of the commodity between themselves, it is clear that a rise or fall in wages, although it determines the rate of surplus value (profit), does not affect the value of the commodity or the PRICE (AS MONETARY EXPRESSION OF THE VALUE OF A COMMODITY). The proportion in which a whole is divided between two SHAREHOLDERS makes the whole neither larger nor smaller. It is, therefore, an erroneous preconception to assume that a *rise in wages raises the prices of commodities*; it only makes profit (surplus value) fall. Even the exceptions cited by Ricardo, where a rise in wages is supposed to make the exchange values of some commodities fall and those of others rise, are wrong so far as *value* is concerned and only correct for *cost prices.*[6]

[XII-662] Since the rate of surplus value (profit) is determined by the relative height of wages, how is the latter determined? Apart from competition, by the price of the necessary means of subsistence. This, in turn, depends on the productivity of labour, which increases with the fertility of the land (Ricardo assumes capitalist production here). Every "IMPROVEMENT" reduces the prices of commodities, of the means of subsistence. Wages,or the VALUE OF LABOUR, thus rise and fall in inverse proportion to the development of the productive power of labour, in so far as the latter produces NECESSARIES which enter into the AVERAGE consumption of the working class. The rate of surplus value (profit) falls or rises, therefore, in direct proportion to the development of the productive power of labour, because this development reduces or raises wages.

The rate of profit (surplus value) cannot fall unless wages rise, and cannot rise unless wages fall.

The value of wages has to be reckoned not according to the

quantity of the means of subsistence received by the worker, but according to the quantity of labour which these means of subsistence cost (in fact, the proportion of the working day which he appropriates for himself), that is according to the *relative share* of the total product, or rather of the total value of this product, which the worker receives. It is possible that, reckoned in terms of use values (quantity of commodities or money), his wages rise (as productivity increases) and yet the value of the wages may fall and vice versa. It is one of Ricardo's great merits that he examined relative or proportionate wages, and established them as a definite category. Up to this time, wages had always been regarded as something simple and consequently the worker was considered an animal. But here he is considered in his social relationships. The position of the classes to one another depends more on PROPORTIONATE WAGES than on the ABSOLUTE AMOUNT OF WAGES.

Now these propositions have to be substantiated by quotations from Ricardo.

* "The *value* of the deer, the produce of the hunter's *day's labour*, would be exactly equal to the value of the fish, the produce of the fisherman's *day's labour*. The comparative value of the fish and the game, would be entirely regulated by the quantity of labour realised in each; *whatever might be the quantity of production,* or however *high or low general wages or profits might be.* If ... the fisherman ... employed ten men, whose annual labour cost £100 and who *in one day* obtained by *their* labour twenty salmon: If ... the hunter also employed ten men, whose *annual labour* cost £100 and who *in one day* procured him ten deer; then the natural price of a deer would be two salmon, whether *the proportion of the whole produce bestowed on the men who obtained* [it], were large or small. The *proportion* which might be paid for *wages,* is of the utmost importance in the question of *profits;* for it must at once be seen, that profits would be high or low, exactly in proportion as wages were low or high; but it could not in the least affect the relative value of fish and game, as wages would be high or low at the same time in both occupations" * (Сн. I, "On Value", pp. 20-21).

It can be seen that Ricardo derives the whole value of the commodity from the LABOUR of the MEN EMPLOYED. It is their own labour or the product of that labour or the value of this product, which is divided between them and capital.

* "No alteration in the wages of labour could produce any alteration in the relative value of these commodities; for suppose them to rise, no *greater quantity of labour* would be required in any of these occupations, but it would be *paid* for at a *higher price....* Wages might rise twenty per cent., and profits consequently fall in a greater or less proportion, without occasioning the least alteration in the relative value of these commodities" * (l.c., [p.] 23).

* "There can be no rise in the *value of labour* without a fall of profits. If the corn is to be *divided* between the farmer and the labourer, the *larger the proportion* that is given to the latter, the less will remain for the former. So if cloth or cotton goods be *divided* between the workman and his employer, the *larger the proportion* given to the former, the less remains for the latter" * (l.c., [p.] 31).

[XII-663] * "Adam Smith, and all the writers who have followed him, have, without one exception that I know of, maintained that *a rise in the price of labour* would be uniformly followed by *a rise in the price of all commodities.* I hope I have succeeded in showing, that there are no grounds for such an opinion" * (l.c. [p.] 45).

* "A rise of wages, from the circumstance of the labourer being more liberally rewarded, or from a difficulty of procuring the necessaries on which wages are expended, does not, except in some instances, produce the effect of raising price, but has a great effect in lowering profits." *

The position is different, however, when the RISE OF WAGES is due to "AN ALTERATION IN THE VALUE OF MONEY". * "In the one case" * // namely, in the last-mentioned case //, *"no *greater proportion of the annual labour of the country* is devoted to the *support of* [the] *labourers*; in the other case, a larger portion is so devoted" * (l.c. [p.] 48).

([We see from the following passage] that Ricardo deliberately identifies VALUE with COST OF PRODUCTION:

* "Mr. Malthus appears to think that it is a part of my doctrine, that the *cost* and *value* of a thing should be the same;—it is, if he means by cost 'cost of production' including profits" * (l.c., [p.] 46 [note]).)

* "With a rise in the price of food and necessaries, the natural price of labour will rise; with a fall in their price, the natural price of labour will fall" * (l.c., [p.] 86).

* "The *surplus produce* remaining, after satisfying the wants of the existing population, must necessarily be in proportion to the *facility of production*, viz., to the *smaller number of persons* employed in production" * ([p.] 93).

* "Neither the farmer who cultivates that quantity of land, which regulates price, nor the manufacturer, who manufactures goods, sacrifice any portion of the produce for rent. The *whole value of their commodities is divided* into *two portions* only: one constitutes the profits of stock, the other the wages of labour" * (l.c., [p.] 107). * "Suppose the price of silks, velvets, furniture, and any other commodities, not required by the labourer, to rise in consequence of more labour being expended on them, would not that affect profits? Certainly not: for nothing can affect profits but a rise in wages; silks and velvets are not consumed by the labourer, and therefore cannot raise wages" * (l.c., [p.] 118).

* "If the labour of ten men will, on land of a certain quality, obtain 180 qrs of wheat, and its value be £4 per qr, or £720..." (p. 110) "...in all cases, the same sum of £720 must be divided between wages and profits.... Whether wages or profits rise or fall, it is this sum of £720 from which they must both be provided. On the one hand, profits can never rise so high as to absorb so much of this £720 that enough will not be left to furnish the labourers with absolute necessaries; on the other hand, wages can never rise so high as to leave no portion of this sum to profits" * (l.c., [p.] 113).

* "Profits *depend on high or low wages,* wages on the price of necessaries, and the price of necessaries chiefly on the price of food, because all other requisites may be increased almost without limit" * (l.c., [p.] 119).

* "Although a greater value is produced" * (with a deterioration of the land) * "a *greater proportion of what remains of that value,* after paying rent, is consumed by the *producers*" * // he identifies LABOURERS with PRODUCERS here [19] //, * "and it is this, *and this alone*, which regulates profits" * (l.c., [p.] 127).

* "It is the essential quality of an *improvement* to *diminish the quantity of labour* before required to produce a commodity; and this diminution cannot take place

without a *fall of its price or relative value"* (l.c., [p.] 70). * "Diminish the cost of production of hats, and their price will ultimately fall to their new natural price, although the demand should be doubled, trebled, or quadrupled. Diminish the cost of subsistence of men, by diminishing the natural price of the food and clothing, by which life is sustained, and wages will ultimately fall, notwithstanding that the demand for labourers may [XII-664] very greatly increase"* (l.c., [p.] 460).

* "In proportion as less is appropriated for wages, more will be appropriated for profits, and vice versa"* (l.c., [p.] 500).

* "It has been one of the objects of this work to shew, that with every fall in the real value of necessaries, the wages of labour would fall, and that the profits of stock would rise—in other words, that of any given *annual value a less portion would be paid to the labouring class,* and a larger portion to those *whose funds employed this class."* *

// It is only in this statement, which has now become a commonplace, that Ricardo expresses the NATURE OF CAPITAL, though he may not be aware of it. It is not *accumulated labour employed by the labouring class, by the labourers themselves, but it is "funds", "accumulated labour", "employing this class", employing present, immediate labour.* //

* "Suppose *the value* of the commodities produced in a particular manufacture to be £1,000, and to *be divided* between *the master* and *his* labourers"* (here again [he expresses] the nature of capital; the capitalist is the MASTER, the workers are HIS LABOURERS) * "in the proportion of £800 to labourers, and £200 to the master; if the value of these commodities should fall to £900, and £100 be saved from the wages of labour, in consequence of the fall of necessaries, the net income of the masters would be in no degree impaired"* ([pp. 511-]12).

* "If the shoes and clothing of the labourer, could, by improvements in machinery, be produced by one-fourth of the labour now necessary to their production, they would probably fall 75 per cent.; but so far is it from being true, that the labourer would thereby be enabled permanently to consume four coats, or four pair of shoes, instead of one, that it is probable his *wages would in no long time be adjusted* by the effects of competition, and the stimulus to population, to the *new value of the necessaries* on which they were expended. If these improvements extended to all the objects of the labourer's consumption, we should find him probably at the end of a very few years, in possession of only a small, if any, addition to his enjoyments, although the exchangeable value of those commodities, compared with any other commodity, had sustained a very considerable reduction; and though they were the produce of a very considerably diminished quantity of labour"* (l.c., [p.] 8).

* "When wages rise, it is always at the expense of profits, and when they fall, profits always rise"* (l.c., [p.] 49l, note).

* "It has been my endeavour to shew throughout this work, that the rate of profits can never be increased but by a fall in wages, and that there can be no permanent fall of wages but in consequence of a fall of the necessaries on which wages are expended. If, therefore, by the *extension of foreign* trade, or by *improvements in machinery,* the food and necessaries of the labourer can be brought to market, at a reduced price, profits will rise. If, instead of growing our own corn, or manufacturing the clothing and other necessaries of the labourer, we discover a new market from which we can supply ourselves with these commodities at a cheaper price, wages will fall and profits rise; but if the commodities obtained at a

cheaper rate, by the extension of foreign commerce, or by the improvement of machinery, be exclusively the commodities consumed by the rich, no alteration will take place in the rate of profits. The rate of wages would not be affected, although wine, velvets, silks, and other expensive commodities should fall 50 per cent., and consequently profits would continue unaltered. Foreign trade, then, though highly beneficial to a country, as it increases the amount and variety of the objects on which revenue may be expended, and affords, by the abundance and cheapness of commodities, incentives to saving" * (and * why not incentives to spending?), "and to the *accumulation of capital*, has no tendency to raise the profits of stock, *unless the commodities imported be of that description on which the wages of labour are expended.* The remarks which have been made respecting foreign trade, apply equally to home trade. The rate of profits is *never increased"* *

//he has just said the very opposite; evidently he means NEVER UNLESS BY THE IMPROVEMENTS MENTIONED THE VALUE OF LABOUR IS DIMINISHED//

* "by a *better distribution of labour*, by the *invention of machinery*, by the *establishment of roads and canals*, or by *any means of abridging labour in the manufacture or in the conveyance of goods.* These are causes which operate on price, and never fail to be highly beneficial to consumers; since they enable them with the same labour, to obtain in exchange a greater quantity of the commodity to *which the improvement* is applied; but they have no effect whatever on profit. On the other hand, every [XII-665] diminution in the wages of labour raises profits, but produces no effect on the price of commodities. One is advantageous to all classes, for all classes are consumers";*

(but how is it ADVANTAGEOUS TO THE LABOURING CLASS? For Ricardo presupposes that if these commodities enter into the consumption of the wage earner they reduce wages, and if these commodities become cheaper without reducing wages they are not commodities on which wages are expended)

* "the other is beneficial only to producers; they gain more, but every thing remains at its former price." *

(Again, how is this possible, since Ricardo presupposes that the DIMINUTION IN WAGES OF LABOUR WHICH RAISES PROFITS, takes place precisely because the price of the NECESSARIES has fallen and therefore by no means "EVERY THING REMAINS AT ITS FORMER PRICE".)

* "In the first case they get the same as before; but *every thing*" * (wrong again; should read EVERY THING, NECESSARIES EXCLUDED) * "on which their gains are expended, is diminished in exchangeable value" * (p[p]. 137-38).

It is evident that this *passus* is rather INCORRECT. But apart from this formal aspect, the statements are only true if one reads "RATE OF SURPLUS VALUE" for RATE OF PROFIT, and this applies to the whole of this investigation into relative surplus value. Even in the case of luxury articles, such IMPROVEMENTS can raise the general rate of profit, since the rate of profit in these spheres of production, as in all others, bears a share in the levelling out of all particular rates of profit into the AVERAGE rate of profit. If in such cases, as a result of the above-mentioned influences, the value of the constant capital falls proportionately to the variable, or the period of turnover is reduced (i.e. a CHANGE takes place in the circulation process), then the rate of profit rises. Furthermore, the influence of FOREIGN TRADE is expounded in an entirely one-sided way. The development of the product into a commodity is fundamental to capitalist production and this is intrinsically bound up with the expansion of the market, the creation of the world market, and therefore FOREIGN TRADE.

Apart from this, Ricardo is right when he states that all IMPROVEMENTS, be they brought about through the division of labour, improvements in machinery, the perfection of means of communication, foreign trade—in short all measures that reduce the necessary labour time involved in the manufacture or transport of commodities increase the surplus value (HENCE PROFIT) and thus enrich the capitalist class because, and in so far as, these "IMPROVEMENTS" reduce THE VALUE OF LABOUR.

Finally, in this section, we must quote a few passages in which Ricardo analyses the NATURE OF *PROPORTIONAL* WAGES.

* "If I have to hire a labourer for a week, and instead of ten shillings I pay him eight, no variation having taken place in the value of money, the labourer can probably obtain more food and necessaries, with his eight shillings, than he before obtained for ten: but this is owing, not to a rise in the *real value of his wages,* as stated by Adam Smith, and more recently by Mr. Malthus, but to a fall in the value of the things, on which his wages are expended, things perfectly distinct; and yet *for calling this a fall in the real value of wages,* I am told that I adopt new and unusual language, not reconcilable with the true principles of the science" * (l.c., [pp.] 11-12).

* "It is not by the *absolute quantity of produce* obtained by either class, that we can correctly judge of the rate of profit, rent, and wages, but by the quantity of labour required to obtain that produce. By improvements in machinery and agriculture, the whole produce may be doubled; but if wages, rent, and profit be also doubled, these three will bear *the same proportions to one another as before,* and neither could be said to have *relatively varied.* But if wages partook not of the whole of this increase; if they, instead of being doubled, were only increased one-half; ... it would, I apprehend, be correct for me to say, that ... wages had fallen while profits had risen; for if we had an invariable standard by which to measure the *value* of this produce, we should find that a less value had fallen to the class of labourers..., and a greater to the class of capitalists, than had been given before" * (l.c., [p.] 49). * "It will not the less be a real fall, because they" (the wages) "might furnish him with a greater quantity of cheap commodities than his former wages" * (l.c., [p.]51).

De Quincey points out the contrast between some of the propositions developed by Ricardo and those of the other economists. By the economists before Ricardo:

*"When it was asked, what determined the value of all commodities: it was answered that this value was chiefly determined by wages. When again it was

asked—what determined wages? it was recollected that wages must be adjusted to the value of the commodities upon which they were spent; and the answer was in effect that wages were determined by the value of commodities" * (*Dialogues of Three Templars on Political Economy, chiefly in Relation to the Principles of Mr. Ricardo,* [XII-666] *The London Magazine,* Vol. IX, 1824, [p.] 560).

The same *Dialogues* contains the following passage about the law governing the measurement OF VALUE BY THE QUANTITY OF LABOUR and BY THE VALUE OF LABOUR:

* "So far are the two formulae from presenting merely two different expressions of the same law, that the very best way of expressing negatively Mr. Ricardo's law (viz. A is to B in value as the quantities of the producing labour) would be to say—A is not to B in value as the *values* of the producing labour" * [l.c., p. 348].

(If the organic composition of the capital in A and B were the same, then it could in fact be said that their *relation* to one another is proportionate to the VALUES OF THE PRODUCING LABOUR. For the ACCUMULATED LABOUR in each would be in the same proportion as the IMMEDIATE LABOUR in each. The quantities of paid labour in each, however, would be proportionate to the total quantities of IMMEDIATE LABOUR in each. Assume the composition to be $80c + 20v$ and the rate of surplus value=50%. If one capital=[£]500 and the other=300, then the product in the first case=550 and in the second =330. The products would then be as $5 \times 20 = 100$ (wages) to $3 \times 20 = 60$; $100:60 = 10:6 = 5:3$. $550:330 = 55:33$ or as $^{55}/_{11}:^{33}/_{11}$ ($5 \times 11 = 55$ and $3 \times 11 = 33$); i.e. as 5:3. But even then one would only know their relation to one another and not their true values, since many different values correspond to the ratio 5:3.)

"If the price is 10s., then WAGES and PROFITS, TAKEN AS A WHOLE, CANNOT EXCEED TEN SHILLINGS. BUT DO NOT THE WAGES AND PROFITS AS A WHOLE, THEMSELVES, ON THE CONTRARY, PREDETERMINE THE PRICE? NO; THAT IS THE OLD SUPERANNUATED DOCTRINE" (Thomas de Quincey, *The Logic of Political Economy,* Edinburgh, 1844,[a] [p.] 204). "The new political economy has shown THAT ALL PRICE IS GOVERNED BY THE PROPORTIONAL QUANTITY OF THE PRODUCING LABOUR, AND BY THAT ONLY. BEING ITSELF ONCE SETTLED, THEN, *ipso facto,*[b] PRICE SETTLES THE FUND OUT OF WHICH BOTH WAGES AND PROFITS MUST DRAW THEIR SEPARATE DIVIDENDS" (l.c., [p.] 204). "ANY CHANGE THAT CAN DISTURB THE EXISTING RELATIONS BETWEEN WAGES AND PROFITS, MUST ORIGINATE IN WAGES" (l.c., [p.] 205). "Ricardo's doctrine of rent is new in so far as he poses the question whether in fact it sets aside the LAW OF ACTUAL VALUE" [20] (l.c., [p.] 158).

---

a In the manuscript: "1845".— *Ed.*
b By virtue of this.— *Ed.*

5) Theory of Profit

It has already been shown in some detail, that the laws of surplus value—or rather of the rate of surplus value—(assuming the working day as given) do not so directly and simply coincide with, nor are they applicable to, the laws of profit, as Ricardo supposes. It has been shown that he wrongly identifies surplus value with profit and that these are only identical in so far as the total capital consists of variable capital or is laid out directly in wages; and that therefore what Ricardo deals with under the name of "profit" is in fact surplus value. Only in this case can the total product simply be resolved into wages and surplus value. Ricardo evidently shares Smith's view, that the *total value* of the annual product resolves itself into revenues. Hence also his confusion of value with cost price.

It is not necessary to repeat here that the rate of profit is not directly governed by the same laws as the rate of surplus value.

Firstly: We have seen that the rate of profit can rise or fall as a result of a fall or rise in rent, independently of ANY CHANGE IN THE VALUE OF LABOUR.

Secondly: The ABSOLUTE AMOUNT OF PROFIT=the ABSOLUTE AMOUNT OF SURPLUS VALUE. The latter, however, is determined not only by the rate of surplus value but just as much by the number of workers employed. The same AMOUNT OF PROFIT is therefore possible, with a falling rate of surplus value and a rising number of workers and vice versa, etc.

Thirdly: With a *given* rate of surplus value, the rate of profit depends on the ORGANIC COMPOSITION OF CAPITAL.

Fourthly: With a *given surplus value* (the ORGANIC COMPOSITION OF CAPITAL per 100 is also assumed to be given) the rate of profit depends on the *relative value* of the different parts of the capital, which may be differently affected, partly by ECONOMY OF POWER etc. in the use of the means of production, partly by VARIATIONS in VALUE which may affect one part of capital while they leave the rest untouched.

Finally, one has to take into account the differences in the COMPOSITION of capital arising from the process of circulation.

[XII-667] Some of the observations that occur in Ricardo's writing should have led him to the distinction between surplus value and profit. Because he fails to make this distinction, he appears in some passages to descend to the vulgar view—as has already been indicated in the analysis of CH. I, "On Value"—the view that profit is a mere addition over and above the value of the commodity; for instance when he speaks of the determination of profit on capital in which the fixed capital predominates, etc.[a] This was the source of much nonsense among his successors. This vulgar view is bound to arise, if the proposition (which in practice is correct) that on the average *capitals of equal size yield equal profits* or that profit depends on the size of the capital employed, is not connected by a series of intermediary links with the general laws of value etc.: in short, if profit and surplus value are treated as identical, which is only correct for the aggregate capital. Accordingly Ricardo has no means for determining a *general rate of profit.*

Ricardo realises that the *rate of profit* is *not* modified by those VARIATIONS OF THE VALUE OF COMMODITIES which affect all parts of capital *equally* as, for example, VARIATIONS IN THE VALUE OF MONEY. He should therefore have concluded that *it is affected* by such VARIATIONS IN THE VALUE OF COMMODITIES which do *not* affect all parts of capital *equally;* that therefore VARIATIONS in the rate of profit may occur while the VALUE OF LABOUR remains unchanged, and that even the rate of profit may move in the opposite direction to VARIATIONS IN THE VALUE OF LABOUR. Above all, however, he should have kept in mind that here the SURPLUS PRODUCE, or what is for him the same thing, SURPLUS VALUE, or again the same thing, SURPLUS LABOUR, when he is considering it *sub specie*[b] profit, is not calculated in proportion to the variable capital alone, but in proportion to the *total capital advanced.*

With reference to a CHANGE in the VALUE OF MONEY, he says:

* "The variation in the value of money, however great, makes no difference in the *rate of profits;* for suppose the goods of the manufacturer to rise from £1,000 to £2,000, or 100%, if *his capital,* on which the variations of money have as much effect as on the value of produce, if his machinery, buildings, and stock in trade rise also 100 per cent.... his *rate of profits* will be the same.... If, with a capital of a given value, he can, by economy in labour, double the quantity of produce, and it fall to half its former price, it *will bear the same proportion to the capital that produced it* which it did before, and *consequently* profits will still be at the same rate. If, at the same time that he doubles the quantity of produce by the employment of the same capital, the value of money is by any accident lowered one half, the produce will sell for twice the money [value] that it did before; but the capital employed to produce it will also be of twice its former money value; and therefore in this case too, *the value of the produce will bear the same proportion to the value of the capital as it did before*" * (l.c., [pp.] 51-52).

If Ricardo means SURPLUS PRODUCE when he writes PRODUCE in the last passage then this is correct. For the rate of profit =

---

[a] See present edition, Vol. 31, pp. 406-08.— *Ed.*
[b] From the viewpoint of.— *Ed.*

$\dfrac{\text{SURPLUS PRODUCE (VALUE)}}{\text{capital}}$. Thus if the SURPLUS PRODUCE $= 10$ and the capi-

tal $= 100$, the rate of profit $= 10/100 = {}^{1}/_{10} = 10\%$. If however he means the total product, then the way he puts it is not accurate. In that case by proportion of the VALUE OF THE PRODUCE TO THE VALUE OF CAPITAL, he evidently means nothing but the excess of the value of the commodity over the value of the capital advanced. In any case, it is obvious that *here* he does not identify profit with surplus value or the rate of profit with the rate of surplus

value, $= \dfrac{\text{SURPLUS VALUE}}{\text{VALUE OF LABOUR}}$ or $\dfrac{\text{SURPLUS VALUE}}{\text{VARIABLE CAPITAL}}$.

Ricardo says on p. *518* (l.c., CH. XXXII):

> * "The *raw produce* of which commodities are made, is supposed to have fallen in price, and, therefore, commodities will fall on that account. True, they will fall, but their fall will not be attended with any diminution in the money income of the producer. If he sell his commodity for less money, it is only because *one of the materials from which it is made has fallen in value.* If the clothier sell his cloth for £900 instead of £1,000, his income will not be less, if the wool from which it is made, has declined £100 in value" * (l.c., [p.] 518).

(The particular point with which Ricardo is actually dealing, the effect in a practical CASE, does not concern us here. But a sudden DEPRECIATION of wool would of course affect (adversely) the MONEY INCOME of those CLOTHIERS who had on their hands a large STOCK of ready-made cloth manufactured at a time when wool was dearer and which has to be sold after the price [XII-668] of wool has dropped.) If, as Ricardo assumes here, the CLOTHIERS set in motion the same amount of labour as before //they could set in motion a much greater amount of labour because a part of the capital which was previously EXPENDED *only* on raw material is now at their disposal and can be EXPENDED on raw material+LABOUR//, it is clear that their "MONEY INCOME" taken in absolute terms, "WILL NOT BE LESS" but their *rate of profit* will be *greater* than previously; for—say it was 10%, i.e. £100—the same amount as before would now have to be reckoned on £900 instead of 1,000. In the first case the rate of profit $= 10\%$. In the second $= {}^{1}/_{9} = 11{}^{1}/_{9}\%$. Since Ricardo moreover presupposes that the RAW PRODUCE OF WHICH COMMODITIES ARE MADE has fallen generally, the GENERAL RATE OF PROFIT would rise and not only the RATE OF PROFIT in one TRADE. It is all the more strange that Ricardo does not realise this, because he understands it when the opposite takes place.

For in CH. VI "On Profits" Ricardo deals with the CASE where, as a result of an increase in the price of NECESSARIES owing to the cultivation of worse land and the consequent rise in differential rent, firstly wages rise and secondly all RAW PRODUCE from the SURFACE OF THE EARTH. (This assumption is by no means necessary; cotton may very well fall in price, so can silk and even wool and linen, although the price of corn may be rising.)

In the first place he says that the *surplus value* (he calls it profit) of the farmer will fall because the value of the product of the 10 men whom he employs, continues to be £720 and from this fund of 720 he has to hand over more in WAGES. And he continues:

*"But the *rate of profits* will fall still more, because the *capital* of the farmer ... consists in a great measure of raw produce, such as his corn and hay-ricks, his unthreshed wheat and barley, his horses and cows, which would all rise in price in consequence of the *rise of produce.* His *absolute profits* would fall from £480 to £445 15s.; but if from the cause which I have just stated, his capital should rise from £3,000 to £3,200, *the rate of his profits* would, when corn was at £5 2s. 10d., be under 14 per cent. If a manufacturer had also employed £3,000 in his business, he would be obliged in consequence of the rise of wages, to increase his capital, in order to be enabled to carry on the same business. If his commodities sold before for £720 they would continue to sell at the same price; but the wages of labour, which were before £240, would rise when corn was at £5 2s. 10d., to £274 5s. In the first case he would have a balance of £480 as profit on £3,000, in the second he would have a profit only of £445 15s., on an increased capital, and therefore his profits would conform to the altered rate of those of the farmer"* (l.c., [pp.] 116-17).

In this passage, therefore, Ricardo distinguishes between ABSOLUTE PROFITS (= SURPLUS VALUE) and RATE OF PROFITS and also shows that the rate of profit falls more as a result of the change in the value of the capital advanced, than the ABSOLUTE PROFITS (SURPLUS VALUE) fall as a result of the RISE IN THE VALUE OF LABOUR. The RATE OF PROFITS would have also fallen, if the VALUE OF LABOUR [had] remained *the same,* because *the same* ABSOLUTE PROFIT would have to be calculated on a greater capital. The reverse result, i.e. a rise in the rate of profit (as distinct from a rise in SURPLUS VALUE or ABSOLUTE PROFIT), would take place in the first instance cited from him, where the value of the RAW PRODUCE falls. It is evident, therefore, that rises and falls in the rate of profit may also be brought about by circumstances other than the rise and fall in the absolute profit and the rise and fall in its rate, reckoned on the capital laid out in wages. In connection with the last quoted passage Ricardo writes:

*"Articles of jewellery, of iron, of plate, and of copper, would not *rise,* because none of the raw produce from the surface of the earth enters into their composition"* (l.c., [p.] 117).

The prices of these commodities would not rise, but the rate of profit in these TRADES would rise above that in the others. For in the latter, a smaller surplus value (because of the rise in wages) would correspond to a capital outlay that had grown in value for two reasons: firstly, because the outlay in wages had increased; secondly, because the outlay in raw materials had increased. In the second case [XII-669] there is a smaller surplus value on a capital outlay in which only the variable part has grown because of the rise in wages.

In these passages, Ricardo himself throws overboard his whole theory of profit, which is based on the false identification of the rate of surplus value with the rate of profit.

* "In every case, agricultural, as well as manufacturing profits are lowered by a rise in the *price of raw produce,* if it be accompanied by a rise of wages" * (l.c., [pp.] 113-14).

It follows from what Ricardo himself has said, that, even if [the rise in the price of raw produce] is not ACCOMPANIED BY A RISE OF WAGES, the RATE OF PROFITS WOULD BE LOWERED BY AN ENHANCEMENT OF THAT PART OF THE ADVANCED CAPITAL CONSISTING OF RAW PRODUCE.

* "Suppose the price of silks, velvets, furniture, and any other commodities, not required by the labourer, to rise in consequence of more labour being *expended on them, would not that affect profits?* Certainly not: for *nothing can affect profits but a rise in wages*; silks and velvets are not consumed by the labourer, and therefore cannot raise wages" * (l.c., [p.] 118).

CERTAINLY, THE RATE OF PROFITS IN THOSE particular TRADES WOULD FALL, ALTHOUGH THE VALUE OF LABOUR—WAGES—REMAINED THE SAME. The raw material used by the silk manufacturers, piano manufacturers, furniture manufacturers, etc. would have become dearer, and therefore the proportion borne by the same surplus value to the capital laid out would have fallen and HENCE THE RATE OF PROFIT. And the *general rate of profit* consists of the AVERAGE of the particular rates of profit in all BRANCHES OF BUSINESS. Or, in order to make the same average profit as before, these manufacturers would raise the price of their commodities. Such a nominal rise in prices does not directly affect the rate of profit, but the EXPENDITURE OF PROFIT.

Ricardo returns once more to the case considered above, where the surplus value (ABSOLUTE PROFIT) falls, because the price of the NECESSARIES (and along with these, also rent) rises.

* "I must again observe, that the *rate of profits* would fall much more rapidly than I have estimated in my calculation: for the *value of the produce* being what I have stated it under the circumstances supposed, the value of *the farmer's stock* would be *greatly increased from its necessarily consisting of many of the commodities which had risen in value.* Before corn could rise from £4 to £12, *his capital* would probably be doubled in exchangeable value, and be worth £6,000 instead of £3,000. If then his profit were £180, or 6 per cent. on his *original capital,* profits would not at that time be really at *a higher rate* than 3 per cent.; for £6,000 at 3 per cent. gives £180; and on *those terms only could a new farmer with £6,000 money in his pocket enter into the farming business.* Many trades would derive some advantage, more or less, from the

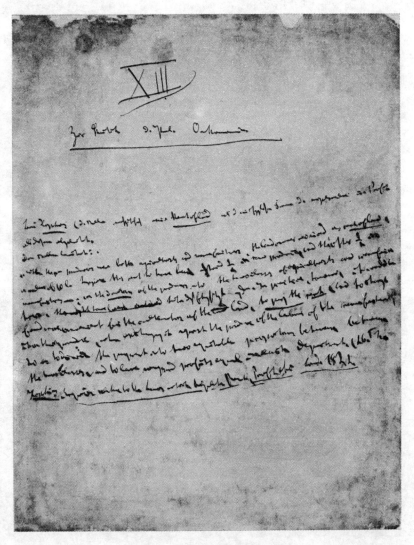

Front cover page of Notebook XIII,
Economic Manuscript of 1861-1863

same source. The brewer, the distiller, the clothier, the linen manufacturer, would be *partly compensated for the diminution of their profits, by the rise in the value of their stock of raw and finished materials*; but a manufacturer of hardware, of jewellery, and of many other commodities, as well as those whose capitals uniformly consisted of money, would be subject to the *whole fall in the rate of profits*, without any compensation whatever" * (l.c., [pp.] 123-24).

What is important here is only something of which Ricardo is not aware, namely, that he throws overboard his identification of profit with surplus value and [admits] that the rate of profit can be affected by a VARIATION IN THE VALUE OF THE CONSTANT CAPITAL independently of the VALUE OF LABOUR. Moreover, his illustration is only partially correct. The gain which the FARMER, CLOTHIER, etc., would derive from the rise in price of the STOCK OF COMMODITIES they have on hand and on the market, would of course cease as soon as they had sold these commodities. The increased value of their capital would similarly no longer represent a gain for them, when this capital was used up and had to be reproduced. They would then all find themselves in the position of the new farmer cited by Ricardo himself, who would have to advance a capital of £6,000 in order to make a profit of 3%. On the other hand, [XIII-670] the JEWELLER, MANUFACTURER OF HARDWARE, MONEY DEALER etc.—although at first they would not [receive] any compensation for their losses—would realise a rate of profit of more than 3%, for only the capital laid out in wages would have risen in value whereas their constant capital remained unchanged.

One further point of importance in connection with this compensation of the falling profit by the rise in value of the capital, mentioned by Ricardo, is that for the capitalist—and generally, as far as the division of the product of annual labour is concerned—it is a question not only of the distribution of the product among the various SHAREHOLDERS in the REVENUE, but also of the division of this product into capital and REVENUE.

Formation of the General Rate of Profit.
(AVERAGE PROFITS or "USUAL PROFITS")

Ricardo is by no means theoretically clear here.

* "I have already remarked, that the *market price* of a commodity may *exceed* its *natural or necessary price*, as it may be produced in less abundance than the new demand for it requires. This, however, is but a *temporary* effect. The high profits on capital employed in producing that commodity, will naturally attract capital to that trade; and as soon as the requisite funds are supplied, and the quantity of the commodity is duly increased, *its price will fall, and the profits of the trade will conform*

to the general level. A *fall in the general rate of profits* is by no means incompatible with *a partial rise of profits in particular employments.* It is through the inequality of profits, that capital is moved from one employment to another. Whilst then general profits are falling, and gradually settling at a lower level in consequence of the rise of wages, and the increasing difficulty of supplying the increasing population with necessaries, the profits of the farmer may, for an interval of some little duration, be above the former level. An extraordinary stimulus may be also given for a certain time, to a particular branch of foreign and colonial trade." * (l.c., [pp.] 118-19).

 * "It should be recollected that prices always vary in the market, and in the first instance, through the comparative state of demand and supply. Although cloth could be furnished at 40s. per yard, and give the *usual profits of stock,* it may rise to 60 or 80s. from a general change of fashion.... The makers of cloth will for a time have unusual profits, but capital will naturally flow to that manufacture, till the supply and demand are again at their fair level, when the price of cloth will again sink to 40s., its natural or necessary price. In the same manner, with every increased demand for corn, it may rise so high as to afford more than the general profits to the farmer. If there be plenty of fertile land, the price of corn will again fall to its former standard, after the requisite quantity of capital has been employed in producing it, and profits will be as before; but if there be not plenty of fertile land, if, to produce this additional quantity, more than the usual quantity of capital and labour be required, corn will not fall to its former level. Its natural price will be raised, and the farmer, instead of obtaining permanently larger profits, will find himself obliged to be satisfied with the diminished rate which is the inevitable consequence of the rise of wages, produced by the rise of necessaries" * (l.c., [pp.] 119-20).

If the *working day* is given (or if only such DIFFERENCES occur IN THE WORKING DAY IN DIFFERENT TRADES AS ARE COMPENSATED BY THE PECULIARITIES OF DIFFERENT LABOUR) then the *general rate of surplus value,* i.e. OF SURPLUS LABOUR, is given since wages are ON AN AVERAGE the same. Ricardo is preoccupied with this idea, and he confuses the GENERAL RATE OF SURPLUS VALUE with the GENERAL RATE OF PROFITS. I have shown that with the same GENERAL RATE OF SURPLUS VALUE, the *rates of profits* IN DIFFERENT TRADES must be very different, if the commodities are to be sold at their respective *values.* The *general rate of profits* is formed through the total surplus value produced being calculated on the total capital of society (of the class of capitalists). Each capital, therefore, in each particular TRADE, represents a *portion* of a total capital of the same [XIII-671] *organic composition,* both as regards constant and variable capital, and circulating and fixed capital. As such a portion, it draws its dividends from the SURPLUS VALUE created by the aggregate capital, in accordance with its size. The surplus value thus distributed, the amount of surplus value which falls to the share of a block of capital of given size, for example 100, during a given period of time, for example one year, constitutes the AVERAGE PROFIT or the GENERAL RATE OF PROFIT, and as such it enters into the costs of production OF EVERY TRADE. If this share=15, then the USUAL PROFIT=15% and the cost price=115. It can be less if, for instance, only a part of the capital advanced enters as wear and tear into the valorisation process. But it is always=to the capital consumed+15, the AVERAGE profit on the capital advanced. If in one case 100 entered into the product and in another only 50, then in the first case the cost price=100+15=115 and in the second case it=50+15=65; thus both capitals would have sold their commodities at *the same cost price*, i.e. at a price which yielded the same RATE OF PROFIT to both. It is evident, that the emergence, realisation, creation of the *general rate of profit* necessitates the *transformation of values* into *cost prices* that are *different* from these values. Ricardo on the contrary assumes the identity of values and cost prices, because he confuses the rate of profit with the rate of surplus value. Hence he has not the faintest notion of the GENERAL CHANGE which takes place in the PRICES of commodities, in the course of the establishment of a GENERAL RATE OF PROFIT, before there can be any talk of a GENERAL RATE OF PROFIT. He accepts this RATE OF PROFITS as something pre-existent which, therefore, even plays a part in his determination of *value*. (See CH. I, "On Value".) The GENERAL RATE OF PROFIT *having been presupposed,* he only concerns himself with the exceptional modifications in prices which are necessary for the *maintenance,* for the continued existence of this GENERAL RATE OF PROFIT. He does not realise at all that in order to *create* the GENERAL RATE OF PROFITS VALUES must first be transformed into COST PRICES and that therefore, when he presupposes a GENERAL RATE OF PROFITS, he is no longer dealing directly with the *VALUES* OF COMMODITIES.

Moreover, the passage under consideration, *only* [expresses] the Smithian concept and even this in a one-sided way, because Ricardo is preoccupied with his notion of a GENERAL RATE OF SURPLUS VALUE. According to him, the rate of profit rises above the [average] LEVEL only in particular TRADES, because there the MARKET PRICE rises above the NATURAL PRICE owing to the relation between SUPPLY and DEMAND, underproduction or overproduction. Competition, influx of new capital into one TRADE or withdrawal of old capital from another, will then equalise MARKET PRICE and NATURAL PRICE and *reduce* the profit of the particular TRADE to the GENERAL LEVEL. Here the REAL LEVEL OF PROFITS is assumed as *constant* and presupposed as given, and it is only a question of *reducing* the profit to this level in particular TRADES in which it has risen above or fallen below it, as a result of the action of SUPPLY and DEMAND. Ricardo, moreover, always assumes that the commodities whose prices yield more than the AVERAGE PROFIT stand *above* their value and that those which yield less than the average profit stand *below* their value. If competition makes their *market value* conform to their *value,* then the LEVEL is established.

According to Ricardo, the LEVEL itself can only rise or fall if wages fall or rise (for a relatively long period), that is to say, if the *rate of relative surplus value* falls or rises; and this occurs without any change in prices. (Yet Ricardo himself admits here that there can be very significant variations in prices IN DIFFERENT TRADES, according to the ratio of circulating and fixed capital.)

But even when a GENERAL RATE OF PROFITS is established and therefore *cost prices,* the RATE OF PROFITS in particular TRADES may rise, because the *hours of work* in them *are longer* and consequently the RATE OF ABSOLUTE SURPLUS VALUE rises. That competition between the workers cannot level this out, is proved by the *intervention of the state.* The rate of profit will rise in these particular TRADES without the MARKET PRICE rising above the NATURAL PRICE. Competition between capitals, however, can and in the long run will prevent this excess profit from accruing entirely to the capitalists in these particular TRADES. They will have to reduce the prices of their commodities below their "NATURAL PRICES", or the other TRADES will raise *their prices* a little (or if they do not actually raise them, because a fall in *value* of these commodities may supervene, then [XIII-672] at any rate they will not lower them as much as the development of the productive power of labour in their own TRADES required). The GENERAL LEVEL will rise and the cost prices will change.

Furthermore: if a new TRADE comes into being in which a disproportionate amount of living labour is employed in relation to accumulated labour, in which therefore the composition of capital is far below the AVERAGE COMPOSITION which determines the AVERAGE PROFIT, the relations of SUPPLY and DEMAND in this new TRADE may make it possible to sell its output above its *cost price,* at a price approximating more closely to its *actual value.* Competition can level this out, only through the raising of the GENERAL LEVEL, because capital on the whole realises, sets in motion, a greater quantity of *unpaid surplus labour.* The relations of SUPPLY and DEMAND do not, in the first instance as Ricardo maintains, cause the commodity to be sold *above its value,* but merely cause it to be sold above its cost price, at a price approximating *to its value.* The equalisation can therefore bring about not its reduction to the old LEVEL, but the establishment of a *new LEVEL.*

The same applies, for example, to COLONIAL TRADE, where as a result of slavery and the bounty of nature, the VALUE OF LABOUR is lower than in the old COUNTRY (or perhaps because, in fact or in law, landed property has not developed there). If capitals from the mother country are freely TRANSFERABLE TO THIS NEW TRADE, then they will reduce the specific SURPLUS PROFIT in this TRADE, but will raise the GENERAL LEVEL OF PROFIT (as Adam Smith observes quite correctly).

On this point, Ricardo always helps himself out with the phrase: But in the old TRADES the quantity of labour employed has nevertheless remained the same, and so have wages. The GENERAL RATE OF PROFIT is, however, determined by the ratio of unpaid labour to paid labour and to the capital advanced not in this or that TRADE, but in all TRADES to which the CAPITAL MAY BE FREELY TRANSFERRED. The ratio may stay the same in $^9/_{10}$; but if it alters in $^1/_{10}$, then the GENERAL RATE OF PROFIT in the $^{10}/_{10}$ must change. Whenever there is an increase in the quantity of unpaid labour set in motion by a capital of a given size, the effect of competition can only be that capitals of equal size draw equal dividends, equal shares in this increased surplus labour; but not that the dividend of each individual capital remains the same or is reduced to its former share in surplus labour, despite the increase of surplus labour in proportion to the total capital advanced. If Ricardo makes this assumption he has no grounds whatsoever for contesting Adam Smith's view that the rate of profit is reduced merely by the growing competition between capitals due to their accumulation. For he himself assumes here that the rate of profit is reduced simply by competition, although the RATE OF SURPLUS VALUE is increasing. This is indeed connected with his second false assumption, that (leaving out of account the lowering or raising of wages) the RATE OF PROFITS can never rise or fall, except as a result of temporary deviations of the MARKET PRICE from the NATURAL PRICE. And what is NATURAL PRICE? That price = ADVANCES + AVERAGE PROFIT. Thus one arrives again at the assumption that AVERAGE PROFIT can only fall or rise in the same way as the RELATIVE SURPLUS VALUE.

Ricardo is therefore wrong when, contradicting Adam Smith, he says:

* "Any change from one foreign trade to another, or from home to foreign trade, cannot, in my opinion, affect the rate of profits"* (l.c., [p.] 413).

He is equally wrong in supposing that the RATE OF PROFITS does not affect cost prices because it does not affect VALUES.

Ricardo is wrong in thinking that, IN CONSEQUENCE OF A FAVOURED FOREIGN TRADE, the GENERAL LEVEL [of profits] must always be re-established by reducing [profits in a branch of foreign trade] to the former LEVEL and not by raising the general level of profits.

* "They contend, that the equality of profits will be brought about by the general rise of profits; and I am of opinion, that the profits of the favoured trade will speedily subside to the general level" * ([pp.] 132-33).

Because of his completely wrong conception of the rate of profit, Ricardo misunderstands entirely the influence of FOREIGN TRADE, when it does not directly lower the price of the LABOURERS' FOOD. He does not see how enormously important it is for England, for example, to secure [XIII-673] cheaper raw materials for industry, and that in this case, as I have shown previously,[a] the *rate of profit* rises *although prices fall*, whereas in the reverse case, with *rising prices*, the rate of profit can fall, even if wages remain the same in both cases.

* "It is *not*, therefore, in consequence of the extension of the market that the rate of profit is raised" * (l.c., [p.] 136).

The RATE OF PROFIT does not depend on the price of the individual commodity but on the amount of surplus labour which can be realised with a given capital. Elsewhere Ricardo also fails to recognise the importance of the *market* because he does not understand the nature of money.

Law of the Diminishing Rate of Profit

(In connection with the above it must be noted that Ricardo commits all these BLUNDERS, because he attempts to carry through his identification of the rate of surplus value with the rate of profit by means of forced abstraction. The *vulgus* has therefore concluded that theoretical truths are abstractions which are at variance with reality, instead of seeing, on the contrary, that Ricardo does not carry true abstract thinking far enough and is therefore driven into false abstraction.[21])

This is one of the most important points in the Ricardian system.

The rate of profit has a tendency to fall. Why? Adam Smith says: As a result of the growing ACCUMULATION and the growing competition between capitals which accompanies it. Ricardo retorts: Competition can level out profits in DIFFERENT TRADES (we have seen above that he is not consistent in this); but it cannot lower the general rate of profit. This would only be possible if, as a result of the ACCUMULATION of capital, the capital grew so much

---

[a] See present edition, Vol. 31, pp. 430-37.— *Ed.*

more rapidly than the POPULATION, that the demand for labour were *constantly* greater than its SUPPLY, and therefore wages—both nominal and real wages and in terms of use value—were constantly rising in value and in use value. This is not the case. Ricardo is not an optimist who believes such fairy-tales.

But because for Ricardo the *rate of profit* and the *rate of surplus value*—that is, relative surplus value, since he assumes the length of the working day to be constant—are identical terms, a permanent fall in profit or the tendency of profit to fall can only be explained as the result of the *same causes* that bring about a permanent fall or tendency to fall in the *rate of surplus value,* i.e. in that part of the day during which the worker does not work for himself but for the capitalist. What are these causes? If the length of the working day is assumed to remain constant, then the part of it during which the worker works for nothing for the capitalist can only fall, diminish, if the part during which he works for himself grows. And this is only possible (assuming that LABOUR is paid at its *VALUE*), if the *value* of the NECESSARIES—the means of subsistence on which the worker spends his wages—increases. But as a result of the development of the productive power of labour, the value of industrial commodities is constantly decreasing. The diminishing rate of profit can therefore only be explained by the fact that the value of FOOD, the principal component part of the means of subsistence, is constantly rising. This happens because agriculture is becoming less productive. This is the same presupposition which, according to Ricardo's interpretation, explains the existence and growth of rent. The continuous fall in profits is thus bound up with the continuous rise in the rate of rent. I have already shown that Ricardo's view of rent is wrong. This then cuts out one of the grounds for his explanation of the FALL IN THE RATE OF PROFITS. But secondly, it rests on the false assumption that the RATE OF SURPLUS VALUE and the RATE OF PROFIT are identical, that therefore a fall in the RATE OF PROFIT is identical with a fall in the RATE OF SURPLUS VALUE, which in fact could only be explained in Ricardo's way. And this puts an end to his theory. The rate of profit falls, although the RATE OF SURPLUS VALUE remains the same or rises, because the proportion of variable capital to constant capital decreases with the development of the productive power of labour. The rate of profit thus falls, not because labour becomes less productive, but because it becomes more productive. Not because the worker is less exploited, but because he is more exploited, whether the ABSOLUTE SURPLUS TIME grows or, when the state prevents this, the RELATIVE SURPLUS TIME grows, for capitalist production is inseparable from falling RELATIVE VALUE OF LABOUR. Thus Ricardo's theory rests on two false presuppositions:

1) The false supposition that the existence and growth of rent is determined by the diminishing productivity of agriculture;

2) The false assumption that the rate of profit=the rate of relative surplus value and can only rise or fall in inverse proportion to a fall or rise in wages.

[XIII-674] I shall now place together the statements in which Ricardo expounds the view that has just been described.

First, however, some comments on the way in which, given his concept of rent, Ricardo thinks that rent gradually swallows up the rate of profit.

We shall use the tables on page 574,[a] but with the necessary modifications.

In these tables it is assumed that the capital employed$=60c+40v$, the surplus labour$=50\%$, the *value* of the product therefore$=£120$, whatever the productivity of labour. Of this £10=profit and £10=absolute rent. Say, the £40 represents wages for 20 men (for a week's labour for example or rather because of the rate of profit, say, a year's labour; but this does not matter here at all). According to Table *A*, where land I determines the market value, the number of tons=60, therefore 60 tons$=£120$, 1 ton$=£^{120}/_{60}=£2$. The wages, £40, thus=20 tons [of coal] or qrs of grain. This then is the necessary wage for the number of workers employed by the capital of 100. Now if it were necessary to descend to an inferior type of soil, where a capital of 110 (60 constant capital and the 20 workers which this sets in motion, that is, 60 constant capital and 50 variable capital) was required, in order to produce 48 tons. In this case the surplus value$=£10$, and the price per ton$=£2^1/_2$. If we descended to an even worse type of land where £120=40 tons, the price per ton$=^{120}/_{40}=£3$. In this case there would be no surplus value on the worse type of land. What the 20 men produce always=the value of £60 (£3=1 working day of a given length). Thus if wages grow from 40 to 60, the surplus value disappears altogether. It is assumed throughout that 1 qr is the necessary wage FOR ONE MAN. Assume that in both these cases a capital of only 100 is to be laid out. Or, which is the same thing, whatever capital may be laid out, what is the proportion for 100? For instead of calculating that, if the same number of workers and the same constant capital is employed as before, the capital outlay will amount to 110 or 120,

---

we shall calculate on the basis of the same organic composition (not measured in value but in amount of labour employed and amount of constant capital) how much constant capital and how great a number of workers a capital of 100 contains (in order to keep to the comparison of 100 with the other classes).

The proportion $110:60=100:54^6/_{11}$ and $110:50=100:45^5/_{11}$. 20 men set in motion 60 constant capital; so how many [men] set in motion $54^6/_{11}$?

The situation is as follows: The value obtained from employing a number of workers (say 20) is £60. In this case 20 qrs or tons=£40 will fall to the share of the workers employed, if the value of the ton or qr=£2. If the value of a ton rises to £3, the surplus value disappears. If it rises to $2^1/_2$, then that $^1/_2$ of the surplus value disappears, which constituted the absolute rent.

In the first case, where a capital of £120 (60c and 60v) is laid out the product=£120=40 tons (40×3).

In the second case, where a capital of 110 (60c and 50v) is laid out the product=£120=48 tons ($48×2^1/_2$).

In the first case, if the capital laid out were £100 (50c and 50v) the product=100=$33^1/_3$ tons ($£3×33^1/_3=100$).

Moreover, since only the land has deteriorated while the capital has undergone no change, the proportionate number [of workers] who set in motion the constant capital of 50 will be the same as that previously setting in motion the capital of 60. Thus if the latter was set in motion by 20 men (who received £40 while the value of 1 ton=£2) it will now be set in motion by $16^2/_3$ men, who receive £50 since the value of a ton has risen to £3. As before, 1 man receives 1 ton or 1 qr=£3, for $16^2/_3×3=50$. If the value created by $16^2/_3$ men=50, then that created by 20 men=£60. Thus the assumption that a day's labour of 20 men=£60 remains unchanged.

Now let us take the 2nd case. With a capital outlay of 100, the product=$109^1/_{11}=43^7/_{11}$ tons ($2^1/_2×43^7/_{11}=109^1/_{11}$). The constant capital=$54^6/_{11}$ and the variable=$45^5/_{11}$. How many men does the £$45^5/_{11}$ represent?

$18^2/_{11}$ men. [XIII-675] For if the value of a day's labour of 20 men=£60, then that of $18^2/_{11}$ men=$54^6/_{11}$, hence the value of the product=£$109^1/_{11}$.

It can be seen that in both cases the same capital sets in motion fewer men who, however, cost more. They work for the same length of time, but the surplus [labour] time decreases or disappears altogether, because they produce a smaller amount of product using the same amount of labour (and this product consists of their NECESSARIES), therefore they use more labour time for the production of 1 ton or 1 qr although they work *the same* length of time as before. In his calculations, Ricardo always presupposes that the capital must set in motion *more labour* and that therefore a *greater* capital, i.e. 120, 110, must be laid out instead of the previous 100. This is only correct if *the same quantity* is to be produced, i.e. 60 tons in the cases cited above, instead of 40 tons being produced IN CASE I, with an outlay of 120, and 48 in case II with an outlay of 110. With an outlay of 100, therefore, $33^1/_3$ tons are produced in case I and $43^7/_{11}$ tons in case II. Ricardo thus departs from the correct view point, which is not that more workers must be employed in order to create the same product, but that a given number of workers create a smaller product, a greater share of which is in turn taken up by wages.

We shall now compile two tables, firstly Table A from page 574 and the new table which follows from the data given above.

A

	Capital	Tons	TV [Total value]	MV [Market value] per ton	IV [Individual value] per ton	DV [Differential value] per ton	CP [Cost price] per ton	AR [Absolute rent]	DR [Differential rent]	AR [Absolute rent]
	[£]		£	£	£	£	£	£	£	tons
I)	100	60	120	2	2	0	$1^5/_6$	10	0	5
II)	100	65	130	2	$1^{11}/_{13}$	$^2/_{13}$	$1^9/_{13}$	10	10	5
III)	100	75	150	2	$1^9/_{15}$	$^2/_5$	$1^7/_{15}$	10	30	5
	300	200	400					30	40	15

	DR [Differential rent]	REN-TAL	REN-TAL	COMPOSITION OF CAPITAL	Surplus value	Number of workers	Wages	Wages	Rate of profit
	tons	£	tons		%		£	tons	%
[I)]	0	10	5	$60c+40v$	50	20	40	20	10
[II)]	5	20	10	$60c+40v$	ditto	ditto			
[III)]	15	40	20	$60c+40v$	ditto	ditto			
	20	70	35						

If this table were constructed in the reverse direction, according to Ricardo's DESCENDING LINE: that is beginning from III and if at the same time one assumed that the more fertile land which is cultivated first, pays no rent, then we would, in the first place, have a capital of 100 in III, [which] produces a value of 120, consisting of 60 constant capital and 60 newly added labour. According to Ricardo, one would further have to assume, that the rate of profit stood at a higher level than entered in Table A, since, when the ton of coal (qr of wheat)=£2, the 20 men received 20 tons=£40; now that, as a result of the fall in the value, the ton=£1$^9/_{15}$, or £1 12s., the 20 men receive only £32 (=20 tons). The capital advanced to employ the same number of workers would amount to 60c and 32v=£92 and the produced value=120, since the value of the work carried out by the 20 men=£60 as before. Accordingly, a capital of 100 would produce a value of 130$^{10}/_{23}$, for 92:120=100:130$^{10}/_{23}$ (or 23:30=100:130$^{10}/_{23}$). Moreover this capital of 100 would be composed as follows: 65$^5/_{23}$c and 34$^{18}/_{23}$v. Thus the capital would be 65$^5/_{23}$c+34$^{18}/_{23}$v; the value of the product=130$^{10}/_{23}$. The *number of workers* would be 21$^{17}/_{23}$ and the rate of surplus value 87$^1/_2$%.

1) So we would have:

	Capital	TV [Total value]	Number of tons	MV [Market value per ton]	IV [Individual value] per ton	DV [Differential value per ton]
	[£]	[£]		£	£	
III)	100	130$^{10}/_{23}$	81$^{12}/_{23}$	1$^9/_{15}$	1$^9/_{15}$	0

	Rent	Profit	Rate of profit	Composition of capital	Surplus value	Number of workers
	£		%		%	
[III)]	0	30$^{10}/_{23}$	30$^{10}/_{23}$	65$^5/_{23}$c+34$^{18}/_{23}$v	87$^1/_2$	21$^{17}/_{23}$

Expressed in tons, wages=21$^{17}/_{23}$ tons and profit=19$^1/_{46}$ tons. [XIII-676] Continuing on the Ricardian assumption, let us now suppose that as a result of the increasing population, the market price rises so high that class II must be cultivated, where the value per ton=£1$^{11}/_{13}$.

In this case it is impossible to assume as Ricardo wants that the 21$^{17}/_{23}$ workers produce always the same value, i.e. £65$^5/_{23}$ (wages added to surplus value). For the *number of workers* whom III can employ, and therefore exploit, decreases—according to his own assumption—hence also the total amount of surplus value.

At the same time, the composition of the AGRICULTURAL CAPITAL always remains the same. Whatever their wages may be, 20 workers are always required (with a given length of the working day) in order to set in motion 60c.

Since these 20 workers receive 20 tons and the ton=$£1^{11}/_{13}$, 20 workers cost $£20$ $(1+^{11}/_{13})=£20+£16^{12}/_{13}=£36^{12}/_{13}$.

The value which these 20 workers produce, whatever the productivity of their labour, $=60$; thus the capital advanced$=96^{12}/_{13}$, the value$=120$, and profit$=£23^{1}/_{13}$. The profit on a capital of 100 will therefore be $23^{17}/_{21}$ and the composition: $61^{19}/_{21}c+38^{2}/_{21}v$. $20^{40}/_{63}$ workers [are] employed. Since the total value $123^{17}/_{21}$, and the individual value per ton in class III$=£1^{9}/_{15}$, of how many tons does the product consist? $77^{8}/_{21}$ tons. The *rate of surplus value* is $62^{1}/_{2}\%$. But III sells the ton at $£1^{11}/_{13}$. This results in a differential value of $4^{12}/_{13}$s. or $£^{16}/_{65}$ per ton, and on $77^{8}/_{21}$ tons it amounts to $(77^{8}/_{21})$ $(4^{12}/_{13}$s.$)=£19^{20}/_{21}$s. Instead of selling its product at $123^{17}/_{21}$, III sells at $123^{17}/_{21}+£19^{20}/_{21}$s. (or $£19^{1}/_{21})=£142$ $17^{1}/_{7}$s. The $£19$ $^{20}/_{21}$s. constitutes the rent.

Thus we would have the following for III:

Capital	Tons	Actual total value	Total market value	IV [Individual value per ton]	MV [Market value per ton]
[£]		£	£	£	[£]
III) 100	$77^{8}/_{21}$	$123^{17}/_{21}$	$£142$ $17^{1}/_{7}$s.	$1^{9}/_{15}$	$1^{11}/_{13}$

DV [Differential value per ton]	Surplus value	Rate of profit	Number of workers	Composition of capital	Rent	Rent in tons
		%	%			
[III)] $+4^{12}/_{13}$s.	$62^{1}/_{2}$	$23^{17}/_{21}$	$20^{40}/_{63}$	$61^{19}/_{21}c+38^{2}/_{21}v$	$£19^{20}/_{21}$s.	10 tons and fraction

The wages measured in tons $=20$ $^{40}/_{63}$ tons. And the profit$=12$ $^{113}/_{126}$ tons.

We now pass on to class II; there is no rent here. Market value and individual value are equal. The number of tons produced by II$=67^{4}/_{63}$.

Thus we have the following *for II*:

Capital	Tons	TV [Total value]	MV [Market value per ton]	IV [Individual value per ton]
[£]		[£]	[£]	[£]
II) 100	$67^{4}/_{63}$	$123^{17}/_{21}$	$1^{11}/_{13}$	$1^{11}/_{13}$

DV [Differential value per ton]	Surplus value %	Rate of profit [%]	Number of workers	Composition of capital	Rent
[II)] 0	$62^1/_2$	$23^{17}/_{21}$	$20^{40}/_{63}$	$61^{19}/_{21}\,c+38^2/_{21}\,v$	0

Wages measured in tons=$20^{40}/_{63}$ and profit=$12^{113}/_{126}$ tons.

[XIII-677] For the 2nd CASE, in which class II is introduced and rent comes into existence, we have the following:

2) Capital [£]	Tons [£]	ATV [Actual total value] [£]	TMV [Total market value] [£]	MV [Market value per ton] £	IV [Individual value per ton] [£]	DV [Differential value per ton] [£]
III) 100	$77^8/_{21}$	$123^{17}/_{21}$	£142 $17^1/_7$s.	$1^{11}/_{13}$	$1^9/_{15}$	$+4^{12}/_{13}$s.
II) 100	$67^4/_{63}$	$123^{17}/_{21}$	$123^{17}/_{21}$	$1^{11}/_{13}$	$1^{11}/_{13}$	0

Composition of capital	Number of workers	Surplus value %	Rate of profit [%]	Wages in tons	Profit in tons	Rent £	Rent in tons
[III)] $61^{19}/_{21}c+38^2/_{21}v$	$20^{40}/_{63}$	$62^1/_2$	$23^{17}/_{21}$	$20^{40}/_{63}$	$12^{113}/_{126}$	£19$^{20}/_{21}$s.	$10^{20}/_{63}$
[II)] $61^{19}/_{21}c+38^2/_{21}v$	$20^{40}/_{63}$	$62^1/_2$	$23^{17}/_{21}$	$20^{40}/_{63}$	$12^{113}/_{126}$	0	0

Let us now pass on to the 3rd CASE and, like Ricardo, let us assume that mine I, a poorer mine, must and can be worked, because the *market value* has risen to £2. Since 20 workers are required for a constant capital of 60 and their wages are now £40, we have the same composition of capital as in Table *A p. 574*, i.e. $60c+40v$, and as the value produced by the 20 workers always=60, the total value of the product produced by a capital of 100=120, whatever its productivity. The rate of profit in this case=20 and the surplus value=50%. Measured in tons, the profit=10 tons. We must now see what changes occur in III and II as a result of this change in the market value and the introduction of I, which determines the rate of profit.

Although III works the most fertile land he can with 100 only employ 20 workers, costing him £40, for a constant capital of 60 requires 20 workers. The number of workers employed with a capital of 100 therefore falls to 20. And the actual total value of the product now=120. But how many tons have been produced by III when the individual value of one ton=£$1^9/_{15}$? 75 tons, since 120 divided by $^{24}/_{15}$ (£$1^9/_{15}$)=75. The number of tons produced by

III decreases because he can employ *less* labour with the same capital, not *more* (as Ricardo wrongly declares, because he always considers merely how much labour is required in order to create *the same* output; and not *how much living labour* can be employed with the new composition of capital though this is the only important point). But he sells these 75 tons at 150 (instead of at 120, which is their value) and so the rent rises to £30 in III. So far as II is concerned, the value of the product here ditto=120 etc. But, as the individual value per ton=$1^{11}/_{13}$, 65 tons are produced (for 120 divided by $^{24}/_{13}$ ($1^{11}/_{13}$)=65). In short, we arrive here at Table *A from p. 574.* But since for our purpose we need new headings here, now that I is introduced and the market value has risen to £2 we set out the table anew.

3)	Capital	Tons	ATV [Actual total value]	TMV [Total market value]	MV [Market value per ton]	IV [Individual value per ton]	DV [Differential value per ton]
	[£]		[£]	[£]	£	£	
III)	100	75	120	150	2	$1^9/_{15}$	8s.
II)	100	65	120	130	2	$1^{11}/_{13}$	$3^1/_{13}$s.
I)	100	60	120	120	2	2	0

	Composition of capital	Number of workers	Surplus value	Rate of profit	Wages in tons	Profit in tons	Rent	Rent in tons
			%	%			£	
[III)]	$60c+40v$	20	50	20	20	10	30	15
[II)]	$60c+40v$	20	50	20	20	10	10	5
[I)]	$60c+40c$	20	50	20	20	10	0	0
							40	20

[XIII-678] In short, this CASE III) corresponds to Table A p. 574 (apart from absolute rent which appears as a part of profit here) only the order is reversed.

Let us now go on to the newly assumed CASES.[a] First of all the class which still yields a profit. Let it be called Ib. With a capital of 100 it only yields $43^7/_{11}$ tons.

The value of a ton has risen to £$2^1/_2$. The composition of the capital=$54^6/_{11}c+45^5/_{11}v$. The value of the product=£$109^1/_{11}$. £$45^5/_{11}$ is enough to pay $18^2/_{11}$ men. And since the value of a day's

---

[a] See this volume, pp. 74-77.— *Ed.*

labour of 20 men=£60, that of $18^2/_{11}$ men=$54^6/_{11}$. The value of the product therefore=$109^1/_{11}$. The *rate of profit*=$£9^1/_{11}$=$3^7/_{11}$ tons. The *rate of surplus value* is 20%.

Since the organic composition of the capitals in III, II, I is the same as in Ib and they must pay the same wages, they too can employ only $18^2/_{11}$ men with £100, these men produce a total value of $54^6/_{11}$, and therefore a surplus value of 20% and a rate of profit of $9^1/_{11}$% as in Ib. The total value of the product here, as in Ib,=$£109^1/_{11}$.

But since the individual value of a ton in III=$£1^9/_{15}$, III produces (or its product=) $£109^1/_{11}$ divided by $1^9/_{15}$ or $^{24}/_{15}$=$68^2/_{11}$ tons. Moreover, the difference between the market value of a ton and the individual value amounts to $£2^1/_2$–$£1^9/_{15}$. That is £2 10s.—£1 12s.=18s. And on $68^2/_{11}$ tons this=18 (68+$^2/_{11}$)s.=1,227$^3/_{11}$s.=£61 7$^3/_{11}$s. Instead of selling at $£109^1/_{11}$, III sells at £170 $9^1/_{11}$s. And this excess=the rent of III. This rent, expressed in tons,=$24^6/_{11}$ tons.

Since the individual value of a ton in II=$£1^{11}/_{13}$, II produces $109^1/_{11}$ divided by $1^{11}/_{13}$ and this=$59^1/_{11}$ tons. The difference between the market value of one ton in II and its [individual] value is £2 10s.−£1 16$^{12}/_{13}$s. or (−$£1^{11}/_{13}$), which=$13^1/_{13}$s. And on $59^1/_{11}$ tons, this=$13^1/_{13}$ (59+$^1/_{11}$)s.=£38 12$^8/_{11}$s. And this is the rent. The total market value=£147 14$^6/_{11}$s. The rent expressed in tons=$15^5/_{11}$ tons.

Finally, since the individual value of a ton in I=£2, $£109^1/_{11}$=$54^6/_{11}$ tons. The difference between the market value and the individual value=$£2^1/_2$–£2=10s. And on $54^6/_{11}$ tons this=(54+$^6/_{11}$) 10s.=540s.+$^{60}/_{11}$s.=£27+5$^5/_{11}$s. The total market value therefore=£136 7$^3/_{11}$s. And the value of the rent expressed in tons=$10^4/_5$ tons,[22] if we omit a fraction ($5^5/_{11}$s.).

Bringing together all the data for CASE 4), one gets the following: [XIII-679]

4) Capital	Tons	ATV [Actual total value]	TMV [Total market value]	MV [Market value per ton]	IV [Individual value per ton]	DV [Differential value per ton]
[£]		£	£	£	£	
III) 100	$68^2/_{11}$	$109^1/_{11}$	£170 $9^1/_{11}$s.	$2^1/_2$	$1^9/_{15}$	18s.
II) 100	$59^1/_{11}$	$109^1/_{11}$	£147 $14^6/_{11}$[s.]	$2^1/_2$	$1^{11}/_{13}$	$13^1/_{13}$s.
I) 100	$54^6/_{11}$	$109^1/_{11}$	£136 $7^3/_{11}$[s.]	$2^1/_2$	2	10s.
Ib) 100	$43^7/_{11}$	$109^1/_{11}$	$£109^1/_{11}$	$2^1/_2$	$2^1/_2$	0

Composition of capital	Number of workers	Surplus value	Rate of profit	Wages [in] tons	Profit [in] tons	Rent	Rent [in] tons
		%	%			£	
[III)] $54^6/_{11}c+45^5/_{11}v$	$18^2/_{11}$	20	$9^1/_{11}$	$18^2/_{11}$	$3^7/_{11}$	£61 $7^3/_{11}$s.	$24^6/_{11}$
[II)] $54^6/_{11}c+45^5/_{11}v$	$18^2/_{11}$	20	$9^1/_{11}$	$18^2/_{11}$	$3^7/_{11}$	£38 $12^8/_{11}$s.	$15^5/_{11}$
[I)] $54^6/_{11}c+45^5/_{11}v$	$18^2/_{11}$	20	$9^1/_{11}$	$18^2/_{11}$	$3^7/_{11}$	£27 $5^5/_{11}$s.	$10^4/_5$
[Ib)] $54^6/_{11}c+45^5/_{11}v$	$18^2/_{11}$	20	$9^1/_{11}$	$18^2/_{11}$	$3^7/_{11}$	0	0

Finally let us look at the last CASE in which, according to Ricardo, the *entire profit* disappears and there is no surplus value.

In this case the value of the product rises to £3, so that if 20 men are employed, their wage=£60=the value produced by them. The composition of the capital=$50c+50v$. Now *$16^2/_3$ men* are employed. If the value produced by 20 men=60, then that produced by $16^2/_3$ men=£50. The wages, therefore, swallow up the whole value. Now, as before, a man receives 1 ton. The value of the product=100 and therefore the number of tons produced=$33^1/_3$ tons, of which $^1/_2$ merely replaces the value of the constant capital and the other half the value of the variable capital.

Since in III, the individual value of a ton=$1^9/_{15}$ or £$^{24}/_{15}$, how many tons does III produce? 100 divided by $^{24}/_{15}$, i.e. $62^1/_2$ tons, whose value=100. The difference, however, between market value and individual value=£$3-£1^9/_{15}$=£$1^6/_{15}$ or £$1^2/_5$. On $62^1/_2$ tons this=£$87^1/_2$. Hence the total market value of the product=£$187^1/_2$. And the rent in tons=$29^1/_6$ tons.

In II the individual value of a ton=£$1^{11}/_{13}$. Hence the differential value=£$3-£1^{11}/_{13}$=£$1^2/_{13}$. Since the individual value of a ton here=£$1^{11}/_{13}$ or £$^{24}/_{13}$, the capital of 100 produces 100 divided by $^{24}/_{13}$=$54^1/_6$ tons. On this number of tons, that difference=£62 10s. And the market value of the product=£162 10s. Expressed in tons, the rent=$20^5/_6$ tons.

In I the individual value of a ton=£2. The differential value therefore=$3-2$=£1. Since the individual value of a ton=£2 here, a capital of 100 produces 50 tons. This makes a difference of £50. The market value of the product=150 and the rent in tons=$16^2/_3$ tons.

We now come *to Ib*, which until now has not carried a rent. Here the individual value=£$2^1/_2$. Hence differential value=$3-£2^1/_2$=£$^1/_2$ or 10s. And since the individual value of a ton is here=$2^1/_2$ or £$^5/_2$, [£]100 produces 40 tons. The differential value on these=£20, so that the total market value=120. And the rent expressed in tons=$6^2/_3$ tons.

Let us now construct CASE 5) in which, according to Ricardo, profit disappears.
[XIII-680]

5)	Capital	Tons	ATV [Actual total value]	MV [Market value per ton]	IV [Individual value per ton]	DV [Differential value per ton]
	$[£]$		$[£]$	£	$[£]$	£
III)	100	$62^1/_2$	100	3	$1^9/_{15}$	$1^2/_5$
II)	100	$54^1/_6$	100	3	$1^{11}/_{13}$	$1^2/_{13}$
I)	100	50	100	3	2	1
Ib)	100	40	100	3	$2^1/_2$	$^1/_2$
Ia)	100	$33^1/_3$	100	3	3	0

	Composition of capital	Number of workers	Surplus value	Rate of profit	Wages [in tons]	Rent £	Rent in tons
[III)]	$50c+50v$	$16^2/_3$	0	0	$16^2/_3$	$87^1/_2$	$29^1/_6$
[II)]	$50c+50v$	$16^2/_3$	0	0	$16^2/_3$	$62^1/_2$	$20^5/_6$
[I)]	$50c+50v$	$16^2/_3$	0	0	$16^2/_3$	50	$16^2/_3$
[Ib)]	$50c+50v$	$16^2/_3$	0	0	$16^2/_3$	20	$6^2/_3$
[Ia)]	$50c+50v$	$16^2/_3$	0	0	$16^2/_3$	0	0

On the following page I shall now put all five CASES in tabular form [see pp. 84-85].

[XII-683] If in the first place we examine *Table E*) on the previous page, we see that the position in the last class, Ia, is very clear. In this case wages swallow up the whole product and the whole value of the labour. Surplus value is non-existent, hence there is neither profit nor rent. The value of the product=the value of the capital advanced, so that the workers—who are here in possession of their own capital—can invariably reproduce their wages and the conditions of their labour, but no more. In this last class it cannot be said that the rent swallows up the profit. There is no rent and no profit because there is no surplus value. Wages swallow up the surplus value and therefore the profit.

In the 4 other classes the position is *prima facie* by no means clear. If there is no surplus value, how can rent exist? Moreover, the productivity of labour on the types of land Ib, I, II and III has not altered at all. The *non-existence* of surplus value must therefore be sheer illusion.

[XIII-681]

The Movement of the Rent According to Ricardo
(with Certain Corrections)

	Capital [£]	Tons	Actual total value £	Total market value £	Market value per ton £	Individual value per ton £	Differential value per ton £	Composition of capital
A) (Only the best class, III, is cultivated.) Non-existence of rent.								
III)	100	$81^{12}/_{23}$	$130^{10}/_{23}$	$130^{10}/_{23}$	$1^9/_{15}$	$1^9/_{15}$	0	$65^5/_{23}c + 34^{18}/_{2}$
B) Second class, II, is added. Rent comes into existence on land (mine) III								
III)	100	$77^8/_{21}$	$123^{17}/_{21}$	£142 $17^1/_7$ s.	$1^{11}/_{13}$	$1^9/_{15}$	$+4^{12}/_{13}$ s.	$61^{19}/_{21}c + 38^2$
II)	100	$67^4/_{63}$	$123^{17}/_{21}$	$123^{17}/_{21}$	$1^{11}/_{13}$	$1^{11}/_{13}$	0	$61^{19}/_{21}c + 38^2$
Total 200		$144^4/_9$	$247^{13}/_{21}$	£266 $13^1/_3$ s.				
C) Third class, I, is added. Rent comes into existence on land (mine) II								
III)	100	75	120	150	2	$1^9/_{15}$	8s.	$60c + 40v$
II)	100	65	120	130	2	$1^{11}/_{13}$	$3^1/_{13}$s.	$60c + 40v$
I)	100	60	120	120	2	2	0	$60c + 40v$
Total 300		200	360	400				
D) Fourth class, Ib, is added. Rent comes into existence on land (mine) I								
III)	100	$68^2/_{11}$	$109^1/_{11}$	£170 $9^1/_{11}$s.	$2^1/_2$	$1^9/_{15}$	18s.	$54^6/_{11}c + 45^5/$
II)	100	$59^1/_{11}$	$109^1/_{11}$	£147 $14^6/_{11}$s.	$2^1/_2$	$1^{11}/_{13}$	$13^1/_{13}$s.	$54^6/_{11}c + 45^5/$
I)	100	$54^6/_{11}$	$109^1/_{11}$	£136 $7^3/_{11}$s.	$2^1/_2$	2	10s.	$54^6/_{11}c + 45^5/$
Ib)	100	$43^7/_{11}$	$109^1/_{11}$	£109 $^1/_{11}$	$2^1/_2$	$2^1/_2$	0	$54^6/_{11}c + 45^5/$
Total 400		$225^5/_{11}$	$436^4/_{11}$	£563 $12^8/_{11}$s.				
E) Fifth class, Ia, is added. Surplus value and profit disappear altogether								
III)	100	$62^1/_2$	100	$187^1/_2$	3	$1^9/_{15}$	$1^2/_5$	$50c + 50v$
II)	100	$54^1/_6$	100	$162^1/_2$	3	$1^{11}/_{13}$	$1^2/_{13}$	$50c + 50v$
I)	100	50	100	150	3	2	1	$50c + 50v$
Ib)	100	40	100	120	3	$2^1/_2$	$^1/_2$	$50c + 50v$
Ia)	100	$33^1/_3$	100	100	3	3	0	$50c + 50v$
Total 500		240	500	720				

Number of workers	Rate of surplus value %	Profit £	Profit in tons	Wages in tons	Money rent £	Rent in tons	
		[XIII-682] Only the most fertile land or mine is cultivated					A)
							B)
$1^{17}/_{23}$	$87^{1}/_{2}$	$30^{10}/_{23}$	$19^{1}/_{46}$	$21^{17}/_{23}$	0	0	
$0^{40}/_{63}$	$62^{1}/_{2}$	$23^{17}/_{21}$	$12^{113}/_{126}$	$20^{40}/_{63}$	£19 $^{20}/_{21}$s.	$10^{20}/_{63}$	
$0^{40}/_{63}$	$62^{1}/_{2}$	$23^{17}/_{21}$	$12^{113}/_{126}$	$20^{40}/_{63}$	0	0	
$1^{17}/_{63}$		$47^{13}/_{21}$	$25^{50}/_{63}$	$41^{17}/_{63}$	£19 $^{20}/_{21}$s.	$10^{20}/_{63}$	
							C)
20	50	20	10	20	30	15	
20	50	20	10	20	10	5	
20	50	20	10	20	0	0	
60		60	30	60	40	20	
							D)
$8^{2}/_{11}$	20	$9^{1}/_{11}$	$3^{7}/_{11}$	$18^{2}/_{11}$	£61 $7^{3}/_{11}$s.	$24^{6}/_{11}$	
$8^{2}/_{11}$	20	$9^{1}/_{11}$	$3^{7}/_{11}$	$18^{2}/_{11}$	£38 $12^{8}/_{11}$s.	$15^{5}/_{11}$	
$8^{2}/_{11}$	20	$9^{1}/_{11}$	$3^{7}/_{11}$	$18^{2}/_{11}$	£27 $5^{5}/_{11}$s.	$10^{4}/_{5}$	
$8^{2}/_{11}$	20	$9^{1}/_{11}$	$3^{7}/_{11}$	$18^{2}/_{11}$	0	0	
$2^{8}/_{11}$		$36^{4}/_{11}$	$14^{6}/_{11}$	$72^{8}/_{11}$	£127 $5^{5}/_{11}$s.	$50^{4}/_5$	
							E)
$6^{2}/_{3}$	0	0	0	$16^{2}/_{3}$	$87^{1}/_{2}$	$29^{1}/_{6}$	
$6^{2}/_{3}$	0	0	0	$16^{2}/_{3}$	$62^{1}/_{2}$	$20^{5}/_{6}$	
$6^{2}/_{3}$	0	0	0	$16^{2}/_{3}$	50	$16^{2}/_{3}$	
$6^{2}/_{3}$	0	0	0	$16^{2}/_{3}$	20	$6^{2}/_{3}$	
$6^{2}/_{3}$	0	0	0	$16^{2}/_{3}$	0	0	
$3^{1}/_{3}$				$83^{1}/_{3}$	220	$73^{1}/_{3}$	

Furthermore, another phenomenon becomes apparent and this, *prima facie*, is equally inexplicable. The rent in tons [of coal] or [in quarters] of corn for III amounts to $29^1/_6$ tons or qrs, whereas in Table A, where only land III was cultivated, where there was no rent and where, moreover, $21^{17}/_{23}$ men were EMPLOYED whereas now only $16^2/_3$ men are employed, the profit (which absorbed the entire surplus value) only amounted to $19^1/_{46}$ tons.

The same contradiction is apparent in II, where the rent in *Table E*)=$20^5/_6$ tons or qrs while in *Table B*) the profit, which absorbed the entire surplus value ($20^{40}/_{63}$ men being EMPLOYED, instead of $16^2/_3$ men now), amounted to only $12^{113}/_{126}$ tons or qrs.

Similary in I, where the rent in *Table E*)=$16^2/_3$ tons or qrs, while in Table C the profit of I), which absorbs the entire surplus value,=only 10 tons (20 men being EMPLOYED, instead of the present $16^2/_3$).

Finally in Ib, where the rent in *Table E*)=$6^2/_3$ tons or qrs, while the profit of Ib in *Table D*), where the profit absorbed the entire surplus value,=only $3^7/_{11}$ tons or qrs (while $18^2/_{11}$ MEN were EMPLOYED, instead of the $16^2/_3$ now being employed). It is, however, clear, that whereas the rise in market value above the individual value of the products of III, II, I, Ib can alter the distribution of the product, shifting it from one class of SHAREHOLDERS to the other, it can by no means increase the product which represents the surplus value over and above the wages. Since the productivity of the various types of land has remained the same, as has the productivity of capital, how can III to Ib become more productive in tons or qrs through the entry into the market of the less productive type of land or mine Ia?

The riddle is solved in the following manner:

If a day's labour of 20 men=£60, then that of $16^2/_3$ men produces £50. And since in land of class III, the labour time contained in $1^9/_{15}$ or £$^{24}/_{15}$ is represented in 1 ton or 1 qr, £50 will be represented in $31^1/_4$ tons or qrs. $16^2/_3$ tons or qrs have to be deducted from this for wages, thus leaving $14^7/_{12}$ tons as *surplus value*.

Furthermore, because the market value of a ton has risen from $1^9/_{15}$ or £$^{24}/_{15}$ to £3, $16^2/_3$ tons or qrs out of the product of $62^1/_2$ tons or qrs, will suffice to replace the value of the constant capital [£50]. On the other hand, so long as the ton or qr produced on III itself determined the market value, and the latter was therefore equal to its individual value, $31^1/_4$ tons or qrs were required in order to replace a constant capital of £50. Out of the $31^1/_4$ tons or qrs—the part of the product which was necessary to replace the capital when the value of a ton was $£^{24}/_{15}$—only $16^2/_3$ are now required. Thus $31^1/_4 - 16^2/_3$ tons or qrs, [XIII-684] i.e. $14^7/_{12}$ tons or qrs, become available and fall to the share of rent.

If one now adds the surplus value produced by $16^2/_3$ workers with a constant capital of $£50$ on III, which amounts to $14^7/_{12}$ tons or qrs,

to $14^7/_{12}$ tons or qrs, the part of the product which instead of replacing the constant capital now takes on the form of SURPLUS PRODUCE, then the total surplus PRODUCE amounts to $28^{14}/_{12}$ tons or qrs $= 29^2/_{12} = 29^1/_6$ qrs or tons. And this is EXACTLY the ton or corn rent of III in *Table E*). The apparent contradiction in the amount of ton or corn rent in classes II, I, Ib in *Table E*) is solved in exactly the same way.

Thus it becomes evident that the *differential rent*—which arises on the better types of land owing to the difference between market value and individual value of the products raised on them—in its *material form* as *rent in kind, surplus product, rent in tons* or *corn* in the above example, is made up of *two elements* and due to two *transformations.* [Firstly:] The surplus product which represents the surplus labour of the workers or the surplus value, is changed from the form of profit to the form of rent, and therefore falls to the LANDLORD instead of the capitalist. Secondly: a part of the product which previously—when the product of the better type of land or mine was being sold at its own value—was needed to *replace the value of the constant capital,* is now, when each portion of the product possesses a higher market value, free and appears in the form of SURPLUS PRODUCE, thus falling to the LANDLORD instead of the capitalist.

The *rent in kind* in so far as it is differential rent comes into being as the result of two processes: the transformation of the surplus PRODUCE into rent, and not into profit, and the transformation of a *portion* of the product which was previously allotted for the replacement of the value of the constant capital into surplus PRODUCE, and thus into rent. The latter circumstance, that a part of the product is converted into rent instead of capital, has been overlooked by Ricardo and all his followers. They only see the transformation of surplus PRODUCE into rent, but not the transformation of a part of the product which previously fell to the share of capital (not of profit) into surplus PRODUCE.

The *nominal value* of the *surplus PRODUCE* thus constituted or of the *differential rent,* is determined (according to the presupposition made) by the value of the product produced on the worst land or in the worst mine. But this market value only instigates the different distribution of this product, it does not bring it about.

These same two elements are [present] in all excess profit, for instance, if as a result of new machinery, etc., a cheaply produced product is sold at a higher market value than its own value. A part of the surplus labour of the workers appears as surplus product (excess profit) instead of as profit. And a part of the product which—if the product were sold at its own lower value—would have to replace the value of the capitalist's constant capital, now becomes free, has not got to replace anything, becomes surplus product and therefore swells the profit.

It was assumed throughout this discussion, that the product whose price (according to market value) had risen did not enter *naturaliter*[a] into the composition of the constant capital, but only into wages, only into the variable capital. If the former were the case, Ricardo says that this would cause the rate of profit to fall even more and the rent to rise. This has to be examined. We have assumed until now, that the *value* of the product has to replace the value of the constant capital, i.e. the £50 in the case cited above. Thus if 1 ton or qr costs £3, it is obvious that not so many tons or qrs are required for the replacement of this value than would be needed if the ton or qr cost only £$1^9/_{15}$, etc. But supposing that the coal or the corn or whatever other product of the earth, the product produced by AGRICULTURAL CAPITAL, itself enters *naturaliter* into the formation of the constant capital. Let us assume for instance that it makes up half of the constant capital. In this case it is clear that whatever the price of the coal or the corn [XIII-685] a constant capital of definite size, in other words, one which is set in motion by a definite number of workers, always requires a definite portion of the total product *in natura* for its replacement—since the composition of agricultural capital has, according to the assumption, remained *unchanged* in its proportionate amounts of accumulated and living labour.

If, for example, half the constant capital consists of coal or corn and half of other commodities, then the constant capital of 50 will consist of £25 of other commodities and £25 (or $15^5/_8$ qrs or tons), when the value of a ton=£$^{24}/_{15}$ or £$1^9/_{15}$. And however the market value of a ton or a qr may change, $16^2/_3$ men require a constant capital of £$25+15^5/_8$ qrs or tons, for the nature of the constant capital remains the same, ditto the proportionate number of workers required to set it in motion.

---

[a] In kind.—*Ed.*

Now if, as in *Table E*), the value of a ton or qr rises to £3, then the constant capital required for the $16^2/_3$ men=£25+£3 $(15+^5/_8)$=£25+£45+£$^{15}/_8$=£71$^7/_8$. And since the $16^2/_3$ men cost £50, they would require a total capital outlay of £71$^7/_8$+ +£50=£121$^7/_8$.

The *correlation of values* within the AGRICULTURAL capital would have changed while organic composition remained the same. It would be 71$^7/_8c$+50v (for $16^2/_3$ workers). For [£]100 the composition would be 58$^{38}/_{39}c$+41$^1/_{39}v$. Slightly more than 13$^2/_3$ workers (that is, leaving out of account the fraction $^1/_{117}$). Since $16^2/_3$ workers set in motion 15$^5/_8$ qrs or tons constant capital, 13$^{79}/_{117}$ workers set in motion 12$^{32}/_{39}$ tons or qrs=£38$^6/_{13}$. The remainder of the constant capital=£20$^{20}/_{39}$, would consist of other commodities. Whatever the circumstances, 12$^{32}/_{39}$ tons or qrs would always have to be deducted from the product in order to replace that part of constant capital into which they enter *in natura.* Since the value produced by 20 workers=£60, that produced by 13$^{79}/_{117}$=£41$^1/_{39}$. Wages in *Table E*), however, ditto amount to 41$^1/_{39}$. Therefore no surplus value.

The total number of tons would be 1) [51$^{11}/_{39}$ tons,[23] of which] 12$^{32}/_{39}$ tons are again reproduced; a further 13$^{79}/_{117}$ are for the workers, altogether 26$^{58}/_{117}$. 6$^{98}/_{117}$ tons, at £3 a ton, are used to replace the remainder of the constant capital. That is altogether 33$^1/_3$ tons. This would leave 17$^{37}/_{39}$ tons for the rent.

To shorten the matter, let us take the most extreme case, the one most favourable to Ricardo, i.e. that the constant capital, just as the variable, consists purely of AGRICULTURAL PRODUCE whose value rises to £3 per qr or ton, when class Ia governs the market.

The technological composition of the capital remains the same; that is, the *ratio* between living labour or number of workers (since the normal working day has been assumed to be constant) represented by the variable capital and the *quantity of the means of labour* required, which now, according to our assumption, consist of tons of coal or qrs of corn, remains constant for a given number of workers.

Since with the original composition of the capital, of 60c+40v, and the price per ton of £2, 40v represented 20 workers or 20 qrs, or tons, 60c represented 30 tons; and since these 20 workers produced 75 tons on III, 13$^1/_3$ workers (and 40v=13$^1/_3$ tons or workers if the ton costs £3) produce 50 *tons* and set in motion a constant capital [XIII-686] of $^{60}/_3$=20 tons or qrs.

Moreover, since 20 workers produce a value of £60, 13$^1/_3$ produce £40.

Since the capitalist must pay £60 for the 20 tons and 40 for the $13^1/_3$ workers, but the latter only produce a value of £40, the value of the product=£100; the outlay=£100. Surplus value and profit=0.

But because the productivity of III has remained the same, as has already been said, $13^1/_3$ men produce 50 tons or qrs. The outlay in kind of tons, or qrs, however, only amounts to 20 tons for constant capital and $13^1/_3$ tons for wages, i.e. $33^1/_3$ tons. The 50 tons thus leave a SURPLUS PRODUCE of $16^2/_3$ and this forms the rent.

But what do the $16^2/_3$ represent?

Since the *value* of the product=100 and the product itself=50 tons, the value of the ton produced here would IN FACT be £2=$^{100}/_{50}$. And so long as the product *in natura* is greater than what is required for the replacement of the capital in kind, the individual value of a ton must remain smaller than its market value according to this criterion.

The FARMER must pay £60 in order to replace the 20 tons, and he reckons the 20 tons at £3, since this is the market value per ton and a ton is sold at this price. Similarly he must pay £40 for the $13^1/_3$ workers, or for the tons or qrs which he pays to the workers. Thus the workers only receive $13^1/_3$ tons in the transaction.

In actual fact, however, so far as class III is concerned, the 20 tons cost £40 and the $13^1/_3$ cost only $26^2/_3$. But the $13^1/_3$ workers produce a value of £40, and therefore a surplus value of £$13^1/_3$. At £2 per ton, this=$6^4/_6$ or $6^2/_3$ tons. And since the 20 tons cost only £40 on III, this leaves an excess of £20=10 tons.

The $16^2/_3$ tons rent are thus=$6^2/_3$ tons surplus value which is converted into rent and 10 tons capital which is converted into rent. But because the market value per ton has risen to £3, the 20 tons cost the farmer £60 and the $13^1/_3$ cost him £40, while the $16^2/_3$ tons, that is the excess of the market value over the [individual] value of his product, appear as rent, and=£50.

How many tons are produced by $13^1/_3$ men in class II? 20 men produce 65 here, $13^1/_3$ therefore—$43^1/_3$ tons. The value of the product=100, as above. Of the $43^1/_3$ tons, however, $33^1/_3$ or $33^4/_{12}$ are required for the replacement of the capital. This leaves $43^1/_3-33^4/_{12}$—10 tons as surplus product or rent.

But this rent of 10 tons can be explained as follows: the value of the product of II=100, the product=$43^1/_3$ [tons], thus the value of

a ton=$\dfrac{100}{43+^1/_3}$ =£2 $6^2/_{13}$[s.]. The $13^1/_3$ workers therefore cost

$30^{10}/_{13}$, and this leaves a surplus value of £9 $4^8/_{13}$. Moreover, the

20 tons constant capital cost $46^2/_{13}$ and of the 60 that are paid for this, there remain $13^{11}/_{13}$. Together with the surplus value this comes to £23 $1^7/_{13}$.

Only in class Ia, where $33^1/_3$ tons or qrs, that is the total product, is required *in natura* to replace constant capital and wages, there is IN FACT neither surplus value, nor SURPLUS PRODUCE, nor profit, nor rent. So long as this is not the case, so long as the product is greater than is necessary to replace the capital *in natura*, there will be conversion of profit (surplus VALUE) and capital into rent. Conversion of capital into rent takes place when a part of the product is freed, which, with a lower value, would have had to replace the capital, or [when] a part of the product which would have been converted into capital and surplus value falls to rent.

At the same time it is evident that if constant capital becomes dearer as a result of dearer AGRICULTURAL PRODUCE, the rent is very much reduced, for example, the rent of III and II [in Table E] from 50 tons=£150 with a market value of £3, to $26^2/_3$ tons, i.e. almost to half. Such a reduction is inevitable [XIII-687] since the number of workers employed with the same capital of 100 is reduced for two reasons, firstly, because wages rise, i.e. the value of the variable capital rises, secondly, because the value of the means of production, the constant capital, rises. In itself, the rise in wages necessitates that out of the 100 less can be laid out in labour, hence relatively less (if the value of the commodities that enter into the constant capital remains the same) can be laid out in constant capital; thus £100 represents less accumulated and less living labour TOGETHER. In addition, however, the rise in the value of the commodities which enter into the constant capital, reduces the amount of accumulated labour and for this reason of living labour, which can be employed for the same sum of money, as the technological ratio between accumulated and living labour remains the same. But since, with the same productivity of the land and a given technological composition of the capital, the total product depends on the quantity of labour employed, as the latter decreases, so the rent must also decrease.

This only becomes evident when *profit* disappears. So long as there is a profit, the rent can increase despite the absolute decrease in the product in *all* classes, as shown in the table on *p. 681*.[a] It is after all obvious that as soon as rent alone exists, the decrease in the product, HENCE in the SURPLUS PRODUCE, must hit rent

---

[a] See this volume, pp. 84-85.— *Ed.*

itself. This would occur more rapidly at the outset, if the value of the constant capital increased with that of variable capital.

But this apart, the table on *p. 681* shows that with declining fertility in agriculture, the growth of differential rent is always accompanied, *even on the better classes of land,* by a diminishing volume of total product in proportion to a capital outlay of a definite size, say 100. Ricardo has no inkling of this. The rate of profit decreases, because the same capital, say 100, sets in motion *less* labour and pays more for this labour, thus yielding an ever smaller surplus. The actual product, however, like the surplus value, depends on the number of workers employed by the capital, when the productivity is given. This is overlooked by Ricardo. He ditto ignores the manner in which the rent is formed: not only by transforming SURPLUS VALUE into rent, but also capital into SURPLUS VALUE. Of course this is only an apparent transformation of capital into SURPLUS VALUE. Each particle of SURPLUS PRODUCE would represent SURPLUS VALUE or SURPLUS labour, if the market value were determined by the value of the product of III etc. Ricardo, moreover, only considers that in order to produce the same volume of product, more labour has to be employed, but disregards the fact that with the same capital, an ever diminishing quantity of living labour is employed, of which an ever greater part is NECESSARY LABOUR and an ever smaller part SURPLUS LABOUR, and this is the decisive factor for the determination of both the rate of profit and the quantity of product produced.

ALL THIS CONSIDERED, it must be said that even if rent is taken to be purely differential rent, Ricardo has not made the slightest advance over his predecessors. His important achievement in this field is, as De Quincey pointed out, the *scientific* formulation of the question. In solving it Ricardo accepts the traditional views. Namely:

"Ricardo's doctrine of rent is new in so far as he poses the question whether in fact it sets aside the LAW OF ACTUAL VALUE" [20] (Thomas de Quincey, *The Logic of Political Economy,* Edinburgh, 1844, [p.] 158).

On p. *163* of the same work, Quincey says further:

* "...Rent is that portion of the produce from the soil (or *from any agency of production*) which is paid to the landlord for the *use of its differential powers,* as measured by comparison with those of similar agencies operating on the same market." *

Furthermore on *p. 176*:

"The objections against Ricardo are that the owners of No. 1 will not give it away for nothing. But in the *period*" // this *mythical* period //, "when only No. 1 is being cultivated "NO SEPARATE CLASS OF OCCUPANTS AND TENANTS DISTINCT FROM THE CLASS OF OWNERS [XIII-688] CAN HAVE BEEN FORMED."[a]

So according to De Quincey this law of "landownership" [is valid] so long as there is *no* landownership in the modern sense of the word.

Now to the relevant quotations from Ricardo.

(First the following note on *differential rent*: In reality, the ASCENDING and DESCENDING LINES alternate, run across one another and intertwine.

But it cannot by any means be said that if for individual short periods (such as 1797-1813) the DESCENDING LINE clearly predominates, that *because of this,* the rate of profit must fall (in so far, that is, as the latter is determined by the rate of surplus value). Rather I believe that during that period, the rate of profit in England rose by way of exception, despite the greatly increased prices of wheat and AGRICULTURAL PRODUCE GENERALLY. I do not know of any English statistician who does not share this view on the rise in the rate of profit during that period. Individual economists, such as Chalmers, Blake, etc. have advanced special theories based on this fact.[b] First, I must add that it is foolish to attempt to explain the rise in the price of wheat during that period by the depreciation of money. No one who has studied the history of the prices of commodities during that period, can agree with this. Besides, the rise in prices begins much earlier and reaches a high level before any kind of DEPRECIATION of money occurs. As soon as it appears it must simply be allowed for. If one asks why the rate of profit rose despite the rising corn prices, this is to be explained from the following circumstances: Prolongation of the working day, the direct consequence of the newly introduced machinery; depreciation of the manufactured goods and colonial commodities which enter into the consumption of the workers; reduction of wages (although the nominal wage rose) *below* their traditional average level (this FACT is acknowledged for that period; *P. J. Stirling* in *The Philosophy of Trade etc.*, Edinburgh, 1846, who, on the whole, accepts Ricardo's theory of rent, seeks, however, to prove that the *immediate* consequence of a permanent (that is, not accidental, dependent on the seasons) rise in the price of corn, is

---

[a] Marx gives here, in his own words, a brief summary of the idea developed by De Quincey.— *Ed.*

[b] Cf. Th. Chalmers, *On Political Economy in Connexion with the Moral State and Moral Prospects of Society,* 2nd ed., Glasgow, 1832 and W. Blake, *Observations on the Effects Produced by the Expenditure of Government during the Restriction of Cash Payments,* London, 1823.— *Ed.*

always reduction in the AVERAGE wage[a]; finally, the rise in the rate of profit was due to rising *nominal* prices of commodities, because loans and government expenditure increased the demand for capital even more rapidly than its supply, and this enabled the manufacturers to retrieve part of the product paid to the landowning rentiers and OTHER MEN on a FIXED INCOME in the form of rent, etc. This transaction is of no concern to us here, where we are considering the basic relationships, and therefore are concerned only with 3 classes: LANDLORDS, CAPITALISTS and WORKMEN. On the other hand it plays a significant part in practice, under appropriate circumstances as *Blake* has shown.[24])

// Incidentally, when speaking of the law of the *falling rate of profit* in the course of the development of capitalist production, we mean by profit, the total sum of surplus value which is seized in the first place by industrial capitalist, [irrespective of] how he may have to share this later with the money-lending capitalist (in the form of interest) and the LANDLORD (in the form of rent). Thus here

$$\text{the rate of profit} = \frac{\text{surplus value}}{\text{capital advanced}}.$$

The rate of profit in this sense may fall, although, for instance, the industrial profit rises proportionately to interest or vice versa, or although rent rises proportionately to industrial profit or vice versa. If P=the profit, P'=the industrial profit, I interest and R rent, then $P=P'+I+R$. And it is clear, that whatever the absolute magnitude of P, P', I, R can increase or decrease as compared with one another, independently of the magnitude of P or the rise and fall of P. The reciprocal rise of P', I and R only represents an altered distribution of P among different persons. A further examination of the circumstances on which this distribution of P depends but which does not coincide with a rise or fall of P itself, does not belong here, but into a consideration of the competition between capitals. That, however, R can rise to a level higher even than that of P, if it were only divided into P' and I, is therefore—as has already been explained—due to an *illusion* which arises from the fact that a part of the product whose [market] value is rising, becomes free and is converted into rent instead of being reconverted into constant capital. //

[XIII-689] // Mr. *Hallett* from Brighton exhibited "PEDIGREE NURSERY WHEAT" at the 1862 EXHIBITION.[25] * "Mr. Hallett insists that ears of corn, like racehorses, must be carefully reared, instead of, as is done ordinarily, grown in higgledy-piggledy

---

[a] P. J. Stirling, *The Philosophy of Trade; or, Outlines of a Theory of Profits and Prices...*, Edinburgh, London, 1846, pp. 209-10.— *Ed.*

fashion, with no regard to the theory of natural selection. In illustration of what good education may do even with wheat, some remarkable examples are given. In 1857, Mr. Hallett planted an ear of the first quality of the red wheat, exactly $4^3/_8$ inches long, and containing 47 grains. From the produce of the small crops ensuing, he again selected, in 1858, the finest ear, $6^1/_2$ inches long, and with 79 grains; and this was repeated, in 1859, again with the best offspring, this time $7^3/_4$ inches long, and containing 91 grains. The next year, 1860, was a bad season for agricultural education, and the wheat refused to grow any bigger and better; but the year after, 1861, the best ear came to be $8^3/_4$ inches long, with no less than 123 grains on the single stalk. Thus the wheat had increased, in five years, to very nearly double its size, and to a threefold amount of productiveness in number of grains. These results were obtained by what Mr. Hallett calls the 'natural system' of cultivating wheat; that is, the planting of single grains at such a distance—about 9 inches from each other—every way—as to afford each sufficient space for full development.... He asserts that the corn produce of England may be doubled by adopting 'pedigree wheat' and the 'natural system' of cultivation. He states that from single grains, planted at the proper time, one only on each square foot of ground, he obtained plants consisting of 23 ears on the average, with about 36 grains in each ear. The produce of an acre at this rate was, accurately counted, 1,001,880 ears of wheat; while, when sown in the ordinary fashion, with an expenditure of more than 20 times the amount of seed, the crop amounted to only 934,120 ears of corn, or 67,760 ears less..." //

"With the progress of society the *natural price of labour* has always a *tendency to rise, because one of the principal commodities by which its natural price is regulated, has a tendency to become dearer, from the greater difficulty of producing it.* As, however, the improvements in agriculture, the discovery of new markets, whence provisions may be imported, may for a time counteract the tendency to a rise in the price of necessaries, and may even occasion their natural price to fall, so will the same causes produce the correspondent effects on the natural price of labour"* (l.c., [pp.] 86-87). *"The natural price of all commodities, excepting raw produce and labour, has a tendency to fall, in the progress of wealth and population; for though, on one hand, they are enhanced in real value, from the rise in the natural price of the raw material of which they are made, this is more than counterbalanced by the improvements in machinery, by the better division and distribution of labour, and by *the increasing skill*, both *in science and art,* of the *producers"* * (l.c., [p.] 87).

*"As population increases, these necessaries will be constantly rising in price, because more labour will be necessary to produce them.... Instead, therefore, of the money wages of labour falling, they would rise; but they would not rise sufficiently to enable the labourer to purchase as many comforts and necessaries as he did before the rise in the price of those commodities.... Notwithstanding, then, that the labourer would be really worse paid, yet *this increase in his wages would necessarily diminish the profits of the manufacturer*; for his goods would sell at no higher price, and yet the expense of producing them would be increased.... It appears, then, that *the same cause which raises rent, the increasing difficulty of providing* an *additional quantity of food with the same proportional quantity of labour, will also raise wages*; and therefore if money be of an unvarying value, both rent and wages will have a tendency to rise with the progress of wealth and population"* * (l.c., [pp.] 96-97). *"But there is this essential difference between the rise of rent and the rise of wages. The rise in the money value of rent is accompanied by an [XIII-690] increased share of the produce: not only is the landlord's money rent greater, but his corn rent also.... The fate of the labourer will be less happy; he will receive

more money wages, it is true, but his corn wages will be reduced; and not only his command of corn, but his general condition will be deteriorated, by his finding it more difficult to maintain the market rate of wages above their natural rate" * (l.c., [pp.] 97-98).

* "Supposing corn and manufactured goods always to sell at the same price, profits would be high or low in proportion as wages were low or high. But suppose corn to rise in price because more labour is necessary to produce it; that cause will not raise the price of manufactured goods in the production of which no additional quantity of labour is required ... if, as is absolutely certain, wages should rise with the rise of corn, then their [the manufacturers'] profits would necessarily fall" * (l.c., [p.] 108). But it may be asked, * "whether the *farmer at least* would not have the same rate of profits, although he should pay an additional sum for wages? Certainly not: for he will not only have to pay, in common with the manufacturer, an increase of wages to each labourer he employs, but he will be obliged *either to pay rent, or to employ an additional number of labourers to obtain the same produce*; and the rise in the price of the raw produce will be proportioned only to that rent, or that additional number, and will not compensate him for the rise of wages" * (l.c., [p.] 108).

* "We have shewn that in *early stages of society,* both the landlord's and the labourer's share of the *value* of the produce of the earth, would be but small; and that it would increase in proportion to the progress of wealth, and the difficulty of procuring food" * (l.c., [p.] 109).

These "EARLY STAGES OF SOCIETY" are a peculiar bourgeois fantasy. In these EARLY STAGES, the LABOURER is either slave or SELF-SUSTAINING PEASANT, etc. In the first case he belongs to the LANDLORD, together with the land; in the second case he is his own LANDLORD. In neither case does *any capitalist* stand between the LANDLORD and the LABOURER. The subjugation of agriculture to capitalist production, and *hence* the transformation of SLAVES or PEASANTS into WAGE LABOURERS and the intervention of the capitalist between LANDLORD and LABOURER—which is only the final result of capitalist production—is regarded by Ricardo as a phenomenon belonging to the "EARLY STAGES OF SOCIETY".

* "The natural tendency of profits then is to fall; for, in the progress of society and wealth, the additional quantity of food required is obtained by the sacrifice of more and more labour. This tendency, this gravitation as it were of profits, is happily checked at repeated intervals by the improvements of machinery, connected with the production of necessaries, as well as by discoveries in the science of agriculture which enable us to relinquish a portion of labour before required, and therefore to lower the price of the prime necessary of the labourer" * (l.c., [pp. 120-]21).

In the following sentence, Ricardo says in plain terms that by RATE OF PROFITS he understands the RATE OF SURPLUS VALUE:

* "Although a greater *value* is produced, a *greater proportion of what remains of that value,* after paying rent, is consumed by the producers, and *it is this,* and *this alone, which regulates profits*" * (l.c., [p.] 127).

In other words, apart from rent, the rate of profit=the excess of the value of the commodity over the value of the labour which is paid during its production, or that part of its value which is consumed by the PRODUCERS. Ricardo calls only the workers PRODUCERS.[19] He assumes that the PRODUCED VALUE is produced by them. He thus defines surplus value here, as that part of the value created by the workers which the capitalist retains.

But if Ricardo identifies RATE OF SURPLUS VALUE with RATE OF PROFIT—and at the same time assumes, as he does, that the working day is of given length—then the TENDENCY of the RATE OF PROFIT to fall can only be explained by the same factors which make the RATE OF SURPLUS VALUE fall. But, with a given working day, the rate of surplus value can only fall if the RATE OF WAGES is rising PERMANENTLY. This is only possible if the VALUE of NECESSARIES is rising PERMANENTLY. And this only if agriculture is constantly deteriorating, in other words, if Ricardo's theory of rent is accepted. Since Ricardo identifies RATE OF SURPLUS VALUE with RATE OF PROFIT, [XIII-691] and since the rate OF SURPLUS VALUE can only be reckoned in relation to variable capital, capital laid out in wages, Ricardo, like Adam Smith, assumes that the *value of the whole product*—after deduction of rent—is divided between WORKMEN and CAPITALISTS, into WAGES and PROFITS. This means that he makes the false presupposition that the whole of the capital advanced consists only of variable capital. Thus, for example, after the passage quoted above, he goes on:

* "When poor lands are taken into cultivation, or when more capital and labour are expended on the old land, with a less return of produce, the effect must be permanent. A greater proportion of that part of the produce which remains to be divided after paying rent, between the owners of stock and the labourers, will be apportioned to the latter" * (l.c., [pp.] 127-28).

The passage continues:

* "Each man may, and probably will, have a less absolute quantity; but as more labourers are employed in proportion to the whole produce retained by the farmer, the value of a greater proportion of the whole produce will be absorbed by wages, and consequently the value of a smaller proportion will be devoted to profits" * (l.c., [p.] 128).

And shortly before:

* "The remaining quantity of the produce of the land, after the landlord and labourer are paid, necessarily belongs to the farmer, and *constitutes the profits of his stock*" * (l.c., [p.] 110).

At the end of the section (CH. VI) "On Profits", Ricardo says that his thesis on the FALL OF PROFITS remains true, even if—which is wrong—it were assumed, that the *prices of commodities* rose with a rise in the MONEY WAGES of the LABOURERS.

*"In the Chapter on Wages, we have endeavoured to shew that the *money price of commodities would not be raised by a rise of wages....* But if it were otherwise, if the prices of commodities were permanently raised by high wages, the proposition would not be less true, which asserts that high wages invariably affect the employers of labour, by depriving them of a portion of their real profits. Supposing the hatter, the hosier, and the shoemaker, each paid £10 more wages in the manufacture of a particular quantity of their commodities, and that the price of hats, stockings, and shoes, rose by a sum sufficient to repay the manufacturer the £10, *their situation would be no better than if no such rise took place.* If the hosier sold his stockings for £110 instead of £100, his profits would be precisely the same money amount as before; but as he would obtain in exchange for this equal sum, one-tenth less of hats, shoes, and every other commodity, and as he *could with his former amount of saving"* * (that is with the same capital) *"employ fewer labourers at the increased wages,* and purchase fewer raw materials at the increased prices, he would be in no better situation than if his money profits had been really diminished in amount, and every thing had remained at its former price"* (l.c., [p.] 129).

Whereas elsewhere in his argument Ricardo always only stressed that in order to produce *the same quantity of product* on worse land, *more labourers* have to be paid, here at last he stresses what is decisive for the rate of profit, namely, that with the same AMOUNT OF CAPITAL FEWER LABOURERS ARE EMPLOYED AT INCREASED WAGES. Apart from this, he is not quite right in what he says. It makes no difference to the capitalist, if the price of HATS etc. rises by 10%, but the LANDLORD would have to give up more of his rent. His rent may have risen for example, from 10 to £20. But he gets proportionately fewer HATS etc. for his £20 than for the 10.

Ricardo says quite rightly:

"In an improving state of society, the net produce of land is always diminishing in proportion to its gross produce" (l.c., [p.] 198).

By this he means that the rent initially rises IN AN IMPROVING STATE OF SOCIETY. The real reason is that IN AN IMPROVING STATE OF SOCIETY, the variable capital decreases in proportion to the constant capital.

Regarding the *origin of surplus value*:

*"In the form of money ... capital is productive of no profit; in the form of materials, machinery, and food, for which it might be exchanged, *it would* be *productive of revenue..."** (l.c., p. 267). *"The capital of the stockholder can [XIII-692] never be made productive—*it is, in fact, no capital.* If he were to sell his stock, and employ the capital he obtained for it, productively, he could only do so by detaching the capital of the buyer of his stock from a productive employment"* (l.c., p. 289, note).

That with the PROGRESS of production, the constant capital grows in proportion to the variable, Ricardo himself admits, but only in the form that the FIXED CAPITAL grows in proportion to the CIRCULATING.

* "In rich and powerful countries, where large capitals are invested in machinery, more distress will be experienced from a revulsion in trade, than in poorer countries *where there is proportionally a much smaller amount of fixed, and a much larger amount of circulating capital,* and where consequently *more work is done by the labour of men.* It is not so difficult to withdraw a circulating as a fixed capital, from any employment in which it may be engaged. It is often impossible to divert the machinery which may have been erected for one manufacture, to the purposes of another; but the clothing, the food, and the lodging of the labourer in one employment may be devoted to the support of the labourer in another;" *

(here, therefore, circulating capital comprises only variable capital, capital laid out in wages)

* "or the same labourer may receive the same food, clothing and lodging, whilst his employment is changed. This, however, is an evil to which a rich nation must submit; and it would not be more reasonable to complain of it, than it would be in a rich merchant to lament that his ship was exposed to the dangers of the sea, whilst his poor neighbour's cottage was safe from all such hazard" * (l.c., [p.] 311).

Ricardo himself mentions one reason for the rise in rent, which is quite independent of the RISE IN THE PRICE OF AGRICULTURAL PRODUCE:

* "Whatever capital becomes fixed on the land, must necessarily be the landlord's, and not the tenant's, at the expiration of the lease. Whatever compensation the landlord may receive for this capital, on re-letting his land, *will appear in the form of rent;* but no rent will be paid, if, with a given capital, more corn can be obtained from abroad, than can be grown on this land at home" * (l.c., [p.] 315, note).

On the same subject Ricardo says:

* "In a former part of this work, I have noticed the difference between rent, properly so called, and the remuneration paid to the landlord under that name, for the advantages which the expenditure of his capital has procured to his tenant; but I did not perhaps sufficiently distinguish the difference which would arise from the different modes in which this capital might be applied. As a part of this capital, when once expended in the improvement of a farm, is inseparably amalgamated with the land, and tends to increase its productive powers, the *remuneration paid to the landlord for its use is strictly of the nature of rent,* and is subject to all the laws of rent. Whether the improvement be made at the expense of the landlord or the tenant, it will not be undertaken in the first instance, unless there is a strong probability that the return will at least be equal to the *profit* that can be made by the disposition of any other equal capital; but when once made, the return obtained will *ever after be wholly of the nature of rent,* and will be subject to all the variations of rent. Some of these expenses, however, only give advantages to the land for a limited period, and do not add permanently to its productive powers: being bestowed on buildings, and other perishable improvements, they require to be constantly renewed, and therefore do not obtain for the landlord any permanent addition to his real rent" * (l.c., p. 306, *note*).

Ricardo says:

* "In all countries, and at all times, *profits depend* on the quantity of labour requisite to provide necessaries for the labourers, on that land or with that capital which yields no rent" * (l.c., [p.] 128).

According to this, the profit of the farmer on that land—the worst land, which according to Ricardo pays no rent—regulates THE GENERAL RATE OF PROFIT. The reasoning is this: the product of the worst land is sold at its *value* and pays no rent. We see here exactly, therefore, how much surplus value remains for the capitalist after deduction of the value of that part of the product which is merely an equivalent for the worker. And this surplus value is the profit. This is based on the assumption that *cost price* and *value* are identical, that this product, because it is sold at its cost price, is sold at its value.

This is incorrect, historically and theoretically. I have shown[a] that, where there is capitalist production and where landed property exists, the land or mine of the worst type cannot pay a rent, because its produce is sold *below its value* if it is sold at the market value of corn (which is not regulated by it). For the market value only covers its *cost price*. But what regulates this cost price? The rate of profit of the NON-AGRICULTURAL CAPITAL, into whose determination the price of corn naturally enters as well, however far removed the latter may be from being its sole determinant. Ricardo's assertion would only be correct if VALUES and COST PRICES were [XIII-693] identical. Historically too, as the capitalist mode of production appears later in agriculture than in industry, AGRICULTURAL PROFIT is determined by INDUSTRIAL, and not the other way about. The only correct point is that on the land which pays a profit but no rent, which sells its product at the cost price, the AVERAGE RATE OF PROFITS becomes *apparent,* is tangibly presented, but this does not mean at all that the AVERAGE PROFITS are thereby *regulated*; that would be a very different matter.

The *rate of profit* can fall, without any rise in the *rate of interest* and *rate of rent*.

*"From the account which has been given of the profits of stock, it will appear, that *no accumulation of capital will permanently lower profits,*" *

(By PROFITS Ricardo means here that part of surplus value which the capitalist appropriates, but by no means the [entire] surplus value; and wrong as it is to say that accumulation can cause the surplus value to fall, so it is right that accumulation can cause a fall in profit.)

*"*unless there be some permanent cause for the rise of wages.*... If the necessaries of the workman could be constantly increased with the same facility, there could be no *permanent alteration* in *the rate of profits or wages,*" * (this should read: IN THE RATE OF SURPLUS VALUE AND THE VALUE OF LABOUR) *"to whatever amount capital might be

---

[a] See present edition, Vol. 31, pp. 509.— Ed.

accumulated. *Adam Smith*, however, uniformly *ascribes the fall of profits to the accumulation of capital, and to the competition which will result from it*, without ever adverting to the increasing difficulty of providing food for the additional number of labourers which the additional capital will employ"* (l.c., [pp.] 338-39).

The whole thing would only be right if profit=SURPLUS VALUE. Thus Adam Smith says that the RATE OF PROFIT FALLS with the accumulation of capital, because of the growing competition between the capitalists; Ricardo says that it does so because of the growing DETERIORATION OF AGRICULTURE (increased price of NECESSARIES). We have refuted his view, which would only be correct if RATE OF SURPLUS VALUE and RATE OF PROFIT were identical, and therefore the RATE OF PROFIT could not fall unless the RATE OF WAGES rose (provided the working day remained unchanged). Smith's view rests on his compounding VALUE out of WAGES, PROFITS and RENTS (in accordance with his false view, which he himself refuted). According to him, the accumulation of capitals forces the reduction in ARBITRARY PROFITS—for which there is no inherent measure—through the reduction in the prices of commodities; [they,] according to this conception, being merely a nominal addition to the prices of commodities. Ricardo is of course theoretically right when he maintains, in opposition to Adam Smith, that the accumulation of capitals does not alter the determination of the value of commodities; but Ricardo is quite wrong when he seeks to refute Adam Smith by asserting that *overproduction* in one country is impossible. Ricardo denies the PLETHORA OF CAPITAL, which later became an established axiom in English political economy. Firstly he overlooks that in reality, where not only the capitalist confronts the WORKMAN, but CAPITALIST, WORKMAN, LANDLORD, MONEYED INTEREST, [people receiving] FIXED INCOMES from the state etc., confront one another, the fall in the prices of commodities which hits both the industrial capitalists and the WORKMEN, benefits the other classes. Secondly [he overlooks] that the output level is by no means arbitrarily chosen, but the more capitalist production develops, the more it is forced to produce on a scale which has nothing to do with the IMMEDIATE DEMAND but depends on a constant expansion of the world market. He has recourse to Say's absurd assumption that the capitalist produces not for the sake of profit, for exchange value, but directly for consumption, for use value—for his own consumption. He overlooks the fact that the commodity has to be converted into money. The DEMAND of the workers does not suffice, since profit arises precisely from the fact that the DEMAND of the workers is smaller than the value of their product, and that it [profit] is all the greater the smaller, relatively, is this DEMAND. The DEMAND of the

CAPITALISTS among themselves is equally insufficient. Overproduction does not call forth a *lasting* fall in profit, but it is *lastingly periodic*. It is followed by periods of underproduction etc. Overproduction arises precisely from the fact that the mass of the people can never consume more than the AVERAGE QUANTITY OF NECESSARIES, that their consumption therefore does not grow correspondingly with the productivity of labour. But the whole of this section belongs to the *competition of capitals*. All that Ricardo says on this isn't worth a rap. (This is contained in CH. XXI, "Effects of Accumulation on Profits and Interest".)

* "There is only one case, and that will be *temporary*, in which the accumulation of capital with a low price of food may be attended with a fall of profits; and that is, when the funds for the maintenance of labour increase much more rapidly than population;—wages will then be high, and profits low" * (p. 343).

Ricardo directs against *Say* the following ironical remarks on the relation between PROFITS and INTEREST:

* "M. Say allows, that the rate of interest depends on the rate of profits; but it does not therefore follow, that the rate of profits depends on the rate of interest. One is the cause, the other the effect, and it is impossible for any circumstances to make them change places" * (l.c., [p.] 353, *note*).ᵃ

However, the same causes which bring down profits can make INTEREST rise, and vice versa.²⁶

* "M. Say acknowledges that the *cost of production* is the foundation of price, and yet in various parts of his book he maintains that price is regulated by the proportion which demand bears to supply" * (l.c., [p.] 411).

Ricardo should have seen from this that [XIII-694] the COST OF PRODUCTION⁶ is something very different from the QUANTITY OF LABOUR EMPLOYED FOR THE PRODUCTION OF A COMMODITY. Instead he continues:

* "The real and ultimate regulator of the relative value of any two commodities, is the cost of their production" * (l.c.).
* "And does not Adam Smith agree in this opinion" //that prices are regulated neither by wages nor profits// "when he says, that 'the *prices* of commodities, or the *value* of gold and silver as compared with commodities, depend upon the proportion between the *quantity of labour* which is necessary in order to bring a certain quantity of gold and silver to market, and that which is necessary to bring thither a certain quantity of any other sort of goods?'ᵇ That quantity will not be affected, whether profits be high or low, or wages low or high. *How then can prices be raised by high profits?*" * (pp. 413-14).

In the passage quoted, Adam Smith means by PRICES nothing other than THE MONETARY EXPRESSION OF THE *VALUES* OF COMMODITIES. That

---

ᵃ Cf. also this volume, p. 181.— *Ed.*
ᵇ A. Smith, *An Inquiry into the Nature and Causes of the Wealth of Nations*, Book II, Ch. II.— *Ed.*

these and the gold and silver against which they exchange, are determined by the RELATIVE QUANTITIES OF LABOUR REQUIRED FOR PRODUCING THOSE TWO SORTS OF COMMODITIES //COMMODITIES ON THE ONE SIDE, GOLD and SILVER ON THE OTHER//, in no way contradicts the fact that the *actual* prices of commodities, i.e. their COST PRICES "CAN BE RAISED BY HIGH PROFITS". Although not all prices simultaneously, as Smith thinks. But as a result of HIGH PROFITS, some commodities will rise higher above their value, than if the AVERAGE PROFITS were LOW, while another group of commodities will sink to a smaller extent below their value.[27]

THEORY OF ACCUMULATION

First we shall compare Ricardo's propositions, which are widely scattered over the whole of his work.

*"...All the productions of a country are consumed; but it makes the greatest difference imaginable whether they are consumed by *those who reproduce*, or *by those who do not reproduce another value*. When we say that *revenue is saved*, and *added to capital*, what we mean is, that the *portion of revenue*, so *said to be added to capital*, is *consumed by productive instead of unproductive labourers*." * (This is the same distinction as Adam Smith makes.) * "There can be no greater error than in supposing that *capital is increased by non-consumption*. If the price of labour should rise so high, that notwithstanding the increase of capital, no more could be employed, I should say that such *increase of capital would be still unproductively consumed*" * (p. 163, note).

Here, therefore—as with Adam Smith and others—[it is] only [a question] of whether [the products] are CONSUMED by workers or not. But it is at the same time also a question of the INDUSTRIAL CONSUMPTION of the commodities which form constant capital, and are consumed as instruments of labour or materials of labour, or are consumed in such a way that through this consumption they are transformed into instruments of labour or materials of labour. The conception that accumulation OF CAPITAL=CONVERSION OF REVENUE INTO WAGES, in other words, that it=ACCUMULATION OF VARIABLE CAPITAL—is one-sided, that is, incorrect. This leads to a wrong approach to the whole question of accumulation.

Above all it is necessary to have a clear understanding of the *reproduction of constant capital*. We are considering the *annual* reproduction here, taking the year as the time measure of the process of reproduction.

A large part of the constant capital—the *fixed capital*—enters into the annual process of labour without entering into the annual valorisation process. It is not consumed and, therefore, does not need to be reproduced. Because it enters into the production process and remains in contact with living labour it is *kept* in existence—and along with its use value, also its exchange value. The greater this part of capital is in a particular country in one year, the greater, relatively, will be its purely formal reproduction (preservation) in the following year, providing that the production process is renewed, continued and kept flowing, even if only on the same scale. Repairs and so on, which are necessary to maintain the fixed capital, are reckoned as part of its original labour costs. This has nothing in common with preservation in the sense used above.

A second part of the constant capital is consumed annually in the production of commodities and must therefore also be reproduced. This includes the whole of that part of fixed capital which enters annually into the valorisation process, as well as the whole of that part of constant capital which consists of circulating capital, raw materials and *matières instrumentales*.[a]

As regards this second part of constant capital, the following distinctions must be made:

[XIII-695] A large part of what *appears* as constant capital— means and materials of labour—in one sphere of production, is *simultaneously* the product of another, parallel sphere of production. For example, yarn which forms part of the constant capital of the weaver, is the product of the spinner, and may still have been in the process of becoming yarn on the previous day. When we use the term *simultaneous* here, we mean produced during *the same* year. The same commodities in different phases pass through various spheres of production in the course of the same year. They emerge as products from one sphere and enter another as commodities constituting constant capital. And as constant capital they are all consumed during the year; whether only their value enters into the commodity, as in the case of fixed capital, or their use value too, as with circulating capital. While the commodity produced in one sphere of production enters into another, to be consumed there as constant capital—in addition to the same commodity entering a *succession* of spheres of production—the various elements or the various phases of this commodity are being produced *simultaneously*, side by side. In the course of the same year, it is continuously consumed as constant capital in one sphere and in another parallel sphere it is produced as a commodity. The same commodities which are thus consumed as constant capital in the course of the year are also, in the same way, continuously being produced during the same year. A machine is

---

a Instrumental materials.— *Ed.*

wearing out in sphere A). It is simultaneously being produced in sphere B). The constant capital that is consumed during a year in those spheres of production which produce the means of subsistence, is *simultaneously* being produced in other spheres of production, so that *during the course* of the year or *by the end of the year* it is renewed *in natura*. Both of them, the means of subsistence as well as this part of the constant capital, are the products of new labour employed during the year. In the spheres producing the means of subsistence, as I have shown earlier,[a] that *portion of the value* of the product which replaces the constant capital in these spheres, forms the REVENUE of the *producers* of this constant capital.

But there is also a further portion of the constant capital which is *consumed annually,* without entering as a component part into the spheres of production which produce the means of subsistence (consumable goods). Therefore, it cannot be replaced [by products] from these spheres. We mean instruments of labour, raw materials and *matières instrumentales*, i.e. that portion of constant capital which is itself consumed industrially in the creation or production of constant capital, that is to say, machinery, raw materials and *matières instrumentales*. This part, as we have seen,[b] is replaced *in natura* either directly out of the product of these spheres of production themselves (as in the case of seeds, livestock and to a certain extent coal) or through the exchange of a portion of the products of the various spheres of production manufacturing constant capital. In this case capital is exchanged for capital. The existence and consumption of this portion of constant capital increases not only the mass of products, but also the *value* of the annual product. The *portion of the value* of the *annual* product which=the value of this section of the consumed constant capital, buys back *in natura* or withdraws from the annual product that part of it, which must replace *in natura* the constant capital that is consumed. For example, the value of the seed sown determined the portion of the value of the harvest (and thus the quantity of corn) which must be returned to the land, to production, as constant capital. This portion would not be reproduced without the labour newly added during the course of the year; but it is in fact *produced* by the labour of the year before, or past labour and—in so far as the productivity of labour remains unchanged—the *value* which it adds to the annual product is not the result of

---

[a] See present edition, Vol. 30, pp. 429-41 and Vol. 31, p. 135.— *Ed*
[b] Ibid., Vol. 30, pp. 442-51 and Vol. 31, pp. 83-94, 143-51.— *Ed.*

this year's labour, but of that of the previous year. The greater, *proportionately*, is the constant capital employed in a country, the greater will also be the part of the constant capital which is consumed in the production of the constant capital, and which not only expresses itself in a greater quantity of products, but also raises the value of this quantity of products. This *value*, therefore, is the result not only of the current year's labour, but equally the result of the labour of the previous year, of past labour, although *without* the IMMEDIATE ANNUAL LABOUR it would not reappear, any more than would the product of which it forms a part. If this portion [of constant capital] grows, not only does the annual mass of products grow, but also their *value*, even if the ANNUAL LABOUR remains the same. This growth is one form of the *accumulation of capital*, which it is essential to understand. And nothing could be further removed from such an understanding than Ricardo's proposition:

* "The labour of a million of men in manufactures, will always produce the same value, but will not always produce the same riches" * (l.c., [p.] 320).

These million MEN—with a given working day—will not only produce very different quantities of commodities depending on the productivity of labour, but the value of these quantities of commodities will be very different, according to whether they are produced with much or little constant capital, that is, whether much or little value originating in the *past* labour of *previous years* is added to them.

For the sake of simplicity, when we speak of the reproduction of constant capital we shall in the first place assume that the productivity of labour, and consequently the mode of production, remain the same. At a given level of production, the constant capital which has to be replaced is a definite quantity *in natura*. If productivity remains the same, then the value [XIII-696] of this quantity also remains constant. If there are changes in the productivity of labour which make it possible to reproduce the same quantity, at greater or less cost, with more or less labour, then similarly changes will occur in the value of the constant capital, which will affect the SURPLUS PRODUCE after deduction of the constant capital.

For example, supposing 20 qrs [of wheat] at £3=£60 were required for sowing. If $1/3$ less labour is used to reproduce a qr it would now cost only £2. 20 qrs have to be deducted from the product, for the sowing, as before; but their share in the value of the whole product only amounts to £40. The replacement of the same constant capital thus requires a smaller portion of value, a smaller share in kind out of the total product, although, as previously, 20 qrs have to be returned to the land as seed.[28]

If the constant capital consumed annually by one nation were 10 million and that consumed by another were only 1 million and the annual labour of 1 million men=£100 million, then the value of the product of the first nation=110 and of the second only 101 million. It would be, moreover, not only possible, but certain, that the individual commodity of nation I would be cheaper than of nation II, because the latter would produce a much smaller quantity of commodities with the same amount of labour, much smaller than the difference between 10 and 1. It is true that a greater portion of the value of the product goes to the replacement of capital in nation I as compared with nation II, and therefore also a greater portion of the total product. But the total product is also much greater.

In the case of factory-made commodities, it is known that a million [workers] in England produce not only a much greater product but also a product of much greater value than in Russia for example, although the individual commodity is much cheaper. In the case of agriculture, however, the same relation between capitalistically developed and relatively undeveloped nations does not appear to exist. The product of the more backward nation is cheaper than that of the capitalistically developed nation, in terms of its *money price*. And yet the product of the developed nation appears to be produced by much less (annual) labour than that of the backward one. In England, for example, less than $^1/_3$ [of the people] are employed in agriculture, while in Russia it is $^4/_5$; in the former $^5/_{15}$, in the latter $^{12}/_{15}$. These figures are not to be taken *à la lettre*.[a] In England, for instance, a large number of people in NON-AGRICULTURAL INDUSTRY—in engineering, trade, transport etc.—are engaged in the production and distribution of elements of AGRICULTURAL PRODUCTION, but this is not the case in Russia. The proportion of persons engaged in agriculture cannot therefore be directly determined by [the number] of INDIVIDUALS IMMEDIATELY EMPLOYED in AGRICULTURE. In countries with a capitalist mode of production, many people participate *indirectly* in AGRICULTURAL PRODUCTION, who in less developed countries are directly included in it. The difference therefore appears to be greater than it is. For the civilisation of the country as a whole, however, this difference is very important, even in so far as it only means that a large

---

section of the workers involved in agriculture do not participate in it directly; they are thus saved from the narrow parochialism of country life and belong to the industrial population.

But *d'abord à part*[a] this point and also the fact that most AGRICULTURAL PEOPLES are forced to sell their product *below* its value whereas in countries with advanced capitalist production the AGRICULTURAL PRODUCE rises to its value. At any rate, a portion of the value of the constant capital enters into the value of the product of the ENGLISH agriculturist, which does not enter into the product of the RUSSIAN AGRICULTURIST. Let us assume that this portion of value=a day's labour of 10 men, and that one English worker sets this constant capital in motion. I am speaking of that part of the constant capital of the AGRICULTURAL PRODUCE, which is not replaced by new labour, such as is the case, for example, with agricultural implements. If 5 Russian workers were required in order to produce the same product which one Englishman produces with the help of the constant capital, and if the constant capital used by the Russian were equal to 1 [day's labour], then the English product=$10+1=11$ working days, and that of the Russian=$5+1=6$. If the Russian soil were so much more fertile than the English, that without the application of any constant capital or with a constant capital that was $^1/_{10}$ the size, it could produce as much corn as the Englishman with a constant capital 10 times as great, then the *values* of the same quantities of English and Russian corn would compare as 11:6. If the qr of Russian corn were sold at £2, then the English would be sold at £$3^2/_3$, for $2:3^2/_3=6:11$. The money price and the value of the English corn would thus be much higher than that of the Russian, but nevertheless, the English corn would be produced with less labour, since the *past* labour, which reappears in the quantity as well as in the value of product, costs no additional new labour. This would always be the case, if the Englishman uses less IMMEDIATE LABOUR than the Russian, but the greater constant capital which he uses—and which costs him *nothing,* although it has cost something and must be paid for—does not raise the productivity of labour to such an extent that it compensates for the natural fertility of the Russian soil. The money prices of AGRICULTURAL PRODUCE can, therefore, be higher in countries of capitalist production than in [XIII-697] less developed countries, although in fact it costs less labour. It contains more IMMEDIATE+PAST LABOUR, but this PAST LABOUR costs nothing. The product would be cheaper if the difference in

---

[a] Let us leave aside for the moment.— *Ed.*

natural fertility did not intervene. This would also explain the higher money price of the labourer's wage.

Up to now we have only spoken of the reproduction of the capital involved. The labourer replaces his wage with a SURPLUS PRODUCE or SURPLUS VALUE, which forms the profit (including rent) of the capitalist. He replaces that part of the annual product which serves him anew as wages. The capitalist has consumed his profit during the course of the year, but the labourer has created a portion of the product which can again be consumed as profit. That part of the constant capital which is consumed in the production of the means of subsistence, is replaced by constant capital which has been produced by new labour, during the course of the year. The producers of this new portion of constant capital realise their revenue (profit and wages) in that part of the means of subsistence which=the part of the value of the constant capital consumed in their production. Finally, the constant capital which is consumed in the production of constant capital, in the production of machinery, raw materials and *matière instrumentale,* is replaced *in natura* or through the exchange of capital, out of the total product of the various spheres of production which produce constant capital.

What then is the position with regard to the *increase* of capital, its *accumulation* as distinct from reproduction, the *transformation of* REVENUE into capital?

In order to simplify the question, it is assumed that the productivity of labour remains the same, that no CHANGES occur in the mode of production, that therefore the same quantity of labour is required to produce the same quantity of commodities, and consequently that the *increase* in capital costs the same amount of labour as the production of capital of the same AMOUNT cost the previous year.

A portion of the surplus value must be transformed into capital, instead of being consumed as revenue. It must be converted partly into constant and partly into variable capital. And the proportion in which it is divided into these two different parts of capital, depends on the given organic composition of the capital, since the mode of production remains unaltered and also the proportional value of both parts. The higher the development of production, the greater will be that part of surplus value which is transformed into constant capital, compared with that part of the surplus value which is transformed into variable capital.

To begin with, a portion of the surplus value (and the corresponding SURPLUS PRODUCE in the form of means of subsistence) has to be transformed into variable capital, that is to say, new labour has to be bought with it. This is only possible if the number of labourers grows or if the labour time during which they work, is prolonged. The latter takes place, for instance, when a part of the labouring population was only employed for half or $^2/_3$, or also, when for longer or shorter periods, the working day is absolutely prolonged, this however, must be paid for. But that cannot be regarded as a method of accumulation which can be continuously used. The labouring population can increase, when previously unproductive labourers are turned into productive ones, or sections of the population who did not work previously, such as women and children, or PAUPERS, are drawn into the production process. We leave this latter point out of account here. Finally, together with the growth of the population in general, the labouring population can grow absolutely. If accumulation is to be a steady, continuous process, then this absolute growth in population—although it may be decreasing in relation to the capital employed—is a necessary condition. An *increasing population* appears to be the basis of accumulation as a continuous process. But this presupposes an AVERAGE wage which permits not only reproduction of the labouring population but also its constant growth. Capitalist production provides for unexpected contingencies by overworking one section of the labouring population and keeping the other *in petto,* as a reserve army consisting of partially or entirely pauperised people.

What then is the position with regard to the other portion of the surplus value which has to be converted into constant capital? In order to simplify this question, we shall leave out of account foreign trade and consider a self-sufficing nation. Let us take an example. Let us assume that the surplus value produced by a linen weaver=£10,000, and that he wants to convert into capital ONE HALF of it, i.e. £5,000. Let $^1/_5$ of this be laid out in wages in accordance with the organic composition [of capital] in mechanised weaving. In this case we are disregarding the turnover of capital, which may perhaps enable him to carry on with an amount sufficient for 5 weeks, after which he would sell [his product] and so receive back from circulation the capital for the payment of wages. We are assuming that in the course of the year he will gradually lay out IN WAGES (for 20 men) £1,000 which he must hold in reserve with his BANKER. Then £4,000 are to be converted into constant capital. Firstly he must purchase as much yarn as 20 men can weave during the year. (The turnover of the circulating part of capital is disregarded throughout.) Further, he must increase the number of looms in his factory, ditto perhaps install an additional steam-engine or enlarge the existing one, etc. But in order to purchase all these things, he must find yarn, looms etc. available on the market. He must convert his £4,000 into yarn, looms, coal, etc., [XIII-698] i.e. he must buy them. In order to buy them, they must be available. Since we have assumed that the reproduction of the old capital has taken place under the old conditions, the spinner of yarn has spent the whole of his capital in order to supply the amount of yarn required by the weavers during the previous year. How then is he to satisfy the ADDITIONAL DEMAND BY AN ADDITIONAL SUPPLY OF YARN? The position of the manufacturer of machines, who supplies looms, etc., is just the same. He has produced only sufficient new looms in order to cover the average consumption in weaving. But the weaver who is keen on accumulation, orders yarn for £3,000 and for £1,000 looms, coal (since the position of the coal producer is the same), etc. Or IN FACT, he gives £3,000 to the spinner, and £1,000 to the machinery manufacturer and the coal merchant, etc., so that they will transform this money into yarn, looms and coal for him. He would thus have to wait until this process is completed before he could begin with his accumulation—his production of new linen. This would be interruption number I.

But now the owner of the spinning-mill finds himself in the same position with the £3,000 as the weaver with the 4,000, only he deducts his profit right away. He can find an ADDITIONAL NUMBER OF SPINNERS, but he needs flax, spindles, coal, etc. Similarly the coal producer [needs] new machinery or implements apart from the additional workers. And the owner of the engineering works who is supposed to supply the new looms, spindles, etc. [needs] iron and so forth, apart from ADDITIONAL LABOURERS. But the position of the flax-grower is the worst of all, since he can supply the ADDITIONAL QUANTITY OF FLAX only in the following year.

So that accumulation can be a continuous process and the weaver able to transform a portion of his profit into constant capital every year, without long-winded complications and interruptions, he must find AN ADDITIONAL QUANTITY OF YARN, looms, etc. available on the market. He [the weaver], the spinner, the producer of coal, etc. require additional workers, only if they are able to obtain flax, spindles and machines on the market.

A part of the constant capital which is calculated to be used up annually and enters as wear and tear into the value of the product, is in fact *not* used up. Take, for example, a machine which lasts 12 years and costs £12,000; its AVERAGE wear and tear, which has to be charged each year,=£1,000. Thus, since £1,000 is incorporated into the product each year, the value of £12,000 will have been reproduced at the end of the 12 years and a new machine of the same kind can be bought for this price. The repairs and patching up which are required during the 12 years are reckoned as part of the production costs of the machine and have nothing to do with the question under discussion. In fact, however, reality differs from this calculation of averages. The machine may perhaps run more smoothly in the 2nd year than in the first. And yet after 12 years it is no longer usable. It is the same as with an animal whose AVERAGE life is 10 years, but this does not mean that it dies by $^1/_{10}$ each year, although at the end of 10 years it must be replaced by a new individual. Naturally, during the course of *a particular year,* a certain quantity of machinery, etc. always reaches the stage when it must actually be replaced by new machines. Each year, therefore, a certain quantity of old machinery, etc. has in fact to be replaced *in natura* by new machines, etc. And the AVERAGE annual PRODUCTION OF MACHINERY, etc., corresponds with this. The value with which they are to be paid for, lies READY; it is derived from the [proceeds of the] commodities, according to the reproduction period (of the machines). But the FACT remains, that although a large part of the value of the annual product, of the value which is paid for it each year, is needed to replace, for example, the old machines after 12 years, it is by no means actually required to replace $^1/_{12}$ *in natura* each year, and IN FACT this would not be feasible. This fund may be used partly for wages or for the purchase of raw material, before the commodity, which is constantly thrown into circulation but does not immediately return from circulation, is sold and paid for. This cannot, however, be the case throughout the whole year, since the commodities which complete their turnover during the year realise their whole value, and must therefore replace the wages, raw material and used up machinery contained in them, as well as pay SURPLUS VALUE. Hence where much constant capital, and therefore also much fixed capital, is employed, that part of the value of the product which replaces the wear and tear of the fixed capital, provides an *accumulation fund,* which can be invested by the person controlling it, as new fixed capital (or also circulating capital), without any deduction whatsoever having to be made from the SURPLUS VALUE for this part of the accumulation. (See MacCulloch.[29]) This accumulation fund does not exist at levels of production and in nations where there is not much fixed capital. This is an important point. It is a fund for the continuous introduction of improvements, expansions etc. But the point we want to make here is the following: Even if the total capital employed in machine-building were only large enough to replace the annual wear and tear of machinery, it would produce much more machinery each year than required, since in part the wear and tear merely exists nominally, and in reality it only has to be replaced *in natura* after a certain number of years. The capital thus employed, therefore yields annually a mass of machinery which is available for new capital investments and anticipates these new capital investments. For example, the factory of the machine-builder begins production, say, this year. He supplies £12,000 worth of machinery during the year. If he were merely to replace the machinery produced by him, he would only have to produce machinery worth £1,000 in each of the 11 following years and even this annual production would not be annually consumed. An even smaller part [of his production would be used], if he invested the whole of his capital. A continuous expansion of production in the branches of industry which use these machines is required in order to keep his capital employed and merely to reproduce it annually [XIII-699]. (An even greater [expansion is required] if he himself accumulates.) Thus even the mere reproduction of the capital invested in this sphere requires continuous accumulation in the remaining spheres of production. But because of this, one of the elements of continuous accumulation is always available on the market. Here, in one sphere of production—even if only the existing capital is reproduced in this sphere—exists a continuous supply of commodities for accumulation, for new, additional industrial consumption in other spheres.

As regards the £5,000 profit or surplus value which is to be transformed into capital, for instance by the weaver, there are 2 possibilities—always assuming that he *finds available* on the market *the labour* which he must buy with part of the £5,000, i.e. 1,000 in order to transform the £5,000 into capital according to the conditions prevailing in his sphere of production. This part is transformed into variable capital and is laid out IN WAGES. But in order to employ this labour, he requires yarn, additional *matières instrumentales* and ADDITIONAL MACHINERY (unless the working day is prolonged). //In that case the machinery is merely used up faster, its reproduction period is curtailed, but at the same time more SURPLUS VALUE is produced; and though the value of the machinery has to be distributed over the commodities produced during a shorter period far more commodities are being produced, so that despite this more rapid depreciation of the machine, a smaller portion of machine value enters into the value or price of the individual commodity. In this case, no *new* capital has to be laid out directly in machinery. It is only necessary to replace the value of the machinery a little more rapidly. But in this case *matières instrumentales* require THE ADVANCE OF ADDITIONAL CAPITAL.// Either the weaver finds these, his conditions of production, on the market; then the purchase of these commodities only differs from that of other commodities by the fact that he buys commodities for *industrial consumption* instead of for *individual* consumption. Or he does not find these conditions of production on the market; then he must order them (as for instance machines of a new design), just as he has to order articles for his private consumption which are not readily available on the market. If the raw material (flax) were only produced to order //as, for instance, indigo, jute etc. are produced by the Indian Ryots to orders and with advances from English merchants//, then the linen weaver could not accumulate in his own business during that year. On the other hand, assuming, that the spinner converts the £5,000 into capital and that the weaver does not accumulate, then the spun yarn— although all the conditions for its production were in supply on the market—will be unsaleable and the £5,000 have IN FACT been transformed into yarn but not into capital.

(*Credit*, which does not concern us further here, is the means whereby accumulated capital is not just used in that sphere in which it is created, but wherever it has the best chance of being turned to good account. Every capitalist will however prefer to invest his accumulation as far as possible in his own TRADE. If he invests it in another, then he becomes a MONEYED CAPITALIST and instead of profit he draws only interest—unless he goes in for speculative transactions. We are, however, concerned with AVERAGE ACCUMULATION here and only [assume] for the sake of illustration that [it] is invested in a particular TRADE.)

If, on the other hand, the flax-grower had expanded his production, that is to say, had accumulated, and the spinner and weaver and machine-builder, etc. had not done so, then he would have superfluous flax in store and would probably produce less in the following year.

//At present we are leaving individual consumption completely out of account and are only considering the mutual relations between producers. If these relations exist, then in the first place the producers constitute a market for the capitals which they must replace for one another. The newly employed, or more fully employed workers constitute a market for some of the means of subsistence; and since the surplus value increases in the following year, the capitalists can consume an increasing part of their revenue, TO A CERTAIN EXTENT therefore they also constitute a market for one another. Even so, a large part of the annual product may still remain unsaleable.//

The question has now to be formulated thus: *assuming general accumulation,* in other words, assuming that capital is accumulated to some extent in all TRADES—this is IN FACT ⸱ condition of capitalist production and is just as much the urge of the capitalist as a capitalist, as the urge of the hoarder is the piling up of money (it is also a necessity if capitalist production is to go ahead)—what are the *conditions* of this general accumulation, what does it amount to? Or, since the linen weaver may be taken to represent the capitalist in general, what are the *conditions* in which he can uninterruptedly reconvert the £5,000 surplus value into capital and steadily continue the process of accumulation year in, year out? The accumulation of the £5,000 means nothing but the transformation of this money, this amount of value, into capital. The *conditions for the accumulation of capital are thus the very same as those for its original production or for reproduction in general.*

These conditions, however, were: that labour was bought with one part of the money, and with the other, commodities (raw material, machinery, etc.) which could be *consumed industrially* by this labour. //Some commodities can only be consumed industrially, such as machinery, raw material, semi-finished goods, etc.; others, such as houses, horses, wheat, grain (from which brandy or starch, etc., is made), can be consumed industrially or individually.// These commodities can only be purchased, if they are available on the [XIII-700] *market* as commodities—in the intermediate stage when production is completed and consumption has not as yet begun, in the hands of the seller, in the stage of circulation—or if they can be procured to order (or produced as is the case with the construction of new factories etc.). Commodities were available—this was presupposed in the production and reproduction of capital—as a result of the division of labour carried out in capitalist production on a social scale (DISTRIBUTION OF LABOUR AND CAPITAL BETWEEN THE DIFFERENT TRADES); as a result of *parallel* production and reproduction which takes place *simultaneously* over the whole field. This was the condition of the *market,* of the production and the reproduction of capital. The greater the capital, the more developed the productivity of labour and the scale of capitalist production in general, *the greater is also the volume of commodities found on the market, in circulation, in transition between production and consumption* (individual and industrial), and the greater the certainty that each particular capital will find its conditions for reproduction readily available on the market. This is all the more the case, since it is in the nature of capitalist production that: 1) each particular capital operates on a scale which is not determined by individual demand (orders, etc., private needs), but by the endeavour to realise as much labour and therefore as much surplus labour as possible and to produce the largest possible quantity of commodities with a given capital; 2) each individual capital strives to capture the largest possible share of the market and to supplant its competitors and exclude them from the market — *competition of capitals.* // The greater the development of the means of communication, the more can the stocks on the market be reduced. //

* "There will, indeed, where production and consumption are comparatively great, naturally be, at any given moment, a *comparatively great surplus* in the intermediate state, in the market, on its way from having been produced to the hands of the consumer; unless indeed the quickness with which things are sold off should have increased so as to counteract what would else have been the consequence of the increased production" * (*An Inquiry into those Principles respecting the Nature of Demand and the Necessity of Consumption, lately Advocated by Mr. Malthus etc.*, London, 1821, [pp.] 6-7).

The accumulation of new capital can therefore proceed only under the same conditions as the reproduction of already existing capital. // We disregard here the case in which more capital is accumulated than can be invested in production, and for example lies fallow in the form of money at the bank. This results in loans abroad, etc., in short, speculative investments. Nor do we consider the case in which it is impossible to sell the mass of commodities produced, crises, etc. This belongs into the section on competition.[30] Here we examine only the forms of capital in the various phases of its process, assuming throughout, that the commodities are sold at their value. // The weaver can reconvert the £5,000 surplus value into capital, if besides labour for £1,000 he finds yarn, etc. READY on the market or is able to obtain it to order; this presupposes the production of a SURPLUS PRODUCE consisting of commodities which enter into his constant capital, particularly of those which require a longer period of production and whose volume cannot be increased rapidly, or cannot be increased at all during the course of the year, such as raw material, for example flax. // What comes into play here is the merchants' capital, which keeps warehouses stocked with goods READY to meet growing individual and industrial consumption; but this *is only a form of intermediary agency,* hence does not belong here, but into the consideration of the competition of capitals. // Just as the production and reproduction of existing capital in one *sphere* presupposes *parallel* production and reproduction in other spheres, so accumulation or the formation OF ADDITIONAL CAPITAL IN ONE TRADE presupposes *simultaneous or parallel* creation OF ADDITIONAL PRODUCTION IN OTHER TRADES. Thus the scale of production in all spheres which supply constant capital must grow simultaneously (in accordance with the AVERAGE participation—determined by the demand—of each particular sphere in the general growth of production) and all spheres which do not produce FINISHED PRODUCE for individual consumption, supply constant capital. Of the greatest importance, is the increase in machinery (tools), *raw material,* and *matières instrumentales,* for, if these preconditions are present, all other industries into which they enter, whether they produce semifinished or finished goods, only need to set in motion more labour.

It seems therefore, that for accumulation to take place, continuous *surplus production* in all spheres is necessary.

This will have to be more closely defined.

Then there is the second essential question:

The *surplus value* [or] in this case the part of *profit* (including rent; if the LANDLORD wants to accumulate, to transform rent into capital, it is always the *industrial capitalist* who gets hold of the surplus value; this applies even when the worker transforms a portion of his revenue into capital), which is reconverted into capital, consists only of *labour newly added* during [XIII-701] the past year. The question is, whether this new capital is entirely expended on wages, i.e. exchanged only against new labour.

The following speaks for this: All value is originally derived from labour. All constant capital is originally just as much the product of labour as is variable capital. And here we seem to encounter again the direct genesis of capital from labour.

An argument against it is: Can one suppose that the formation of additional capital takes place under worse conditions of production than the reproduction of the old capital? Does a reversion to a lower level of production occur? This would have to be the case if the new value [were] spent only on IMMEDIATE LABOUR, which, *without fixed capital,* etc., would thus also first have to produce this fixed capital, just as originally, labour had first to create its constant capital. This is sheer NONSENSE. But this is the *assumption made by Ricardo, etc.* This needs to be examined more closely.

The first question is this:

Can the capitalist transform a part of the surplus value into capital by employing it *directly* as capital instead of *selling* the surplus value, or rather the surplus PRODUCE in which it is expressed? An affirmative answer to this question would already imply that the whole of the surplus value to be transformed into capital is *not* transformed into variable capital, or is not laid out in wages.

With that part of the AGRICULTURAL PRODUCE which consists of corn or livestock, this is clear from the outset. Some of the corn which belongs to that part of the harvest representing the SURPLUS PRODUCE or the SURPLUS VALUE of the FARMER (similarly some of the livestock), instead of being sold, can at once serve again as a condition of production, as seed or draught animals. The same applies to that part of the manure produced on the land itself, which at the same time can circulate in COMMERCE as a commodity, that is to say, can be sold. This part of the SURPLUS PRODUCE which falls to the share of the FARMER as SURPLUS VALUE, as profit, can be at once transformed by him into a condition of production within his own branch of production, it is thus *directly* converted into capital. This part is not expended on WAGES; it is not transformed into variable capital. It is withdrawn from individual consumption without being consumed *productively* in the sense used by Smith and Ricardo. It is consumed *industrially*, but as raw material, not as means of subsistence either of productive or of unproductive workers. Corn, however, serves not only as means of subsistence for productive worker, etc., but also as *matière instrumentale*[a] for livestock, as raw material for spirits, starch, etc. Livestock (for fattening or draught animals) in turn serves not only as means of subsistence, but its fur, hide, fat, bones, horns, etc. supply raw materials for a large number of industries, and it also provides motive power, partly for agriculture itself and partly for the transport industry.

In all industries, in which the *period of reproduction* extends over more than a year, as is the case with a major part of livestock, timber, etc., but whose products at the same time have to be continuously reproduced, thus requiring the application of a certain amount of labour, accumulation and reproduction coincide in so far as the newly *added* labour, which includes not only paid but also unpaid labour, must be accumulated *in natura*, until the product is ready for sale. (We are not speaking here of the accumulation of the profit which according to the general rate of profit is added each year—this is not *real* accumulation, but only a

---

[a] Here: fodder.— *Ed.*

method of accounting. We are concerned here with the accumulation of the total labour which is repeated in the course of several years, during which not only paid, but also unpaid labour is accumulated *in natura* and at once reconverted into capital. The accumulation of profit is in such cases however independent of the quantity of newly added labour.)

The position is the same with *commercial crops* (whether they provide raw materials or *matières instrumentales*). Their seeds and that part of them which can be used again as manure, etc., represent a portion of the total product. Even if this were *unsaleable*, it would not alter the fact that as soon as it re-enters as a condition of production, it forms a part of the total value and as [XIII-702] such constitutes constant capital for new production.

This settles one major point—the question of raw materials and means of subsistence (FOOD), in so far as they are actually AGRICULTURAL PRODUCE. Here therefore, accumulation coincides *directly* with reproduction on a larger scale, so that a part of the SURPLUS PRODUCE serves again as a means of production in its own sphere, *without being exchanged for wages or other commodities.*

The second important question relates to *machinery.* Not the machines which produce commodities, but the machines which produce machines, the *constant capital* of the machine-producing industry. Given this machinery, the extractive industries require nothing but labour in order to provide the raw material, iron, etc. for the production of containers and machines. And with the latter are produced the machines for working up the raw materials themselves. The difficulty here is not to get entangled in a *cercle vicieux* of presuppositions. For, in order to produce more machinery, more material is required (iron etc., coal etc.) and in order to produce this, more machinery is required. Whether we assume that industrialists who build machine-building machines and industrialists who manufacture machines (with the machine-building machines) are in one and the same category, does not alter the situation. This much is clear: One part of the SURPLUS PRODUCE is embodied in machine-building machines (at least it is up to the manufacturers of machines to see that this happens). These need not be sold but can re-enter the new production *in natura*, as constant capital. This is therefore a second category of SURPLUS PRODUCE which enters directly (or through exchange within the same sphere of production) as constant capital into the new production (accumulation), without having gone through the process of first being transformed into variable capital.

The question whether a part of the SURPLUS VALUE can be directly transformed into constant capital, resolves, in the first place, into the question whether a part of the SURPLUS PRODUCE, in which the SURPLUS VALUE is expressed, can directly re-enter its own sphere of production as a condition of production, without first having been alienated.

The general law is as follows:

Where a part of the product, and therefore also of the SURPLUS PRODUCE (i.e. the use value in which the SURPLUS VALUE is expressed) can re-enter as a condition of production—as instrument of labour or material of labour—into the sphere of production from which it came, directly, without an intermediary phase, ACCUMULATION within this sphere of production can and must take place in such a way that a part of the SURPLUS PRODUCE, instead of being sold, is as a condition of reproduction re-incorporated into the process directly (or through exchange with other specialists in the same sphere of production who are similarly accumulating), so that accumulation and reproduction on a larger scale coincide here *directly.* They must coincide everywhere, but not in this direct manner.

This also applies to a part of the *matières instrumentales.* For example to the coal produced in a year. A part of the SURPLUS PRODUCE can itself be used to produce more coal and can therefore be used up again directly by its producer, without any intermediary phase, as constant capital for production on a larger scale.

In industrial areas there are machine-builders who build whole factories for the manufacturers. Let us assume $1/10$ is SURPLUS PRODUCE or unpaid labour. Whether this $1/10$, the SURPLUS PRODUCE, consists of factory buildings which are built for a third party and are sold to them, or of factory buildings which the producer builds for himself—sells to himself—clearly makes no difference. The only thing that matters here is whether the *kind of use value* in which the SURPLUS labour is expressed, can re-enter as condition of production into the sphere of production [XIII-703] of the capitalist to whom the SURPLUS PRODUCE belongs. This is yet another example of how important is the analysis of *use value for the determination of economic phenomena.*

Here, therefore, we already have a considerable portion of the SURPLUS PRODUCE, and *hinc*[a] of the SURPLUS VALUE, which can and must be transformed directly into constant capital, in order to be *accumulated* as *capital* and without which no ACCUMULATION of capital can take place at all.

_____
[a] Therefore.— *Ed.*

Secondly, we have seen that where capitalist production is developed, that is, where the productivity of labour, the constant capital and particularly that part of constant capital which consists of fixed capital are developed, the mere reproduction of fixed capital in all spheres and the parallel reproduction of the existing capital which produces fixed capital, forms an accumulation fund, that is to say, provides machinery, i.e. constant capital, for production on an extended scale.

Thirdly: There remains the question: Can a part of the SURPLUS PRODUCE be re-transformed into capital (that is constant capital) through an (intermediary) exchange between the producer, for example of machinery, implements of labour, etc. and the producer of raw material, iron, coal, metals, timber, etc., that is, through the exchange of various components of constant capital? If, for example, the manufacturer of iron, coal, timber, etc., buys machinery or tools from the machine-builder and the machine-builder buys metal, timber, coal, etc. from the primary producer, then they replace or form new constant capital through this exchange of the reciprocal component parts of their constant capital. The question here is: to what extent is the SURPLUS PRODUCE converted in this way?

We saw earlier,[a] that in the simple reproduction of the capital which has been posited *in advance,* the portion of the constant capital which is used up in the reproduction of *constant capital* is replaced either directly *in natura* or through exchange between the producers of constant capital—an exchange of capital against capital and not of REVENUE against REVENUE or REVENUE against capital. Moreover, the constant capital which is used up or consumed industrially in the production of consumable goods—commodities which enter into individual consumption—is replaced by new products of the same kind, which are the result of *newly added* labour, and therefore resolve into REVENUE (wages and profit). Accordingly, therefore, in the spheres which produce consumable goods, the portion of the mass of products, which=the portion of their value which replaces their constant capital, represents the REVENUE of the producers of constant capital; while, on the other hand, in the spheres which produce constant capital, the part of the mass of products which represents newly added labour and therefore forms the REVENUE of the producers of this constant capital, represents the constant capital (replacement capital) of the producers of the means of subsistence.

---

[a] See present edition, Vol. 30, pp. 441-51 and Vol. 31, pp. 83-94, 143-51.— *Ed.*

This presupposes, therefore, that the producers of constant capital exchange their surplus PRODUCE (which means here, the excess of their product over that part of it which= *their* constant capital) against means of subsistence, and consume its value individually. This SURPLUS PRODUCE, however, 1)=wages (or the reproduced FUND for wages), and this portion must continue to be allocated (by the capitalist) for paying out WAGES, that is, for individual consumption (and assuming a minimum wage, the worker too can only convert the WAGES he receives, into means of subsistence); 2)=the profit of the capitalist (including rent). If this portion is large enough, it can be consumed partly individually and partly industrially. And in this latter case, an exchange of products takes place between the producers of constant capital; this is, however, no longer an exchange of the portion of their products representing their constant capital which has to be mutually replaced between them, but is an exchange of a part of their SURPLUS PRODUCE, REVENUE (*newly added* labour) which is directly transformed into constant capital, thus increasing the amount of constant capital and expanding the scale of reproduction. In this case, too, therefore, a part of the existing SURPLUS PRODUCE, that is, of the labour which has been newly added during the year, is transformed directly into constant capital, without first having been converted into variable capital. This demonstrates again that the industrial consumption of the SURPLUS PRODUCE—or accumulation—is by no means identical with the conversion of the entire SURPLUS PRODUCE into WAGES paid to productive workers.

It is quite possible that the manufacturer of machines sells (part of) his commodity to the producer, say, of cloth. The latter pays him in money. With this money he purchases iron, coal, etc. instead of means of subsistence. But when one considers the process as a whole, it is evident that the producers of means of subsistence cannot purchase any replacement machinery or replacement raw materials, unless the producers of the replacements of constant capital buy their means of subsistence from them, in other words, unless this circulation is fundamentally an exchange between means of subsistence and constant capital. The separation of the acts of buying and selling can of course cause considerable disturbances and complications in this compensatory process.

[XIII-704] If a country cannot itself produce the amount of machinery required for the accumulation of capital, then it buys it from abroad. Ditto, if it cannot itself produce a sufficient quantity of means of subsistence (for WAGES) and the raw material. As soon as international trade intervenes, it becomes quite obvious that a part of the SURPLUS PRODUCE of a country—in so far as it is intended for accumulation—is not transformed into wages, but directly into constant capital. But then there may remain the notion that over there, in the foreign country, the money thus laid out is spent entirely on wages. We have seen that, even leaving foreign trade out of account, this is not so and cannot be so. The proportion in which the SURPLUS PRODUCE is divided between variable and constant capital, depends on the average composition of capital, and the more developed capitalist production is, the smaller, *relatively*, will be the part which is directly laid out in wages. The idea that, because the SURPLUS PRODUCE is solely the product of the labour newly added during the year, it can therefore only be converted into variable capital, i.e. only be laid out in wages, corresponds altogether to the false conception that because the product is only the result, or the materialisation, of labour, its value is resolved only into revenue—wages, profit, and rent—the false conception of Smith and Ricardo.

A large part of constant capital, namely, the fixed capital, may enter directly into the process of the production of means of subsistence, raw materials, etc., or it may serve either to shorten the circulation process, like railways, roads, navigation, telegraphs, etc. or to store and accumulate stocks of commodities like docks, warehouses, etc., alternatively it may increase the yield only after a long period of reproduction, as for instance levelling operations, drainage, etc. The direct consequences for the reproduction of the means of subsistence, etc. will be very different according to whether a greater or smaller part of the SURPLUS PRODUCE is converted into one of these types of fixed capital.

If *surplus production* of constant capital is assumed—that is greater production than is required for the replacement of the former capital and therefore also for the production of the former quantity of means of subsistence—surplus production or accumulation in the spheres using the machinery, raw materials, etc. encounters no further difficulties. If sufficient surplus labour is available, they [the manufacturers] will find on the market all the means for the formation of new capital, for the transformation of their surplus money into new capital. But the whole process of accumulation in the first place resolves itself into *surplus production*, which on the one hand corresponds to the natural growth of the population, and on the other hand, forms an inherent basis for the phenomena which appear during *crises*. The criterion of this surplus production is *capital* itself, the scale on which the conditions of production are available and the unlimited desire of the capitalists to enrich themselves and to enlarge their capital, but by no means *consumption*, which from the outset is inhibited, since the majority of the population, the working people, can only expand their consumption within very narrow limits, whereas the demand for labour, although it grows *absolutely*, decreases *relatively*, to the same extent as capitalism develops. Moreover, all equalisations are *accidental* and although the proportion of capital employed in individual spheres is equalised by a continuous process, the continuity of this process itself equally presupposes the constant disproportion which it has continuously, often violently, to even out.

Here we need only consider the forms which capital passes through in the various stages of its development. The real conditions within which the actual process of production takes place are therefore not analysed. It is assumed throughout, that the commodity is sold at its value. We do not examine the competition of capitals, nor the credit system, nor the actual composition of society, which by no means consists only of two classes, workers and industrial capitalists, and where therefore consumers and producers are not identical categories. The first category, that of the consumers (whose revenues are in part not primary, but secondary, derived from profit and wages), is much broader than the second category, and therefore the way in which they spend their revenue, and the very size of the revenue give rise to very considerable modifications in the economy and particularly in the circulation and reproduction process of capital. Nevertheless, just as the examination of money[a]—both in so far as it represents a form altogether different from the natural form of commodities, and also in its form as means of payment—has shown that it contained the possibility of crises, the examination of the general nature of capital, even without going further into the actual relations which all constitute prerequisites for the real process of production, reveals this still more clearly.

[XIII-705] The conception (which really belongs to Mill), adopted by Ricardo from the tedious Say (and to which we shall return when we discuss that miserable individual), that *overproduction* is not possible or at least that NO GENERAL GLUT OF THE MARKET is possible, is based on the proposition that *products* are exchanged *against products*,[b] or as Mill put it, on the "metaphysical equilibrium

---

[a] See K. Marx, *A Contribution to the Critique of Political Economy.* Part One (present edition, Vol. 29, pp. 333-34, 373-74, 378-79).— *Ed.*

[b] J.-B. Say, *Traité d'économie politique...*, 2nd ed., Vol. 2, Paris, 1814, p. 382. See also this volume, pp. 130-34, 307.— *Ed.*

of sellers and buyers",[31] and this led to [the conclusion] that demand is determined only by production, or also that DEMAND and OFFER are identical. The same proposition exists also in the form, which Ricardo liked particularly, that ANY AMOUNT OF CAPITAL can BE EMPLOYED PRODUCTIVELY in any country.

* "M. Say," * writes Ricardo in Ch. XXI (*Effects* of Accumulation on Profits and Interest), * "has ... most satisfactorily shewn, that there is no amount of capital which may not be employed in a country, because *demand is only limited by production.* No man *produces, but with a view to consume* or *sell, and he never sells, but* with an *intention to purchase some other commodity,* which may be immediately useful to him, or which may contribute to future production. By producing, then, he necessarily becomes either the consumer of his own goods, or the purchaser and consumer of the goods of some other person. It is not to be supposed that he should, for any length of time, be ill-informed of the commodities which he can most advantageously produce, to attain the object which he has in view, namely, the *possession of other goods*; and, therefore, it is not probable, that he will *continually*" * (the point in question here is not eternal life) * "produce a commodity for which there is no demand" * ([pp.] 339-40.)

Ricardo, who always strives to be consistent, discovers that his authority, Say, is playing a trick on him here. He makes the following comment in a footnote to this passage:

* "Is the following quite consistent with M. Say's principle? 'The more disposable capitals are abundant in proportion to the extent of employment for them, the more will the rate of interest on loans of capital fall.' (*Say,* Vol. 2, p. 108). If capital to any extent can be employed by a country, how can it be said to be abundant, compared with the extent of employment for it?" * (l.c., [p.] 340, note).

Since Ricardo cites Say, we shall criticise Say's theories later, when we deal with this humbug himself.

Meanwhile we just note here: In reproduction, just as in the accumulation OF CAPITAL, it is not only a question of replacing *the same* quantity of use values of which capital consists, on the former scale or on an enlarged scale (in the case of accumulation), but of replacing the *value* of the capital advanced along with the usual rate of profit (surplus value). If, therefore, through any circumstance or combination of circumstances, the market prices of the commodities (of all or most of them, it makes no difference) fall far below their cost prices, then reproduction of capital is curtailed as far as possible. Accumulation, however, stagnates even more. SURPLUS VALUE amassed in the form of money (gold or notes) could only be transformed into capital at a loss. It therefore lies idle as a hoard in the banks or in the form of credit money, which in essence makes no difference at all. The same hold up could occur for the opposite reasons, if the *real prerequisites* of reproduction were missing (for instance if grain became more expensive or because not enough constant capital had been accumulated *in natura*). There occurs a stoppage in reproduction, and thus in the flow of circulation. Purchase and sale get bogged down and unemployed capital appears in the form of idle money. The same phenomenon (and this usually precedes crises) can appear when SURPLUS CAPITAL is produced at a very rapid rate and its reconversion into productive capital increases the demand for all the elements of the latter to such an extent, that actual production cannot keep pace with it; this brings about a rise in the prices of all commodities, which enter into the formation of capital. In this case the rate of interest falls sharply, however much the profit may rise and this fall in the rate of interest then leads to the most risky speculative ventures. The interruption of the reproduction process leads to the decrease in variable capital, to a fall in wages and in the quantity of labour employed. This in turn reacts anew on prices and leads to their further fall.

It must never be forgotten, that in capitalist production what matters is not the immediate use value but the exchange value and, in particular, the expansion of surplus value. This is the driving motive of capitalist production, and it is a pretty conception that—in order to reason away the contradictions of capitalist production—abstracts from its very basis and depicts it as a production aiming at the direct satisfaction of the consumption of the producers.

Further: since the circulation process of capital is not completed in one day but extends over a fairly long period until the capital returns to its original form, since this period coincides with the period within which market prices [XIII-706] equalise with cost prices, and great upheavals and CHANGES take place in the *market* in the course of this period, since great CHANGES take place in the productivity of labour and therefore also in the *real value* of commodities, it is quite clear, that between the starting-point, the prerequisite capital, and the time of its return at the end of one of these periods, great catastrophes must occur and elements of crisis must have gathered and develop, and these cannot in any way be dismissed by the pitiful proposition that products exchange for products. The *comparison* of value in one period with the value of the same commodities in a later period is no scholastic illusion, as Mr. Bailey maintains,[a] but rather forms the fundamental principle of the circulation process of capital.

---

[a] See [S. Bailey,] *A Critical Dissertation on the Nature, Measures and Causes of Value...*, London, 1825, pp. 71-93.— *Ed.*

When speaking of the *destruction of capital* through crises, one must distinguish between two factors.

In so far as the reproduction process is checked and the labour process is restricted or in some instances is completely stopped, *real* capital is destroyed. Machinery which is not used is not capital. Labour which is not exploited is equivalent to lost production. Raw material which lies unused is no capital. Buildings (also newly built machinery) which are either unused or remain unfinished, commodities which rot in warehouses—all this is destruction of capital. All this means that the process of reproduction is checked and that the *existing* means of production are not really used as means of production, are not put into operation. Thus their use value and their exchange value go to the devil.

Secondly, however, the *destruction of capital* through crises means the DEPRECIATION of *values* which prevents them from later renewing their reproduction process as capital on the same scale. This is the ruinous effect of the fall in the prices of commodities. It does not cause the destruction of any use values. What one loses, the other gains. Values used as capital are prevented from acting again as *capital* in the hands of the same person. The old capitalists go bankrupt. If the value of the commodities from whose sale a capitalist reproduces his capital=£12,000, of which say £2,000 were profit, and their price falls to £6,000, then the capitalist can neither meet his contracted obligations nor, even if he had none, could he, with the £6,000, restart his business on the former scale, for the commodity prices have risen once more to the level of their cost prices. In this way, £6,000 has been destroyed, although the buyer of these commodities, because he has acquired them at half their cost price, can go ahead very well once business livens up again, and may even have made a profit. A large part of the nominal capital of the society, i.e. of the *exchange value* of the existing capital, is once for all destroyed, although this very destruction, since it does not affect the use value, may very much expedite the new reproduction. This is also the period during which MONIED INTEREST enriches itself at the cost of INDUSTRIAL INTEREST. As regards the fall in the purely nominal capital, state bonds, shares, etc.—in so far as it does not lead to the bankruptcy of the state or of the share company, or to the complete stoppage of reproduction through undermining the credit of the industrial capitalists who hold such securities—it amounts only to the transfer of wealth from one hand to another and will, on the whole, act favourably upon reproduction, since the parvenus into whose hands these stocks or shares fall cheaply, are mostly more enterprising than their former owners.

To the best of his knowledge, Ricardo is always consistent. For him, therefore, the statement that no *overproduction* (of commodities) is possible, is synonymous with the statement that no PLETHORA or SUPERABUNDANCE OF CAPITAL is possible.*

"There cannot, then, be accumulated in a country any amount of capital which cannot be employed productively, until wages rise so high in consequence of the rise of necessaries, and so little consequently remains for the profits of stock, that the motive for accumulation ceases" (l.c., [p.] 340).

"It follows then ... that there is no limit to demand—no limit to the employment of capital while it yields any profit, and that *however abundant capital may become*, there is no other adequate reason for a *fall of profit* but a rise of wages, and further it may be added, that the only adequate and permanent cause for the rise of wages is the increasing difficulty of providing food and necessaries [XIII-707] for the increasing number of workmen" (l.c., [pp.] 347-48).[a]

What then would Ricardo have said to the stupidity of his successors, who deny overproduction in one form (as a GENERAL GLUT OF COMMODITIES IN THE MARKET) and who, not only admit its existence in another form, as overproduction OF CAPITAL, PLETHORA OF CAPITAL, SUPERABUNDANCE OF CAPITAL, but actually turn it into an essential point in their doctrines?

Not a single responsible economist of the post-Ricardian period denies the PLETHORA OF CAPITAL. On the contrary, all of them regard it as the cause of crises (in so far as they do not explain the latter by factors relating to credit). Therefore, they all admit overproduction in one form but deny its existence in another. The only remaining question thus is: what is the relation between these two forms of overproduction, i.e. between the form in which it is denied and the form in which it is asserted?

Ricardo himself did not actually know anything of crises, of general crises of the world market, arising out of the production process itself. He could explain that the crises which occurred between 1800 and 1815, were caused by the rise in the price of corn due to poor harvests, by the DEPRECIATION of paper money, the DEPRECIATION of colonial products etc., because, in consequence of the continental blockade,[32] the market was forcibly contracted for

*A distinction must be made here. When Adam Smith explains the fall in the rate of profit from a SUPERABUNDANCE OF CAPITAL, an ACCUMULATION OF CAPITAL, he is speaking of a *permanent* effect and this is wrong. As against this, the transitory SUPERABUNDANCE OF CAPITAL, overproduction and crises are something different. Permanent crises do not exist.

---

[a] Marx quotes these two passages in English.— *Ed.*

political and not economic reasons. He was also able to explain the crises after 1815, partly by a bad year and a shortage of corn, and partly by the fall in corn prices, because those causes which, according to his own theory, had forced up the price of corn during the war when England was cut off from the continent, had ceased to operate; partly by the transition from war to peace which brought about "SUDDEN CHANGES IN THE CHANNELS OF TRADE". (See CH. XIX—"On Sudden Changes in the Channels of Trade"—of his *Principles*.) Later historical phenomena, especially the almost regular periodicity of crises on the world market, no longer permitted Ricardo's successors to deny the FACTS or to interpret them as accidental. Instead—apart from those who explain everything by credit, but then have to admit that they themselves are forced to presuppose the SUPERABUNDANCE OF CAPITAL—they invented the nice distinction between PLETHORA OF CAPITAL and OVERPRODUCTION. Against the latter, they arm themselves with the phrases and good reasons used by Ricardo and Smith, while by means of the first they attempt to explain phenomena that they are otherwise unable to explain. Wilson, for example, explains certain crises by the PLETHORA of fixed capital, while he explains others by the PLETHORA of circulating capital.[a] The PLETHORA of capital itself is affirmed by the best economists (such as Fullarton[b]), and has already become a matter of course to such an extent, that it can even be found in the learned Roscher's compendium[c] as a self-evident fact.

The question is, therefore, what is the PLETHORA OF CAPITAL and how does it differ from OVERPRODUCTION? (In all fairness, however, it must be said, that other economists, such as Ure, Corbet, etc., declare OVERPRODUCTION to be the *usual condition in large-scale industry*, so far as the home country is concerned and that it thus only leads to crises UNDER CERTAIN CIRCUMSTANCES, in which the foreign market also contracts.) According to the same economists, capital=money or commodities. Overproduction of capital thus=overproduction of money or of commodities. And yet these two phenomena are supposed to have nothing in common with each other. Even the overproduction of money [is of] no [avail], since money for them is a commodity, so that the entire phenomenon resolves into one

---

[a] See J. Wilson, *Capital, Currency, and Banking...*, London, 1847.—*Ed.*

[b] See J. Fullarton, *On the Regulation of Currencies...*, London, 1844, pp. 161-66, especially p. 165. See also K. Marx, *Outlines of the Critique of Political Economy (Rough Draft of 1857-58)* (present edition, Vol. 29, p. 225).—*Ed.*

[c] See W. Roscher, *Die Grundlagen der Nationalökonomie*, Stuttgart and Augsburg, 1858, S. 368-70.—*Ed.*

of overproduction of commodities which they admit under one name and deny under another. Moreover, the statement that there is overproduction of fixed or of circulating capital, is based on the fact that commodities are here no longer considered in this simple form, but in their designation as capital. This, however, is an admission that in capitalist [XIII-708] production and its phenomena—e.g. OVERPRODUCTION—it is a question not only of the simple relationship in which the product appears, is designated, as *commodity,* but of its designation within the social framework; it thereby becomes something *more* than, and also different from, a commodity.

Altogether, the phrase PLETHORA OF CAPITAL instead of *overproduction of commodities* in so far as it is not merely a prevaricating expression, or unscrupulous thoughtlessness, which admits the existence and necessity of a particular phenomenon when it is called *a,* but denies it as soon as it is called *b,* in fact therefore showing scruples and doubts only about the *name* of the phenomenon and not the phenomenon itself; or in so far as it is not merely an attempt to avoid the difficulty of explaining the phenomenon, by denying it in one form (under one name) in which it contradicts existing prejudices and admitting it in a form only in which it becomes meaningless—apart from these aspects, the transition from the phrase *"overproduction of commodities"* to the phrase *"PLETHORA OF CAPITAL"* is indeed an *advance.* In what does this consist? In [expressing the fact], that the producers confront one another not purely as owners of commodities, but as capitalists.

A few more passages from Ricardo:

*"One would be led to think ... that Adam Smith concluded we were *under some necessity"* * (this is indeed the case) * *of producing a surplus* of corn, woollen goods, and hardware, and that the capital which produced them could not be otherwise employed. It is, however, always a matter of choice in what way a capital shall be employed, and therefore there can never, *for any length of time,* be a surplus of any commodity; for if there were, it would fall below its natural price, and capital would be removed to some more profitable employment"* ([pp.] 341-42, *note*).
* *"Productions are always bought by productions, or by services; money is only the medium by which the exchange is effected."* *

(That is to say, money is merely a means of circulation, and exchange value itself is merely a fleeting aspect of the exchange of product against product—which is wrong.)

*"Too much of a particular commodity may be produced, of which there may be such a glut in the market, as not to repay the capital expended on it; *but this cannot be the case with all commodities"* * (l.c., [pp.] 341-42).
* *"Whether these increased productions, and the consequent demand which they occasion,* shall or shall not lower profits, depends solely on the rise of wages; and the rise of

wages, excepting for a limited period, on the facility of producing the food and the necessaries of the labourer" * (l.c., [p.] 343).

* "When merchants engage their capitals in foreign trade, or in the carrying trade, it is always from choice, and never from necessity: it is because in that trade their profits will be somewhat greater than in the home trade" * (p. 344).

So far as crises are concerned, all those writers who describe the real movement of prices, or all experts, who write in the actual situation of a crisis, have been right in ignoring the allegedly theoretical twaddle and in contenting themselves with the idea that what may be true in abstract theory—namely, that no GLUTS in the MARKET and so forth are possible—is, nevertheless, wrong in practice. The constant recurrence of crises has in fact reduced the rigmarole of Say and others to a phraseology which IS now only USED IN TIMES OF PROSPERITY BUT IS THROWN TO THE WINDS IN TIMES OF CRISIS.

[XIII-709] In the crises of the world market, the contradictions and antagonisms of bourgeois production are strikingly revealed. Instead of investigating the nature of the conflicting elements which erupt in the catastrophe, the apologists content themselves with denying the catastrophe itself and insisting, in the face of its regular and periodic recurrence, that if production were carried on according to the textbooks, crises would never occur. Thus the apologetics consist in the falsification of the simplest economic relations, and particularly in clinging to the concept of unity in the face of contradiction.

If, for example, purchase and sale—or the metamorphosis of commodities—represent the unity of two processes, or rather the movement of one process through two opposite phases, and thus essentially the unity of the two phases, the movement is essentially just as much the separation of these two phases and their becoming independent of each other. Since, however, they belong together, the independence of the two correlated aspects can only *show itself* forcibly, as a destructive process. It is just the *crisis* in which they assert their unity, the unity of the different aspects. The independence which these two linked and complimentary phases assume in relation to each other is forcibly destroyed. Thus the crisis manifests the unity of the two phases that have become independent of each other. There would be no crisis without this inner unity of factors that are apparently indifferent to each other. But no, says the apologetic economist. Because there is this unity, there can be *no* crises. Which in turn means nothing but that the unity of contradictory factors excludes contradiction.

In order to prove that capitalist production cannot lead to general crises, all its conditions and distinct forms, all its principles and *differentiae specificae*—in short *capitalist production* itself—are denied. In fact it is demonstrated that if the capitalist mode of production had not developed in a specific way and become a unique form of social production, but were a mode of production dating back to the most rudimentary stages, then its peculiar contradictions and conflicts and hence also their eruption in crises would not exist.

Following Say, Ricardo writes: "Productions are always bought by productions, or by services; money is only the medium by which the exchange is effected" [p. 341].

Here, therefore, firstly *commodity*, in which the contradiction between exchange value and use value exists, becomes mere product (use value) and therefore the exchange of commodities is transformed into mere barter of products, of simple use values. This is a return not only to the time before capitalist production, but even to the time before there was simple commodity production; and the most complicated phenomenon of capitalist production—the world market crisis—is flatly denied, by denying the first condition of capitalist production, namely, that the product must be a commodity and therefore express itself as money and undergo the process of metamorphosis. Instead of speaking of wage labour, the term "services" is used. This word again omits the specific characteristic of wage labour and of its use—namely, that it increases the value of the commodities against which it is exchanged, that it creates surplus value—and in doing so, it disregards the specific relationship through which money and commodities are transformed into capital. "*Service*" is labour seen only as use value (which is a side issue in capitalist production) just as the word "product" fails to express the essence of *commodity* and its inherent contradiction. It is quite consistent that *money* is then regarded merely as the medium in the exchange of products, and not as an essential and necessary form of existence of the commodity which must manifest itself as exchange value, as general social labour. Since the transformation of the commodity into mere use value (product) obliterates the essence of [XIII-710] exchange value, it is just as easy to deny, or rather it is necessary to deny, that *money* is an essential aspect of the commodity and that in the process of metamorphosis it is *independent* of the original form of the commodity.

Crises are thus reasoned out of existence here by forgetting or denying the first prerequisite of capitalist production: the existence of the product as a commodity, the duplication of the commodity in commodity and money, the consequent separation which takes place in the exchange of commodities and finally the relation of money or commodities to wage labour.

Incidentally, those economists are no better who (like John Stuart Mill) want to explain the crises by these simple *possibilities* of crisis contained in the metamorphosis of commodities—such as the separation between purchase and sale. These definitions which explain the possibility of crises, by no means explain their actual occurrence. They do not explain *why* the phases of the process come into such conflict that their inner unity can only assert itself through a crisis, through a violent process. This *separation* appears in the crisis; it is the elementary form of the crisis. To *explain* the crisis on the basis of this, its elementary form, is to explain the existence of the crisis by describing its most abstract form, that is to say, to explain the crisis by the crisis.

Ricardo says: "No man produces, but with a view to consume *or sell,* and he never sells, but with an intention to *purchase* some other commodity, which may be immediately useful to him, or which may contribute to *future production.* By producing, then, he necessarily becomes either the consumer of his own goods,[a] or the purchaser and consumer of the goods of some person. It is not to be supposed that he should, *for any length of time,* be ill-informed of the commodities which he can most advantageously produce, to attain the object which he has in view, namely, the *possession of other goods;* and, *therefore,* it is not probable that he will *continually* produce a commodity for which there is no demand" [pp. 339-40].[b]

This is the childish babble of a Say, but it is not worthy of Ricardo. In the first place, no capitalist produces in order to consume his product. And when speaking of capitalist production, it is right to say that: "no man produces with a view to consume his own product", even if he uses portions of his product for industrial consumption. But here the point in question is private consumption. Previously it was forgotten that the product is a commodity. Now even the social division of labour is forgotten. In a situation where men produce for themselves, there are indeed no crises, but neither is there capitalist production. Nor have we ever heard that the ancients, with their slave production ever knew crises, although individual producers among the ancients too, did go bankrupt. The first part of the alternative is nonsense. The second as well. A man who has produced, does not have the choice of selling or not selling. He must *sell.* In the crisis there arises the very situation in which he cannot sell or can only sell below the cost price or must even sell at a positive loss. What difference does it make, therefore, to him or to us that he has

---

[a] After this word Marx gives in brackets its English equivalent.—*Ed.*

[b] Cf. this volume, p. 125.—*Ed.*

produced in order to sell? The very question we want to solve is
what has thwarted this good intention of his? Further:

"he never *sells,* but with an intention to *purchase* some other commodity, which
may be immediately useful to him, or which may contribute to future production".[a]

What a cosy description of bourgeois conditions! Ricardo even
forgets that a person may *sell* in order to *pay,* and that these
forced sales play a very significant role in the crises. The
capitalist's immediate object in selling, is to turn his commodity, or
rather his commodity capital, back into *money capital,* and thereby
to *realise* his profit. Consumption—REVENUE—is by no means the
guiding motive in this process, although it is for the person who
only sells *commodities* in order to transform them into means of
subsistence. But this is not capitalist production, in which revenue
appears as the result and not as the determining purpose.
Everyone *sells* first of all in order to sell, that is to say, in order to
transform commodities into money.

[XIII-711] During the crisis, a man may be very pleased, if he
has *sold* his commodities without immediately thinking of a
purchase. On the other hand, if the value that has been realised is
again to be used as capital, it must go through the process of
reproduction, that is, it must be exchanged for labour and
commodities. But the crisis is precisely the phase of disturbance
and interruption of the process of reproduction. And this
disturbance cannot be explained by the fact that it does not occur
in those times when there is no crisis. There is no doubt that no
one "WILL CONTINUALLY PRODUCE A COMMODITY FOR WHICH THERE IS NO DEMAND"
([pp. 339-]40), but no one is talking about such an absurd
hypothesis. Nor has it anything to do with the problem. The
immediate purpose of capitalist production is not "THE POSSESSION OF
OTHER GOODS", but the APPROPRIATION OF VALUE, OF MONEY, OF ABSTRACT WEALTH.

Ricardo's statements here are also based on James Mill's
proposition on the "metaphysical equilibrium of purchases and
sales", which I examined previously[31]—an equilibrium which sees
only the unity, but not the separation in the processes of purchase
and sale. Hence also Ricardo's assertion (following James Mill):

* "Too much of a *particular* commodity may be produced, of which there may
be such a glut in the market, as not to repay the capital expended on it; but this
cannot be the case with respect to *all* commodities" * ([pp.] 341-42).

Money is not only "THE MEDIUM BY WHICH THE EXCHANGE IS EFFECTED"
([p.] 341), but at the same time THE MEDIUM BY WHICH THE EXCHANGE OF
PRODUCE WITH PRODUCE BECOMES DISSOLVED INTO TWO ACTS, INDEPENDENT OF EACH

---

[a] Cf. this volume, p. 125.— *Ed.*

OTHER, AND DISTANT FROM EACH OTHER, IN TIME AND SPACE. With Ricardo, however, this false conception of money is due to the fact that he concentrates exclusively on the *quantitative determination* of exchange value, namely, that it=a definite quantity of labour time, forgetting on the other hand the *qualitative* characteristic, that individual labour must present itself as *abstract general social* labour only through its alienation.* [a]

That only *particular* commodities, and not *all* kinds of commodities, can form "A GLUT IN THE MARKET" and that therefore overproduction can always only be partial, is a poor way out. In the first place, if we consider only the nature of the commodity, there is nothing to prevent *all commodities* from being superabundant on the market, and therefore all falling below their price.[34] We are here only concerned with the factor of crisis. That is all commodities, apart from *money*. [The proposition] *the* commodity must be converted into money, only means that *all* commodities must do so. And just as the difficulty of undergoing this metamorphosis exists for an individual commodity, so it can exist for all commodities. The general nature of the metamorphosis of commodities—which includes the separation of purchase and sale just as it does their unity—instead of excluding the *possibility* of a GENERAL GLUT, on the contrary, contains the possibility of a GENERAL GLUT.

Ricardo's and similar types of *raisonnements*[b] are moreover based not only on the relation of *purchase and sale*, but also on that of *demand* and *supply*, which we have to examine only when considering the competition of capitals. As Mill says purchase is sale, etc., therefore demand is supply and supply demand. But they also fall apart and can become independent of each other. At a given moment, the supply of all commodities can be greater than the demand for all commodities, since the demand for the *general commodity*, money, exchange value, is greater than the demand for all particular commodities, in other words the motive to turn the commodity into money, to realise its exchange value, prevails over the motive to transform the commodity again into use value.

* [XIII-718] (That Ricardo [regards] money merely as *means of circulation* is synonymous with his regarding *exchange value* as a merely transient form, and altogether as something purely formal in bourgeois or capitalist production, which is consequently for him not a specific definite mode of production, but simply *the* mode of production.) [33]

---

[a] After this word Marx gives in brackets its English equivalent.— *Ed.*
[b] Reasoning.— *Ed.*

If the relation of demand and supply is taken in a wider and more concrete sense, then it comprises the relation of *production* and *consumption* as well. Here again, the *unity* of these two phases, which does exist and which forcibly asserts itself during the crisis, must be seen as opposed to the *separation* and *antagonism* of these two phases, separation and antagonism which exist just as much, and are moreover typical of bourgeois production.

With regard to the contradiction between partial and universal overproduction, in so far as the existence of the former is affirmed in order to evade the latter, the following observation may be made:

Firstly: Crises are usually preceded by a general INFLATION in PRICES of all articles of capitalist production. All of them therefore participate in the subsequent CRASH, and at their prices before the CRASH, OVERBURDENING THE MARKET. The market can absorb a larger volume of commodities at falling prices, at prices which have fallen below their cost prices, than it could absorb at their former prices. The excess of commodities is always relative; in other words it is an excess at particular prices. The prices at which the commodities are then absorbed are ruinous for the producer or merchant.

[XIII-712] *Secondly*:

For a crisis (and therefore also for overproduction) to be general, it suffices for it to affect the principal commercial goods.

Let us take a closer look at how Ricardo seeks to deny the possibility of A GENERAL GLUT in THE MARKET:

* "Too much of a particular commodity may be produced, of which there may be such a glut in the market, as not to repay the capital expended on it; but this cannot be the case with respect to all commodities; the demand for corn is limited by the mouths which are to eat it, for shoes and coats by the persons who are to wear them; but though a community, or a part of a community, may have as much corn, and as many hats and shoes, as it is able or may wish to consume, *the same cannot be said of every commodity produced by nature or by art*. Some would consume more wine, if they had the ability to procure it. Others having enough of wine, would wish to increase the quantity or improve the quality of their furniture. Others might wish to ornament their grounds, or to enlarge their houses. The wish to do all or some of these is implanted in every man's breast; *nothing is required but the means, and nothing can afford the means, but an increase of production*" * (l.c., [pp.] 341-42).

Could there be a more childish *raisonnement*? It runs like this: more of a particular commodity may be produced than can be consumed of it; but this cannot apply to *all* commodities at the same time. Because the needs, which the commodities satisfy, have no limits and all these needs are not satisfied at the same time. On the contrary. The fulfilment of one need makes another, so to speak, latent. Thus nothing is required, but the means to satisfy these wants, and these means can only be provided through an increase in production. Hence no general overproduction is possible.

What is the purpose of all this? In periods of overproduction, a large part of the nation (especially the working class) is less well provided than ever with corn, shoes, etc., not to speak of wine and FURNITURE. If overproduction could only occur when all the members of a nation had satisfied even their most urgent needs, there could never, in the history of bourgeois society up to now, have been a state of general overproduction or even of partial overproduction. When, for instance, THE MARKET IS GLUTTED BY SHOES OR CALICOES OR WINES OR COLONIAL PRODUCE, does this perhaps mean that $^4/_6$ of the nation have more than satisfied their needs in shoes, CALICOES, etc.? What after all has overproduction to do with absolute needs? It is only concerned with demand that is backed by ability to pay. It is not a question of absolute overproduction— overproduction as such in relation to the absolute need or the desire to possess commodities. In this sense there is neither partial nor general overproduction; and the one is not opposed to the other.

But—Ricardo will say—WHEN THERE are A LOT OF PEOPLE, WHO WANT SHOES AND CALICOES, WHY DO THEY NOT PROCURE THEMSELVES THE MEANS OF OBTAINING THEM BY PRODUCING SOMETHING WHEREWITH TO BUY SHOES AND CALICOES? Would it not be even simpler to say: Why do they not produce shoes and CALICOES for themselves? An even stranger aspect of overproduction is that the workers, the actual producers of the VERY COMMODITIES WHICH GLUT THE MARKET STAND IN WANT OF THEM. It cannot be said here that they should produce things in order to OBTAIN them, for they have produced them and yet they have not got them. Nor can it be said that a particular commodity GLUTS THE MARKET, because no one is in want of it. If, therefore, it is even impossible to explain that *partial* overproduction arises because the demand for the commodities WHICH GLUT THE MARKET has been more than satisfied, it is quite impossible to explain away *universal* overproduction by declaring that needs, unsatisfied needs, exist for many of the commodities which are on the market.

Let us keep to the example of the weaver of CALICO.[a] So long as reproduction continued uninterruptedly—and therefore also the phase of this reproduction in which the product existing as a saleable commodity, the calico, was reconverted into money, at its

___

[a] See this volume, pp. 109-12. There the reference is to a linen weaver.— *Ed.*

value—so long, shall we say, the workers who produced the CALICO, also consumed a part of it, and with the expansion of reproduction, that is to say, with accumulation, they were consuming more of it, or also more workers were employed in the production of CALICO, who also consumed part of it.

Now before we proceed further, the following must be said:

The *possibility* of crisis, which became apparent in the simple metamorphosis of the commodity, is once more demonstrated, and further developed, by the disjunction between the process of production (direct) and the process of circulation.[a] As soon as these processes do not merge smoothly into one another [XIII-713] but become independent of one another, the crisis is there.

The possibility of crisis is indicated in the metamorphosis of the commodity like this:

Firstly, the commodity which actually exists as use value, and nominally, in its price, as exchange value, must be transformed into money. $C—M$. If this difficulty, the sale, is solved then the purchase, $M—C$, presents no difficulty, since money is directly exchangeable for everything else. The use value of the commodity, the usefulness of the labour contained in it, must be assumed from the start, otherwise it is no commodity at all. It is further assumed that the individual value of the commodity=its social value, that is to say, that the labour time materialised in it=the socially *necessary* labour time for the production of this commodity. The possibility of a crisis, in so far as it shows itself in the simple form of metamorphosis, thus only arises from the fact that the differences in form—the phases—which it passes through in the course of its progress, are in the first place necessarily complimentary and secondly, despite this intrinsic and necessary correlation, they are distinct parts and forms of the process, independent of each other, diverging in time and space, separable and separated from each other. The possibility of crisis therefore lies solely in the separation of sale from purchase. It is thus only in the form of commodity that the commodity has to pass through this difficulty here. As soon as it assumes the form of money it has got over this difficulty. Subsequently however this too resolves into the separation of sale and purchase. If the commodity could not be withdrawn from circulation in the form of money or its retransformation into commodity could not be postponed—as with direct barter—if purchase and sale coincided, then the

---

[a] See K. Marx, *A Contribution to the Critique of Political Economy.* Part One (present edition, Vol. 29, pp. 324-34).— *Ed.*

possibility of crisis would, under the assumptions made, disappear. For it is assumed that the commodity represents use value for other owners of commodities. In the form of direct barter, the commodity is not exchangeable only if it has no use value or when there are no other use values on the other side which can be exchanged for it; therefore, only under these two conditions: either if one side has produced *useless* things or if the other side has nothing *useful* to exchange as an equivalent for the first use value. In both cases, however, no exchange whatsoever would take place. *But in so far as exchange did take place,* its phases would not be separated. The buyer would be seller and the seller buyer. The *critical* stage, which arises from the form of the exchange—in so far as it is circulation—would therefore cease to exist, and if we say that the simple form of metamorphosis comprises the possibility of crisis, we only say that in this form itself lies the possibility of the rupture and separation of essentially complimentary phases. But this applies also to the content. In direct barter, the bulk of production is intended by the producer to satisfy his own needs, or, where the division of labour is more developed, to satisfy the needs of his fellow producers, needs that are known to him. What is exchanged as a commodity is the surplus and it is unimportant whether this surplus is exchanged or not. In *commodity production* the conversion of the product into money, the sale, is a *conditio sine qua* [*non*]. Direct production for personal needs does not take place. Crisis results from the impossibility to sell. The difficulty of transforming the *commodity*—the particular product of individual labour—into its opposite, *money,* i.e. abstract general social labour, lies in the fact that *money* is not the particular product of individual labour, and that the person who has effected a sale, who therefore has commodities in the form of money, is not compelled to buy again at once, to transform the money again into a particular product of individual labour. In barter this contradiction does not exist: no one can be a seller without being a buyer or a buyer without being a seller. The difficulty of the seller—on the assumption that his commodity has use value—only stems from the ease with which the buyer can defer the retransformation of money into commodity. The difficulty of converting the commodity into money, of selling it, only arises from the fact that the commodity must be turned into money but the money need not be immediately turned into commodity, and therefore *sale* and *purchase* can be separated. We have said that this *form* contains the *possibility* of crisis, that is to say, the possibility that elements which are correlated, which are inseparable, are separated and consequently are forcibly reunited, their coherence is violently asserted against their mutual independence. [XIII-714] *Crisis* is nothing but the forcible assertion of the unity of phases of the production process which have become independent of each other.

The general, abstract possibility of crisis denotes no more than the *most abstract form* of crisis, without content, without a compelling motivating factor. Sale and purchase may fall apart. They thus represent *crisis* potentia and their coincidence always remains a critical factor for the commodity. The transition from one to the other may, however, proceed smoothly. The *most abstract form of crisis* (and therefore the formal possibility of crisis) is thus the *metamorphosis of the commodity* itself; the contradiction of exchange value and use value, and furthermore of money and commodity, comprised within the unity of the commodity, exists in metamorphosis only as an involved movement. The factors which turn this possibility of crisis into [an actual] crisis are not contained in this form itself; it only implies that *the* framework for a crisis exists.

And in a consideration of the bourgeois economy, that is the important thing. The world trade crises must be regarded as the real concentration and forcible adjustment of all the contradictions of bourgeois economy. The individual factors, which are condensed in these crises, must therefore emerge and must be described in each sphere of the bourgeois economy and the further we advance in our examination of the latter, the more aspects of this conflict must be traced on the one hand, and on the other hand it must be shown that its more abstract forms are recurring and are contained in the more concrete forms.

It can therefore be said that the crisis in its first form is the metamorphosis of the commodity itself, the falling asunder of purchase and sale.

The crisis in its second form is the function of money as a means of payment, in which money has 2 different functions and figures in two different phases, divided from each other in time. Both these forms are as yet quite abstract, although the second is more concrete than the first.

To begin with therefore, in considering the *reproduction process* of capital (which coincides with its circulation) it is necessary to prove that the above forms are simply repeated, or rather, that only here they receive a content, a basis on which to manifest themselves.

Let us look at the movement of capital from the moment in

which it leaves the production process as a commodity in order once again to emerge from it as a commodity. If we abstract here from all the other factors determining its content, then the total commodity capital and each individual commodity of which it is made up, must go through the process $C—M—C$, the metamorphosis of the commodity. The general possibility of crisis, which is contained in this form—the falling apart of purchase and sale—is thus contained in the movement of capital, in so far as the latter is *also* commodity and nothing but commodity. From the interconnection of the metamorphoses of commodities it follows, moreover, that one commodity is transformed into money because another is retransformed from the form of money into commodity. Furthermore, the separation of purchase and sale appears here in such a way that the transformation of one capital from the form of commodity into the form of money, must correspond to the retransformation of the other capital from the form of money into the form of commodity. The first metamorphosis of one capital [must correspond] to the second [metamorphosis] of the other; one capital leaves the production process as the other capital returns into the production process. This intertwining and coalescence of the processes of reproduction or circulation of different capitals is on the one hand necessitated by the division of labour, on the other hand it is accidental; and thus the definition of the content of crisis is already fuller.

Secondly, however, with regard to the possibility of crisis arising from the form of money as *means of payment,* it appears that capital may provide a much more concrete basis for turning this possibility into reality. For example, the weaver must pay for the whole of the constant capital whose elements have been produced by the spinner, the flax-grower, the machine-builder, the iron and timber manufacturer, the producer of coal, etc. In so far as these latter produce constant capital that only enters into the production of constant capital, without entering into the cloth, the final commodity, they replace each other's means of production through the exchange of capital. Supposing the [XIII-715] weaver now sells the cloth for £1,000 to the *merchant* but in return for a bill of exchange so that money figures as *means of payment.* The weaver for his part hands over the bill of exchange to the *banker,* to whom he may thus be repaying a debt or, on the other hand, the banker may negotiate the bill for him. The flax-grower has sold to the spinner in return for a bill of exchange, the spinner to the weaver, the machine manufacturer to the weaver, the iron and timber manufacturer to the machine manufacturer, the coal producer to the spinner, weaver, machine manufacturer, iron and timber supplier. Besides, the iron, coal, timber and flax producers have paid one another with bills of exchange. Now if the merchant does not pay, then the weaver cannot pay his bill of exchange to the banker. The flax-grower has drawn on the spinner, the machine manufacturer on the weaver and the spinner. The spinner cannot pay because the weaver [can]not pay, neither of them pay the machine manufacturer, and the latter does not pay the iron, timber or coal supplier. And all of these in turn, as they cannot realise the value of their commodities, cannot replace that portion of value which is to replace their constant capital. Thus the general crisis comes into being. This is nothing other than the *possibility of crisis* described when dealing with money as a means of payment; but here—in capitalist production—we can already see the connection between the mutual claims and obligations, the sales and purchases, through which the possibility can develop into actuality.

In any *case*: If purchase and sale do not get bogged down, and therefore do not require forcible adjustment—and, on the other hand, money as means of payment functions in such a way that claims are mutually settled, and thus the contradiction inherent in money as a means of payment is not realised—if therefore neither of these two abstract forms of crisis become real, no crisis exists. No crisis can exist unless sale and purchase are separated from one another and come into conflict, or the contradictions contained in money as a means of payment actually come into play; crisis, therefore, cannot exist without manifesting itself at the same time in its simple form, as the contradiction between sale and purchase and the contradiction of money as a means of payment. But these are merely *forms*, general possibilities of crisis, and hence also forms, abstract forms, of actual crisis. In them, the existence of crisis appears in its simplest forms, and, in so far as this form is itself the simplest content of crisis, in its simplest content. But the content is not yet *substantiated*. Simple circulation of money and even the circulation of money as a means of payment— and both come into being long *before* capitalist production, while there are no crises—are possible and actually take place without crises. These forms alone, therefore, do not explain why their crucial aspect becomes prominent and why the contradiction contained in them potentially becomes a real contradiction.

This shows the economists' enormous *fadaise*,[a] when they are no

---

[a] Vulgarity, commonness.— *Ed.*

longer able to explain away the phenomenon of overproduction and crises, are content to say that these forms contain the possibility of *crises,* that it is therefore *accidental* whether or not crises occur and consequently their occurrence is itself merely a *matter of chance.*

The contradictions inherent in the circulation of commodities, which are further developed in the circulation of money—and thus, also, the possibilities of crisis—reproduce themselves, automatically, in capital, since developed circulation of commodities and of money, in fact, only takes place on the basis of capital.

But now the further development of the potential CRISIS has to be traced—the real crisis can only be educed from the real movement of capitalist production, competition and credit—in so far as crisis arises out of the special aspects of capital which are *peculiar* to it as capital, and not merely comprised in its existence as commodity and money.

[XIII-716] The mere (direct) *production process* of capital in itself, cannot add anything new in this context. In order to exist at all, its conditions are presupposed. The first section dealing with capital—the *direct* process of production—does not contribute any new element of crisis. Although it *does* contain such an element, because the production process implies appropriation and hence production of surplus value. But this cannot be shown when dealing with the production process itself, for the latter is not concerned with the *realisation* either of the reproduced value or of the surplus value.

This can only emerge in the *circulation process* which is in itself also a *process of reproduction.*

Furthermore it is necessary to describe the circulation or reproduction process *before* dealing with the already existing capital— *capital and profit*—since we have to explain, not only how capital produces, but also how capital is produced. But the actual movement starts from the existing capital—i.e. the actual movement denotes developed capitalist production, which starts from and presupposes its own basis. The process of reproduction and the predisposition to crisis which is further developed in it, are therefore only partially described under this heading and require further elaboration in the chapter on "Capital and Profit".[35]

The circulation process as a whole or the reproduction process of capital as a whole is the unity of its production phase and its circulation phase, so that it comprises both these processes or phases. Therein lies a further developed possibility or abstract form of crisis. The economists who deny crises consequently assert only the unity of these two phases. If they were only separate, without being a unity, then their unity could not be established by force and there could be no crisis. If they were only a unity without being separate, then no violent separation would be possible implying a crisis. Crisis is the forcible establishment of unity between elements that have become independent and the enforced separation from one another of elements which are essentially one. [XIII-716]

[XIII-770a] [36] Therefore:

1) The general *possibility* of crisis is given in the process of *metamorphosis of capital* itself, and in two ways: in so far as money functions as *means of circulation,* there is the separation *of purchase and sale,* and in so far as money functions as *means of payment,* it has two different aspects, it acts as *measure of value* and as *realisation of value.* These two aspects become separated. If in *the interval* between them the value has changed, if the commodity at the moment of its sale is not *worth* what it was *worth* at the moment when money was acting as a measure of value and therefore as a measure of the reciprocal obligations, then the obligation cannot be met from the *proceeds of the sale of the commodity,* and therefore the whole series of transactions which retrogressively depend on this one transaction, cannot be settled. If even for only *a limited period of time* the commodity cannot be sold then, although its value has not altered, *money* cannot function as *means of payment,* since it must function as such in a *definite given period of time.* But as the same sum of money acts for a whole series of reciprocal transactions and obligations here, *inability to pay* occurs not only at one, but at many points, hence a *crisis* arises.

These are the *formal possibilities* of crisis. The form mentioned first is possible without the latter—that is to say, crises are possible without credit, without money functioning as a means of payment. But the second form is not possible without *the first*—that is to say, without the separation between purchase and sale. But in the latter case, the crisis occurs not only because the commodity is unsaleable, but because it is not saleable within a *particular period of time,* and the crisis arises and derives its character not only from the *unsaleability* of the commodity, but from the *non-fulfilment of a whole series of payments* which depend on the sale of this particular commodity within this particular period of time. This is the *actual* form of money crises.

If the *crisis* appears, therefore, because purchase and sale become separated, it becomes a *money crisis,* as soon as money has developed as *means of payment,* and this *second form* of crisis follows as a matter of course, when the *first occurs.* In investigating why the general *possibility of crisis* becomes a *reality,* in investigating the *conditions* of crisis, it is therefore quite superfluous to concern oneself with the *forms* of crisis which arise out of the development of money as *means of payment.* This is precisely why economists like to suggest that this *obvious* form is the *cause* of crises. (In so far as the development of money as means of payment is linked with the development of credit and of OVERCREDIT the causes of the latter have to be examined, but this is not yet the place to do it.)

2) In so far as crises arise from *changes in prices* and *revolutions in prices,* which do not coincide with *changes in the values* of commodities, they naturally cannot be investigated during the examination of capital in general, in which the prices of commodities are assumed to be *identical* with the *values* of commodities.

3) The *general possibility* of crisis is the formal *metamorphosis* of capital itself, the separation, in time and space, of purchase and sale. But this is never the *cause* of the crisis. For it is nothing but the *most general form of crisis,* i.e. the crisis[37] itself in *its most generalised expression.* But it cannot be said that the *abstract form of crisis* is *the cause of crisis.* If one asks what its cause is, one wants to know why *its abstract form,* the form of its possibility, turns from possibility into *actuality.*

4) The *general conditions* of crises, in so far as they are independent of *price fluctuations* (whether these are linked with the credit system or not) as distinct from fluctuations in value, must be explicable from the general conditions of capitalist production.

First phase. The *reconversion of money into capital.* A definite level of *production or reproduction* is assumed. Fixed capital can be regarded here as given, as remaining unchanged and not entering into the *valorisation process.* Since the reproduction of raw material is not dependent solely on the labour employed on it, but on the productivity of this labour which is bound up with *natural conditions,* it is possible for the volume, [XIV-771a][38] the *amount* of the product of *the same* quantity of labour, to fall (as a result of BAD SEASONS). *The value of the raw material therefore rises; its volume decreases,* in other words the *proportions* in which the money has to be reconverted into the *various component parts* of capital in order to continue production on the former scale, are upset. More must be expended on *raw material,* less remains for *labour,* and it is not possible to absorb the same quantity of labour as before. Firstly this is *physically impossible,* because of the deficiency in raw material. *Secondly,* it is impossible because a greater *portion of the value of the product* has to be converted into raw material, thus leaving less for conversion into *variable capital.* Reproduction cannot be *repeated* on the same scale. A part of *fixed capital* stands idle and a part of the workers is thrown out on the streets. The *rate of profit* falls because the value of constant capital has risen as against that of variable capital and less variable capital is employed. The fixed charges—interest, rent—which were based on the anticipation of a *constant* rate of profit and exploitation of labour, remain the same and in part *cannot be paid.* Hence *crisis.* Crisis of labour and crisis of capital. This is therefore a *disturbance in the reproduction process* due to the increase in the value of that part of constant capital which has to be replaced out of the value of the product. Moreover, although the *rate of profit* is decreasing, there is a *rise in the price of the product.* If this product enters into other spheres of production as a means of production, the *rise in* its *price* will result in the same DERANGEMENT in *reproduction* in these spheres. If it enters into general consumption as a means of subsistence, it either enters also *into the consumption of the workers* or *not.* If it does so, then its effects will be the same as those of a DERANGEMENT in *variable capital,* of which we shall speak later. But in so far as it enters into *general consumption* it *may* result (if its consumption is not reduced) in a diminished *demand* for other products and consequently *prevent their reconversion* into money at their value, thus disturbing the *other aspect* of their reproduction— not the *reconversion of money* into productive capital but the *reconversion* of commodities into money. In any case, the *volume of profits* and the *volume of wages* is reduced in this branch of production thereby reducing a *part of the necessary* RETURNS from the sale of commodities from other branches of production.

Such a *shortage of raw material* may, however, occur not only because of the *influence of* SEASONS or of the *natural productivity* of the labour which supplies the raw material. For if an *excessive portion* of the *surplus value, of the surplus capital,* is laid out in machinery, etc. in a particular branch of production, then, although the [raw] MATERIAL would have been sufficient for the *old level of production,* it will be insufficient for the *new.* This therefore arises from the DISPROPORTIONATE conversion of SURPLUS CAPITAL into its various elements. It is a CASE of *surplus production of fixed capital* and gives rise to exactly the same phenomena as occur in the first case. (See the previous page.)

[XIV-861a] [39]
Or they [the crises] are due to an *overproduction of fixed capital* and therefore a relative underproduction of circulating capital.

Since *fixed capital*, like *circulating*, consists of commodities, it is quite ridiculous that the same economists who admit the *overproduction of fixed capital*, deny the *overproduction of commodities*.

5) *Crises arising from disturbances in the first phase of reproduction*; that is to say, interrupted conversion of commodities into money or *interruption of sale*. In the case of crises of the first sort the crisis arises from interruptions in the *flowing back* of the elements of productive capital.

[XIII-716] Before embarking on an investigation of the new forms of crisis,[40] we shall resume our consideration of Ricardo and the above example.[a]

(A *crisis* can arise: 1) in the course of the *reconversion* [of money] *into productive capital*, [2)] through *changes in the value* of the elements of productive capital, particularly of *raw material*, for example when there is a decrease in the quantity of cotton harvested. Its *value* will thus rise. We are not as yet concerned with prices here but with *values*.)

So long as the owner of the weaving-mill reproduces and accumulates, his workers, too, purchase a part of his product, they spend a part of their wages on calico. Because he produces, they have the MEANS to purchase a part of his product and thus to some extent give him the MEANS to sell it. The worker can only buy—he can represent a DEMAND only for—commodities which enter into individual consumption, for he does not himself turn his labour to account nor does he himself possess the means to do so—the instruments of labour and materials of labour. This already, therefore, excludes the majority of producers (the workers themselves, where capitalist production prevails) as consumers, buyers. They buy neither raw material nor means of labour; they buy only means of subsistence (commodities which enter directly into individual consumption). Hence nothing is more ridiculous than to speak of the identity of producers and consumers, since for an extraordinarily large number of TRADES—all those that do not supply articles for direct consumption—the mass of those who participate in production are entirely excluded from the *purchase* of their own products. They are never *direct* consumers or buyers of this large part of their own products,

---

[a] See this volume, pp. 110 et seq.—*Ed.*

although they pay a portion of the value of these products in the articles of consumption that they buy. This also shows the ambiguity of the word consumer and how wrong it is to identify it with the word buyer. As regards industrial consumption, it is precisely the workers who consume machinery and raw material, using them up in the labour process. But they do not use them up for themselves and they are therefore not *buyers* of them. Machinery and raw material are for them neither use values nor commodities, but objective conditions of a process of which they themselves are the subjective conditions.

[XIII-717] It may, however, be said that their EMPLOYER represents them in the purchase of the means and materials of labour. But he represents them under different conditions from those in which they would represent themselves. Namely, on the market. He must sell a quantity of commodities which represents surplus value, unpaid labour. They [the workers] would only have to sell the quantity of commodities which would reproduce the value advanced in production—the value of the means of labour, the materials of labour and the wages. He therefore requires a wider market than they would require. It depends, moreover, on him and not on them, whether he considers the conditions of the market sufficiently favourable to begin reproduction.

They are therefore producers without being consumers—even when no interruption of the reproduction process takes place—in relation to all articles which have to be consumed not individually but industrially.

Thus nothing is more absurd as a means of denying crises, than the assertion that the consumers (buyers) and producers (sellers) are identical in capitalist production. They are entirely distinct categories. In so far as the reproduction process takes place, this identity can be asserted only for one out of 3,000 producers, namely, the capitalist. On the other hand, it is equally wrong to say that the consumers are producers. The LANDLORD (rent) does not produce, and yet he consumes. The same applies to the whole of the MONIED INTEREST.

The apologetic phrases used to deny crises are important in so far as they always prove the opposite of what they are meant to prove. In order to deny crises, they assert unity where there is conflict and contradiction. They are therefore important in so far as one can say: they prove that there would be no crises if the contradictions which they have erased in their imagination, did not exist in fact. But in reality crises exist because these contradictions exist. Every reason which they put forward against crisis is an exorcised contradiction, and, therefore, a real contradiction, which can cause crises. The desire to convince oneself of the non-existence of contradictions, is at the same time the expression of a pious wish that the contradictions, which are really present, *should* not exist.

What the workers in fact produce, is surplus value. So long as they produce it, they are able to consume. As soon as they cease [to produce it], their consumption ceases, because their production ceases. But that they are able to consume is by no means due to their having produced an equivalent for their consumption. On the contrary, as soon as they produce merely such an equivalent, their consumption ceases, they have no equivalent to consume. Their work is either stopped or curtailed, or at all events their wages are reduced. In the latter case—if the level of production remains the same—they do not consume an equivalent of what they produce. But they lack these means not because they do not produce enough, but because they receive too little of their product for themselves.

By reducing these relations simply to those of consumer and producer, one leaves out of account that the wage labourer who produces and the capitalist who produces are two producers of a completely different kind, quite apart from the fact that some consumers do not produce at all. Once again, a *contradiction* is denied, by abstracting from a contradiction which really exists in production. The mere relationship of wage labourer and capitalist implies:

1) that the majority of the producers (the workers) are non-consumers (non-buyers) of a very large part of their product, namely, of the means and materials of labour;

2) that the majority of the producers, the workers, can consume an equivalent for their product only so long as they produce more than this equivalent, that is, so long as they produce SURPLUS VALUE or SURPLUS PRODUCE. They must always be *overproducers*, produce over and above their needs, in order to be able to be consumers or buyers within the [XIII-718] limits of their needs.[41]

As regards this class of producers, the unity between production and consumption is, at any rate *prima facie*, false.

When Ricardo says that the only limit to DEMAND is production itself, and that this is limited by capital,[a] then this means, in fact, when stripped of false assumptions, nothing more than that capitalist production finds its measure only in capital; in this

---

[a] D. Ricardo, *On the Principles of Political Economy, and Taxation*, 3rd ed., London, 1821, pp. 339 and 347 (see this volume, pp. 125 and 128).—*Ed.*

context, however, the term capital also includes the labour capacity which is incorporated in (bought by) capital as one of its conditions of production. The question is whether capital as such is also the limit for consumption. At any rate, it is so in a negative sense, that is, more cannot be consumed than is produced. But the question is, whether this applies in a positive sense too, whether— on the basis of capitalist production—as much can and must be consumed as is produced. Ricardo's proposition, when correctly analysed, says the very opposite of what it is meant to say— namely, that production takes place without regard to the existing limits to consumption, but is limited only by capital itself. And this is indeed characteristic of this mode of production.

Thus according to the assumption, the market is GLUTTED, for instance with COTTONS,[a] so that part of it remains unsold or all of it, or it can only be sold well below its price. (For the time being, we shall call it *value*, because while we are considering circulation or the reproduction process, we are still concerned with value and not yet with cost price, even less with market price.)

It goes without saying that, in the whole of this observation, it is not denied that too much may be produced in individual spheres and *therefore* too little in others; partial crises can thus arise from DISPROPORTIONATE PRODUCTION (PROPORTIONATE PRODUCTION is, however, always only the result of DISPROPORTIONATE PRODUCTION on the basis of competition) and a general form of this DISPROPORTIONATE PRODUCTION may be overproduction of fixed capital, or on the other hand, overproduction of circulating capital.* Just as it is a condition for the sale of commodities at their value, that they contain only the socially necessary labour time, so it is for an entire sphere of production of capital, that only the necessary part of the total labour time of society is used in the particular sphere, only the labour time which is required for the satisfaction of social need (DEMAND). If more [is used], then, even if each individual commodity only contains the necessary labour time, the total contains more than the socially necessary labour time; in the same way, although the individual commodity has use value, the total sum of commodities loses some of its use value under the conditions assumed.

---

* [XIII-720] (When spinning-machines were invented, there was overproduction of yarn in relation to weaving. This disproportions disappeared when mechanical looms were introduced into weaving.)[42]

---

[a] After this word Marx gives in brackets its German equivalent.— *Ed.*

However, we are not speaking of crisis here in so far as it arises from DISPROPORTIONATE production, that is to say, the disproportion in the distribution of social labour between the individual spheres of production. This can only be dealt with in connection with the competition of capitals. In that context it has already been stated[a] that the rise or fall of market value which is caused by this DISPROPORTION, results in the TRANSFER or WITHDRAWAL OF CAPITAL FROM ONE TRADE TO another, the MIGRATION OF CAPITAL FROM ONE TRADE TO another. This equalisation itself however already implies as a precondition the opposite of equalisation and may therefore comprise *crisis*; the crisis itself may be a form of equalisation. Ricardo, etc., admit this form of crisis.

When considering the production process[43] we saw that the whole aim of capitalist production is appropriation of the greatest possible amount of surplus labour, in other words, the realisation of the greatest possible amount of immediate labour time with the given capital, be it through the prolongation of the labour day or the reduction of the necessary labour time, through the development of the productive power of labour by means of cooperation, division of labour, machinery, etc., in short, large-scale production, i.e. mass production. It is thus in the nature of capitalist production, to produce without regard to the limits of the market. During the examination of reproduction, it is, in the first place, assumed that the mode of production remains the same and it remains the same, moreover, for a period while production expands. The volume of commodities produced is increased in this case, because more capital is employed and not because capital is employed more productively. But the mere quantitative increase in [XIII-719] capital at the same time implies that its productive power grows. If its quantitative increase is the result of the development of productive power, then the latter in turn develops on the assumption of a broader, extended capitalist basis. Reciprocal interaction takes place in this case. Reproduction on an extended basis—accumulation—even if originally it appears only as a quantitative expansion of production—the use of more capital under the same conditions of production—at a certain point, therefore, always represents also a qualitative expansion in the form of greater productivity of the conditions under which reproduction is carried out. Consequently the volume of products increases not only in simple proportion to the growth of capital in

---

[a] See present edition, Vol. 31, pp. 431-35.— *Ed.*

expanded reproduction—accumulation. Now let us return to our example of CALICO.

The stagnation in the market, WHICH IS GLUTTED WITH CALICOES, hampers the reproduction process of the weaver. This disturbance first affects his workers. Thus they are now to a smaller extent, or not at all, consumers of his commodity—COTTONS—and of other commodities which entered into their consumption. It is true, that they need COTTONS, but they cannot buy it because they have not the MEANS, and they have not the MEANS because they cannot continue to produce and they cannot continue to produce because too much has been produced, TOO MANY COTTONS GLUT THE MARKET. Neither Ricardo's advice "TO INCREASE THEIR PRODUCTION", nor his alternative "TO PRODUCE SOMETHING ELSE" can help them.[a] They now form a part of the temporary surplus population, of the SURPLUS PRODUCTION OF LABOURERS, in this CASE of COTTON PRODUCERS, because there is a SURPLUS PRODUCTION OF COTTONS UPON THE MARKET.

But apart from the workers who are directly employed by the capital invested in COTTON weaving, a large number of other producers are hit by this interruption in the reproduction process of COTTON: SPINNERS, COTTON DEALERS (OR COTTON CULTIVATORS), MECHANICS (PRODUCERS OF SPINDLES AND LOOMS, etc.), IRON, COAL PRODUCERS, etc. Reproduction in all these spheres would also be impeded because the reproduction of COTTONS is a condition for their own reproduction. This would happen even if they had not *overproduced* in their own spheres, that is to say, had not produced beyond the limit set and justified by the cotton industry when it was working smoothly. All these industries have this in common, that their REVENUE (wages and profit, in so far as the latter is consumed as REVENUE and not accumulated) is not consumed by them in their own product but in the product of other spheres, which produce articles of consumption, CALICO among others. Thus the consumption of and the demand for CALICO fall just because there is too much of it on the market. But this also applies to all other commodities on which, as articles of consumption, the REVENUE of these *indirect* producers of COTTON is spent. Their MEANS for buying CALICO and other articles of consumption shrink, contract, because there is too much CALICO on the market. This also affects other commodities (articles of consumption). They are now, all of a sudden, *relatively* overproduced, because the means with which to buy them and therefore the demand for them, have contracted. Even if there has

---

[a] D. Ricardo, *On the Principles of Political Economy, and Taxation*, 3rd ed., London, 1821, pp. 342, 339-40 (see this volume, pp. 125, 133, 136).—*Ed.*

been no overproduction in these spheres, now they are over-producing.

If overproduction has taken place not only in CALICOES, but also in LINENS, SILKS, and WOOLLENS, then it can be understood how overproduction in these few, but leading articles, calls forth a more or less general (*relative*) overproduction on the whole market. On the one hand there is a superabundance of all the means of reproduction and a superabundance of all kinds of unsold commodities on the market. On the other hand bankrupt capitalists and destitute, starving workers.

This ARGUMENT, HOWEVER, CUTS TWO WAYS. If it is easily understood how overproduction of some leading articles of consumption must bring in its wake the phenomenon of a more or less general overproduction, it is by no means clear how overproduction of these articles can arise. For the phenomenon of general over-production is derived from the interdependence not only of the workers directly employed in these industries, but of all branches of industries which produce the elements of their products, the various stages of their constant capital. In the latter branches of industry, overproduction is an effect. But whence does it come in the former? For the latter continue to produce so long as the former go on producing, and along with this continued produc-tion, a general growth in REVENUE, and therefore in their own consumption, seems assured.

[XIII-720] [a] If one were to answer the question by pointing out that the constantly expanding production // it expands annually for two reasons; firstly because the capital invested in production is continually growing; secondly because the capital is constantly used more productively; in the course of reproduction and accumulation, small improvements are continuously building up, which eventually alter the whole level of production. There is a piling up of improvements, a cumulative development of produc-tive powers// requires a constantly expanding market and that production expands more rapidly than the market, then one would merely have used different terms to express the phenome-non which has to be explained—concrete terms instead of abstract terms. The market expands more slowly than production; or in the cycle through which capital passes during its reproduction—a cycle in which it is not simply reproduced but reproduced on an extended scale, in which it describes not a circle but a spiral— there comes a moment at which the market manifests itself as too

---

[a] See this volume, p. 150.— *Ed.*

narrow for production. This occurs at the end of the cycle. But it merely means: the market is GLUTTED. Overproduction is MANIFEST. If the expansion of the market had kept pace with the expansion of production THERE WOULD BE NO GLUT in the MARKET, NO OVERPRODUCTION. However, the mere admission that the market must expand with production, is, on the other hand, again an admission of the possibility of overproduction, for the market is limited externally in the geographical sense, the internal market is limited as compared with a market that is both internal and external, the latter in turn is limited as compared with the world market, which however is, in turn, limited at each moment of time, [though] in itself capable of expansion. The admission that the market must expand if there is to be no overproduction, is therefore also an admission that there can be overproduction. For it is then possible—since market and production are two independent factors—that the expansion of one does *not* correspond with the expansion of the other; that the limits of the market are not extended rapidly enough for production, or that new markets— new extensions of the market—may be rapidly outpaced by production, so that the expanded market becomes just as much a barrier as the narrower market was formerly.

Ricardo is therefore consistent in denying the necessity of *an expansion of the market* simultaneously with the expansion of production and growth of capital. All the available capital in a country can also be advantageously employed in that country. Hence he polemises against Adam Smith, who on the one hand put forward *his* (Ricardo's) view and, with his usual rational instinct, contradicted it as well. Adam Smith did not yet know the phenomenon of overproduction, and crises resulting from over-production. What he knew were only credit and money crises, which automatically appear, along with the credit and banking system. In fact he sees in the accumulation of capital an unqualified increase in the general wealth and well-being of the nation. On the other hand, he regards the mere fact that the internal market develops into an external, colonial and world market, as proof of a so-to-speak relative overproduction (existing in itself) in the internal market. It is worth quoting Ricardo's polemic against him at this point:

* "When merchants engage their capitals in foreign trade, or in the carrying trade, it is always from choice, and never from necessity: it is because in that trade their profits will be somewhat greater than in the home trade. Adam Smith has justly observed 'that the desire of food is limited in every man by the narrow capacity of the human stomach'," *

// Adam Smith is very much mistaken here, for he excludes the luxury products of AGRICULTURE. //

* " 'but the desire of the conveniences and ornaments of building, dress, equipage, and household furniture, seems to have no limit or certain boundary.' ª *Nature* then" * (Ricardo continues) * "has necessarily *limited the amount of capital which can* at any *time be profitably engaged in agriculture*" *

// Is that why there are nations which export AGRICULTURAL PRODUCE? As if it were impossible, despite NATURE, to sink all possible capital into agriculture in order to produce, in England for example, melons, figs, grapes, etc., flowers, and birds and game, etc. And as if the raw materials of industry were not produced by means of AGRICULTURAL CAPITAL. // (See, for example, the capital that the Romans put into artificial fish culture alone.)

* "*but she has placed no limits*" * (as if nature had anything to do with the matter!) * "*to the amount of capital* that may be employed in procuring 'the conveniences and ornaments' of life. To procure these gratifications in *the greatest abundance* is *the object in view*, and it is only because foreign trade, or the carrying trade, will accomplish it better, that men engage in them in preference to manufacturing the commodities required, or a substitute for them, at home. If, however, from peculiar circumstances, we were precluded from engaging capital in foreign trade, or in the carrying trade, we should, though with less advantage, employ it at home; and *while there* is *no limit* to the desire of 'conveniences, ornaments of building, dress, equipage, and [XIII-721] household furniture', *there can be no limit to the capital that may be employed in procuring them*, except that which bounds our power to *maintain the workmen who are to produce them.*

"Adam Smith, however, speaks of the carrying trade as one, not of choice, but of necessity; as if the capital engaged in it would be inert if not so employed, as *if the capital in the home trade could overflow*, if not confined to a limited amount. He says, 'when the capital stock of any country is increased to such a degree, *that it cannot be all employed in supplying the consumption*, and *supporting the productive labour of that particular country*,'" * (this passage is printed in italics by Ricardo himself) * " 'the *surplus part* of it naturally disgorges itself into the carrying trade, and is employed in performing the same offices to other countries'...ᵇ But could not this portion of the productive labour of Great Britain be employed in preparing some other sort of goods, with which something more in demand at home might be purchased? And if it could not, might we not employ this productive labour, though with less advantage, in making those goods in demand at home, or at least some substitute for them? If we wanted velvets, might we not attempt to make velvets; and if we could not succeed, might we not make more cloth, or some other object desirable to us?

"We manufacture commodities, and with them buy goods abroad, because we can obtain a *greater quantity*" * // the qualitative difference does not exist! // * "than we could make at home. Deprive us of this trade, and we immediately manufacture again for ourselves. But this opinion of Adam Smith is at variance with all his general doctrines on this subject. 'If' " * (Ricardo now cites Smith) * " 'If a foreign

---

ª A. Smith, *An Inquiry into the Nature and Causes of the Wealth of Nations,* Book I, Ch. XI, Part 2.— *Ed.*

ᵇ *Ibid.,* Book II, Ch. V.— *Ed.*

country can supply us with a commodity, cheaper than we ourselves can make it, better buy it of them with some part of the produce of our own industry, employed in a way in which we have some advantage. *The general industry of the country being always in proportion to the capital which employs it*'," * //in very different proportion// (this sentence too is emphasised by Ricardo) * "'will not thereby be diminished, but only left to find out the way in which it can be employed with the greatest advantage.'ᵃ

// "Again. 'Those, therefore, who have the command of more food than they themselves can consume, are always willing to *exchange the surplus*, or, what is the same thing, the price of it, for gratifications of another kind. What is over and above satisfying the limited desire, is given for the amusement of *those desires which cannot be satisfied, but seem to be altogether endless*. The poor, in order to obtain food, exert themselves to gratify those fancies of the rich; and to obtain it more certainly, they vie with one another in the cheapness and perfection of their work. The number of workmen increases with the increasing quantity of food, or with the growing improvement and cultivation of the lands; and as the nature of their business admits of the utmost subdivisions of labours, the quantity of materials which they can work up increases in a much greater proportion than their numbers. Hence arises a demand for every sort of material which human invention can employ, either usefully or ornamentally, in building, dress, equipage, or household furniture; for the fossils and minerals contained in the bowels of the earth, the precious metals, and the precious stones.'ᵇ

"It follows then from these admissions that *there is no limit to demand—no limit to the employment of capital while it yields any profit*, and that *however abundant capital may become*, there is no other adequate reason for a fall of profit but a rise of wages, and further it may be added, that the only adequate and permanent cause for the rise of wages is the increasing difficulty of providing food and necessaries for the increasing number of workmen"* (l. c., [pp.] 344-48).

The world OVERPRODUCTION in itself leads to error. So long as the most urgent needs of a large part of society are not satisfied, or *only* the most immediate needs are satisfied, there can of course be absolutely no talk of an *overproduction of products*—in the sense that the amount of products is excessive in relation to the need for them. On the contrary, it must be said that on the basis of capitalist production, there is constant *underproduction* in this sense. The limits to production are set by the profit of the capitalist and in no way by the needs of the producers. But overproduction of products and overproduction of *commodities* are two entirely different things. If Ricardo thinks that the *commodity* form makes no difference to the product, and furthermore, that *commodity circulation* differs only formally from barter, that in this context the exchange value is only a fleeting form of the exchange of things, and that money is therefore merely a formal means of circulation—then this in fact is in line with his presupposition that

---

ᵃ A. Smith, *An Inquiry into the Nature and Causes of the Wealth of Nations*, Book IV, Ch. II.— *Ed.*

ᵇ Ibid., Book I, Ch. XI, Part 2.— *Ed.*

the bourgeois mode of production is the absolute mode of production, hence it is a mode of production without any definite specific characteristics, its distinctive traits are merely formal. He cannot therefore admit that the bourgeois mode of production contains within itself a barrier to the free development of the productive forces, a barrier which comes to the surface in crises and, in particular, in *overproduction*—the basic phenomenon in crises.

[XIII-722] Ricardo saw from the passages of Adam Smith, which he quotes, approves, and therefore also repeats, that the limitless "DESIRE" for all kinds of use values is always satisfied on the basis of a state of affairs in which the mass of producers remains more or less restricted to necessities—"FOOD" and other "NECESSARIES"—that consequently this great majority of producers remains more or less excluded from the consumption of wealth—in so far as wealth goes beyond the bounds of the NECESSARIES.

This was indeed also the case, and to an even higher degree, in the ancient mode of production which depended on slavery. But the ancients never thought of transforming the SURPLUS PRODUCE into capital. Or at least only to a very limited extent. (The fact that the hoarding of treasure in the narrow sense was widespread among them shows how much SURPLUS PRODUCE lay completely idle.) They used a large part of the SURPLUS PRODUCE for unproductive expenditure on art, religious works and *travaux publics.*[a] Still less was their production directed to the release and development of the material productive forces—division of labour, machinery, the application of the powers of nature and science to private production. In fact, by and large, they never went beyond handicraft labour. The wealth which they produced for private consumption was therefore relatively small and only appears great because it was amassed in the hands of a few persons, who, incidentally, did not know what to do with it. Although, therefore, there was no *overproduction* among the ancients, there was *overconsumption* by the rich, which in the final periods of Rome and Greece turned into mad extravagance. The few trading peoples among them lived partly at the expense of all these *essentiellement* poor nations. It is the unconditional development of the productive forces and therefore mass production on the basis of a mass of producers who are confined within the bounds of the NECESSARIES on the one hand and, on the other, the barrier set up by

---

[a] Public works.— *Ed.*

the capitalists' profit, which [forms] the basis of modern over-production.

All the objections which Ricardo and others raise against overproduction, etc., rest on the fact that they regard bourgeois production either as a mode of production in which no distinction exists between purchase and sale—direct barter—or as *social* production, implying that society, as if according to a plan, distributes its means of production and productive forces in the degree and measure which is required for the fulfilment of the various social needs, so that each sphere of production receives the *quota* of social capital required to satisfy the corresponding need. This fiction arises entirely from the inability to grasp the specific form of bourgeois production and this inability in turn arises from the obsession that bourgeois production is production as such, just like a man who believes in a particular religion and sees it as *the* religion, and everything outside of it only as *false* religions.

On the contrary, the question that has to be answered is: since, on the basis of capitalist production, everyone works for himself and a particular labour must at the same time appear as its opposite, as abstract general labour and in this form as social labour—how is it possible to achieve the necessary balance and interdependence of the various spheres of production, their dimensions and the proportions between them, except through the constant neutralisation of a constant disharmony? This is admitted by those who speak of adjustments through competition, for these adjustments always presuppose that there is something to adjust, and therefore that harmony is always only a result of the movement which neutralises the existing disharmony.

That is why Ricardo admits that a GLUT of certain commodities is possible. What is supposed to be *impossible* is only A SIMULTANEOUS, GENERAL GLUT in THE MARKET. The possibility of overproduction in any particular sphere of production is therefore not denied. It is the *simultaneity* of this phenomenon for *all* spheres of production which is said to be impossible and therefore makes impossible [general] overproduction and thus a GENERAL GLUT in THE MARKET (this expression must always be taken *cum grano salis*,[a] since in times of general overproduction, the overproduction in some spheres is always only the *result*, the *consequence*, of overproduction in the leading articles of commerce; [it is] always only *relative*, i.e. overproduction because overproduction exists in other spheres).

Apologetics turns this into its very opposite. [There is only]

---

[a] Literally: with a grain of salt; figuratively: with skepticism.— *Ed.*

overproduction in the leading articles of commerce, in which alone, active overproduction shows itself—these are on the whole articles which can only be produced on a mass scale and by factory methods (also in agriculture), because overproduction exists in those articles in which relative or passive overproduction manifests itself. According to this, overproduction only exists because overproduction is not universal. The *relativity* of overproduction— that actual overproduction in a few spheres calls forth overproduction in others—is expressed in this way: There is no *universal* overproduction, because if overproduction were universal, all spheres of production would retain the same relation to one another; therefore *universal* overproduction=PROPORTIONATE PRODUCTION which excludes overproduction. And this is supposed to be an argument against universal overproduction. [XIII-723] For, since *universal overproduction* in the absolute sense would not be overproduction but only a greater than usual development of the productive forces in all spheres of production, it is alleged that *actual overproduction*, which is precisely not this non-existent, self-abrogating overproduction, does *not* exist—although it only exists because it is not this.

If this miserable sophistry is more closely examined, it amounts to this: Suppose, that there is overproduction in iron, cotton goods, LINENS, SILKS, WOOLLENS, etc.; then it cannot be said, for example, that too little coal has been produced and that this is the reason for the above overproduction. For that overproduction of iron, etc. involves an exactly similar overproduction of coal, as, say, the overproduction of woven cloth does of yarn. //Overproduction of yarn as compared with cloth, iron as compared with machinery, etc. could occur. This would always be a relative overproduction of constant capital.// There cannot, therefore, be any question of the underproduction of those articles whose overproduction is implied because they enter as an element, raw material, *matière instrumentale* or means of production, into those articles (the "PARTICULAR COMMODITY OF WHICH TOO MUCH MAY BE PRODUCED, OF WHICH THERE MAY BE SUCH A GLUT IN THE MARKET, AS NOT TO REPAY THE CAPITAL EXPENDED ON IT" [a]), whose positive overproduction is precisely the FACT TO BE EXPLAINED. Rather, it is a question of other articles which belong directly to [other] spheres of production and [can] neither [be] subsumed under the leading articles of commerce which, according to the assumption, have been OVERPRODUCED, nor be attributed to spheres in which, because they supply the *intermediate*

---

[a] See this volume, pp. 130, 134, 136.— *Ed.*

product for the leading articles of commerce, production must have reached at least the same level as in the final phases of the product—although there is nothing to prevent production in those spheres from having gone even further ahead thus causing an overproduction within the overproduction. For example, although sufficient coal must have been produced in order to keep going all those industries into which coal enters as necessary condition of production, and therefore the *overproduction* of coal is implied in the *overproduction* of iron, yarn, etc. (even if coal was produced only in proportion to the production of iron and yarn), it is *also* possible that more coal was produced than was required even for the overproduction of iron, yarn, etc. This is not only possible, but very probable. For the *production of coal and yarn* and of all other spheres of production which produce only the conditions or earlier phases of a product to be completed in another sphere, is governed not by the immediate demand, by the immediate production or reproduction, but by the *degree, measure, proportion*[a] in which these are expanding. And it is SELF-EVIDENT that in this calculation, the target may well be overshot. Thus not enough has been produced of other articles such as, for example, pianos, precious stones, etc., they have been *underproduced.* //There are, however, also cases where the overproduction of non-leading articles is not the result of overproduction, but where, on the contrary, *underproduction* is the cause of overproduction, as for instance when there has been a failure in the grain crop or the cotton crop, etc.//

The absurdity of this statement becomes particularly marked if it is applied to the international scene, as it has been by Say and others after him.[44] For instance, that England has not *overproduced* but Italy has *underproduced.* There would have been no over-production, if Italy 1) had enough capital to replace the English capital exported to Italy in the form of commodities; 2) if Italy had invested this capital in such a way that it produced those particular articles which are required by English capital—partly in order to replace itself and partly in order to replace the REVENUE yielded by it. Thus the fact of the actually existing *overproduction* in *England*—in relation to the *actual* production in Italy—would not have existed, but only the fact of *imaginary underproduction* in *Italy*; imaginary because it [XIII-724] presupposes a capital in Italy and a development of the productive powers that does not exist there, and secondly because it makes the equally utopian

---

[a] Marx uses an English word in parenthesis after a German one.— *Ed.*

assumption, that this capital which does *not* exist in Italy, has been employed in exactly the way required to make ENGLISH SUPPLY AND ITALIAN DEMAND, English and Italian production, complementary to each other. In other words, this means nothing but: there would be no overproduction, if demand and supply corresponded to each other, if the capital were distributed in such proportions in all spheres of production, that the production of one article involved the consumption of the other, and thus its own consumption. There would be no overproduction, if there were no overproduction. Since, however, capitalist production can allow itself free rein only in certain spheres, under certain conditions, there could be no capitalist production at all if it had to develop *simultaneously* and *evenly* in all spheres. Because absolute over-production takes place in certain spheres, relative overproduction occurs also in the spheres where there has been no overproduction.

This explanation of overproduction in one field by underpro-duction in another field therefore means merely that if production were proportionate, there would be no overproduction. Ditto, if demand and supply corresponded to each other. Ditto, if all spheres provided equal opportunities for capitalist production and its expansion—division of labour, machinery, export to distant markets, etc., including mass production, if all countries which traded with one another possessed the same capacity for produc-tion (and indeed for different and complementary production). Thus overproduction takes place because all these pious wishes are not fulfilled. Or, in even more abstract form: There would be no overproduction in one place, if overproduction took place to the same extent everywhere. But there is not enough capital to overproduce so universally, and therefore there is [no] universal overproduction. Let us examine this fantasy more closely:

It is admitted that there can be overproduction in each *particular* TRADE. The only circumstance which could prevent overproduction in *all* [trades] simultaneously is, according to the assertions made, the fact that commodity exchanges against commodity—i.e. RECOURSE [is taken] TO THE SUPPOSED conditions OF BARTER. But this loop-hole is blocked by the very fact that TRADE is not BARTER, and that therefore the seller of a commodity is not necessarily AT THE SAME TIME THE BUYER OF ANOTHER. This whole subterfuge then rests on abstracting from *money* and from the fact that we are not concerned with the exchange of products, but with the circulation of commodities, an essential part of which is the separation of purchase and sale.[45]

//The circulation of capital contains within itself the *possibilities* of interruptions. In the reconversion of money into its conditions of production, for example, it is not only a question of transforming money into the same use values (in kind), but for the repetition of the reproduction process [it is] essential that these use values can again be obtained at their old value (at a lower value would of course be even better). A very significant part of these elements of reproduction, which consists of raw materials, can however rise in price for two reasons: *Firstly*, if the instruments of production increase more rapidly than the amount of raw materials that can be provided at THE GIVEN TIME. *Secondly*, as a result of the variable character of the SEASONS. That is why weather conditions, as Tooke rightly observes, play such an important part in modern industry.[a] (The same applies to the means of subsistence in relation to wages.) The reconversion of money into commodity can thus come up against difficulties and can create the possibilities of crisis, just as well as can the conversion of commodity into money. When one examines simple circulation— not the circulation of capital—these difficulties do not arise.// (There are, besides, a large number of other factors—conditions, possibilities of crises, which can only be examined when considering the concrete conditions, particularly the competition of capitals and credit.[30])

[XIII-725] The *overproduction of commodities* is denied but the *overproduction of capital* is admitted. Capital itself however consists of commodities or, in so far as it consists of money, it must be reconverted, into commodities *d'une manière ou d'une autre*,[b] in order to be able to function as capital. What then does *overproduction of capital* means? Overproduction of amounts of value destined to produce surplus value (or, if one considers the material content, overproduction of commodities destined for reproduction)—that is, *reproduction on too large a scale*, which is the same as overproduction pure and simple.

Defined more closely, this means nothing more than that too much has been produced for the purpose of *enrichment*, or that too great a part of the product is intended not for consumption as REVENUE, but *for making more money* (for accumulation); not to satisfy the personal needs of its owner, but to give him money, abstract social riches and capital, more power over the labour of

---

[a] Th. Tooke, *A History of Prices, and of the State of the Circulation, from 1839 to 1847 Inclusive...*, London, 1848, pp. 3-35.— *Ed.*

[b] Of one kind or another.— *Ed.*

others, i.e. to increase this power. This is what one side says. (Ricardo denies it.[a]) And the other side, how does it explain the overproduction of commodities? By saying that production IS NOT DIVERSIFIED ENOUGH, that certain articles of consumption have not been produced in sufficiently large quantities. That it is not a matter of industrial consumption is obvious, for the manufacturer who overproduces linen, thereby necessarily increases his demand for yarn, machinery, labour, etc. It is therefore a question of personal consumption. Too much linen has been produced, but perhaps too few oranges. Previously the existence of money was denied, in order to show [that there was no] separation between sale and purchase. Here the existence of capital is denied, in order to transform the capitalists into people who carry out the simple operation *C—M—C* and who produce for individual consumption and not *as* capitalists with the aim of enrichment, i.e. the reconversion of part of the surplus value into capital. But the statement that there is *too much capital*, after all means merely that too little is consumed as REVENUE, and that more cannot be consumed in the given conditions. (*Sismondi.*[46]) Why does the producer of linen demand from the producer of corn, that he should consume more linen, or the latter demand that the linen manufacturer should consume more corn? Why does the man who produces linen not himself convert a larger part of his REVENUE (surplus value) into linen and the FARMER into corn? So far as each individual is concerned, it will be admitted that his desire for capitalisation (apart from the limits of his needs) prevents him from doing this. But for all of them collectively, this is not admitted.

(We are entirely leaving out of account here that element of crises which arises from the fact that commodities are reproduced more cheaply than they were produced. HENCE the depreciation of the commodities on the market.)

In world market crises, all the contradictions of bourgeois production erupt collectively; in particular crises (*particular* in their content and in extent) the eruptions are only sporadical, isolated and one-sided.

Overproduction is specifically conditioned by the general law of the production of capital: to produce to the limit set by the productive forces (that is to say, to exploit the maximum amount of labour with the given amount of capital), without any consideration for the actual limits of the market or the needs

---

[a] See this volume, pp. 127-28.— *Ed.*

backed by the ability to pay; and this is carried out through continuous expansion of reproduction and accumulation, and therefore constant reconversion of REVENUE into capital, while [XIII-726] on the other hand, the mass of the producers remain tied to the AVERAGE level of needs, and must remain tied to it according to the nature of capitalist production.

In Cн. VIII, "On Taxes", Ricardo says:

"When the annual productions of a country more than replace its annual consumption, it is said to increase its capital; when its annual consumption is not at least replaced by its annual production, it is said to diminish its capital. Capital may therefore be increased by an increased production, or by a diminished unproductive consumption" ([pp.] 162-63).

By "UNPRODUCTIVE CONSUMPTION" Ricardo means here, as he says in the note on p. 163, consumption by unproductive workers, "BY THOSE WHO DO NOT REPRODUCE ANOTHER VALUE". By increase in the annual production, therefore, is meant increase in the annual industrial consumption. This can be increased by the direct expansion of it, while non-industrial consumption remains constant or even grows, or by reducing non-industrial consumption.

"When we say," writes Ricardo in the same note, *"that revenue is saved, and added to capital, what we mean is, that the portion of revenue, so said to be added to capital, is consumed by productive instead of unproductive labourers."* *

I have shown that the conversion of REVENUE into capital is by no means synonymous with the conversion of REVENUE into variable capital or with its expenditure on wages.[a] Ricardo however thinks so. In the same note he says:

"If the price of labour should rise so high, that notwithstanding the increase of capital, no more could be employed, I should say that such increase of capital would be still unproductively consumed." *

It is therefore not the consumption of REVENUE by productive workers, which makes this consumption "productive", but its consumption by workers who produce surplus value. According to this, capital increases only when it commands *more labour*.

Cн. *VII.* "On Foreign Trade".

" There are two ways in which capital may be accumulated: it may be saved either in consequence of increased revenue, or of diminished consumption. If my profits are raised from £1,000 to £1,200 while my expenditure continues the same, I accumulate annually £200 more than I did before. If I save £200 out of my expenditure, while my profits continue the same, the same effect will be produced; £200 per annum will be added to my capital" ([p.] 135).

"If, by the introduction of machinery, the *generality of the commodities on which revenue was expended* fell 20 per cent. in value, I should be enabled to save as

---

[a] See this volume, pp. 103-23.— Ed.

effectually as if my revenue had been raised 20 per cent.; but in one case the *rate of profits* is stationary, in the other it is raised 20 per cent.—If, by the introduction of cheap foreign goods, I can save 20 per cent. from my expenditure, the effect will be precisely the same as if machinery had lowered the expense of their production, but profits would not be raised" * ([p.] 136).

(That is to say, they would NOT BE RAISED IF THE CHEAPER GOODS ENTERED NEITHER INTO THE VARIABLE NOR THE CONSTANT CAPITAL.)

Thus with the *same expenditure of* REVENUE accumulation is the result of the rise in the rate of profit (but accumulation depends not only on the rate of profit but on the amount of profit); with a *constant rate of profit* accumulation is the result of decreasing EXPENDITURE, which is however assumed by Ricardo to occur because of the reduced price (whether this is brought about by machinery or FOREIGN TRADE) of "COMMODITIES ON WHICH REVENUE WAS EXPENDED".

CH. XX, "Value and Riches, their Distinctive Properties".

*"The wealth" * (Ricardo takes this to mean *use values*) * "of a country may be increased in two ways: it may be increased by *employing* a *greater portion of revenue in the maintenance of productive labour,*—which will not only add to the *quantity*, but to the *value* of the mass of commodities; or it may be increased, *without employing any additional quantity of labour,* by *making the same quantity more productive,*—which will add to the abundance, but not to the value of commodities. In the first case, a country would not only become rich, but the value of its riches would increase. It *would become rich by parsimony*; by diminishing its expenditure on objects of luxury and enjoyment; and *employing those savings in reproduction*.

[XIII-727] "In the second case, there will not necessarily be either *any diminished expenditure on luxuries and enjoyments,* or any *increased quantity of productive labour employed, but with the same labour more would be produced*; wealth would increase, but not value. Of these two modes of increasing wealth, the last must be preferred, since it produces the same effect without the privation and diminution of enjoyments, which can never fail to accompany the first mode. *Capital is that part of the wealth of a country which is employed with a view to future production, and may be increased in the same manner as wealth.* An *additional capital* will be equally efficacious in the production of future wealth, whether it *be obtained from improvements in skill and machinery,* or from *using more revenue reproductively*; for wealth always depends on the quantity of commodities produced, without any regard to the facility with which the instruments employed in production may have been procured. A certain quantity of clothes and provisions will maintain and employ the same number of men, and will therefore procure the same quantity of work to be done, whether they be produced by the labour of 100 or 200 men; but they will be of twice the value if 200 have been employed on their production" * ([pp.] 327-28).

Ricardo's first proposition was:

Accumulation grows,

if the rate of profit rises, while EXPENDITURE remains the same; or when the rate of profit remains the same, if EXPENDITURE (in terms of VALUE) decreases, because the commodities on which the REVENUE is expended become cheaper.

Now he puts forward another antithetical proposition.

Accumulation grows, capital is accumulated in amount and value, if a larger part of the REVENUE is withdrawn from individual consumption and directed to industrial consumption, if more productive labour is set in motion with the portion of REVENUE thus saved. In this case accumulation is brought about by PARSI-MONY.

Or EXPENDITURE remains the same, and no additional productive labour is employed; but the same labour produces more, its productive power is raised. The elements which make up the productive capital, raw materials, machinery, etc. //previously it was the commodities UPON WHICH REVENUE IS EXPENDED; now it is the commodities EMPLOYED AS INSTRUMENTS IN PRODUCTION// are produced with the same labour in greater quantities, better and therefore cheaper. In this case, accumulation depends neither on a rising rate of profit, nor on a greater portion of REVENUE being converted into capital as a result of PARSIMONY, nor on a smaller portion of the REVENUE being spent unproductively as a result of a reduction in the price of those commodities on which REVENUE is expended. It depends here on labour becoming more productive in the spheres of production which produce the elements of capital itself, thus lowering the price of the commodities which enter into the production process as raw materials, instruments, etc.

If the productive power of labour has been increased through greater production of fixed capital in proportion to variable capital, then not only the amount, but also the *value* of reproduction will rise, since a part of the value of the fixed capital enters into the annual reproduction. This can occur simultaneously with the growth of the population and with an increase in the number of workers employed, although the number of workers steadily declines *relatively*, in proportion to the constant capital which they set in motion. There is therefore a growth, not only OF WEALTH, but OF VALUE, and a larger quantity of living labour is set in motion, although the labour has become more productive and the quantity of labour in proportion to the quantity of commodities produced, has decreased. Finally, variable and constant capital can grow in equal degree with the natural, annual increase in population while the productivity of labour remains the same. In this case, too, capital will accumulate in volume and in value. These last points are all disregarded by Ricardo.

In the same chapter Ricardo says:

"The labour of a million of men in manufactures, will always produce the same value, but will not always produce the same riches."

(This is quite wrong. The value of the product of a MILLION OF MEN does not depend solely on their labour but also on the value of the capital with which they work; it will thus vary considerably, according to the amount of the already produced productive powers with which they work.)

* "By the invention of machinery, by improvements in skill, by a better division of labour, or by the discovery of new markets, where more advantageous exchanges may be made, a million of men may produce double, or treble the amount of riches, of 'necessaries, conveniences, and amusements', in one state of society, that they could produce in another, but they will not on that account add any thing to value" *

(they certainly will, since their past [XIII-728] labour enters into the new reproduction to a much greater extent),

* "for every thing rises or falls in value, in proportion to the facility or difficulty of producing it, or, in other words, in proportion to the quantity of labour employed on its production." *

(Each individual commodity may become cheaper but the value of the increased total mass of commodities [will] rise.)

* "Suppose with a given capital, the labour of a certain number of men produced 1,000 pair of stockings, and that by inventions in machinery, the same number of men can produce 2,000 pair, or that they can continue to produce 1,000 pair, and can produce besides 500 hats; then the value of the 2,000 pair of stockings,[a] and 500 hats, will be neither more nor less than that of the 1,000 pair of stockings before the introduction of machinery; for they will be the produce of the same quantity of labour." *

(N.B. provided the NEWLY INTRODUCED MACHINERY costs *nothing.*)

* "But the *value of the general mass of commodities will nevertheless be diminished*; for, although the value of the increased quantity produced, in consequence of the improvement, will be the same exactly as the value would have been of the less quantity that would have been produced, had no improvement taken place, *an effect is also produced on the portion of goods still unconsumed, which were manufactured previously to the improvement*; the value of those goods will be reduced, inasmuch as they must fall to the level, quantity for quantity, of the goods produced under all the advantages of the improvement: and the society will, notwithstanding the increased quantity of commodities, notwithstanding its augmented riches, and its augmented means of enjoyment, *have a less amount of value. By constantly increasing the facility of production, we constantly diminish the value of some of the commodities before produced*, though by the same means we not only add to the national riches, but also to the power of future production" * ([pp.] 320-22).

Ricardo says here that the progressive development of the productive powers causes the DEPRECIATION of the commodities produced under less favourable conditions, whether they are still on the market, or functioning as capital in the production process.

---

[a] Further Ricardo has: "or of the 1,000 pair of stockings".— *Ed.*

But, although the value of one part of the commodities will be reduced, it does not by any means follow from this that "THE VALUE OF THE GENERAL MASS OF COMMODITIES WILL BE DIMINISHED". This would be the only effect if, 1) the value of the machinery and commodities that have been newly added as a result of the IMPROVEMENTS, is smaller than the loss in value suffered by previously existing goods of the same kind; 2) if one leaves out of account the fact that with the development of the productive forces, the number of spheres OF PRODUCTION is also steadily increasing, thus creating possibilities for capital investment which previously did not exist at all. Production not only becomes cheaper in the course of the development, but it is also *diversified.*

CH. IX, "Taxes on Raw Produce".

*"With respect to the third objection against taxes on raw produce, namely, that the raising wages, and lowering profits, is a discouragement to accumulation, and acts in the same way as a natural poverty of soil; I have endeavoured to shew in another part of this work that *savings may be as effectually made from expenditure as from production; from a reduction in the value of commodities, as from a rise in the rate of profits.* By increasing my profits from [£]1,000 to £1,200, whilst *prices* continue the same, my power of increasing my capital by savings is increased, but it is not increased so much as it would be if *my profits continued as before,* whilst commodities were so lowered in price, that £800 would procure me as much as £1,000 purchased before"* ([pp.] 183-84).

The total value of the product (or rather that part of the product which is divided between capitalist and worker) can decrease, without causing a fall in the NET INCOME, in terms of the amount of value it represents. (It may even rise proportionally.) This in:

CH. XXXII, "Mr. Malthus's Opinions on Rent".

*"The whole argument, however, of Mr. Malthus, is built on an infirm basis: it supposes, because the *gross income* of the country is diminished, that, therefore, the net income must also be diminished, in the same proportion. It has been one of the objects of his work to shew, that with every fall in the real value of necessaries, the wages of labour would fall, and that the profits of stock would rise—in other words, that of any given annual value a less portion would be paid to the labouring class, and a larger portion to those whose funds employed this class. Suppose the value of the commodities produced in a particular manufacture to be £1,000 and to be divided between the master and his labourers, in the proportion of £800 to labourers, and £200 to the master; [XIII-729] if the value of these commodities should fall to £900, and £100 be saved from the wages of labour,[a] the net income of the masters would be in no degree impaired, and, therefore, he could with just as much facility pay the same amount of taxes, after, as before the reduction of price"* ([pp.] 511-12).

---

a Further Ricardo has: "in consequence of the fall of necessaries".—*Ed.*

Cн. V, "On Wages".

* "Notwithstanding the tendency of wages to conform to their natural rate, their market rate may, in an improving society, for an indefinite period, be constantly above it; for no sooner may the impulse, which an increased capital gives to a new demand for labour be obeyed, than another increase of capital may produce the same effect; and thus, if the increase of capital be gradual and constant, the demand for labour may give a continued stimulus to an increase of people" * ([p.] 88).

From the capitalist standpoint, everything is seen upside down. The number of the labouring population and the degree of the productivity of labour determine both the reproduction of capital and the reproduction of the population. Here, on the contrary, it appears that *capital* determines the population.

Cн. IX, "Taxes on Raw Produce".

* "An accumulation of capital naturally produces an increased competition among the employers of labour, and a consequent rise in its price" * ([p.] 178).

This depends on the proportion in which the various component parts of CAPITAL grow as a result of its ACCUMULATION. Capital can be accumulated and the demand for labour can decrease absolutely or relatively.

According to Ricardo's theory of rent, the rate of profit has a tendency to fall, as a result of the accumulation of capital and the growth of the population, because the NECESSARIES rise in value, or agriculture becomes less productive. Consequently accumulation has the tendency to check accumulation, and the *law of the falling rate of profit*—since agriculture becomes relatively less productive as industry develops—hangs ominously over bourgeois production. On the other hand, Adam Smith regarded the falling rate of profit with satisfaction. Holland is his model. It compels most capitalists, except the largest ones, to employ their capital in industry, instead of living on interest and is thus a spur to production. The dread of this pernicious tendency assumes tragi-comic forms among Ricardo's disciples.

Let us here compare the passages in which Ricardo refers to this subject.

Cн. V, "On Wages".

* "In different stages of society, the accumulation of capital, or of the means of employing labour, is more or less rapid, and *must in all cases depend on the productive powers of labour*. The productive powers of labour are generally greatest when there is an abundance of fertile land: at such periods accumulation is often so rapid, that labourers cannot be supplied with the same rapidity as capital" ([p.] 92).

"It has been calculated, that under favourable circumstances population may be doubled in twenty-five years; but under the same favourable circumstances, the whole capital of a country might possibly be doubled in a shorter period. In that

12*

case, wages during the whole period would have a tendency to rise, because the demand for labour would increase still faster than the supply.

"In new settlements, where the arts and knowledge of countries far advanced in refinement are introduced, it is probable that capital has a tendency to increase faster than mankind: and if the deficiency of labourers were not supplied by more populous countries, this tendency would very much raise the price of labour. In proportion as these countries become populous, and land of a worse quality is taken into cultivation, the tendency to an increase of capital diminishes; *for the surplus produce remaining, after satisfying the wants of the existing population, must necessarily be in proportion to the facility of production, viz. to the smaller number of persons employed in production.* Although, then, it is probable, that under the most favourable circumstances, the power of production is still greater than that of population, it will not long continue so; for the land being limited in quantity, and differing in quality, with every increased portion of capital employed on it, there will be a decreased rate of production, whilst *the power of population continues always the same*"* ([pp.] 92-93).

(The latter statement is a parson's fabrication. THE POWER OF POPULATION DECREASES with the POWER OF PRODUCTION). First it should be noted here that Ricardo admits that "THE ACCUMULATION OF CAPITAL ... MUST IN ALL CASES DEPEND ON THE PRODUCTIVE POWERS OF LABOUR", LABOUR therefore is *prius*[a] and not capital.

Further, according to Ricardo, it would appear that IN long SETTLED, industrially developed COUNTRIES more people are engaged in agriculture than are in the colonies—while in fact it is the other way about. In proportion to the output [XIII-730], England, for example, uses fewer AGRICULTURAL LABOURERS THAN ANY OTHER COUNTRY, NEW OR OLD, although a larger section of the NON-AGRICULTURAL POPULATION participates indirectly in AGRICULTURAL PRODUCTION. But even this is by no means proportionate to the extra numbers of the directly AGRICULTURAL POPULATION in the less developed countries. Supposing even that in England grain is dearer, and the costs of production are higher. More capital is employed. More past labour, even though less living labour is used in AGRICULTURAL PRODUCTION. But the reproduction of this capital, although its value is reproduced in the product, costs less labour because of the already existing basis of production.

Ch. VI, "On Profits".

First, however, a few observations. [The amount of] surplus value, as we saw, depends not only on the rate of surplus value but on the number of workers simultaneously employed, that is to say, on the size of the variable capital.

Accumulation for its part is not determined—directly—by the *rate of surplus value*, but by the ratio of surplus value to the TOTAL

---

[a] Primary.— *Ed.*

AMOUNT OF THE CAPITAL ADVANCED, that is, by the rate of profit, and not so much by the rate of profit as by the *total* AMOUNT OF PROFIT. This, as we have seen, is for the total capital of society identical with the aggregate AMOUNT OF SURPLUS VALUE, but for individual capitals employed IN THE DIFFERENT TRADES MAY VARIATE VERY MUCH FROM THE AMOUNT OF SURPLUS VALUE PRODUCED BY THEM. If we consider the accumulation of capital *en bloc*,[a] then profit=surplus value and the rate of

$$\text{profit} = \frac{\text{surplus value}}{\text{capital}},$$ or rather surplus value reckoned on a capital of 100.

If the rate of profit (per cent) is given, then the total AMOUNT OF PROFIT depends on the size of the capital advanced, and therefore accumulation too in so far as it is determined by profit.

If the total sum of capital is given then the total AMOUNT OF PROFIT depends on the rate of profit.

A small capital with a higher rate of profit may therefore yield more PROFIT than a larger capital with a lower rate of profit.

Let us suppose:

1)

	Capital [£]	Rate of profit %	Total profit [£]
	100	10	10
(100×2)	200	$^{10}/_2$ or 5	10
(100×3)	300	$^{10}/_2$ or 5	15
(100×1$^1/_2$)	150	5	7$^1/_2$

2)

	Capital [£]	Rate of profit %	Total profit [£]
	100	10	10
2×100	(200)	$\frac{10}{2^1/_2} = 4$	8
2$^1/_2$×100	(250)	4	10
3×100	[(300)]	4	12

3)

Capital [£]	Rate of profit [%]	Total profit [£]
500	10	50
5,000	1	50
3,000	1	30
10,000	1	100

---

[a] As a whole.— *Ed.*

If the multiplier of the capital and the divisor of the rate of profit are the same, that is to say, if the size of the capital increases in the same proportion as the rate of profit falls, then the total PROFIT remains unchanged. 100 at 10% amounts to 10, and 2×100 at $^{10}/_2$ or 5% also amounts to 10. In other words, the amount of PROFIT remains unchanged if the rate of profit falls in the same proportion in which capital accumulates (grows).

If the rate of profit falls more rapidly than the capital grows, then the amount of PROFIT decreases. 500 at 10% yields a total PROFIT of 50. But six times as much, 6×500 or 3,000 at $^{10}/_{10}$% or 1% yields only 30.

Finally, if capital grows faster than the rate of profit falls, the amount of PROFIT increases in spite of the falling rate of profit. Thus 100 at 10% profit yields a profit of 10. But 300 (3×100) at 4% (i.e. where the rate of profit has fallen by 60 per cent) yields a total profit of 12.

Now to the passages from Ricardo.

CH. VI, "On Profits".

* "The *natural tendency of profits then is to fall*; for, in the progress of society and wealth, the additional quantity of food required is obtained by the sacrifice of more and more labour. This tendency, this *gravitation as it were of profits*, is *happily checked* at repeated intervals by the improvements in machinery, connected with the production of necessaries, as well as by discoveries in the science of agriculture which enable us to relinquish a portion of labour before required, and [XIII-731] therefore to lower the price of the prime necessaries of the labourer. The rise in the price of necessaries and in the wages of labour is however limited; for as soon as wages should be equal ... to £720, the whole receipts of the farmer, there *must be an end of accumulation*; *for no capital can then yield any profit whatever*, and no *additional labour can be demanded*, and consequently *population will have reached its highest point*. Long indeed before this period, the *very low rate of profits will have arrested all accumulation*, and almost the whole produce of the country, after paying the labourers, will be the property of the owners of land and the receivers of tithes and taxes" * ([pp.] 120-21).

This, as Ricardo sees it, is the bourgeois "Twilight of the Gods" — the Day of Judgement.

* "Long before this state of prices was become permanent, *there would be no motive for accumulation*; *for no one accumulates but with a view to make his accumulation productive*, and [...] consequently such a state of prices never could take place. The *farmer and manufacturer can no more live without profit, than the labourer without wages*. Their *motive* for accumulation will *diminish with every diminution of profit*, and will *cease altogether when their profits are so low* as not to afford them *an adequate compensation* for their trouble, and the *risk which* they *must necessarilly encounter in employing their capital productively*" ([p.] 123).

"I must again observe, that the rate of profits would fall much more rapidly ... for the value of the produce being what I have stated it under the circumstances supposed, the value of the farmer's stock would be greatly increased from its necessarily consisting of many of the commodities which had risen in value. Before corn could rise from £4 to £12, *his capital would probably be doubled in exchangeable value*, and be worth £6,000 instead of £3,000. If then his profit were £180, or 6 per cent. on his original capital, profits would not at that time be really at a higher *rate* than 3 per cent.; for £6,000 at 3 per cent. gives £180; and on *those terms* only could a *new farmer with £6,000 money* in his pocket *enter into the farming business"* ([pp. 123-]24).

"We should also expect that, however *the rate of the profits of stock* might diminish *in consequence of the accumulation of capital on the land,* and the rise of wages, yet that *the aggregate amount of profits would increase.* Thus supposing that, with repeated accumulations of £100,000, the rate of profit should fall from 20 to 19, to 18, to 17 per cent., a constantly diminishing rate, we should expect that the whole amount of profits received by those successive owners of capital would be always progressive; that it would be greater when the capital was £200,000, than when £100,000; still greater when £300,000; and so on, *increasing, though at a diminishing rate, with every increase of capital.* This *progression however is only true for a certain time:* thus 19 per cent. on £200,000 is more than 20 on £100,000; again 18 per cent. on £300,000 is more than 19 per cent. on £200,000; but after capital has accumulated to a large amount, and profits have fallen, the *further accumulation diminishes the aggregate of profits.* Thus suppose the accumulation should be £1,000,000, and the profits 7 per cent. the whole amount of profits will be £70,000; now if an addition of £100,000 capital be made to the million, and profits should fall to 6 per cent., £66,000 or a diminution of £4,000 will be received by the owners of stock, although the whole amount of stock will be increased from £1,000,000 to £1,100,000.

"*There can, however, be no accumulation of capital, so long as stock yields any profit at all, without its yielding not only an increase of produce, but an increase of value.* By employing £100,000 additional capital, no part of the former capital will be rendered less productive. The produce of the land and labour of the country must increase, and its value will be raised, not only by the value of the addition which is made to the former quantity of productions, but by the new value which is given to the whole produce of the land, by the increased difficulty of producing the last portion of it. When the accumulation of capital, however, becomes very great, notwithstanding this increased value, it will be so distributed that a less value than before will be appropriated to profits, while that which is devoted to rent and wages will be increased" ([pp.]124-26).

"Although a greater value is produced, a greater proportion of what remains of that value, after paying rent, is consumed by the producers, and it is this, and this alone, which regulates profits. Whilst the land yields abundantly, wages may temporarily rise, and the producers may consume more than their accustomed proportion; but the stimulus which will thus be given to population, will *speedily reduce the labourers to their usual consumption.* But when poor lands are taken into cultivation, or when more capital and labour are expended on the old land, with a less return of produce, the effect must be permanent" ([p.] 127).

[XIII-732] "The effects then of accumulation will be different in different countries, and will depend chiefly on the fertility of the land. However extensive a country may be where the land is of a poor quality, and where the importation of food is prohibited, the most moderate accumulations of capital will be attended with great reductions in the rate of profit, and a rapid rise in rent; and on the contrary a small but fertile country, particularly if it freely permits the importation of food, may accumulate a large stock of capital without any great diminution in the rate of profits, or any great increase in the rent of land" * ([pp.] 128-29).

[It can] also [happen] as a result of *taxation* that * "*sufficient surplus produce* may not be left to stimulate the exertions of those who usually augment by their savings the capital of the State" * (CH. XII, "Land-Tax", [p.] 206).

// CH. XXI, "Effects of Accumulation on Profits and Interest // * "There is only one case, and that will be temporary, in which the accumulation of capital with a low price of food may be attended with a fall of profits; and that is, when the *funds for the maintenance of labour increase much more rapidly than population;*—wages will then be high, and profits low. If every man were to forego the use of luxuries, and be intent only on accumulation, a quantity of necessaries might be produced, for which there could not be any immediate consumption. *Of commodities so limited in number, there might undoubtedly be a universal glut,* and consequently there might neither be demand for an additional quantity of such commodities, nor profits on the employment of more capital. If men ceased to consume, they would cease to produce" * ([p.] 343).

Thus Ricardo on accumulation and the law of the falling rate of profit.

RICARDO'S MISCELLANEA

Gross and Net Income

Net income, as opposed to gross income (which=the total product or the value of the total product), is the form in which the Physiocrats originally conceived surplus value. They consider rent to be its sole form, since they think of industrial profit as merely a kind of wage; later economists who blur the concept of PROFIT by calling it WAGES for the SUPERINTENDENCE OF LABOUR, ought to agree with them.

NET REVENUE is therefore in fact the excess of the product (or the excess of its value) over that part of it which replaces the capital outlay, comprising both constant and variable capital. It thus consists simply of profit and rent, the latter, in turn, is only a separate portion of the profit, a portion accruing to a class other than the capitalist class.

The direct purpose of capitalist production is not the production of commodities, but of surplus value or profit (in its developed form); the aim is not the product, but the SURPLUS PRODUCE. Labour itself, from this standpoint, is only productive in so far as it creates profit or SURPLUS PRODUCE for capital. If the worker does not create profit, his labour is unproductive. The mass of productive labour employed is only of interest to capital in so far as through it—or in proportion to it—the mass of surplus labour grows. Only to this extent is what we called necessary labour time, necessary. In so far as it does not have this result, it is superfluous and to be suppressed.

It is the constant aim of capitalist production to produce a maximum of surplus value or surplus product with the minimum capital outlay; and to the extent that this result is not achieved by overworking the workers, it is a tendency of capital to seek to produce a given product with the least possible expenditure— ECONOMY OF POWER AND EXPENSE. It is therefore the economic tendency of capital which teaches humanity to husband its strength and to achieve its productive aim with the least possible expenditure of means.

In this conception, the workers themselves appear as that which they are in capitalist production—mere means of production, not an end in themselves and not the aim of production.

NET INCOME is not determined by the value of the total product, but by the excess of the value of the total product over the value of the capital outlay, or by the size of the SURPLUS PRODUCE in relation to the total product. Provided this surplus grows the aim of capitalist production has been achieved even if the value decreases [XIII-733] or, if along with the value, the total quantity of the product also decreases.

Ricardo expressed these tendencies consistently and ruthlessly. Hence much howling against him on the part of the philanthropic philistines.

In considering NET INCOME, Ricardo again commits the error of resolving the total product into REVENUE, WAGES, PROFITS and RENT, and disregarding the constant capital which has to be replaced. But we will leave this out of account here.

CH. XXXII, "Mr. Malthus's Opinions on Rent".

* "It is of importance to distinguish clearly between gross revenue and net revenue, for it is from the net revenue of a society that all taxes must be paid. Suppose that all the commodities in the country, all the corn, raw produce, manufactured goods, etc. which could be brought to market in the course of the year, were of the value of 20 millions, and that in order to obtain this value, the labour of a certain number of men was necessary, and that the absolute necessaries of these labourers required an expenditure of 10 millions. I should say that the gross revenue of such society was 20 millions, and its net revenue 10 millions. It does not follow from this supposition, that the labourers should receive only 10 millions for their labour; they might receive 12, 14, or 15 millions, and in that case they would have 2, 4, or 5 millions of the net income. The rest would be divided between landlords and capitalists; but the whole net income would not exceed 10 millions. Suppose such a society paid 2 millions in taxes, its net income would be reduced to 8 millions" * ([pp.] 512-13).

[CH. XXVI, "Gross and Net Income".]

* "What would be the advantage resulting to a country from a great quantity of productive labour, if, whether it employed that quantity or a smaller, its net rent and profits together would be the same. The *whole produce of the land and labour of*

every country is divided into three portions: of these, one portion is devoted to wages, another to profits, and the other to rent." *

(This is wrong because the portion WHICH IS DEVOTED TO REPLACE THE CAPITAL (WAGES EXCLUDED) EMPLOYED IN PRODUCTION has been forgotten.)

* "It is from the two last portions only, that any deductions can be made for taxes, or for savings; *the former, if moderate, constituting always the necessary expenses of production."* *

(Ricardo himself makes the following comment on this passage in a note on p. 416:

* "Perhaps this is expressed too strongly, as more is generally allotted to the labourer under the name of wages, than the absolutely necessary expenses of production. In that case a part of the net produce of the country is received by the labourer, and may be saved or expended by him; or it may enable him to contribute to the defence of the country.)

"To an individual with a capital of £20,000, whose profits were £2,000 per annum, it would be a matter quite indifferent whether his capital would employ a hundred or a thousand men, whether the commodity produced, sold for £10,000, or for £20,000, provided, in all cases, his profits were not diminished below £2,000. *Is not the real interest of the nation similar?* Provided *its net real income, its rent and profits be the same, it is of no importance whether the nation consists of ten or 12 millions of inhabitants.* Its power of supporting fleets and armies, and all species of unproductive labour, must be in proportion to its net, and not in proportion to its gross income. If five millions of men could produce as much food and clothing as was necessary for ten millions, food and clothing for five millions would be the net revenue. Would it be of any advantage to the country, that to produce this same net revenue, seven millions of men should be required, that is to say, that seven millions should be employed to produce food and clothing sufficient for 12 millions? The food and clothing of five millions would be still the net revenue. The employing a greater number of men would enable us neither to add a man to our army and navy, nor to contribute one guinea more in taxes" * ([pp.] 416-17).

To gain a better understanding of Ricardo's views, the following passages must also be considered:

* "There is this advantage always resulting from a relatively low price of corn,—that the division of the actual production is more likely to increase the *fund for the maintenance of labour,* inasmuch as more will be allotted, under the name of profit, to the productive class, and less under the name rent, to the *unproductive class"* * ([p.] 317).

PRODUCTIVE CLASS here refers only to the INDUSTRIAL CAPITALISTS.

* "Rent is a creation of value ... but not a creation of wealth. If the price of corn, from the difficulty of producing any portion of it, should rise from £4 to £5 per qr, a million of qrs will be of the value of £5,000,000 instead of £4,000,000, ... the society altogether will be possessed of greater value, and in that sense rent is a creation of value. But this value is so far nominal, that it adds nothing to the wealth, that is to say, the necessaries, conveniences, and enjoyments of the society. We should have precisely the same quantity, and no more of commodities, and the same million quarters of corn as before; but the effect of its being rated at £5 per quarter, instead of £4, *would be to transfer a portion of the value of* [the] *corn and*

commodities from their former possessors to the landlords. Rent then is a creation of value, but not a creation of wealth; *it adds nothing to the resources of a country"* * ([pp.] 485-86).

[XIII-734] Supposing that through the import of foreign corn the price of corn falls so that rent is decreased by 1 million. Ricardo says that as a result the MONEY INCOMES of the CAPITALISTS will increase, and then continues:

* "But it may be said, that the capitalist's income will not be increased; that the million deducted from the landlord's rent, will be paid in additional wages to labourers! Be it so; ... the situation of the society will be improved, and they will be able to bear the same money burthens with greater facility than before; it will only prove what is still more desirable, that the situation of another class, *and by far the most important class in society,* is the one which is chiefly benefited by the new distribution. All that they receive more than 9 millions, *forms part of the net income of the country,* and it cannot be expended without adding to its revenue, its happiness, or its power. Distribute then the net income as you please. Give a little more to one class, and a little less to another, yet you do not thereby diminish it; a greater amount of commodities will be still produced with the same labour, although the amount of the gross money value of such commodities will be diminished; but the net money income of the country, that fund from which taxes are paid and enjoyments procured, would be much more adequate, than before, to maintain the actual population, to afford it enjoyments and luxuries, and to support any given amount of taxation" * ([pp.] 515-16).

Machinery

Сн. I (Sect. V), "On Value".

* "Suppose ... a machine which could in any particular trade be employed to do the work of one hundred men for a year, and that it would last only for one year. Suppose too, the machine to cost £5,000, and the wages annually paid to one hundred men to be £5,000, it is evident that it would be a matter of indifference to the manufacturer whether he bought the machine or employed the men. But suppose labour to rise, and consequently the wages of one hundred men for a year to amount to £5,500, it is obvious that the manufacturer would now no longer hesitate, it would be for his interest to buy the machine and get his work done for £5,000. But will not the machine rise in price, will not that also be worth £5,500 in consequence of the rise of labour? It would rise in price if *there were no stock employed on its construction, and no profits to be paid to the maker of it.* If for example, the machine were the produce of the labour of one hundred men, working one year upon it with wages of £50 each, and its price were consequently £5,000; should those wages rise to £55, its price would be £5,500, but this cannot be the case; less than one hundred men are employed or it could not be sold for £5,000, for out of the £5,000 must be paid the profits of stock which employed the men. Suppose then that only eighty-five men were employed at an expense of £50 each, or £4,250 per annum, and that the £750 which the sale of the machine would produce over and above the wages advanced to the men, constituted the profits of the engineer's stock. When wages rose 10 per cent. he would be obliged to employ an *additional capital* of £425 and would therefore employ £4,675 instead of £4,250,

on which capital he would only get a profit of £325 if he continued to sell his machine for £5,000; but this is precisely the case of all manufacturers and capitalists; the rise of wages affects them all. If therefore the maker of the machine should raise the price of it in consequence of a rise of wages, an unusual quantity of capital would be employed in the construction of such machines, till their price afforded only the common rate of profits. We see then that machines would not rise in price, in consequence of a rise of wages. The manufacturer, however, who in a general rise of wages, can have recourse to a machine which shall not increase the charge of production on his commodity, would enjoy peculiar advantages if he could continue to charge the same price for his goods; but he, as we have already seen, would be obliged to lower the price of his commodities, or capital would flow to his trade till his profits had sunk to the general level. Thus *then is the public benefited by machinery: these mute agents are always the produce of much less labour than that which they displace, even when they are of the same money value"* ([pp.] 38-40).

This point is quite right. At the same time it provides the answer to those who believe that the workers DISPLACED by machines find employment in machine manufacture itself. This view, incidentally, belongs to an epoch in which the MECHANIC ATELIER was still based entirely on the division of labour, and machines were not as yet employed on the production of machines. Suppose the annual wage of one man=£50, then that of 100=£5,000. If these 100 men are replaced by a machine which costs, similarly, £5,000, then this machine must be the product of the labour of less than 100 men. For besides paid labour it contains unpaid labour which forms the profit of the machine manufacturer. If it were the product of 100 men, then it would contain only paid labour. If the rate of profit were 10%, then approximately 4,545 of the £5,000 would represent the capital advanced and 454 the profit. At [a wage of] £50, 4,545 would only represent $90\frac{9}{10}$ men.

[XIII-735][47] [But] the capital of 4,545 by no means represents only variable capital (capital laid out directly in wages). It represents [also] raw materials and the wear and tear of the fixed capital employed by the machine manufacturer. The machine costing £5,000, which [replaces] 100 men whose wages=£5,000, thus represents the product of far fewer than 90 men. Moreover, the machine can only be employed profitably, if it // at least that portion of it which enters annually with interest into the product, i.e. into its value // is the (annual) product of far fewer MEN than it replaces.

Every rise in wages increases the variable capital that has to be laid out, although the *value of the product*—since this=the variable capital+the surplus labour—remains the same (for the number of workers which the variable capital sets in motion remains *the same*); the value produced or reproduced by the variable capital remains the same.

Ch. XX, "Value and Riches, their Distinctive Properties". Natural agents add nothing to the value of commodities, on the contrary, they reduce it. But by doing so they add to the surplus value, which alone interests the capitalists.

* "In contradiction to the opinion of Adam Smith, M. Say, in the fourth chapter,[a] speaks of the value which is given to commodities by *natural agents*, such as the sun, the air, the pressure of the atmosphere, etc., which are sometimes substituted for the labour of man, and sometimes concur with him in producing. But these natural agents, though they add greatly to *value in use*, never add exchangeable value, of which M. Say is speaking,[b] to a *commodity*: as soon as by *the aid of machinery*, o r *by the knowlegde of natural philosophy*, you oblige natural agents to do the work which was before done by man, the exchangeable value of such work falls accordingly" * ([pp.] 335-36).

The machine costs something. Natural agents as such cost nothing. They cannot, therefore, add any value to the product; rather they diminish its value in so far as they replace capital or labour, immediate or accumulated labour. Inasmuch as natural philosophy teaches how to replace human labour by natural agents, without the aid of machinery or only with the same machinery as before (perhaps even more cheaply, as with the steam boiler, many chemical processes, etc.), it costs the capitalist, and society as well, nothing and cheapens commodities absolutely.

Ricardo continues the above-quoted passage thus:

* "If ten men turned a corn mill, and it be discovered that by the assistance of wind, or of water, the labour of these ten men may be spared, the flour which is the produce partly of the work performed by the mill, would immediately fall in value, in proportion to the quantity of labour saved; and *the society would be richer by the commodities which the labour of the ten men could produce, the funds destined for their maintenance being in no degree impaired*" * ([p.] 336).

Society would in the first place be richer by the diminished price of flour. It would either consume more flour or spend the money formerly destined for flour upon some other commodity, either existing, or called into life, because a new fund for consumption had become free. Of this part of the revenue, formerly spent on flour and now, consequent upon the diminished price of flour, become free for any other application, it may be said that it was "destined"—by virtue of the whole economy of the society—for a certain thing, and that it is now freed from that "destiny". It is the same as if new capital had been accumulated. And in this way, the application of machinery and natural agents frees capital and enables previously "latent needs" to be satisfied.

---

[a] See J.-B. Say, *Traité d'économie politique...*, Vol. 1, Paris, 1814, p. 31.—*Ed.*
[b] Cf. this volume, p. 365.—*Ed.*

On the other hand, it is wrong to speak of "THE FUNDS DESTINED FOR THE MAINTENANCE" OF THE TEN MEN THROWN OUT OF EMPLOYMENT BY THE NEW DISCOVERY. For the first FUND which is saved or created through the DISCOVERY is that part of the REVENUE which society previously paid for flour and which it now saves as a result of the diminished price of flour. The second FUND which is saved, however, is that which the miller previously paid for the TEN MEN NOW DISPLACED. This "FUND" indeed, as Ricardo notes, is IN NO WAY IMPAIRED by the DISCOVERY and the DISPLACEMENT of the 10 MEN. But the FUND has no NATURAL *connexus* with the 10 MEN. They may become PAUPERS, starve, etc. One thing only is certain, that 10 MEN of the NEW GENERATION who should take the place of these 10 MEN in order to turn the mill, must now be absorbed in other EMPLOYMENT; and so the relative population has increased (independently of the AVERAGE INCREASE OF POPULATION) in that the mill is now driven and the 10 men who would otherwise have had to turn it ARE EMPLOYED IN PRODUCING SOME OTHER COMMODITY. The invention of machinery and the EMPLOYMENT OF NATURAL AGENTS thus set free capital and men (workers) and create together with freed capital freed hands (FREE HANDS, as Steuart calls them [a]), whether [XIII-736] [for] newly created spheres of production or [for] the old ones which are expanded and operated on a larger scale.

The miller with his freed capital will build new mills or will lend out his capital if he cannot spend it himself as capital.

On no account, however, is there a FUND "*DESTINED*" FOR THE TEN MEN DISPLACED. We shall return [b] to this absurd assumption: namely that, if the introduction of machines (or NATURAL AGENTS) does not (as is partly the case in AGRICULTURE, when horses take the place of men or stock-raising takes the place of corn growing) reduce the quantity of means of subsistence which can be laid out in wages, the FUND which has thus been set free must necessarily be laid out as variable capital (as if there was no possibility of exporting means of subsistence, or spending them on unproductive workers, or [as if] wages in certain spheres could not rise, etc.) and must even be paid out to the DISPLACED LABOURERS. Machinery always creates a relative SURPLUS POPULATION. a reserve army of workers, which greatly increases the power of capital.

In the note on P. 335, Ricardo also makes the following observation directed against Say:

---

[a] J. Steuart, *An Inquiry into the Principles of Political Oeconomy...*, Vol. I, Dublin, 1770, p. 396. Cf. also K. Marx, *Outlines of the Critique of Political Economy...* (present edition, Vol. 29, p. 164) and present edition, Vol. 30, p. 357.— *Ed.*

[b] See this volume, pp. 183-90.— *Ed.*

* "Though Adam Smith, who defined riches to consist in the abundance of necessaries, conveniences and enjoyments of human life, would have allowed that *machines* a n d *natural agents* might very greatly add to the riches of a country, he would not have allowed that they add *any thing to the value of those riches.*" *

NATURAL AGENTS, INDEED, ADD NOTHING TO VALUE, so long as there are no CIRCUMSTANCES in which they give occasion for the CREATION OF RENT. But machines invariably add *their own value* to the already existing value and 1) in so far as their existence facilitates the further transformation of circulating into fixed capital, and makes it possible to carry on this transformation on an ever growing scale, they increase not only RICHES but also the *value* which is added by past labour to the product of the annual labour; 2) since machines make possible the absolute growth of population and with it the growth of the mass of the annual labour, they increase the value of the annual product in this second way.

// In CH. XXI, "On Profits and Interest" (pp. 352 and 353, note), Ricardo directs against Say the following remarks:

* "M. Say allows, that *the rate of interest depends on the rate of profits*; but it does not therefore follow, *that the rate of profits depends on the rate of interest.* One is the cause, the other the effect, and it is impossible for *any circumstances* to make them change places." *

The last is definitely not correct "UNDER CERTAIN CIRCUMSTANCES".// [a]
CH. XXXI, "On Machinery".

This section, which Ricardo added to his THIRD EDITION, bears witness to his *bonne foi*[b] which so essentially distinguishes him from the vulgar economists.

* "It is more incumbent on me to declare my opinions on this question" // viz. "the influence of machinery on the interests of the different classes of society" //, "because they have, on further reflection, undergone a considerable change; and although I am not aware that I have ever published any thing respecting machinery which it is necessary for me to retract, yet I have in other ways" * (as a Member of Parliament?) [48] * "given my support to doctrines which I now think erroneous; it, therefore, becomes a duty in me to submit my present views to examination, with my reasons for entertaining them" ([p.] 466).

"Ever since I first turned my attention to questions of political economy, I have been of opinion, that such an application of machinery to any branch of production, as should have the effect of saving labour, was a general good, accompanied only with that portion of inconvenience which in most cases attends the removal of capital and labour from one employment to another." *

// This INCONVENIENCE is great enough for the worker, if, as in modern production, it is perpetual. //

* "It appeared to me, that provided the landlords had the same money rents, they would be benefited by the reduction in the prices of some of the commodities

_____

[a] Cf. this volume, p. 102.— *Ed.*
[b] Honesty.— *Ed.*

on which those rents were expended, and which reduction of price could not fail to be the consequence of the employment of machinery. The capitalist, I thought, was eventually benefited precisely in the same manner. He, indeed, who made the discovery of the machine, or who first applied it, would enjoy an additional advantage, by making great profits for a time; but, in proportion as the machine came into general use, the price of the commodity produced, would, from the effects of competition, sink to its cost of production, when the capitalist would get the same money profits as before, and he would only participate in the general advantage, [XIII-737] as a consumer, by being enabled, with the same money revenue, to command an additional quantity of comforts and enjoyments. *The class of labourers also,* I thought, *was equally benefited by the use of machinery,* as they would have the means of buying more commodities with the same money wages, and I thought that *no reduction of wages would take place, because the capitalist would have the power of demanding and employing the same quantity of labour as before,* although he might be under the necessity of employing it in the production of a new, or at any rate of a different commodity. If, by improved machinery, with the employment of the same quantity of labour, the quantity of stockings could be quadrupled, and the demand for stockings were only doubled, some labourers would necessarily be discharged from the stocking trade; but *as the capital which employed them was still in being, and as it was the interest of those who had it to employ it productively,* it appeared to me that it would be employed on the production of some other commodities, useful to the society, for which there could not fail to be a demand.... As then, it appeared to me that *there would be the same demand for labour as before,* and that wages would not be lower, I thought that the labouring class would, equally with the other classes, participate in the advantage, from the general cheapness of commodities arising from the use of machinery. These were my opinions, and they continue unaltered, as far as regards the landlord and the capitalist; but I am convinced, that *the substitution of machinery for human labour, is often very injurious to the class of labourers"* ([pp.] 466-68).

In the first place, Ricardo starts from the false assumption that machinery is always introduced into spheres of production in which the capitalist mode of production already exists. But the mechanised loom originally replaced the hand-loom weaver, the spinning jenny the hand spinner, the mowing, threshing and sowing machines often the SELF-LABOURING PEASANT, etc. In this case, not only is the labourer displaced, but his instrument of production too ceases to be capital (in the Ricardian sense). This entire or complete devaluation of the old capital also takes place when machinery revolutionises manufacture previously based on the simple division of labour. It is ridiculous to say in this case that the "old capital" continues to make THE SAME DEMAND ON LABOUR as before.

THE "CAPITAL" WHICH WAS EMPLOYED BY THE HAND-LOOM WEAVER, HAND SPINNER, ETC., HAS CEASED BEING "IN BEING".

But suppose, for the sake of simplicity, that the machinery is introduced //there is, of course, no question here of the employment of machinery IN NEW TRADES// only into spheres where capitalist production (manufacture) is already [dominant] or it may be introduced into the workshop already based on machinery, thus increasing the mechanisation of the labour processes or bringing into use improved machinery, which makes it possible either to dismiss a section of the workers previously employed or to produce a greater product while employing *the same* number of workers as before. The latter is OF COURSE the most favourable case.

In order to reduce CONFUSION, we must distinguish here between: 1) the FUNDS of the capitalist who employs machinery and dismisses workers; 2) the FUNDS of society, that is, of the consumers of the commodities produced by this capitalist.

Ad 1) So far as the capitalist who introduces the machinery is concerned, it is wrong and absurd to say that he can lay out the same amount of capital in wages as before. (Even if he borrows, it is still equally wrong, not for him, but for society.) One part of his capital he will convert into machinery and other forms of fixed capital; another part into *matières instrumentales* which he did not need before, and a larger part into raw materials, if we assume that he produces more commodities with fewer workers, thus requiring more raw material. The proportion of variable capital— that is to say, of capital laid out in wages—to constant capital has decreased in his branch of business. And this *reduction in the proportion will be permanent* (indeed, the decrease in variable capital relatively to constant will even continue at a *faster* rate as a result of the productive power of labour developing along with accumulation), even if his business on the new scale of production expands to such an extent that he can re-employ the total number of dismissed workers, and employ even more workers than before. // The demand for labour in his business will grow with the accumulation of his capital, but to a much smaller degree than his capital accumulates, and his capital will in absolute terms never again require the same amount of labour as before. The immediate result, however, will be that a section of the workers is thrown on to the street. //

But it may be said that indirectly the demand for workers will remain the same, for more workers will be required for the construction of machines. But Ricardo himself has already shown [a] that machinery never costs as much labour as the labour which it displaces. It is possible for the hours of labour in the mechanic ateliers to be lengthened FOR SOME TIME [XIII-738] and that, in the first instance, not a man more may be employed in them. Raw material—cotton for example—can come from America and

---

[a] See this volume, pp. 177-78.— *Ed.*

China and it makes no difference whatsoever to the Englishmen who have been thrown out of work, whether the demand for NIGGERS[a] or COOLIES grows. But even assuming that the raw materials are supplied within the country, more women and children will be employed in agriculture, more horses, etc., and perhaps more of one product and less of another will be produced. But there will be no demand for the dismissed workers, for in agriculture, too, the same process which creates a constant relative SURPLUS POPULATION is taking place.

Prima facie it is not likely that the introduction of machinery will set free any of the capital of the manufacturer when he makes his first investment. It merely provides a new type of investment for his capital, its immediate result, according to the assumption, is the dismissal of workers and the conversion of part of the variable capital into constant capital.

Ad 2) So far as the general public is concerned, in the first place, REVENUE is set free as a result of the lowering in price of the commodity produced by means of the machine; *capital*—directly— only in so far as the manufactured article enters into constant capital as an element of production. // If it entered into the AVERAGE consumption of the worker, it would, according to Ricardo, bring in its wake a reduction in REAL WAGES[b] also in the other branches of industry. // A part of the REVENUE thus set free, will be consumed in the same article, either because the reduction in price makes it accessible to new classes of consumers (in this case, incidentally, it is not the REVENUE which is set free that is EXPENDED ON THE ARTICLE), or because the old consumers consume more of the cheaper article, for instance 4 pairs of cotton stockings instead of one pair. Another part of the REVENUE thus set free may serve to expand the TRADE into which the machinery has been introduced, or it may be used in the formation of a new TRADE producing A DIFFERENT COMMODITY, or it may serve to expand a TRADE which already existed before. For whatever purpose the REVENUE thus set free and reconverted into capital is used, it will in the first place hardly be sufficient to absorb that part of the increased population which each year streams into each TRADE, and which is now debarred from entering the old TRADE. It is, however, also possible for a portion of the freed REVENUE to be exchanged against foreign products or to be consumed by unproductive workers. But *by no*

---

[a] See pp. VIII-IX of the Preface.— *Ed.*
[b] Cf. this volume, pp. 37, 40, 52, 58-59.— *Ed.*

means does a *necessary* CONNEX *exist between the revenue that has been set free and the workers that have been set free of* REVENUE.

3) The absurd fundamental notion, however, which underlies Ricardo's view, is the following:

The capital of the manufacturer who introduces machinery is not SET FREE. It is merely utilised in a *different* manner, namely, in such a manner that it is not, as before, transformed into wages for the DISCHARGED WORKING MEN. A part of the variable capital is converted into constant capital. Even if some of it were set free, it would be absorbed by spheres in which the DISCHARGED LABOURERS could not *work* and where, at the most, their *remplaçants*[a] could find refuge.

By expanding old spheres of production or opening up new ones the REVENUE set free—in so far as it is not offset by greater consumption of the cheaper article or is not exchanged against foreign luxury articles—only gives the necessary VENT (IF IT DOES SO!) for that part of the annual population increase that is for the time being debarred from the old TRADE into which the machinery has been introduced.

But the absurdity which lies concealed at the root of Ricardo's notions, is this:

The means of subsistence which were previously consumed by the workers [now] discharged, remain after all in existence and are still on the market. The workers, on the other hand, are also available on the market. Thus there are, on the one hand, means of subsistence (and therefore means of payment) for workers, δυνάμει[b] variable capital, and on the other, unemployed workers. Hence the FUND is there to set them in motion. Consequently they will find employment.

Is it possible that even such an economist as Ricardo can babble such hair-raising NONSENSE?

According to this, no human being who is capable of work and willing, could ever starve in bourgeois society, when there are means of subsistence on the market, at the disposal of the society, to pay him FOR ANY OCCUPATION WHATEVER. These means of subsistence, in the first place, do not by any means confront those workers as capital.

Assume that 100,000 workers have suddenly been thrown out on the streets by machinery. Then in the first place there is no doubt whatsoever [XIII-739] that the AGRICULTURAL PRODUCTS on the

---

a Substitutes.— *Ed.*
b Potential.— *Ed.*

market, which on the average suffice for the whole year and which were previously consumed by these workers, are still on the market as before. If there were no demand for them—and if, at the same time, they were not exportable—what would happen? As the supply relative to the demand would have grown, they would fall in price, and as a result of this fall in price, their consumption would rise, even if the 100,000 [workers] were starving to death. The price need not even fall. Perhaps less of these means of subsistence is imported or more of them exported.

Ricardo imagines quixotically that the entire bourgeois social mechanism is arranged so NICELY that if, for instance, 10 men are discharged from their work, the means of subsistence of these workers—now set free—must definitely be consumed *d'une façon ou d'une autre*[a] by the identical 10 men and that otherwise they could not be sold; as if a mass of semi-employed or completely unemployed were not for ever crawling around at the bottom of this society—and as if the capital existing in the form of means of subsistence were a fixed amount. If the market price of corn fell due to the decreasing demand, then the capital available in the shape of corn would be *diminished* (money capital) and would exchange for a smaller portion of the society's MONEY REVENUE, in so far as it is not exportable. And this applies even more to manufactures. During the many years in which the HAND-LOOM WEAVERS WERE GRADUALLY STARVING, the production and export of English cotton cloth increased enormously. At the same time (1838-41) the prices OF PROVISIONS rose. And the weavers had only rags in which to clothe themselves and not enough food to keep body and soul together. The constant artificial production of a SURPLUS POPULATION, which disappears only in times of feverish PROSPERITY, is one of the necessary conditions of production of modern industry. There is nothing to prevent a part of the money capital lying idle and without employment and the prices of the means of subsistence falling because of relative *surproduction* while at the same time WORKING MEN who have been DISPLACED by machinery, ARE BEING STARVED.

It is true that IN THE LONG RUN the labour that has been released together with the portion of REVENUE or capital that has been released, will FIND its vent in a new trade or by the expansion of the old one, but this is of more benefit to the *remplaçants of the DISPLACED MEN* than to the displaced men themselves. New ramifications of more or less unproductive branches of labour are continually being formed and in these REVENUE is directly

---

[a] In one way or another.— *Ed.*

expended. Then there is the formation of fixed capital (railways, etc.) and the LABOUR OF SUPERINTENDENCE which this opens up; the manufacture of luxuries, etc.; foreign trade, which increasingly diversifies the articles on which REVENUE is spent.

From his absurd standpoint, Ricardo therefore assumes that the introduction of machinery harms the workers only when it diminishes the GROSS PRODUCE (and therefore GROSS REVENUE), a case which may occur, it is true, in large-scale agriculture, with the introduction of horses which consume corn in place of the workers, with the transition from corn-growing to sheep-raising, etc.; but it is quite preposterous [to extend this case] to industry proper, whose ability to sell its GROSS PRODUCT is by no means restricted by the internal market. (Incidentally, while one section of the workers starves, another section may be better fed and clothed, as may also the unproductive workers and the middle strata between worker and capitalist.)

It is wrong, in itself, to say that the increase (or the quantity) of articles entering into REVENUE as such, forms a FUND for the workers or forms capital for them. A portion of these articles is consumed by unproductive workers or non-workers, another portion may be transformed by means of foreign trade, from its coarse form, the form in which it serves as wages, into a form in which it enters into the REVENUE of the wealthy, or in which it serves as an element of production of constant capital. Finally, a portion will be consumed by the discharged workers themselves in the WORKHOUSE, or in prison, or as alms, or as stolen goods, or as payment for the prostitution of their daughters.

In the following pages I shall briefly compare the passages in which Ricardo develops this nonsense. As he says himself, he received the impetus for it from *Barton's* work,[a] which must therefore be examined, after citing those passages.

[XIII-740] It is self-evident, that in order to employ a certain number of workers each year, a certain quantity of FOOD and NECESSARIES must be produced annually. In large-scale agriculture, stock-raising, etc., it is possible for the NET INCOME (profit and rent) to be increased while the GROSS INCOME is reduced, that is to say, while the quantity of NECESSARIES intended for the maintenance of the workers is reduced. But that is not the question here. The quantity of articles entering into consumption or, to use Ricardo's expression, the quantity of articles of which the GROSS REVENUE

---

[a] J. Barton, *Observations on the Circumstances which Influence the Condition of the Labouring Classes of Society*, London, 1817. See this volume, pp. 201-08.— *Ed.*

consists, can be increased, without a consequent increase in that portion of this quantity which is transformed into variable capital. This may even decrease. In this case more is consumed as REVENUE by capitalists, LANDLORDS and their RETAINERS, the unproductive classes, the state, the middle strata (merchants), etc. What lies behind the view taken by Ricardo (and Barton) is that he originally set out from the assumption that every accumulation of capital = an increase in variable capital, that the demand for labour therefore increases directly, in the same proportion, as capital is accumulated. But this is wrong, since with the accumulation of capital a change takes place in its organic composition and the constant part of the capital grows at a faster rate than the variable. This does not, however, prevent REVENUE from constantly growing, in value and in quantity. But it does not result in a proportionately larger part of the total product being laid out in wages. Those classes and sub-classes who do not live directly from their labour become more numerous and live better than before, and the number of unproductive workers increases as well.

Since, in the first place, it has nothing to do with the question, we will not concern ourselves with the REVENUE of the capitalist who transforms a part of his variable capital into machinery (and therefore also puts more into raw material relatively to the amount of labour employed in all those spheres of production where raw material is an element of the valorisation process). His REVENUE and that part of his capital which has actually gone into the production process exist, at first, in the form of *products* or rather *commodities* which he produces himself, for example yarn if he is a spinner. AFTER THE INTRODUCTION OF MACHINERY he transforms one part of these commodities—or the money for which he sells them—into machinery, *matières instrumentales* and raw materials whereas, previously, he paid it out as wages to the workers, thus transforming it indirectly into means of subsistence for the workers. With some exceptions in agriculture, he will produce more of these commodities than before, although his *discharged* workers have ceased to be consumers, i.e. DEMANDERS, of his own articles, though they were so before. More of these commodities will now be present on the market, although for the workers THROWN ON THE STREET, they have ceased to exist or have ceased to exist in their previous quantity. Thus, so far as his own product is concerned, in the first place, even if it enters into the consumption of the workers, its increased production in no way contradicts the fact that a part of it has ceased to exist as capital for the workers.

A larger part of it (of the total product) on the other hand must now replace that portion of the constant capital which resolves into machinery, *matières instrumentales* and raw materials, that is to say, it must be exchanged against more of these ingredients of reproduction than formerly. If the increase in commodities through machinery and the decrease in a previously existing demand (*namely in the demand of the workers that have been discharged*) for the commodities produced by this machinery were contradictory, then IN MOST CASES, no machinery could in fact be introduced. The mass of commodities produced and the portion of these commodities which is reconverted into wages, therefore, have no definite relationship or necessary connection, when we consider the capital of which a part is transformed into machinery instead of into wage labour.

So far as society in general is concerned, the replacement or rather the extension of the limits of its REVENUE takes place first of all on account of the articles whose price has been lowered by the introduction of machinery. This REVENUE may continue to BE SPENT as REVENUE, and if a considerable part of it is transformed into capital, the increased population—apart from the artificially created SURPLUS POPULATION—is already there to absorb that part of the REVENUE which is transformed into variable capital.

Prima facie, therefore, what this comes to is only: the production of all other articles, particularly in the spheres which produce articles entering into the consumption of the workers—despite the DISCHARGING of the 100 MEN, etc.—continues on the same scale as before; quite certainly at the moment when the workers are discharged. In so far, therefore, as the dismissed workers represented a demand for these articles, the demand has decreased, although the supply has remained the same. If the reduced demand is not made good, the price will fall // or instead of a fall in price a larger stock may remain on the market for the following year //. If the article is not produced for export, too, and if the decrease in demand were to persist, then reproduction would decrease, but it does not follow that the capital employed in this sphere [XIII-741] must necessarily decrease. Perhaps more meat or commercial crops or luxury foods are produced [and] less wheat or more oats for horses, etc., or fewer FUSTIAN JACKETS and more bourgeois frock-coats. But none of these consequences need necessarily materialise, if, for instance, as a result of the cheapening of COTTONS, the employed workers are able to spend more on food, etc. The same quantity of commodities and even more of them—including those consumed by the workers—can be produced, although less capital, a smaller portion of the total product, is transformed into variable capital, that is laid out in wages.

Neither is it the case that part of the capital of the producers of these articles has been set free. At worst the demand for their commodities would have decreased, and the reproduction of their capital impeded by the reduced price of their commodities. Hence their own REVENUE would immediately decrease, as it would with any fall in the prices of commodities. But it cannot be said that any particular part of their commodities had previously confronted the discharged workers as capital and was now "set free" along with the workers. What confronted them as capital, was a part of the commodities now being produced with machinery; this part came to them in the form of money and was exchanged by them for other commodities (means of subsistence), which did not face them as capital, but confronted their money as commodities. This is therefore an entirely different relationship. The FARMER, etc., whose commodity they bought with their wages, did not confront them as capitalist and did not employ them as workers. They *have only ceased to be buyers for him,* which may possibly—IF NOT COUNTERBALANCED BY OTHER CIRCUMSTANCES—bring about a temporary DEPRECIATION in his capital, but does not set free any capital for the discharged workers. The capital that employed them "IS STILL IN BEING", but no longer in a form in which it resolves into wages, or only indirectly and to a smaller extent.

Otherwise anyone who through some bad luck ceased to have money, would inevitably set free sufficient capital FOR HIS OWN EMPLOYMENT.

By GROSS REVENUE Ricardo means that part of the product which replaces wages and SURPLUS VALUE (PROFITS and RENT); by NET REVENUE he means the SURPLUS PRODUCE = the SURPLUS VALUE. He forgets here, as throughout his work, that a portion of the GROSS PRODUCE must replace the value of the machinery and raw material, in short, of the constant capital.

Ricardo's subsequent treatment is of interest, partly because of some of the observations he makes in passing, partly because, *mutatis mutandis,* it is of practical importance for large-scale AGRICULTURE, particularly sheep-rearing, and shows the limitations of capitalist production. Not only is its determining purpose not production *for* the producers (WORKMEN), but its exclusive aim is NET REVENUE (PROFIT and RENT), even if this is achieved at the cost of the volume of production—at the cost of the volume of commodities produced.

* "My mistake arose from the supposition, that whenever the *net income* of a society increased, its *gross income* would also increase; I now, however, see reason to be satisfied that *the one fund, from which landlords and capitalists derive their revenue, may increase,* while the other, *that upon which the labouring class mainly depend, may diminish,* and therefore it follows, if I am right, that the *same cause* which may increase the net revenue of the country, may at the same time *render the population redundant,* and deteriorate the condition of the labourer" * ([p.] 469).

First it is noteworthy that Ricardo here admits that causes which further the wealth of the capitalists and LANDLORDS, "MAY ... RENDER THE POPULATION REDUNDANT" so that the REDUNDANCY of the population or OVERPOPULATION is presented here as the result of the process of enrichment itself, and of the development of productive forces which conditions this process.

So far as the FUND is concerned, out of which the capitalists and LANDLORDS draw their REVENUE and on the other hand the FUND from which the workers draw theirs, to begin with, it is the total product which forms this common FUND. A large part of the products which enter into the consumption of the capitalists and LANDLORDS, does not enter into the consumption of the workers. On the other hand, almost all, IN FACT *plus ou moins* all products which enter into the consumption of the workers also enter into that of the LANDLORDS and CAPITALISTS, their RETAINERS and HANGERS-ON, including dogs and cats. One cannot suppose that there are two essentially distinct fixed FUNDS in existence. The important point is, what aliquot PARTS each of these groups draws from the common FUND. The aim of capitalist production is to obtain as large an amount of SURPLUS PRODUCE or SURPLUS VALUE as possible with a given amount of WEALTH. This aim is achieved by constant capital growing more rapidly in proportion to variable capital or by setting in motion the greatest possible [XIII-742] constant capital with the least possible variable capital. In much more general terms than Ricardo conceives here, the same CAUSE effects an increase in the FUNDS out of which CAPITALISTS and LANDLORDS draw their REVENUE, by a decrease in the FUND out of which the workers draw theirs.

It does not follow from this that the FUND from which the workers draw their REVENUE is diminished *absolutely*; only that it is diminished *relatively*, in proportion to the total result of their production. And that is the only important factor in the determination of the portion which they appropriate out of the wealth they themselves created.

* "A capitalist we will suppose employs a capital of the value of £20,000 and that he carries on the joint business of a farmer, and a manufacturer of necessaries. We will further suppose, that £7,000 of this capital is invested in fixed capital, viz. in buildings, implements, etc., and that the remaining £13,000 is

employed as circulating capital in the support of labour. Let us suppose, too, that profits are 10%, and consequently that the capitalist's capital is every year put into its original state of efficiency, and yields a profit of £2,000. Each year the capitalist begins his operations, by having food and necessaries in his possession of the value of £13,000, all of which he sells in the course of the year to his own workmen for that sum of money, and, during the same period, he pays them the like amount of money for wages: *at the end of the year* they replace in his possession food and necessaries of the value of £15,000, £2,000 of which he consumes himself, or disposes of as may best suit his pleasure and gratification." *

// The *nature of* SURPLUS VALUE is very palpably expressed here. (The passage [is on] pp. 469-70.) //

* "As far as these products are concerned, the *gross produce* for that year is £15,000 and the net produce £2,000. Suppose now, that the following year the capitalist employs half his men in constructing a machine, and the other half in producing food and necessaries as usual. During that year he would pay the sum of £13,000 in wages as usual, and would sell food and necessaries to the same amount to his workmen; but what would be the case the following year? While the machine was being made, only one-half of the usual quantity of food and necessaries would be obtained, and they would be only one-half the value of the quantity which was produced before. The machine would be worth £7,500, and the food and necessaries £7,500, and, therefore, the capital of the capitalist would be as great as before; for he would have besides these two values, his fixed capital worth £7,000, making in the whole £20,000 capital, and £2,000 profit. After deducting this latter sum for his own expenses, he would have a no greater circulating capital than £5,500 with which to carry on his subsequent operations; and, therefore, his means of employing labour, would be reduced in the proportion of £13,000 to £5,500, and, consequently, *all the labour which was before employed by £7,500, would become redundant.*" *

(This would, however, also be the case if by means of the machine which costs £7,500, exactly the same quantity of products were produced as previously with a variable capital of £13,000. Suppose the wear and tear of the machine $=^1/_{10}$ in one year, $= £750$, then the value of the product—previously £15,000— $= £8,250$. (Apart from the wear and tear of the original fixed capital of £7,000, whose replacement Ricardo does not mention at all.) Of these £8,250, £2,000 would be profit, as previously out of the £15,000. The lower price would be advantageous to the FARMER in so far as he himself consumes FOOD and NECESSARIES as REVENUE. It would also be advantageous to him in so far as it enables him to reduce the wages of the workers he employs thus releasing a portion of his variable capital. It is this portion, which TO A CERTAIN DEGREE could employ new labour, but only because the *real wage* of the workers who have been retained had fallen. A small number of those who have been discharged could thus—at the cost of those who had been retained—be re-employed. The fact however that the product would be just as great as before, would not help the dismissed workers. If the wage remained the same, no part of the variable capital would be [released]. The fact that the product of £8,250 represents the same amount of NECESSARIES and FOOD as previously £15,000 does not cause its value to rise. The farmer would have to sell it for £8,250, partly in order to replace the wear and tear of his machinery and partly in order to replace his variable capital. In so far as this lowering of the price of FOOD and NECESSARIES did not bring about a fall in wages in general, or a fall in the INGREDIENTS ENTERING INTO THE REPRODUCTION OF THE CONSTANT CAPITAL, the REVENUE of society would have expanded only in so far as IT IS EXPENDED ON FOOD AND NECESSARIES. A section of the unproductive and productive workers, etc., would live better. *Voilà tout.*[a] (They could also save, but that is always ACTION IN THE FUTURE.) The discharged workers would remain on the street, although the *physical* possibility of their maintenance existed just as much as before. Moreover, the same capital would be employed in the reproduction process as before. But a *part of the product* (whose value had fallen), which previously existed as *capital* has now become *revenue.*)

* "The reduced quantity of labour which the capitalist can employ, must, indeed, with the assistance of the machine, and after deductions for its repair, produce a value equal to £7,500, it must replace the circulating capital with a profit of £2,000 on the whole capital; but if this be done, [XIII-743] if the net income be not diminished, of what importance is it to the capitalist, whether the gross income be of the value of £3,000, of £10,000, or of £15,000?" *

(This is perfectly correct. The GROSS INCOME is of absolutely no importance to the capitalist. The only thing which is of interest to him is the NET INCOME.)

* "In this case, then, although the net produce will not be diminished in value, although its power of purchasing commodities may be greatly increased, the gross produce will have fallen from a value of £15,000 to a value of £7,500 and as *the power of supporting a population, and employing labour, depends always on the gross produce of a nation, and not on its net produce,*" *

// hence Adam Smith's partiality for GROSS PRODUCE, a partiality to which Ricardo objects. See *Ch. XXVI*, "On Gross and Net Revenue", which Ricardo opens with the words:

* "Adam Smith constantly magnifies the advantages which a country derives from a large gross, rather than a large net income" * ([p.] 415). //

* "there will *necessarily be a diminution in the demand for labour, population will become redundant,* and the situation of the labouring classes will be that of distress and poverty." *

(LABOUR therefore BECOMES REDUNDANT, because the DEMAND FOR LABOUR DIMINISHES, AND THAT DEMAND DIMINISHES IN CONSEQUENCE OF THE DEVELOPMENT IN THE PRODUCTIVE POWERS OF LABOUR. In Ricardo the passage [is on] *p. 471.*)

---

[a] That is all.— *Ed.*

* "As, however, the *power of saving from revenue to add to capital, must depend on the efficiency of the net revenue,* to satisfy the wants of the capitalist, it *could not fail to follow from the reduction in the price of commodities consequent on the introduction of machinery,* that with the same wants" //but his wants enlarge// "he would *have increased means of saving,—increased facility of transferring revenue into capital."* *

// According to this, first one part of capital is transformed into REVENUE, TRANSFERRED TO REVENUE—not in terms of value, but as regards the use value, the material elements of which the capital consists—in order later TO TRANSFER a part of the REVENUE back into CAPITAL. For example, when £13,000 was laid out in variable capital a part of the product amounting to £7,500, entered into the consumption of the workers whom the FARMER employed, and this part of the product formed part of his capital. Following upon the introduction of machinery, for example, according to our supposition, the same amount of product is produced as previously, but its value does not amount to £15,000, as previously, but only to £8,250; and a larger part of this cheaper product enters into the REVENUE of the FARMERS or the REVENUE of the buyers of FOOD and NECESSARIES. They now consume a part of the product as REVENUE which was previously consumed industrially, as capital, by the FARMER, although his LABOURERS (since dismissed) consumed it as REVENUE as well. As a result of this growth in REVENUE—which has come about because a part of the product which was previously consumed as capital is now consumed as REVENUE—new capital is formed and revenue is reconverted into capital. //

* "But with every increase of capital he would employ more labourers;" *

(this *in any case* not in proportion to the INCREASE of capital, not TO THE WHOLE EXTENT OF THAT INCREASE. PERHAPS HE WOULD BUY MORE HORSES, OR GUANO, OR NEW IMPLEMENTS)

* "and, therefore, a *portion of the people thrown out of work in the first instance, would be subsequently employed*; and *if the increased production, in consequence of the employment of the machine, was so great as to afford, in the shape of net produce, as great a quantity of food and necessaries as existed before in the form of gross produce,* there would be *the same ability to employ the whole population,* and, therefore, there would not *necessarily*" //but possibly, and probably!// "*be any redundancy of people*" * ([pp.] 469-72).

In the last lines, Ricardo thus says what I observed above. In order that REVENUE is transformed in this way into capital, capital is first transformed into REVENUE. Or, as Ricardo puts it: First the NET PRODUCE is increased at the expense of the GROSS PRODUCE in order then to reconvert a part of the NET PRODUCE into GROSS PRODUCE. PRODUCE IS PRODUCE. NET or GROSS makes no difference //although this antithesis may also mean that the *excess over and above the outlay* increases, that therefore the NET PRODUCE grows although the total product, i.e. the GROSS PRODUCE, diminishes//. The produce only becomes one or the other, according to the determinate form which it assumes in the process of production.

* "All I wish to prove, is, that the discovery and use of machinery may be attended with a diminution of gross produce; and whenever that is the case, it will be injurious to the labouring class, as some of their number will be thrown out of employment, and *population will become redundant, compared with the funds which are to employ it*" * ([p.] 472).

But THE SAME MAY, AND IN MOST INSTANCES [XIII-744] WILL BE THE CASE, EVEN IF THE GROSS PRODUCE REMAINS THE SAME OR ENLARGES; ONLY THAT PART OF IT, FORMERLY ACTING AS VARIABLE CAPITAL, IS NOW BEING CONSUMED AS REVENUE. It is superfluous for us to go into Ricardo's absurd example of the CLOTHIER who reduces his production because of the introduction of machinery (pp. 472-74).

* "If these views be correct, it follows,
"1st) That the discovery, and useful application of machinery, *always leads to the increase* of the *net produce of the country,* although it may not, and will not, after an inconsiderable interval, increase the *value of that net* produce" ([p.] 474).

It will always increase that value whenever it diminishes the value of labour.

"2dly) That the increase of the net produce of a country is compatible with a diminution of the gross produce, and that the motives for employing machinery are always sufficient to insure its employment, if it will increase the net produce, although it may, and frequently must, diminish both the quantity of the gross produce, and its value" ([p.] 474).
"3dly) That the opinion entertained by the labouring class, that the employment of machinery is frequently detrimental to their interests, is not founded on prejudice and error, but is conformable to the correct principles of political economy" ([p.] 474).
"4thly) That if the improved means of production, in consequence of the use of machinery, should increase the net produce of a country in a degree so great as not to diminish the gross produce, (I mean always quantity of commodities and not value,) then the situation of all classes will be improved. The landlord and capitalist will benefit, not by an increase of rent and profit, but by the advantages resulting from the expenditure of the same rent, and profit, on commodities, very considerably reduced in value," *

(this sentence contradicts the whole of Ricardo's doctrine, according to which the lowering in the price of NECESSARIES, and therefore OF WAGES, RAISES PROFITS, whereas machinery, which permits more to be extracted from the same land with less labour, MUST LOWER RENT),

* "while the situation of the labouring class will also be considerably improved; 1st, *from the increased demand for menial servants;*" *

(this is indeed a fine result of machinery, that a considerable section of the female and male labouring class is turned into servants)

* "2ndly, from the stimulus to savings from revenue, which such an abundant net produce will afford; and 3dly, from the low price of all articles of consumption on which their wages will be expended" // and in consequence of which their wages will be reduced * // (pp. 474-75).

The entire apologetic bourgeois presentation of machinery does not deny,

1) that machinery—sometimes here, sometimes there, but continually— MAKES A PART OF THE POPULATION REDUNDANT, throws a section of the labouring population on the street. It creates a SURPLUS POPULATION, thus leading to lower wages in certain spheres of production, here or there, not because the population grows more rapidly than the means of subsistence, but because the rapid growth in the means of subsistence, due to machinery, enables more machinery to be introduced and *therefore* reduces the *immediate demand for labour*. This comes about not because the social FUND diminishes, but because of the growth of this fund, the part of it WHICH IS SPENT IN WAGES falls relatively.

2) Even less does this apologetics deny the subjugation of the workers who operate the machines and the *misère* of the manual workers or craftsmen who are displaced by machinery and perish.

What it [asserts]—and PARTLY correctly—is [firstly] that as a result of machinery (of the development of the productive powers of labour in general) the NET REVENUE (PROFIT and RENT) grows to such an extent, that the bourgeois needs more MENIAL SERVANTS than before; whereas previously he had to lay out more of his product in PRODUCTIVE LABOUR, he can now lay out more in UNPRODUCTIVE LABOUR, [so that] servants and other workers living on the unproductive class increase in number. This progressive transformation of a section of the workers into servants is a fine prospect. For them it is equally consoling that because of the growth in the NET PRODUCE, more spheres are opened up for UNPRODUCTIVE LABOUR, who live on their product and whose interest in their exploitation coincides *plus ou moins* with that of the directly exploiting classes.

Secondly, that because of the spur given to accumulation, on the new basis requiring less living labour in proportion to past labour, the workers who were dismissed and pauperised, or at least that part of the population increase [XIII-745] which replaces them, are either absorbed in the expanding engineering-works themselves, or in supplementary TRADES which machinery has made necessary and brought into being, or IN NEW FIELDS OF EMPLOYMENT OPENED BY THE NEW CAPITAL, AND SATISFYING NEW WANTS. This then is another wonderful prospect: the LABOURING CLASS has to bear all the "TEMPORARY INCONVENIENCES"—THROWING OUT OF LABOUR, DISPLACEMENT OF LABOUR AND CAPITAL—but wage labour is nevertheless not to be abolished, on the contrary it will be reproduced on an ever growing scale, growing absolutely, even though decreasing relatively to the growing total capital which employs it.

Thirdly: that consumption becomes more *refined* due to machinery. The reduced price of the immediate necessities of life allows the scope of luxury production to be extended. Thus the 3rd fine prospect opens before the workers: in order TO WIN THEIR NECESSARIES, THE SAME AMOUNT OF THEM, THE SAME NUMBER OF LABOURERS WILL ENABLE THE HIGHER CLASSES TO EXTEND, REFINE, AND diversify THE CIRCLE OF THEIR ENJOYMENTS, AND THUS TO WIDEN THE ECONOMICAL, SOCIAL, AND POLITICAL GULF SEPARATING THEM FROM THEIR BETTERS. FINE PROSPECTS, THESE, AND VERY DESIRABLE RESULTS, FOR THE LABOURER, OF THE DEVELOPMENT OF THE PRODUCTIVE POWERS OF HIS LABOUR.

Furthermore, Ricardo then shows that it [is in] the interest of the labouring classes,

"THAT AS MUCH OF THE REVENUE AS POSSIBLE SHOULD BE DIVERTED FROM EXPENDITURE ON LUXURIES, TO BE EXPENDED ON MENIAL SERVANTS" ([p.] 476). For whether I [purchase] furniture or keep MENIAL SERVANTS, I thereby present a demand for a definite amount of commodities and set in motion approximately the same amount of PRODUCTIVE LABOUR in one case as in the other; but in the latter case, I ADD [a new demand] "TO THE FORMER DEMAND FOR LABOURERS, AND THIS ADDITION WOULD TAKE PLACE ONLY BECAUSE I CHOSE THIS MODE OF EXPENDING MY REVENUE" ([pp. 475-]76).

The same applies to the maintenance OF LARGE FLEETS AND ARMIES ([p.] 476).

* "Whether it" (the revenue) "was expended in the one way or in the other, there would be *the same quantity of labour employed in production*; for the food and clothing of the soldier and sailor would require the same amount of industry to produce it as the more luxurious commodities; but in the case of the war, there would be the additional demand for men as soldiers and sailors; and, consequently, a war which is supported out of the revenue, and not from the capital of a country, is favourable to the increase of population" ([p.] 477).

"There is one other case that should be noticed of the possibility of an *increase in the amount of the net revenue of a country*, and *even of its gross revenue*, with a diminution of demand for labour, and that is, when the labour of horses is substituted for that of man. If I employed one hundred men on my farm, and if I found that the food bestowed on fifty of those men, could be diverted to the support of horses, and afford me a greater return of raw produce, after allowing for the interest of the capital which the purchase of the horses would absorb, it would be advantageous to me to substitute the horses for the men, and I should accordingly do so; but this would not be for the interest of the men, and unless the income I obtained, was so much increased as to enable me to employ the men as well as the horses, it *is evident that the population would become redundant,* and the labourers' condition would sink in the general scale. It is evident, he could not, under any circumstances, be employed in agriculture;" (why not? if the field of agriculture were enlarged?) "but if the produce of the land were increased by the substitution of horses for men, he might be employed in manufactures, or as a menial servant"* ([pp.] 477-78).

There are two tendencies which constantly cut across one another; to employ as little labour as possible, in order to produce the same or a greater quantity of commodities, in order to produce the same or a greater NET PRODUCE, SURPLUS VALUE, NET REVENUE; secondly, to employ the largest possible number of workers (although as few as possible in proportion to the quantity of commodities produced by them), because—at a given level of productive power—the mass of SURPLUS VALUE and of SURPLUS PRODUCE grows with the amount of labour employed. The one tendency throws the labourers on to the streets and makes a part of the POPULATION REDUNDANT, the other absorbs them again and extends WAGE SLAVERY absolutely, so that the lot of the worker is always fluctuating but he never escapes from it. The worker, therefore, justifiably regards the development of the productive power of his own labour as hostile to himself; the capitalist, on the other hand, always treats him as an element to be eliminated from production. These are the contradictions with which Ricardo struggles in this chapter. What he forgets to emphasise [XIII-746] is the constantly growing number of the middle classes, those who stand between the WORKMAN on the one hand and the capitalist and LANDLORD on the other. The middle classes maintain themselves to an ever increasing extent directly out of REVENUE, they are a burden weighing heavily on the WORKING base and increase the social security and power of the UPPER TEN THOUSAND.

According to the bourgeoisie the perpetuation of WAGE SLAVERY through the application of machinery is a "vindication" of the latter.

*"I have before observed, too, that *the increase of net incomes, estimated in commodities, which is always the consequence of improved machinery,* will lead to new savings and accumulations. *These savings,* it must be remembered, are *annual,* and must soon create a *fund, much greater than the gross revenue, originally lost by the discovery of the machinery,* when the demand for labour will be as great as before, and the situation of the people will be still further improved by the increased savings which the increased net revenue will still enable them to make"* ([p.] 480).

First GROSS REVENUE declines and NET REVENUE increases. Then a portion of the INCREASED NET REVENUE is transformed into capital again and hence into GROSS REVENUE. Thus the workman must constantly enlarge the power of capital, and then, after VERY SERIOUS DISTURBANCES, obtain permission to repeat the process on a larger scale.

* "With every increase of capital and population, food will generally rise, on account of its being more difficult to produce" * ([pp.] 478-79).

It then goes straight on:

* "The consequence of a rise of food will be a rise of wages, and every rise of wages will have a tendency to determine *the saved capital in a greater proportion than before to the employment of machinery. Machinery and labour are in constant competition, and the former can frequently not be employed until labour rises*" * ([p.] 479).

The machinery is thus a means to prevent a RISE OF LABOUR.

* "To elucidate the principle, I have been supposing that improved machinery is *suddenly* discovered and extensively used; but the truth is, that these discoveries are gradual, and rather operate in *determining the employment of the capital which is saved and accumulated, than in diverting capital from its actual employment*" * ([p.] 478).

THE TRUTH IS, THAT IT IS NOT SO MUCH THE DISPLACED LABOUR AS, RATHER, THE NEW SUPPLY OF LABOUR—THE PART OF THE GROWING POPULATION WHICH WAS TO REPLACE IT—WHICH, BY THE NEW ACCUMULATIONS, GETS FOR ITSELF NEW FIELDS OF EMPLOYMENT OPENED.

* "In America and many other countries, where the food of man is easily provided, there is not nearly such great temptation to employ machinery" * (nowhere is it used on such a massive scale and also, so to speak, for domestic needs as in America) * "as in England, where food is high, and costs much labour for its production." *

// How little the employment of machinery is dependent on the PRICE OF FOOD is shown precisely by America, which employs relatively much more machinery than England, WHERE THERE IS ALWAYS A REDUNDANT POPULATION. The use of machinery *may*, however, depend on the relative scarcity OF LABOUR as, for instance, in America, where a comparatively small population is spread over immense tracts of land. Thus we read in *The Standard* of *September 19, 1862,* in an article on the Exhibition[25]:

* "Man is a machine-making animal.... If we consider the American as a representative man, the definition [...] is perfect. It is one of the cardinal points of an American's system to do nothing with his hands that he can do by a machine. From rocking a cradle to making a coffin, from milking a cow to clearing a forest, from sewing on a button to voting for a President, almost, he has a machine for everything. He has invented a machine for saving the trouble of masticating food.... *The exceeding scarcity of labour* and its consequent high value" // despite the low value of food //, "as well as a certain innate 'cuteness have stimulated this inventive spirit.... The machines produced in America are, generally speaking, inferior in value to those made in England ... they are rather, as a whole, *makeshifts to save labour* than inventions to accomplish former impossibilities" * // And the steam ships? // ... "In the UNITED STATES department of the *Exhibition is *Emery's cotton-gin.* For many a year after the introduction of cotton to America the crop was very small; because not only was the demand rather limited, but the difficulty of cleaning the crop by manual labour rendered it anything but remunerative. When Eli Whitney, however invented the saw [XIII-747] cotton-gin there *was an immediate increase* in *the breadth planted,* and that increase has up to the present time gone on

almost in an arithmetical progression. In fact, it is not too much to say that Whitney made the cotton trade. With modifications more or less important and useful his gin has remained in use ever since; and until the invention of the present improvement and addition Whitney's original gin was quite as good as the most of its would-be supplanters. By the present machine, which bears the name of Messrs. Emery, of Albany, N.Y., we have no doubt that Whitney's gin, on which it is based, will be almost entirely supplanted. It is as simple and more efficacious; it delivers the cotton not only cleaner, but in sheets like wadding, and thus the layers as they leave the machine are at once fit for the cotton press and the bale.... In [the] American Court proper there is little else than machinery: *The cow-milker* ... *a belt-shifter* ... *a hemp carding and spinning machine,* which at one operation reels the sliver direct from the bale.... *A machine for the manufacture of paper-bags,* which it cuts from the sheet, pastes, folds, and perfects at the rate of 300 a minute.... Hawes's *clothes-wringer,* which by two indiarubber rollers presses from clothes the water, leaving them almost dry, saves time, but does not injure the texture ... *bookbinder's machinery....* *Machines for making shoes.* It is well known that the uppers have been for a long time made up by machinery in this country, but here are machines for putting on the sole, others for cutting the sole to shape, and others again for trimming the heels.... A *stone-breaking machine* is very powerful and ingenious, and no doubt will come extensively into use for ballasting roads and crushing ores.... A *system of marine signals* by Mr. W. H. Ward of Auburn, New York.... *Reaping and mowing machines* are an American invention coming into very general favour in England. McCormick's the best.... Hansbrow's California Prize Medal *Force Pump,* in simplicity and efficiency the best in the Exhibition ... it will throw more water with the same power than any pump in the world.... *Sewing machines....*" * // [a]

* "The same cause that raises labour, does not raise the value of machines, and, therefore, *with every augmentation of capital, a greater proportion of it is employed on machinery. The demand for labour will continue to increase with an increase of capital, but not in proportion to its increase; the ratio will necessarily be a diminishing ratio*" * ([p.] 479).

In the last sentence Ricardo expresses the correct law of growth of capital, although his reasoning is very one-sided. He adds a note to this, from which it is evident that he follows *Barton* here, whose work we will therefore examine briefly. But first one more comment: When Ricardo discussed REVENUE EXPENDED either on MENIAL SERVANTS or LUXURIES, he wrote:

* "In both cases the net revenue would be the same, and so would be the gross revenue, but the *former would be realised in different commodities*" * ([p.] 476).

Similarly the GROSS PRODUCE, in terms of value, may be the same, but it may "BE REALISED"—and this would strongly affect the WORKMEN—"*IN DIFFERENT COMMODITIES*" according to whether it had to replace more variable or constant capital.

Barton's work is called:

---

[a] "America in the Exhibition", *The Standard,* No. 11889, September 19, 1862.— *Ed.*

John Barton, *Observations on the Circumstances which Influence the Condition of the Labouring Classes of Society*, London, 1817.

Let us first gather together the small number of theoretical propositions to be found in Barton's work.

* "The demand for labour depends on *the increase of circulating, and not of fixed capital.* Were it true *that the proportion between these two sorts of capital is the same at all times, and in all countries,* then, indeed, it follows that the *number of labourers employed is in proportion to the wealth of the State.* But such a position has not the semblance of probability. As arts are cultivated, and civilization is extended, *fixed capital bears a larger and larger proportion to circulating capital.* The amount of fixed capital employed in the production of a piece of British muslin is at least a hundred, probably a thousand times greater than that employed in the production of a similar piece of Indian muslin. And the [XIII-748] proportion of circulating capital employed is a hundred or a thousand times less. It is easy to conceive that, under certain circumstances, the whole of the annual savings of an industrious people might be added to fixed capital, in which case they would have no effect in increasing the demand for labour" * (l.c. pp. 16-17).

(Ricardo comments on this passage in a note on p. 480:

* "It is not easy, I think, to conceive that under any circumstances, an increase of capital should not be followed by an increased demand for labour; the most that can be said is, that the *demand will be in a diminishing ratio.* Mr. Barton, in the above publication, has, I think, taken *a correct view* of some of the effects of an increasing amount of fixed capital on the condition of the labouring classes. His Essay contains much valuable information." *)

To Barton's above proposition we must add the following:

* "Fixed capital, when once formed, ceases to affect the demand for labour," * (incorrect, since it necessitates reproduction, even if only at intervals and gradually) * "but during its formation it gives employment to just as many hands as an equal amount would employ, either of circulating capital, or of revenue" * (p. 56).

And:

* "The demand for labour absolutely depends on the joint amount of revenue and circulating capital" * ([pp. 34-]35).

Indisputably, Barton has very great merit.

Adam Smith believes that the DEMAND FOR LABOUR grows in direct proportion to capital accumulation. Malthus derives surplus population from capital not being accumulated (that is, reproduced on a growing scale) as rapidly as the population. Barton was the first to point out that the different organic component parts of capital do not grow evenly with accumulation and development of the productive forces, that on the contrary, in the process of this growth, that part of capital which resolves into wages decreases in proportion to that part (he calls it fixed capital) which, in relation to its size, alters the DEMAND FOR LABOUR only to a very small degree. He is therefore the first to put forward the important proposition: "THAT THE NUMBER OF LABOURERS EMPLOYED IS" *NOT* "IN PROPORTION TO THE

WEALTH OF the STATE"; that relatively more workers are employed in an industrially undeveloped country than in one which is industrially developed.

In the 3rd edition of his *Principles*, CH. XXXI, "On Machinery", Ricardo—having followed exactly in Smith's footsteps in his earlier editions—now takes up Barton's correction on this point, and moreover, in the same *one-sided* formulation in which Barton gives it. The only point in which he makes an advance—and this is important—is that, unlike Barton, he not only says that the demand for labour does *not* grow *proportionally* with the development of machinery, but that the machines themselves "MAKE POPULATION REDUNDANT",[a] i.e. create surplus population. But he wrongly limits this EFFECT to the case in which the NET PRODUCE is increased at the cost of the GROSS PRODUCE. This only occurs in agriculture, but he also transfers it into industry. *In nuce,*[b] however, the whole of the absurd theory of population was thus overthrown, in particular also the claptrap of the vulgar economists, that the workers must strive TO KEEP THEIR MULTIPLICATION BELOW THE STANDARD OF THE ACCUMULATION OF CAPITAL. The opposite follows from Barton's and Ricardo's presentation, namely that to keep down THE LABOURING POPULATION, DIMINISHING THE SUPPLY OF LABOUR, AND, CONSEQUENTLY, RAISING ITS PRICE, WOULD ONLY *ACCELERATE* THE APPLICATION OF MACHINERY, THE CONVERSION OF CIRCULATING INTO FIXED CAPITAL, AND, HENCE, MAKE THE POPULATION ARTIFICIALLY "REDUNDANT"; THAT REDUNDANCY EXISTS, GENERALLY, NOT IN REGARD TO THE QUANTITY OF [the means] OF SUBSISTENCE, BUT THE MEANS OF EMPLOYMENT, THE ACTUAL DEMAND FOR LABOUR.

[XIII-749] Barton's error or deficiency lies in his conceiving the organic differentiation or composition of capital only in the form in which it appears in the *circulation process*—as fixed and circulating capital—a difference which the Physiocrats had already discovered, which Adam Smith had developed further and which became a prepossession among the economists who succeeded him; a prepossession in so far as they see *only* this difference—which was handed down to them—in the organic composition of capital. This difference, which arises out of the process of circulation, has a considerable effect on the reproduction of wealth in general, and therefore also on that part of it which forms the LABOUR FUND. But that is not decisive here. The difference between fixed capital such as machinery, buildings, breeding cattle, etc., and circulating capital, does not *directly* lie in their relation to

---

[a] See this volume, pp. 191-93, 195, and 197.— *Ed.*
[b] Literally: in a nutshell; here: essentially.— *Ed.*

wages, but in their mode of circulation and reproduction.

The *direct relation* of the different component parts of capital to living labour is not connected with the phenomena of the circulation process. It does not arise from the latter, but from the *immediate process of production,* and is the relation of *constant* to *variable capital,* whose difference is based *only* on their relationship to living labour.

Thus Barton says for example: The DEMAND FOR LABOUR does not depend on *fixed capital,* but only on *circulating* capital. But a part of circulating capital, *raw material* and *matières instrumentales,* is not exchanged against living labour, any more than is machinery, etc. In all branches of industry in which raw material enters as an element into the valorisation process—in so far as we consider only that portion of the fixed capital which enters into the commodity—it forms the *most important* part of that portion of capital which is not laid out in wages. Another part of the circulating capital, namely of the commodity capital, consists of articles of consumption which enter into the REVENUE of the non-productive class (i.e. [not of] the working class). The growth of these two parts of *circulating* capital therefore does not influence the demand for labour any more than does that of fixed capital. Furthermore, the part of the circulating capital which resolves into *matières brutes*[a] and *matières instrumentales* increases in the same or even greater proportion as that part of capital which is fixed in machinery, etc.

On the basis of the distinction made by Barton, *Ramsay* goes further. He improves on Barton but retains his method of approach. Indeed he reduces the distinction to constant and variable capital, but continues to call constant capital *fixed* capital, although he includes raw materials, etc., and [calls] variable capital circulating capital, although he excludes from it all circulating capital which is not directly laid out in wages. More on this later, when we come to Ramsay.[b] It does, however, show the intrinsic necessity of the process.

Once the distinction between constant capital and variable capital has been grasped, a distinction which arises simply out of the immediate process of production, out of the relationship of the different component parts of capital to living labour, it also becomes evident that in itself it has nothing to do with the absolute amount of the consumption goods produced, although

---

a Raw materials.— *Ed.*

b See pp. XVII—1086-1087 of the manuscript (present edition, Vol. 33).— *Ed.*

plenty with the way in which these are realised—*this way, however, of realising the gross revenue in different commodities is not, as Ricardo has it, and Barton intimates it, *the cause,* but the *effect* of the immanent laws of capitalistic production, leading to a diminishing proportion, if compared with the total amount of produce, of that part of it which forms the fund for the reproduction of the labouring class.* If a large part of the capital consists of machinery, raw materials, *matières instrumentales,* etc., then a smaller portion of the working class as a whole will be employed in the reproduction of the means of subsistence [XIII-750] which enter into the consumption of the workers. This relative DIMINUTION in the reproduction of variable capital, however, is not the reason for the relative DECREASE IN THE DEMAND FOR LABOUR, but on the contrary, its effect. Similarly: A larger section of the workers employed in the production of articles of consumption 'which enter into REVENUE in general will produce articles which enter into the consumption—the EXPENDITURE OF the REVENUE—of CAPITALISTS, LANDLORDS AND THEIR RETAINERS (STATE, CHURCH, etc.), than that which [will produce] articles destined for the REVENUE of the workers. But this again is effect, not cause. A change in the social relation of workers and capitalists, a revolution in the conditions governing capitalist production, would change this at once. THE REVENUE WOULD BE "REALISED IN DIFFERENT COMMODITIES", TO USE AN EXPRESSION OF RICARDO'S. There is nothing in the, so-to-speak, physical conditions of production which forces the above to take place. *The workmen, if they were dominant, if [they were] allowed to produce for themselves, would very soon, and without any great exertion, bring the capital (to use a phrase of the vulgar economists) up to the standard of their wants.* The very great difference is whether the available means of production confront the workers as capital and can therefore be employed by them *only* in so far as it is necessary for the increased production of SURPLUS VALUE AND SURPLUS PRODUCE FOR THEIR EMPLOYERS, in other words whether the means of production employ *them,* or whether they, as subjects, employ the means of production—in the accusative case—in order to produce wealth for themselves. It is of course assumed here that capitalist production has already developed the productive powers of labour in general to a sufficiently high level for this revolution to take place.

//Take for example 1862 (the present autumn). The plight of the Lancashire LABOURERS OUT OF EMPLOYMENT, on the other hand, "THE DIFFICULTY OF FINDING EMPLOYMENT FOR MONEY" ON THE London MONEY MARKET, this has almost made necessary the formation of fraudulent companies, since it [is] difficult to obtain 2% for money. According to Ricardo's theory "SOME OTHER EMPLOYMENT OUGHT TO HAVE BEEN OPENED", for on the one hand there is capital in London, and on the other, unemployed workers in Manchester.//

Barton explains further, that the accumulation of capital increases the DEMAND FOR LABOUR only very slowly, unless the population has grown to such an extent *previously*, that the RATE OF WAGES is low.

"The *proportion which the* WAGES OF LABOUR AT ANY GIVEN TIME BEAR TO THE WHOLE PRODUCE OF LABOUR, determine the APPROPRIATION OF CAPITAL IN ONE (FIXED) OR THE OTHER (CIRCULATING) WAY" (l.c., p. 17).

"For if the rate of wages should decline, while the price of goods remained the same, or if goods should rise, while wages remained the same, the PROFIT of the EMPLOYER would increase, and HE would be INDUCED TO HIRE MORE HANDS. If on the other hand, WAGES should rise in proportion to commodities, the MANUFACTURER would keep as few HANDS as possible.—He would aim at performing every thing by machinery" (pp. 17-18).

"WE HAVE GOOD EVIDENCE THAT POPULATION ADVANCED MUCH MORE SLOWLY UNDER A GRADUAL RISE OF WAGES during the EARLIER PART of the last CENTURY, than during the LATTER PART of the same CENTURY WHILE THE REAL PRICE OF LABOUR FELL RAPIDLY" ([p.] 25).

"A RISE OF WAGES, OF ITSELF, THEN, NEVER INCREASES THE LABOURING POPULATION; A FALL OF WAGES may sometimes increase it very rapidly. Suppose that the Englishman's demands should sink to the level of the Irishman's. Then the manufacturer would engage more [workers] IN PROPORTION TO THE DIMINISHED EXPENSE OF MAINTENANCE" (l.c., [p.] 26).

"IT IS THE DIFFICULTY OF FINDING EMPLOYMENT, MUCH MORE THAN THE INSUFFICIENCY OF THE RATE OF WAGES, WHICH DISCOURAGES MARRIAGE" ([p.] 27).

"IT IS ADMITTED THAT EVERY INCREASE OF WEALTH HAS THE TENDENCY TO CREATE A FRESH DEMAND FOR LABOUR; but as LABOUR, of all commodities, requires the greatest length of time for its production"

//for the same reason, the RATE OF WAGES can remain below the AVERAGE for long periods, because of all commodities, LABOUR is the most difficult TO WITHDRAW FROM THE MARKET AND THUS TO BRING DOWN TO THE LEVEL OF THE ACTUAL DEMAND//

"SO, OF ALL COMMODITIES, [XIII-751] IT IS THE MOST RAISED BY A GIVEN INCREASE OF DEMAND; and as every RISE OF WAGES PRODUCES A TENFOLD REDUCTION OF PROFITS, it is evident that the *accumulation of capital* can operate *only in an inconsiderable degree* IN ADDING TO THE EFFECTUAL DEMAND FOR LABOUR, *UNLESS PRECEDED BY SUCH AN INCREASE OF POPULATION AS SHALL HAVE THE EFFECT OF KEEPING DOWN THE RATE OF WAGES*" ([p.] 28).[a]

Barton puts forward various propositions here:

First: It is not the rise of wages in itself which increases the labouring population, but a fall in wages may very easily and rapidly make it rise. Proof: First half of the 18th century, gradual

---

[a] Marx gives these quotations with some alterations.— *Ed.*

rise in wages, slow movement in population; in the second half of the 18th century, on the other hand, sharp fall in real wages, rapid increase in the labouring population. Reason: It is not the INSUFFICIENT RATE OF WAGES which prevents MARRIAGES, but the DIFFICULTY OF FINDING EMPLOYMENT.

Secondly: The FACILITY OF FINDING EMPLOYMENT stands, however, in inverse ratio to the rate of wages. For capital is transformed into circulating or fixed capital, that is to say, capital which EMPLOYS labour or capital which DOES NOT EMPLOY IT, in inverse proportion to the high or low level of wages. If wages are low, then the demand for labour is great because it is then profitable for the EMPLOYER to use much labour, and he can employ *more* with the same circulating capital. If wages are high, then the MANUFACTURER employs as few HANDS as possible and seeks to do everything with the aid of machines.

Thirdly: The accumulation of capital by itself raises the demand for labour only slowly, because each increase in this demand, IF [labour is] scarce, causes [the price] of labour to rise rapidly and brings about a fall of profit which is ten times greater than the rise in wages. Accumulation can have a rapid effect on the demand for labour only if *accumulation was preceded by a large increase in the labouring population,* and wages are therefore very low so that even a rise of wages still leaves them low because the demand mainly absorbs unemployed workers rather than competing for those fully employed.

This is all, *cum grano salis,*[a] correct so far as fully developed capitalist production is concerned. But it does not explain this development itself.

And even Barton's historical proof therefore contradicts that which it is supposed to prove.

During the first half of the 18th century, wages rose gradually, the population grew slowly and [there was] no machinery; moreover, compared with the following half of the century, little other fixed capital [was employed].

During the second half of the 18th century, however, wages fell continuously, population grew amazingly—and [so did] machinery. But it was precisely the machinery which on the one hand made the existing population REDUNDANT, thus reducing wages, and on the other hand, as a result of the rapid development of the world market, absorbed the population again, made it REDUNDANT once more and then absorbed it again; while at the same time, it

---

a Literally: with a grain of salt; figuratively: with scepticism.— *Ed.*

speeded up the accumulation of capital to an extraordinary extent, and increased the *amount* of variable capital, although variable capital fell relatively, both compared with the total value of the product and also compared with the number of workers it employed. In the first half of the 18th century, however, large-scale industry did not as yet exist, but only *manufacture based on the division of labour*. The principal component part of capital was still variable capital laid out in wages. The productive powers of labour developed, but slowly, compared with the second half of the century. The demand for labour, and therefore also wages, rose almost proportionately to the accumulation of capital. England was as yet essentially an AGRICULTURAL NATION and a very extensive HOME MANUFACTURE—spinning and weaving—which was carried on by the agricultural population, continued to exist, and even to expand. A numerous proletariat could not as yet come into being, any more than there could exist industrial millionaires at the time. In the first half of the 18th century, variable capital was relatively dominant; in the second, fixed capital; but the latter requires a large mass of human material. Its introduction on a large scale MUST BE PRECEDED BY AN INCREASE OF POPULATION. The whole course of things, however, contradicts Barton's presentation, inasmuch as it is evident that a general CHANGE in the mode of production took place. The laws which correspond to large-scale industry are not identical with those corresponding to manufacture [XIII-752]. The latter constitutes merely a phase of development leading to the former.

But in this context some of Barton's historical data—comparing the development in England during the first half and the second half of the 18th century—are of interest, partly because they show the movement of wages, and partly because they show the movement in corn prices.

"The following STATEMENT will shew" (the "WAGES increased from the middle of the 17th, till near the middle of the 18th century, for the price of corn declined within that space of time not less than 35%"), "WHAT PROPORTION THE *WAGES OF HUSBANDRY* HAVE BORNE TO THE PRICE OF CORN during the last 70 years.

PERIODS	WEEKLY PAY	WHEAT PER QR	WAGES IN PINTS OF WHEAT
1742-1752	6s. 0d.	30s. 0d.	102
1761-1770	7 6	42 6	90
1780-1790	8 0	51 2	80
1795-1799	9 0	70 8	65
1800-1808	11 0	86 8	60" (pp. [25-]26).

"From a table of the number of BILLS FOR THE INCLOSING OF LAND PASSED IN EACH SESSION SINCE THE REVOLUTION,[49] given IN THE LORD'S REPORT ON THE POOR LAWS"[50] (1816?), "it appears that in 66 years from 1688 to 1754, that number of BILLS was 123; in the 69 years[a] from 1754 to 1813 it was 3,315.—THE PROGRESS OF CULTIVATION was then about 25 times more rapid during the last period than the former. But during the first 66 years MORE AND MORE CORN WAS GROWN CONTINUALLY FOR EXPORTATION; whereas, during the GREATER PART of the last 69 years, we not only consumed all that we had formerly sent abroad, but likewise imported AN INCREASING, and at last A VERY LARGE QUANTITY, for our own consumption ... the increase of population in the former period, as compared with the latter, was still slower than the PROGRESS OF CULTIVATION MIGHT APPEAR TO INDICATE" ([pp.] 11-12).

"In the year 1688, the population of England and Wales was computed by Gregory King, from the number of houses, at $5^1/_2$ millions."[b] The population in 1780 is put down by Mr. Malthus at 7,700,000.[c] In 92 years then it had increased 2,200,000—in the succeeding 30 years it increased something more than 2,700,000. But of the first increase there is every probability, that the far greater part took place from 1750 to 1780" ([p.] 13).

Barton calculates from good sources that

"the number of inhabitants in 1750 [was] 5,946,000, MAKING AN INCREASE since the revolution of 446,000, or 7,200 per annum" ([pp.] 13-14). "At the LOWEST ESTIMATE then the PROGRESS OF POPULATION OF LATE YEARS has been 10 times more rapid than A CENTURY AGO. Yet it is impossible to believe, that the accumulation of capital has been ten times greater" ([p.] 14).

It is not a question of how great a quantity of means of subsistence is produced annually, but how large a portion of living labour enters into the annual production of fixed and circulating capital. This determines the size of the variable capital in relation to constant.

Barton explains the REMARKABLE INCREASE in population which took place almost all over Europe during the last 50 to 60 YEARS, from the INCREASED PRODUCTIVENESS of the AMERICAN MINES, since this abundance of PRECIOUS METALS raised commodity prices more than wages, thus IN FACT, lowering the latter and causing the rate of profit to rise ([pp.] 29-35).[d]

---

[a] Barton has 69, though in fact the period from 1754 to 1813 comprises only 59 years.— Ed.

[b] See G. King, *Natural and Political Observations and Conclusions upon the State and Condition of England*, 1696. In: G. Chalmers, *An Estimate of the Comparative Strength of Great Britain...*, London, 1804, p. 36.— Ed.

[c] See T. R. Malthus, *An Essay on the Principle of Population...*, 5th ed., Vol. II, London, 1817, p. 92 (Malthus has: "7,721,000").— Ed.

[d] See present edition, Vol. 31, p. 10.— Ed.

[XIII-753] i) MALTHUS (THOMAS ROBERT)[51]

The writings of Malthus which have to be considered here are:
1) *The Measure of Value Stated and Illustrated etc.*, London, 1823.
2) *Definitions in Political Economy etc.*, London, 1827 (as well as the same work published by *John Cazenove* in London in 1853 with Cazenove's NOTES and SUPPLEMENTARY REMARKS).
3) *Principles of Political Economy etc.*, 2nd ED., London, 1836 (first [edition] 1820 or thereabout, to be looked up).
4) Also to be taken into consideration the following work by a Malthusian[a] (i.e. a Malthusian in contrast to the Ricardians): *Outlines of Political Economy etc.*, London, 1832. In his *Inquiry into the Nature and Progress of Rent* (1815)[52] Malthus still says the following about Adam Smith:

* "Adam Smith was evidently led into this train of argument,[53] from his habit of considering *labour*" * (that is, the * value of labour) "as *the standard measure of value*, and corn as the measure of labour... That neither labour nor any other commodity can be an accurate measure of real value in exchange, is now considered as one of the most incontrovertible doctrines of political economy; and, indeed, follows from the very definition of value in exchange" * [p. 12].

But in his *Principles of Political Economy* (1820), Malthus borrows this "STANDARD MEASURE OF VALUE" from Smith to use it against Ricardo, though Smith himself never used it when he was really analysing his subject matter.[54] Malthus himself, in his book on the RENT[52] already referred to, adopted Smith's other definition concerning the determination of value by the QUANTITY OF CAPITAL (ACCUMULATED LABOUR) AND (IMMEDIATE) LABOUR NECESSARY FOR THE PRODUCTION OF AN ARTICLE.

One cannot fail to recognise that both Malthus' *Principles* and the 2 other works mentioned, which were intended to amplify certain aspects of the *Principles*, were largely inspired by envy at the success of Ricardo's book[b] and were an attempt by Malthus to regain the leading position which he had attained by skilful plagiarism before Ricardo's book appeared. In addition, Ricardo's definition of value, though somewhat abstract in its presentation, was directed against the interests of the LANDLORDS and their RETAINERS, which Malthus represented even more directly than those of the industrial bourgeoisie. At the same time, it cannot be denied that Malthus presented a certain theoretical, speculative interest. Nevertheless his opposition to Ricardo—and the form

---

a John Cazenove.— *Ed.*
b D. Ricardo, *On the Principles of Political Economy, and Taxation*, London, 1817.— *Ed.*

this opposition assumed—was possible only because Ricardo had got entangled in all kinds of inconsistencies.

The points of departure for Malthus' attack are, on the one hand, the origin of SURPLUS value[55] and [on the other] the way in which Ricardo conceives the equalisation of cost prices[6] in different spheres of the employment of capital as a modification of the law of value itself [as well as] his continual confusion of profit with surplus value (direct identification of one with the other). Malthus does not unravel these contradictions and *quid pro quos* but accepts them from Ricardo in order to be able to overthrow the Ricardian fundamental law of value, etc., by using this confusion and to draw conclusions acceptable to his PROTECTORS.

The real contribution made by Malthus in his 3 books is that he places the main emphasis on the unequal exchange between capital and wage labour, whereas Ricardo does not actually explain how the exchange of commodities according to the law of value (according to the labour time embodied in the commodities) gives rise to the unequal exchange between capital and living labour, between a definite amount of accumulated labour and a definite amount of IMMEDIATE LABOUR, and therefore in fact leaves the origin of surplus value obscure (since he makes capital exchange immediately for labour and not for labour capacity). [XIII-754] *Cazenove*, one of the few later disciples of Malthus, realises this and says in his preface to *Definitions etc.* mentioned above:

"Interchange of commodities and *distribution"* (wages, rent, profits) "must be kept distinct from each other ... the laws of distribution are not altogether dependent upon those relating to interchange"* (PREFACE, [pp.] vi and vii).

Here this can only mean that the relation of wages to profit, the exchange of capital and wage labour, of ACCUMULATED LABOUR AND IMMEDIATE LABOUR, does not *directly* coincide with the LAW of the INTERCHANGE OF COMMODITIES.

If one considers the *utilisation* of money or commodities as capital—that is, not their value but their capitalist *utilisation*—it is clear that *surplus value* is nothing but the excess of labour (the unpaid labour) which is commanded by capital, i.e. which the commodity or money commands over and above the quantity of labour it itself contains. In addition to the quantity of labour it itself contains (=the sum of labour contained in the elements of production of which it is made up+the immediate labour which is added to them), it buys an excess of labour which it does not itself embody. This excess constitutes the surplus value; its size determines the rate of valorisation. And this surplus quantity of living labour for which it is exchanged is the source of profit.

Profit (or rather surplus value) does not result from the exchange of an amount of objectified labour for an equivalent amount of living labour, but from the portion of living labour which is appropriated in this exchange without an equivalent payment in return, that is, from unpaid labour which capital appropriates in this pseudo-EXCHANGE. If one disregards how this process is mediated—and Malthus is all the more justified in disregarding it as the intermediate link is not mentioned by Ricardo—if one considers only the factual content and the result of this process, then valorisation, profit, transformation of money or commodities into capital, arises not from the fact that commodities are exchanged according to the law of value, namely, in proportion to the amount of labour time which they cost, but rather conversely, from the fact that commodities or money (objectified labour) are exchanged for *more* living labour than is embodied or worked up in them. Malthus' sole contribution in the books mentioned is the emphasis he places on this point, which emerges all the less sharply in Ricardo as Ricardo always presupposes the finished product which is divided between the capitalist and the worker without considering exchange, the intermediate process which leads to this division. However, this contribution is cancelled out by the fact that he confuses the *utilisation* of money or the commodity as capital, and hence its *value* in the specific function of capital, with the *value* of the *commodity* as such; consequently he falls back in his exposition, as we shall see, on the fatuous conceptions of the Monetary System, on profit UPON EXPROPRIATION,[56] and gets completely entangled in the most hopeless confusion. Thus Malthus, instead of advancing beyond Ricardo, seeks to drag political economy back to where it was before Ricardo, even to where it was before Adam Smith and the Physiocrats.

"In the same country, and at the same time, the exchangeable value of those commodities which can be resolved into LABOUR and PROFITS alone, would be accurately measured by the quantity of labour which would result from adding to the ACCUMULATED and *immediate labour actually worked up in them+the varying amount of the profits on all the advances estimated in labour. But, this must necessarily be the same as the quantity of labour which they will command" (*The Measure of Value Stated and Illustrated*, London, 1823, [pp.] 15-16).

"The labour which a commodity can command is a standard measure of value" (l.c., [p.] 61).

"I had nowhere seen it stated"* (that is, before his own book *The Measure of Value etc.* appeared), *"that the ordinary *quantity of labour* which a commodity will command must represent and measure the *quantity of labour worked up in it*, with the addition of profits"* (*Definitions in Political Economy etc.*, London, 1827, [p.] 196).

Mr. Malthus wants to include "profit" directly in the definition of *value*, so that it follows immediately from this definition, which is not the case with Ricardo. This shows that he felt where the difficulty lay.

Besides, it is particularly absurd that he declares the *value of the commodity* and its *utilisation* as capital to be identical. When commodities or money (in brief, objectified labour) are exchanged as capital against living labour, they are always exchanged against a [XIII-755] greater quantity of labour than they contain. And if one compares the commodity before this exchange on the one hand, with the product resulting from this exchange with living labour on the other, one finds that the commodity has been exchanged for its own value (equivalent)+a surplus over and above its own value—the surplus value. But it is therefore absurd to say that the value of a commodity=its value+a surplus over and above this value. If the commodity, as a commodity, is exchanged for other commodities and not as capital against living labour, then, in so far as it is exchanged for an equivalent, it is exchanged for the same quantity of objectified labour as is embodied in it.

The only notable thing is therefore that according to Malthus the profit exists already in the value of the commodity, and that it is clear to him that the commodity always commands more labour than it embodies.

* "It is precisely because the labour which a commodity will ordinarily command measures the labour actually worked up in it with the addition of profits, that it is justifiable to consider it" (labour) "as a measure of value. If then the *ordinary value* of *a commodity* be considered as determined by the natural *and necessary conditions of its supply*, it is certain that the labour which it will ordinarily command is alone the measure of these conditions" (*Definitions in Political Economy*, London, 1827, [p.] 214).

"*Elementary costs of production*: an expression exactly equivalent to the conditions of [the] supply" (l.c., ed. by Cazenove, London, 1853, [p.] 14).

"*Measure of the conditions of* [the] *supply*: the quantity of labour for which the commodity will exchange, when it is in its natural and ordinary state" (l.c., ed. by Cazenove, [p.] 14).

"The quantity of labour which a commodity commands represents exactly the quantity of labour worked up in it, with the profits upon the advances, and does therefore really represent and measure those natural and necessary conditions of the supply, those elementary costs of production which determine value" (l.c., ed. by Cazenove, [p.] 125).

"The demand for a commodity, though not proportioned to the *quantity* of any other commodity which the purchaser is willing and able to give for it, is really proportioned to the *quantity of labour* which he will give for it; and for this reason: the *quantity of labour which a commodity will ordinarily command*, represents exactly the effectual demand for it; because it represents exactly *that quantity of labour and profits united necessary to effect its supply*; while the *actual* quantity of labour which a commodity will command when it differs from the *ordinary* quantity, represents the excess or defect of demand arising from temporary causes" * (l.c., ED. by Cazenove, [p.] 135).

Malthus is right in this also. The CONDITIONS OF SUPPLY, i.e. of the production or rather the reproduction of a commodity on the basis of capitalist production, are that it or its value (the money into which it is transformed) is exchanged in the process of its production or reproduction for more labour than is embodied in it, for it is only produced in order to realise a profit. For example, a cotton manufacturer sells his calico. The condition for the SUPPLY of new calico is that he exchanges the money—the exchange value of the calico—for more labour in the process of the reproduction of the calico than was embodied in it or than is represented by the money. For the cotton manufacturer produces calico as a capitalist. What he wants to produce is not calico, but profit. The production of calico is only a means for the production of profit. But what follows from this? The calico he produces contains more labour time, more labour than was contained in the calico ADVANCED. This surplus labour time, this surplus value, is also represented by a SURPLUS PRODUCE, *more* calico than was exchanged for labour. Therefore one part of the product does not replace the calico exchanged for labour, but constitutes SURPLUS PRODUCE which belongs to the manufacturer. Or, if we consider the whole product, each yard of calico contains an aliquot part, or its value contains an aliquot part, for which no equivalent is paid; this represents *unpaid* labour. If the manufacturer sells a yard of calico at its value, that is, if he exchanges it for money or for commodities which contain an equal amount of labour time, he realises a sum of money, or receives a quantity of commodities which cost him nothing. For he sells the calico not for the labour time for which he has paid, but for the labour time embodied in the calico, and [XIII-756] he did not pay for part of this labour time. He receives, for example, labour time=12s. but he only paid 8s. of this amount. When he sells it at its value, he sells it for 12, and thus gains 4s.

As far as the buyer is concerned, the assumption is that, under all circumstances, he pays *nothing but* the value of the calico. This means that he gives a sum of money which contains as much labour time [as] there is in the calico. Three cases are possible. The buyer is a capitalist. The money (i.e. the value of the commodity) with which he pays, also contains a portion of unpaid labour. Thus, if one person sells unpaid labour, the other person buys with unpaid labour. Both realise unpaid labour—one as seller, the other as buyer. Or, the buyer is an INDEPENDENT PRODUCER. In this case he receives equivalent for equivalent. Whether the labour which the seller sells him in the shape of commodities is paid for or not, does not concern him. He receives as much objectified labour as he gives. Or, finally, he is a wage worker. In this case also, like every other buyer—provided the commodities are sold at their value—he receives an equivalent for his money in the shape of commodities. He receives as much objectified labour in commodities as he gives in money. But for the money which constitutes his wages he has given more labour than is embodied in the money. He has replaced the labour contained in it+surplus labour which he gives gratis. He paid for the money above its value, and therefore also pays for the equivalent of the money, the calico, etc., above its value. The COST for him as PURCHASER is thus greater than it is for the SELLER of any commodity although he receives an equivalent of the money in the commodity; but in the money he did not receive an equivalent of his labour; on the contrary, he gave more than the equivalent in labour. Thus the worker is the only one who pays for all commodities above their value even when he buys them at their value, because he buys money, the universal equivalent, above its value for labour. Consequently, no gain accrues to those who sell commodities to the worker. The worker does not pay the seller any more than any other buyer, he pays the value of labour. In fact, the capitalist who sells the commodity produced by the worker back to him, realises a profit on this sale, but only the same profit as he realises on every other buyer. His profit—as far as this worker is concerned—arises not from his having sold the worker the commodity *above* its value, but from his having previously bought it from the worker, as a matter of fact in the production process, *below* its value.

Now Mr. Malthus, who transformed the utilisation of commodities as capital into the value of commodities, quite consistently transforms all buyers into wage workers, in other words he makes them all exchange with the capitalist not commodities, but immediate labour, and makes them all give back to the capitalist more labour than the commodities *contain*, while conversely, the capitalist's profit results from *selling all* the labour contained in the commodities when he has *paid* for only a portion of the labour contained in them. Therefore, whereas the difficulty with Ricardo [arises from] the fact that the law of commodity exchange does not directly explain the exchange between capital and wage labour, but rather seems to contradict it, Malthus solves the difficulty by transforming the purchase (exchange) of commodities into an exchange between capital and wage labour. What Malthus does not understand is the difference between the total sum of labour contained in a particular commodity and the sum of paid labour which is contained in it. It is precisely this difference which constitutes the source of profit. Further, Malthus inevitably arrives at the point of deriving profit from the fact that the seller sells his commodity not only *above* the amount it costs *him* (and the capitalist does this), but above what *it costs*; he thus reverts to the vulgarised conception of profit UPON EXPROPRIATION and derives surplus value from the fact that the seller sells the commodity *above* its value (i.e. for more labour time than is contained in it). What he thus gains as a seller of a commodity, he loses as a buyer of another and it is absolutely impossible to discover what "profit" is to be made in reality from such a general nominal price increase. [XIII-757] It is in particular difficult to understand how society *en masse* can enrich itself in this way, how a real SURPLUS value or SURPLUS PRODUCE can thus arise. An absurd, stupid idea.

Relying on some propositions of Adam Smith—who, as we have seen,[a] naively expresses all sorts of contradictory elements and thus becomes the source, the starting-point, of diametrically opposed conceptions—Mr. Malthus attempts in a confused way, though on the basis of a correct surmise and of the realisation of the existence of an unsolved difficulty, to counterpose a new theory to that of Ricardo and thus to maintain a "FIRST RANK" position. The transition from this attempt to the nonsensical, vulgarised conceptions proceeds in the following way:

If we consider the utilisation of a commodity as capital—that is, in its exchange for living, productive labour—we see that it commands—besides the labour time it itself contains, i.e. besides the equivalent reproduced by the worker—surplus labour time, which is the source of profit. Now if we transfer this *utilisation of the commodity* to its *value*, then each purchaser of a commodity must act as if he were a worker, that is, in buying it, besides the quantity of labour contained in the commodity, he must give for it a surplus quantity of labour. But since other purchasers, *apart from the workers*, are *not* related to commodities as workers // even when the worker appears as a mere purchaser, the old, original difference persists indirectly, as we have seen //, it must be assumed that although they do not directly give more labour than is contained in the commodities, they give a value which contains more labour, and this amounts to the same thing. It is by means of this "surplus labour, or, what amounts to the same thing, the

---

[a] See present edition, Vol. 30, pp. 397-98 and Vol. 31, pp. 7, 439-40.—*Ed.*

value of more labour", that the transition is made. IN FACT, it comes to this: the value of a commodity consists of the value paid for it by the purchaser, and this value=the equivalent (the value) of the commodity+a surplus over and above this value, SURPLUS value. Thus we have the vulgarised view that profit consists in a commodity being *sold more dearly than it was bought.* The purchaser buys it for more labour or for more objectified labour than it costs the seller.

But if the purchaser is himself a capitalist, a seller of commodities, and his money, his means of purchase, represents only goods which have been sold, then it follows that both have sold their goods too dearly and are consequently swindling each other, moreover they are swindling each other to the same extent, provided they both merely realise the general rate of profit. Where are the buyers to come from who will pay the capitalist the QUANTITY of labour equal to that contained in his commodity+his profit? For example, the commodity costs the seller 10s. He sells it for 12s. He thus commands labour not to the value of 10s. only, but of 2s. more. But the buyer also sells his commodity, which costs 10s., for 12s. So that each loses as a buyer what he gained as a seller. The only exception is the working class. For since the price of the product is increased beyond its cost, they can only buy back a part of that product, and thus another part of the product, or the price of another part of the product, constitutes profit for the capitalist. But as profit arises precisely from the fact that the workers can only buy back part of the product, the capitalist (the capitalist class) can never realise his profit as a result of demand from the workers, he cannot realise it by exchanging the whole product against the workers' wage, but rather by exchanging *the whole* of the workers' wage against only part of the product. Additional demand and additional buyers apart from the workers themselves are therefore necessary, otherwise there could not be any profit. Where do they come from? If they themselves are capitalists, sellers, then the mutual swindling within the capitalist class mentioned earlier occurs, since they mutually raise the nominal prices of their commodities and each gains as a seller what he loses as a buyer. What is *required* therefore are *buyers who are not sellers,* so that the capitalist [can] realise his profit and sell his commodities "at their value". Hence the necessity for LANDLORDS, pensioners, sinecurists, priests, etc., not to forget their MENIAL SERVANTS and RETAINERS. How these "purchasers" come into possession [XIII-758] of their means of purchase, how they must first take part of the product from the capitalists without giving any equivalent in order to buy back less than an equivalent with the means thus obtained, Mr. Malthus does not explain. At any rate, what follows from this is his PLEA for the greatest possible increase in the unproductive classes in order that the sellers may find a market, a DEMAND for their SUPPLY. And so it turns out further that the population pamphleteer[57] preaches continuous overconsumption and the maximum possible appropriation of the annual product by idlers, as a condition of production. In addition to the PLEA arising inevitably out of this theory, comes the argument that capital represents the drive *for abstract wealth,* the *drive for valorisation,* which can only be put into effect by means of a class of buyers representing the *drive to spend, to consume, to squander,* namely, the unproductive classes, who are buyers without being sellers.

There developed on this basis a fine old row between the MALTHUSIANS and the RICARDIANS in the 20s (from 1820 to 1830 was in general the great metaphysical period in English political economy).[a] Like the MALTHUSIANS, the RICARDIANS deem it necessary that the worker should not himself appropriate his product, but that part of it should go to the capitalist, in order that he, the worker, should have an *incentive for production,* and that the development of wealth should thus be ensured. But they rage against the view of the MALTHUSIANS that LANDLORDS, STATE AND CHURCH SINECURISTS, AND A WHOLE LOT OF IDLE RETAINERS, MUST FIRST LAY HOLD—WITHOUT ANY EQUIVALENT—OF A PART OF THE CAPITALIST'S PRODUCE (just as the capitalist does in respect of the workers) therewith to buy their own goods from the capitalist with a profit for the latter, although this is exactly what the RICARDIANS affirm with regard to the workers. In order that accumulation may increase and with it the demand for labour, the worker must relinquish as much of his product as possible gratis to the capitalist, so that the latter can transform the NET REVENUE, which has been increased in this way, back again into capital. The same sort [of argument is used by] the MALTHUSIAN. As much as possible should be taken away gratis from the industrial capitalists in the form of rent, taxes, etc., to enable them to sell what remains to their involuntary "SHAREHOLDERS" at a profit. The worker must not be allowed to appropriate his own product, otherwise he would lose the incentive to work, say the RICARDIANS along with the MALTHUSIANS. The industrial capitalist must relinquish a portion of his product to the classes which only

---

consume—*fruges consumere nati*[a]—in order that these in turn may exchange it again, on unfavourable terms, with the capitalist. Otherwise the capitalist would lose the incentive for production, which consists precisely in the fact that he makes a big profit, that he sells his commodities far above their value. We shall return to this comic struggle later.[b]

First of all, some evidence showing that Malthus arrives at a very common conception:

*"Whatever may be the number of intermediate acts of barter which may take place in regard to commodities—whether the producers send them to China, or sell them in the place where they are produced: the question as to an adequate market for them, depends exclusively upon *whether the producers can replace their capitals with ordinary profits,* so as to enable them successfully to go on with their business. *But what are their capitals?* They are, as Adam Smith states, the tools to work with, the materials to work upon, and the means of commanding the necessary quantity of labour."*

(And this, he affirms, is ALL THE LABOUR WORKED UP IN THE COMMODITY. Profit is a *surplus* over and above the LABOUR EXPENDED in the production of the commodity. IN FACT, therefore, a NOMINAL SURCHARGE OVER and above THE COST OF THE COMMODITY.) And in order that there may remain no doubt about his meaning, he quotes Colonel Torrens' [*An Essay*] *on the Production of Wealth* (CH. VI, p. 349) approvingly as confirming his own views:

*"Effectual demand consists in the power and inclination, on *the part of consumers*"* //the antithesis of buyers and sellers becomes that of CONSUMERS and PRODUCERS//, [XIII-759] *"to give for commodities, either by immediate or circuitous barter, some greater proportion of all the ingredients of capital than their production costs"* (*Definitions* [*in Political Economy*], ED. by Cazenove, pp. 70-71).

And Mr. Cazenove himself, the publisher of, apologist for and commentator on the Malthusian *Definitions,* says:

*"Profit does not depend upon the *proportion in which commodities are exchanged with each other,*"*

(for if commodity exchange between capitalists alone were taken into account, the Malthusian theory, in so far as it does not speak of exchange with workers, who have *no* other COMMODITY apart from their LABOUR to exchange with the capitalists, would appear nonsensical [since profit would be] merely a reciprocal SURCHARGE, a nominal SURCHARGE ON THE PRICES OF THEIR COMMODITIES. Commodity exchange must therefore be disregarded and people who produce *no* commodities must exchange money)

[a] Born to consume the fruits (Horace, *Epistolae,* Liber primus, Epistola II, 27).—*Ed.*
[b] See this volume, pp. 233-41.—*Ed.*

* "seeing that the same proportion may be maintained under every variety of profit, *but upon the proportion which goes to wages,* or is required to cover the prime cost, and which is in all cases determined by the degree in which the *sacrifice made by the purchaser,* or the *labour's worth which he gives,* in order to acquire a commodity, *exceeds that made by the producer, in order to bring it to market"* * (Cazenove, l.c., p. 46).

In order to achieve these wonderful results, Malthus has to make some very great theoretical preparations. *D'abord,*[a] seizing on that side of Adam Smith's theory according to which the value of a commodity=the QUANTITY OF LABOUR WHICH IT COMMANDS, OR BY WHICH IT IS COMMANDED, OR AGAINST WHICH IT EXCHANGES, he must cast all the objections raised by Adam Smith himself, by his followers and also by Malthus, to the effect that the *value* of a commodity—value—can be the measure of value.

The Measure of Value Stated and Illustrated, London, 1823, is a real example of feeble-minded thought, which winds its way in a casuistical and self-stupefying manner through its own inner confusion, and whose difficult, clumsy style leaves the unprejudiced and incompetent reader with the impression that the difficulty of making sense out of the confusion does not lie in the contradiction between confusion and clarity, but in a lack of understanding on the part of the reader.

Malthus has first of all to obliterate Ricardo's differentiation between "VALUE OF LABOUR" and "QUANTITY OF LABOUR"[b] and to reduce Smith's juxtaposition of the two to the one false aspect.

* "Any given *quantity of labour* must be *of the same value* as the *wages* which command it, or for which it actually exchanges" * (*The Measure of Value Stated and Illustrated,* London, 1823, [p.] 5).

The purpose of this phrase is to equate the expressions "QUANTITY OF LABOUR" and "VALUE OF LABOUR".

This phrase itself is a mere tautology, AN ABSURD TRUISM. Since WAGES or that "FOR WHICH IT" (A QUANTITY OF LABOUR) "EXCHANGES" constitute the *value* of this quantity of labour, it is tautologous to say: the *value* of a certain quantity of labour is equal to the *wages* or to the amount of money or commodities for which this labour exchanges. In other words, this means nothing more than: the exchange value of a definite quantity of labour=its exchange value—otherwise CALLED WAGES. But //apart from the fact that it is not labour, but labour capacity, which exchanges directly for WAGES; it is this confusion that makes the nonsense possible// it by no means follows from this that a definite quantity of labour=the

---

[a] First of all.— *Ed.*
[b] See this volume, pp. 32-35.— *Ed.*

quantity of labour embodied in the WAGES, or in the money or the commodities which represent the WAGES. If a labourer works for 12 hours and receives the product of 6 hours as wages, then the product of the 6 hours constitutes the VALUE of 12 hours labour (because the WAGES [represent] THE EXCHANGEABLE COMMODITY FOR [12 hours labour]). It does not follow from this that 6 hours of labour=12 hours, or that the commodities in which 6 hours of labour are embodied [are] equal to the commodities in which 12 hours of labour are embodied. It does not follow that the value of WAGES=the value of the product in which the labour is embodied. It follows only that the VALUE OF LABOUR (because it is measured by the VALUE of the labour capacity, not by the labour carried out), the [XIII-760] VALUE OF A GIVEN QUANTITY OF LABOUR contains less labour than it buys; that, consequently, the *value of the commodities* in which this purchased labour is embodied, is very different from the value of the commodities with which this GIVEN QUANTITY OF LABOUR WAS PURCHASED, OR BY WHICH IT WAS COMMANDED. Mr. Malthus draws the opposite conclusion. Since the *value* of a given quantity of labour=its value, it follows, according to him, that the value in which this quantity of labour is embodied=the value of the WAGES. It follows further from this that the immediate labour (that is, after deducting the means of production) which is absorbed by and contained in a commodity, creates no greater value than that which is paid for it; [that it] only reproduces the VALUE OF the WAGES. The necessary consequence ensuing from this is that profit cannot be explained if the value of commodities is determined by the amount of labour embodied in them, but must rather be explained in some other way; provided the profit a commodity realises is to be included in the value of that commodity. For the labour worked up in a commodity consists 1) of the labour contained in the machinery, etc., used, which consequently reappears in the value of the product; 2) of the labour contained in the RAW material used up. The amount of labour contained in these two elements before the new commodity is produced is obviously not increased merely because they become production elements of a new commodity. There remains therefore 3) the labour embodied in the WAGES which is exchanged for living labour. However, according to Malthus, this latter is not greater than the objectified labour AGAINST WHICH IT IS EXCHANGED. HENCE, a commodity contains no portion of unpaid labour but only labour which replaces an equivalent. HENCE it follows that if the value of a commodity were determined by the labour embodied in it, it would yield no profit. If it does yield a profit, then this profit is a *surplus* in the price over and above the labour embodied in the commodity. Therefore, in order to be sold at its value (which includes the profit), a commodity must command A QUANTITY OF LABOUR=THE QUANTITY OF LABOUR WORKED UP IN ITSELF+A SURPLUS OF LABOUR, REPRESENTING THE PROFIT REALISED IN THE PURCHASE OF THE COMMODITY.

Moreover, in order to make LABOUR, not the QUANTITY of LABOUR required for production, but LABOUR as a commodity, serve as a measure of value, Malthus asserts that *"THE VALUE OF LABOUR IS CONSTANT"* (*The Measure of Value etc.*, [p.] 29, note). //There is nothing original in this; it is a mere paraphrase and further elaboration of a passage of *Adam Smith,* Book I, CH. V (ed. by Garnier, t. I, [pp.] 65[-66]) [Vol. I, p. 58].[58]

"Equal quantities of labour, at all times and places, may be said to be of equal value to the labourer. In his ordinary state of health, strength and spirits, in the ordinary degree of his skill and dexterity, he must always lay down the same portion of his ease, his liberty, and his happiness. The price which he pays must always be the same, whatever may be the quantity of goods which he receives in return for it. Of these, indeed, it may sometimes purchase a greater and sometimes a smaller quantity; but it is their value which varies, not that of the labour which purchases them. At all times and places that is *dear* which it is difficult to come at, or which it costs much labour to acquire; and that *cheap* which is to be had easily, or with very little labour. Labour alone, therefore, never varying in its own value, is alone the ultimate and real standard by which the value of all commodities can at all times and places be estimated and compared." [a] //

//Further, Malthus' discovery—of which he is very proud and which he claims he was the first to make—namely, that value=the quantity of labour embodied in a commodity+a QUANTITY OF LABOUR which represents the profit; [this discovery] seems likewise to be quite simply a combination of two sentences from Smith. (Malthus never escapes plagiarism.)

"The real value of all the different component parts of price is measured by the quantity of labour which they can, each of them, purchase or command. Labour measures the value, not only of that part of price which resolves itself into *labour,* but of that which resolves itself into *rent,* and of that which resolves itself into *profit*" (ed. by Garnier, t. I, l. I, ch. VI, p. 100) [Vol. I, p. 86].

[XIII-761] Malthus writes in this context:

"If the demand for labour rises, [it appeared that] the GREATER EARNINGS OF THE LABOURER were CAUSED, NOT BY A RISE IN THE VALUE OF LABOUR, BUT BY A FALL IN THE VALUE OF THE PRODUCE FOR WHICH THE LABOUR WAS EXCHANGED. And in the CASE of an ABUNDANCE of labour, THE SMALL EARNINGS OF THE LABOURER were CAUSED BY A RISE IN THE VALUE OF THE PRODUCE AND NOT BY A FALL IN THE VALUE OF LABOUR" [b] (*The Measure of Value etc.*, [p.] 35) (cf. ibid., pp. 33-34).

---

[a] Cf. present edition, Vol. 28, p. 529, and Vol. 30, p. 383.—*Ed.*
[b] Marx quotes Malthus with some alterations.—*Ed.*

Bailey ridicules most excellently Malthus' *proof* that the VALUE OF LABOUR is CONSTANT (Malthus' further demonstration, not that of Smith; nor is the sentence [about] the INVARIABLE VALUE OF LABOUR):

* "In the same way any article might be proved to be of invariable value; for instance, 10 yards of cloth. For whether we gave £5 or £10 for the 10 yards, the sum given would always be equal in value to the cloth for which it was paid, or, in other words, of invariable value in relation to cloth. But that which is given for a thing of invariable value, must itself be invariable, whence the 10 yards of cloth must be of invariable value... It is just the same kind of futility to call wages invariable in value, because though variable in quantity they command the same portion of labour, as to call the *sum* given for a hat, of invariable value, because, although sometimes more and sometimes less, it always purchases the hat" * (*A Critical Dissertation on the Nature, Measures, and Causes of Value etc.*, London, 1825, [pp. 145,] 146-47).

In the same work, Bailey bitingly derides the insipid, impressive-sounding tables with which Malthus "illustrates" his MEASURE OF VALUE. In his *Definitions in Political Economy* (London, 1827), in which Malthus gives FULL VENT to his annoyance over Bailey's sarcasm, he seeks, amongst other things, to prove the INVARIABLE VALUE OF LABOUR, as follows:

"A LARGE CLASS OF COMMODITIES, such as RAW PRODUCTS, rises in the PROGRESS of SOCIETY as compared with labour, while MANUFACTURED ARTICLES FALL. So it is not FAR FROM the TRUTH TO SAY, that the AVERAGE MASS OF COMMODITIES WHICH A GIVEN QUANTITY OF LABOUR WILL COMMAND IN THE SAME COUNTRY, DURING THE COURSE OF SOME CENTURIES, MAY NOT VERY ESSENTIALLY VARY" (*Definitions etc.*, London, 1827, [p.] 206).

Malthus' proof that a rise in the MONEY PRICE OF WAGES must lead to an all-round rise in the money price of commodities is of just the same quality as his proof of the "INVARIABLE VALUE OF LABOUR":

* "If the money wages of labour universally rise, the value of money proportionally falls; and when the value of money falls ... the prices of goods always rise" * (*Definitions*, l.c., [p.] 34).

It has to be proved that, when the VALUE OF MONEY COMPARED WITH LABOUR falls, then the VALUE OF ALL COMMODITIES COMPARED WITH MONEY rises, or that the VALUE OF MONEY, NOT ESTIMATED IN LABOUR, BUT IN THE OTHER COMMODITIES, FALLS. And Malthus proves this by presupposing it.

Malthus bases his polemic against Ricardo's definition of value entirely on the principles first advanced by Ricardo himself, to the effect that VARIATIONS in the *exchangeable values of commodities, independent of the labour worked up in them, are produced by the different composition of capital as resulting from the process of circulation—different proportions of circulating and fixed capital, different degrees of durability in the fixed capitals employed, different returns of circulating capitals. * In short,

Ricardo's confusion of cost price with VALUE [a] and, by regarding the equalisation of cost prices, which are independent of the MASS OF LABOUR EMPLOYED IN THE PARTICULAR SPHERES OF PRODUCTION, as modifications of VALUE itself, he throws the whole principle overboard. Malthus seizes on these contradictions in the determination of value by labour time—contradictions that were first discovered and emphasised by Ricardo himself—not in order to solve them but in order to relapse into quite meaningless conceptions and to pass off the mere *formulation* of contradictory phenomena, their expression in speech, as their solution. We shall see the same method employed during the dissolution of the Ricardian school, i.e. by Mill and McCulloch,[b] who, in order to reason the contradictory phenomena out of existence, seek to bring them into direct conformity with the general law by gabble, by scholastic and absurd definitions and distinctions, with the result, by the way, that the foundation itself vanishes.

The passages in which Malthus uses the material provided by Ricardo against the law of value, and turns it against him, are the following:

* "It is observed by Adam Smith that corn is an annual crop, butchers' meat a crop which requires 4 or 5 years to grow; and consequently, if we compare two quantities of corn and beef which are of equal exchangeable value, it is certain that a difference of 3 or 4 additional years profit at 15% upon the capital employed in the production of the beef would, exclusively of any other considerations, make up in value for a much smaller quantity [XIII-762] of labour, and thus we might have 2 commodities of the same exchangeable value, while the accumulated and immediate labour of the one was 40 or 50% less than that of the other. This is an event of daily occurrence in reference to a vast mass of the most important commodities in the country; and if profits were to fall from 15% to 8%, the value of beef compared with corn would fall above 20%" * (*The Measure of Value Stated etc.*, [pp.] 10[-11]).

Since capital consists of commodities, and a large proportion of the commodities which enter into it or constitute it have a price (or EXCHANGEABLE VALUE in the ordinary sense) which consists neither of ACCUMULATED nor of IMMEDIATE LABOUR, but—in so far as we are discussing only this particular commodity—of a purely nominal increase in the value CAUSED BY THE ADDITION OF THE AVERAGE PROFITS, Malthus says:

* "Labour is not the only element worked up in capital" (*Definitions*, ed. by Cazenove, [p.] 29).

"What are the *costs of production?* ... the quantity of *labour in kind required to be worked up in the commodity,* and in the tools and materials consumed in its

---

[a] See present edition, Vol. 31, pp. 415-23.— *Ed.*
[b] See this volume, pp. 274-93, 353-70.— *Ed.*

production *with such an additional quantity* as is equivalent to the ordinary profits upon the advances for the time that they have been advanced" (l.c., [pp.] 74-75).

"On the same grounds Mr. Mill is quite incorrect, in calling capital hoarded labour. It may, perhaps, be called *hoarded labour and profits*, but certainly not hoarded labour alone, unless we determine to call profits labour" (l.c., [pp. 60-]61).

"To say that the values of commodities are regulated or determined by the quantity of labour and capital necessary to produce them, is essentially false. To say that they are regulated *by the quantity of labour and profits* necessary to produce them, is essentially true" * (l.c., [p.] 129).

In this connection *Cazenove* adds a note on p. 130:

* "The expression Labour and Profits is liable to this objection, that the two are not correlative terms, labour being an agent and profits a result; the one a cause, the other a consequence. On this account *Mr. Senior* has substituted for it the expression: '*Labour and Abstinence*'... It must be acknowledged, indeed, that it is not the abstinence, but the *use* of the capital productively, which is the cause of profits." *

(According to Senior:

* "He who converts his revenue into capital, *abstains from the enjoyment* which its expenditure would afford him." * a)

Marvellous explanation. The value of the commodity consists of the labour contained in it + profit; of the labour contained in it and the labour not contained in it, but which must be paid for.

Malthus continues his polemic against Ricardo:

"Ricardo's assertion, that as the VALUE OF WAGES RISES PROFITS PROPORTIONABLY FALL AND vice versa, can be true only on the assumption that commodities in which the same quantity of labour has been worked up are always of the same value, and this will be found to be true in one case out of 500; and necessarily so because the progress of civilisation and IMPROVEMENT continually increases the QUANTITY OF FIXED CAPITAL EMPLOYED and renders more VARIOUS and UNEQUAL the TIMES OF THE RETURNS OF THE CIRCULATING CAPITAL" (*Definitions*, London, 1827, [pp.] 31-32).

(The same point is made on pp. [53-]54 in Cazenove's EDITION where Malthus actually says:

The NATURAL STATE OF THINGS falsifies Ricardo's measure of value because this * state "in the progress of civilisation and improvement tends continually to increase the quantity of fixed capital employed, and to render more various and unequal the times of the returns of the circulating capital".)

"Mr. Ricardo himself admits of considerable exceptions to his rule; but if we examine the classes which come under his exceptions, that is, where the quantities of fixed capital employed are different and of different degrees of duration, and where the periods of the returns of the circulating capital employed are not the same, we shall find that they are so numerous, that the rule may be considered as the exception, and the exceptions the rule" * ([p.] 50).

---

a See N. W. Senior, *Political Economy*. In: *Encyclopaedia Metropolitana...*, London, 1850, p. 60. Here Marx quotes Senior from Cazenove.— *Ed.*

In accordance with what has been said above, Malthus also declares VALUE to be [59]:

* "The estimation in which a commodity is held, founded upon its *cost to the purchaser* or the *sacrifice* which he must make in order to acquire it, which sacrifice is measured by the *quantity of labour that he gives in exchange for* it, o r what *comes to the same thing,* by the *labour* which it will command" * (*Definitions,* ED. by Cazenove, [pp. 8-]9).

Cazenove also emphasises as a difference between Malthus and Ricardo:

[XIII-763] * "Mr. Ricardo has, with Adam Smith, adopted labour as the true standard of cost; but he has applied it to the *producing* cost only; ...it is equally applicable as a measure of *cost to the purchaser*" * (l.c., [pp.] 56-57).

In other words: the value of a commodity is equal to the sum of money which the purchaser must pay, and this sum is best estimated in terms of the amount of COMMON LABOUR which can be bought with it.

Malthus *presupposes* the *existence of profit* in order to be able to measure its value by an external standard. He does not deal with the question of the origin and intrinsic possibility of profit. But what determines the sum of money is, naturally, not explained. It is the quite ordinary idea of the matter that is prevalent in everyday LIFE. A mere triviality expressed in high-flown language. In other words, it means nothing more than that *cost price* and *value* are identical, a confusion which, in the case of Adam Smith, and still more in the case of Ricardo, contradicts their real analysis, but which Malthus elevates into a law. It is the conception of value held by the philistine who, being a captive of competition, only knows the outward appearance of value. What then determines the cost price? The ADVANCES+profit. And what determines profit? Where do the FUNDS for the profit come from, where does the SURPLUS PRODUCE in which the SURPLUS VALUE manifests itself come from? If it is simply a matter of a nominal increase of the money price, then nothing is easier than to increase the value of commodities. And what determines the value of the ADVANCES? The *value* of the labour contained in it, says Malthus. And what determines this? The *value* of the commodities on which the wages are spent! And the value of these commodities? The value of the labour+profit. And so we keep going round and round in a circle. Granting that the worker is in fact paid the value of his labour, that is, that the commodities (or sum of money) which constitute his WAGES=the value of the commodities (or sum of money) in which his labour is realised, so that if he receives 100 thaler in wages he also adds only 100 thaler [of value] to the raw material, etc.—in short, to the ADVANCES—then profit can only arise from a surcharge added by the seller over and above the *real* value of the commodity. All sellers do this. Thus, in so far as capitalists engage in exchange amongst themselves, nobody gains from this surcharge, and least of all is a surplus fund thus produced from which they can draw their REVENUE. Only the capitalists whose commodities are consumed by the working class will make a real and not an imaginary profit, by selling commodities back again to the workers at a higher price than they paid the workers for them. The commodities for which they paid the workers 100 thaler will be sold back again to them for 110. That means that they will only sell $^{10}/_{11}$ of the product back to the workers and retain $^{1}/_{11}$ for themselves. But what else does that mean but that the worker who, for example, works for 11 hours, gets paid for only 10; that he is given the product of only 10 hours, while the capitalist receives one hour or the product of one hour without giving any equivalent. And what does it mean but that profit—as far as the working class is concerned—is made by their working for the capitalists *for nothing* part of the time, that therefore "the *quantity* of labour" DOES NOT COME TO THE SAME THING AS the "VALUE OF LABOUR". The other capitalists however would only be making an imaginary profit, since they would not have this expedient. How little Malthus understood Ricardo's first propositions, how completely he failed to comprehend that a profit is possible in other ways than by means of a SURCHARGE is shown conclusively by the following passage:

* "Allowing that the first commodities, if completed and brought into use immediately, might be the result of pure labour, and that their value would therefore be determined by the quantity of that labour; yet it is quite impossible that such commodities should be *employed as capital* to assist in the production of other commodities, *without the capitalist being deprived of the use of his advances for a certain period, and requiring a remuneration in the shape of profits.* In the early periods of society, on account of the comparative scarcity of these advances of labour, this remuneration would be high, and would affect the value of such commodities to a considerable degree, owing to the high rate of profits. In the more advanced stages of society, the value of capital and commodities is largely affected by profits, on account of the greatly increased quantity of fixed capital employed, and the greater length of time for which much of the circulating capital is advanced before the capitalist is repaid by the returns. In *both cases,* the *rate at which commodities exchange with each other,* is *affected by the varying amount of profits...*" * (*Definitions,* ED. by Cazenove, [p.] 60).

The concept of *relative* wages is one of Ricardo's greatest contributions. It consists in this—that the *value of the wages* (and consequently of the *profit*) depends absolutely on the proportion of that part of the working day during which the *worker works for himself* (producing or reproducing his wage) to that part of his time which belongs to the capitalist. This is important economically, IN FACT it is only another way of expressing the real theory of surplus value.[a] It is important further in regard to the social relationship between the two [XIII-764] classes. Malthus smells a rat and is therefore constrained to protest.

* "No writer that I have met with, anterior to Mr. Ricardo, ever used the term *wages,* or real wages, as implying *proportions."* *

(Ricardo speaks of the *value* of WAGES, which is indeed also presented as the part of the product accruing to the worker.)[b]

* "*Profits,* indeed, imply proportions; and the *rate of profits had always justly been estimated by a percentage upon the value of the advances."* *

//What Malthus understands by VALUE OF ADVANCES is very hard, and for him even impossible, to say. According to him, the VALUE of a commodity=the ADVANCES contained in it+PROFIT. Since the ADVANCES, apart from the IMMEDIATE LABOUR, also consist of COMMODITIES, the VALUE of the ADVANCES=the ADVANCES IN THEM+PROFIT. Profit thus =profit UPON THE ADVANCES+PROFIT. And so on, *ad infinitum.*//

* "But wages had uniformly been considered as rising or falling, not according to any *proportion* which they might bear to the whole produce obtained by a certain quantity of labour, but by the greater or smaller quantity of any particular produce received by the labourer, or by the greater or smaller power which such produce would convey, of commanding the necessaries and conveniencies of life" * (*Definitions,* London, 1827, [pp.] 29-30).

Since the production of *exchange value*—its valorisation—is the immediate aim of capitalist production, [it is important to know] how to measure it. Since the value of the CAPITAL ADVANCED is expressed in money (real money of account), the rate of increase is measured by the amount of capital itself, and a capital (a sum of money) of a certain size—100—is taken as a standard.

* "Profit of capital," * says Malthus, * "consists of the difference between the value of the capital advanced, and the value of the commodity when sold and used" * (*Definitions in Political Economy,* London, 1827, pp. 240-41).

Productive and unproductive labour.

---

[a] See this volume, pp. 52-59.— *Ed.*
[b] Ibid., pp. 37, 40, 52-53, 184.— *Ed.*

* "Revenue is expended with a view to immediate support and enjoyment, and capital is expended with a view to profit" (*Definitions*, London, 1827, [p.] 86).

"A labourer and a menial servant are two instruments used for purposes distinctly different, one to assist in obtaining wealth, the other to assist in consuming it" * (l.c., [p.] 94).[60]

The following is a good definition of the PRODUCTIVE LABOURER:

The PRODUCTIVE LABOURER he that *DIRECTLY AUGMENTS "HIS MASTER'S WEALTH"* (*Principles of Political Economy*, [2nd ed., p.] 47 [note]).

// In addition the following passage should be noted:

* "The only productive consumption, properly so called, is the consumption and destruction of wealth by capitalists with a view to reproduction... The workman whom the capitalist employs certainly consumes that part of his wages which he does not save, as revenue, with a view to subsistence and enjoyment; and not as capital, with a view to production. *He is a productive consumer to the person who employs him,* and to the state, *but not, strictly speaking, to himself"* * (*Definitions*, ED. by Cazenove, [p.] 30).//

Accumulation.

* "No political economist of the present day can by *saving* mean mere hoarding; and beyond this contracted and inefficient proceeding, no use of the term in reference to the national wealth can well be imagined, but that which must arise from a different application of what is saved, founded upon a real distinction between the different kinds of labour maintained by it" (*Principles of Political Economy*, [2nd ed., pp.] 38-39).

"*Accumulation of Capital*: the employment of a portion of revenue as capital. *Capital may therefore increase without an increase of stock or wealth* (*Definitions*, ED. by Cazenove, [p.] 11).

"Prudential habits with regard to marriage carried to a considerable extent, among the labouring classes of a country mainly depending upon manufactures and commerce, *might injure it"* * (*Principles of Political Economy*, [2nd ed., p.] 215).

This from the preacher of CHECKS against overpopulation.

* "It is the *want of necessaries* which mainly stimulates the working classes to produce luxuries; and were this stimulus removed or greatly weakened, so that the necessaries of life could be obtained with very little labour, instead of more time being devoted to the production of conveniences, there is every reason to think that less time would be so devoted" * (*Principles of Political Economy*, [2nd ed., p.] 334).

Most important for the exponent of overpopulation, however, is this passage:

* "From the nature of a population, an increase of labourers cannot be brought into the market, in consequence of a particular demand, till after the lapse of 16 or 18 years, and the conversion of revenue into capital by saving, may take place much more rapidly: a *country is always liable to an increase in the quantity of the funds* for the maintenance of labour faster than the increase of population" * (l.c., [pp.] 319-20).

[XIII-765] *Cazenove* rightly remarks:

* "When capital is employed in *advancing to the workman his wages, it adds nothing to the funds for the maintenance of labour*, but simply consists in the application of a certain proportion of those funds already in existence, for the purposes of production"* (*Definitions in Political Economy*, [ed. by Cazenove, p.] 22, note).

CONSTANT AND VARIABLE CAPITAL

"*ACCUMULATED LABOUR*" (it should really be called MATERIALISED LABOUR, objectified labour): * "the labour worked up in the raw materials and tools applied to the production of other commodities" (*Definitions in Political Economy*, ed. by Cazenove, [p.] 13).

"The labour worked up in commodities, the labour worked up in the capital necessary to their production should be designated by the term *accumulated labour*, as contradistinguished from the *immediate labour employed by the last capitalist*" * (l.c., [pp.] 28[-29]).

It is indeed very important to make this distinction. In Malthus, however, it leads to nothing.

He does make an attempt to reduce the SURPLUS VALUE or AT LEAST ITS RATE (which, by the way, he always confuses with PROFIT and RATE OF PROFIT) to its relation to variable capital, that part of capital which is expended on IMMEDIATE LABOUR. This attempt, however, is childish and could not be otherwise in view of his conception of VALUE. In his *Principles of Political Economy*, he says:

"Suppose that capital is wholly expended in wages. £100 EXPENDED IN IMMEDIATE LABOUR. The RETURNS at the end of the year 110, 120, or 130; IT IS EVIDENT THAT IN EACH CASE THE PROFITS WILL BE *DETERMINED BY THE PROPORTION OF THE VALUE OF THE WHOLE PRODUCE WHICH IS REQUIRED TO PAY THE LABOUR EMPLOYED.* IF THE VALUE OF THE PRODUCE IN [the] MARKET=110, the PROPORTION REQUIRED TO PAY THE LABOURERS=$10/11$ of the VALUE of the PRODUCE, and PROFITS=10%. If the value of the produce be 120, the proportion for LABOUR=$10/12$, and profits 20%; if 130, the PROPORTION REQUIRED TO PAY THE LABOUR ADVANCED=$10/13$, and PROFITS=30%. Now suppose that the ADVANCES of the CAPITALIST do not consist of LABOUR alone. *The capitalist expects an equal profit upon all the parts of the capital which he advances.* Assume that $1/4$ of his ADVANCES [are] for (IMMEDIATE) LABOUR, [and] $3/4$ consist of ACCUMULATED LABOUR and PROFITS, with ANY ADDITIONS WHICH MAY ARISE from RENTS, TAXES and other OUTGOINGS. Then [it will be] STRICTLY TRUE THAT *THE PROFITS OF THE CAPITALIST WILL VARY WITH THE VARYING VALUE of this $1/4$ of his PRODUCE COMPARED WITH THE QUANTITY OF LABOUR EMPLOYED.* As an instance let us suppose that a FARMER employs in the CULTIVATION £2,000, 1,500 of which [he expends] IN SEED, KEEP OF HORSES, WEAR AND TEAR OF HIS FIXED CAPITAL, INTEREST UPON HIS FIXED AND CIRCULATING CAPITALS, RENTS, TITHES, TAXES, etc., and £500 on IMMEDIATE LABOUR; and [that] the RETURNS [obtained] at the end of the year are worth 2,400. His profits [will be] 400 on 2,000=20%. It is straight away OBVIOUS *THAT IF WE TOOK $1/4$ OF THE VALUE OF THE PRODUCE, namely £600, and COMPARED IT WITH*

THE AMOUNT PAID IN THE WAGES OF IMMEDIATE LABOUR, THE RESULT WOULD SHOW EXACTLY THE SAME RATE OF PROFITS" ([2nd ed., pp.] 267-68).[a]

Here Malthus lapses into LORD DUNDREARYISM.[61] What he wants to do (he has an inkling that SURPLUS VALUE, HENCE profit, has a definite relation to variable capital, the portion of capital expended on wages) is to show THAT "PROFITS ARE DETERMINATED BY THE PROPORTION OF THE VALUE OF THE WHOLE PRODUCE WHICH IS REQUIRED TO PAY THE LABOUR EMPLOYED". He begins correctly in so far as he assumes that the whole of the capital consists of variable capital, capital expended on wages. In this case, profit and SURPLUS VALUE are in fact identical. But even in this case he confines himself to a very SILLY REFLECTION. If the capital expended equals 100 and the profit is 10%, the value of the product is, accordingly, 110 and the profit is $\frac{1}{10}$ of the capital expended (HENCE 10% if calculated on the capital), and $\frac{1}{11}$ of the value of the total product, in the value of which its own value is included. Thus profit constitutes $\frac{1}{11}$ of the value of the total product and the capital expended forms $\frac{10}{11}$ of this value. In relation to the total, 10% profit can be so expressed that the part of the value of the total product which is not made up of profit=$\frac{10}{11}$ of the total product; or, a product of 110 which includes 10% profit consists of $\frac{10}{11}$ outlay, on which the profit is made. This brilliant mathematical effort amuses him so much that he repeats the same calculation using a profit of 20%, 30%, etc. But so far we have merely a tautology. The profit is a PERCENTAGE on the capital expended, the value of the total product includes the value of the profit and the capital expended [XIII-766] is the value of the total product—the value of the profit. Thus 110−10=100. And 100 is $\frac{10}{11}$ of 110. But let us proceed.

Let us assume a capital consisting not merely of variable but also of constant capital. "The capitalist expects an equal profit upon all the parts of the capital which he advances." This however contradicts the proposition advanced above that profit (it should be called SURPLUS VALUE) is determined by the proportion of the capital expended on wages. BUT NEVER MIND. Malthus is not the man to contradict either the "expectations" or the notions of "the capitalist". But now comes his *tour de force.* Assume a capital of [£]2,000, $\frac{3}{4}$ of which or 1,500 is constant capital, $\frac{1}{4}$, or 500, is variable capital. The profit=20%. Thus the profit=400 and the value of the product=2,000+400=2,400. But 600:400=$66\frac{2}{3}$. The value of the total product=1,000 and the part laid out in wages=$\frac{6}{10}$ of this. But what about Mr. Malthus' calculation? If one takes $\frac{1}{4}$ of the total product, it=600; $\frac{1}{4}$ of the capital

---

[a] Marx quotes Malthus with alterations.— *Ed.*

expended=500=the portion expended on wages; and 100=$^1/_4$ of the profit=that part of the profit falling to this amount of wages. And this is supposed to prove "THAT THE PROFITS OF THE CAPITALIST WILL VARY WITH THE VARYING VALUE of this $^1/_4$ of his produce COMPARED WITH THE QUANTITY OF LABOUR EMPLOYED".[62] It proves nothing more than that a profit of a given PERCENTAGE, e.g. of 20%, on a given capital—say of 4,000—yields a profit of 20% on each aliquot part of the capital; that is a tautology. But it proves absolutely nothing about a definite, *special*, distinguishing relationship of this profit to the part of the capital expended on wages. If, instead of [$^1/_4$] taken by Mr. Malthus, I take $^1/_{24}$ of the total product, i.e. 100 (out of 2,400), then this 100 contains 20% profit, or $^1/_6$ of it is profit. The capital would be [£]$83^1/_3$ and the profit [£]$16^2/_3$. If the $83^1/_3$ were equal, for instance, to a horse which was employed in production, then it could be demonstrated according to Malthus' recipe that the profit would VARY WITH THE VARYING VALUE of the horse or the $28^4/_5$ part of the total product.

Such are the *misères*[a] Mr. Malthus comes out with when he stands on his own feet and cannot plagiarise Townsend, Anderson or anyone else. What is really remarkable and pertinent (apart from what is characteristic of the man) is the inkling that SURPLUS VALUE must be calculated on the part of capital expended on wages.

// Given a definite rate of profit, the GROSS PROFIT, the amount of profit, always depends on the size of the capital advanced. Accumulation, however, is then determined by the part of this amount which is reconverted into capital. But this part, since it=the gross profit—the REVENUE consumed by the capitalist, will depend not only on the value of this amount, but on the cheapness of the commodities which the capitalist can buy with it; partly on the cheapness of the commodities which he consumes and which he pays for out of his REVENUE, partly on the cheapness of the commodities which enter into his constant capital. Wages here are assumed as given—since the rate of profit is likewise assumed as given. //

MALTHUS' THEORY OF VALUE

The value of labour is supposed not to vary (derived from Adam Smith[b]) but only the value of the commodities I acquire for it. Wages are, say, 2s. a day in one case, 1s. in another. In the first

---

[a] Wretched things.— *Ed.*

[b] See A. Smith, *An Inquiry into the Nature and Causes of the Wealth of Nations,* Vol. I, Edinburgh, 1814, pp. 48-50, and this volume, pp. 221-22.— *Ed.*

case, the capitalist pays out twice as many shillings for the same labour time as in the second. But in the 2nd case, the worker performs twice as much labour for the same product as in the first, since in the 2nd [case] he works a whole day for 1s. and in the first case only half a day. Mr. Malthus believes that the capitalist pays sometimes more shillings, sometimes less, for the same labour. He does not see that the worker, correspondingly, performs either less or more labour for a given amount of produce.

* "Giving more produce for a given quantity of labour, or getting more labour for a given quantity of produce, are one and the same thing in his" (Malthus') "'view'; instead of being, as one would have supposed, just the contrary" * (*Observations on Certain Verbal Disputes in Political Economy, Particularly Relating to Value, and to Demand and Supply,* London, 1821, [p.] 52).

It is stated very correctly, in the same work (*Observations on Certain Verbal Disputes etc.,* London, 1821) that labour as a measure of value, in the sense in which Malthus borrows it from Adam Smith, would be just as good a measure of value as any other commodity and that it would not be so good a measure as money in fact is. Here it would be in general a question only of a measure of value in the sense in which money is a measure of value.

[XIII-767] In general, it is never the *measure of value* (in the sense of money) which makes commodities commensurable (see Part I of my book, p. 45[a]):

"On the contrary, it is only the commensurability of commodities as objectified labour time which converts gold into money."

Commodities as values constitute one *substance,* they are mere representations of the same substance—social labour. The *measure of value* (money) presupposes them as values and refers solely to the expression and size of this value. The *measure of value* of commodities always refers to the transformation of value into price and already presumes the value. The passage in the *Observations* ALLUDED to reads as follows:

* "Mr. Malthus says: 'In the *same* place, and at the *same* time, the different quantities of day-labour, which different commodities can command, will be exactly in proportion to their relative values in exchange',[b] and vice versa. If this is true of labour, it is just as true of any thing else" (l.c., [p.] 49). "Money does very well as a measure at the same time and place... But it" (Malthus' proposition) "seems *not* to be true of labour. Labour is not a measure even at the same time and place. Take a

---

[a] K. Marx, *A Contribution to the Critique of Political Economy.* Part One (present edition, Vol. 29, pp. 306-07).— *Ed.*

[b] T. R. Malthus, *Principles of Political Economy...,* London, 1820, p. 121.— *Ed.*

portion of corn, such as is at the same time and place said to be of equal value with a given diamond; will the corn and the diamond, paid in specie, command equal portions of labour? It may be said, No; but the diamond will buy *money,* which will command an equal portion of labour ... the test is of no use, for it cannot be applied without being *rectified* by the application of the other test, which it professed to supersede. We can only infer, that the corn and the diamond will command equal quantities of labour, *because* they are of equal value, in money. But we were told to infer, that two things were of equal value, because they would command equal quantities of labour" * (l.c., [pp. 49-]50).

OVERPRODUCTION. *"UNPRODUCTIVE CONSUMERS"*, ETC.

Malthus' theory of value gives rise to the whole doctrine of the necessity for continually rising unproductive consumption which this exponent of overpopulation (because of shortage of means of subsistence) preaches so energetically. The value of a commodity=the value of the materials, machinery, etc., advanced+the quantity of direct labour which the commodity contains; this, according to Malthus, =the *value* of the WAGES contained in the commodity+a price increment on these advances according to the GENERAL RATE OF PROFITS. This nominal price increment represents the profit and is a condition of SUPPLY, that is, the reproduction of the commodity. These elements constitute the PRICE FOR THE PURCHASER as distinct from the PRICE FOR THE PRODUCER, and the PRICE FOR THE PURCHASER is the real value of the commodity. The question now arises — how is this price to be realised? Who is to pay it? And from what funds is it to be paid?

In dealing with Malthus we must make a distinction (which he has neglected to make). One section of capitalists produce goods which are *directly* consumed by the workers; another section produce either goods which are *only indirectly* consumed by them, in so far, for example, as they are part of the capital required for the production of NECESSARIES, as raw materials, machinery, etc., or commodities which *are not consumed* by the workers *at all,* entering only into the REVENUE of the non-workers.

Let us first of all consider the capitalists who produce the articles which are consumed by the workers. These capitalists are not only buyers of labour, but also sellers of their own products to the workers. If the quantity of labour contributed by the worker is valued at 100 thaler the capitalist pays him 100 thaler. And this is the only value added to the raw material, etc., by the labour which the capitalist has bought. Thus the worker receives the value of his labour and only gives the capitalist an equivalent of that value IN RETURN. But although the worker nominally receives the value, he actually receives a smaller quantity of commodities than he has

16*

produced. In fact, he receives back only a part of his labour objectified in the product. Let us assume for the sake of simplicity—as Malthus does quite frequently—that capital consists only of capital laid out in wages. If 100 thaler are advanced to the worker in order to produce commodities, and these 100 thaler are the *value* of the labour purchased and the sole value which it adds to the product—then the capitalist sells these commodities for 110 thaler, and the worker, with his 100 thaler, can buy back only $^{10}/_{11}$ of the product; $^{1}/_{11}$ remains in the hands of the capitalist, to the value of 10 thaler, or the amount of surplus produce in which this surplus value of 10 thaler is embodied. If the capitalist sells the product for 120, then the worker receives only $^{10}/_{12}$ and the capitalist $^{2}/_{12}$ of the product and its value. If he sells it for 130 (30%), then the worker [receives] only $^{10}/_{13}$ and the capitalist $^{3}/_{13}$ of the product. If he sells it at 50% profit, i.e. for 150, the worker receives $^{2}/_{3}$ and the [XIII-768] capitalist $^{1}/_{3}$ of the product. The higher the price at which the capitalist sells, the lower the share of the worker, and the higher his own share in the value of the product and therefore also in the quantity of the product. And the less the worker can buy back of the value or of the product with the value of his labour. It makes no difference to the situation if, in addition to variable capital, constant capital is also advanced, for example, if, in addition to the 100 thaler wages, there is another 100 for raw materials, etc. In this case, if the rate of profit is 10, then the capitalist sells the goods for 220 instead of for 210 (namely, 100 constant capital and 120 the product of labour).

// Sismondi's *Nouveaux principes etc.* first published in 1819.[a] // Here, as regards the *class of capitalists A,* who produce articles which are directly consumed by the workers—necessaries, we have a case where as a result of the nominal surcharge—the normal profit increment added to the price of the advances—a surplus fund is in fact created for the capitalist, since, in this roundabout way, he gives back to the worker only a part of his product while appropriating a part for himself. But this result follows not because he sells the entire product to the worker at the increased value, but precisely because the increase in the value of the product makes the worker unable to buy back the whole product with his wages, and allows him to buy back only part of it. Consequently, it is clear that demand by the workers can never suffice for the realisation of the surplus of the purchase price over and above the cost price,[63] i.e. the realisation of the profit and the

---

"value" of the commodity. On the contrary, a profit fund only exists because the worker is unable to buy back his whole product with his WAGES, and his DEMAND, therefore, does not correspond to the SUPPLY. Thus capitalist A has in hand a certain quantity of products of a certain value, 20 thaler in the present case, which he does not require for the replacement of the capital, and which he can now partly spend as REVENUE, and partly use for accumulation. N.B. The extent to which he has such a fund in hand depends on the value of the surcharge he adds over and above the COST PRICE and which determines the proportions in which he and the worker share the total product.

Let us now turn to the class of capitalists B, who supply raw materials, machinery, etc., in short constant capital, to class A. The class B can sell *only* to class A, for they cannot sell their products back to the workers WHO HAVE NOTHING TO DO WITH capital (RAW MATERIAL, MACHINERY, etc.), or to the capitalists who produce luxury goods (all goods which are not NECESSARIES and which are not IN THE COMMON USE OF THE LABOURING CLASS), or to the capitalists who produce the constant capital required for the production of luxury goods.

Now we have seen that, in the capital advanced by A, 100 is included as constant capital. If the rate of profit=10%, the manufacturer of this constant capital has produced it at a cost price of $90^{10}/_{11}$, but sells it for 100 ($90^{10}/_{11}:9^{1}/_{11}=100:10$). Thus he makes his profit by imposing a SURCHARGE on class A. And thereby he receives from their product of 220 his 100 instead of only $90^{10}/_{11}$, with which, we will assume, he buys IMMEDIATE LABOUR. B does not by any means make his profit from his workers whose product, valued at $90^{10}/_{11}$, he cannot sell back to them for 100, because they do not buy his goods at all. Nevertheless, they are in the same position as the workers of A. For $90^{10}/_{11}$ they receive a quantity of goods which has only nominally a value of $90^{10}/_{11}$, for every part of A's product is made uniformly dearer, or each part of its value represents a smaller part of the product because of the profit surcharge. (This surcharging can only be carried out up to a certain point, for the worker must receive enough goods to be able to live and to reproduce his labour capacity. If capitalist A were to add a surcharge of 100% and to sell commodity which costs 200 for 400, the worker would be able to buy back only $^{1}/_{4}$ of the product (if he receives 100). And if he needed half of the product in order to live, the capitalist would have to pay him 200. Thus he would retain only 100 (100 go to constant capital and 200 to wages). It would therefore be the same as if he sold [the commodity] for 300, etc.)

B makes his profit fund not (directly) through his workers, but through his sales to A. A's product not only serves to realise his profit, but constitutes his own profit fund. It is clear that A cannot realise the profit he makes on his workers by selling to B, and that B cannot provide SUFFICIENT DEMAND for his product (enabling him to sell it at its value) any more than his own workers can. On the contrary, a retroaction takes place here. [XIII-769] The more he raises the profit surcharge, the greater, in relation to his workers, is the portion of the total product which he appropriates and of which he deprives B.

B adds a surcharge of the same size as A. B pays his workers $90^{10}/_{11}$ thaler as he did before, although they get less goods for this sum. But if A takes 20% instead of 10, he [B] likewise takes 20% instead of 10 and sells for $109^{1}/_{11}$ instead of 100. As a result, this part of the outlay increases for A.

A and B may even be considered as a single class. (B belongs to A's expenditure and the more A has to pay to B from the total product, the less remains for him.) Out of the capital of 200, *B* owns $90^{10}/_{11}$ and *A 100.* Between them they expend $190^{10}/_{11}$ and make a profit of $19^{1}/_{11}$. B can never buy back from A to the tune of more than 100 and this includes his profit of $9^{1}/_{11}$. As stated, both of them together have a REVENUE of $19^{1}/_{11}$.

As far as *classes C and D* are concerned, C being the capitalists who produce the constant capital necessary for the production of LUXURIES, and D being those who directly produce the LUXURIES, in the first place it is clear that the IMMEDIATE DEMAND for C is ONLY FORMED by D. D is the PURCHASER of C. And C can only realise profit if he sells his goods to D too dearly by means of a nominal surcharge over and above the cost price. D must pay C more than is necessary for C to REPLACE ALL THE INGREDIENTS OF his COMMODITIES. D for his part makes a profit surcharge partly on the advances made by C and partly on the capital expended directly on wages by D. From the profits which C makes out of D, he can buy some of the commodities made by D, although he cannot expend all his profit in this way, for he also needs NECESSARIES for himself, and not only for workers for whom he exchanges the capital realised from D. In the first place, the realisation of the commodities by C depends directly on their SALE to D; secondly, after THAT SALE is EFFECTED, the value of the commodities sold by D cannot be realised as a result of the DEMAND arising from C's profit, any more than [the total value of A's commodities can be realised] as a result of the DEMAND coming from B. For the profit made by C is made out of D, and if C spends it again on commodities made by D instead of on others, his demand can still never be greater than the profit he makes out of D. It must always be much smaller than C's capital, than his total DEMAND, and it never constitutes a SOURCE of profit for D (the most he can do is a little swindling of C by means of the surcharge on the commodities he sells back to him) for C's profit comes straight out of D's pocket.

Further it is clear that, in so far as the capitalists—whether of class C or of D—mutually sell each other commodities within each class, nobody gains anything or realises a profit thereby. A certain capitalist, *m*, sells to *n* for 110 [thaler] commodities which cost only 100, but *n* does the same to *m*. After the exchange as before, each of them owns a quantity of goods the cost price of which is 100. For 110 each receives goods which cost only 100. The surcharge gives him no greater command over the commodities of the other seller than it gives the other over his. And as far as value is concerned, it would be the same as if every *m* and *n* were to give himself the pleasure of baptising his commodities 110 instead of 100 without exchanging them at all.

It is clear further that the nominal SURPLUS VALUE in D (for C is included in it) does not constitute real SURPLUS PRODUCE. The fact that the worker receives less NECESSARIES for 100 thaler because of the surcharge imposed by A can, at first, be a matter of indifference to D. He has to expend 100 as he did before in order to employ a certain number of workers. He pays the workers the value of their labour and they add nothing more to the product, they only give him an equivalent. He can obtain a surplus over and above this equivalent only by selling to a third person and by selling his commodity above the COST PRICE. In reality, the product of a mirror manufacturer contains both SURPLUS VALUE and SURPLUS PRODUCE just as that of the FARMER. For the product contains unpaid labour (SURPLUS VALUE) and this unpaid labour is embodied in the product just as much as is the paid [labour]. It is embodied in SURPLUS PRODUCE. One part of the mirrors costs him nothing although it has value, because labour is embodied in it in exactly the same way as in that part of the mirrors which replaces the capital advanced. This SURPLUS VALUE exists as SURPLUS PRODUCE *before* the sale of the mirrors and is not [brought into being] only through this sale. If, on the contrary, the worker by his IMMEDIATE labour had only provided an equivalent for the ACCUMULATED LABOUR which he received in the form of WAGES, then neither [XIII-770] [64] the [surplus] PRODUCE nor the SURPLUS VALUE corresponding to it would exist. But according to Malthus, who declares that the worker only gives back an equivalent, things [are] different.

[It is clear] that class D (including C) cannot artificially create for itself a SURPLUS fund in the same way as class A, namely, [by] selling its commodities back to the workers at a higher price than the workers were paid for producing them, thus appropriating part of the total product after replacing the capital expended. For the workers are not buyers of the commodities made by D. No more can the SURPLUS fund of this class [arise] from the sale of commodities or their mutual exchanges. It can be achieved only by the sale of its product to class A and to class B. [Because] the capitalists of class D sell commodities worth 100 for 110, capitalist A can buy only $^{10}/_{11}$ of their product for 100 and they retain $^{1}/_{11}$ of their output, which they can either consume themselves or exchange for commodities produced by [other members of] their own class D.

[According to Malthus] things happen in the following way to all capitalists who do not themselves directly produce NECESSARIES and therefore [do not] sell back to the workers the major, or at least a significant, portion of their products.

Let us say that their (constant) capital = 100. If the capitalist pays another 100 in wages, he is paying the workers the value of their labour. To this 100 the workers add a value of 100, and the total value (the COST PRICE) of the product is therefore 200. Where then does the profit come from? If the AVERAGE RATE OF PROFIT = 10%, then the capitalist sells commodities worth 200 for 220. If he really sells them for 220, then it is clear that 200 is sufficient for their reproduction — 100 for raw materials, etc., 100 for wages, and he pockets 20, which he can dispose of as REVENUE or use to accumulate capital.

But to whom does he sell the commodities at 10% above their "production value", which, according to Malthus, is different from the "sale value" or real value, so that profit, in fact, is equal to the difference between production value and sale value, is equal to sale value − production value? These capitalists cannot realise any profit through exchange or sale amongst themselves. If A sells B for 220 commodities worth 200, then B plays the same trick on A. The fact that these commodities change hands does not alter either their value or their quantity. The quantity of commodities which belonged formerly to A is now in the possession of B, and vice versa. The fact that what was previously 100 is now called 110, makes no difference. The PURCHASING POWER EITHER OF A OR OF B has in no way altered.

But, according to the hypothesis, these capitalists cannot sell their commodities to the workers.

They must, therefore, sell them to the capitalists who produce NECESSARIES. These, indeed, have a real SURPLUS fund at their disposal resulting from their exchange with the workers. The creation of a nominal SURPLUS VALUE has, in fact, placed SURPLUS PRODUCE in their possession. And this is the only SURPLUS fund which has existed up to now. The other capitalists can only acquire a SURPLUS fund by selling their commodities above their production value to those capitalists who possess a SURPLUS fund.

As for the capitalists who produce the constant capital required for the production of NECESSARIES, we have already seen that the producer of NECESSARIES must perforce buy from them. These PURCHASES enter into his production costs. The higher his profit, the dearer are the advances to which the same rate of profit is added. If he sells at 20% instead of at 10, then the producer of his constant capital likewise adds 20% instead of 10. And instead of demanding 100 for $90^{10}/_{11}$, he demands $109^1/_{11}$ or, in round figures, 110, so that the value of the product is now 210, 20% of which=42, so that the value of the whole product=252. Out of this the worker receives 100. The capitalist now receives more than $^1/_{11}$ of the total product as profit, whereas previously he received only $^1/_{11}$ when he sold the product for 220. The total amount of the product has remained the same, but the portion at the disposal of the capitalist has increased both in value and in quantity.

As for those capitalists who produce neither NECESSARIES nor the capital required for their production, their profit [can] only be made by sales to the first two classes of capitalists. If the latter take 20%, then the other capitalists will take [the same].

[Exchange by] the first class of capitalists and exchange between the two classes of capitalists are, however, two very different things. [As a result of exchange] with the workers, the first class has established a real SURPLUS fund of NECESSARIES, SURPLUS PRODUCE, [which as an increment] of capital is in their hands to dispose of, so that they can accumulate part of it and [spend] part of it [as revenue] either on NECESSARIES or on LUXURIES. SURPLUS VALUE here, in fact, [represents] [XIV-771][65] SURPLUS labour and SURPLUS PRODUCE, although this is achieved by the CLUMSY, roundabout method of a SURCHARGE on prices. Let us assume that the value of the product of the workers producing NECESSARIES, in fact, only=100. Since, however, $^{10}/_{11}$ of this is sufficient to pay the wages, it follows that the capitalist only needs to spend $90^{10}/_{11}$, upon which he makes a profit of $9^1/_{11}$. But if he pays the workers £100 and sells them the product for 110, under the illusion that value of labour and quantity of labour are identical, he still retains $^1/_{11}$ of the product as he did previously. The fact that this is now worth £10 instead of $9^1/_{11}$ represents no gain for him, for he has now advanced 100 as capital, not $90^{10}/_{11}$.

But as far as the other classes of capitalists are concerned, they have no real SURPLUS PRODUCE, nothing in which surplus labour time is embodied. They sell the product of labour worth 100 for 110 and merely by the addition of a surcharge this capital is supposed to be transformed into capital+REVENUE.

BUT HOW STANDS THE CASE NOW, AS LORD DUNDREARY [61] WOULD SAY, BETWEEN THESE TWO CLASSES OF CAPITALISTS?

The producers of NECESSARIES sell SURPLUS PRODUCT [66] valued at 100 for 110 (because they paid 100 in wages instead of $90^{10}/_{11}$). But they are the only ones who have SURPLUS PRODUCE in their possession. If the other capitalists likewise sell them products valued at 100 for 110, then they do in fact replace their capital and make a profit. Why? Because NECESSARIES to the value of 100 suffice for them to pay their workers, they can therefore keep 10 for themselves. Or rather because they in fact receive NECESSARIES to the value of 100, but $^{10}/_{11}$ of this is sufficient to pay their workers, since they are in the same position as capitalists in classes A and B. These, on the other hand, receive IN RETURN only an amount of produce representing a value of 100. The fact that its nominal cost is 110 is of no significance to them, for it neither embodies a greater amount quantitatively, as use value, than was produced by the labour time contained in the £100, nor can it add 10 to a capital of 100. This would be only possible if the commodities were resold. Although the capitalists of both classes sell to one another for 110 [commodities] worth 100, only in the hands of the second class has 100 really the significance of 110. In actual fact, the capitalists of the other class only receive the value of 100 for 110. And they only sell their SURPLUS PRODUCE for a higher price because for the articles on which they spend their REVENUE they have to pay *more* than they are worth. In fact, however, the SURPLUS VALUE realised by the capitalists of the 2nd class is limited only to a share in the SURPLUS PRODUCE realised by the first class, for they themselves do not create any SURPLUS PRODUCE.

In connection with this increased cost of LUXURIES, it occurs just in time to Malthus that ACCUMULATION and not EXPENDITURE is the immediate object of capitalist production. As a result of this unprofitable trade, in the course of which the capitalists of class A lose a portion of the fruits wrung out of the workers, they are compelled to moderate their demand for LUXURIES. But if they do so, and increase their accumulation, then effective demand falls, the market for the NECESSARIES they produce shrinks, and this market cannot expand to its full extent on the basis of the demand on the part of the workers and the producers of constant capital. This leads to a fall in the price of NECESSARIES, but it is only through a rise of these prices, through the nominal surcharge on them—and in proportion to this surcharge—that the capitalists of class A are able to extract SURPLUS PRODUCE from the workers. If the price were to fall from 120 to 110, then their SURPLUS PRODUCE (and their SURPLUS VALUE) would fall from $^2/_{12}$ to $^1/_{11}$, and consequently the market, the demand for [the commodities offered by] the producers of LUXURIES, would decline as well, and by a still greater proportion.

In the course of exchange with the second class, the first class sells real SURPLUS PRODUCE after having replaced its capital. The second [class], on the other hand, merely sells its capital in order to turn its capital into capital+REVENUE by this trade. The whole of production is thus only kept going (and this is especially the case with regard to its expansion) by means of *increasing the prices of NECESSARIES*; to this, however, would correspond a price for LUXURIES in inverse proportion to the amount of luxuries actually produced. Class II, which sells for 110 commodities of the value of 100, likewise does not gain by this exchange. For in actual fact, the 110 which it gets back is also only worth 100. But this 100 (in NECESSARIES) replaces capital+profit, while the other 100 [in luxuries] is merely called 110. Thus [it would] amount to class I receiving LUXURIES to the value of 100. It buys for 110 LUXURIES to the value of 100. For the other class, however, 110 is worth 110, because it pays 100 for the labour (thus replacing its capital) and therefore retains a surplus of 10.

[XIV-772] It is difficult to understand how any profit at all can be derived if those who engage in mutual exchange sell their commodities by overcharging one another at the same rate and cheating one another in the same proportion.

This incongruity would be remedied if, in addition to exchange by one class of capitalists with its workers and the mutual exchange between the capitalists of the different classes, there also existed a *third class of purchasers*—a *deus ex machina*[a]—a class which

---

[a] Literally: a god from a machine (in the classical theatre the actors playing gods appeared on the stage with the help of some special gear); figuratively speaking: a person that appears suddenly and unexpectedly and provides a solution to an apparently insoluble difficulty.— *Ed.*

paid the nominal value of commodities without itself selling any commodities, without itself playing the same trick in return; that is, a class which transacted $M-C$, but not $M-C-M$; [a class] which bought not in order to get its capital back plus a profit, but in order to consume the commodities; a class which bought without selling. In this case the capitalists would realise a profit not by exchange amongst themselves but 1) by exchange between them and the workers, by selling back to them a portion of the total product for the same amount of money as they paid the workers for the total product (after deducting the constant capital) and 2) from the portion of NECESSARIES as well as LUXURIES sold to the 3rd sort of purchaser. Since these pay 110 for 100 without selling 100 for 110 in their turn, a profit of 10% would be made in actual fact and not simply nominally. The profit would be made in dual fashion by selling as little as possible of the total product back to the workers and as much as possible to the 3rd class, who pay ready money, who, without themselves selling, buy in order to consume. But buyers who are not at the same time sellers, must be consumers who are not at the same time producers, that is *unproductive consumers,* and it is this class of unproductive consumers which, according to Malthus, solves the problem. But these unproductive consumers must, at the same time, be consumers able to pay, constituting REAL DEMAND, and the money they possess and spend annually must, moreover, suffice to pay not only the production value of the commodities they buy and consume, but also the nominal profit surcharge, the surplus value, the difference between the sale value and the production value. This class will represent consumption for consumption's sake in society, in the same way as the capitalist class represents production for production's sake, the one representing "the PASSION FOR EXPENDITURE", the other "the PASSION FOR ACCUMULATION" (*Principles of Political Economy,* [2nd ed., p.] 326). The urge for accumulation is kept alive in the capitalist class by the fact that their RETURNS are constantly larger than their outlays, and profit is indeed the stimulus to accumulation. In spite of this enthusiasm for accumulation, they are not driven to overproduction, or at least, not at all easily, since the UNPRODUCTIVE CONSUMERS not only constitute a gigantic outlet for the products thrown on to the market, but do not themselves throw any commodities on to the market, and therefore, no matter how numerous they may be, they constitute no competition for the capitalists, but, on the contrary, all represent demand without supply and thus help to make up for the preponderance of supply over demand on the part of the capitalists. But where do the annual financial resources of this class come from? There are, in the first place, the *landed proprietors,* who collect a great part of the value of the annual product under the title of rent and spend the money thus taken from the capitalists in consuming the commodities produced by the capitalists, in the purchase of which they are cheated. These landed proprietors do not have to engage in production and do not ON AN AVERAGE do so. It is significant, that in so far as they spend money on labour, they do not employ productive workers but MENIAL SERVANTS, mere fellow-consumers of their FORTUNE, who help to keep the prices of NECESSARIES up, since they buy without helping to increase their SUPPLY or the supply of any other kind of commodity. But these landed proprietors do not suffice to create "AN ADEQUATE DEMAND". Artificial means must be resorted to. These consist of heavy *taxation,* of a mass of sinecurists in State and Church, of large armies, pensions, tithes for the priests, an impressive national debt, and from time to time, expensive wars. These are the "remedies" (*Principles of Political Economy,* [2nd ed., p.] 408 et seq.).

The 3rd class, proposed by Malthus as a "remedy", the class which buys without selling and consumes without producing, thus receives first of all an important part of the value of the annual product without *paying for it* and enriches the producers by the fact that the latter must first of all advance the third class money gratis for the purchase of their commodities, in order [XIV-773] to draw it back again by selling the third class commodities above their value, or by receiving more value in money than is embodied in the commodities they supply to this class. And this transaction is repeated every year.

Malthus correctly draws the conclusions from his basic theory of value. But this theory, for its part, suits his purpose remarkably well—an apologia for the existing state of affairs in England, for LANDLORDISM, "STATE AND CHURCH", PENSIONERS, TAX-GATHERERS, TENTHS, NATIONAL DEBT, STOCK-JOBBERS, BEADLES, PARSONS AND MENIAL SERVANTS ("NATION-AL EXPENDITURE") assailed by the RICARDIANS as so many useless and SUPERANNUATED DRAWBACKS of bourgeois production and as NUISANCES. *Quand même,*[a] Ricardo championed bourgeois production in so far as it [signified] the most unrestricted development of the social productive forces, unconcerned for the fate of those who participate in production, be they capitalists or workers. He insisted upon the *historical* justification and necessity of this stage

---

[a] For all that.— *Ed.*

of development. His very lack of a historical sense of the past meant that he regarded everything from the historical standpoint of his time. Malthus also wishes to see the freest possible development of capitalist production, however only in so far as the condition of this development is the poverty of its main basis, the working classes, but at the same time he wants it to adapt itself to the "consumption needs" of the aristocracy and its branches in State and Church, to serve as the material basis for the antiquated claims of the representatives of interests inherited from feudalism and the absolute monarchy. Malthus wants bourgeois production as long as it is not revolutionary, constitutes no historical factor of development but merely creates a broader and more comfortable material basis for the "old" society.

On the one hand, therefore, [there is] the working class, which, according to the population principle, is always REDUNDANT in relation to the means of subsistence available to it, over-population arising from underproduction; then [there is] the capitalist class, which, as a result of this population principle, is always able to sell the workers' own product back to them at such prices that they can only obtain enough to keep body and soul together; then [there is] an enormous section of society consisting of parasites and gluttonous drones, some of them masters and some servants, who appropriate, partly under the title of rent and partly under political titles, a considerable mass of wealth gratis from the capitalists, whose commodities they pay for above their value with money extracted from these same capitalists; the capitalist class, driven into production by the urge for accumulation, the economically unproductive sections representing prodigality, the mere urge for consumption. This is moreover [advanced as] the only way to avoid overproduction, which exists alongside over-population in relation to production. The [best][a] remedy for both [is declared to be] overconsumption by the classes standing outside production. The disproportion between the labouring population and production is eliminated by part of the product being devoured by non-producers and idlers. The disproportion arising from overproduction by the capitalists [is eliminated] by means of overconsumption by those who enjoy wealth.

We have seen how childishly weak, trivial and meaningless Malthus is when, basing himself on the weak side of Adam Smith, he seeks to construct a counter-theory to Ricardo's theory, which is

---

[a] The word is illegible in the manuscript. It may also read "ultimate" ("letztes").— Ed.

based on Adam Smith's stronger sides.[a] One can hardly find a more comical exertion of impotence than Malthus' book on value.[b] However, as soon as he comes to practical conclusions and thereby once again enters the field which he occupies as a kind of economic Abraham a Santa Clara, he is QUITE AT HIS EASE. For all that, he does not abandon his innate plagiarism even here. Who at first glance would believe that Malthus' *Principles of Political Economy* is simply the Malthusianised translation of Sismondi's *Nouveaux principes d'économie politique*? But this is the case. Sismondi's book appeared in 1819. A year later, Malthus' English caricature of it saw the light of day. Once again, with Sismondi, as previously with Townsend and Anderson,[c] he found a theoretical basis for one of his stout economic pamphlets, in the production of which, incidentally, he also turned to advantage the new theories learned from Ricardo's *Principles*.

[XIV-774] While Malthus assailed in Ricardo that tendency of capitalist production which is revolutionary in relation to the old society, he took, with unerring parsonical instinct, only that out of Sismondi which is reactionary in relation to capitalist production and modern bourgeois society.

I exclude Sismondi from my historical survey here because a critique of his views belongs to a part of my work dealing with the real movement of capital (competition and credit)[67] which I can only tackle after I have finished this book.

Malthus' adaptation of Sismondi's views can easily be seen from the heading of one of the CHAPTERS in the *Principles of Political Economy*:

"[Of the] *Necessity of a Union of the Powers of Production with the Means of Distribution, in order to ensure a continued Increase of Wealth"* ([2nd ed.,] p. 361).

"THE POWERS OF PRODUCTION ALONE do not secure THE CREATION OF A PROPORTIONATE DEGREE OF WEALTH. SOMETHING ELSE seems to be necessary *in order to call these powers fully into action. This is an effectual and unchecked demand for all that is produced. And what appears to contribute most to the attainment of this object, is such a *distribution of produce,* and such an adaptation of this produce to the wants of those who are to consume it, as constantly to increase the exchangeable value of the whole mass"* (*Principles of Political Economy*, [2nd ed., p.] 361).

---

a See this volume, pp. 231-33.— *Ed.*

b T. R. Malthus, *The Measure of Value Stated and Illustrated...*, London, 1823.— *Ed.*

c See present edition, Vol. 30, pp. 231-33 and Vol. 31, pp. 204-05, 268-69, 344-47.— *Ed.*

Furthermore, in the same Sismondian manner and directed against Ricardo:

> * "The *wealth* of a country depends partly upon the *quantity of produce* obtained by its labour, and partly upon such an adaptation of this quantity to the wants and powers of the existing population as is calculated to give it *value*. Nothing can be more certain than that it is not determined by either of them alone" (l.c., [p.] 301).

> "But where wealth and value are perhaps the most nearly connected, is in the *necessity of the latter to the production of the former*" * (l.c.).

This is aimed especially against Ricardo: Ch. XX, "Value and Riches, Their Distinctive Properties". There Ricardo says, among other things:

> * "Value, then, essentially differs from riches, for value depends not on abundance, but on the difficulty or facility of production" * (l.c., [p.] 320).[a]

// Value, incidentally, can also increase with the "facility of production". Let us suppose that the number of men in a country rises from 1 million to 6 million. The million men worked 12 hours. The 6 million have so developed the productive powers that each of them produces as much again in 6 hours. In these circumstances, according to Ricardo's own views, wealth would have been increased sixfold and value threefold. //

> * "Riches do not depend on value. A man is rich or poor, according to the abundance of necessaries and luxuries which he can command" ([p.] 323). "It is through confounding the ideas of value and wealth, or riches that it has been asserted, that by diminishing the quantity of commodities, that is to say of the necessaries, conveniences, and enjoyments of human life, riches may be increased. If value were the measure of riches, this could not be denied, because by scarcity the value of commodities is raised; but ... if riches consist in necessaries and enjoyments, then they cannot be increased by a diminution of quantity" * (l.c., [pp.] 323-24).

In other words, Ricardo says here: wealth consists of *use values* only. He transforms bourgeois production into mere production of use value, a very pretty view of a mode of production which is dominated by *exchange value*. He regards the specific form of bourgeois wealth as something merely formal which does not affect its content. He therefore also denies the contradictions of bourgeois production which break out in crises. Hence his quite false conception of money. Hence, in considering the production process of capital, he ignores completely the circulation process, in so far as it includes the metamorphosis of commodities, the necessity of the transformation of capital into money. At any rate nobody has better and more precisely than Ricardo elaborated the

---

[a] D. Ricardo, *On the Principles of Political Economy, and Taxation*, 3rd ed., London, 1821.— *Ed.*

point that bourgeois production is not production of wealth for the PRODUCERS (as he repeatedly calls the workers)[19] and that therefore the production of bourgeois wealth is something quite different from the production of "ABUNDANCE", "OF NECESSARIES AND LUXURIES" FOR THE MAN WHO PRODUCES THEM, as this would have to be the case if production were only a means for satisfying the needs of the producers through production dominated by use value alone. Nevertheless, the same *Ricardo* says:

* "If we lived in one of Mr. Owen's parallelograms,[68] and enjoyed all our productions in common, then no one could suffer in consequence of abundance, but *as long as society is constituted as it now is,* abundance will often be injurious to producers, and scarcity beneficial to them" * (*On Protection to Agriculture,* 4th ed., London, 1822, [p.] 21).

[XIV-775] Ricardo regards bourgeois, or more precisely, capitalist production as the *absolute form* of production, whose specific forms of production relations can therefore never enter into contradiction with, or enfetter, the aim of production— ABUNDANCY—which includes both mass and variety of use values, and which in turn implies a profuse development of man as producer, an all-round development of his productive capacities. And this is where he lands in an amusing contradiction: when we are speaking of VALUE and RICHES, we should have only society as a whole in mind. But when we speak of CAPITAL and LABOUR, then it is self-evident that "GROSS REVENUE" only exists in order to create "NET REVENUE". In actual fact, what he admires most about bourgeois production is that its definite forms—compared with previous forms of production—provide scope for the boundless development of the productive forces. When they cease to do this, or when contradictions appear within which they do this, he denies the contradictions, or rather, expresses the contradiction in another form by representing *wealth as such*—the mass of use values in itself—without regard to the producers, as the *ultima Thule.*[a]

Sismondi is profoundly conscious of the contradictions in capitalist production[b]; he is aware that, on the one hand, its forms—its production relations—stimulate unrestrained development of the productive power and of wealth; and that, on the

---

[a] A remote goal or end (literally: the farthest Thule, a land considered by the ancients to be the northernmost part of the habitable world).— *Ed*

[b] See J. C. L. Simonde de Sismondi, *Nouveaux principes d'économie politique...,* 2nd. ed., Vol. 1, Paris, 1827, p. 371, and also K. Marx, *Outlines of the Critique of Political Economy...* (present edition, Vol. 28, pp. 337-38).— *Ed.*

other hand, these relations are conditional, that their contradictions of use value and exchange value, commodity and money, purchase and sale, production and consumption, capital and wage labour, etc., assume ever greater dimensions as productive power develops. He is particularly aware of the fundamental contradiction: on the one hand, unrestricted development of the productive power and increase of wealth which, at the same time, consists of commodities and must be turned into cash; on the other hand, the system is based on the fact that the mass of producers is restricted to the NECESSARIES. HENCE, according to Sismondi, crises are not accidental, as Ricardo maintains, but essential outbreaks— occurring on a large scale and at definite periods—of the immanent contradictions. He wavers constantly: should the State curb the productive forces to make them adequate to the production relations, or should the production relations be made adequate to the productive forces? He often retreats into the past, becomes a *laudator temporis acti,*[a] or he seeks to exorcise the contradictions by a different adjustment of REVENUE in relation to capital, or of distribution in relation to production, not realising that the relations of distribution are only the relations of production seen *sub alia specie.*[b] He forcefully *criticises* the contradictions of bourgeois production but does not *understand* them, and consequently does not understand the process whereby they can be resolved. However, at the bottom of his argument is indeed the inkling that *new* forms of the appropriation of wealth must correspond to productive forces and the material and social conditions for the production of wealth which have developed within capitalist society; that the bourgeois forms are only transitory and contradictory forms, in which wealth attains only an antithetical existence and appears everywhere simultaneously as its opposite. It is wealth which always has poverty as its prerequisite and only develops by developing poverty as well.

We have now seen how nicely Malthus appropriates Sismondi. Malthus' theory is expressed in an exaggerated and even more nauseating form in *On Political Economy in Connexion with the Moral State and Moral Prospects of Society,* 2ND ED., London, 1832, by *Thomas Chalmers* (PROFESSOR OF DIVINITY). Here the parsonic element is more in evidence not only theoretically but also practically, since this MEMBER of the "ESTABLISHED CHURCH"[69] defends

---

[a] Eulogiser of the past (Horace, *Ars poetica,* 173).— *Ed.*
[b] From a different aspect.— *Ed.*

it "economically" with its "LOAVES AND FISHES" and the whole complex of institutions with which this CHURCH stands or falls.[a]

The passages in Malthus (referred to above) having reference to the workers are the following:

* "The consumption and demand occasioned by the workmen employed in productive labour can never *alone* furnish a motive to the accumulation and employment of capital" (*Principles of Political Economy*, [2nd ed., p.] 315).

"No farmer will take the trouble of superintending the labour of ten additional men merely because his whole produce will then sell in the market at an advanced price just equal to what he had paid his additional labourers. There must be something in the previous state of the demand and supply of the commodity in question, or in its price, antecedent to and independent of the demand occasioned by the new labourers, in order to warrant the employment of an additional number of people in its production" (l.c., [p.] 312).

"The demand created by the productive labourer himself can never be an *adequate* demand, [XIV-776] because it does not go to the *full extent of what he produces.* If *it did, there would be no profit,* consequently no motive to employ him. The very *existence of a profit upon any commodity* presupposes a demand *exterior* to that of the labour which has produced it" ([p.] 405, note).

"As a great increase of consumption among the working classes must greatly increase the cost of production, it must lower profits, and diminish or destroy the motive to accumulate" (l.c., [p.] 405).

"It is the *want of necessaries* which mainly stimulates the working classes to produce luxuries; and were this stimulus removed or greatly weakened, so that the necessaries of life could be obtained with very little labour, instead of more time being devoted to the production of conveniences, there is every reason to think that less [time] would be so devoted" * (l.c., [p.] 334).

Malthus is interested not in concealing the contradictions of bourgeois production, but on the contrary, in emphasising them, on the one hand, in order to prove that the poverty of the working classes is necessary (as it is, indeed, for this mode of production) and, on the other hand, to demonstrate to the capitalists the necessity for a well-fed Church and State hierarchy in order to create an ADEQUATE DEMAND. He thus shows that for "CONTINUED PROGRESS OF WEALTH" [p. 314] neither increase of population nor accumulation of capital suffices (l.c., [pp.] 319-20), nor FERTILITY OF the SOIL ([p.] 331 et seq.), nor "INVENTIONS TO SAVE LABOUR", nor the extension of the "FOREIGN MARKETS" (l.c., [pp. 351-]52 and 359).

* "Both labourers and capital may be redundant, compared with the means of employing them profitably" * (l.c., [p.] 414).

Thus he emphasises the possibility of general overproduction in opposition to the view of the RICARDIANS (inter alia l.c., p. 326).

---

[a] See K. Marx, *Outlines of the Critique of Political Economy...* (present edition, Vol. 28, pp. 519-21).— *Ed.*

The principal propositions dealing with this matter are the following:

*"The demand is always determined by *value,* and supply by *quantity*"* (*Principles of Political Economy,* [2nd ed., p.] 316).

"Commodities are exchanged not only for commodities but also for PRODUCTIVE LABOUR and PERSONAL SERVICES and in relation to them, and also to money, there can be a general GLUT of commodities" (l.c.).[a]

*"Supply must always be proportioned to *quantity,* and demand to value" (*Definitions in Political Economy,* ed. by Cazenove, [p.] 65).

"'It is evident,' says James Mill, 'that whatever a man has produced, and does not wish to keep for his own consumption, is a stock which he may give in exchange for other commodities. His will, therefore, to purchase, and his means of purchasing, in other words, his demand, is exactly equal to the amount of what he has produced, and does not mean to consume.'[b] It is quite obvious that his means of purchasing other commodities are not proportioned to the *quantity* of his own commodity which he has produced, and wishes to part with; but to its *value in exchange*; and unless the value of a commodity in exchange be proportioned to its quantity, it cannot be true that the demand and supply of every individual are always equal to one another" (l.c., [pp. 64-]65).

"If the demand of every individual were equal to his supply, in the correct sense of the expression, it would be a proof that he could always sell his commodity for the costs of production, including fair profits; and then even a *partial* glut would be impossible. The argument proves too much ... supply must always be proportioned to *quantity,* and demand to *value*"* (*Definitions in Political Economy,* London, 1827, [p.] 48, note).

"Here, by DEMAND Mill understands HIS (the DEMANDER'S) *means of purchasing. But these means of purchasing other commodities are not proportioned to the *quantity* of his own commodity which he has produced and wishes to part with; but to its *value in exchange*; and unless the value of a commodity in exchange be proportioned to its quantity, it cannot be true that the demand and supply of every individual are always equal to one another"* (l.c., [pp.] 48-49).

"It is wrong for Torrens to say THAT 'INCREASED SUPPLY IS THE ONE AND ONLY CAUSE OF INCREASED EFFECTUAL DEMAND'.[c] If it were, how difficult would it be for MANKIND TO RECOVER ITSELF, UNDER A TEMPORARY DIMINUTION OF FOOD AND CLOTHING. But FOOD AND CLOTHING diminished IN QUANTITY will rise in value; *the money price of the remaining food and clothing will for a time rise in a greater degree than in [proportion to] the diminution of its quantity, while the money price of labour may remain the same. The necessary consequence [will be] the power of setting in motion a greater quantity of productive industry than before"* ([pp.] 59-60).

"All commodities of a nation may fall together compared with money or labour" (l.c., [p.] 64 et seq.). "Thus a general GLUT is possible" (l.c.). "Their prices can all fall below their costs of production" (l.c.)[d]

[XIV-777] For the rest, only the following passage from Malthus, which deals with the circulation process, need be noted.

---

[a] Marx quotes Malthus with some alterations.— *Ed.*

[b] Cf. this volume, p. 290.— *Ed.*

[c] Cf. ibid., p. 268.— *Ed.*

[d] In this paragraph Marx paraphrases some of the ideas expressed by Malthus.— *Ed.*

* "If we reckon the value of the fixed capital employed as a part of the advances, we must reckon the remaining value of such capital at the end of the year as a part of the annual returns ... in reality his" * (the capitalist's) * "*annual advances consist only* of his circulating capital, the wear and tear of his fixed capital with the interest upon it, and the interest of that part of his circulating capital which consists of the money employed in making his annual payments as they are called for" * (*Principles of Political Economy*, [2nd ed., p.] 269).

The SINKING FUND, i.e. the FUND FOR WEAR AND TEAR OF THE FIXED CAPITAL, is, in my opinion, at the same time A fund FOR ACCUMULATION.[a]

I wish to quote yet a few passages from a Ricardian book directed against Malthus' theory. As regards the attacks from the capitalist point of view which are made in the book against Malthus' UNPRODUCTIVE CONSUMERS IN GENERAL AND LANDLORDS IN PARTICULAR I shall demonstrate elsewhere that they can be used word for word against the capitalists from the workers' standpoint. (This is to be included in the section "The Relationship Between Capital and Wage Labour Presented from an Apologetic Standpoint".[70])

* "Considering, that an increased employment of capital will not take place unless a rate of profits equal to the former rate, or greater than it, can be ensured, and considering, that the mere addition to capital does not of itself tend to ensure such a rate of profits, but the reverse, Mr. Malthus, and those who reason in the same manner as he does, proceed to look out for some source, independent [of] and extrinsic to production itself, whose progressive increase may keep pace with the progressive increase of capital, and from which continual additional supplies of the requisite rate of profits may be derived" * (*An Inquiry into those Principles, Respecting the Nature of Demand and the Necessity of Consumption, lately Advocated by Mr. Malthus etc.*, London, 1821, [pp.] 33-34).

According to Malthus, the "UNPRODUCTIVE CONSUMERS" are such a source (l.c., [p.] 35).

* "Mr. Malthus sometimes talks as if there were two *distinct funds,* capital and revenue, supply and demand, production and consumption, which must take care to keep pace with each other, and neither outrun the other. As if, *besides the whole mass of commodities produced,* there was required another mass, fallen from Heaven, I suppose, to purchase them with... The fund for consumption, such as he requires, can only be had at the expense of production" (l.c., [pp.] 49-50).

"We are continually puzzled, in his" (Malthus') "speculations, between the object of increasing production and that of checking it. When a man is in want of a *demand,* does Mr. Malthus recommend him to pay some other person to take off his goods? Probably not" (l.c., [p.] 55. Certainly yes).

"The object of selling your goods is to make a certain amount of money; it never can answer to part with that amount of money for nothing, to another person, that he may bring it back to you, and buy your goods with it: you might as well have just burnt your goods at once, and you would have been in the same situation" * (l.c., [p.] 63).

[It is] right in regard to Malthus. But because it is one and the same fund— "THE WHOLE MASS OF COMMODITIES PRODUCED"—which consti-

---

[a] See this volume, p. 112.— *Ed.*

tutes the production fund and the consumption fund, the fund of
supply and the fund of demand, the fund of capital and the fund
of REVENUE, it does not by any means follow that it is irrelevant how
the total fund is divided between these various categories.

The anonymous author does not understand what Malthus
means when he speaks of the "DEMAND" of the workers being
"INADEQUATE" for the capitalist.

* "As to the *demand* from labour, that is, either the giving labour in exchange
for goods, or ... the giving, in exchange for present, complete products, a future
and accruing addition of value... This is the real demand that it is material to the
producers to get increased, etc." * (l.c., [p.] 57).

What Malthus means is not the OFFER OF LABOUR (which our author
calls DEMAND FROM LABOUR) but the DEMAND for commodities which the
WAGES the worker receives enable him to make, the money with
which the worker enters the commodity market as a purchaser.
And Malthus rightly says of this DEMAND that IT CAN NEVER BE ADEQUATE
TO THE SUPPLY OF THE CAPITALIST. *Alias* the worker would be able to buy
back the whole of his product with his WAGES.

[XIV-778] The same writer says:

* "The very meaning of an increased demand by them" (the labourers) "is a
disposition to take less themselves, and leave a larger share for their employers;
and if it is said that this, by diminishing consumption, increases glut, I can only
answer, that glut is synonymous with high profits" * (l.c., [p.] 59).

This is meant to be witty, but in fact it contains the essential
secret of "GLUT".

In connection with Malthus' *Essay on Rent*,[a] our author says:

* "When Mr. Malthus published his *Essay on Rent,* it seems to have been partly
with a view to answer the cry of 'No Landlords', which then 'stood rubric on the
walls', to stand up in defence of that class, and to prove that they were not like
monopolists. That rent cannot be abolished, that its increase is a natural concomitant,
in general, of increasing wealth and numbers, he shewed; but neither did the
vulgar cry of 'No Landlords' necessarily mean, that there ought to be *no such thing*
as rent, but rather that it ought to be equally divided among the people, according
to what was called 'Spence's plan'.[71] But when he proceeds to vindicate landlords
from the odious name of monopolists, from the observation of Smith, 'that they
love to reap where they never sowed',[b] he seems to be fighting for a *name...* There
is too much air of an *advocate* in all these arguments of his" * (l.c., [pp.108-]09).

Malthus' book *On Population* was a lampoon directed against the
French Revolution and the contemporary ideas of reform in

---

[a] T. R. Malthus, *An Inquiry into the Nature and Progress of Rent, and the Principles
by Which It Is Regulated,* London, 1815.— *Ed.*

[b] A. Smith, *An Inquiry into the Nature and Causes of the Wealth of Nations,* Book I,
Chapter VI. See also Matthew 25:24, 26.— *Ed.*

England (Godwin,[a] etc.). It was an apologia for the poverty of the working classes. The *theory* was plagiarised from Townsend[b] and others.

His *Essay on Rent* was a piece of polemic writing in support of the LANDLORDS against INDUSTRIAL CAPITAL. The theory [was taken from] Anderson.[c] His *Principles of Political Economy* was a polemic work written in the interests of the capitalists against the workers and in the interests of the aristocracy, CHURCH, TAX-EATERS, toadies, etc., against the capitalists. The *theory* [was taken from] Adam Smith. Where [he inserts] his own inventions, [it is] pitiable. It is on Sismondi that he bases himself in further elaborating the theory.

A book in which Malthus' principles are elaborated:

Outlines of Political Economy (being a plain and short view of the laws relating to the production, distribution, and consumption of wealth etc.), London, 1832.

D'abord the author[d] explains the practical reasons governing the opposition of the Malthusians to the determination of value by labour time.

* "That labour is the sole source of wealth, seems to be a doctrine as dangerous as it is false, as it unhappily affords a handle to those who would represent all property as belonging to the working classes, and the share which is received by others as a robbery or fraud upon them" * (l.c., [p.] 22, note).

In the following sentence it emerges more clearly than in Malthus that the author confuses the *value* of commodities with the *utilisation* of commodities, or of money as capital. In the latter sense it correctly expresses the origin of SURPLUS VALUE.

* "The *value of capital*, the quantity of labour which it is worth or will command, is always greater than [that] which it has cost, and the difference constitutes the profit or remuneration to its owner" * (l.c., [p.] 32).

The following, too, which is taken from Malthus, is correct as an explanation of why profit is to be reckoned as part of the *production costs* of capitalist production:

* "Profit upon the capital employed" // "unless this profit were obtained, there would be no adequate motive to produce the commodity" // "is an essential condition of the supply, and, as such, constitutes a component part of the *costs of production*" * (l.c., [p.] 33).

In the following passage we have, on the one hand, the correct statement that profit upon capital directly arises out of the

---

a See W. Godwin, *An Enquiry Concerning Political Justice.*, London, 1793.— *Ed.*
b See present edition, Vol. 30, pp. 204-05.— *Ed.*
c Ibid., Vol. 31, pp. 344-47, 351-52.— *Ed.*
d John Cazenove.— *Ed.*

exchange of capital for labour, and on the other hand, the Malthusian thesis that profit is made in *selling*.

* "A man's profit does not depend upon his command of the *produce* of other men's labour, but upon his command of *labour itself.*" * (Here the correct distinction is made between the exchange of one commodity for another and the exchange of the commodity as capital for labour.) "If" (when THE *VALUE OF MONEY* falls a) * "he can sell [XIV-779] his goods at a higher price, *while his workmen's wages remain unaltered*, he is clearly benefited by the rise, whether other goods rise or not. A smaller proportion of what he produces is sufficient to put that labour into motion, and a larger proportion consequently remains for himself" * ([pp.] 49-50).

The same thing happens when, for example, as a result of the introduction of new machinery, chemical processes, etc., the capitalist produces commodities below their old value and either sells them at their old value or, at any rate, above the individual value to which they have fallen. It is true that when this happens, the worker does not directly work a shorter period for himself and a longer one for the capitalist, but in the reproduction process, A SMALLER PROPORTION OF WHAT HE PRODUCES IS SUFFICIENT TO PUT THAT LABOUR INTO MOTION. In actual fact, the worker therefore exchanges a greater part of his IMMEDIATE LABOUR than previously for his own REALISED LABOUR. For example, he continues to receive what he received previously, £10. But this £10, although it represents the same amount of labour to society, is no longer the product *of the same amount of labour time* as previously, but may represent one hour less. So that, IN FACT the worker works longer for the capitalist and a shorter period for himself. It is as if he received only £8, which, however, represented the same mass of use values as a result of the increased productivity of his labour.

The author remarks in connection with Mill's arguments regarding the IDENTITY OF DEMAND AND SUPPLY, discussed earlier [b]:

* "The supply of each man depends upon the *quantity* which he brings to market: his demand for other things depends upon the *value* of his supply. The former is certain; it depends upon himself: the latter is uncertain; it depends upon others. The former may remain the same, while the latter may vary. A 100 qrs of corn, which a man brings to market, may at one time be worth 30sh., and [at] another time 60sh., the qr. The *quantity of supply* is in both instances the same; but the man's demand or power of purchasing other things is twice as great in the latter as in the former case" * (l.c., [pp.] 111-12).

About the relationship of labour and machinery, the author writes the following:

* "When commodities are multiplied by a more judicious distribution of labour,

---

a In the manuscript: "rises".— *Ed.*
b See this volume, pp. 124-25, 134, 135, 250, 290-93.— *Ed.*

no greater amount of demand than before is required in order to maintain all the labour which was previously employed," *

(HOW SO? IF THE DISTRIBUTION OF LABOUR IS MORE JUDICIOUS, MORE COMMODITIES WILL BE PRODUCED BY THE SAME LABOUR; HENCE [the] SUPPLY WILL GROW, AND DOES ITS ABSORPTION NOT REQUIRE AN INCREASED AMOUNT OF DEMAND? DOES ADAM SMITH NOT RIGHTLY SAY THAT DIVISION OF LABOUR DEPENDS UPON THE EXTENT OF THE MARKET?[a] In actual fact, the difference as regards DEMAND from outside is the same except [that demand] on a larger scale [is required] when machinery is used. But *"a more judicious distribution of labour" may require the same or even a greater number of labourers than before, while the introduction of machinery must under all circumstances diminish the proportion of the capital laid out in immediate labour)

"whereas, when machinery is introduced, if there be not an increased amount of demand, or a fall in wages or profits, *some of the labour will undoubtedly be thrown out of employment.* Let the case be supposed of a commodity worth £1,200, of which £1,000 consists of the wages of 100 men, at £10 each, and £200 [of] profits, at the rate of 20%. Now, let it be imagined that the same commodity can be produced by the labour of 50 men, and a machine which has cost the labour of 50 more, and which requires the labour of 10 men to keep it in constant repair; the producer will then be able to reduce the price of the article to £800, and still continue to obtain the same remuneration for the use of his capital.

The wages of 50 men at £	500	
of 10 men to keep it in repair	100	
Profit 20% on circulating capital	500	⎫
On fixed	500	⎬ 200
		⎭

800" *

(The "10 MEN TO KEEP IT IN REPAIR" represent here the annual wear and tear. Otherwise the calculation would be wrong, since the LABOUR OF REPAIRING would then have to be added to the original production costs of the machinery.) (Previously the manufacturer had to lay out £1,000 annually, but the product was [worth] £1,200. Now he has laid out £500 on machinery once and for all; he has not therefore to lay out this sum again IN ANY OTHER WAY. What he has to lay out is £100 annually for REPAIR and 500 in wages (since there are no RAW MATERIALS in this example). He has to lay out only 600 per annum, but he makes a profit of 200 on his total capital just as he did previously. The amount and rate of

[a] See A. Smith, *An Inquiry into the Nature and Causes of the Wealth of Nations*, Book I, Chapter III.— *Ed.*

profit remain the same. But his annual product amounts to only
£800.)

* "Those who used to pay £1,200 for the commodity will now have £400 to
spare, which they can lay out either on something else, or in purchasing more of
the same commodity. If it be laid out in the [XIV-780] *produce* of immediate
labour, it will give employment to no more than 33.4 men, whereas the number
thrown out of employment by this introduction of the machine will have been 40,
for

The wages of 33.4 men at [£] 10,
are £334

Profits 20%   66

£400." *

(In other words this means: If the £400 is expended on
commodities which are the product OF IMMEDIATE LABOUR and if the
wages per man=£10, then the commodities which cost £400 must
be the product of less than 40 men. If they were the product of 40
men, then they would contain only PAID LABOUR. The value of labour
(or the QUANTITY OF LABOUR REALISED in the WAGES)=the value of the
product (THE QUANTITY OF LABOUR REALISED IN THE COMMODITY). But the
commodities worth £400 contain *unpaid* labour, which is precisely
what constitutes the profit. They must therefore be the product of
less than 40 men. If the profit=20%, then only $^5/_6$ of the product
can consist of paid labour, that is, approximately £334=33.4 MEN at
10 per MAN. The other 6th, roughly 66, represents the unpaid
labour. Ricardo has shown in exactly the same way that machinery
itself, when its money price is as high as the price of the IMMEDIATE
LABOUR it displaces, can never be the product of so much LABOUR.[a])

* "If it" (viz. the £400) "be laid out in the purchase of more of the same
commodity, or of any other, where the same species and quantity of fixed capital
were used, it would employ only 30 men, for—

The wages of 25 men at £10 each, are   250

5 men to keep [it] in repair   50

Profits on £250 circulated and 250 fixed capital   100

£400." *

(That is to say, in the CASE where machinery is introduced, the
production of commodities costing £800 involves an outlay of 500

---

[a] See this volume, pp. 177-78.— *Ed.*

on machinery. Thus for the production of 400 [worth of commodities] only 250 [is spent on machinery]. Furthermore, 50 workers are needed to operate machinery worth 500, therefore 25 workers ([their wages]=£250) for machinery worth 250; further for REPAIR (the maintenance of the machine) 10 men are needed if the machinery costs 500, consequently 5 men ([whose wages come to] £50) are needed for machinery costing 250. Thus [we have] 250 fixed capital and 250 circulating capital—a total of 500, on which there is a profit of 20%=100. The product is therefore=300 WAGES and 100 PROFIT=£400. Thirty workers are employed in producing the commodities. Here it has been assumed all along that the capitalist (who manufactures the commodities) either borrows capital out of the (£400) savings which the consumers have deposited at the bank, or that—apart from the £400 which have been saved from the REVENUE of the consumers—he himself possesses capital. For clearly with a capital of 400 he cannot lay out 250 on machinery and 300 on wages.)

* "When the total sum of £1,200 was spent on the produce of immediate labour, the division was £1,000 wages, £200 profits" * (100 workers [whose] wages=£1,000). * "When it was spent partly in [the] one way and partly in the other ... the division was £934 wages and £266 profits" * (i.e. 60 workers in the machine shop and 33.4 IMMEDIATE LABOUR making a total of 93.4 workers [whose wages]=£934); * "and, as in the third supposition, when the whole sum was spent on the joint produce of [the] machine and labour, the division was £900 wages" * (i.e. 90 workers) * "and £300 profits" (l.c., [pp.] 114-17).

[XIV-781] "The capitalist cannot, after the introduction [of the machine], employ as much labour as he did before, without accumulating further capital" (l.c., [p.] 119); "but the revenue which is saved by the consumers of the article after its price has fallen, will, by increasing their consumption of that or something else, create a demand for some though not for all the labour which has been displaced by the machine" (l.c., [p.] 119).

"Mr. McCulloch conceives that the introduction of machines into any employment necessarily occasions an equal or greater demand for the disengaged labourers in some other employment. In order to prove this, he supposes that the annuity necessary to replace the value of the machine by the time it is worn out, will every year occasion an increasing demand for labour.[a] But as the successive annuities added together up to the end of the term, can only equal the original cost of the machine, and the interest upon it during the time it is in operation, in what way it can ever create a demand for labour, beyond what it would have done had no machine been employed, it is not easy to understand" * (l.c. [pp. 119-20]).

The SINKING FUND itself can, indeed, be used for accumulation in the interval when the wear and tear of the machine is shown in the books, but does not actually affect its work. But in any case, the DEMAND FOR LABOUR created in this way is much smaller than if the

[a] See J. R. MacCulloch, The Principles of Political Economy..., Edinburgh, London, 1825, pp. 181-82. Cf. also this volume, p. 353.— Ed.

whole capital (invested in machinery) were laid out in wages, instead of merely the ANNUITY. MacPeter[a] is an ass—as always. This passage is only noteworthy, because it contains the idea that the SINKING FUND is itself a fund for accumulation.[b]

[XIV-782] k) DISINTEGRATION OF THE RICARDIAN SCHOOL

1) ROBERT TORRENS, *AN ESSAY ON THE PRODUCTION OF WEALTH ETC.*, LONDON, 1821

Observation of competition—the phenomena of production— shows that capitals of equal size yield an equal amount of profit ON AN AVERAGE, or that, given the AVERAGE RATE OF PROFIT (and the term, AVERAGE RATE OF PROFIT, has no other meaning), the amount of profit depends on the amount of capital advanced.

Adam Smith has noted this FACT. Its connection with the theory of value which he put forward caused him no pangs of conscience—especially since in addition to what one might call his esoteric theory,[72] he advanced many others, and could recall one or another at his pleasure. The sole reflection to which this question gives rise is his polemic against the view which seeks to resolve profit into WAGES OF SUPERINTENDENCE, SINCE, APART FROM ANY OTHER CIRCUMSTANCE, the labour OF SUPERINTENDENCE does not increase in the same measure as the scale of production and, moreover, the value of the capital advanced can increase, for instance, as a result of the dearness of raw materials, without a corresponding growth in the scale of production.[c] He has no immanent law to determine the *AVERAGE PROFIT* or its amount. He merely says that competition reduces this *x*.

Ricardo (apart from a few merely chance remarks) directly identifies profit with SURPLUS VALUE everywhere. Hence with him, commodities sell at a *profit* not because they are sold *above* their value, but because they are sold *at their value.* Nevertheless, in considering VALUE (in CHAPTER I of the *Principles*) he is the first to reflect at all on the relationship between the *determination of the value* of commodities and the phenomenon that capitals of equal size yield equal profits. They can only do this inasmuch as the commodities they produce—although they *are* not *sold* at *equal prices* (one can, however, say that their output has equal prices

---

[a] Marx writes about McCulloch in a mocking manner (German "dummer Peter" means an ass).— *Ed.*

[b] See this volume, p. 112.— *Ed.*

[c] See present edition, Vol. 30, pp. 397-98.— *Ed.*

Page 782 of Notebook XIV of the Economic Manuscript
of 1861-1863

provided the value of that part of constant capital which is not consumed is added to the product)—yield the *same* SURPLUS VALUE, the same surplus of price over the price of the capital outlay. Ricardo moreover is the first to draw attention to the fact that capitals of equal size are by no means of equal organic composition. The difference in this composition he defined in the way traditional since Adam Smith, namely as CIRCULATING and FIXED CAPITAL, that is, only the differences arising from the process of circulation. He certainly does not directly say that it is a *prima facie* contradiction of the law of value that capitals of unequal organic composition, which consequently set unequal amounts OF IMMEDIATE LABOUR in motion, produce commodities of the same value and yield the same SURPLUS VALUE (which he identifies with profit). On the contrary he begins his investigation of value by assuming capital and a general rate of profit. He identifies *cost price*[6] with *value* from the very outset, and does not see that from the very start this assumption is a *prima facie* contradiction of the law of value. It is only on the basis of this assumption—which contains the main contradiction and the real difficulty—that he comes to a particular case, *changes in the level of wages,* their rise or fall. For the rate of profit to remain uniform the rise or fall in wages, to which corresponds a fall or rise in profit, must have unequal effects on capitals of different organic composition. If wages rise, then profits fall, and also the prices of commodities in whose production a relatively large amount of fixed capital is employed. Where the opposite is the case, the results are likewise opposite. Under these circumstances, therefore, the *"EXCHANGEABLE VALUES"* of the commodities are not determined by the labour time required for their respective production. In other words, this definition of an equal rate of profit (and Ricardo arrives at it only in individual cases and in this roundabout way) yielded by capitals of different organic composition *contradicts* the law of value or, as Ricardo says, constitutes an *exception* to it, whereupon Malthus rightly remarks that in the PROGRESS OF [XIV-783] INDUSTRY, the rule becomes the exception and the exception the rule.[a] The contradiction itself is not clearly expressed by Ricardo, namely, not in the form: although one of the commodities contains more unpaid labour than the other—for the amount of unpaid labour depends on the amount of paid labour, that is, the amount of IMMEDIATE LABOUR employed provided the rate of exploitation of the workers is equal—they nevertheless yield equal values, or the same surplus

---

[a] See this volume, pp. 224-25.— *Ed.*

of unpaid over paid labour. The contradiction however occurs with him in a particular form: in certain cases, *wages,* variations in wages, affect the cost price (he says, the EXCHANGEABLE VALUES) of commodities.

Equally, differences in the time of turnover of capital—whether the capital remains in the process of production (even if not in the labour process) [73] or in circulation for a longer period, requiring not more work, but more time for its RETURN—these differences have just as little effect on the equality of profit, and this again contradicts (is, according to Ricardo, an *exception* to) the law of value.

He has therefore presented the problem very one-sidedly. Had he expressed it in a general way, he would also have had a general solution.

But his great contribution remains: Ricardo has a notion that there is a difference between value and cost price, and, in certain cases, even though he calls them *exceptions* to the law, he formulates the contradiction that capitals of unequal organic composition (that is, in the last analysis, capitals which do not exploit the same amount of living labour) yield equal SURPLUS VALUE (profit) and—if one disregards the fact that a portion of the fixed capital enters into the labour process without entering into the valorisation process—equal values, commodities of equal value (or rather [of equal] *cost price,* but he confuses this).[a]

As we have seen,[b] *Malthus* uses this in order to deny the validity of the Ricardian law of value.

At the very beginning of his book, *Torrens* takes this discovery of Ricardo as his point of departure, not, however, to solve the problem, but to present the "phenomenon" as the law of the phenomenon.

"Supposing that capitals of DIFFERENT DEGREES OF DURABILITY are employed. If a WOOLLEN and a SILK MANUFACTURER were each to employ a capital of £2,000 and if the former were to employ £1,500 IN DURABLE MACHINES, and £500 IN WAGES and MATERIALS; while the latter employed only £500 IN DURABLE MACHINES, and £1,500 IN WAGES and MATERIALS. Supposing that $^1/_{10}$ of these fixed capitals is annually consumed, and that the rate of profit is 10%; then, as THE RESULTS OF THE WOOLLEN MANUFACTURER'S CAPITAL OF £2,000, must, TO GIVE HIM THIS PROFIT, be £2,200, and as the value of his fixed capital has been reduced by the process of production from £1,500 to £1,350, THE GOODS PRODUCED must SELL FOR £850. And, IN LIKE MANNER, as the fixed capital of the SILK MANUFACTURER is by the PROCESS OF PRODUCTION reduced $^1/_{10}$, or from £500 to £450, *the silks produced must, in order to yield him the *customary rate of profit* upon his whole capital of £2,000, sell

---

a See present edition, Vol. 31, pp. 415-23.— *Ed.*
b See this volume, pp. 210, 222-25.— *Ed.*

for £1,750 ... when capitals equal in amount, but of different degrees of durability, are employed, the articles produced, *together with the residue of capital*, in *one occupation*, will be equal in exchangeable value to the things produced, and the residue of capital, in *another occupation*"* (p[p. 28-]29).

Here the phenomenon manifested in competition is merely mentioned, registered. Ditto A "CUSTOMARY RATE OF PROFIT" *is presupposed* without explaining how it comes about, or even the feeling that this ought to be explained.

"EQUAL CAPITALS, or, in other words, EQUAL QUANTITIES OF ACCUMULATED LABOUR, WILL OFTEN PUT IN MOTION DIFFERENT QUANTITIES OF IMMEDIATE LABOUR; but this changes nothing in substance" (p[p. 29-]31),[a]

namely, in the fact that the value of the product+the RESIDUE OF THE CAPITAL NOT CONSUMED, yield equal values, or, what is the same thing, equal profits.

The merit of this passage does not consist in the fact that Torrens here merely registers the phenomenon once again without explaining it, but in the fact that he defines the difference by stating that equal capitals set in motion unequal quantities of living labour, though he immediately SPOILS it by declaring it to be a "special" case. If the value=the labour worked up, realised in a commodity, then it is clear that—if the commodities are sold at their value—the SURPLUS VALUE contained in them can only=the unpaid, or SURPLUS LABOUR, which they contain. But this SURPLUS LABOUR—given the same rate of exploitation of the worker—cannot be equal in the case of capitals WHICH PUT IN MOTION DIFFERENT QUANTITIES OF IMMEDIATE LABOUR, whether it is the immediate production process or the period of circulation which is the cause of this difference. It is therefore to Torrens' credit that he expresses this. What does he conclude from it? That here [XIV-784] within capitalist production the law of value suddenly changes. That is, that the law of value, which is abstracted from capitalist production, contradicts capitalist phenomena. And what does he put in its place? Absolutely nothing but the crude, thoughtless, verbal expression of the phenomenon which has to be explained.

"In the early period of society"

(that is, precisely when exchange value in general, the product as commodity, is hardly developed at all, and consequently when there is no law of value either)

"it is the TOTAL QUANTITY OF LABOUR, ACCUMULATED AND IMMEDIATE, EXPENDED ON PRODUCTION, that determines the relative value of commodities. But as soon as STOCK has ACCUMULATED, and there emerges a *class of capitalists* distinct from *that*

---

[a] Here and below cf. present edition, Vol. 29, p. 196.— *Ed.*

of labourers, WHEN THE PERSON, WHO UNDERTAKES ANY BRANCH OF INDUSTRY, DOES NOT PERFORM HIS OWN WORK, BUT ADVANCES SUBSISTENCE AND MATERIALS TO OTHERS, THEN IT IS THE *AMOUNT OF CAPITAL,* OR THE *QUANTITY OF ACCUMULATED LABOUR* EXPENDED IN PRODUCTION, that determines the EXCHANGEABLE POWER OF COMMODITIES" (l.c., [pp.] 33-34).

"As long as two capitals [are] equal, their products are of equal value, *HOWEVER WE MAY VARY THE QUANTITY OF IMMEDIATE LABOUR WHICH THEY PUT IN MOTION,* OR WHICH *THEIR PRODUCTS MAY REQUIRE.* If they are unequal, their PRODUCTS are OF UNEQUAL VALUE, THOUGH THE TOTAL QUANTITY OF LABOUR EXPENDED UPON EACH SHOULD BE PRECISELY EQUAL" ([p.] 39). "Therefore after the *SEPARATION OF CAPITALISTS AND LABOUR[ERS],* it is the *AMOUNT OF CAPITAL,* THE QUANTITY OF ACCUMULATED LABOUR, and not, *as before this separation,* THE SUM OF ACCUMULATED AND IMMEDIATE LABOUR, EXPENDED ON PRODUCTION, which determines the exchange value" (l.c., [pp. 39-40]).[a]

Here again, he merely states the phenomenon that capitals of equal size yield equal profits or that the cost price of commodities is equal to the price of the capital advanced + the AVERAGE profit; there is at the same time a HINT that—SINCE EQUAL CAPITALS PUT IN MOTION DIFFERENT QUANTITIES OF LABOUR—this *phenomenon* is, *prima facie,* inconsistent with the determination of the value of commodities by the amount of labour time embodied in them. The remark that this phenomenon of capitalist production only manifests itself when capital comes into existence—[when] the classes of capitalists and workers [arise, and] the objective conditions of labour acquire an independent existence as capital—is tautology.

But *how* the separation of the [factors necessary] for the production of commodities—into capitalists and workers, capital and wage labour—upsets the law of value of commodities, is merely "inferred" from the uncomprehended phenomenon.

Ricardo sought to prove that, apart from certain exceptions, the separation between capital and wage labour does not change anything in the determination of the value of commodities. Basing himself on the exceptions noted by Ricardo, Torrens rejects the law. He reverts to Adam Smith (against whom the Ricardian demonstration is directed) according to whom the value of commodities was determined by the labour time embodied in them "IN THE EARLY PERIOD" when men confronted one another simply as owners and exchangers of goods, but not when capital and property in land have been evolved. This means (as I observed in Part One[b]) that the law which applies to commodities *qua* commodities, no longer applies to them once they are regarded as

---

a Marx quotes Torrens with some alterations.—*Ed.*

b See K. Marx, *A Contribution to the Critique of Political Economy.* Part One (present edition, Vol. 29, pp. 299-300).—*Ed.*

capital or as products of capital, or as soon as there is, in general, an advance from the commodity to capital. On the other hand, the product wholly assumes the form of a commodity only—as a result of the fact that the entire product has to be transformed into exchange value and that also all the ingredients necessary for its production enter it as commodities—in other words it wholly becomes a commodity only with the development and on the basis of capitalist production. Thus the law of the commodity is supposed to be valid for a type of production which produces no commodities (or only to a limited extent) and not to be valid for a type of production which is based on the product as a commodity. The law itself, as well as the commodity as the general form of the product, is abstracted from capitalist production and yet it is precisely in respect of capitalist production that the law is held to be invalid.

The proposition regarding the influence of the separation of "CAPITAL and LABOUR" on the determination of value—apart from the tautology that capital cannot determine prices so long as it does not as yet exist—is moreover a quite superficial translation of a fact manifesting itself on the surface of capitalist production. So long as each person works himself with his own tools and sells his product himself //but in reality, the necessity to sell products on a [XIV-785] social scale never coincides with production carried on with the producer's own conditions of labour //, *his* costs comprise the cost of both the tools and the *labour* he performs. The cost to the capitalist consists in the capital he advances—in the sum of values he EXPENDS on production—not in labour, which he does not perform, and which only costs *him* what he pays for it. This is a very good reason for the capitalists to calculate and distribute the (social) SURPLUS VALUE amongst themselves according to the size of their capital outlay and not according to the quantity OF IMMEDIATE LABOUR WHICH A GIVEN CAPITAL PUTS IN MOTION. But it does not explain where the SURPLUS VALUE—which has to be distributed and is distributed in this way—comes from.

Torrens adheres to Ricardo in so far as he maintains that the value of a commodity is determined by the quantity of labour, but he declares [that it is] only "THE QUANTITY OF ACCUMULATED LABOUR" EXPENDED UPON THE PRODUCTION OF COMMODITIES which determines their value. Here, however, Torrens lands himself in a fine mess.

For example, the value of woollen cloth is determined by the ACCUMULATED LABOUR contained in the loom, the wool, etc., and the WAGES, which constitute the ingredients of its production, *accumulated labour,* which, in this context, means nothing else but REALISED

LABOUR, objectified labour time. However, once the woollen cloth is ready and production is over, the IMMEDIATE LABOUR EXPENDED on the woollen cloth has likewise been transformed into ACCUMULATED or REALISED LABOUR. Then why should the value of the loom and of the wool be determined by the REALISED LABOUR (which is nothing but IMMEDIATE LABOUR REALISED IN AN OBJECT, IN A RESULT, IN A USEFUL THING) they contain, and the value of the woollen cloth not be so determined? If the woollen cloth in turn becomes a component part OF PRODUCTION in say dyeing or tailoring, then it is "ACCUMULATED LABOUR", and the value of the coat is determined by the value of the WAGES of the workers, their tools and the woollen cloth, the value of which is determined by the "ACCUMULATED LABOUR" contained in it. If I regard a commodity as *capital,* that means in this context as a condition of production, then its value resolves itself into IMMEDIATE LABOUR, which is called "ACCUMULATED LABOUR" because it exists in an objectified form. On the other hand, if I regard the same commodity as a commodity, as a product and result of the [production] process, then it is definitely not determined by the LABOUR which is accumulated in it, but by the LABOUR accumulated in its conditions of production.

It is indeed a fine *cercle vicieux*[a] to seek to determine the value of a commodity by the value of the capital, since the value of the capital = the value of the commodities of which it is made up. *James Mill* is right as against this fellow when he says:

"*CAPITAL IS COMMODITIES.* If the value of commodities, then, depends upon the value of capital, it depends upon the value of commodities." [74]

One thing more is to be noted here. Since [according to Torrens] the value of a commodity is determined by the value of the capital which produces it, or, in other words, by the quantity of LABOUR, the LABOUR ACCUMULATED and REALISED in this capital, then only two possibilities ensue.

The commodity contains: first, the value of the fixed capital used up; second, the value of the raw material or the quantity of labour contained in the fixed capital and raw material; third, the quantity of labour which is objectified in the money or in the commodities which function as WAGES.[b]

Now there are two [possibilities].

The "accumulated" labour contained in the fixed capital and raw material remains the same after the process of production as it was before. As far as the 3rd part of the "ACCUMULATED LABOUR"

---

a Vicious circle.— *Ed.*

b See this volume, pp. 263-64.— *Ed.*

ADVANCED is concerned, the worker replaces it by his IMMEDIATE LABOUR, that is, the "IMMEDIATE LABOUR" added to the raw material, etc., represents just as much ACCUMULATED LABOUR in the commodity as was contained in the WAGES. Or it represents more. If it represents more, the commodity contains more ACCUMULATED LABOUR than the capital advanced did. Then profit arises precisely out of the surplus of ACCUMULATED LABOUR contained in the commodity over that contained in the CAPITAL ADVANCED. And the *value* of [XIV-786] the commodity is determined, as previously, by the quantity of labour (ACCUMULATED+IMMEDIATE) contained in it (in the commodity the latter type of labour likewise constitutes ACCUMULATED, and no longer IMMEDIATE [labour]. It is IMMEDIATE [labour] in the production process, and ACCUMULATED [labour] in the product).

Or immediate labour only represents the quantity embodied in the WAGES, is only an equivalent of it. (If it were less than this, the point to be explained would not be why the capitalist makes a profit but how it comes about that he makes no loss.) Where does the profit come from in this case? Where does the SURPLUS VALUE, i.e. the excess of the value of the commodity over the value of the component parts of production, or over that of the capital outlay, arise? Not in the production process itself—so that merely its realisation takes place in the process of EXCHANGE, or in the circulation process—but in the EXCHANGE process, in the circulation process. We thus come back to Malthus and the crude mercantilist conception of "PROFIT UPON EXPROPRIATION".[75] And it is this conception at which Mr. Torrens consistently arrives, although he is, on the other hand, sufficiently inconsistent to explain this *payable value* not by means of an inexplicable fund dropped down from the skies, namely, a fund which provides not only an equivalent for the commodity, but a surplus over and above this equivalent, and is derived from the MEANS of the purchaser, who is always able to pay for the commodity above its value without selling it above its value—thus reducing the whole thing to thin air. Torrens, who is not as consistent as Malthus, does not have recourse to such a fiction, but, on the contrary, asserts that "EFFECTUAL DEMAND"—the sum of values paid for the product—arises from *SUPPLY* alone, and is therefore likewise a commodity; and thus, since the two sides are both buyers and sellers, it is impossible to see how they can mutually cheat one another AT THE SAME RATE.

* "The effectual demand for any commodity is always determined, and under any given rate of profit, is constantly commensurate with the quantity of the ingredients of capital, or of the things required in its production, which consumers may be able and willing to offer in exchange for it" (l.c., p. 344).

"Increased supply is the *one and only cause of increased effectual demand"* *
([p.] 348).

Malthus, who quotes this passage from Torrens, is quite justified
in protesting against it (*Definitions in Political Economy,* London,
1827, p. 59).[a]

But the following passages about *production costs,* etc., demonstrate that Torrens does indeed arrive at such absurd conclusions:

> *"*Market price*" * (Malthus calls it PURCHASING VALUE) "always includes the
> * customary rate of profit for the time being. *Natural price,* consisting of the *cost of
> production,* or, in other words, *of the capital expended* in raising or fabricating
> commodities, cannot include the rate of profit" * (l.c., [p.] 51).
> "The farmer expends 100 qrs OF CORN and obtains IN RETURN 120 qrs. In this
> case, 20 qrs constitute the profit; [but] it would be absurd to call this EXCESS, or
> profit, A PART OF THE EXPENDITURE... Likewise the MANUFACTURER obtains IN RETURN
> A QUANTITY OF FINISHED WORK OF A HIGHER *EXCHANGEABLE VALUE* than the
> MATERIALS, etc." ([pp.] 51-53).
> * "Effectual demand consists in the power and inclination, *on the part of the
> consumers,* to give for commodities, either by immediate or circuitous barter, *some
> greater proportion* of all the ingredients of capital than their production costs" * (l.c.,
> [p.] 349).

120 qrs of corn are most certainly more than 100 qrs. But—if
one merely considers the use value and the process it goes
through, that is, in reality, the vegetative or physiological
[XIV-787] process, as is the case here—it would be wrong to say,
not indeed, with regard to the 20 qrs, but with regard to the
elements which go to make them up, that they do [not] enter into
the *production process.* If this were so, they could never emerge
from it. In addition to the 100 qrs of corn—the seeds[76]—various
chemical ingredients supplied by the manure, salts contained in
the soil, water, air, light, are all involved in the process which
transforms 100 qrs of corn into 120. The transformation and
absorption of the elements, the ingredients, the conditions—the
EXPENDITURE OF NATURE, which transforms 100 qrs into 120—takes
place in the *production process* itself and the elements of these
20 qrs enter into this process itself as physiological "EXPENDITURE",
the result of which is the transformation of 100 qrs into 120 qrs.

Regarded merely from the standpoint of use value, these 20 qrs
are not mere profit. The inorganic components have been merely
assimilated by the organic components and transformed into
organic material. Without the addition of matter—and this is the
physiological EXPENDITURE—the 100 qrs would never become 120.
Thus it can in fact be said even from the point of view of mere
use value, that is, regarding corn as corn—what enters into corn

---

[a] See this volume, p. 250.— *Ed.*

in inorganic form, as EXPENDITURE, appears in *organic* form, as the actual result, the 20 qrs, i.e. as the surplus of the corn harvested over the corn sown.

But these considerations, in themselves, have as little to do with the question of profit, as if one were to say that lengths of wire which, in the labour process, are stretched to a thousand times the length of the metal from which they are fabricated, yield a thousandfold *profit* since their length has been increased a thousandfold. In the CASE of the wire, the length has been increased, in the CASE of CORN, the quantity. But neither increase in length nor increase in quantity constitutes *profit*, which is applicable solely to exchange value, although exchange value manifests itself in a SURPLUS PRODUCE.

As far as exchange value is concerned, there is no need to explain further that the value of 90 qrs of corn can be equal to (or greater than) the value of 100, that the value of 100 can be greater than that of 120, and that of 120 greater than that of 500.

Thus, on the basis of one example which has *nothing* to do with profit, with the surplus in the *value* of the product over the *value* of the capital outlay, Torrens draws conclusions about profit. And even considered physiologically, as use value, his example is wrong since, in actual fact, the 20 qrs of corn which form the SURPLUS PRODUCE already exist *d'une manière ou d'une autre*[a] in the production process, although in a different form.

Finally, Torrens blurts out the brilliant old conception that profit is profit UPON EXPROPRIATION. One of Torrens' merits is that he has at all raised the controversial question: what are *production costs*. Ricardo continually confuses the *values* of commodities with their *production costs* (in so far as they = the cost price) and is consequently astonished that *Say*, although he believes that prices are determined by production costs, draws different conclusions.[b] Malthus, like Ricardo, asserts that the price of a commodity is determined by the production costs, and, like Ricardo, he includes the profit in the production costs. Nevertheless, he defines value in a different way, not by the quantity of labour contained in the commodity, but by the quantity of labour it can command.

The ambiguities surrounding the concept of *production costs* arise from the very nature of capitalist production.

Firstly: The *cost to the capitalist* of the commodity (he produces) is, naturally, what it *costs him.* It costs him nothing—that is, he

---

[a] In one way or another.— *Ed.*
[b] See this volume, p. 102.— *Ed.*

EXPENDS NO VALUE UPON IT—apart from the value of the *capital ADVANCED.* If he lays out £100 on raw materials, machinery, WAGES, etc., in order to produce the commodity, it costs him £100, *ni plus ni moins.*[a] Apart from the labour embodied in these ADVANCES, apart from the *accumulated labour* that is contained in the capital expended and determines the value of the commodities expended, it costs him no labour. What the IMMEDIATE LABOUR costs him is the WAGES he pays for it. Apart from these WAGES, the IMMEDIATE LABOUR costs him nothing, and apart from IMMEDIATE LABOUR he advances nothing EXCEPT THE VALUE OF THE CONSTANT CAPITAL.

[XIV-788] It is in this sense that Torrens understands production costs, and this is the sense in which every capitalist understands them when he calculates his profit, WHATEVER ITS RATE MAY BE.

Production costs are here = the ADVANCES OF THE CAPITALIST = THE VALUE OF THE CAPITAL ADVANCED = THE QUANTITY OF the LABOUR CONTAINED IN THE ADVANCED COMMODITIES. Every economist, including Ricardo, uses *this* definition of production costs, whether they are called ADVANCES or EXPENSES, etc. This is what Malthus calls THE PRODUCING PRICE as opposed to the PURCHASER'S price. The transformation of SURPLUS VALUE into *profit* corresponds to this definition of ADVANCES.

Secondly: According to the first definition, the production costs are the price which the capitalist *pays* for the manufacture of the commodity DURING THE PROCESS OF PRODUCTION, therefore they are what the commodity costs *him.* But what the production of a commodity *costs* the capitalist and what the *production of the commodity itself costs,* are two entirely different things. The labour (REALISED and IMMEDIATE) which the capitalist *pays* for the production of the commodity and the labour which is necessary in order to *produce* the commodity are entirely different. Their difference constitutes the difference between the VALUE ADVANCED and the VALUE EARNED; between the purchase price of the commodity for the capitalist and its sale price (that is, if it is sold at its value). If this difference did not exist, then neither money nor commodities would ever be transformed into capital. The source of profit would disappear together with the SURPLUS VALUE. The *production costs of the commodity itself* consist of the value of the capital consumed in the process of its production, that is, the quantity of objectified labour embodied in the commodity + the *quantity OF IMMEDIATE LABOUR WHICH IS EXPENDED UPON IT.* The total *amount* of "REALISED" + "IMMEDIATE LABOUR" consumed in it constitutes the *production costs of the*

---

[a] Neither more nor less.— *Ed.*

commodity itself. The commodity can only be produced by means of the industrial consumption of this quantity OF REALISED AND IMMEDIATE LABOUR. This is the precondition for its emergence out of the process of production as a *product,* as a *commodity* and as a use value. And no matter how profit and wages may vary, these immanent production costs of the commodity remain the same so long as the technological conditions of the real labour process remain the same, or, what amounts to the same thing, as long as there is no variation in the existing development of the productive powers of labour. In this sense, the *production costs of a commodity* = its *value.* The living labour EXPENDED UPON THE COMMODITY and the living labour PAID BY THE CAPITALIST are two different things. HENCE *de prime abord* the production costs of a commodity to the capitalist (HIS ADVANCES) differ from the *production costs of the commodity* itself, its value. THE EXCESS OF ITS VALUE (that is, what the commodity itself costs) OVER AND BEYOND THE VALUE OF THE ADVANCES (that is, what it costs the capitalist) constitutes the profit WHICH, THEREFORE, RESULTS NOT FROM SELLING THE COMMODITY BEYOND ITS VALUE, BUT BEYOND THE VALUE OF THE ADVANCES PAID BY THE CAPITALIST.

The production costs thus defined, the immanent production costs of the commodity, which are equal to its value, i.e. to the total amount of labour time (REALISED AND IMMEDIATE) required for its production, remain the fundamental condition for its production and remain unchangeable so long as the productive powers of labour remain unchanged.

Thirdly: I have however previously shown[a] that, in each separate TRADE OR PARTICULAR OCCUPATION, the capitalist does not by any means sell his commodities—which are also the product of a particular TRADE, OCCUPATION or SPHERE OF PRODUCTION—at the value contained in them, and that, therefore, the AMOUNT OF ITS PROFIT IS NOT IDENTICAL WITH THE AMOUNT OF SURPLUS VALUE, OF SURPLUS LABOUR or UNPAID LABOUR REALISED IN THE COMMODITIES HE SELLS. On the contrary, he can, ON THE AVERAGE, only realise as much SURPLUS VALUE in the commodity as devolves on it as the product of an aliquot part of the social capital. If the social capital = 1,000 and the capital in a particular [XIV-789] OCCUPATION amounts to 100, and if the TOTAL AMOUNT OF SURPLUS VALUE (HENCE OF THE SURPLUS PRODUCE IN WHICH THAT SURPLUS VALUE IS REALISED) = 200, that is, 20%, then the capital of 100 in this particular OCCUPATION would sell its commodity for 120, *whatever might be the value of that commodity, whether 120, less, or more; whether, therefore, the unpaid labour contained in his commodity

---

[a] See present edition, Vol. 31, pp. 262-65, 269, 301-06.— *Ed.*

forms $^1/_5$ of the labour advanced upon it, or whether it do[es] not.*

This is the *cost price*, and when one speaks of *production costs* in the proper sense (in the economic, capitalist sense), then the term denotes THE VALUE OF THE ADVANCES + THE VALUE OF THE AVERAGE PROFITS.[6]

It is clear that, however much the cost price of an individual commodity may diverge from its value, it is determined by the *value* of the total product of the social capital. It is through the equalisation of the profits of the different capitals that they are connected with one another as aliquot parts of the aggregate social capital, and as such aliquot parts they draw dividends out of the COMMON FUNDS OF SURPLUS VALUE (SURPLUS PRODUCE), or SURPLUS LABOUR, OR UNPAID LABOUR. This does not alter in any way the value of the commodity; it does not alter the fact *that, whether its cost price is equal to, greater or smaller than its value, it can never be produced *without its value* being produced, that is to say, without the total amount of realised and immediate labour required for its production being expended upon it.* This quantity of labour, NOT ONLY OF PAID, BUT OF UNPAID LABOUR, must be expended on it, and nothing in the general relationship between capital and LABOUR is altered by the fact THAT IN SOME OCCUPATIONS PART OF THE UNPAID LABOUR IS APPROPRIATED BY "BROTHER CAPITALISTS"[77] INSTEAD OF BY THE CAPITALIST WHO PUTS THE LABOUR IN MOTION IN THAT PECULIAR DEPARTMENT OF INDUSTRY. Further, it is clear *that whatever the relation between the value and the cost price of a commodity, the latter will always change, rise or fall, according with the changes of value, that is to say, the quantity of labour required for the production of the commodity*. It is furthermore clear that *part of the profit must always represent surplus value, unpaid labour, realised in the commodity itself, because, on the basis of capitalistic production, in all commodities there is more labour worked up than has been paid by the capitalist putting that labour in motion. Some part of the profit may consist of labour not worked up in the commodity yielded by a definite trade, or resulting from a given sphere of production; but, then, there is some other commodity, resulting from some other sphere of production, whose cost price falls below its value, or in whose cost price less unpaid labour is accounted for, paid for, than is contained in it.*

It is clear, therefore, that although the *cost prices of most commodities must differ from their values, and hence the "costs of production" [of these commodities must differ] from the total quantity of labour contained in them, nevertheless, those costs of production and those cost prices are not only determined by the values of [the] commodities [and] confirm the law of value instead of contradicting it, but, moreover, that the very existence of costs of production and cost prices can be conceived only on the foundation of value and its law, and becomes a meaningless absurdity without that premiss.*

At the same time one perceives how economists who, on the one hand, observe the actual phenomena of competition and, on the other hand, do not understand the relationship BETWEEN THE LAW OF VALUE AND THE LAW OF COST PRICE, resort to the fiction that capital, not labour, determines the value of commodities or RATHER that there is no such thing as value.[a]

[XIV-790] Profit enters into the *production costs of commodities*; it is rightly included in the "natural price" of commodities by Adam Smith, because, in conditions of capitalist production, the commodity—*in the long run, on the average—is not brought to market if it does not yield the cost price=the value of the advances + the average profit.*[b] Or, as Malthus puts it—although he does not understand the origin of profit, ITS REAL CAUSE[c]— because the profit, and therefore the cost price WHICH includes IT, IS (on the basis of capitalist production) *a condition of the *supply* of the commodity. To be produced, to be brought to the market, the commodity must at least fetch that market price, that cost price to the seller, whether its own value be greater or smaller than that cost price.* It is a matter of indifference to the capitalist whether his commodity contains more or less UNPAID LABOUR than other commodities, *if into its price enters so much of the general stock of unpaid labour, or the surplus produce in which it is fixed, as every other equal quantity of capital will draw from that common stock.* In this respect, the capitalists are "communists". In competition, each naturally tries to secure more than the AVERAGE PROFIT, which is only possible if others secure less. It is precisely as a result of this struggle that the AVERAGE PROFIT is established.

A part of the SURPLUS VALUE realised in profit, i.e. that part which assumes the form of interest on capital laid out (whether borrowed or not), appears to the capitalist as *outlay,* as *production cost* which he has as a *capitalist,* just as profit in general is the immediate aim of capitalist production. But in interest (especially on borrowed

---

[a] See K. Marx, *Outlines of the Critique of Political Economy...* (present edition, Vol. 29, pp. 143-45, 196-98); Vol. 30, p. 101, and also this volume, pp. 264-67, 393-94.— *Ed.*

[b] See present edition, Vol. 31, pp. 440-43.— *Ed.*

[c] See this volume, pp. 210-12, 218, 225-26.— *Ed.*

capital), this appears also as the actual precondition of his production.

At the same time, this reveals the significance of the distinction between the forms of production and of distribution. Profit, a form of distribution, is here simultaneously a form of production, a condition of production, A NECESSARY INGREDIENCY OF THE PROCESS OF PRODUCTION. How absurd it is, therefore, for John Stuart Mill and others to conceive bourgeois forms of production as absolute, but the bourgeois forms of distribution as historically relative, HENCE TRANSITORY. I shall return to this later.[a] The form of distribution is simply the form of production seen *sub alia specie*.[b] The *differentia specifica*—and therefore also the specific limitation—which sets bounds to bourgeois distribution, enters into production itself, as a determining factor, which overlaps and dominates production. The fact that bourgeois production is compelled by its own immanent laws, on the one hand, to develop the productive forces as if production did not take place on a narrow restricted social foundation, while, on the other hand, it can develop these forces only within these narrow limits, is the deepest and most hidden cause of crises, of the crying contradictions within which bourgeois production is carried on and which, even at a cursory glance, reveal it as only a transitional, historical form. This is grasped rather crudely but nonetheless correctly by Sismondi, for example, as a contradiction between production for the sake of production and distribution which *eo ipso*[c] makes absolute development of productivity impossible.[d]

Mill was the first to present Ricardo's theory in systematic form, even though he did it only in rather abstract outlines. What he tries to achieve is formal logical consistency. The *disintegration* of the Ricardian school therefore begins with him. With the master what is new and significant develops vigorously amid the "manure" of contradictions out of the contradictory phenomena. The underlying contradictions themselves testify to the richness of the living foundation from which the theory itself developed. It is

---

[a] See this volume, pp. 498-99.— *Ed.*
[b] From a different aspect.— *Ed.*
[c] By the very fact.— *Ed.*
[d] See this volume, pp. 247-48.— *Ed.*

different with the disciple. His raw material is no longer reality, but the new theoretical form in which the master had sublimated it. It is in part the theoretical disagreement of opponents of the new theory and in part the often paradoxical relationship of this theory to reality which drive him to seek to refute his opponents and explain away reality. In doing so, he entangles himself in contradictions and with his attempt to solve these he demonstrates the beginning disintegration of the theory which he dogmatically espouses. On the one hand, Mill wants to present bourgeois production as the absolute form of production and seeks therefore to prove that its real contradictions are only apparent ones. On the other hand, [he seeks] to present the Ricardian theory as the absolute theoretical form of this mode of production and ditto to disprove the theoretical contradictions, both the ones pointed out by others and the ones he himself cannot help seeing. Nevertheless in a way Mill advances the Ricardian view beyond the bounds reached by Ricardo. He supports the same historical interests as Ricardo—those of industrial capital against landed property—and he draws the practical conclusions from the theory—that of rent for example—more ruthlessly, against the institution of landed property which he would like to see more or less directly transformed into state property.[a] This conclusion and this side of Mill do not concern us here.

Ricardo's disciples, just as Ricardo himself, fail to make a distinction between *surplus value* and *profit*. Ricardo only becomes aware of the problem as a result of the different influence which the variation of wages can exercise on capitals of different organic composition (and [he considers] different organic composition only with regard to the circulation process). It does not occur to them that, even if one considers not capitals in DIFFERENT OCCUPATIONS but *each* capital separately, in so far as it does not consist exclusively of variable capital, of capital laid out in wages only, rate of profit and rate of surplus value are different things, that therefore profit must be a more developed, specifically modified form of surplus value. They perceive the difference only in so far as it concerns equal profits—AVERAGE RATE OF PROFIT—for capitals in DIFFERENT SPHERES OF PRODUCTION AND DIFFERENTLY COMPOSED OF FIXED AND CIRCULATING INGREDIENTS. In this connection Mill only repeats in a vulgarised form what Ricardo says in CHAPTER I, "On Value". The only new consideration which occurs to him in relation to this question is this:

---

[a] See present edition, Vol. 31, p. 379, and also K. Marx, *The Poverty of Philosophy. Answer to the "Philosophy of Poverty" by M. Proudhon* (present edition, Vol. 6, p. 203).— *Ed.*

Mill remarks that "*TIME AS SUCH*" (i.e. not labour time, but simply *time*) produces nothing, consequently it does not produce "VALUE". How does this fit in with the law of value according to which capital, because it requires a longer time for its RETURNS, yields, as Ricardo says, the same profit as capital which employs more immediate labour but returns more rapidly? One perceives that Mill deals here only with a quite individual case which, expressed in general terms, would read as follows: How does the cost price, and the [XIV-792] AVERAGE RATE OF PROFIT which it presupposes (HENCE equal value of commodities containing very UNEQUAL quantities of labour), fit in with the fact that profit is nothing but a part of the labour time contained in the commodity, the part which is appropriated by the capitalist without an equivalent? On the other hand, in the case of the AVERAGE RATE OF PROFIT and cost price, criteria which are quite extrinsic and external to the determination of value are advanced, for example, that the capitalist whose capital takes longer to bring in a RETURN because, as in the case of WINE, it must remain longer in the production process (or, in other cases, longer in the circulation process) must be compensated for the time in which he cannot valorise his capital. But how can the time in which no valorisation takes place create value?

Mill's passage concerning "*time*" reads:

*"Time can do nothing ... how then can it add to value? Time is a mere abstract term. It is a word, a sound. And it is the very same logical absurdity to talk of an abstract unit measuring value, and of time creating it" * (*Elements etc.*, 2ND ED., p. 99).[a][78]

In reality, what is involved in the grounds for compensation between CAPITALS IN DIFFERENT SPHERES OF PRODUCTION is not the production of surplus value, but *its division between different categories of capitalists.* Viewpoints are here advanced which have nothing whatever to do with the determination of value as such. Everything which compels capital in A particular SPHERE OF PRODUCTION to renounce conditions which would produce a *greater amount of surplus value* in other spheres, is regarded here as *grounds for compensation.* Thus, if more fixed and less circulating capital is employed, if more constant than variable capital is employed, if it must remain longer in the circulation process, and finally, if it must remain longer in the production process without being subjected to the labour process—a thing which always happens when breaks of a technological character occur in the production

---

[a] Quoted from [S. Bailey,] *A Critical Dissertation...*, p. 217.— *Ed.*

process in order to expose the developing product to the working of natural forces, for example, wine in the cellar. Compensation ensues in all these cases and the last mentioned is the one which Mill seizes on, thus tackling the difficulty in a very circumscribed and isolated way. A part of the surplus value produced in other spheres is transferred to the capitals more unfavourably placed with regard to the direct exploitation of labour, simply in accordance with their size (competition brings about this equalisation so that each separate capital appears only as an aliquot part of social capital).[a] The phenomenon is very simple as soon as the relationship of surplus value and profit as well as the equalisation of profits in a general rate of profit is understood. If, however, it is to be explained directly from the law of value without any intermediate link, that is, if the profit which a particular capital yields in a particular TRADE is to be explained on the basis of the surplus value contained in the commodities it produces, [in other words on the basis of] the *unpaid labour* (consequently also on the basis of the LABOUR directly WORKED UP in the commodities themselves), this is a much more difficult problem to solve than that of squaring the circle, which can be solved algebraically.[79] It is simply an attempt to present that which does not exist as in fact existing. But it is in this *direct* form that Mill seeks to solve the problem. Thus no solution of the matter is possible here, only a sophistic explaining away of the difficulty, that is, only scholasticism. Mill begins this process. In the case of an unscrupulous blockhead like *McCulloch*, this manner assumes a swaggering shamelessness.[b] Mill's solution cannot be better summed up than it is in the words of *Bailey*:

* "Mr Mill has made a curious attempt to resolve the *effects of time* into *expenditure of labour*. 'If,' says he," * (p. 97 of the *Elements*, 2ND ED., 1824) * "'the wine which is put in the cellar is increased in value $1/10$ by being kept a year, $1/10$ more of labour may be correctly *considered* as having been expended upon it.' ...a fact can be correctly considered as having taken [XIV-793] place only when it really has taken place. In the instance adduced, no human being, by the terms of the supposition, has approached the wine, or spent upon it a moment or a single motion of his muscles" * (*A Critical Dissertation on the Nature, Measures, and Causes of Value etc.*, London, 1825, [pp.] 219-20).

Here the contradiction between the general law and further developments in the concrete circumstances is to be resolved not by the discovery of the connecting links but by directly subordinat-

---

a See present edition, Vol. 31, pp. 259-65, 302-05, 430-39; this volume, pp. 67-71, and the manuscript, Notebook XVIII, p. 1190 (Vol. 33).— *Ed.*

b See this volume, pp. 361-64, and also Vol. 31, p. 416.— *Ed.*

ing and immediately adapting the concrete to the abstract. This moreover is to be brought about by a verbal fiction, BY CHANGING *vera rerum vocabula*.[a] (These are indeed "VERBAL DISPUTES",[b] they are "VERBAL", however, because real contradictions which are not resolved in a real way, are to be solved by phrases.) When we come to deal with McCulloch, it will be seen that this manner, which appears in Mill only in embryo, did more to undermine the whole foundation of the Ricardian theory than all the attacks of its opponents.[c]

Mill resorts to this type of argument only when he is quite unable to find any other expedient. But as a rule his method is quite different. Where the economic relation—and therefore also the categories expressing it—includes opposites, contradictions, and even the unity of the opposites, he emphasises the aspect of the *unity* of the contradictions and denies the *contradictions*. He transforms the unity of opposites into the direct identity of opposites.

For example, a commodity conceals the contradiction of use value and exchange value. This contradiction develops further, presents itself and manifests itself in the duplication of the commodity into commodity and money. This duplication appears as a process in the metamorphosis of commodities in which selling and buying are different aspects of a single process and each act of this process simultaneously includes its opposite. In the first part of this work, I mentioned that Mill disposes of the contradiction by concentrating only on the *unity* of buying and selling; consequently he reduces circulation to barter, then, however, smuggles categories borrowed from circulation into barter.[d] See also what I wrote there about Mill's *theory of money*, in which he employs similar methods.[e]

In James Mill we find the unsatisfactory divisions— "Production", "Distribution", "Interchange", "Consumption".[f] [80]

Wages:

"Instead, however, of waiting till the commodity is produced, and the value of it is realised, it has been found to suit *much better* the convenience of the labourers to

---

a The correct names of things.— *Ed.*
b See this volume, pp. 298-305.— *Ed.*
c Ibid., pp. 360-62.— *Ed.*
d See K. Marx, *A Contribution to the Critique of Political Economy*. Part One (present edition, Vol. 29, p. 333).— *Ed.*
e Ibid., pp. 409-12.— *Ed.*
f See J. Mill, *Élémens d'économie politique*, Paris, 1823, pp. 7, 13, 85, 237.— *Ed.*

receive their share *in advance*. The shape under which it has been found most convenient [for all parties] that they should receive it, is that of wages. When the share of the commodity which belongs to the labourer has been all received in the shape of wages, the commodity itself belongs to the capitalist, he having, in reality, *bought the share of the labourer* and paid for it in advance" (*Élémens d'économie politique*, French translation by [J. T.] Parisot, Paris, 1823, p[p. 33-]34).

It is highly characteristic of Mill that, just as *money* for him is an expedient invented for convenience's sake, *capitalist relations* are likewise invented for the same reason. These specific social relations of production are invented for "convenience's" sake. Commodities and money are transformed into capital because the worker has ceased to engage in exchange as a commodity producer and commodity owner; instead of selling commodities he is compelled to sell his labour itself ([to sell] directly his labour capacity) as a commodity to the owner of the objective conditions of labour. This separation is the prerequisite for the relationship of capital and wage labour in the same way as it is the prerequisite for the transformation of money (or of the commodities by which it is represented) into capital. Mill presupposes the *separation,* the *division*; he presupposes the relationship of capitalist and wage worker, in order to present as a matter of convenience the situation in which the worker sells *no product,* no commodity, but his share of the product (in the production of which he has no say whatsoever and which proceeds *independently* of him) before he has produced it. [XIV-794] Or, more precisely, the worker's share of the product is paid for—transformed into money—by the capitalist before the capitalist HAS DISPOSED OF, or realised, the product in which the worker has a share.

This view is aimed at circumventing the specific difficulty, along with the specific form of the relationship. Namely, the difficulty of the Ricardian system according to which the worker sells his *labour* directly (not his labour capacity). For: the value of a commodity is determined by the labour time required for its production; how does it happen that this law of value does not hold good in the greatest of all exchanges, which forms the foundation of capitalist production, the exchange between capitalist and wage worker? Why is the quantity OF REALISED LABOUR received by the worker as WAGES not equal to the quantity of IMMEDIATE LABOUR which he gives in exchange for his WAGES? To SHIFT THIS DIFFICULTY, Mill transforms the wage worker into a commodity owner who sells the capitalist his *product, his commodity*—since his *share* of the product, of the commodity, is *his* product, his *commodity,* a value produced by him in the form of a particular commodity. He resolves the difficulty by transforming the transaction between capitalist and wage worker, which includes the contradiction between REALISED and IMMEDIATE LABOUR, into a COMMON transaction between commodity owners, owners of REALISED LABOUR. Although by resorting to this artifice Mill has indeed made it impossible for himself to grasp the specific nature, the *differentia specifica* of the proceedings which take place between capitalist and wage worker, he has not reduced the difficulty in any way, but has increased it, because the peculiarity of the result is now no longer comprehensible in terms of the peculiarity of the commodity which the worker sells (and the specific feature of this commodity is that its use value is itself a factor of exchange value, its use therefore creates a greater exchange value then it itself contained).

According to Mill, the worker is a seller of commodities like any other. For example, he produces 6 yards of linen. Of these 6, 2 yards are assumed to be equal to the value of the labour which he has added. He thus sells 2 yards of linen to the capitalist. Why then should he not receive the full value of the 2 yards, like any other seller of 2 yards of linen, since he is now a seller of linen like any other? Rather the contradiction with the law of value now expresses itself much more crassly than before. He does not sell a particular commodity differing from all other commodities. He sells labour embodied in a product, that is, a commodity which as such is not specifically different from any other commodity. If now the price of a yard [of linen]—that is, the quantity of money containing the same amount of labour time as the yard [of linen]—is 2s., why then does the worker receive 1s. instead of 2? But if the worker received 2s., the capitalist would not secure any SURPLUS VALUE and the whole Ricardian system would collapse. We would have to return to PROFIT UPON EXPROPRIATION.[75] The 6 yards would cost the capitalist 12s., i.e. their value, but he would sell them for 13s.

Or linen, and any other commodity, is sold at its value when the capitalist sells it, but *below* its value when the worker sells it. Thus the law of value would be destroyed by the transaction between worker and capitalist. And it is precisely in order to avoid this that Mill resorts to his fictitious argument. He wants to transform the relationship between worker and capitalist into the ordinary one between sellers and buyers of commodities. But why should not the ordinary law of value of commodities apply to this transaction? [It may be said however that] the worker is paid "in advance". Consequently this is not after all the ordinary relationship of buying and selling commodities. What does this "payment in advance" mean in this context? The worker who, for example, is paid weekly, "*advances*" his labour and produces the share of the weekly product which belongs to him—his weekly labour embodied in a product—(both according to Mill's assumption and in practice) before he receives "payment" for this share from the capitalist. The capitalist "advances" raw materials and instruments, the worker the "labour", and as soon as the wages are paid at the end of the week, he *sells* a commodity, his commodity, his share of the total commodity, to the capitalist. But, Mill will say, the capitalist pays the 2 [XIV-795] yards of linen due to the worker, i.e. turns them into cash, transforms them into money, before he himself sells the 6 yards of linen and transforms them into money. But what if the capitalist is working on orders, if he sells the goods before he produces them? Or to express it more generally, what difference does it make to the worker—in this case the seller of 2 yards of linen—if the capitalist buys these 2 yards from him in order to sell them again, and not to consume them? Of what concern are the buyer's motives to the seller? And how can motives, moreover, modify the law of value? To be consistent, each seller would have to dispose of his commodities below their value, for he is disposing of his products to the buyer in the form of a use value, whereas the buyer hands over value in the form of money, the cash form of the product. In this case, the linen manufacturer would also have to *underpay* the yarn merchant and the machine manufacturer and the colliery owner and so on. For they sell him commodities which he only intends to transform into money, whereas he pays them "in advance" the *value* of the component parts entering into his commodity not only before the commodity is sold, but before it is even produced. The worker provides him with linen, a commodity in a marketable form, in contrast to other sellers whose commodities, machinery, raw materials, etc., have to go through a process before they acquire a saleable form. It is a pretty kettle of fish for such an inveterate Ricardian as Mill, according to whom purchase and sale, supply and DEMAND are identical terms, and money a mere formality, if the transformation of the commodity into money—and nothing else takes place when the 2 yards of linen are sold to the capitalist—includes the fact that the seller has to sell the commodity below its value, and the buyer, with his money, has to buy it above its value.

[Mill's argument] therefore amounts to the absurdity that, in this transaction, the buyer buys the commodity in order to resell it at a profit and that, consequently, the seller must sell the commodity *below* its value—and with this the whole theory of value falls to the ground. This second attempt by Mill to resolve a Ricardian contradiction, in fact destroys the whole basis of the system, especially its great merit that it defines the relationship between capital and wage labour as a direct exchange between HOARDED and IMMEDIATE LABOUR, that is, that it grasps its specific features.

In order to extricate himself, Mill would have to go further and to say that it is not merely a question of the simple transaction of the purchase and sale of commodities; that, on the contrary, in so far as it involves payment or the turning into money of the worker's product, which is equal to his share of the total product, the relationship between worker and capitalist is similar to that prevailing between the LENDING CAPITALIST OR DISCOUNTING CAPITALIST (the MONIED CAPITALIST) and the INDUSTRIAL CAPITALIST. It would be a pretty state of affairs to presuppose interest-bearing capital—a special form of capital—in order to deduce the general form of capital, capital which produces profit; that is, to present a derived form of surplus value (which already presupposes capital) as the cause of the appearance of surplus value. In that case, moreover, Mill would have to be consistent and in place of all the definite laws concerning wages and the RATE OF WAGES elaborated by Ricardo, he would have to derive them from the RATE OF INTEREST, and if he did that it would indeed be impossible to explain what determines the RATE OF INTEREST, since, according to the RICARDIANS AND ALL OTHER ECONOMISTS WORTH NAMING, the rate of interest IS DETERMINED BY THE RATE OF PROFIT.

The proposition concerning the *"share"* of the worker in his own product is in fact based on this: If one considers not simply the isolated transaction between capitalist and worker, but the EXCHANGE which takes place between both in the COURSE OF REPRODUCTION, and if one considers the real content of this process instead of the form in which it appears, then it is in fact evident that what the capitalist pays the worker (as well as the part of capital which confronts the worker as constant capital) is nothing but a part of the worker's product itself and, indeed, a part which does not have to be transformed into money, but which has already been sold, has already been transformed into money, since WAGES are paid in money, not *in naturalibus.* Under slavery, etc., the false appearance brought about by the previous transformation of the product into money—in so far as it is expended on WAGES—does not arise; it is therefore obvious that what the slave receives as wages is not, in fact, something that the SLAVE-OWNER "ADVANCES" him, but simply the portion of the realised labour of the SLAVE that returns to him in the form of means of subsistence. The same applies to the capitalist. He "advances" something only in appearance. Since he pays for the work only after it has been done, he advances or rather [XIV-796] *pays* the worker as WAGES a part of the product produced by the worker and already transformed into money. A part of the worker's product which the capitalist appropriates, which is *deducted beforehand,* returns to the worker in the form of WAGES—as an advance on the new product, if you like. It is quite unworthy of Mill to cling to this *appearance* of the transaction in order to explain the transaction itself (this sort of thing might suit McCulloch, Say or Bastiat). The capitalist can ADVANCE the worker NOTHING EXCEPT WHAT HE HAS TAKEN previously FROM THE worker, i.e. what HAS BEEN ADVANCED TO HIM BY OTHER PEOPLE'S LABOUR. Malthus himself says that what the capitalist advances CONSISTS not "OF CLOTH" and "OTHER COMMODITIES", but "*OF LABOUR*",[a] that is, precisely of that which he himself does not perform. He advances the worker's own labour to the worker.

However, the whole paraphrase is of no use to Mill, for it does not help him to avoid resolving the question: how can the exchange between HOARDED and IMMEDIATE LABOUR (and this is the way the exchange process between capital and labour is perceived by Ricardo and by Mill and others after him) correspond to the law of value, which it contradicts directly? One can see from the following passage that it is of no help to Mill:

> "In *what proportion* are the products divided between the labourer and the capitalist, or what share [of the labourer] determines the rate of wages? ([Mill, *Élémens d'économie politique*,] ED. by Parisot, p. 34). The determination of the shares of the labourer and the CAPITALIST is the subject of a *bargain* between them. All bargains, when left in freedom, are determined by competition, and the terms alter according to the *state of supply and demand*" (l.c., [pp.] 34-35).[b]

The worker is paid for his "share" of the product. This is said in order to transform him into an ordinary seller of a *commodity* (a product) vis-à-vis capital and to eliminate the specific feature of this relationship. The worker's share of the product is *his* product, that is, the share of the product in which his newly added labour is realised. *Quod non.*[c] On the contrary, we now ask which is his "share" of the product, that is, *which* is *his* product? For the part of the product which belongs to him is *his* product, which he sells. We are now told that *his* product and his *product* are two quite different things. We must establish, first of all, what his product (in other words, his share of the product, that is, the part

---

[a] T. R. Malthus, *The Measure of Value Stated and Illustrated...*, pp. 17-18.— *Ed.*
[b] Marx quotes Mill with some alterations.— *Ed.*
[c] But this is not the case.— *Ed.*

of the product that belongs to him) is. His product is thus a mere phrase, since the [quantity of] value which he receives from the capitalist is not determined by his own production. Mill has thus merely removed the difficulty one step. He has got no farther than he was at the beginning.

There is a *quid pro quo* here. Supposing that the exchange between capital and wage labour is a continuous activity—as it is if one does not isolate and consider one individual act or element of capitalist production—then the worker receives a part of the value of his product which he has replaced+that part of the value which he has given the capitalist for nothing. This is repeated continuously. Thus he receives in fact continuously a portion of the value of his own product, a part of, or a share in, the value he has produced. Whether his WAGES are high or low is not determined by his share of the product but, on the contrary, his share of the product is determined by the amount of his WAGES. He actually receives a share of the value of the product. But the share he receives is determined by the VALUE OF LABOUR, not conversely, the VALUE OF LABOUR—by his share in the product. The VALUE OF LABOUR is determined by the labour time required by the worker for his own reproduction; it is determined by the sale of his labour capacity to the capitalist. This virtually determines his share of the product as well. It does not happen the other way round, that his share of the product is determined first, and as a result, the amount or VALUE of his WAGES. This is precisely one of Ricardo's most important and most emphasised propositions, for otherwise the price of labour would be determined by the price of the commodity it produces, whereas, according to Ricardo, the price of labour determines nothing but the *rate of profit.*

And how does Mill determine the "share" of the product which the worker receives? By demand and supply, competition between workers and capitalists. What Mill says applies to all commodities:

"The determination of the shares" (read: in the value of commodities) "of the labourer and the capitalist" (seller and buyer) "is the subject of a bargain between [XIV-797] them. All bargains, when left in freedom, are determined by competition, and the terms alter according to the state of supply and demand." [a]

Here we have the gist of the matter.[b] [This is said by] Mill who, as a zealous Ricardian, proves that although demand and supply can, to be sure, determine the vacillations of the market price

---

[a] Marx quotes Mill with some alterations. Cf. this volume, p. 283.— *Ed.*

[b] In the manuscript: Also das des Pudels Kern! (Goethe, *Faust*, Act I, Scene 4, "Faust's Study").— *Ed.*

either above or below the *value* of the commodity, they cannot determine that value itself, that these are meaningless words when applied to the determination of value, for the determination of demand and supply presupposes the determination of value! In order to determine the VALUE OF LABOUR, the *value* of a commodity, Mill now resorts to something for which Say had already reproached Ricardo [14]: determination by demand and supply.[a]

But even more.

Mill does not say which of the two parties represents supply and which DEMAND—which is of no importance to the matter here. Still, since the capitalist offers money and the worker offers something for the money, we will assume that DEMAND is on the side of the capitalist and supply on that of the worker. But what then does the worker "sell"? What does he supply? His "share" of the product which does not [yet] exist? But it is just his share in the future product which has to be determined by competition between him and the capitalist, by the "demand and supply" relationship. One of the sides of this relationship—supply—cannot be something which is itself the result of the struggle between demand and supply. What then does the worker offer for sale? His *labour*? If this is so, then Mill is back again at the original difficulty he sought to evade, the EXCHANGE *between* HOARDED *and* IMMEDIATE LABOUR. And when he says that what is happening here is not the exchange of equivalents, or that the value of LABOUR, the commodity sold, is not measured by "the labour time" itself, but by competition, by demand and supply, then he admits that Ricardo's theory breaks down, that his opponents are right, that the determination of the value of commodities by labour time is false, because the value of the most important commodity, labour itself, contradicts this law of value of commodities. As we shall see later, *Wakefield* says this quite explicitly.[b] Mill can turn and twist as he will, he cannot extricate himself from the dilemma. At best, to use his own mode of expression, competition causes the workers to offer a *definite quantity of labour* for a price which, according to the relation of demand and supply, is equal to a larger or smaller part of the product which they will produce with this quantity of labour. That this *price*, this *sum of money*, which they receive in this way, is equal to a larger or smaller part of the value of the product to be manufactured, does not, however, *de prime abord*,[c] in

---

[a] See this volume, pp. 290-93.— *Ed.*
[b] Ibid., p. 371.— *Ed.*
[c] Here: as a matter of course.— *Ed.*

any way prevent a *definite amount of living labour* (IMMEDIATE LABOUR) from being exchanged for a greater or lesser amount of *money* (ACCUMULATED LABOUR, existing moreover in the form of exchange value). It does not therefore prevent the exchange of unequal quantities of labour, that is, of less HOARDED LABOUR for more IMMEDIATE LABOUR. This was precisely the phenomenon that Mill had to explain and he wished to clear the problem up without violating the law of value. The phenomenon is not changed in the slightest, much less explained, by declaring that the proportion in which the worker exchanges his IMMEDIATE LABOUR for money *is expressed* at the end of the production process in the ratio of the value paid him to the value of the product he has produced. The original *unequal* exchange between capital and LABOUR thus only *appears* in a different form.

How Mill boggles at direct EXCHANGE between LABOUR and capital—which Ricardo takes as his point of departure without any embarrassment at all—is also shown by the way he proceeds. Thus he says:

[XIV-798] "Let us begin by supposing that there is a certain number of capitalists and a certain number of labourers. The *proportion, in which the commodities produced are divided between them, has fixed itself at some particular point.* Let us next suppose that the labourers have increased in number without any increase in the *quantity of capital.* The additional labourers must endeavour to supplant those who have forestalled the employment. They must *offer to work for a smaller reward.* Wages, therefore, decline ... and vice versa... If the ratio which capital and population bear to one another remains the same, the wage rate will remain the same" (l.c., p. 35 et seq. passim).

What has to be determined is "the proportion in which they" (capitalists and workers) "divide the product". In order to establish this by competition, Mill *assumes* that this proportion "*has fixed itself* at some particular *point*". In order to establish the "share" of the worker by means of competition, he *assumes* that it is determined *before* competition "at some particular point". Moreover, in order to demonstrate how competition alters the division of the product which is *determined* "at some particular point", he assumes that workers "*offer to work for a smaller reward*" when their number grows more rapidly than the quantity of capital. Thus he says here outright that what the workers supply consists of "l a b o u r" and that they offer this labour for a "*reward*", i.e. money, a definite quantity of "HOARDED LABOUR". In order to avoid direct exchange between labour and capital, direct *sale of labour*, he has recourse to the theory of the "division of the product". And in order to explain the proportion in which the product is divided, he presupposes *direct sale* of labour for money, so that this original EXCHANGE between CAPITAL and LABOUR is later *expressed* in the proportion of [the share] the worker receives of his product, and not that the original EXCHANGE is determined by his share of the product. And finally, if the number of workers and the amount of capital remain the same, then the "wage rate" will remain *the same*. But what is the wage rate when demand and supply balance? That is the point which has to be explained. It is not explained by declaring that this rate *is altered* when the equilibrium between demand and supply is upset. Mill's tautological circumlocutions only demonstrate that he feels there is a snag here in the Ricardian theory which he can only overcome by abandoning the theory altogether.

Against Malthus, Torrens, and others. Against the determination of the value of commodities by the value of capital, Mill remarks correctly:

*"Capital *is* commodities. If the value of commodities, then, depends upon the value of capital, it depends upon the value of commodities; the value of commodities depends upon itself"* (*Elements etc.*, 1ST ED. London, 1821, [p.] 74).

Demand, supply, overproduction.[81] // Mill does not gloss over the contradiction between capital and labour. The *rate of profit* must be high so that the social class which is free from immediate labour may be important; and for that purpose wages must be relatively low. It is necessary that the mass of the labourers should not be masters of their own time and should be slaves of their own needs, so that human (social) capacities can develop freely in the classes for which the working class serves merely as a basis. The working class represents lack of development in order that other classes can represent human development. This IN FACT is the contradiction in which bourgeois [XIV-799] society develops, as has every hitherto existing society, and this is declared to be a *necessary law*, i.e. the existing state of affairs is declared to be absolutely reasonable.

"*Man's perfectibilité*, or the power of advancing continually from one degree of knowledge, and of happiness, to another, seem, in a great measure, to depend upon the existence of a class of men which have *their time at their command*; that is, who are rich enough to be freed from all solicitude with respect to the means of living in a certain state of enjoyment. It is by this class of men that knowledge is cultivated and enlarged; it is also by this class that it is diffused; it is this class of men whose children receive the best education, and are prepared for all the higher and more delicate functions of society, as legislators, judges, administrators, teachers, inventors in all the arts, and superintendents in all the more important works, by which the dominion of the human species is extended over the powers of nature" (l.c., [*Élémens d'économie politique*, tr. by Parisot, Paris, 1823, p.] 65).

"To enable a considerable proportion of the community to enjoy the advantages of *leisure*, the *return to capital* must *evidently* be *large*" (l.c., [p.] 67).

In addition to the above. Mill, as a Ricardian, defines LABOUR and CAPITAL simply as *different forms* of labour.

* "Labour and Capital—the one, *immediate labour*... the other, *hoarded* labour" * ([*Elements of Political Economy*,] 1st Engl. ed., London, 1821, p. 75).

In another passage he says:

"Of these two *species of labour*, [two things] are to be observed. They are *not always paid according to the same rate*" ([*Élémens d'économie politique*,] ed. by Parisot, [p.] 100).

Here he comes to the point. Since what pays for IMMEDIATE labour is always HOARDED LABOUR, CAPITAL, the fact that it is not paid at *the same rate* means nothing more than that more IMMEDIATE LABOUR is exchanged for less HOARDED LABOUR, and that this is "*always*" the case, since otherwise HOARDED LABOUR would not be exchanged as "capital" for IMMEDIATE LABOUR and would not only fail to yield the *very high return* desired by Mill, but would yield none at all. The passage quoted thus contains the admission (since Mill along with Ricardo regards the exchange between CAPITAL and LABOUR as a direct exchange of HOARDED and IMMEDIATE LABOUR), that they are exchanged in *unequal proportions,* and that in respect of them the law of value—according to which equal quantities of labour are exchanged for one another—breaks down.

Mill advances as a basic law what Ricardo actually assumes in order to develop his theory of rent[a]:

"The rate of agricultural profits determines the rate of all other profits" ([*Elements of Political Economy*,] 2nd ed., London, 1824, [p.] 78).[b]

This is fundamentally wrong, since capitalist production develops first of all in industry, not in agriculture, and only embraces the latter by degrees, so that it is only as a result of the advance of capitalist production that THE AGRICULTURAL PROFITS BECOME EQUALISED TO THE INDUSTRIAL profits and only as a result of this equalisation do the former [influence] the latter. Hence it is in the first place wrong historically. But secondly, once this EQUALISATION is an accomplished fact—that is, presupposing a level of development of agriculture in which capital, in accordance with the rate of profit, flows from industry to agriculture and vice versa—it is equally wrong to state that from this point on AGRICULTURAL PROFITS become the determining force, instead of the influence being reciprocal. Incidentally, in order to develop the concept of rent, Ricardo himself assumes the opposite. The price of corn rises; as a

---

a See this volume, pp. 99-101.— *Ed.*

b Marx quotes Mill with some alterations.— *Ed.*

result agricultural *profits* do not *fall* (as long as there are no new supplies either from inferior lands or from additional, less productive investments of capital)—for the rise in the price of corn more than compensates the farmer for the loss he incurs by the rise in wages following on the rise in the price of corn—but *profits fall* in industry, where no such compensation or over-compensation takes place. Consequently the *industrial profit rate* falls and HENCE capital which yields this lower rate of profit can therefore BE EMPLOYED on inferior lands. This would not be the case if the old profit rate prevailed. Only because the decline of industrial profits thus reacts on the agricultural profit yielded by THE WORSE LANDS, does AGRICULTURAL PROFIT GENERALLY fall, [XIV-800] and a part of it is detached in the form of rent from the profit THE BETTER SOILS yield. This is the way Ricardo describes the process, according to which, therefore, INDUSTRIAL PROFIT determines AGRICUL-TURAL profit. If AGRICULTURAL PROFIT were to rise again as a result of improvements in agriculture, then industrial profit would also rise. But this does not by any means exclude the fact that—as originally the *decline in industrial profit* causes a decline in AGRICULTURAL profit—*a rise* in industrial profit may bring about a rise in AGRICULTURAL PROFIT. This is always the case when INDUSTRIAL PROFIT rises *independently of the price of corn* and of other AGRICULTURAL NECESSARIES which enter into the wages of the workers, that is, [when it rises] as a result of the fall in the value of commodities which constitute constant capital, etc. Rent moreover cannot possibly be explained if industrial profit does *not* regulate AGRICULTURAL profit. THE *AVERAGE RATE* OF PROFIT in industry is established as a result of equalisation of the profits of capitals and the consequent transformation of the values into *cost prices*.[6] These cost prices— the value of the capital advanced+AVERAGE PROFIT—are the *prerequi-site* received by agriculture from industry, since the equalisation of profits cannot take place in agriculture owing to landownership. If then the value of AGRICULTURAL PRODUCE is higher than the cost price determined by the *INDUSTRIAL AVERAGE PROFIT* would be, the excess of this value over the cost price constitutes the absolute rent. But in order that this excess of value over cost price can be measured, the *cost price* must be the *prius*; it must therefore be imposed on agriculture as a law by industry.

A passage from Mill must be noted:

"That which is *productively* consumed is always capital. This is a particularly strange property of productive consumption. Whatever is consumed productively *is* capital, and it *becomes* capital because of the consumption" (l.c., [*Élémens d'économie politique*,] ED. by Parisot, [pp. 241-]242).

"A demand means the *will to purchase* and *means of purchasing*... The *equivalent object*" (means of purchasing) "which a man brings is the *instrument* of demand. The extent of his demand is measured by the value of this object. The demand and the equivalent are convertible terms, and one may be substituted for the other... His" (a man's) "will, therefore, to *purchase*, and his *means of purchasing*, in other words, his demand, is exactly equal to the [value] of what he has produced, and does not mean to consume" (l.c., ED. by Parisot, [pp.] 252-53).[a]

One sees here how the direct identity of demand and supply (HENCE the impossibility of a GENERAL GLUT) is proved. The product constitutes demand and the extent of this demand, moreover, is measured by the value of the product. The same abstract "reasoning" with which Mill demonstrates that buying and selling are but identical and do not differ; the same tautological phrases with which he shows that prices depend on the amount of money in circulation; the same methods used to prove that supply and demand (which are only more developed forms of buyer and seller) must balance each other. The logic is always the same. If a relationship includes opposites, it comprises not only opposites but also the *unity* of opposites. It is therefore a *unity without opposites.* This is Mill's logic, by which he eliminates the "contradictions".

Let us begin with *supply.* What I supply is *commodities,* a unity of use value and exchange value, for example, a definite quantity of iron=£3 (which=a definite quantity of labour time). According to the assumption I am a manufacturer of iron. I supply a use value—iron—and I supply a value, namely, the value expressed in the price of the iron, that is, in £3. But there is the following little difference. A definite quantity of iron is *in reality* placed on the market by me. The *value* of the iron, on the other hand, exists only as its *price* which must first be realised by the buyer of the iron, who represents, as far as I am concerned, the *demand* for iron. The demand of the seller of iron consists in the demand for the *exchange value* of the iron, which, although it is embodied in the iron, is not realised. It is possible for the same *exchange value* to be represented by very different quantities of iron. The supply of use value and the supply of value to be realised are thus by no means identical, since quite different quantities of use value [XIV-801] can represent the same quantity of exchange value.

The same value—£3—can be represented by 1, 3 or 10 tons [of iron]. The quantity of iron (use value) which I supply and the quantity of value I supply, are by no means proportionate to one another, since the latter quantity can remain unchanged no matter how much the former changes. No matter how large or small the

---

[a] Marx quotes Mill with some alterations.— *Ed.*

quantity of iron I supply may be, it is assumed that I always want to realise the value of the iron, which is independent of the actual quantity of iron and in general of its existence as a use value. The value supplied (but not yet realised) and the quantity of iron which is realised, do not correspond to each other. No grounds exist therefore for assuming that the possibility of selling a commodity at its value corresponds in any way to the quantity of the commodity I bring to market. For the buyer, my commodity exists, above all, as use value. He buys it as such. But what he needs is a definite quantity of iron. His need for iron is just as little determined by the quantity produced by me as the value of my iron is commensurate with this quantity.

It is true that the man who buys has in his possession merely the *converted form* of a commodity—money—the commodity in the form of exchange value, and he can act as a buyer only because he or others have earlier acted as sellers of commodities which now exist in the form of money. This, however, is no reason why he should reconvert his money into my commodity or why his need for my commodity should be determined by the quantity of it that I have produced. In so far as he demands my commodity, he may want either a smaller quantity than I supply, or the entire quantity, but *below* its value. His DEMAND does not have to correspond to my supply any more than the quantity I supply and the value at which I supply it are identical.

However, the inquiry into demand and supply does not belong here.

In so far as I supply iron, I do not demand iron, but money. I supply a particular use value and demand its value. My supply and demand are therefore as different as use value and exchange value. In so far as I supply a *value* in the iron itself, I demand the *realisation of this value.* My supply and demand are thus as different as something conceptual is from something real. Further, the quantity I supply and its value stand in no proportion to each other. The demand for the quantity of use value I supply is however measured not by the value I wish to realise, but by the quantity which the buyer requires at a definite price.

Yet another passage from Mill:

"It is evident, that each man contributes to the general supply the whole of what he has produced and does not mean to consume. In whatever shape any part of the annual produce has come into his hands, if he proposes to consume no part of it himself, he wishes to dispose of the whole; and the whole, therefore, becomes matter of supply: if he consumes a part, he wishes to dispose of all the rest, and all the rest becomes matter of supply" (l.c., p. 253).

In other words, this means nothing else but that all commodities placed on the market constitute supply.

"As every man's demand, therefore,=that part of the annual produce, or, in other words,=that part of the wealth, which he has to dispose of" [a]

// *Halte là!*[b] His demand is equal to the *value* (when it is realised) of the portion of products which he wants to dispose of. What he wants to dispose of is a certain quantity of use value; what he wishes to have is the *value* of this use value. Both things are ANYTHING BUT IDENTICAL //

"and each man's supply is exactly the same thing",

//by no means; his demand does not consist in what he wishes to dispose of, i.e. the product, but in the demand for the value of this product; on the other hand, his supply really consists of this product, whereas the value is only conceptually supplied//

"the supply and demand of every individual are of necessity equal" [pp. 253-54].

(That is, the *value* of the commodity supplied by him and the *value* which he asks for it but does not possess are equal; *provided* he sells the commodity at its value, the value supplied (in the form of commodity) and the value received (in the form of money) are equal. But it does not follow that, because he wants to sell the commodity at its value, he actually does so. A quantity of commodities is supplied by him, and is on the market. He tries to get the value for it.)

"Demand and supply are terms [XIV-802] related in a peculiar manner. A commodity which is supplied, is always, at the same time, a commodity which is the *instrument* of demand. A commodity which is the instrument of demand, is always, at the same time, a commodity added to the stock of supply. Every commodity is always *at one and the same time* matter of demand and matter of supply. Of two men who perform an exchange, the one does not come with only a supply, the other with only a demand; the *supply which he brings* is the instrument of his demand; and his demand and supply are of course exactly equal to one another. But if the demand and supply of every individual are always equal to one another, then the demand and supply of all the individuals in the nation, taken aggregately, must be equal. Whatever, therefore, be the amount of the annual produce, it never can exceed the amount of the annual demand. The whole of the annual produce is divided into a number of shares equal to that of the people to whom it is distributed. The whole of the demand is equal to as much of the whole of the shares as the owners do not keep for their own consumption. But the whole of the shares is equal to the whole of the annual produce" (l.c., [pp.] 254-55).

Once Mill has *assumed* that supply and demand are equal for each individual, then the whole long-winded excursus to the effect

---

[a] Marx quotes Mill with some alterations.— *Ed.*
[b] Stop!— *Ed.*

that supply and demand are also equal for *all* individuals, is quite superfluous.

How Mill was regarded by contemporary RICARDIANS can be seen, for instance, from the following:

"There is thus at least one case" //they say with regard to Mill's definition of the value of labour// "in which the price" (the price of labour) "is permanently determined by supply and demand relations" (Prévost, *Reflexions* [*du traducteur*] *sur le système de Ricardo*, appended to *Discours sur* [*l'origine, les progrès, les objets particuliers, et l'importance de*] *l'économie politique*, by McCulloch, translated by G-me Prévost, Geneva, [Paris,] 1825, [p.] 187).[a]

In the work cited, *McCulloch* says that Mill's object is

"to give a strictly *logical deduction* of the principles of political economy" (p. 88). Mill "touches on almost every topic of discussion. He has disentangled and simplified the most complex and difficult questions, has placed the various principles which compose the science in their natural order" (l.c.).

One can conclude from his logic that he takes over the quite illogical Ricardian structure, which we analysed earlier,[b] and naïvely regards it on the whole as a "natural order".

As far as the above-mentioned *Prévost* is concerned, who made Mill's EXPOSITION of the Ricardian system the basis of his *Réflexions etc.*, a number of his objections are founded on sheer, callow misunderstanding of Ricardo.

But the following remark about rent is noteworthy:

"One may entertain a doubt about the influence of *inferior land* on the determination of prices, if one bears in mind, as one should, its *relative area*" (Prévost, l.c., p. 177).

Prévost cites the following from *Mill,* which is also important for my argument,[c] since Mill himself here thinks of one example where *differential rent* arises because the NEW DEMAND, the ADDITIONAL DEMAND, IS SUPPLIED BY A BETTER, NOT BY A WORSE SOIL, consequently, the ASCENDING LINE.

"MR. *Mill* USES this comparison: 'Suppose that all the land cultivated in the country were of one uniform quality, and yielded the same return to every portion of the capital employed upon it, with the exception of one acre; that acre, we shall suppose, yields six times as much as any other acre'" (Mill, *Elements etc.*, 2ND ED., p. 71). "It is certain—as MR. Mill demonstrates—that the farmer who rents this last acre, cannot increase his rent"[82] (that is, cannot make a higher profit than the other farmers; it is very badly expressed) "and that five-sixths of the product will go to the landowner."

---

[a] This and the following passages from Prévost and McCulloch's *Discours...* are quoted in French in the manuscript. Below, in analysing Prévost's views, Marx uses quite a few French expressions.— *Ed.*

[b] See present edition, Vol. 31, pp. 389-94, 397.— *Ed.*

[c] Ibid., pp. 461-62, 489, 522-25.— *Ed.*

(Thus there is here differential rent without the lowering of the rate of profit and without any increase in the price of agricultural products.) (This must happen all the more frequently, since the *situation* [XIV-803] must *improve* continuously with the industrial development of the country, the growth of its means of communication and the increase in population, irrespective of the natural fertility, and the relatively better location has the same effect as [greater] natural fertility.)

"But had the ingenious author thought of making a similar supposition in the opposite case, he would have realised that the result would be different. Let us suppose that all the land was of equal quality with the exception of one acre of inferior land. The profit on the capital on this single acre amounted to one-sixth of the profit yielded by every other acre. Does he believe that the profit on several million acres would be reduced to one-sixth of their accustomed level? It is probable that this solitary acre would have no effect at all, because the various products (particularly corn), when they come onto the market, would not be markedly affected by such a *minute* amount. That is why we say that the assertions of Ricardo's supporters about the effect of inferior soil should be modified by taking the *relative areas* of land of different quality into account" (Prévost, l.c., [pp.] 177-78).

//*Say,* in his notes to Ricardo's book translated by Constancio, makes only *one* correct remark about *foreign trade.*[83] Profit can also be made by cheating, one person gaining what the other loses. Loss and gain within a *single* country cancel each other out. But not so with trade between different countries. And even according to Ricardo's theory, 3 days of labour of one country can be exchanged against one of another country—a point *not* noted by Say. Here the law of value undergoes essential modification. The relationship between working days of different countries may be similar to that existing between SKILLED, COMPOSED LABOUR and UNSKILLED, SIMPLE [labour] within a country. In this case, the richer country exploits the poorer one, even where the latter gains by the exchange, as John Stuart Mill explains in his *Some Unsettled Questions etc.*[84]//

"We admit that, in general, the rate of agricultural profit determines that of industrial profit. But at the same time we must point out that the latter also reacts of necessity on the former. If the price of corn rises to a certain point, industrial capitals turn to agriculture, and necessarily depress agricultural profits" (Prévost, l.c., [p.] 179).

The point is correct, but is conceived in a much too limited sense. See above.[a]

The RICARDIANS insist that profit can fall only as a result of a rise in wages, because NECESSARIES rise in price with [the growth of]

---

[a] See this volume, pp. 288-89.— *Ed.*

population; this, however, is a consequence of the accumulation of capital, since inferior soils are cultivated as a result of this accumulation. But Ricardo himself admits that profits can also fall when capitals increase faster than population, when the competition of capitals causes wages to rise. This [corresponds to] Adam Smith's theory.[a] *Prévost* says:

"When the growing demand of the capitals increases the price of the labourer, that is, *wages*, does it not then appear that there are no grounds for asserting that the growing supply of these selfsame capitals never causes the price of capitals, in other words, *profit*, to fall?" (l.c., [p.] 188).

Prévost builds on the false Ricardian foundation—which can only explain falling profits as a result of decreasing SURPLUS VALUE, and therefore decreasing SURPLUS LABOUR, and consequently as a result of greater value or *rising cost of the* NECESSARIES *consumed by the labourer,* that is, increasing VALUE OF LABOUR, ALTHOUGH THE REAL RETRIBUTION OF THE LABOURER, INSTEAD OF BEING ASCENDING, DECLINES—on this basis he seeks to prove that a CONTINUAL decline in profits is not inevitable. He says *first*:

"To begin with, the state of prosperity increases profits"

(namely, agricultural profits, for the population increases with the state of prosperity, HENCE the demand for AGRICULTURAL PRODUCE, HENCE SURPLUS PROFITS of the FARMER)

"and this happens long before new land is taken into cultivation. The increased area under cultivation does indeed affect rent and decreases profits. But although profit is thus directly decreased, it still remains as high as before the advance... Why is the cultivation of land of inferior quality undertaken at certain times? It is undertaken in the expectation of a profit which is *at least equal to the customary profit*. And what circumstance can lead to the realisation of such a profit on this kind of land? Increase [XIV-804] of population. It presses on ... the existing means of subsistence, thereby raising the prices of food (especially of corn) so that agricultural capitals obtain high profits. The other capitals pour into agriculture, but since the soil is limited in area, this competition has its limits and the point is reached when *even higher profits can be made than in trade or manufacture* through the cultivation of inferior soils. If there is a sufficient area of inferior land available, then agricultural profit must be adjusted to the last capitals applied to the land. If one proceeds from the rate of profit prevailing at the beginning of the increasing prosperity" (division of profit into profit and rent), "then it will be found that profit has no tendency to decline. It rises with the increase in the population until agricultural profit rises to such a degree that it can suffer a considerable reduction (as a result of the cultivation of new land) without ever sinking below its original rate, or, to be more precise, below the average rate determined by various circumstances" ([pp.] 190-92).

Prévost obviously misunderstands the Ricardian view. As a result of prosperity, the population increases, HENCE THE PRICES OF AGRICULTUR-

___

[a] Ibid., pp. 72-73, 100-02.—*Ed.*

AL PRODUCTS, HENCE AGRICULTURAL PROFITS. (Although it is not easy to see why, if this rise is constant, rents should not be increased after the leases run out and [why] these AGRICULTURAL SURPLUS PROFITS should not be collected in the form of rent even before the inferior land is cultivated.) But the same rise in [the price of] AGRICULTURAL PRODUCE which causes AGRICULTURAL PROFITS to go up, increases wages IN ALL INDUSTRIES and consequently brings about a fall in INDUSTRIAL PROFITS. Thus A NEW RATE OF PROFIT arises in industry. If at the existing market prices the inferior lands even pay only this LOWER RATE OF PROFIT, capitals can be transferred to the inferior land. They will be attracted to it by the high AGRICULTURAL PROFITS and the high market price of corn. As Prévost says, they may, before a sufficient amount of capital has been transferred, even yield higher profits than the INDUSTRIAL PROFIT, which has declined. But as soon as the ADDITIONAL SUPPLY is adequate, the market price falls, so that the inferior soils only yield THE ORDINARY INDUSTRIAL PROFIT. The additional amount yielded by the product of the better [soils] is converted into rent. This is the Ricardian conception, whose basic premises are accepted by *Prévost* and from which he reasons. Corn is now dearer than it was before the rise in AGRICULTURAL PROFIT. But the SURPLUS PROFIT which it brought the farmer is transformed into rent. In this way, therefore, profit also declines on the better land to the LOWER RATE OF INDUSTRIAL PROFIT brought about by the RISE in [the price of] AGRICULTURAL PRODUCE. There is no reason for assuming that as a consequence profits do not have to fall below their "original rate" if no other modifying circumstances intervene. Other circumstances *may*, of course, intervene. According to the assumption, after the RISE in [the price of] NECESSARIES, AGRICULTURAL PROFIT is in any case higher than INDUSTRIAL profit. If, however, as a result of the development of productive power, the part of the workers' NECESSARIES supplied by industry has fallen to such a degree that wages (even though they are paid at their AVERAGE VALUE) do not rise as much as they would have done without the intervention of these paralysing circumstances, proportionally to the increased [price of] AGRICULTURAL PRODUCE; if, furthermore, the same development of productive power has reduced the price of the products of the extractive industries, ditto of AGRICULTURAL RAW MATERIALS which are not used as food (although the supposition is not very likely), INDUSTRIAL PROFIT need not fall, though it would be lower than AGRICULTURAL PROFIT. A decline of the latter as a result of a TRANSFER OF CAPITAL TO AGRICULTURE and the building-up of rent, [XIV-805] would only restore the old rate OF PROFIT.

Prévost tries a different approach.

"Soils of inferior quality ... are only put into cultivation if they yield profits as high as—or even higher than—the profit yielded by industrial capitals. Under these conditions, the price of corn or of other agricultural products often remains very high despite the newly cultivated land. These high prices press on the working population, since rises in wages do not correspond exactly to rises in the prices of the goods used by wage workers. They are more or less a burden to the whole population, since nearly all commodities are affected by the rise in wages and in the prices of essential goods. This general pressure, linked with the increasing mortality brought about by too large a population, results in a decline in the number of wage workers and, consequently, in a rise in wages and a decline in agricultural profits. Further development now proceeds in the opposite direction to that taken previously. Capitals are withdrawn from the inferior soils and reinvested in industry. But the population principle soon begins to operate once again. As soon as poverty has been ended, the number of workers increases, their wages decline, and profits rise as a consequence. Such fluctuations follow one another repeatedly without bringing about a change in the average of profit. Profit may decline or rise for other reasons or as a result of these causes; it may alternately go up and down, and yet it may not be possible to attribute the average rise or fall to the necessity for cultivating new soils. The population is the regulator which establishes the natural order and keeps profit within certain limits" (l.c., [pp.] 194-96).

Although confused, this is correct according to the "population principle". It is however not in line with the assumption that agricultural profits rise until the ADDITIONAL SUPPLY required by the population has been produced. If this presupposes a constant increase in the prices of AGRICULTURAL PRODUCE, then it leads not to a decrease in population, but to a GENERAL LOWERING OF THE RATE OF PROFIT, HENCE OF ACCUMULATION, and, consequently, to a decrease OF POPULATION. According to the Ricardian-Malthusian view, the population would grow more slowly. But Prévost's basis is: that the process would depress wages below their AVERAGE level, this fall in wages and the poverty of the workers causes the price of corn to fall and HENCE profits to rise again.

This latter argument, however, does not belong here, for here it is assumed that the VALUE OF LABOUR is always paid; that is, that the workers receive the means of subsistence necessary for their reproduction.

This [exposition] of Prévost is important, because it demonstrates that the Ricardian view—along with the view he adopted from Malthus—can indeed explain fluctuations in the rate of profit, but cannot explain (constant) falls in the same without repercussions, for upon reaching a certain level the rise in corn prices and the drop in profit would force wages below their level, bringing about a violent decrease in the population, and therefore a fall in the prices of corn and other NECESSARIES, and this would lead again to a rise in profits.

The period between 1820 and 1830 is metaphysically speaking the most important period in the history of English political economy—theoretical tilting for and against the Ricardian theory, a whole series of anonymous polemical works, the most important of which are quoted here, especially in relation to those matters which concern our subject. At the same time, however, it is a characteristic of these polemical writings that all of them, in actual fact, merely revolve around the definition of the concept of value and its relation to capital.

a) *Observations on Certain Verbal Disputes in Political Economy, Particularly Relating to Value, and to Demand and Supply*, London, 1821

This is not without a certain acuteness. The title *Verbal Disputes* is characteristic.

Directed in part against Smith and Malthus, but also against Ricardo.

The real SENSE of this work is that

* "disputes ... are entirely owing to the use of words in different senses by different persons; to the disputants looking, like the knights in the story, at different sides of the shield" * ([pp.] 59-60).

This kind of scepticism always heralds the dissolution of a theory, it is the harbinger of a frivolous and unprincipled eclecticism designed for domestic use.

First of all in relation to Ricardo's theory of value:

* "There is an obvious difficulty in supposing that *labour* is what we mentally allude to, when we talk of value or [of] real price, as opposed to nominal price; for we often want to speak of the *value or price of labour itself*. Where by labour, as the real price of a thing, we mean the labour which *produced* the thing, there is another difficulty besides; for we often want to speak of *the value or price of land*, but land is not produced by labour. This definition, then, will only apply to *commodities*" * (l.c., [p.] 8).

As far as labour is concerned, the objection to Ricardo is correct in so far as he presents capital as the immediate purchaser of labour and consequently speaks directly of the VALUE OF LABOUR, while what is bought and sold is the temporary use of labour capacity, itself a product. Instead of the problem being resolved, it is only emphasised here that a problem remains unsolved.

It is also quite correct that "THE VALUE OR PRICE OF LAND", which is not produced by labour, appears directly to contradict the concept of value and cannot be derived directly from it. This proposition is [all the more] insignificant when used against Ricardo, since its author does not attack Ricardo's theory of rent in which precisely Ricardo sets forth how the nominal value of land is evolved on the basis of capitalist production and does not contradict the definition of value. The value of land is nothing but the price which is paid for capitalised rent. Much more far-reaching developments have therefore to be presumed here than can be deduced *prima facie* from the simple consideration of the commodity and its value, just as from the simple concept of productive capital one cannot evolve fictitious capital,[85] the object of gambling on the stock exchange, which is actually nothing but the selling and buying of entitlement to a certain part of the annual tax revenue.

The second objection—that Ricardo transforms value, which is a *relative* concept, into an *absolute* concept—is made the chief point of the attack on the whole Ricardian system in another polemical work (written by Bailey), which appeared later. In considering this latter work, we will also cite relevant passages from the *Observations.*[a]

A very pertinent observation about the source from which capital, which pays labour, arises, is contained in an incidental remark unconsciously made by the author, who on the contrary wants to use it to prove what is said in the following sentence not underlined [by me], namely, that the SUPPLY OF LABOUR itself constitutes a CHECK on the tendency OF LABOUR TO SINK TO ITS NATURAL PRICE.

*"*An increased supply of labour is an increased supply of that which is to purchase labour. If we say, then, with Mr. Ricardo, that labour is at every moment *tending* to what he calls its natural price,[b] we must only recollect, that the increase made in its supply, in order to *tend* to that, is itself one of the causes of [the] counteracting power, which prevents the tendency from being *effectual"* * (l.c., [pp.] 72-73).

No analysis is possible unless the AVERAGE PRICE OF LABOUR, i.e., the VALUE OF LABOUR, is made the point of departure; just as little would it be possible if one failed to take the VALUE OF COMMODITIES in general

---

[a] See this volume, pp. 312 20, 324.— *Ed.*
[b] Ibid., pp. 35-40.— *Ed.*

as the point of departure. Only on this basis is it possible to understand the real phenomena of price fluctuations.

[XIV-807] *"It is not meant to be asserted by him" (Ricardo), "that two particular lots of two different articles, as a hat and a pair of shoes, exchange with one another when *those two particular lots* were produced by equal quantities of labour. By '*commodity*' we must here understand '*description of commodity*', not a particular individual hat, pair of shoes, etc. The whole labour which produces all the hats in England is to be considered, to this purpose, as divided among all the hats. This seems to me not to have been expressed at first, and in the general statements of this doctrine"* (l.c., [pp.] 53-54). For example, Ricardo speaks of "A PORTION OF [the] LABOUR OF THE ENGINEER IN MAKING MACHINES" contained, for instance, in a pair of stockings.[a] *"Yet the 'total labour' that produced each single pair of stockings, if it is of a single pair we are speaking, includes the *whole* labour of the engineer, not a 'portion'; for one machine makes many pairs, and none of those pairs could have been done without any part of the machine"* (l.c., [p.] 54).

The last *passus* is based on a misunderstanding. The whole machine enters into the labour process, but only a part of it enters the valorisation process.

Apart from this, some things in the remark are correct.

We start with the *commodity*, this specific social form of the product, as the foundation and prerequisite of capitalist production. We take individual products and analyse those distinctions of form which they have as commodities, which stamp them as commodities. In earlier modes of production—*preceding* capitalist production—a large part of the output never enters into circulation, is never placed on the market, is not produced as commodities, and does not become commodities. On the other hand, at that time a large part of the products which enter into production are not commodities and do not enter into the process as commodities. The transformation of products into commodities only occurs in individual cases, is limited only to the surplus of production, etc., or only to individual spheres of production (manufactured products), etc. A whole range of products neither enter into the process as articles to be sold, nor arise from it as such. Nevertheless, the *prerequisite,* the *starting-point,* of the formation of capital and of capitalist production is the development of the product into a commodity, commodity circulation and consequently money circulation within certain limits, and consequently trade developed to a certain degree. It is as such a prerequisite that we treat the commodity, since we proceed from it as the simplest element in capitalist production. On the other hand, the product, the result of capitalist production, is the

---

[a] D. Ricardo, *On the Principles of Political Economy, and Taxation,* 3rd ed., London, 1821, p. 18.— *Ed.*

commodity. What appears as its element is later revealed to be its own product. Only on the basis of capitalist production does the commodity become the general form of the product and the more this production develops, the more do the products in the form of commodities enter into the process as ingredients. The commodity, as it emerges in capitalist production, is different from the commodity taken as the element, the starting-point of capitalist production. We are no longer faced with the individual commodity, the individual product. The individual commodity, the individual product, manifests itself not only as a real product but also as a commodity, as a *part* both really and conceptually of production as a whole. Each individual commodity [represents] a definite portion of capital and of the surplus value created by it.

The value of the capital advanced+the surplus labour appropriated, for example, a value of £120 (if £100 is the capital and the surplus labour=£20), is, as far as its value is concerned, contained in the total product, let us say, in 1,200 yards of cotton. Each yard=$£^{120}/_{1,200}=^{1}/_{10}$ of £1=2s. It is not the individual commodity which appears as the result of the process, but the mass of the commodities in which the value of the total capital has been reproduced+a surplus value. The total value produced divided by the number of products determines the value of the individual product and it becomes a commodity only as such an aliquot part. It is no longer the labour expended on the individual particular commodity (in most cases, it can no longer be calculated, and may be greater in the case of one commodity than in that of another) but a proportional part of the total labour—the average of the total value [divided] by the number of products—determines the value of the individual product and establishes it as a commodity. Consequently, the total mass of commodities must also be sold, each commodity at its value, determined in this way, in order to replace the total capital together with a surplus value. If only 800 out of the 1,200 yards were sold, then the capital would not be replaced, still less would there be a profit. But each yard would *also* have been sold below its value, for its value is determined not in isolation but as an aliquot part of the total product.

[XIV-808] * "If you call labour a commodity, it is not like a commodity which is first produced in order to exchange, and then brought to market where it must exchange with other commodities according to the respective quantities of each which there may be in the market at the time; labour is *created* at the moment it is brought to market; nay, it is brought to market before it is created" * (l.c., [pp.] 75-76).

What is in fact brought to market is not LABOUR, but the LABOURER. What he sells to the capitalist is not his labour but the TEMPORARY USE OF HIMSELF AS A WORKING POWER. This is the immediate object of the contract which the capitalist and the worker conclude, the purchase and sale which they transact.

Where payment is for piece-work, TASK-WORK, instead of according to the time for which the labour capacity is placed at the disposal of the employer, this is only another method of determining the time. It is measured by the product, a definite quantity of products being considered as a standard representing the socially necessary labour time. In many branches of industry in London where TASK-WORK is the rule, payment is thus made by the hour, but disputes often arise as to whether this or that piece of work constitutes "an hour" or not.

Irrespective of the individual form, it is the case not only with regard to TASK-WORK, but GENERALLY, that, although labour capacity is sold on definite TERMS before its USE, it is only *paid for* after the work is completed, whether it is paid daily, weekly, etc. Here money becomes the *means of payment* after it has served previously as an abstract means of purchase, because the nominal transfer of the commodity to the buyer is distinct from the actual transfer. The sale of the commodity—labour capacity—the legal transfer of the use value and its actual alienation, do not occur at the same time. The realisation of the price therefore takes place later than the sale of the commodity (see *the first part* of my book, p. 122).[a] It can also be seen that here it is the worker, not the capitalist, who does the advancing, just as in the case of the renting of a house, it is not the tenant but the landlord who advances use value. The worker will indeed be paid (or at least he may be, if the goods have not been ordered beforehand and so on) before the commodities produced by him have been sold. But *his* commodity, his labour capacity, has been consumed industrially, has been transferred into the hands of the buyer, the capitalist, before he, the worker, has been paid. And it is not a question of what the buyer of a commodity wants to do with it, whether he buys it in order to retain it as a use value or in order to sell it again. It is a question of the *direct* transaction between the first buyer and seller.

* "In different stages of society, the accumulation of *capital,* or [of] the *means of employing labour,* is more or less rapid, and must in all cases depend on the

---

[a] K. Marx, *A Contribution to the Critique of Political Economy.* Part One (present edition, Vol. 29, pp. 374-76).— *Ed.*

productive powers of labour. The productive powers of labour are generally greatest where there is an abundance of fertile land" * (Ricardo, [*On the Principles of Political Economy,*] 3RD ED., [London,] 1821, [p.] 92).ª

The following remark on this passage of Ricardo's:

* "If, in the first sentence, *the productive powers of labour mean the smallness of that aliquot part of any produce that goes to those whose manual labour produced it,* the sentence is nearly identical, because the *remaining aliquot part is the fund whence capital can,* if the owner pleases, *be accumulated"* * [l.c.].

(This is a tacit admission that from the standpoint of the capitalist * "*productive powers of labour* mean the smallness of that aliquot part of any produce that goes to those whose manual labour produced it".* This sentence is very nice.)

* "But then this does not generally happen where there is most fertile land." *

(This is SILLY. Ricardo presupposes capitalist production. He does not investigate whether it develops more freely with FERTILE OR RELATIVELY UNFERTILE LAND. Where it exists, it is most productive where land is most fertile. Just as the social productive forces, the natural productive powers of labour, that is, those labour finds in inorganic nature, appear as the productive POWER of capital. Ricardo himself, in the passage cited above, rightly identifies PRODUCTIVE POWERS OF LABOUR with LABOUR PRODUCTIVE OF CAPITAL, PRODUCTIVE OF THE WEALTH THAT COMMANDS LABOUR, NOT OF THE WEALTH THAT BELONGS TO LABOUR. *His expression,* "CAPITAL, OR THE MEANS OF EMPLOYING LABOUR", is, in fact, the only one in which he grasps the real nature of capital.[86] He himself is so much the prisoner of a [XIV-809] capitalist standpoint that this conversion, this *quid pro quo,* is for him a matter of course. The objective conditions of labour— created, moreover, by labour itself—RAW MATERIALS AND WORKING INSTRUMENTS, ARE NOT *MEANS EMPLOYED BY LABOUR AS ITS MEANS,* BUT, ON THE CONTRARY, THEY ARE *THE MEANS OF EMPLOYING LABOUR.* They are not employed by labour; they employ labour. For them labour is a MEANS by which they are accumulated as capital, not a means to provide products, WEALTH for the worker.)

* "It does in North America, but that is an artificial state of things" * (that is, A CAPITALISTIC STATE OF THINGS). * "It does not in Mexico. It does not in New Holland.ᵇ The productive powers of labour are indeed, in *another* sense, greatest where there is much fertile land, viz. the power of man, if he chooses it, to raise much *raw produce* in proportion to the whole labour he performs. It is, indeed, a *gift of nature, that men can raise more food than the lowest quantity that they could maintain and keep up the population on"* *;

ª Here and below (pp. 303, 304) cf. present edition, Vol. 30, p. 254.— *Ed.*
ᵇ Old name of Australia.— *Ed.*

(This is the basis of the doctrine of the *Physiocrats*. The physical basis of SURPLUS VALUE is this "GIFT OF NATURE", most obvious in agricultural labour, which originally satisfied nearly all human needs.[a] It is not so in manufacturing labour, because the product must first be sold as a commodity. The Physiocrats, the first to analyse SURPLUS VALUE, understand it in its natural form.)

* "but '*surplus produce*' (the term used by Mr. Ricardo, p. 93), generally means the excess of the whole price of a thing above that part of it which goes to the labourers who made it;" *

(the fool does not see that where the LAND is FERTILE, the PART OF THE PRICE OF THE PRODUCE THAT GOES TO THE LABOURER, ALTHOUGH THAT PART [may] BE SMALL, BUYS A SUFFICIENT QUANTITY OF NECESSARIES; THE PART THAT GOES TO THE CAPITALIST IS GREATEST):

* "a point which is settled by human arrangement, and not fixed" * (l.c., [*Observations on Certain Verbal Disputes...*, pp.] 74-75).

If the last, concluding *passus* has any meaning at all, it is that "SURPLUS PRODUCE" in the capitalist sense must be strictly distinguished from the productivity of industry as such. The latter is of interest to the capitalist only in so far as it realises profit for him. Therein lies the narrowness and limitation of capitalist production.

* "When the demand for an article exceeds that which is, with reference to the present rate of supply, the effectual demand; and when, consequently, the price has risen, either additions can be made to the rate of supply at the same rate of cost of production as before; in which case they will be made till the article is brought to exchange at the same rate as before with other articles: or, secondly, *no* possible additions can be made to the former rate of supply: and then the price, which has risen, will not be brought down, but continue to afford, as Smith says,[b] a greater rent, or profits, or wages (or all three), to the particular land, capital, or labour, employed in producing the article, or, thirdly, the additions which can be made will require proportionally *more* land, or capital, or labour, or all three, than were required *for the periodical production*" * (*note these words*) * "of the amount previously supplied. Then the addition will not be made till the demand is strong enough, 1) to pay this increased price for the addition; 2) to pay the same increased price upon the old amount of supply. For the person who has produced the additional quantity will be no more able to get a high price for it than those who produced the former quantity... There will then be *surplus profits* in this trade... The *surplus profits* will be either in the hands of some particular producers only ... or, if the *additional* produce cannot be *distinguished* from the rest, will be a surplus shared by all... People will give something to belong to a trade in which such *surplus profits* can be made... What they so give, is rent" * (p. 79 et seq.).

Here, one need only say that in this book RENT is for the first time regarded as the general FORM of consolidated *surplus profit*.

---

[a] See present edition, Vol. 30, pp. 355-61, 368-71.— *Ed.*

[b] See A. Smith, *An Inquiry into the Nature and Causes of the Wealth of Nations*, Book I, Ch. VII.— *Ed.*

[XIV-810] * "'Conversion of revenue into capital' is another of these *verbal* sources of controversy. One man means by it, that the capitalist lays out part of the profits he has made by his capital, in making additions to his capital, instead of spending it for [his] private use, as he might else have done: another man means by it, that a person lays out as capital something which he never got as profits, or any capital of his own, but received as rent, wages, salary" * (l.c., [pp.] 83-84).

This last passage—"ANOTHER OF THESE *VERBAL SOURCES* OF CONTROVERSY. ONE MAN MEANS BY IT ... ANOTHER MAN MEANS BY IT..."—testifies to the method used by this smart-alec.

b) *An Inquiry into those Principles, Respecting the Nature of Demand and the Necessity of Consumption, lately Advocated by Mr. Malthus etc.*, London, 1821

[A] RICARDIAN [work]. Good against Malthus. Demonstrates the infinite narrow-mindedness to which the clairvoyance of these fellows is reduced as soon as they examine not LANDED PROPERTY, but capital. NEVERTHELESS, it is one of the best of the polemical works of the decennium mentioned.

* "If the capital employed in cutlery is increased as 100:101, and can only produce an increase of cutlery in the same proportion, the degree in which it will increase the command which its producers have over things in general, no increased production of *them* having by the supposition taken place, will *be in a less proportion*; and this, and not the increase of the quantity of cutlery, constitutes the employers' profits or the increase of their wealth. But if the like addition of 1% had been *making at the same time to the capitals of all other trades,* and *with the like result as to produce,* this [conclusion] would not follow: for the rate at which each article would exchange with the rest would remain unaltered, and therefore a given portion of each would give the same command as before over the rest" * (l.c., [p.] 9).

D'abord,[a] if there has been no increase of production (and of the capital devoted to production) except in the CUTLERY TRADE, as is assumed, then the RETURN will not be "*IN A LESS PROPORTION*", but * an absolute loss. There are then only three courses open to the cutlery monger. Either he must exchange his increased produce as he would have done his less produce, and so his increased production would result in a positive loss. Or he must try to get new consumers; if amongst the old circle, this could only be done by withdrawing customers from another trade and shifting his loss upon other shoulders; or he must enlarge his market beyond his former limits; but neither the one nor the other operation depends on his good will, nor on the mere existence of an

---

a First of all.— *Ed.*

increased quantity of knives. Or, in the last instance, he must carry over his production to another year and diminish his new supply for that year, which, if his addition of capital did exist not only in additional wages, but in additional fixed capital, will equally result in a loss.

Furthermore: If all other capitals have accumulated at the same rate, it does not follow at all that their production has increased at the same rate. But if it has, it does not follow that they want one per cent more of cutlery, as their demand for cutlery is not at all connected, either with the increase of their own produce, or with their increased power of buying cutlery.* What follows is merely the tautology: If the INCREASED CAPITAL used in each particular TRADE is * proportionate to the rate in which the wants of society increase the demand for each particular commodity, then the increase of one commodity secures a market for the increased supply of other commodities.*

Here, therefore, is presupposed: 1) *capitalist production,* in which the production OF each particular TRADE and ITS INCREASE are NOT IMMEDIATELY REGULATED, BY THE WANTS OF SOCIETY, AND [XIV-811] CONTROLLED BY IT, BUT BY THE productive forces at the disposal of each individual CAPITALIST, INDEPENDENT OF THE WANTS OF SOCIETY;

2) It is assumed that nevertheless production is *proportional* [to the requirements] as though capital were EMPLOYED IN THE DIFFERENT TRADES directly by society in accordance with its needs.

On this assumption—if capitalist production were entirely socialist production—a *contradictio in adjecto*ᵃ—no overproduction could, in fact, occur.

By the way, in the various TRADES in which *the same accumulation* of capital takes place //and this too is an unfortunate assumption that capital ACCUMULATES AT AN *EQUAL RATE* IN DIFFERENT TRADES//, the amount of products corresponding to the increased capital employed may vary greatly, since the productive powers in the DIFFERENT TRADES or the total use values produced in relation to the labour employed differ considerably. The same value is produced in both cases, but the quantity of commodities in which it is represented is very different. It is quite incomprehensible, therefore, why TRADE A, because the value of its output has increased by 1% while the mass of its products has grown by 20%, must find a market in TRADE B where the value has likewise increased by 1%, but the quantity of its output only by 5%. Here,

---

ᵃ Literally: a contradiction in terms; here: logical absurdity, nonsense.— *Ed.*

the author has failed to take into consideration the difference between use value and exchange value.

Say's earth-shaking discovery that "commodities can only be bought with commodities" [a] simply means that money is itself the converted form of the commodity. It does not prove by any means that because I can buy only with commodities, I can buy with *my* commodity, or that my purchasing power is related to the *quantity* of commodities I produce. The same *value* can be embodied in very different quantities [of commodities]. But the use value— consumption—depends not on value, but on the quantity. It is quite unintelligible why I should buy 6 knives because I can get them for the same price that I previously paid for 1. Apart from the fact that the workers do not sell commodities, but labour, a great number of people who do not produce commodities at all buy things with money. Buyers and sellers of commodities are not identical. The LANDLORD, the MONEYED CAPITALIST and others obtain in the form of *money* commodities produced by other people. They are buyers without being sellers of "commodities". Buying and selling occurs not only between industrial capitalists, but they also sell to workers; and likewise to owners of REVENUE who are not commodity producers. Finally, the purchases and sales transacted by them as capitalists are very different from the purchases they make as REVENUE-SPENDERS.

* "Mr. Ricardo (2nd ed., p. 359),[b] after quoting the doctrine of Smith about the cause of the fall of profits, adds: 'Mr. Say has, however, most satisfactorily shown, that there is no capital which may not be employed in a country, because demand is only *limited* by production.'" *

(This is very wise. *LIMITED*, indeed. * Nothing can be demanded which *cannot* be produced upon demand, or which the demand finds not ready made in the market. Hence, because demand is *limited* by production, it does by no means follow that *production is, or was, limited by demand,* and can never overstep the demand, particularly the demand at the market price.* This is Say-like acumen.)

* " 'There cannot be accumulated' (p. 360) 'in a country any amount of capital which cannot be employed *productively*' (meaning, I assume," *—says the author in brackets—* "with profit to the owner) 'until wages rise so high *in consequence* of the rise of necessaries, and so little consequently remains for the profits of stock, that the motive for accumulation ceases.'" *

---

[a] J. B. Say, *Traité d'économie politique...*, 2nd ed., Vol. 2, Paris, 1814, p. 382. See also this volume, pp. 124-26, 130-31.— *Ed.*

[b] *On the Principles of Political Economy, and Taxation*, London, 1819.— *Ed.*

(Ricardo here equates "PRODUCTIVELY" and "PROFITABLY", whereas it is precisely the fact that in capitalist production "PROFITABLY" alone is "PRODUCTIVELY", that constitutes the difference between it and absolute production, as well as its limitations. In order to produce "productively", production must be carried on in such a way that the mass of PRODUCERS are excluded from the DEMAND for a part of the PRODUCE. Production has to be carried on in opposition to a class [XIV-812] whose consumption stands in no relation to its production—since it is precisely in the excess of its production over its consumption that the profit of capital consists. On the other hand, production must be carried on for classes which consume without producing. It is not enough merely to give the SURPLUS PRODUCE a form in which it becomes an object of demand for these classes. On the other hand, the capitalist himself, if he wishes to accumulate, must not [be] a DEMANDER of his own products, in so far as they make up the REVENUE to the extent that he is their PRODUCER. Otherwise he cannot accumulate. That is why Malthus opposes to the capitalist classes whose task is not ACCUMULATION but EXPENDITURE. And while on the one hand all these contradictions are assumed, it is assumed on the other that production proceeds without any friction just as if these contradictions did not exist at all. Purchase is divorced from sale, commodity from money, use value from exchange value. It is assumed however that this separation does not exist, but that there is barter. Consumption and production are separated; [there are] producers who do not consume and consumers who do not produce. It is assumed that consumption and production are identical. The capitalist directly produces exchange value in order to increase his profit, and not for the sake of consumption. It is assumed that he produces directly for the sake of consumption and only for it. [If] it is assumed that the contradictions existing in bourgeois production—which, in fact, are reconciled by a process of adjustment which, at the same time, however, manifests itself as a crisis, violent fusion of disconnected factors operating independently of one another and yet correlated—if it is assumed that they do not exist, then these contradictions obviously cannot come into play. In every TRADE each individual capitalist produces IN PROPORTION TO HIS CAPITAL irrespective of the WANTS OF SOCIETY and especially irrespective of the COMPETITIVE SUPPLY of capitals in the same TRADE. It is assumed that he produces as if he were fulfilling orders placed by society. If there were no foreign trade, then LUXURIES could be produced AT HOME, WHATEVER their COST. In that case, labour, with the exception of [the branches producing] NECESSARIES, would, in actual fact, be very unproductive. HENCE accumulation of capital [would proceed at a low rate]. Thus every country would be able to employ all the capital accumulated there, since according to the assumption very little capital would have been accumulated.)

* "The latter sentence limits (not to say contradicts) the former, if 'which may not be employed', in the former, means 'employed productively', or rather, 'profitably'. And if it means simply 'employed', the proposition is useless; because neither Adam Smith nor any body else, I presume, denied that it might be 'employed', if you did not care what profits it brought" * (l.c., [pp.] 18-19).

Ricardo says indeed that all capital in a given LAND, AT WHAT[EVER] RATE ACCUMULATED, MAY BE EMPLOYED PROFITABLY; on the other hand he says THAT THE VERY FACT OF THE ACCUMULATION OF CAPITAL CHECKS ITS "PROFITABLE" EMPLOYMENT, BECAUSE IT MUST RESULT IN LESSENING PROFITS, THAT IS, THE RATE OF ACCUMULATION.

* "The very meaning of an increased demand by them" (the labourers) "is a disposition to take less themselves, and leave a larger share for their employers; and if it is said that this, by diminishing consumption, increases glut, I can only answer, that glut is synonymous with high profits" * (l.c., [p.] 59).[a]

This is indeed the secret basis of GLUT.

* "The labourers do not, considered as consumers, derive any benefit from machines, while flourishing (as Mr. Say says [in his] *Letters to Malthus*, 4th ed., p. 60) [87] unless the article, which the machines cheapen, is one that can be brought, by cheapening, within their use. Threshing-machines, windmills, may be a great thing for them in this view; but the invention of a veneering machine, [or] a block machine, or a lace frame, does not mend *their* condition much" (l.c., [pp.] 74-75).

"The habits of [the] labourers, where division of labour has been carried very far, are applicable only to the particular line they have been used to; *they are a sort of machines.* Then, there is a long period of idleness, that is, of labour lost; of wealth cut off at its root. It is quite useless to repeat, like a parrot, that things have a tendency to find their level. We must look about us, and see that they [XIV-813] *cannot* for a long time find a level; that when they do, it will be a far lower level than they set out from" * (l.c., [p.] 72).

This RICARDIAN, following Ricardo's example, recognises correctly crises resulting FROM A SUDDEN CHANGE IN THE CHANNELS OF TRADE.[88] This was the case in England after the war of 1815. And consequently, whenever a crisis occurred, all later economists declared that the *most obvious cause* of the particular crisis was the only possible cause of all crises.

The author also admits that the credit system may be a cause of crises (p. 81 et seq.) (As if the credit system itself did not arise out of the DIFFICULTY of EMPLOYING CAPITAL "PRODUCTIVELY", i.e. "PROFITABLY".) The English, for example, are forced to lend their capital to other countries in order to create a market for their commodities.

---

[a] Cf. this volume, p. 252.— *Ed.*

Overproduction, the credit system, etc., are means by which capitalist production seeks to break through its own barriers and to produce over and above its own *limits*. Capitalist production, on the one hand, has this driving force; on the other hand, it only tolerates production commensurate with the profitable employment of existing capital. HENCE crises arise, which simultaneously drive it onward and beyond [its own limits] and force it to put on seven-league boots, in order to reach a development of the productive forces which could only be achieved very slowly within its own *bornes*.[a]

What the author writes about Say is very true. This should be dealt with in connection with Say (see p. 134, *Notebook VII*[89]).

*"He" * (the worker) * "will agree *to work part of his time for the capitalist,* or, what comes to the same thing, to consider part of the whole produce, when raised and exchanged, as belonging to the capitalist. He must do so, or the capitalist would not have afforded him this assistance." *

(Namely capital. Very fine that it *comes to the same thing whether the capitalist owns the whole produce and pays part of it as wages to the labourer, or whether the labourer leaves, makes over to the capitalist part of his (the labourer's) produce.)

"But as the capitalist's *motive was gain,* and as these advantages always depend, in a certain degree, on the *will* to save, as well as on the *power,* the capitalist will be disposed to afford an additional portion of these assistances; and as he will find fewer people in want of this additional portion, than were in want of the original portion, he must expect to have a less share of the benefit to himself; he must be content to make a *present*" (!!!) "(as it were) to the labourer, of part of the benefit his assistance occasions, or else he would not get the other part; the profit is reduced, then, by competition" * (l.c., [pp.] 102-03).

This is very fine. If, as a consequence of the development of the productive powers of labour, capital accumulates so quickly that the demand for labour increases WAGES and the worker works for LESS TIME gratis for the capitalist and SHARES TO SOME DEGREE IN THE BENEFITS OF HIS MORE PRODUCTIVE LABOUR — THE CAPITALIST MAKES HIM A *"PRESENT"*!

The same author demonstrates in great detail that high wages are a poor ENCOURAGEMENT for workers, although, speaking of the LANDLORDS, he CONSIDERS that LOW PROFIT is A DISCOURAGEMENT for the CAPITALISTS (see p. 13, Notebook XII[90]).

"Adam Smith thought that *accumulation or increase of stock in general lowered the rate of profits in general, on the same principle which makes the increase of stock in any particular trade lower the profits of that trade. But such increase of stock in a particular trade *means* an increase more *in proportion* than stock is at the same time increased in other trades" * (l.c., [p.] 9).

---

[a] Limits.— *Ed.*

Against Say. (Notebook XII, p. 12.[44])

* "The immediate market for capital, or *field* for capital, may be said to be labour. The amount of capital which can be invested at a given moment, in a given country, or the world, so as to return not less than a given rate of profits, seems principally to depend on the *quantity of labour*, which it is possible, by laying out that capital, to induce the then existing number of human beings to perform" (l.c., [p.] 20).

[XIV-814] *"Profits* do not depend on *price*, they depend on price compared with outgoings" (l.c., [p.] 28).

"The proposition of M. Say [91] does not at all prove that *capital* opens a market for itself, but only that capital and labour open a market for one another" * (l.c., [p.] 111).

c) *Dialogues of Three Templars on Political Economy, chiefly in Relation to the Principles of Mr. Ricardo* ([*The*] *London Magazine*, Vol. IX, 1824) (author: Thomas De Quincey)

Attempt at a refutation of all the attacks made on Ricardo. That he is aware of what is at issue is to be seen from this sentence:

"All difficulties of political economy will be found reducible to this: * What is the ground of exchangeable value?" * (l.c., [*Dialogues of Three Templars...*, p.] 347).[a]

In this work, the inadequacies of the Ricardian view are often pointedly set forth, although the dialectical depth is more affected than real. The real difficulties, which arise not out of the determination of VALUE, but from Ricardo's inadequate elaboration of his ideas on this basis, and from his arbitrary attempt to make concrete relations directly fit the simple relation of value, are in no way resolved or even grasped. But the work is characteristic of the period in which it appeared. It shows that in political economy consistency and thinking were still taken seriously at that time.

(A later work by the same author: *The Logic of Political Economy*, Edinburgh, 1845,[92] is weaker.)

De Quincey very clearly outlines the differences between the Ricardian view and those which preceded it, and does not seek to mitigate them by re-interpretation or to abandon the essential features of the problems in actual fact while retaining them in a purely formal, verbal way as happened later on, thus opening the door wide to easy-going, unprincipled eclecticism.

One more point in the Ricardian doctrine which is especially emphasised by De Quincey and which should be mentioned here

---

[a] Marx quotes De Quincey with some alterations.— *Ed.*

because it plays a role in the polemic against Ricardo to which we shall refer below, is that the command which one commodity has over other commodities (its purchasing power; in fact, its value expressed in terms of another commodity) is altogether different from its *real value.*

> "It is quite wrong to conclude *that the real value is great because the quantity it buys is great, or small because the quantity it buys is small... If A doubles its value, it will not therefore command double the former quantity of B. It may do so: and it may also command 500 times more or 500 times less...* No man has ever denied that A *by doubling its own value will command a double quantity of all things which have been stationary in value. But the question is whether universally, [by] doubling its value, A will command a double quantity"* (l.c., [p.] 552 et seq. *passim*).

d) *A Critical Dissertation on the Nature, Measures, and Causes of Value; Chiefly in Reference to the Writings of Mr. Ricardo and His Followers.* By the Author of Essays on the Formation and Publication of Opinions (Samuel Bailey), London, 1825

This is the main work directed against Ricardo. (Also aimed against Malthus.) It seeks to overturn the foundation of the doctrine— VALUE.[a] It is definitely worthless except for the definition of the "MEASURE OF VALUE", or RATHER, of money in this function.[b] Compare also the same author's: *A Letter to a Political Economist; Occasioned by an Article in the Westminster Review on the Subject of Value etc.,* London, 1826.

Since, as has been mentioned,[c] this work basically agrees with *Observations on Certain Verbal Disputes in Political Economy,* it is here necessary to add the relevant passages from these *Observations.*

The author of the *Observations* accuses Ricardo of having transformed VALUE from a relative attribute of commodities in their relationship to one another, into something absolute.

The only thing that Ricardo can be accused of in this context is that, in elaborating the concept of value, he does not clearly distinguish between the various aspects, between the exchange value of the commodity, as it *manifests itself, appears* in the process of commodity exchange, and the existence of the commodity as

---

[a] See present edition, Vol. 31, pp. 469-80.— *Ed.*
[b] See this volume, pp. 319-25.— *Ed.*
[c] Ibid., p. 299.— *Ed.*

value as distinct from its existence as an object, product, use value. [XIV-815] It is said in the *Observations*:

* "If the absolute quantity of labour, which produces the greater part of commodities, or all except one, is increased, would you say that the value of that one is unaltered? since it will exchange for less of every commodity besides. If, indeed, it is meant to be asserted that the *meaning* of increase or diminution of value, is increase or diminution in the quantity of labour that produced the commodity spoken of, the conclusions I have just been objecting to might be true enough. But to say, as Mr. Ricardo does, that the comparative quantities of labour that produce two commodities are the cause of the rate at which the two commodities will exchange with each other, i.e. of the exchangeable value of each,—is very different from saying that the *exchangeable value of either means* the quantity of labour which produced it, understood without any reference to the other, or to the existence of the other" (*Observations etc.*, p. 13).

"Mr. Ricardo tells us indeed that 'the inquiry to which he wishes to draw the reader's attention relates to the effects of the variations in the *relative* value of commodities, and not in their *absolute* value'[a]; as if he there considered that there *is* such a thing as exchangeable value which is not relative" (l.c., [pp. 9-]10).

"That Mr. Ricardo has departed from his original use of the term value, and *has made of it something absolute, instead of relative,* is still more evident in his chapter entitled: 'Value and Riches, their distinctive Properties'. The question there discussed has been discussed also by others, and is simply verbal and useless" * (l.c., [p.] 15 et seq.).

Before dealing with this author, we shall add the following about Ricardo. In his CHAPTER ON "Value and Riches", he argues that social wealth does not depend on the value of the commodities produced, although this latter point is decisive for EVERY INDIVIDUAL PRODUCER. It should have been all the more clear to him that a form of production whose exclusive aim is SURPLUS VALUE, in other words, which is based on the relative poverty of the mass of the PRODUCERS, cannot possibly be the absolute form of the production of wealth, as he constantly asserts.

Now to the "OBSERVATIONS"[b] of the "VERBAL" wiseacre.

If all commodities except one increase in value because they cost more labour time than they did before, smaller amounts of these commodities will be exchanged for the single commodity whose labour time remains unchanged. Its *exchange value,* in so far as it is realised in other commodities—that is, its exchange value expressed in the *use values* of all other commodities—has been reduced. "Would you then say that the exchange value of that one is *unaltered?*" This is merely a formulation of the point at issue, and it calls neither for a positive nor for a negative reply. The same result would occur if the labour time required for the production

---

[a] D. Ricardo, *On the Principles of Political Economy, and Taxation*, 3rd ed., London, 1821, p. 15. See also present edition, Vol. 31, p. 399.— *Ed.*

[b] *Observations on Certain Verbal Disputes...— Ed.*

of the one commodity were reduced and that of all the others remained unchanged. A given quantity of this particular commodity would exchange for a reduced quantity of all the other commodities. The same phenomenon occurs in both cases although from directly opposite causes. Conversely, if the labour time required for the production of commodity A remained unchanged, while that of all others were reduced, then it would exchange for larger amounts of all the other commodities. The same would happen for the opposite reason, if the labour time required for the production of A increased and that required for all other commodities remained unchanged. Thus, sometimes commodity A exchanges for smaller quantities of all the other commodities, and this for either of two different and opposite reasons. At other times it exchanges for larger quantities of all the other commodities, again for two different and opposite reasons. But, *nota bene,* it is assumed that it always exchanges at *its value,* consequently for an *equivalent.* It always realises its value in the quantity of use values of the other commodities for which it exchanges, no matter how much the quantity of these use values varies. From this it obviously follows: that the rate at which commodities exchange for one another as use values, although it is an *expression* of their value, their *realised* value, is not their value itself, since the same proportion of value can be represented by quite different quantities of use values. Value as an aspect of the commodity is not expressed in its own use value, or in its existence as use value. Value *manifests itself* when commodities are expressed in other use values, that is, [it manifests itself] in the rate at which these other use values are exchanged for them. If 1 ounce of gold = 1 ton of iron, that is, if a small quantity of gold exchanges for a large quantity of iron, is therefore the value of the ounce of gold expressed in iron greater than the value of the iron expressed in gold? That commodities exchange for one another in proportion to the labour embodied in them, means that they are equal, alike, in so far as they represent the same quantity of labour. Consequently it means likewise that every commodity, considered in itself, is something *different* from its [XIV-816] own use value, from its own existence as use value.

The *value* of the same commodity can, without changing, be expressed in infinitely *different* quantities of use values, always according to whether I express it in the use value of this or of that commodity. This does not alter the value, although it does alter the way it is expressed. In the same way, all the various quantities of different use values in which the value of commodity A can be expressed, are equivalents and are related to one another not only as values, but as equal values, so that when these very unequal quantities of use value replace one another, the value remains completely unchanged, as if it had not found expression in quite different use values.

When commodities are exchanged in the proportion in which they represent equal amounts of labour time, then it is their existence as objectified labour time, as embodied labour time, which manifests their *substance,* the *identical element* they contain. As such, they are *qualitatively* the same, and differ only *quantitatively,* according to whether they represent smaller or larger quantities of *the same* substance, i.e. labour time. They are *values* as expressions of the same element; and [they are] equal values, *equivalents,* in so far as they represent an equal amount of labour time. They can only be compared as magnitudes, because they are already homogeneous magnitudes, qualitatively identical.

It is as manifestations of this substance that these different things constitute *values* and are related to one another as values; their different *magnitudes of value,* their immanent measure of value are thus also given. And only *because of this* can the value of a commodity be represented, expressed, in the use values of other commodities as its equivalents. Hence the *individual commodity* as *value,* as the *embodiment of this substance,* is different from itself as use value, as an object, quite apart from the expression of its value in other commodities. As the embodiment of labour time, it is *value* in general, as the embodiment of a definite quantity of labour time, it is a definite *magnitude of value.*

It is therefore typical of our wiseacre when he says: * If we *mean* that, we do n o t *mean* that and vice versa. Our "meaning" has nothing at all to do with the essential characters of the thing we consider. If we speak of the *value in exchange* of a thing, we *mean* in the first instance of course the *relative quantities* of all other commodities that can be exchanged with the first commodity. But, on further consideration, we shall find that for the proportion, in which one thing exchanges with an infinite mass of other things, which have nothing at all in common with it—and even if there are natural or other similarities between those things, they are not considered in the exchange—[for the proportion] to be a *fixed proportion,* all those various heterogeneous things must be considered as proportionate representations, expressions of the *same* common *unity,* [of] an element quite different from their natural existence or appearances. We shall then furthermore find, that if our view has any sense, the value of a commodity is something by which it not only differs from or is related to other commodities, but is a quality by which it differs from its own existence as a thing, a value in use.

"The rise of value of article A, only meant *value estimated* in articles B, C, etc., i.e. value in exchange for articles B, C, etc." (l.c., p. 16).

To *estimate* the value of A, a book for instance, in B, coals, and C, wine, A, B, C must be as *value* something different from their existences as books, coals or wine. To estimate a value of A in B, A must have a value independent of the estimation of that value in B, and both must be equal to a third thing, expressed in both of them.*

It is quite wrong to say that the value of a commodity is thereby transformed from something *relative* into something *absolute*. On the contrary, as a use value, the commodity appears as something independent. On the other hand, as value it appears as something merely *posited*,[93] something merely determined by its relation to socially necessary, equal, simple labour time. It is to such an extent relative that when the labour time required for its reproduction changes, its value changes, although the labour time really contained in the commodity has remained unaltered.

[XIV-817] How deeply our wiseacre has sunk into *fetishism* and how he transforms what is relative into something positive, is demonstrated most strikingly in the following passage:

*"*Value* is a *property of things, riches* of men. Value, in this sense, necessarily implies exchange, riches do not"* (l.c., [p.] 16).

RICHES here are use values. These, as far as men are concerned, are, of course, RICHES, but it is through its *own* PROPERTY, its own qualities, that a thing is a use value and therefore an element of wealth for men. Take away from grapes the qualities that make them grapes, and their use value as grapes disappears for men and they cease to be an element of wealth for men. RICHES which are identical with use values are PROPERTIES OF THINGS THAT ARE MADE USE OF BY MEN AND WHICH EXPRESS A RELATION TO THEIR WANTS. But "VALUE" is supposed to be a "PROPERTY OF THINGS".

As values, commodities are *social* magnitudes, that is to say, something absolutely different from their "PROPERTIES" AS "THINGS". As VALUES, they constitute only relations of men in their PRODUCTIVE ACTIVITY. VALUE indeed "IMPLIES EXCHANGES", but EXCHANGES are EXCHANGES OF THINGS BETWEEN MEN; EXCHANGES which in no way affect the things as such. A thing retains the same "PROPERTIES" whether it be owned by A or by B. In actual fact, the concept "VALUE" presupposes "EXCHANGES" of the products. Where labour is communal, the relations of men in their social production do not manifest themselves as *"values" of "things". Exchange of products as commodities is a certain method of exchanging labour, and [the form] of the dependence of the labour of each upon the labour of the others, a certain mode of social labour or social production.*

In the first part of my book,[a] I mentioned that it is characteristic of labour based on private exchange that the social character of labour "manifests itself" in a perverted form—as the "PROPERTY" of things; that a social relation appears as a relation between things (between PRODUCTS, VALUES IN USE, COMMODITIES). This *appearance* is accepted as something real by our fetish-worshipper, and he actually believes that the exchange value of things is determined by their PROPERTIES AS THINGS, and is altogether A NATURAL PROPERTY of things. No scientist to date has yet discovered what natural qualities make definite proportions of snuff tobacco and paintings "equivalents" for one another. Thus he, the WISEACRE, transforms value into something absolute, "A PROPERTY OF THINGS", instead of seeing in it only something relative, the relation of things to social labour, social labour based on private exchange, a relation in which things are defined not as independent entities, but as mere expressions of social production.

But to say that "VALUE" is not an absolute, is not conceived as AN ENTITY, is quite different from saying that commodities must impart to their VALUE OF EXCHANGE a *separate* expression which is *different* from and *independent* of their use VALUE and of their existence as real products, in other words, that commodity circulation is bound to evolve money. Commodities express their exchange value in money, first of all in the *price,* in which they all present themselves as materialised forms of *the same* labour, as only quantitatively different expressions of *the same* substance. The fact that the *exchange value* of the commodity *assumes an independent existence* in money is itself the result of the process of exchange, the development of the contradiction of use value and exchange value embodied in the commodity, and of another no less important contradiction embodied in it, namely, that the definite, particular labour of the private individual must manifest itself as its opposite, as equal, necessary, general labour and, in this form, social labour. The representation of the commodity as money implies not only that the different magnitudes of commodity values are measured by expressing the values in the use value of one exclusive

---

[a] K. Marx, *A Contribution to the Critique of Political Economy.* Part One (see present edition, Vol. 29, pp. 275-76, 289-90).— *Ed.*

commodity, but at the same time that they are all expressed in a form in which they exist as the embodiment of *social labour* and are therefore exchangeable for every other commodity, that they are translatable at will into any use value desired. Their representation as money—in the price—therefore appears first only as something nominal, a representation which is realised only through actual sale.

Ricardo's mistake is that he is concerned only with the *magnitude of value*. Consequently his attention is concentrated on [XIV-818] the *relative quantities of labour* which the different commodities represent, or which the commodities as values embody. But the labour embodied in them must be represented as *social* labour, as alienated individual labour. In the price this representation is nominal; it becomes reality only in the sale. This transformation of the labour of private individuals contained in the commodities into *uniform social labour,* consequently into labour which can be expressed in all use values and can be exchanged for them, this *qualitative* aspect of the matter which is contained in the representation of exchange value as money, is not elaborated by Ricardo. This circumstance—the necessity of *presenting* labour contained in commodities as *uniform social labour,* i.e. as money—is overlooked by Ricardo.

For its part, the development of capital already *presupposes* the full development of the exchange value of commodities and consequently its independent existence as money. The point of departure in the process of the production and circulation of capital, is the independent form of value which maintains itself, increases, measures the increase against its original amount, whatever CHANGES the commodities in which it manifests itself may undergo, and quite irrespective of whether it presents itself in the most varied use values and changes the commodities which serve as its embodiment. The relation between the value preposited to production and the value which results from it—capital as preposited value is capital in contrast to profit—constitutes the all-embracing and decisive factor in the whole process of capitalist production. It is not only an independent expression of value as in money, but dynamic value, value which maintains itself in a process in which use values pass through the most varied forms. Thus in capital the independent existence of value is raised to a higher power than in money.

From this we can judge the wisdom of our "VERBAL" WISEACRE, who treats the independent existence of exchange value as a figure of speech, a MANNER OF TALKING, a SCHOLASTIC INVENTION.

* "Value, or *valeur* in French, is not only used absolutely instead of relatively as a quality of things, but is even used by some as a measurable commodity, 'Possessing a value', 'Transferring a portion of value'" * (a very important factor with regard to fixed capital), * "'the sum, or totality of values', etc. I do not know what this means" * (l.c., [p.] 57).

The fact that the value which has become independent acquires only a relative expression in money, because money itself is a commodity, and HENCE OF A CHANGEABLE VALUE, makes no difference but is a shortcoming which arises from the nature of the commodity and the necessity of expressing its exchange value, as distinct from its use value. OUR MAN has made it abundantly clear that he DOES "NOT KNOW" this. This is shown by the kind of criticism which would like to talk out of existence the difficulties innate in the contradictory functions of things themselves, by declaring them to be the result of reflexions or of conflicting DEFINITIONS.

* "'The *relative* value of two things' is open to two meanings: the rate at which two things exchange or would exchange with *each other,* or the comparative portions of a *third* for which each exchanges or would exchange" * (l.c., [p.] 53).

D'abord,[a] this is a fine definition. If 3 lbs of coffee EXCHANGE for 1 lb. of tea TODAY OR WOULD EXCHANGE TOMORROW, it does not at all mean that equivalents HAVE BEEN EXCHANGED FOR EACH OTHER. According to this, a commodity could always be EXCHANGED only at its value, for its value would constitute any quantity of some other commodity for which it had been accidentally exchanged. *This, however, is not what people generally *mean*, when they say that 3 lbs of coffee have been exchanged for their equivalent in tea.[b] They suppose that after, as before, the exchange, a *commodity of the same value* is in the hands of either of the exchangers. The rate at which two commodities exchange does not determine their value, but their value determines the rate at which they exchange.* If value were nothing more than the quantity of commodities for which commodity A is accidentally exchanged, how is it possible *to express the value of A in the commodity B, C, etc.? Because [XIV-819] then, as there is no *immanent* measure common to the two, the value of A could not be expressed in B before it had been exchanged against B.*

Relative value means first of all *magnitude of value* in contradistinction to the quality of being *value* at all. For this reason, the latter is not something absolute. It means, secondly, the value of one commodity expressed in the use value of another commodity.

---

[a] To begin with.— *Ed.*
[b] In the manuscript: "sugar".— *Ed.*

This is *only a relative* expression of its value, namely, *in relation to the commodity in which it is expressed. The value of a pound of coffee is only relatively expressed in tea[a]; to express it absolutely—even in a relative way, that is to say, not in regard to the time of labour, but to other commodities—it ought to be expressed in an infinite series of equations *with all other commodities*. This would be an *absolute* expression of its *relative value*; its absolute expression would be its expression *in* [the] *time of labour*, and by this absolute expression it would be expressed as something relative, but in the absolute relation, by which it *is* value.*

Let us now turn to Bailey.[94]

His book has only one positive merit—that he was the first to give a more accurate definition of the MEASURE OF VALUE, that is, in fact, of one of the functions of money, or money in a particular, determinate form. In order to measure the *value* of commodities—to establish an *external* measure of value—it is not necessary that the value of the commodity in terms of which the other commodities are measured, should be invariable. (It must on the contrary be variable, as I have shown in the first part,[b] because the measure of value is, and must be, a commodity since otherwise it would have no *immanent* measure in common with other commodities.) If, for example, the value of money changes, it changes to an equal degree in relation to all other commodities. Their relative values are therefore expressed in it just as correctly as if the value of money had remained unchanged. The problem of finding an "invariable measure of value" is thereby eliminated.[c] But this problem itself (the interest in comparing the value of commodities in different historical periods, is, indeed, not an *economic* interest as such, [but] an academic interest[d]) arose out of a misunderstanding and conceals a much more profound and important question. "Invariable measure of value" signifies *de prime abord*[e] a measure of value which is itself of invariable value, and consequently, since value itself is a predicate of the commodity, a commodity of invariable value. For example, if gold and silver or corn, or labour, were such commodities, then it would be possible to establish, by comparison with them, the rate

---

a In the manuscript: "sugar".— *Ed.*

b K. Marx, *A Contribution to the Critique of Political Economy.* Part One (see present edition, Vol. 29, pp. 304-07).— *Ed.*

c See present edition, Vol. 31, p. 426.— *Ed.*

d Cf. this volume, pp. 340-41.— *Ed.*

e Primarily.— *Ed.*

at which other commodities are exchanged for them, that is, to measure exactly the variations in the values of these other commodities by their prices in gold, silver, or corn, or their relation to wages. Stated in this way, the problem therefore presupposes from the outset that in the "measure of value" we are dealing simply with the commodity in which the values of all other commodities are expressed, whether it be the commodity by which they are really represented—money, the commodity which functions as money—or a commodity which, because its value remains invariable, would function as the money in terms of which the theoretician makes his calculations. It thus becomes evident that in this context it is in any case a question only of a kind of money which as the measure of value—either theoretically or practically—would itself not be subject to changes in value.

But for commodities to express their exchange value independently in money, in a third commodity, the exclusive commodity, the *values of commodities* must already be presupposed. Now the point is merely to compare them quantitatively. A *homogeneity* which makes them the same—makes them values—which as values makes them qualitatively equal, is already presupposed in order that their value and their differences in value can be represented in this way. For example, if all commodities express their value in gold, then this expression in gold, their gold price, their equation with gold, is an equation on the basis of which it is possible to elucidate and compute their value relation to one another, for they are now expressed as *different quantities of gold* and in this way the commodities are represented in their *prices*, as [XIV-820] comparable magnitudes of the same common denominator.

But in order to be represented in this way, the commodities must *already* be *identical* as *values*. Otherwise it would be impossible to solve the problem of expressing the value of each commodity in gold, if commodity and gold or any two commodities as values were not representations of the same substance, capable of being expressed in one another. In other words, this presupposition is already implicit in the problem itself. Commodities are already presumed as values, as *values* distinct from their use values, before the question of representing this value in a special commodity can arise. In order that two quantities of different use values can be equated as equivalents, it is already presumed that they are *equal* to a third, that they are *qualitatively* equal and only constitute different quantitative expressions of this qualitative equality.

The problem of an "invariable measure of value" was in fact simply a spurious name for the quest for the concept, the nature, *of value* itself, the definition of which could not be another value, and consequently could not be subject to variations as value. This was *labour time, social labour*, as it presents itself specifically in commodity production. A quantity of labour has no value, is not a commodity, but is that which transforms commodities into values, it is their *common substance*; as manifestations of it commodities are *qualitatively equal* and only *quantitatively different*. They [appear] as expressions of definite quantities of social labour time.

Let us assume that gold has an invariable value. If the value of all commodities were then expressed in gold one could measure variations in the values of commodities by their gold prices. But in order to express the value of commodities in gold, commodities and gold must be identical as *values*. Gold and commodities can only be considered to be identical as definite quantitative expressions of this value, as definite magnitudes of value. The invariable value of gold and the variable value of the other commodities would not prevent them, as *value*, from being the same, [consisting of] the same substance. Before the invariable value of gold can help us to make a step forward, the value of commodities must first be expressed, assessed, in gold—that is, gold and commodities must be represented as equivalents, as expressions *of the same substance*.

//In order that the commodities may be measured according to the quantity of labour embodied in them—and the measure of the quantity of labour is time—the different kinds of labour contained in the commodities must be reduced to uniform, simple labour, average labour, ordinary, UNSKILLED LABOUR. Only then can the amount of labour embodied [in] them be measured according to a common measure, according to time. The labour must be qualitatively equal so that its differences become merely quantitative, merely differences of magnitude. This reduction to simple, average labour is not, however, the only determinant of the *quality* of this labour to which as a unity the values of the commodities are reduced. That the quantity of labour embodied in a commodity is the quantity *socially necessary* for its production—the labour time being thus *necessary labour time*—is a definition which concerns only the *magnitude of value*. But the labour which constitutes the substance of value is not only uniform, simple, average labour; it is the labour of a private individual represented in a definite product. However, the product as value must be the embodiment of *social* labour and, as such, be directly convertible from one use value into any other. (The particular use value in which labour is directly represented is irrelevant so that it can be converted from one form into another.) Thus the *labour of individuals* has to be directly represented as its opposite, *social* labour; this transformed labour is, as its immediate opposite, *abstract, general labour*, which is therefore represented in a general equivalent. Only by its alienation does individual labour manifest itself as its opposite. The commodity, however, must have this general expression before it is alienated. This necessity to express individual labour as general labour is equivalent to the necessity of expressing a commodity as money. The commodity receives this expression in so far as the money serves as a measure and expresses the value of the commodity in its *price*. It is only through sale, through its real transformation into money, that the commodity acquires its adequate expression as exchange value. The first transformation is merely a theoretical process, the second is a real one.

[XIV-821] Thus, in considering the existence of the commodity as *money*, it is not only necessary to emphasise that in money commodities acquire a definite *measure* of the magnitude of their value—since all commodities express their value in the use value of *the same* commodity—but that they all become manifestations of social, abstract, general labour; and as such they all possess the same form, they all appear as the direct incarnation of social labour; and as such they all act as social labour, they can be *directly exchanged* for all other commodities in proportion to the magnitude of their value; whereas in the hands of the people whose commodities have been transformed into money, they exist not as exchange value in the form of a particular use value, but as use value (gold, for example) which is merely a bearer of exchange value. A commodity may be sold either below or above its value. This is purely a matter of the *magnitude of its value*. But whenever a commodity is sold, transformed into money, its exchange value acquires an independent existence, separate from its use value. The commodity now exists only as a certain quantity of social labour time, and it proves that it is such by being *directly* exchangeable for any commodity whatsoever and convertible (in proportion to its quantity) into any use value whatsoever. This point must not be overlooked in relation to money any more than the formal transformation undergone by the labour a commodity contains as its element of value. But an examination of money—of that absolute exchangeability which the commodity possesses as money, of its absolute effectiveness as *exchange value* which has nothing to do with magnitude of value—shows that it is not quantitatively, but qualitatively determined and that as a result of the very process through which the commodity itself passes, its *exchange value* becomes independent, and is really represented as a separate aspect alongside its use value as it is already nominally in its price.

This shows, therefore, that the "VERBAL OBSERVER" [95] understands as little of the value and the nature of money as Bailey, since both regard the independent existence of value as a scholastic invention of economists. This independent existence becomes even more evident in capital, which, in one of its aspects, can be called *value in process*—and since value only exists independently in money, [it can accordingly be called] *money in process*, as it goes through a series of processes in which it preserves itself, departs from itself, and returns to itself increased in volume. It goes without saying that the paradox of reality is also reflected in paradoxes of speech which are at variance with COMMON SENSE and with WHAT VULGARIANS MEAN AND BELIEVE they are TALKING OF. The contradictions which arise from the fact that on the basis of commodity production the labour of the individual presents itself as general social labour, and the relations of people as relations between things and as things—these contradictions are innate in the subject-matter, not in its verbal expressions.//

Ricardo often gives the impression, and sometimes indeed writes, as if the QUANTITY OF LABOUR is the solution to the false, or falsely conceived problem of an "INVARIABLE MEASURE OF VALUE" in the same way as corn, money, wages, etc., were previously considered and advanced as *nostra*[a] of this kind. In Ricardo's work this false impression arises because for him the decisive task is the definition of the magnitude of value. Because of this he does not understand the specific form in which labour is an element of value, and fails in particular to grasp that the labour of the individual must present itself as abstract general labour and, in this form, as *social* labour. Therefore he has not understood that the development of money is connected with the nature of value and with the determination of this value by labour time. Bailey's book has rendered a good service in so far as the objections he raises help to clear up the confusion between "MEASURE OF VALUE" expressed in money as a commodity along with other commodities, and the immanent measure and substance of value. But if he had analysed money as a "MEASURE OF VALUE", not only as a quantitative measure

---

[a] Here: secret remedy. See this volume, p. 322.— *Ed.*

but as a qualitative transformation of commodities, he would have arrived at a correct analysis of value. Instead of this, he contents himself with a mere superficial consideration of the external "MEASURE OF VALUE"—which already presupposes VALUE—and remains rooted in a purely frivolous approach to the question.

[XIV-822] There are, however, occasional passages in Ricardo in which he directly emphasises that the quantity of labour embodied in a commodity constitutes the immanent measure of the *magnitude* of its value, of the *differences in the amount* of its value, only because labour is the factor the different commodities have in *common*, which constitutes their uniformity, their substance, the intrinsic foundation of their value. The thing however he failed to investigate is the specific form in which labour plays that role.

* "In making *labour* the *foundation of the value* of commodities, *and* the *comparative quantity of labour* which is necessary to their production, *the rule which determines the respective quantities of goods* which shall be given in exchange for each other, we must not be supposed to deny the accidental and temporary deviations of the actual or market price of commodities from this, their primary and natural price" ([Ricardo, *On the Principles...,*] 3rd ed., [London,] 1821, [p.] 80).

"'To measure ... is to find how many times they'" (the things measured) "'contain ... *unities of the same description.*' [a] A franc is not a measure of value for any thing, but for a quantity of the *same metal* of which francs are made, unless francs, and the thing to be measured, can be referred to *some other measure which is c o m m o n to both*. This, I think, they can be, for they are both the *result of labour*; and, therefore" * (because LABOUR is their *causa efficiens*[b]) *"labour is a *common measure,* by which their *real* as well as their *relative value* may be estimated" * (l.c., [pp.] 333-34).

All commodities can be reduced to LABOUR as their common element. What Ricardo does not investigate is the *specific* form in which LABOUR manifests itself as the common element of commodities. That is why he does not understand money. That is why in his work the transformation of commodities into money appears to be something merely formal, which does not penetrate deeply into the very essence of capitalist production. He says however: only because LABOUR is the common factor of commodities, only because they are all mere manifestations of the same common element, of LABOUR, is LABOUR their MEASURE. It is their measure only because it forms their *substance* as values. Ricardo does not sufficiently differentiate between LABOUR in so far as it is represented in use values or in exchange value. LABOUR as the

---

[a] A. L. C. Destutt-Tracy, *Élémens d'idéologie.* Part I, *Idéologie proprement dite,* 2nd ed., Paris, 1804, p. 187.— *Ed.*

[b] Effective cause.— *Ed.*

foundation of value is not any particular LABOUR, with particular qualities. Ricardo continuously confuses the LABOUR which is represented in use value and that which is represented in exchange value. It is true that the latter species of LABOUR is only the former species expressed in an abstract form.

By *REAL VALUE*, Ricardo, in the *passus* cited above, understands the commodity as the embodiment of a definite amount of labour time. By *RELATIVE VALUE*, he understands the labour time the commodity contains expressed in the use values of other commodities.

Now to *Bailey*.

Bailey clings to the form in which the exchange value of the commodity—as commodity—appears, manifests itself. It manifests itself in a *general form* when it is expressed in the use value of a third commodity, in which all other commodities likewise express their value—a commodity which serves as money—that is, in the *money price* of the commodity. It manifests itself in a *particular form* when the exchange value of any particular commodity is expressed in the use value of any other, that is, as the *corn price, linen price,* etc. In actual fact, the exchange value of the commodity always appears, manifests itself with regard to other commodities, only in the *quantitative relationship* in which they exchange. The individual commodity as such cannot express general labour time, or it can only express it in its equation with the commodity which constitutes money, in its *money price*. But then the value of commodity A is always expressed in a certain quantity of the use value of M, the commodity which functions as money. This is how matters *appear directly*. And Bailey clings to this. The most superficial form of exchange value, that is, the *quantitative relationship* in which commodities exchange with one another, *constitutes*, according to Bailey, their value. The advance from the surface to the core of the problem is not permitted. He even forgets the simple consideration that if y yards of linen$=x$ lbs of straw, this [implies] a parity between two unequal things—linen and straw—making them equal magnitudes. This existence of theirs as things that are equal must surely be different [XIV-823] from their existence as straw and linen. It is not straw and linen that they are equated, but as equivalents. The one side of the equation must, therefore, express the same value as the other. The value of straw and linen must, therefore, be neither straw nor linen, but something common to both and different from both commodities considered as straw and linen. What is it? He does not answer this question. Instead, he wanders off into all the categories of political economy in order to repeat the same monotonous litany over and over again, [namely,] that value is the exchange relation of commodities and consequently is not anything different from this relation.

> * "*If* the *value* of an object *is its power of purchasing,* there must be something to purchase. Value denotes, *consequently,* nothing positive or intrinsic, but merely the *relation* in which two objects stand to each other as *exchangeable commodities*" * ([*A Critical Dissertation...*, pp.] 4-5).

His entire wisdom is, in fact, contained in this passage. * "If *value* is *nothing* but *power of purchasing*" (a very fine definition since "purchasing" [pre]supposes not only value, but the representation of value as "money"), "it denotes",* etc. However let us first clear away from Bailey's proposition the absurdities which have been smuggled in. "PURCHASING" means transforming money into commodities. Money already presupposes VALUE and the development OF VALUE. Consequently, out with the expression "PURCHASING" first of all. Otherwise we are explaining VALUE by VALUE. Instead of PURCHASING we must say "EXCHANGING AGAINST OTHER OBJECTS". It is quite superfluous to say that "THERE MUST BE SOMETHING TO PURCHASE". If the "OBJECT" was to be consumed by its producers as a use value, if it was not merely a means of appropriating other objects, not a "*commodity*", then obviously there could be no question of VALUE. First, it is a matter of an OBJECT. But then the relation "IN WHICH TWO OBJECTS STAND TO EACH OTHER" is transformed into "THE RELATION ... THEY STAND TO EACH OTHER ... AS *EXCHANGEABLE COMMODITIES*". After all, the OBJECTS STAND only in relation OF EXCHANGE or as EXCHANGEABLE OBJECTS TO EACH OTHER. That is why they are "*COMMODITIES*", which is SOMETHING other THAN "OBJECTS". On the other hand, the "relation OF EXCHANGEABLE COMMODITIES" is either nonsense, since "NOT EXCHANGEABLE OBJECTS" are not COMMODITIES, or Mr. Bailey has beaten himself. The OBJECTS SHALL NOT BE EXCHANGED IN ANY PROPORTION WHATEVER, but are to be EXCHANGED as COMMODITIES, that is, they are to stand to one another as EXCHANGEABLE COMMODITIES, that is, as objects each of which has a value, and which are to be exchanged with one another in *proportion to their equivalence.* Bailey thereby admits that the RATE at which they are exchanged, that is, the POWER of each of the commodities to purchase the other, is determined by its *value,* but this value however is not determined by this POWER, which is merely a corollary.

If we strip the passage of everything that is wrong, nonsensical or smuggled in, then it will read like this.

But wait: we must dispose of yet another snare and piece of

nonsense. We have two sorts of expression. AN OBJECT'S "POWER" OF EXCHANGING, etc. (since the term "PURCHASING" is unjustified and makes no sense without the concept of money), and the RELATION IN WHICH AN OBJECT EXCHANGES WITH OTHERS. If "POWER" is to be regarded as something different from "RELATION", then one ought not to say that "POWER OF EXCHANGING" IS "*MERELY THE RELATION*", etc. If it is meant to be *the same thing*, then it is confusing to describe the same thing with two different expressions which have nothing in common with each other. The * *relation* of a thing to another is a relation of the two things and cannot be said to belong to either. *Power of a thing*, on the contrary, is something intrinsic to the thing, although this, its intrinsic quality, may only [XIV-824] manifest itself in its relation to other things. For instance, power of attraction is a power of the thing itself, although that power is "latent" as long as there are no things to attract.* Here an attempt is made to represent the value of the "OBJECT" as something intrinsic to it, and yet as something merely existing as a "RELATION". That is why [Bailey uses] first the word POWER and then the word RELATION.

Accurately expressed it would read as follows:

*"*If* the value of an object is the relation in which it exchanges with other objects, value denotes, *consequently*" (viz., in consequence of the "if"), "nothing, but merely the relation in which two objects stand to each other as exchangeable objects"* (l.c., [pp.] 4-5).

Nobody will contest this tautology. What follows from it, by the way, is that the "VALUE" OF AN OBJECT "DENOTES NOTHING". For example, 1 lb. of COFFEE=4 lbs of COTTON. What then is the value of 1 lb. of COFFEE? 4 lbs of COTTON. And of 4 lbs of COTTON? 1 lb. of COFFEE. Since the value of 1 lb. of coffee is 4 lbs of COTTON, and, on the other hand, the value of 4 lbs of COTTON=1 lb. of COFFEE, then it is clear that the value of 1 lb. of COFFEE=1 lb. of COFFEE (since 4 lbs of COTTON=1 lb. of COFFEE), $a=b$, $b=a$, HENCE $a=a$. What arises from this explanation is, therefore, that the value of a use value=a [certain] quantity of the same use value. Consequently, the value of 1 lb. of COFFEE is nothing else than 1 lb. of coffee. If 1 lb. of COFFEE=4 lbs of cotton, then it is clear that 1 lb. of COFFEE>3 lbs of COTTON and 1 lb. of COFFEE<5 lbs of COTTON. To say that 1 lb. of COFFEE>3 lbs of COTTON and<5 lbs of COTTON, expresses a RELATION between COFFEE and COTTON just as well as saying that 1 lb. of COFFEE=4 lbs of COTTON. The symbol = does not express any more of a relation than does the symbol < or the symbol >, but simply a *different* relation. Why is it then precisely the relation represented by the sign of equality, by =, which expresses the value of the COFFEE in COTTON and that of the COTTON in COTTON? Or is this sign of equality the result of the fact that these two amounts exchange for one another at all? Does this sign = merely express the fact of exchange? It cannot be denied that if COFFEE exchanges for COTTON in any RATIO whatever, they are exchanged for one another, and if the mere FACT of their exchange constitutes the RELATION between the commodities, then the value of the COFFEE is equally well expressed in cotton whether it exchanges for 2, 3, 4 or 5 lbs of cotton. But what is then the word RELATION supposed to mean? COFFEE in itself has no "INTRINSIC, POSITIVE" quality which determines the *rate at which* it exchanges for COTTON. It is not a relation which is determined by any kind of determinant INTRINSIC to coffee and separate from real exchange. What is then the purpose of the word "relation"? What is the relation? THE QUANTITY OF COTTON AGAINST WHICH A QUANTITY OF COFFEE IS EXCHANGED. Then one could not speak of a relation IN WHICH IT EXCHANGES but only of a RELATION IN WHICH IT *IS* OR *HAS BEEN* EXCHANGED. For if the RELATION were determined before the exchange, then the exchange would be determined by the "RELATION" and not the RELATION by the exchange. We must therefore DROP the *relation* as signifying something which *stands over and above* the coffee and the cotton and is distinct from them.

* "If the value of an object is the quantity of another object exchanged with it, value denotes, consequently, nothing, but merely the quantity of the other object exchanged with it." *

As a commodity, a commodity can only express its value in other commodities, since general labour time does not exist for it as a commodity. If the value of one commodity is expressed in another commodity, the value of one commodity is nothing apart from this EQUATION with another commodity. Bailey flaunts this piece of wisdom tirelessly—and all the more tiresomely. As he conceives it, it is a *tautology,* for he says: If the value of any commodity is nothing but its exchange relation with another commodity, it is nothing apart from this relation. He reveals his philosophical profundity in the following passage:

* "As we cannot speak of *the distance of any object* without implying some other object, *between which and the former this relation exists,* so we cannot speak of the value of a commodity but in reference to *another commodity* [XIV-825] *compared with it.* A thing cannot be valuable in itself without reference to another thing" * (Is * social labour, to which the value of a commodity is related, not another thing?) "any more than a thing can be *distant in itself* without reference to another thing" * (l.c., [p.] 5).

If a thing is distant from another, the distance is in fact a relation between the one thing and the other; but at the same time, the distance is something different from this relation between the two things. It is a dimension of space, it is some length which may as well express the distance of two other things besides those compared. But this is not all. If we speak of the distance as a relation between two things, we suppose something "intrinsic", some "property" of the things themselves, which enables them to be distant from each other. What is the distance between the syllable A and a table? The question would be nonsensical. In speaking of the distance of two things, we speak of their difference in space. Thus we suppose both of them to be contained in space, to be points of space. Thus we equalise them as being both existences of space, and only after having them equalised *sub specie spatii*[a] we distinguish them as different points of space. To belong to space is their unity.*[b]

But what is this UNITY of OBJECTS EXCHANGED AGAINST EACH OTHER? This EXCHANGE is not a relation which exists between them as natural things. It is likewise not a relation which they bear as natural things to human needs, for it is not THE DEGREE OF THEIR UTILITY THAT DETERMINES THE QUANTITIES IN WHICH THEY EXCHANGE. What is therefore their identity, which enables them TO BE EXCHANGED IN A CERTAIN MEASURE AGAINST EACH OTHER? As what DO THEY BECOME *EXCHANGEABLE*?

---

* [XV-887] // The following has to be added with regard to Bailey's insipidity:

When he says that A IS DISTANT from B, he does not thereby compare them with one another, equalise them, but *separates* them in space. They do *not* occupy *the same* space. Nevertheless he still declares that both are *spatial* things and are differentiated in virtue of being things which belong in space. He therefore makes them equal in advance, gives them the same unity. However, here it is a question of equation. If I say that the area of the $\triangle$ A is equal to that of the $\square$ B, this means not only that the area of the $\triangle$ is expressed in the $\square$ and that of the $\square$ in the $\triangle$, but it means that if the height of the $\triangle$=h and the base=b, then $A=\frac{h \times b}{2}$ a property which belongs to it itself just as it is a property of the $\square$ that it is likewise $=\frac{h \times b}{2}$.[96] As areas, the $\triangle$ and the $\square$ are here declared to be equal, to be equivalents, although as a triangle and a parallelogram they are different. In order to equate these different things with one another, each must represent *the same common element* regardless of the other. If geometry, like the political economy of Mr. Bailey, contented itself with saying that the equality of the $\triangle$ and of the $\square$ means that the $\triangle$ is expressed in the parallelogram, and the parallelogram in the triangle, it would be of little value.// [XV-887]

---

a Under the aspect of space.— *Ed.*
b Marx wrote this paragraph in English.— *Ed.*

In fact, in all this Bailey is merely a *pedisequuus*[a] of the author of THE "VERBAL OBSERVATIONS".[b]

"It" (value) "cannot alter as to one of the objects compared, without altering as to the other" (l.c., [p.] 5).

This again simply means that the expression of the value of one commodity in another commodity can only change as such an *expression*. And the expression as such presupposes not one but two commodities.

Mr. Bailey is of the opinion that if one were to consider *only two commodities*—in exchange with one another—one would automatically discover the mere relativity of *value*, in his sense.[c] The fool. As if it were not just as necessary to say, in connection with [two] commodities which exchange with one another—two products which are related to one another as *commodities—in what* they are identical, as it would be in the case of a thousand. For that matter, if only two products existed, the products would never become commodities, and consequently the exchange value of commodities would never evolve either. The necessity for the labour in product I to manifest itself as social labour would not arise. Because the product is not produced as an immediate object of consumption for the producers, but only as a *bearer of value*, as a claim, so to speak, to a certain quantity of all materialised social labour, all products as *values* are compelled to assume a form of existence distinct from their existence as use values. And it is this development of the labour embodied in them as social labour, it is the development of their *value*, which determines the formation of money, the necessity for commodities to represent themselves in respect of one another as *money*—which means merely as independent forms of existence of exchange value—and they can only do this by setting apart one commodity from the mass of commodities, and all of them measuring their values in the use value of this excluded commodity, thereby directly transforming the labour embodied in this exclusive commodity into *general, social* labour. Mr. Bailey, with his QUEER way of thinking which only grasps the surface appearance of things, concludes on the contrary: Only *because,* besides commodities, *money* exists, and we are so used [to regarding] the value of commodities not in their relation to one another but as a relation to a *third,* as a [XIV-826] third relation distinct from the *direct* relation, is the *concept of*

---

[a] A servile follower.— *Ed.*
[b] *Observations on Certain Verbal Disputes in Political Economy...*— *Ed.*
[c] See present edition, Vol. 31, pp. 399-403.— *Ed.*

value evolved—and consequently value is transformed from the merely quantitative relation in which commodities are exchanged for one another into something independent of this relation (and this, he thinks, transforms the value of commodities into something absolute, into a scholastic ENTITY existing in isolation from the commodities). According to Bailey, it is not the determination of the product as value which leads to the establishment of money and which expresses itself in *money*, but it is the existence of money which leads to the fiction of the concept of value. Historically it is quite correct that the search for value is at first based on money, the *visible* expression of commodities as value, and that consequently the search for the definition of value is (wrongly) represented as a search for a commodity of "invariable value", or for a commodity which is an "invariable measure of value". Since Mr. Bailey now demonstrates that money as an external measure of value—and expression of value—has fulfilled its purpose, even though it has a *variable* value, he thinks he has done away with the question of the concept of value—which is not affected by the variability of the magnitudes of the value of commodities—and that in fact it is no longer necessary to attribute any meaning at all to value. Because the representation of the value of a commodity in money—in a third, exclusive commodity—does not exclude variation in the value of this third commodity, because the problem of an "invariable measure of value" disappears, the problem of the determination of value itself disappears. Bailey carries on this insipid rigmarole for hundreds of pages, with great self-satisfaction.

The following passages, in which he constantly repeats the same thing, are, in part, *verbotenus*[a] copied from the VERBAL ONE.[b]

"Suppose that only two commodities are IN EXISTENCE, both EXCHANGEABLE in proportion to the *quantity of labour. If A ... should, at a subsequent period, require double the quantity of labour for its production, while B continued to require only the same, A would become of double value to B... But although B continued to be produced by the same labour, it would not continue of the same value, for it would exchange for only half the quantity of A, the only *commodity*, by the supposition, with which it could be compared" (l.c., [p.] 6).

"*It is from this circumstance of constant reference to other commodities*" * (instead of regarding value *merely as a* RELATION *between two commodities*) * "or to *money*, when we *are speaking of the relation between any two commodities*, that the *notion of value*, as *something intrinsic* and *absolute*, has arisen" (l.c., [p.] 8).

---

a Verbatim.— *Ed.*
b *Observations on Certain Verbal Disputes in Political Economy...*— *Ed.*

"What I assert is, that if all commodities were produced under exactly the same circumstances, as for instance, by labour alone, any commodity, which always required the same quantity of labour, could not be *invariable in value*" * // that is, INVARIABLE IN THE *EXPRESSION* OF ITS VALUE IN OTHER COMMODITIES—a tautology //, * "while every other commodity underwent alteration" (l.c., [pp.] 20-21).

"Value is nothing intrinsic and absolute" (l.c., [p.] 23).[a]

"It is impossible to designate, *or* express *the value* of a commodity, except by *a quantity of some other commodity*" (l.c., [p.] 26).

(As impossible as it is to *"designate"* or *"express"* a thought except by a quantity of syllables. Hence Bailey concludes that a thought is—syllables.)

"Instead of regarding value as a *relation between two objects,* they" (Ricardo and his followers) "consider it as a positive result produced by a definite quantity of labour" (l.c., [p.] 30).

"Because the values of A and B, according to their doctrine, are to each other as the quantities of producing labour, or ... are determined by the quantities of producing labour, they appear to have concluded, that the value of A alone, without reference to anything else, is as the quantity of its producing labour. There is no meaning certainly in this last proposition" * (l.c., [pp.] 31-32).

They speak of * "value as a sort of general and independent property" ([p.] 35).

"The value of a commodity must be its value in something" * (l.c.).

We can see why it is so important for Bailey to limit value to *two commodities,* to understand it as the relation between *two commodities.* But a difficulty now arises:

* "The *value of any commodity* denoting *its relation in exchange* to some other commodity" *

(what is in this context the purpose of the "RELATION [XIV-827] IN EXCHANGE"? WHY NOT, ITS "*EXCHANGE*"? But at the same time EXCHANGE is intended to express a *definite* relation, not *merely the* FACT *of* EXCHANGE. HENCE VALUE=RELATION IN EXCHANGE)

* "we may speak of it as money-value, corn-value, cloth-value, according to the commodity with which it is compared; and then there are *a thousand different kinds of value,* as *many kinds of value as there are commodities in existence,* and all are equally *real* and equally *nominal*" * ([p.] 39).

Here we have it. VALUE = PRICE. THERE IS NO DIFFERENCE BETWEEN THEM. And THERE IS NO "INTRINSIC" DIFFERENCE BETWEEN MONEY PRICE AND ANY OTHER EXPRESSION OF PRICE, ALTHOUGH IT IS THE MONEY PRICE AND NOT THE CLOTH PRICE, ETC., WHICH EXPRESSES THE NOMINAL VALUE, THE GENERAL VALUE OF THE COMMODITY.

But although the commodity has a THOUSAND DIFFERENT KINDS OF VALUE, or a THOUSAND DIFFERENT PRICES, AS MANY KINDS OF VALUE AS THERE ARE COMMODITIES IN EXISTENCE, ALL THESE THOUSAND EXPRESSIONS ALWAYS EXPRESS THE

---

[a] Marx here sums up Bailey's argument in his own words.— *Ed.*

SAME VALUE. This proves that all these DIFFERENT EXPRESSIONS ARE EQUIVALENTS which not only can replace one another in this expression, but do replace one another in EXCHANGE itself. This *relation* of the commodity, with the price of which we are concerned, is expressed in a thousand DIFFERENT "RELATIONS IN EXCHANGE" to ALL the DIFFERENT commodities and yet always expresses *the same* relation. Thus this RELATION, which remains the same, is distinct from its thousand DIFFERENT EXPRESSIONS, or VALUE IS DIFFERENT from PRICE, and the PRICES ARE ONLY EXPRESSIONS OF VALUE; MONEY PRICE [is] ITS GENERAL EXPRESSION, OTHER PRICES [are] PARTICULAR EXPRESSIONS. It is not even this simple conclusion that Bailey arrives at. In this context Ricardo is not a fictionist but Bailey is a fetishist in that he conceives value, though not as a property of the individual object (considered in isolation), but as a *relation of objects to one another*, while it is only a representation in objects, an objective expression, of a relation between men, a social relation, the relationship of men to their reciprocal productive activity.

* "Mr. Ricardo, ingeniously enough, avoids a difficulty, which, on a first view, threatens to encumber his doctrine, that value depends on the quantity of labour employed in production. If this principle is rigidly adhered to, it follows that the *value of labour depends on the quantity of labour employed in producing it*—which is evidently absurd. By a dexterous turn, therefore, Mr. Ricardo makes the *value of labour* depend on *the quantity of labour required to produce wages*, or, to give him the benefit of his own language, he maintains that the value of labour *is to be estimated* by the quantity of labour required to produce wages; by which he means the quantity of labour required to produce the money or commodities given to the labourer. This is similar to saying, that the value of cloth is to be estimated, not by the quantity of labour bestowed on its production, but by the quantity of labour bestowed on the production of the silver, for which the cloth is exchanged" * (l.c., [pp.] 50-51).[a]

This is a justified criticism of Ricardo's mistake of making capital exchange directly with labour instead of with labour capacity. It is the same objection which we have already come across in another form.[b] Nothing else. Bailey's comparison cannot be applied to labour capacity. It is not CLOTH, but an organic product such as MUTTON, that he ought to compare with living labour capacity. Apart from the labour involved in tending livestock and that required for the production of their means of subsistence, the labour required for their production is not to be understood as meaning the labour which they themselves perform in the act of consumption, the act of eating, drinking, in short, the

---

[a] Cf. this volume, pp. 34-35, and also present edition, Vol. 30, pp. 47-48.— *Ed.*
[b] See this volume, pp. 298-99.— *Ed.*

appropriation of those products or means of subsistence. It is just the same with labour capacity. The labour required for its production, or reproduction, consists solely of the labour involved in the reproduction of the means of subsistence which the labourer consumes—apart from the labour involved in developing his labour capacity, his *education,* his APPRENTICESHIP, which hardly arises in relation to UNSKILLED LABOUR. The appropriation of these means of subsistence is not "*labour*". [XIV-828] Any more than the labour contained in the CLOTH, in addition to the labour of the weaver and the labour which is contained in the wool, the dye-stuff, etc., comprises the chemical or physical action of the wool in absorbing the dye-stuff, etc., an action which corresponds to the appropriation of the means of subsistence by the worker or the cattle.

Bailey then seeks to invalidate Ricardo's law that the value of labour and profit stand in *inverse* proportion to one another. He seeks, moreover, to invalidate that part of it which is correct. Like Ricardo, he identifies SURPLUS VALUE with PROFIT. He does not mention the one possible exception to this law, namely, when the working day is lengthened and workers and capitalists * share equally in that prolongation, but even then, since the value of the working power will be consumed more quickly—in fewer years—the surplus value rises at the expense of the working man's life, and his working power is depreciated as compared with the surplus value it yields to the capitalist.*

Bailey's REASONING IS OF THE MOST SUPERFICIAL DESCRIPTION. Its starting-point is his concept of value. The value of the commodity is the expression of its value IN A CERTAIN QUANTITY OF OTHER VALUES IN USE (the use value of other commodities). Thus the value of labour=the quantity of other commodities (use values) for which it is exchanged. // THE REAL PROBLEM, HOW IT IS POSSIBLE TO EXPRESS THE VALUE IN EXCHANGE OF A IN THE VALUE IN USE OF B—does not even occur to him.// So long, therefore, as the worker receives the same quantity of commodities, the VALUE OF LABOUR remains unchanged, BECAUSE, AS BEFORE, IT IS EXPRESSED IN THE SAME QUANTITY OF OTHER USEFUL THINGS. Profit, on the other hand, expresses a relation to capital, or else to the total product. The *portion* received by the worker can, however, remain the same although the *proportion* received by the capitalist rises if the productivity of labour increases.[97] It is not clear why, in dealing with capital, we suddenly come to a proportion and of what use this *proportion* is supposed to be to the capitalist, since the value of what he receives is determined not by the proportion, but by ITS "EXPRESSION IN OTHER COMMODITIES".

The point he makes here has, in fact, already been mentioned by Malthus.[a] Wages=A QUANTITY OF *use values*. Profit, on the other hand, is (but Bailey must avoid saying so) A RELATION OF *VALUE*. If I measure wages according to use value and profit according to exchange value, it is quite EVIDENT that neither an inverse nor any other kind of relation exists between them, BECAUSE I SHOULD THEN COMPARE INCOMMENSURABLE MAGNITUDES, THINGS WHICH HAVE NO COMMON UNITY.

But what Bailey says here about the *VALUE OF LABOUR* applies— according to his principle—to the *VALUE OF EVERY OTHER COMMODITY* as well. IT IS NOTHING ELSE BUT A CERTAIN QUANTITY OF OTHER THINGS EXCHANGED AGAINST IT. If I receive 20 lbs of twist for £1, then the value of the £1 always remains the same, and will therefore be always paid, although the labour required to produce 1 lb. of twist can on one occasion be double that required on another. The most ordinary merchant does not believe that he is getting the same value for his £1 when he receives 1 qr of wheat for it in a period of famine and in a period of glut. But the concept of value ends here. And there remains only the unexplained and inexplicable fact that a quantity of A is exchanged against a quantity of B IN ANY PROPORTION WHATEVER. AND WHATEVER THAT PROPORTION MAY BE IT IS AN EQUIVALENT. Even Bailey's formula, *the value of A expressed in B loses thus every sense. If the value of A is expressed in B, it is supposed that the same value is, if expressed once in A, and at another time in B, so that, if [it is] expressed in B, the value of A remains the same as it was before. But with Bailey there is no value of A [that could] be expressed in B, because neither A nor B have a value besides that expression. The value of A [expressed] in B must be something quite different from the value of A in C, as different as B and C are. And it is not the same value, identical in both expressions, but there are two relations of A which have nothing in common with each other, and of which it would be nonsense to say that they are equivalent expressions.

[XIV-829] "A rise or fall in the value of labour implies an increase or decrease in the quantity of the commodity given in exchange for it" (l.c., [p.] 62).

Nonsense! [From Bailey's standpoint] there can be no rise or fall in the value of labour, nor of any other thing. I get today 3 Bs for one A, tomorrow 6 Bs and [the day] after tomorrow 2 Bs. But [according to Bailey] in all these cases the value of A is nothing but the quantity of B for which it has [been] exchanged. It was 3 Bs, it is now 6 Bs. How can its value be said to have risen or fallen? The A expressed in 3 Bs had another value from that expressed in 6 or 2 Bs. But then it is not the identical A which at

---

[a] See this volume, p. 227.— *Ed.*

the identical time has been exchanged for 3 or 2 or 6 Bs. The identical A at the identical time has always been expressed in the same quantity of B. It is only with regard to different times that it could be said the value of A had changed. But it is only with "contemporaneous" commodities that A can be exchanged, and it is only the fact (not even the mere possibility of exchange) of exchange with other commodities which constitutes [according to Bailey] A to be a value. It is only the actual "relation in exchange" which constitutes its value; and the actual "relation in exchange" can of course only take place for the same A at the identical time.* Bailey therefore declares the comparison of commodity values at different periods to be nonsense.[a] But at the same time he should also have declared the *rise or fall of value—[which is] impossible if there is no comparison between its [a commodity's] value at one time and its value at another time*—to be nonsense and consequently, also, the *"rise or fall in the value of labour".

"Labour is an exchangeable thing, or one which commands other things in exchange; but the term profits denotes only a share or *proportion of commodities, not an article which can be exchanged against other articles.* When we ask whether wages have risen, we mean, whether a definite portion of labour exchanges for a greater quantity of other things than before" *

(thus when corn becomes dearer, the value of labour falls because less corn is EXCHANGED for it. On the other hand, if CLOTH becomes cheaper at the same time, the value of labour *rises* simultaneously, because more CLOTH can be EXCHANGED for it. Thus the value of labour both rises and falls at the same time and the two EXPRESSIONS OF ITS VALUE—IN CORN AND [in] CLOTH—ARE NOT IDENTICAL, NOT EQUIVALENT, because its *increased* value CANNOT BE EQUAL to its *reduced value*);

* "but when we ask whether profits have risen, we ... mean ... whether the gain of the capitalist bears a higher ratio to the capital employed" ([pp.] 62-63).

"The value of labour does not entirely depend on the proportion of the whole produce, which is given to the labourers in exchange for their labour, but also on the productiveness of labour" ([pp.] 63-64).

"The proposition, that when labour rises profits must fall, is true only when its rise is not owing to an increase in its productive powers" ([p.] 64).

"If this productive power be augmented, that is, if the same labour produce more commodities in the same time, labour may rise in value without a fall, nay even with a rise of profits" * ([p.] 66).

(Accordingly it can also be said of every other commodity that *a rise in its value does not imply a fall in the value of the other

---

[a] See [S. Bailey,] *A Critical Dissertation on the Nature, Measures, and Causes of Value...*, pp. 71-93. Cf. this volume, pp. 126, 340-41, 347.— Ed.

commodity with which it exchanges, nay, may even imply a rise in value on the other side.* For instance, supposing the same labour which produced 1 qr of corn, now produces 3 qrs. The 3 qrs COST £1, as *the one qr did before. If 2 qrs be now exchanged against £1, the value of money has risen, because it is expressed in 2 qrs instead of one. Thus the purchaser of corn gets a greater value for his money. But the seller who sells for £1 what has cost him only $^2/_3$ gains $^1/_3$. And thus the value of his corn has risen at the same time that the money price of corn has fallen.)

[XIV-830] "Whatever the produce of the labour of 6 men might be, whether 100 or 200 or 300 qrs of corn, yet so long as the proportion of the capitalist was one-fourth of the produce, that fourth part estimated in labour would be invariably the same."

// And so would the $^3/_4$ of the produce accruing to the labourer, if estimated in labour.//

"Were the produce 100 qrs, then, as 75 qrs would be given to 6 men, the 25 accruing to the capitalist would command the labour of two men;"

(and that given to the labourers would command the labour of 6 men)

"if the produce were 300 qrs, the 6 men would obtain 225 qrs, and the 75 falling to the capitalist would still command 2 men and no more."

(Thus the 225 qrs falling to the 6 men would still command 4[a] men and no more.) (Why does the almighty Bailey then forbid Ricardo to estimate the portion of the men, as well as that of the capitalist, in labour, and compare their mutual value as expressed in labour?)

"Thus a rise in the proportion which went to the capitalist would be the same as an increase of *the value of profits estimated in labour*,"

(how can he speak of the *value of profits,* and an increase in their value, if "[the term] profits denotes ... not an article which can be exchanged against other articles" (see above) and, consequently, denotes no "value"? And, on the other hand, is a rise in the *proportion* which went to the capitalist possible without a fall *in the proportion* that goes to the labourer?)

"or, in other words, an increase in their power of commanding labour" ([p.] 69).

(And is this *increase* in the power of the capitalist to appropriate the labour of others not exactly identical with the *decrease* in the power of the labourer to appropriate his own labour?)

---

[a] This is apparently a slip of the pen: it should definitely be "6".— *Ed.*

"Should it be objected to the doctrine of profits and the value of labour rising at the same time, that as *the commodity produced is the only source whence the capitalist and the labourer can obtain their remuneration,* it necessarily follows that [what] one gains the other loses, the reply is obvious. So long as the product continues the same, this is undeniably true; but it is equally undeniable, that if the product be doubled *the portion of both may be increased,* although the *proportion of one is lessened and that of the other is augmented.*" *

(This is just what Ricardo says. The *proportion of both cannot increase, and if the *portion* of both increases, it cannot increase in the same proportion, as otherwise portion and proportion would be identical. The proportion of the one cannot increase but by that of the other decreasing.* [a] [97] However, that Mr. Bailey calls the PORTION OF THE LABOUR "*VALUE*" OF "WAGES", and the *proportion* [of the capitalist] value of "profits", that the same commodity has 2 values for him, one in the hands of the labourer, and the other in the hands of the capitalist, is nonsense of his own.)

"So long as the produce continues the same, this is undeniably true; but it [is] equally undeniable, that if the product be doubled the *portion* of both may be increased, although the *proportion* of one is lessened and that of the other augmented. Now it is an increase in the *portion* of the product assigned to [the] labourer which constitutes a rise in the *value* of his labour"

(because here we understand by *value* a certain quantity of articles);

"but it is an increase in the *proportion* assigned to the capitalist which constitutes a rise in [his] profits"

(because here we understand by *value* the same articles not estimated by their quantity, but by the labour worked up in them).

"*Whence*" *

(that is, because of the absurd use of two measures, in the one case ARTICLES, in the other case * the value of the same articles)

"it clearly follows, that there is nothing inconsistent in the supposition of a *simultaneous rise in both*" * ([p.] 70).

This absurd argument against Ricardo is quite [XIV-831] futile since he merely declares that the VALUE of the two portions must RISE and FALL in inverse proportion to one another.[b] It merely amounts to a repetition by Bailey of his proposition that VALUE IS THE QUANTITY OF ARTICLES EXCHANGED FOR AN ARTICLE. In dealing with *profit* he was bound to find himself in an embarrassing position. For here, the value of capital is compared with the value of the

---

[a] See D. Ricardo, *On the Principles of Political Economy, and Taxation,* 3rd ed., London, 1821, pp. 48 and 107.— *Ed.*

[b] See this volume, pp. 52-56.— *Ed.*

product. Here he seeks refuge in taking *value* to mean the VALUE OF AN ARTICLE ESTIMATED IN LABOUR (in the Malthusian manner[a]).

* "Value is a relation between *contemporary* commodities, because such only admit of being exchanged for each other; and if we compare the value of a commodity at one time with its value at another, it is only a comparison of the relation in which it stood at these different times to some other commodity"* (l.c., [p.] 72).

Consequently, as has been stated, there can be NEITHER [a] RISE NOR [a] FALL [in] VALUE for this ALWAYS involves COMPARING THE VALUE OF A COMMODITY AT ONE TIME WITH ITS VALUE AT ANOTHER. A commodity cannot be sold below its value any more than [above] it, for its value is what it is sold for. VALUE and market price are identical. In fact one cannot speak either of "*CONTEMPORARY*" COMMODITIES, or of *PRESENT* VALUES, but ONLY of *PAST* ONES. What is the value of 1 qr OF WHEAT? The £1 for which it was sold yesterday. For ITS VALUE IS ONLY WHAT IS GOT IN EXCHANGE FOR IT, AND AS LONG AS IT IS NOT EXCHANGED, ITS "RELATION TO MONEY" IS ONLY IMAGINARY. But as soon as the EXCHANGE has been transacted, we have £1 instead of 1 qr [of wheat] and we can no longer speak of the value of 1 qr [of wheat]. In comparing values at different periods, Bailey has in mind merely academic researches into the different values of commodities, for example in the 18th and the 16th centuries. There the difficulty arises from the fact THAT THE SAME MONETARY EXPRESSION OF VALUE—OWING TO THE VICISSITUDES IN THE VALUE OF MONEY ITSELF—DENOTES DIFFERENT VALUES. The difficulty here lies in reducing the MONEY PRICES to VALUES. But what a fool he is! Is it not a fact that, in the process of circulation or the process of reproduction of capital, COMPARING THE VALUE OF ONE PERIOD TO THAT OF ANOTHER is always AN OPERATION UPON WHICH PRODUCTION ITSELF IS BASED?

Mr. Bailey does not understand at all what the expressions—to determine the value of commodities by labour time or by the VALUE OF LABOUR—mean. He simply does not understand the difference.

* "I beg not to be understood as contending, either that the values of commodities are to each other as the *quantities of labour* necessary for their production, or that the values of commodities are to each other as the *values of the labour*: all that I intend to insist upon is, that if the former is true, the latter cannot be false"* (l.c., [p.] 92).

The determination of the value of commodities by the value of another commodity (and in so far as they are determined by the "VALUE OF LABOUR", they are determined by another commodity; for *VALUE OF LABOUR* presupposes labour as a commodity) or its determination by a third entity, which has neither value nor is itself a commodity, but is the substance of value, and that which

---

a See this volume, pp. 211-12, 225-26.— *Ed.*

first turns products into commodities, are for Bailey identical. In the first case, it is a question of a *measure* of the *value* of *commodities*, that is, IN FACT, of *money*, of a commodity in which the other commodities *express* their value. In order that this can happen, the *values* of the commodities must already be *preposited*. The commodity which measures as well as that to be measured must have a *third* element in common. In the second case, this *identity* itself is first posited; later it is EXPRESSED in the PRICE, either MONEY PRICE OR any OTHER PRICE.

Bailey identifies the "invariable measure of value" with the search for an immanent measure of value, that is, the concept of value itself. So long as the two are confused it is even a reasonable instinct which leads to the search for an "invariable measure of value". Variability is precisely the characteristic of value. The term "invariable" expresses the fact that the immanent measure of value must not itself be a commodity, a value, but rather something which constitutes value and which is *therefore* also the immanent *measure* of its [the commodity's] value. Bailey demonstrates [XIV-832] that commodity values can find A MONETARY EXPRESSION and that, if the *value relation of commodities is given*, all commodities can express their value in *one* commodity, although the value of this commodity may change. But it nevertheless always remains the same for the other commodities at a given time, since it changes SIMULTANEOUSLY in relation to all of them. From this *he* concludes that no value relation between commodities is necessary nor is there any need to look for one. Because he finds it reflected in the MONETARY EXPRESSION, he does not need to "understand" how this expression becomes possible, how it is determined, and *what* in fact it expresses.

These remarks, in general, apply to Bailey as they do to Malthus, since he believes that one is concerned with *the same* question, on the same plane, whether one makes QUANTITY OF LABOUR OR VALUE OF LABOUR the measure of value. In the latter case, one presupposes the *values* whose measure is being sought, [their] external measure, [their] representation as value. In the first case one investigates the genesis and immanent nature of value itself. In the second, the development of the commodity into money or the form which exchange value acquires in the process of the exchange of commodities. In the first, we are concerned with *value*, independent of this representation, or rather *antecedent* to this representation. Bailey has this in common with the other fools: to determine the value of commodities means to find their *monetary expression*, AN EXTERNAL MEASURE OF THEIR VALUES. They say, however, impelled by a reasonable instinct, that this measure then must have invariable value, and must itself IN FACT stand *outside the category* of value, whereas Bailey says that one does not need to understand it, since one does find the *expression of value* in practice, and this expression itself has and can have variable value without prejudice to its function.

In particular, he himself has informed us that 100, 200 or 300 qrs can be the product of the labour of 6 men, that is, of the same quantity of labour, whereas "VALUE OF LABOUR" ONLY MEANS for him the ALIQUOT PART of the 100, 200 or 300 qrs which the 6 men receive. This could be 50, 60 or 70 qrs per man.[98] The QUANTITY OF LABOUR and the VALUE OF THE SAME QUANTITY OF LABOUR are therefore, according to Bailey himself, very different expressions. And how can it be the same if the value is expressed first in one thing and then in something essentially different? If the same labour which formerly produced 3 qrs of corn now produces 1 qr, while the same labour which formerly produced 20 yards of CLOTH (or 3 qrs of corn) still produces 20 yards, then, reckoned according to labour time, 1 qr of corn is now equal to 20 yards of CLOTH, or 20 yards of CLOTH to 1 qr of corn, and 3 qrs of CORN=60 yards instead of 20. Thus the values of the quarter of corn and the yard of linen have been altered RELATIVELY. But they have by no means been altered according to the "VALUE OF LABOUR", for 1 qr of corn and 20 yards of CLOTH remain the same use values as before. And it is possible that 1 qr of corn does not command a larger quantity of labour than before.

If we take a single commodity, then Bailey's assertion makes no sense whatever. If the labour time required for the production of shoes decreases and now only one-tenth of the labour time formerly required is necessary, then the value of shoes drops to one-tenth of the former value; and this also holds true when the shoes are *compared* with, or EXPRESSED IN, ALL OTHER COMMODITIES, WHEN THE LABOUR REQUIRED FOR THEIR PRODUCTION HAS REMAINED THE SAME OR HAS NOT DECREASED AT THE SAME RATE. Nevertheless, the value of labour—for example the daily wage in shoemaking as well as in all other INDUSTRIES—may have remained the same; or it may even have increased. Less labour is contained in the individual shoe, hence also less paid labour. But when one speaks of the *value of labour*, one does not mean that for one hour's labour, for a smaller quantity of labour, less is paid than for a greater quantity. Bailey's proposition could have meaning only in relation to the total product of capital. Suppose 200 pairs of shoes are the product of the same capital (and the same labour) which formerly produced

100 pairs. In this case, the value of the 200 pairs is the same as [previously] that of 100 pairs. And it could be said that the 200 pairs of shoes are to 1,000 yards of linen (say the product of £200 of capital) as the *value* of the labour set in motion by the two amounts of capital. In what sense? In the sense in which it would *also* apply [XIV-833] to the relation of the individual pair of shoes to the single yard of linen?

The *value* of labour is the part of the labour time contained in a commodity which the worker himself appropriates; it is the part of the product in which the *labour time which belongs* to the worker *himself is embodied.* If the entire value of a commodity is reduced to paid and unpaid labour time—and if the rate of unpaid to paid labour is the same, that is, if surplus value constitutes the same proportion of total value in all commodities—then it is clear that if the ratio of one commodity to another is proportional to the total quantity of labour they contain, they must also represent *equal* aliquot *parts* of these total quantities of labour, and their ratio must therefore also be as that of the paid labour time in one commodity to the paid labour time in the other.

C:C'=TLT (total labour time) to TLT' (total labour time).

$\frac{TLT}{x}$=the paid labour time in C, and $\frac{TLT'}{x}$=the paid labour time

in C', since it is presupposed that the paid labour time in both commodities constitutes the same *aliquot part* of the total labour time.

$$C:C'=TLT:TLT'$$
$$TLT:TLT'=\frac{TLT}{x}:\frac{TLT'}{x}$$
$$\text{and } C:C'=\frac{TLT}{x}:\frac{TLT'}{x}$$

or the commodities are to one another as *the quantities of paid labour time contained in them,* that is, as the VALUES OF the LABOUR CONTAINED IN THEM.

The VALUE OF LABOUR is then, however, not determined in the way Bailey would like, but by the labour time [contained in the commodity].

Further, disregarding the conversion of values into prices of production and considering only the values themselves, capitals consist of different ALIQUOT PARTS OF VARIABLE AND CONSTANT CAPITAL. HENCE, AS FAR AS VALUES ARE CONSIDERED, THE SURPLUS VALUES ARE NOT EQUAL, OR THE PAID LABOUR IS NOT AN EQUAL ALIQUOT PART OF THE TOTAL LABOUR ADVANCED.

In general, WAGES—or VALUES OF LABOUR—would here be INDICES of the VALUES OF COMMODITIES, not as VALUES, not in so far as WAGES rise or fall, but in so far as the *quantity of paid labour*—represented by WAGES—contained in a commodity would be an INDEX of the *total quantity* of the labour contained in the corresponding commodities.

In a word, the point is that, if the values of commodities are to one another as LT to LT' (the amounts of labour time contained in them), then their ratio is likewise as $\dfrac{LT}{x}$ to $\dfrac{LT'}{x}$, i.e. the amounts of paid labour time embodied in them, *if* the proportion of the paid labour time to the unpaid is the same in all commodities, that is, *if* the paid labour time always=the total labour time, whatever this may be, divided by *x*. But the "if" does not correspond to the real state of affairs. Supposing that the workers in different industries work the same amount of surplus labour time, the relation of paid to actually employed labour time is nevertheless different in different industries, because the ratio of *IMMEDIATE LABOUR* EMPLOYED to *ACCUMULATED LABOUR* EMPLOYED is different. [Let us take two capitals consisting,] for example, [the one of] $50v$ [variable] and $50c$ [constant] and [the other of] $10v$ and $90c$. In both cases, let the unpaid labour=$^{1}/_{10}$. [The value of] the first commodity would accordingly be 105, [of] the second 101. The paid labour time would=$^{1}/_{2}$ of the labour advanced in the first case, and only $^{1}/_{10}$ in the second.

[XIV-834] Bailey says:

* "If the commodities are to each other as the quantities, they must also be to each other as the values of the producing labour; for the contrary would necessarily imply, that the two commodities A and B might be equal in value, although the value of the labour employed in one was greater or less than the value of the labour employed in the other; or that A and B might be unequal in value, if the labour employed in each was equal in value. But this *difference in the value of two commodities*, which were *produced by labour of equal value*, would be inconsistent with *the acknowledged equality of profits*, which Mr. *Ricardo maintains in common with other writers*" * (l.c., [pp.] 79-80).

In this last phrase, he stumbles unconsciously on a real objection to Ricardo, who directly identifies profit with SURPLUS VALUE and VALUES with COST PRICES.[6] Correctly stated, it is—if the commodities are sold at their *value*, they yield *unequal profits*, for then profit=the surplus value embodied in them. And this is correct. But this objection does not refer to the theory of value, but to A BLUNDER OF Ricardo's in applying this theory.

How little Bailey himself, in the above passage, can have correctly understood the problem, is shown in the following statement:

"Ricardo on the other hand maintains *'that labour may rise and fall in value without affecting the value of the commodity'. This is obviously a very different proposition from the other, and depends in fact on the falsity of the other, or on the contrary proposition"* etc. (l.c., [p.] 81).

The fool himself previously asserted that the result of the same labour may be 100, 300 or 200 qrs [of corn]. This determines the relation of a quarter to other commodities irrespective of the changing value of labour, that is, irrespective of how much of the 100, 200 or 300 qrs falls to the labourer himself. The fool would have shown some consistency if he had said: the VALUES OF LABOUR may rise or fall, nevertheless the VALUES OF COMMODITIES are as the VALUES OF LABOUR, because—according to a false assumption—the rise or fall * of wages being general, and the value of wages being always the same *proportionate part* of the whole quantity of labour employed.

"The capability of *expressing* the values of commodities has nothing to do with the *constancy of their values*"

// indeed not! but it has much to do with first finding the value, before expressing it; finding in what way the values in use, so different from each other, fall under the common category and denomination of *values,* so that the value of the one may be expressed in the other //

"either to each other or to the medium employed; neither has the capability of comparing these *expressions of value* anything to do with it".

// If the values of different commodities are expressed in the same third commodity, however variable its value may be, it is of course very easy to compare these *expressions,* already possessed of a common denomination.//

"Whether A is worth 4B or 6B"

(the difficulty consists in equalising A with any portion of B; and this is only possible if there exists a common entity for A and B, or if A and B are different representations of the same entity. If all commodities are to be expressed in gold, [or] money, the difficulty remains the same. There must be a common entity to gold and each of the other commodities)

"and whether C is worth 8B or 12B, are circumstances which make no difference *in the power of expressing* the value of A and C in B, and certainly no difference in the power of comparing the value of A and C when expressed" ([pp.] 104-05).

But how to *express* A in B or in C? To *express* "them" in each other, or, what comes to the same thing, to treat them as equivalent expressions of the same unity, A, B, C must all be considered as something different from what they are as things, products, values in use. A=4B. Then the value of A is *expressed* in 4B, and the value of 4B in A, so that both sides express the same. They are equivalents. They are both *equal* expressions of value. It would be the same if they were unequal ones or A>4B, A<4B. In all these cases they are, as far [XIV-835] as they are values, only different or equal in quantity, but [they are] always quantities of the same quality. The difficulty is to find this quality.

"The requisite condition in the process is, that the commodities to be measured should be reduced to a *common denomination*" *

// for example, in order to compare a △ with any of the other polygons it is only necessary to transform the latter into △, * to express them in triangles. But to do this the △ and the polygon are in fact supposed [to be] *identities*, different figurations of the same [thing]—space //

"which may be done at all times with equal facility; or rather it *is* ready done to our hands, since it is the *prices* of commodities which are recorded, or their relations in value to money" (l.c., [p.] 112).

"*Estimating* value is the same thing as *expressing* it" * (l.c., [p.] 152).

We have the fellow here. We find the VALUES measured, expressed in the PRICES. We can therefore content ourselves with *not* knowing what value is. He confuses the development of the measure of value into money and further the development of money as the standard of price with the discovery of the *concept of value* itself in its development as the immanent measure of commodities in EXCHANGE. He is right in thinking that this money need not be a commodity of invariable value; from this he concludes that no separate determination of value independent of the commodity itself is necessary.

As soon as the value of commodities, as the element they have in common, is given, the measurement of their relative value and the expression of this value coincide. But we can never arrive at the *expression* so long as we do not find the common factor, which is different from the immediate existence of the commodities.

This is shown by the very example he gives, the DISTANCE BETWEEN A and B.[a] When one SPEAKS OF THEIR DISTANCE one ALREADY presupposes that they are POINTS (OR LINES) in SPACE. Having been reduced to POINTS, AND POINTS OF THE SAME LINE, THEIR DISTANCE MAY BE EXPRESSED IN INCHES, OR FEET, etc. THE identity OF THE TWO COMMODITIES A AND B IS, AT FIRST sight, THEIR EXCHANGEABILITY. THEY ARE "EXCHANGEABLE" OBJECTS. AS "EXCHANGEABLE" OBJECTS THEY ARE MAGNITUDES OF THE SAME DENOMINATION. BUT

---

[a] See this volume, p. 330.— *Ed.*

THIS "THEIR" EXISTENCE AS "EXCHANGEABLE" OBJECTS MUST BE DIFFERENT FROM THEIR EXISTENCE AS VALUES IN USE. WHAT IS IT?

Money is already a *representation* of value, and presupposes it. As the *standard* of price money, for its part, already presupposes the (hypothetical) transformation of the commodity into money. If the values of all commodities are represented in money prices, then one can compare them, they are IN FACT already compared. But for the value to be represented as price, the value of commodities must have been expressed previously as money. Money is merely the form in which the value of commodities appears in the process of circulation. But how can one express *x* COTTON in *x* money? This question resolves itself into this—how is it at all possible to express one commodity in another, or how to present commodities as equivalents? Only the elaboration of value, independent of the representation of one commodity in another, provides the answer.

* "Mistake ... that the relation of value can exist between commodities at different periods, which is in the nature of the case impossible; and if no relation exists there can be no measurement" * ([p.] 113).

We have already had the same nonsense before.[a] "THE RELATION OF VALUE BETWEEN COMMODITIES AT DIFFERENT PERIODS" already exists when money acts as means of payment. The whole circulation process is a perpetual comparison of VALUES OF COMMODITIES AT DIFFERENT PERIODS.

* "If it" (money) "is not a good medium of comparison between commodities at different periods,*... [it asserts] its *incapability of performing a function in a case where there is no function for it to perform" * ([p.] 118).

Money has this FUNCTION TO PERFORM as means of payment and as treasure.

All this is simply copied from the "VERBAL OBSERVER"[b] and in fact the secret of the whole nonsense OOZES OUT IN THE FOLLOWING PHRASE which has also convinced me that the "VERBAL OBSERVATIONS" which were very carefully concealed by Bailey, were used by him in the manner of a plagiarist.

[XIV-836] * "Riches are the attribute of men, value is the attribute of commodities. A man or [a] community is rich; a pearl or a diamond is valuable" ([p.] 165).[c]

A pearl or a diamond is valuable *as* a pearl or a diamond, that is, by their qualities, as values in use for men, that is, as *riches.* But there is nothing in a pearl or a diamond by which a relation of

a See ibid., pp. 337, 339-40.— *Ed.*

b The anonymous author of *Observations on Certain Verbal Disputes in Political Economy...*— *Ed.*

c Cf. this volume, p. 316.— *Ed.*

exchange between them is given,* etc.

Bailey now becomes a profound philosopher:

"Difference between LABOUR AS CAUSE AND MEASURE, and in general between CAUSE AND MEASURE OF VALUE" ([p.] 170 et seq.).

There is, in actual fact, a very significant difference (which Bailey does not notice) between "MEASURE" (in the sense of money) and "CAUSE OF VALUE". The "CAUSE" of value transforms use values into VALUE. The external MEASURE OF VALUE already presupposes the existence of VALUE. For example, gold can only MEASURE the VALUE OF COTTON if gold and COTTON—as VALUES—possess a *common factor* which is different from both. The "CAUSE" OF VALUE is the substance of VALUE and hence also its immanent measure.

* "Whatever circumstances ... act with assignable influence, whether mediately or immediately, on the *mind* in the interchange of commodities, may be considered as causes of value"* ([pp.] 182-83).

This in fact means nothing more than: the *cause* of the value of a commodity or of the fact that two commodities are equivalent are the circumstances which cause the seller, or perhaps both the buyer and the seller, to consider something to be the value or the equivalent of a commodity. The "circumstances" which determine the value of a commodity are by no means further elucidated by being described as circumstances which influence the "MIND" of those engaging in exchange.

(These same circumstances (independent of the MIND, but influencing it), which compel the producers to sell their products as *commodities*—circumstances which differentiate one form of social production from another—provide their products with an exchange value which (also in their MIND) is independent of their use value. Their "MIND", their consciousness, may be completely ignorant of, unaware of the existence of, what IN FACT determines the value of their commodities or their products as values. They are placed in conditions which determine their reasoning but they may not know it. Anyone can use money as money without necessarily understanding what money is. Economic categories are reflected in the mind in a very distorted fashion.) He [Bailey] transfers the problem into the mental sphere, because his theory has nothing further to offer. The circumstances which, as such, likewise exist (or perhaps they do not, or perhaps they are incorrectly conceived) in the consciousness of those engaging in exchange.

Instead of explaining what he himself understands by "value" (or "CAUSE OF VALUE") Bailey tells us that it is something which buyers and sellers imagine in the act of exchange.

In fact, however, the following considerations are the basis of the would-be philosophical proposition.

1) The market price is determined by various circumstances which express themselves in the relation of demand and supply and which, as such, INFLUENCE "THE MIND" OF THE OPERATORS ON THE MARKET. This is a very important discovery!

2) In connection with the *conversion of commodity values into cost prices,* "various CIRCUMSTANCES" are taken into account which as "reasons for compensation" influence THE MIND or are reflected in it. All these reasons for compensation, however, affect only the MIND of the CAPITALIST as CAPITALIST and stem from the nature of capitalist production itself, and not from the subjective notions of buyers and sellers. In their mind they exist rather as self-evident "eternal truths".

Like his predecessors, Bailey CATCHES hold of Ricardo's confusion of VALUES and COST PRICES IN ORDER TO PROVE THAT VALUE IS NOT DETERMINED BY LABOUR, BECAUSE COST PRICES ARE DEVIATIONS FROM VALUES. Although this is quite correct in relation to Ricardo's identification, it is incorrect as far as the question itself is concerned.

In this context, Bailey quotes first from Ricardo himself about the CHANGE IN THE RELATIVE VALUES OF [XIV-837] COMMODITIES IN CONSEQUENCE OF A RISE IN THE VALUE OF LABOUR.[a] He quotes further the "effect of time" (different times of production though the labour time remains unchanged), the same CASE which aroused scruples in Mill.[b] He does not notice the real *general* contradiction—THE VERY EXISTENCE OF *AN AVERAGE RATE* OF PROFIT, DESPITE THE DIFFERENT COMPOSITION OF CAPITAL, ITS DIFFERENT TIMES OF CIRCULATION, etc. He simply repeats the particular forms in which the contradiction appears, and which Ricardo himself—and his followers—had *already* noticed. Here he merely echoes what has been previously said but does not advance criticism a step forward.

He emphasises further that the costs of production are the main CAUSE OF "VALUE", and therefore the main element in value. However, he stresses correctly—as was done [by other writers] after Ricardo—that the concept of *production costs* itself varies. He himself in the last analysis expresses his agreement with Torrens that value is determined by the capital advanced,[c] which is correct

---

[a] See present edition, Vol. 31, pp. 405-25.— *Ed.*

[b] See this volume, pp. 276-77, and also K. Marx, *Outlines of the Critique of Political Economy...* (present edition, Vol. 29, pp. 58-60).— *Ed.*

[c] See this volume, pp. 265-66, 270-71, and also K. Marx, *Outlines of the Critique of Political Economy...* (present edition, Vol. 29, p. 196).— *Ed.*

in relation to COST PRICES but meaningless if it is not evolved on the basis of value itself, that is, if the *value* of a commodity is to be derived from a more developed relationship, the *value of capital,* and not the other way round.

His last objection is this: The value of commodities cannot be measured by labour time if the labour time in one TRADE is not the same as in the others, so that the commodity in which, for example, 12 hours of an engineer's labour is embodied has perhaps twice the value of the commodity in which 12 hours of the labour of a FIELD LABOURER is embodied. What this amounts to is the following: A simple working day, for example, is not a measure of value if there are other working days which, compared with DAYS OF SIMPLE LABOUR, have the effect of COMPOSITE [working] DAYS. Ricardo showed that this FACT does not prevent the measurement of commodities by labour time if the relation between SIMPLE and COMPOSITE LABOUR is given.[a] He has indeed not described how this relation develops and is determined. This belongs to the definition of *wages,* and, in the last analysis, can be reduced to the *different values of labour capacity itself,* that is, its varying production costs (determined by labour time).

The passages in which Bailey expresses what has been summarised above are:

* "It is not, indeed, disputed, that the main circumstance, which determines the quantities in which articles of this class" * (where no MONOPOLY exists and where it is possible to INCREASE [output] by expanding INDUSTRY) * "are exchanged, is the *cost of production*; but our best economists do not exactly agree on the meaning to be attached to this term; some contending that the *quantity of labour* expended on the production of an article constitutes its cost; others, that the *capital employed upon it* is entitled to that appellation" (l.c., [p.] 200).

"What the labourer produces without capital, costs him his labour; what the capitalist produces costs him his capital" * ([p.] 201).

(This is the factor which determines Torrens' views. The labour which the capitalist employs, costs him nothing apart from the capital he lays out in wages.)

* "The mass of commodities are determined in value by the capital expended upon them" * ([p.] 206).

Against the determination of the value of commodities simply by the QUANTITY OF LABOUR CONTAINED IN THEM:

* "Now this cannot be true if we can find any instances of the following nature: 1) Cases in which two commodities have been produced by an equal quantity of labour, and yet sell for different quantities of money; 2) Cases in which two

---

[a] D. Ricardo, *On the Principles of Political Economy, and Taxation,* 3rd ed., London, 1821, pp. 13-15.— *Ed.*

commodities, once equal in value, have become unequal in value, without any change in the quantity of labour respectively employed in each" ([p.] 209).

"It is no answer"* (with regard to CASES of the first kind) *"to say, with Mr. Ricardo, that 'the estimation in which different qualities of labour are held, comes soon to be adjusted in the market with sufficient precision for all practical purposes'[a]; or with Mr. Mill, that 'in estimating equal quantities of labour, an allowance would, of course, be included for different degrees of hardness and skill'.[b] Instances of this kind entirely destroy the integrity of the rule" ([p.] 210).

"There are only two possible methods of comparing one quantity of labour with another; one is to compare *them by the time expended,* the *other by the result produced"* * (the latter is done in the TASK-WORK system). *"The former is applicable to all kinds of labour; the latter can be used only in comparing labour bestowed on similar articles. If, therefore, in estimating two different sorts of work, the time spent will not determine the proportion between the [XIV-839][99] quantities of labour, it must remain undetermined and undeterminable"* ([p.] 215).

With reference to 2: *"Take any two commodities of equal value, A and B, one produced by fixed capital and the other by labour, without the intervention of machinery; and suppose, that without any change whatever in the fixed capital or the quantity of labour, there should happen to be a rise in the value of labour; according to Mr. Ricardo's own showing, A and B would be instantly altered in their relation to each other; that is, they would become unequal in value" ([pp.] 215-16).

."To these cases we may add *the effect of time* on value. If a commodity take more time than another for its production, *although no more capital and labour,* its value will be greater. The influence of this cause is admitted by Mr. Ricardo, but Mr. Mill contends",* etc. (l.c. [p. 217]).

Finally Bailey remarks, and this is the only new contribution he makes in this respect:

"The 3 types of commodities" // this is again taken from the author of the VERBAL OBSERVATIONS, I mean the 3 types// (namely, [the commodities produced] under absolute monopoly, or limited monopoly, as is the case with corn, or completely free competition) "cannot be entirely distinguished from one another. *They are all not only promiscuously exchanged for each other, but *blended in production.* A commodity, therefore, may owe part of its value to monopoly, and part to those causes which determine the value of unmonopolised products. An article, for instance, may be manufactured amidst the freest competition out of a raw material, which a complete monopoly enables its producer to sell at 6 times the actual cost" ([p.] 223).[c] "In this case it is obvious, that although the value of the article might be correctly said to be determined by the quantity of capital expended upon it by the manufacturer, yet no analysis could possibly resolve the value of the capital into quantity of labour"* ([pp.] 223-24).

This remark is correct. But monopoly does not concern us here, where we are dealing with two things only, *value* and *cost price.* It is clear that the conversion of value into cost price works in two ways. First, the profit which is added to the capital advanced may

---

[a] D. Ricardo, *On the Principles of Political Economy, and Taxation,.* 3rd ed., London, 1821, p. 13.— Ed

[b] J. Mill, *Elements of Political Economy,* 2nd ed., London, 1824, pp. 91-92.— Ed

[c] Marx quotes Bailey with some alterations.— Ed

be either above or below the *surplus value* which is contained in the commodity itself, that is, it may represent more or less *unpaid* labour than the commodity itself contains. This applies to the variable part of capital and its reproduction in the commodity. But apart from this, the cost price of constant capital—or of the commodities which enter into the value of the newly produced commodity as raw materials, *matières instrumentales* [a] and instruments and conditions of—may likewise be either above or below its value. Thus the commodity comprises a portion of the price which differs from value, and this portion is independent of the quantity of labour newly added, or of the labour whereby these conditions of production with given cost prices are transformed into a new product. It is clear that what applies to the difference between the cost price and the value of the *commodity* as such—as a result of the production process—likewise applies to the *commodity* in so far as, in the form of constant capital, it becomes an ingredient, a precondition, of the production process. Variable capital, whatever difference between value and cost price it may contain, is replaced by a certain quantity of labour which forms a constituent part of the value of the new commodity, irrespective of whether its price expresses its value correctly or stands above or below the value. On the other hand, the difference between cost price and value, in so far as it enters into the price of the new commodity independently of its own production process, is incorporated into the value of the new commodity as a presupposed element. The difference between the cost price and the value of the commodity is thus brought about in two ways: by the difference between the cost price and the value of commodities which constitute the preconditions of the process of production of the new commodity; by the difference between the surplus value which is really added to the conditions of production and the profit which is calculated. But every commodity which enters into another commodity as constant capital, itself emerges as the result, the product, of another production process. And so the commodity appears alternately as a precondition for the production of other commodities and as the result of a process in which the existence of other commodities is the precondition for its own production. In agriculture (cattle-breeding), the same commodity appears at one point of time as a product and at another as a condition of production.

---

[a] Instrumental materials.— *Ed.*

This important deviation of cost prices from values brought about by capitalist production does not alter the fact that cost prices continue to be determined by values.

[XIV-840] 4) McCULLOCH

The vulgariser of Ricardian political economy and simultaneously the most pitiful embodiment of its decline.

He vulgarises not only Ricardo but also James Mill.

He is moreover a vulgar economist in everything and an apologist for the existing state of affairs. His only fear, driven to ridiculous extremes, is the tendency of profit to fall; he is perfectly contented with the position of the workers, and in general, with all the contradictions of bourgeois economy which weigh heavily upon the working class. Here everything is green. He even knows that

* "the introduction of machines into any employment necessarily occasions an equal or greater demand *for the disengaged labourers* in some other employment".*ᵃ

Here HE DEVIATES FROM Ricardo, and in his later writings, he also becomes very MEALY-MOUTHED about the landowners. But HIS WHOLE TENDER ANXIETY is reserved FOR THE POOR CAPITALISTS, CONSIDERING THE TENDENCY OF THE RATE OF PROFIT TO FALL!

"Mr. McCulloch, unlike other exponents of science, SEEMS TO LOOK not * for *characteristic differences,* but only for *resemblances*: and proceeding upon this principle, he is led to confound material with immaterial objects; productive with unproductive labour; capital with revenue; the food of the labourer with the labourer himself; production with consumption; and labour with profits" (Malthus, *Definitions in Political Economy etc.,* London, 1827, [pp.] 69-70).

"Mr. McCulloch, in his *Principles of Political Economy,* London, 1825,¹⁰⁰ divides *value* into *real* and *relative or exchangeable value*; the former, he says, (p. 225) is dependent on the quantity of labour expended in its appropriation or production, and the latter on the *quantity of labour,* or *of any other commodity* for which it will *exchange*; and these two values are, he says (p. 215), *identical* in the ordinary state of things, that is, when the supply of commodities in the market is exactly proportioned to the effectual demand for them. Now, if they be identical, the two quantities of labour which he refers to must be identical also; but, at page 221, he tells us that they are not, for that the one includes profits, while the other excludes them" * ([J. Cazenove,] *Outlines of Political Economy etc.,* London, 1832, [p.] 25).

Namely McCulloch says on page 221 of his *Principles of Political Economy*:

ᵃ J. R. MacCulloch, *The Principles of Political Economy...,* Edinburgh, London, 1825, pp. 181-82. Marx quotes from [J. Cazenove,] *Outlines of Political Economy,* London, 1832, pp. 119-20. Cf. also this volume, p. 257.— Ed.

* "In point of fact, it"* (the commodity) * "will always exchange for more"
//labour than that by which it has been produced//; "*and it is this excess that
constitutes profits.*" *

This is a brilliant example of the methods used by this
archhumbug of a Scotsman.

The arguments of Malthus, Bailey, etc., compel him to
differentiate between REAL VALUE and EXCHANGEABLE or RELATIVE VALUE.
But he does so, basically, in the way he finds the difference dealt
with by Ricardo. REAL VALUE means the commodity examined with
regard to the labour required for *its* production; RELATIVE VALUE
implies the consideration of the proportions of *different commodities* which can be produced in the same amount of time,
which are *consequently* equivalents, and the value of one of which
can therefore be *expressed* in the quantity of use value of the other
which costs the same amount of labour time. The RELATIVE VALUE of
commodities, in this Ricardian sense, is only another expression
for their REAL VALUE and means nothing more than that the
commodities exchange with one another in proportion to the
labour time embodied in them, in other words, that the *labour time
embodied in both is equal.* If, therefore, the market price of a
commodity is equal to its EXCHANGEABLE VALUE (as is the case when
DEMAND and SUPPLY are in equilibrium), then the commodity bought
contains as much labour as that which is sold. It merely realises its
EXCHANGEABLE VALUE, or it is only sold at its EXCHANGEABLE VALUE when
one receives *the same amount of labour* in exchange for it as one hands
over.

McCulloch relates all this, correctly repeating what has already
been said.[a] But he goes too far here since the Malthusian
definition of EXCHANGEABLE VALUE—the quantity of wage labour which
a commodity commands—already sticks in his throat. He therefore defines RELATIVE VALUE as the "QUANTITY OF LABOUR, OR OF ANY OTHER
COMMODITY FOR WHICH A COMMODITY WILL EXCHANGE". Ricardo, in dealing
with RELATIVE VALUE, always speaks only of COMMODITIES EXCLUSIVE OF
LABOUR, BECAUSE IN THE EXCHANGE OF COMMODITIES ONLY A PROFIT IS REALISED,
BECAUSE IN THE EXCHANGE BETWEEN COMMODITY AND LABOUR EQUAL QUANTITIES OF
LABOUR ARE NOT EXCHANGED. By putting the main emphasis right at the
beginning of his book on the fact that the determination of the
value [XIV-841] of a commodity by the labour time embodied in
it differs *toto coelo*[b] from the determination of this value by the

---

[a] See J. R. MacCulloch, *Principles of Political Economy...*, Edinburgh, London, 1825,
p. 211.— *Ed.*

[b] Immensely.— *Ed.*

quantity of labour which it can buy,[a] Ricardo, on the one hand, posits the difference between the quantity of labour contained in a commodity and the quantity of labour which it commands. On the other hand, he excludes the exchange of commodity and labour from the RELATIVE VALUE OF A COMMODITY. BECAUSE, IF A COMMODITY EXCHANGES WITH A COMMODITY, EQUAL QUANTITIES OF LABOUR ARE EXCHANGED. IF IT EXCHANGES WITH LABOUR ITSELF, UNEQUAL QUANTITIES OF LABOUR ARE EXCHANGED, AND CAPITALISTIC PRODUCTION RESTS ON THE INEQUALITY OF THIS EXCHANGE. Ricardo does not explain how this *exception* fits in with the concept of value. This is the reason for the arguments amongst his followers. But his instinct is sound when he makes the *exception.* (In actual fact, there is no exception; it exists only in *his* formulation.) Thus McCulloch goes farther than Ricardo and is apparently more consistent than he.

There is no flaw in his system; it is all of a piece. Whether a commodity is exchanged for a commodity or for labour, this ratio of exchange is in both cases THE *RELATIVE VALUE* OF A COMMODITY. And if the commodities exchanged are sold at their value (i.e. if demand and supply are in equilibrium), this RELATIVE VALUE is always the expression of the *REAL VALUE*. That is, there are equal quantities of labour at both poles of the exchange. Thus "IN THE ORDINARY STATE OF THINGS" a commodity only exchanges for a quantity of wage labour equal to the quantity of labour contained in it. The workman receives in WAGES just as much MATERIALISED LABOUR as he gives back to capital in the form of IMMEDIATE LABOUR. With this the source of SURPLUS VALUE disappears and the whole Ricardian theory collapses. Thus Mr. McCulloch first destroys it under the appearance of making it more consistent.

And what next? He then flits shamelessly from Ricardo to Malthus, according to whom the value of a commodity is determined by the quantity of labour which it buys and which must always be greater than that which the commodity itself contains. The only difference is that in Malthus this is plainly stated to be what it is, *opposition* to Ricardo, and Mr. McCulloch adopts this opposite viewpoint after he has adopted the Ricardian formula with an apparent consistency (that is, with the consistency of incogitancy) which destroys the whole sense of the Ricardian theory. McCulloch therefore does not understand the essential kernel of Ricardo's teaching—how profit is realised because commodities exchange *at their value*—and abandons it. Since

---

[a] D. Ricardo, *On the Principles of Political Economy, and Taxation,* 3rd ed., London, 1821, pp. 1-12.— *Ed.*

EXCHANGEABLE VALUE—which IN "THE ORDINARY STATE OF THE MARKET" is, according to McCulloch, equal to the REAL VALUE but "IN POINT OF FACT" is always greater, since profit is based on this surplus (a fine contradiction and a fine discourse based on a "POINT OF FACT")—is "THE QUANTITY OF LABOUR, OR OF ANY OTHER COMMODITY", for which the commodity is exchanged, hence what applies to "LABOUR" applies to "ANY OTHER COMMODITY". This means that the commodity is not only exchanged for a greater amount of IMMEDIATE LABOUR than it itself contains, but for more MATERIALISED LABOUR IN THE OTHER COMMODITIES than it itself contains; in other words, profit is "profit UPON EXPROPRIATION" and with this we are back again amongst the Mercantilists. Malthus draws this conclusion.[a] With McCulloch this conclusion follows naturally but with the pretence that this constitutes an elaboration of the Ricardian system.

And this total decline of the Ricardian system into twaddle—a decline which prides itself on being its most consistent exposition—has been accepted by the MOB, especially by the CONTINENTAL MOB (with Mr. Roscher naturally amongst them), as the conclusion of the Ricardian system *carried too far*, to its extreme limit; they thus believe Mr. McCulloch that the Ricardian mode of "coughing and spitting",[101] which he uses to conceal his helpless, thoughtless and unprincipled eclecticism, is in fact a scientific attempt to set forth this system consistently.

McCulloch is simply a man who wanted to turn Ricardian economics to his own advantage—an aim in which he succeeded in a most remarkable degree. In the same way *Say* used Smith, but Say at least made a contribution by bringing Smith's theories into a certain formal order and, apart from misconceptions, he occasionally also ventured to advance theoretical objections. Since McCulloch first obtained a professorial chair in London on account of Ricardian economics,[102] in the beginning he had to come forward as a Ricardian and especially to participate in the struggle against the landlords. As soon as he had obtained a foothold and climbed to a position on Ricardo's [XIV-842] shoulders, his main effort was directed to expounding political economy, especially Ricardian economics, within the framework of Whiggism[103] and to eliminate all conclusions which were distasteful to the Whigs. His last works on money, taxes, etc.,[b] are mere PLAIDOYERS on behalf of the Whig Cabinet of the day. In this way

---

[a] See this volume, p. 212, and also present edition, Vol. 30, pp. 405-25.— *Ed.*
[b] See J. R. MacCulloch, *A Treatise on Metallic and Paper Money and Banks,* Edinburgh, London, 1858.— *Ed.*

the man secured a lucrative job. His statistical writings[a] are merely CATCHPENNIES. The incogitant decline and vulgarisation of the theory likewise reveal the fellow himself as "A VULGARIAN", a matter to which we shall have to return BEFORE WE HAVE DONE WITH THAT SPECULATING SCOTSMAN.[b]

In *1828* McCulloch published Smith's *Wealth of Nations,*[c] and the 4th volume of this edition contains his own NOTES and DISSERTATIONS in which, to pad out the volume, he reprints in part some mediocre essays which he had published previously, e.g., on "ENTAIL", etc., and which have absolutely nothing to do with the matter, and in part, his lectures on the history of political economy repeated almost *verbotenus*[d]; he himself says that he "LARGELY DRAWS UPON THEM"; in part, however, he tries in his own way to assimilate the new ideas advanced in the interim by Mill and by Ricardo's opponents.

In his *Principles of Political Economy,*[104] Mr. McCulloch presents us with nothing more than a copy of his "NOTES" and "DISSERTATIONS" which he had already copied from his earlier "scattered manuscripts". But things turned out slightly worse in the *Principles,* for inconsistencies are of less importance in "NOTES" than in an allegedly methodical treatment. Thus the passages quoted above, though they are, in part, taken verbatim from the "NOTES", etc., look rather less inconsistent in these "NOTES" than they do in the *Principles.* // In addition the *Principles* contain plagiarisms of Mill amplified by absurd ILLUSTRATIONS, and REPRINTS of articles on CORN TRADE, etc., which he has repeatedly published, maybe *verbotenus,* under 20 different titles in different periodicals, often even in *the same* periodical AT DIFFERENT PERIODS. //

In the above-mentioned *VOLUME IV* of his EDITION of Adam Smith (London, 1828), Mac says (he repeats the same thing word for word in his *Principles of Political Economy* but without making the distinctions which he still felt to be necessary in the "NOTES"):

*"It is necessary to distinguish between the *exchangeable value...* and the *real* or *cost value* of commodities or products. By the *first,* or the exchangeable value of a commodity or product, is meant its power or capacity of exchanging either for other commodities *or* for labour; and by the *second,* or its real or cost value, is meant the quantity of labour which it required for its production or appropriation,

---

a See J. R. MacCulloch, *A Descriptive and Statistical Account of the British Empire...,* Vols I-II, London, 1854; *A Dictionary, Practical, Theoretical, and Historical, of Commerce and Commercial Navigation,* London, 1847.— *Ed.*

b See this volume, pp. 366-70.— *Ed.*

c A. Smith, *An Inquiry into the Nature and Causes of the Wealth of Nations.* In four volumes, Edinburgh, 1828.— *Ed.*

d Verbatim.— *Ed.*

or rather the quantity which would be required for the production or appropriation of a similar commodity at the time when the investigation is made" (l.c., [pp.] 85-86).

"*A commodity* produced by a certain quantity of labour will" //when the supply of commodities is equal to the effectual demand// "uniformly exchange for, or buy any other commodity produced by the same quantity of labour. It will never, however, exchange for, or buy exactly the same quantity of labour that produced it; but though it will not do this, it will *always* exchange for, or buy the same quantity of labour as any other commodity produced under the same circumstances, or by means of the same quantity of labour, as itself" (l.c., [pp.] 96-97).

"*In point of fact*"* (this phrase is repeated literally in the *Principles,* since, IN POINT OF FACT, this "IN POINT OF FACT" constitutes the whole of his deduction,[a]) *"it" (the commodity) "will always exchange for more" //viz., [for] more labour than that by which it was produced//; "and *it is this excess that constitutes profits.* No capitalist would have *any motive"* * (as if the "MOTIVES" of the buyer was the point in question when dealing with the exchange of commodities and the investigation of their value) *"to exchange the produce of a given quantity of labour already performed [XIV-843] for the produce of the same *quantity of labour to be performed.* This would be to *lend"* //"to exchange" would be to "lend"// "without receiving any interest on the loan"* (l.c., p. 96).

Let us start at the end.

If the capitalist did not get back more labour than the amount he advances in WAGES, HE WOULD "LEND" WITHOUT "PROFIT". What has to be explained is how profit is possible if commodities (LABOUR OR OTHER COMMODITIES) are exchanged at their value. And the answer is that no profit would be possible if equivalents were exchanged. It is assumed, first of all, that capitalist and worker "exchange". And then, in order to explain profit, it is assumed that they do "not" exchange, but that one of the parties lends (i.e. gives commodities) and the other borrows, that is, pays only after he has received the commodities. In other words, in order to explain profit, it is said that the capitalist secures "no interest" if he makes no profit. This is putting the thing wrongly. The commodities in which the capitalist pays WAGES and the commodities which he gets back as a result of the labour, are different *use values.* He does not therefore receive back what he advanced, any more than he does when he exchanges one commodity for another. Whether he buys another commodity, or whether he buys the specific labour which produces the other commodity for him, amounts to the same. For the use value he advances he receives back another use value, as happens in all exchanges of commodities. If, on the other hand, one pays attention only to the value of the commodity, then it is no longer a contradiction TO EXCHANGE "A GIVEN QUANTITY OF LABOUR ALREADY PERFORMED" AGAINST "THE SAME QUANTITY TO BE PERFORMED" (although the capitalist IN

---

[a] See this volume, p. 354.— *Ed.*

FACT pays only after the LABOUR *has been* PERFORMED), NOR [is it a contradiction] TO EXCHANGE A QUANTITY OF LABOUR PERFORMED AGAINST THE SAME QUANTITY OF LABOUR PERFORMED. This latter is an insipid tautology. The first part of the passage implies that "THE LABOUR TO BE PERFORMED" IS MATERIALISED IN ANOTHER VALUE OF USE AS THE LABOUR PERFORMED. In this case there is thus a difference [between the objects to be exchanged] and, consequently, a motive for exchange arising out of the relationship itself, but this is not so in the other case, since A only exchanges for A in so far as in this EXCHANGE it is a matter of the QUANTITY OF LABOUR. This is why Mr. Mac has recourse to the *motive.* The motive of the capitalist is to receive back a greater "QUANTITY OF LABOUR" than he advances. Profit is here explained by the fact that the capitalist has the *motive* to make "profit". But the same thing can be said about the sale of goods by the merchant and about every sale of commodities not for consumption but for gain: *He has no motive to exchange the same quantity of performed labour against the same quantity of performed labour. His motive is to get in return more performed labour than he gives away. Hence he *must* get more performed labour in the form of money or commodities than he gives away in the form of a commodity or of money. He must, therefore, buy cheaper than he sells, and sell dearer than he has bought.* Profit UPON ALIENATION is thus explained, not by the fact that it corresponds to the law of value, but by declaring that buyers and sellers have no "motive" for buying and selling in accordance with the law of value. This is Mac's first "sublime" discovery, it fits beautifully into the Ricardian system, which seeks to show how THE LAW OF VALUE asserts itself DESPITE THE "MOTIVES" OF SELLER AND BUYER. [XIV-844] For the rest, Mac's presentation in the "NOTES" differs from the one in the *Principles* only in the following:

In the *Principles* he makes a distinction between "REAL VALUE" and "RELATIVE VALUE" and says that both are equal "UNDER ORDINARY CIRCUMSTANCES" but "IN POINT OF FACT" they cannot be equal if there is to be a profit. He therefore says merely that the "FACT" contradicts the "principle".

In the "NOTES" he distinguishes three sorts of VALUE: "REAL VALUE", the "RELATIVE VALUE" OF A COMMODITY IN ITS EXCHANGE with OTHER COMMODITIES, and the RELATIVE VALUE OF A COMMODITY EXCHANGED WITH LABOUR. The "RELATIVE VALUE" OF A COMMODITY IN ITS EXCHANGE WITH ANOTHER COMMODITY IS ITS *REAL* VALUE *EXPRESSED* IN ANOTHER COMMODITY, OR IN AN "EQUIVALENT". On the other hand, ITS RELATIVE VALUE IN EXCHANGE WITH LABOUR IS ITS REAL VALUE EXPRESSED IN ANOTHER REAL VALUE THAT IS GREATER THAN ITSELF. That means, its value is the exchange with a greater value, with a non-equivalent. If it were exchanged for an EQUIVALENT IN LABOUR, then there would be no profit. The value of a commodity IN ITS EXCHANGE WITH LABOUR is a greater value.

Problem: The Ricardian definition of value conflicts with the EXCHANGE OF A COMMODITY WITH LABOUR.

Mac's solution: IN THE EXCHANGE OF A COMMODITY WITH LABOUR THE LAW OF VALUE DOES NOT EXIST, BUT ITS CONTRARY. Otherwise profit could not be explained. Profit for him, the RICARDIAN, is to be explained by the law of value.

Solution: The law of value (IN THIS CASE) is profit. "IN POINT OF FACT" Mac only reiterates what the opponents of the Ricardian theory say, namely, that there would be *no profit* if the law of value applied to exchange between capital and LABOUR. Consequently, they say, the Ricardian law of value is invalid. He says that *in this case*, which he must explain by the Ricardian law, the law does not exist and that in this case "VALUE" "MEANS" SOMETHING ELSE.

From this it is obvious how little he understands of the Ricardian law. Otherwise he would have had to say that profit arising in exchange between commodities which are exchanged in proportion to the labour time, is due to the fact that "unpaid" labour is contained in the commodities. In other words, the unequal exchange between capital and labour explains the exchange of commodities at their value and the profit which is realised in the course of this exchange. Instead of this he says: Commodities which contain the same amount of labour time command the same amount OF SURPLUS labour, which is not contained in them. He believes that in this way he has reconciled Ricardo's propositions with those of Malthus, by establishing an identity between the determination of the value of commodities by labour time and the determination of the value of commodities by the LABOUR they COMMAND. But what does it mean when he says that commodities which contain the same amount of labour time command the same amount of *surplus* labour in addition to the labour contained in them? It means nothing more than that a commodity in which a *definite* amount of labour time is embodied commands a definite quantity of surplus labour [that is, more labour] than it itself contains. That this applies not only to commodity A, in which x hours of labour time are embodied, but also to commodity B, in which x hours of labour time are also embodied, follows by definition from the Malthusian formula itself.

The contradiction is therefore solved by Mac in this way: If the Ricardian law of value were really a valid one, then profit, and hence capital and capitalist production, would be impossible. This is exactly what Ricardo's opponents assert. And this is what Mac answers them, how he refutes them. And in so doing, he does not notice the beauty of an explanation of EXCHANGEABLE VALUE IN [exchange with] LABOUR which amounts to saying that *value is exchange for something which has no value.*

[XIV-845] After Mr. Mac has thus abandoned the basis of Ricardian political economy, he proceeds even further and destroys the basis of this basis.

The first difficulty in the Ricardian system was the EXCHANGE OF CAPITAL AND LABOUR—SO AS TO BE CORRESPONDING TO THE "LAW OF VALUE".

The second difficulty was that *capitals of equal magnitude,* no matter what their organic composition, yield *equal profits* or the GENERAL RATE OF PROFIT. This is indeed the unrecognised problem of how VALUES are converted into COST PRICES.

The difficulty arose because *capitals of equal magnitude,* but of unequal composition—WHETHER UNEQUAL PROPORTIONS OF CONSTANT AND VARIABLE CAPITAL, WHETHER OF FIXED AND CIRCULATED CAPITAL, WHETHER OF UNEQUAL TIMES OF CIRCULATION—set in motion *unequal* quantities of immediate labour, and therefore unequal quantities of unpaid labour; consequently they cannot appropriate equal quantities of SURPLUS VALUE or SURPLUS PRODUCE in the process of production. Hence they cannot yield equal profit if profit is nothing but the SURPLUS VALUE CALCULATED IN REGARD TO THE VALUE OF THE WHOLE CAPITAL ADVANCED. If, however, the SURPLUS VALUE were something different from (unpaid) labour, then labour could, after all not be the "FOUNDATION AND MEASURE" OF THE VALUE OF COMMODITIES.[a]

The difficulties arising in this context were discovered by Ricardo himself (although not in their general form) and set forth by him as *exceptions* to the RULE OF VALUE.[b] Malthus used these exceptions to throw the whole rule overboard on the grounds that the exceptions constituted the rule.[c] Torrens, who also criticised Ricardo, indicated the problem at any rate when he said that capitals of equal size set unequal quantities of labour in motion, and nevertheless produce commodities of equal "values", HENCE value cannot be determined by labour.[d] Ditto Bailey,[e] etc. *Mill* for his part accepted the exceptions noted by Ricardo as exceptions,

---

[a] See this volume, p. 325.— *Ed.*
[b] See present edition, Vol. 31, pp. 401-03, and also this volume, pp. 261-62.— *Ed.*
[c] See present edition, Vol. 31, p. 416, and also this volume, pp. 225, 261-62.— *Ed.*
[d] See this volume, pp. 262-64.— *Ed.*
[e] Ibid., pp. 349-50.— *Ed.*

and he had no scruples about them except with regard to one single form.[a] One particular *cause of the equalisation* of the profits of the capitalists he found *incompatible* with the RULE. It was the following. Certain commodities remain in the process of production (for example, wine in the cellar) without any labour being applied to them; there is a period during which they are subject to certain natural processes (for example, prolonged breaks in labour occur in agriculture and in tanning before certain new chemicals are applied—these cases are not mentioned by Mill). These periods are nevertheless considered as profit-yielding. The period of time during which the commodity is not being worked on by labour [is regarded] as labour time (the same thing in general applies where a *longer period of circulation time* is involved). Mill "lied" his way—so to speak—out of the difficulty by saying that one can consider the time in which the wine, for example, is in the cellar as a period when it is soaking up labour, *although* according to the assumption this is, IN POINT OF FACT, not the case.[b] Otherwise one would have to say that "time" creates profit and time as such is "sound and fury".[c] McCulloch uses this balderdash of Mill as a starting-point, or rather he reproduces it in his customary affected, plagiarist manner in a general form in which the latent nonsense becomes apparent and the last vestiges of the Ricardian system, as of all economic thinking whatsoever, are happily discarded.

On closer consideration, all the difficulties mentioned above resolve themselves into the following difficulty.

That part of capital which enters into the production process in the form of commodities, as raw materials or tools, does not add more value to the product than it possessed before production. For it only has value in so far as it is embodied labour and the labour contained in it IS IN NO WAY ALTERED by its entry into the production process. It is to such an extent independent of the production process into which it enters and dependent on the socially determined labour REQUIRED FOR ITS OWN PRODUCTION that its own value changes when more labour time or less labour time than it itself contains is required for its reproduction. As value, this part of capital therefore enters unchanged into the production process and emerges from it unchanged. In so far as it really enters into the production process and is changed, this change affects only its

---

[a] See this volume, p. 276.— *Ed.*

[b] Ibid.— *Ed.*

[c] Goethe, *Faust.* Der Tragödie erster Teil. "Marthens Garten".— *Ed.*

use value, i.e. it undergoes a change as *use value.* And all operations undergone by the raw material or carried out by the instrument of labour are merely processes to which they are submitted as specific kinds of raw material, etc., and particular tools (spindles, etc.), processes which affect their use value, but which, as processes, have nothing to do with their exchange value. Exchange value is maintained in this [XIV-846] CHANGE. *Voilà tout.*[a]

It is different with that part of capital which is exchanged against labour capacity. The use value of labour capacity is *labour,* the element which produces exchange value. Since the labour provided by labour capacity in industrial consumption is greater than the labour which is required for its own reproduction, which provides an equivalent of its wages, the value which the capitalist receives from the worker in exchange is greater than the price he pays for this labour. It follows from this that, if equal rates of exploitation are assumed, of 2 capitals of equal size, that which sets less living labour in motion—whether this is due to the fact that the proportion of variable to constant capital is less from the start, or to the fact that it has a [longer] period of circulation or period of production during which it is not exchanged against labour, does not come into contact with it, does not absorb it—will produce less surplus value, and, in general, commodities of less value. How then can the *values* created be *equal* and the surplus values proportional to the capital advanced? Ricardo was unable to answer this question because, put in this way, it is *absurd* since, in fact, neither equal values nor [equal] surplus values are produced. Ricardo, however, did not understand the genesis of the general rate of profit nor, consequently, the transformation of VALUES into COST PRICES which differ specifically from them.

Mac, however, eliminates the difficulty by basing himself on Mill's insipid "evasion". One gets round the inconvenience by talking out of existence by means of a phrase the' characteristic difference out of which it arose. This is the characteristic difference: The use value of labour capacity is labour; it consequently produces exchange value. The use value of the other commodities is use value as distinct from exchange value, therefore no CHANGE which this use value undergoes can change the predetermined exchange value. One gets round the inconvenience by calling the use values of commodities—exchange value, and the operations in which they are involved as use values, the services they render as use values in production—*labour.* For after all, in

---

[a] That is all.— *Ed.*

ordinary life we speak of working animals, working machines, and even say poetically that the iron works in the furnace, or works under the blows of the hammer. It even screams. And nothing is easier than to prove that every "operation" is labour, for labour is—an operation. In the same way one can prove that everything material experiences sensation, for everything which experiences sensation is—material.

> * "*Labour* may *properly* be defined to be any sort of action or operation, whether performed by man, the lower animals, machinery, or natural agents, that tends to bring about a desirable result" * (l.c., [MacCulloch, *Supplemental Notes and Dissertations to Smith's "Wealth of Nations"*, Vol. IV,] p. 75).

And this does not by any means apply [solely] to instruments of labour. It is in the nature of things that this applies equally to raw materials. Wool undergoes A PHYSICAL ACTION OR OPERATION when it is dyed. In general, nothing can be acted upon physically, mechanically, chemically, etc., in order "TO BRING ABOUT A DESIRABLE RESULT" without the thing itself reacting. It cannot therefore be worked upon without itself working. Thus all commodities which enter into the production process bring about an increase in value not only by retaining their own value, but by creating new value, because they "work" and are not merely objectified labour. In this way, all the difficulties are naturally eliminated. In reality, this is merely a paraphrase, a new name for Say's "productive services of capital", "productive services of land", etc., which Ricardo attacked continuously[a] and against which Mac—*mirabile dictu*[b]— himself polemicises in the same "dissertation" or "note" where he pompously presents his discovery, borrowed from Mill and embellished still further.[c] In criticising Say, McCulloch makes lavish use of recollected passages from Ricardo and remembers that these "productive services" are in fact only the attributes displayed by things as *use values* in the production process. But naturally, all this is changed when he calls these "productive services" by the sacramental name of "*labour*".

[XIV-847] After Mac has happily transformed commodities into workers, it goes without saying that these workers also draw wages and that, in addition to the value they possess as "ACCUMULATED LABOUR", they must be paid wages for their "operations" or "action". These WAGES of the commodities are pocketed by the

---

[a] See K. Marx, *A Contribution to the Critique of Political Economy.* Part One (present edition, Vol. 29, p. 278); D. Ricardo, *On the Principles of Political Economy, and Taxation*, 3rd ed., London, 1821, pp. 329-37.— *Ed.*

[b] Wonderful to tell.— *Ed.*

[c] See this volume, pp. 277, 357-58.— *Ed.*

capitalists [*per*] *procurationem*; they are "WAGES OF ACCUMULATED LABOUR"—alias *profit*.[a] And this is proof that equal profit on equal capitals, whether they set large or small amounts of labour in motion, follows directly from the determination of value by *labour time*.

The most extraordinary thing about all this, as we have already noted, is the way Mac, at the very moment when he is basing himself on Mill and appropriating Say, hurls Ricardian phrases against Say. How literally he copies Say—except that where Say speaks of ACTION, he calls this ACTION LABOUR[b]—can best be seen from the following passages from Ricardo where the latter polemicises against Say:

* "M. Say ... imputes to him" (Adam Smith), "as an error, that 'he attributes to the *labour of man alone*, the power of producing value. A more correct analysis shows us that value is owing to the action of labour, or rather the industry of man, combined with *the action of those agents* which nature supplies, and *with that of capital*. His ignorance of this principle prevented him from establishing the true theory of the influence of machinery in the production of wealth.'[c] In contradiction to the opinion of Adam Smith, M. Say ... speaks of the value which is given to commodities by natural agents, etc. But these natural agents, though they add greatly to *value in use*, never add *exchangeable value*, of which M. Say is speaking" (*Principles*, 3rd ed., [pp.] 334-36).[d] "*Machines* and natural agents might very greatly add to the riches of a country, ... not ... any thing to the value of those riches" ([p.] 335, note).*

Like all economists WORTH NAMING, [including] Adam Smith (although in a fit of humour he once called the ox A PRODUCTIVE LABOURER[e]), Ricardo emphasises that labour as *human activity*, even more, as socially determined *human activity*, is the sole source of value. It is precisely through the consistency with which he treats the value of commodities as a mere "REPRESENTATION" of socially determined labour, that Ricardo differs from the other economists. All these economists understand more or less clearly, but Ricardo more clearly than the others, that the exchange value of *things* is a mere expression, a specific social form, of the productive activity of men, something *toto genere*[f] different from things and their USE as things, whether in industrial or in non-industrial consumption. For them, value is, in fact, simply an

---

[a] Ibid., p. 369.—*Ed.*

[b] See J. R. MacCulloch, *The Principles of Political Economy...*, Edinburgh, London, 1825, p. 211 ff.—*Ed.*

[c] J. B. Say, *Traité d'économie politique...*, Vol. I, 2nd ed., Paris, 1814, pp. LI-LII.—*Ed.*

[d] Cf. this volume, p. 179.—*Ed.*

[e] See present edition, Vol. 31, p. 162.—*Ed.*

[f] Entirely.—*Ed.*

objectively expressed relation of the productive activity of men, of the different types of labour to one another. When he argues against Say, Ricardo explicitly quotes the words of Destutt de Tracy,[a] as expressing his own views:

> *"As it is certain that our physical and moral faculties are alone our original riches, the *employment of those faculties"* * (the faculties of men), *"*labour of some kind"* * (that is, LABOUR as the realisation of the faculties of *men*), *"is our only original treasure, and it is always from this employment, that all those things are created which we call riches... It is certain too, that all *those things only represent the labour which has created them,* and if they have *a value,* or even two distinct values, they can only derive them from ... the labour from which they emanate"* * (Ricardo, l.c., [p.] 334).

Thus commodities, things in general, have value only because they *represent* human [XIV-848] labour, not in so far as they are things in themselves, but in so far as they are incarnations of social labour.

And yet some persons have had the temerity to say that the miserable Mac has taken Ricardo to extremes, he who, in his incogitant efforts to "utilise" the Ricardian theory eclectically along with those opposed to it, *identifies* its *principle* and that of all political economy—*labour itself* as human activity and as socially determined human activity—with the physical, etc., action, which commodities possess as *use values,* as things. He who abandons the very concept of labour itself!

Rendered insolent by Mill's "evasion", he plagiarises Say while arguing against him, and copies precisely those phrases of Say which Ricardo in Chapter 20 [of his book], entitled "Value and Riches", attacks as being fundamentally opposed to his own ideas and those of Smith. (Roscher naturally repeats that Mac has carried Ricardo to extremes.[b]) Mac, however, is sillier than Say, who does not call the "action" of fire, machinery, etc., *labour.* And more inconsistent. While Say attributes the creation of "value" to wind, fire, etc., Mac considers that only those use values, things, which can be monopolised create value, as if it were possible to utilise the wind, or steam, or water as motive power without the possession of windmills, steam-driven machinery or waterwheels! As if those who own, monopolise, the things whose possession alone enables them to employ the natural AGENTS did not also monopolise the NATURAL AGENTS. I can have as much air, water, etc., as I like. But I possess them as productive agents only if I have the commodities, the things, by the

---

    [a] [A. L. C.] Destutt de Tracy, *Élémens d'idéologie*, Part IV, Paris, 1815, pp. 99-100.—*Ed.*

    [b] W. Roscher, *Die Grundlagen der Nationalökonomie...*, pp. 82 and 191.—*Ed.*

use of which these agents will operate as such. Thus Mac is even lower than Say.

This vulgarisation of Ricardo represents the most complete and most frivolous decline of Ricardo's theory.

*"In so far, however, as that result" (the result produced by the action or operation of any thing) "is effected by the labour *or* operation of natural agents, that can neither be monopolised nor appropriated by a greater or smaller number of individuals to the exclusion of others, it has *no value.* What is done by these agents is done *gratuitously*"* (Mac[Culloch, *Supplemental Notes and Dissertations to Smith's "Wealth of Nations"*, Vol. IV], l.c., p. 75).

As if what is done by cotton, wool, iron or machinery, were not also done "gratuitously". The machine costs money, but the operation of the machine is not paid for. No use value of any kind of commodity costs anything after its exchange value has been paid.

"The man who sells oil makes no charge for its natural qualities. In estimating its cost he puts down the value of the labour employed in its pursuit, and such is its value" (Carey, *Principles of Political Economy*, PART I, Philadelphia, 1837, [p.] 47).

In arguing against Say, Ricardo emphasises precisely that the action of the machine, for example, costs just as little as that of wind and water.

*"The services which ... natural agents *and* m a c h i n e r y perform for us ... are serviceable to us ... by adding to value in use; but as *they* perform their work *gratuitously* ... the assistance which they afford us, adds nothing to *value in exchange*"* (Ricardo, [l.c.,] pp. 336-37).

Thus Mac has not understood the most elementary propositions of Ricardo. But the sly dog thinks: if the use value of cotton, machinery, etc., costs *nothing*, is not paid for apart from its exchange value, then, on the other hand, this use value is *sold* by those who use cotton, machinery, etc. They sell what costs them nothing.

[XIV-849] The brutal thoughtlessness of this fellow is evident, for after accepting Say's "principle", he sets forth rent with great emphasis, plagiarising extensively from Ricardo.

Land is a

"natural agent ... monopolised or appropriated by a greater or smaller number of individuals to the exclusion of others"[a]

and its natural, vegetative action or "labour", its productive power, consequently has *value,* and rent is thus ascribed to the productive power of land, as is done by the Physiocrats.[b] This is an outstanding

---

[a] Cf. above on this page.— *Ed.*
[b] See present edition, Vol. 30, pp. 356-61, 363-70.— *Ed.*

example of Mac's way of vulgarising Ricardo. On the one hand, he copies Ricardo's arguments, which only make sense if they are based on the Ricardian assumptions, and on the other hand, he takes from others the direct negation of these assumptions (with the reservation that he uses his "nomenclature" or makes some small changes in the propositions). He should have said: "Rent is the wages of land" pocketed by the landowner.

* "If a capitalist expends the same sum in paying the wages of labourers, in maintaining horses, or in hiring a machine, and if the men, the horses, and the machine can all perform *the same piece of work*, *its* value will *obviously* be the same by whichever of them it may be performed"* ([MacCulloch,] l.c., p. 77).

In other words: the value of the product depends on the value of the capital laid out. This is the problem to be solved. The formulation of the problem is, according to Mac, "obviously" the solution of it. But since the machine, for example, performs a greater piece of work than the men displaced by it, it is even more "obvious" that the product of the machine will not fall but rise in value compared with [the value of the product of] the men who "perform the same work". Since the machine can produce 10,000 pieces of work where a man can only produce 1, and every piece has *the same value*, the product of the machine should be 10,000 times as dear as that "of man".

Moreover, in his anxiety to distinguish himself from Say by stating that *value* is produced not by the action of natural agents but only by the action of monopolised agents, or agents produced by labour, Mac gets into difficulties and falls back on Ricardian phrases. For example,

The * labour of [the] wind produces the desired effect* on the * ship (produces a change in it). "But the *value* of that change is not increased by, and is in no degree dependent on, the operation or labour of the natural agents concerned, but on the *amount of capital,* or the *produce of previous labour,* that co-operated in the production of the effect; just as *the cost of grinding* corn does not depend on the action of the wind or water that turns the mill, but on the amount of capital *wasted* in that operation"* ([p.] 79).

Here, all of a sudden, grinding is viewed as adding value to the corn in so far only as capital—"the produce of previous labour"—is "wasted" in the act of grinding. That is, it is not due to the millstone "working", but to the fact that along with the "waste" of the millstone, the value contained in it, the labour embodied in it, is also "wasted".

After these pretty arguments, Mac sums up the wisdom (borrowed from Mill and Say) in which he brings the concept of value into harmony with all kinds of contradictory phenomena, in the following way:

* "The word *labour* means ... in all discussions respecting *value* ... either the immediate labour of man, or the labour of the capital produced by man, or both" * (l.c., [p.] 84).

Hence LABOUR [XIV-850] is to be understood as meaning the labour of man, then his ACCUMULATED LABOUR, and finally, the *practical application,* that is, the physical, etc., properties of use values evolved in (industrial) consumption. Apart from these properties, use value means nothing at all. Use value operates only in consumption. Consequently, by the exchange value of the products of labour, we understand the use value of these products, for this use value consists only in its *action,* or, as Mac calls it, "*labour*", in consumption, regardless of whether this is industrial consumption or not. However, the types of "operation", "action", or "labour" of use values, as well as their physical measures, are as varied as the use values themselves. But what is the unity, the measure by means of which we compare them? This is established by the general word "labour" which is substituted for these quite different applications of use values, after labour itself has been reduced to the words "operation" or "action". Thus, with the identification of use value and exchange value ends this vulgarisation of Ricardo, which we must therefore consider as the last and most sordid expression of the disintegration of the Ricardian school as such.

* "The *profits of capital* are only another name for the *wages of accumulated labour*" * (Mac[Culloch], *Principles etc.,* 1825,[100] p. 291),

that is, for the wages paid to commodities for the services they render as *use values* in production.

In addition, these WAGES OF ACCUMULATED LABOUR have their own mysterious connotation as far as Mr. McCulloch is concerned. We have already mentioned[a] that, apart from his plagiarism of Ricardo, Mill, Malthus and Say, which constitutes the real basis of his writings, he himself continually REPRINTS and sells his "ACCUMULATED LABOUR" under various titles, always "LARGELY DRAWING" UPON WHAT HE HAD GOT PAID BEFORE. This method of drawing the "WAGES OF ACCUMULATED LABOUR" was discussed at great length as early as *1826* in a special work, and what has not McCulloch done since then—from 1826 to 1862—with regard to DRAWING WAGES FOR ACCUMULATED LABOUR! (This miserable phrase has also been adopted by Roscher in his role of Thucydides.[b][105])

---

[a] See this volume, pp. 357-58.— *Ed.*
[b] See W. Roscher, *Die Grundlagen der Nationalökonomie...,* p. 353.— *Ed.*

The book referred to is called: *Some Illustrations of Mr. McCulloch's Principles of Political Economy*, Edinburgh, 1826, by Mordecai Mullion.[a] It traces how our *chevalier d'industrie*[b] made a name for himself. Nine-tenths of his work is copied from Adam Smith, Ricardo and others, the remaining tenth being culled repeatedly from his own ACCUMULATED LABOUR "MOST SHAMELESSLY AND DAMNABLY REITERATED" [p. 4]. Mullion shows, for example, not only that McCulloch sold *the same articles* to *The Edinburgh Review* and *The Scotsman* and the *Encyclopaedia Britannica* as his own "DISSERTATIONS" and as new works, but also that he published *the same* articles *word for word* and with only a few transpositions and under new titles in different issues of *The Edinburgh Review* over the years. In this respect Mullion says the following about "THIS MOST INCREDIBLE COBBLER" [p. 31], "THIS MOST ECONOMICAL OF ALL THE ECONOMISTS" [p. 66]:

* "Mr. McCulloch's articles are as unlike as may be to the heavenly bodies—but, in one respect, they resemble such luminaries—they have stated times of return" * ([p.] 21).

No wonder he believes in the "WAGES OF ACCUMULATED LABOUR".

Mr. Mac's fame illustrates the power of fraudulent baseness.

[XIV-850a] In order to perceive how McCulloch exploits some of Ricardo's propositions to give himself airs, see, *inter alia*, *The Edinburgh Review* for *March 1824*, where this friend of the WAGES OF ACCUMULATED LABOUR gives vent to a veritable jeremiad about the fall in the rate of profit. (This claptrap is called "Considerations on the Accumulation of Capital".)

"The author ... expresses the fears inspired in him by *the decline in profit* as follows: 'The condition of England however prosperous in appearance, is bad and unsound at bottom; the plague of poverty is secretly creeping on the mass of her citizens, and the foundations of her power and greatness have been shaken... Where the rate of interest is low, as in England, the rate of profit is also low, and the prosperity of the nation has passed its culminating point.' These observations must surprise everybody acquainted with England's splendid situation" (Prévost, l.c., [*Réflexions du traducteur sur le système de Ricardo*,] p. 197).

There was no need for Mr. Mac to distress himself over the fact that "LAND" GETS BETTER "WAGES" THAN "IRON, BRICKS, etc." THE CAUSE MUST BE THAT IT "LABOURS" HARDER.

---

[a] Pseudonym of John Wilson.— *Ed.*
[b] Swindler, crook.— *Ed.*

Wakefield's real contribution to the understanding of capital has already been dealt with in the previous section on the *Conversion of Surplus Value into Capital.*[106] Here we shall only deal with what is directly relevant to the "TOPIC".

* "Treating labour as a commodity, and capital, the produce of labour, as another, then, if the value of these two commodities were regulated by equal quantities of labour, a given amount of labour would, under all circumstances, exchange for that quantity of capital which had been produced by the same amount of labour; *antecedent labour* would always exchange for the same amount of *present labour.* But the value of labour, in relation to other commodities, in so far, at least, as wages depend upon share, is determined, not by equal quantities of labour, but by the proportion between supply and demand" * (Wakefield's edition of Smith's *Wealth of Nations,* VOL. I, London, 1835,[13] p[p. 230-]231, note).

Thus, according to Wakefield, profit would be inexplicable if wages corresponded to the *value* of labour.

In VOLUME II of his edition of Adam Smith's work Wakefield remarks:

* "Surplus produce [107] always constitutes rent: still rent may be paid, which does not consist of surplus produce" * (l.c., [p.] 216).

"If, as in Ireland, * the bulk of a people be brought to live upon potatoes, and in hovels and rags, and to pay, for permission so to live, all [that] they can produce beyond hovels, rags, and potatoes, then, in proportion as they put up with less, the owner of the land on which they live, obtains more, even though the return to capital or labour should remain unaltered. What the miserable tenants give up, the landlord gathers. So a fall in the standard of living amongst the cultivators of the earth is another cause of surplus produce... When wages fall, the effect upon surplus produce is the same as a fall in the standard of living; the whole produce remaining the same, the surplus part is greater; the producers have less, and the landlord more" * ([pp.] 220-21).

In this case, profit is called *rent,* just as it is called *interest* when, for example, as in India, the worker (although nominally independent) works with advances he receives from the capitalist and has to hand over all the SURPLUS PRODUCE to the capitalist.

"The QUANTITY of every commodity must be so regulated that the supply of each commodity shall bear a less proportion to the demand for it than the supply of labour bears to the demand for labour. The difference between the price or value of the commodity, and the price or value of the LABOUR WORKED UP IN IT constitutes the *profit* OR *surplus* which Ricardo cannot explain on the basis of his theory" ([pp.] 72-73).[a]

---

[a] Marx quotes Stirling with some alterations.— *Ed.*

[XIV-851] The same author informs us:

"When the values of commodities relate to each other according to their production costs, this may be called PAR OF VALUE" (p[p. 16-]18).[a]

Thus if demand and supply of labour correspond with one another, then labour would be sold at its *value* (whatever Stirling may understand by value). And if demand and supply of the commodities IN WHICH THE LABOUR IS WORKED UP do correspond, then the commodities would be sold at their *production costs,* by which Stirling understands THE VALUE OF LABOUR. The price of the commodity would then be equal to the VALUE OF the LABOUR WORKED UP IN IT. And the price of labour would be ON A PAR with its own *VALUE.* HENCE THE PRICE OF THE COMMODITY=THE PRICE OF THE LABOUR WORKED UP IN IT. HENCE, THERE WOULD BE NO PROFIT OR SURPLUS. Stirling explains profit, or the SURPLUS, in this way:

The supply of labour in relation to the demand for it must be greater than the supply of commodities in which THE LABOUR IS WORKED UP in relation to the demand for them. The matter must be so arranged that the commodity is sold at a higher price than that paid for the labour contained in it. This is what Mr. Stirling calls explaining the phenomenon of the surplus, whereas it is, in fact, nothing but a paraphrase of what is supposed to be explained. If we go into it further, then there are only 3 possibilities. [1)] The price of labour is ON "a PAR with VALUE", that is, the demand for and supply of labour balance in such a way that the price of labour=the value of labour. In these circumstances, the commodities must be sold *above* their value, or things must be arranged in such a way that the supply is *below* the demand. This is *tout pur*[b] "*profit* UPON ALIENATION",[56] except that the condition is stated under which it is possible. [2)] Or the demand for labour is greater than the supply and the price is higher than its value. In these circumstances, the capitalist has paid the worker more than the value of the commodity, and the buyer must then pay the capitalist a twofold surplus—first to replace the amount he [the capitalist] has *d'abord* paid to the worker and then his profit. [3)] Or the price of labour is *below* its value and the supply of labour above the demand for it. The SURPLUS would then arise from the fact that labour is paid *below its* value and is sold at its *value* or, at least, above its *price.*

---

[a] Here Marx is summarising pages 16-18 of Stirling's book.— *Ed.*
[b] Pure.— *Ed.*

If one strips this of all NONSENSE, then Stirling's SURPLUS is [here] due to the fact that labour is bought by the capitalist *below* its value and is sold again *above* its price in the form of commodities.

The other cases, divested of their ridiculous form—according to which the producer has to "arrange" matters in such a way that he is able to sell his commodity above its value, or above "THE PAR OF VALUE"—mean nothing but that the *market price* of a commodity rises above its value, if the demand for it is greater than the supply. This is certainly not a new discovery and explains one sort of "SURPLUS" which never caused Ricardo or anyone else the slightest difficulty.

7) JOHN STUART MILL, *SOME UNSETTLED QUESTIONS ETC.*, LONDON, 1844

In a previous notebook[a] I have traced in detail how Mill violently attempts to derive Ricardo's law of the *rate of profit* (in inverse proportion to wages) directly from the theory of value without distinguishing between *surplus value* and *profit*.

This whole account of the Ricardian school shows that it declines at 2 points.

1) Exchange between capital and labour corresponding to the law of value.

2) Elaboration of the general rate of profit. Identification of surplus value and profit. Failure to understand the relation between VALUES and COST PRICES.[6]

[XIV-852] l) OPPOSITION TO THE ECONOMISTS (BASED ON THE RICARDIAN THEORY)

During the Ricardian period of political economy its antithesis, communism (Owen) and socialism (Fourier, St. Simon, the latter only IN HIS FIRST BEGINNINGS), [comes] also [into being]. According to our plan,[b] however, we are here concerned only with that opposition which takes as its starting-point the premises of the economists.[108]

---

[a] See present edition, Vol. 31, pp. 35-60.— *Ed.*
[b] See this volume, pp. 7-8.— *Ed.*

It will be seen from the works which we quote that in fact they all derive from the Ricardian form.

1) *THE SOURCE AND REMEDY OF THE NATIONAL DIFFICULTIES ETC. A LETTER TO LORD JOHN RUSSELL,* LONDON, 1821 (ANONYMOUS)

This scarcely known pamphlet (ABOUT 40 PAGES) [which appeared] at a time when MacCulloch, "THIS INCREDIBLE COBBLER",[109] began to make a stir, contains an important advance on Ricardo. It bluntly describes SURPLUS VALUE — or "profit", as Ricardo calls it (often also "SURPLUS PRODUCE"), or "*INTEREST*", as the author of the pamphlet terms it — as "*SURPLUS LABOUR*", the labour which the worker performs gratis, the labour he performs over and above the quantity of labour by which the value of his labour capacity is replaced, i.e. by which he produces an equivalent for his WAGES. Important as it was to reduce VALUE to LABOUR, it was equally important to present SURPLUS VALUE, which manifests itself in SURPLUS PRODUCE, as SURPLUS LABOUR. This was in fact already stated by Adam Smith[a] and constitutes one of the main elements in Ricardo's argumentation. But nowhere did he clearly express it and record it in an *absolute form*.

Whereas the only concern of Ricardo and others is to understand the conditions of capitalist production, and to assert them as the absolute forms of production, the pamphlet and the other works of this kind to be mentioned seize on the mysteries of capitalist production which have been brought to light in order to combat the latter from the standpoint of the industrial proletariat.

* "Whatever may be *due* to the capitalist" * (from the viewpoint of capital) * "he *can only receive* the *surplus labour* of the labourer; for the labourer must *live*" * (l.c., [p.] 23).

To be sure, these conditions of life, the minimum on which the worker can live, and consequently also the quantity of surplus labour which can be squeezed out of him, are relative magnitudes.

* "If capital does not decrease in value as it increases in amount, the capitalists will exact from the labourers the produce of every hour's labour beyond what it is *possible* for the labourer to subsist on: and however horrid and disgusting it may seem, the capitalist may eventually speculate on the food that requires the least labour to produce it, and eventually say to the labourer: 'You sha'n't eat bread, because barley meal is cheaper; you sha'n't eat meat, because it is possible to subsist on beet root and potatoes.' And to this point have we come" ([pp. 23-]24).

"If the labourer can be brought to feed on potatoes instead of bread, it is indisputably true that more can be exacted from his labour; i.e. if when he fed on

---

[a] See present edition, Vol. 30, pp. 385-91, and this volume, p. 41.— *Ed.*

bread he was obliged to *retain for the maintenance of himself and family the labour of Monday and Tuesday,* he will, on potatoes, receive only the half of Monday; and the *remaining half of Monday and the whole of Tuesday* are available either *for the service of the state or the capitalist"* * ([p.] 26).[a]

Here profit, etc., is reduced directly to appropriation of the labour time for which the worker receives no equivalent.

* "It is admitted that the interest paid to the capitalists, whether in the nature of rents, interests of money, or profits of trade, is paid out of the *labour of others"* * ([p.] 23).

Rent, money interest, industrial profit, are thus merely different forms of "interest of capital", which again is reduced to the "surplus labour of the labourer". This surplus labour takes the form of surplus produce. The capitalist is the possessor[b] of the surplus labour or of the surplus produce.

The surplus produce is capital.

* "Suppose ... there is *no surplus labour,* consequently, nothing that can be allowed to accumulate as capital" * ([p.] 4).

And immediately after this he says:

* "the possessors of [the] surplus produce *or* capital" * (l.c.).

The author says, in a quite different sense from the whining Ricardians:

* "The natural and necessary consequence of an increased capital, is its decreasing value" * ([pp. 21-]22).

And in reference to Ricardo:

* "Why set out by telling us that no accumulation of capital will lower profits, because nothing will lower profits but increased wages, when it appears that if population does not increase with capital, wages would increase from the [dis]proportion between capital and labour; and if population does increase, wages would increase from the difficulty of procuring food" * ([p.] 23).

[XIV-853] If the value of capital, that is, the interest of capital, i.e. the surplus labour which it commands, which it appropriates, did not decrease when the amount of capital increases, the [accumulation of] interest from interest would follow in geometrical progression,[c] and just as, calculated in money (see *Price*[d]), this presupposes an *impossible* accumulation (rate of accumulation), so, reduced to its real element—labour, it would swallow up not only the surplus labour, but also the necessary labour as "being due" to

---

[a] Cf. present edition, Vol. 30, p. 204.— *Ed.*

[b] In the manuscript: "Professor".— *Ed.*

[c] See this volume, p. 543.— *Ed.*

[d] R. Price, *An Appeal to the Public on the Subject of the National Debt,* London, 1772, p. 19.— *Ed.*

capital. (We shall return to Price's fantasy in the section on REVENUE AND ITS SOURCES.[110])

* "If it were possible to continue to increase capital and keep up the value of capital, which is proved by the interest of money continuing the same, the interest to be paid for capital would soon exceed the whole produce of labour. ...capital tends in more than arithmetical progression to increase capital. It is admitted that the *interest* paid to the capitalists, whether in the nature of rents, *interests* of money, or *profits* of trade, is paid out of the labour of others. Consequently, if capital go on accumulating, the labour to be given for the use of the capital must go on increasing, interest paid for capital continuing the same, till all the labour of all the labourers of the society is engrossed by the capitalist. But this is impossible to happen: for whatever may be *due* to the capitalist, he can *only receive* the *surplus labour* of the labourer; for the labourer must live" * ([p.] 23).

But it is not clear to him how the VALUE OF CAPITAL DECREASES. He himself says, when dealing with Ricardo, that this recurs because wages rise when capital accumulates more rapidly than the POPULATION grows, or because the *value* of WAGES (not their QUANTITY) increases when the population grows more rapidly than capital accumulates (or even if population *increases simultaneously*) as a result of decreasing productivity of agriculture. But how does he explain it? He does not accept the latter alternative; he assumes that WAGES are reduced more and more to the minimum possible. [A reduction of interest on capital] can only take place, [he] says, because the portion of capital which is exchanged for living labour declines relatively, although the worker is exploited more than, or just as much as, before.

In any case, it is a step forward that the nonsense about the geometrical progression of interest is reduced to its true sense, that is, nonsense.[a]

There are, incidentally, according to the pamphleteer, two ways in which the growth of SURPLUS PRODUCE or SURPLUS LABOUR prevents capital from being forced to give a steadily growing share of its plunder back to the workers.

The first is the conversion of SURPLUS PRODUCE into fixed capital, which prevents the LABOUR fund—or the part of the product consumed by the worker—from necessarily increasing with the accumulation OF CAPITAL.

The second is foreign trade, which enables the capitalist to exchange the SURPLUS PRODUCE for foreign luxury articles and thus to consume it himself. In this way, even that part of the product which exists as NECESSARIES may quite well increase without the need for it to be returned to the workers in the form of a proportionate increase in WAGES.

---

a See this volume, p. 543.— *Ed.*

It should be noted that the first way—which is only effective for a time and then neutralises its own effect (at least as regards the fixed capital consisting of machinery, etc., itself used in the production of NECESSARIES)—implies the transformation of SURPLUS PRODUCE into capital, whereas the 2nd way implies consumption of an ever increasing portion of the surplus PRODUCE by the capitalists—increasing consumption on the part of the capitalists, and *not the reconversion* of SURPLUS PRODUCE into capital. If the same SURPLUS PRODUCE were to remain in the form in which it immediately exists, a larger part of it would have to be exchanged with the workers as variable capital. The result would be an increase in wages and a reduction in the amount of absolute or relative SURPLUS VALUE. Here is the real secret of the necessity for increasing consumption by "the rich", advocated by Malthus, in order that the part of the product which is exchanged for labour and converted into capital, should have great value, yield large profits, absorb a large amount of surplus labour.[a] He does not however propose that the industrial capitalists themselves should increase their consumption, but [allots] this FUNCTION to LANDLORDS, SINECURISTS, etc., because the urge for accumulation and the urge for EXPENDITURE, if united in the same person, would play tricks on each other. It is here also that the erroneousness of the view of Barton, Ricardo,[b] and others stands out. Wages are not determined by that portion of the total product that is either consumed as, or can be converted into, *variable* capital, but by that part of it which is actually converted into variable capital. A part can be consumed by RETAINERS even in its natural form, another can be consumed in the shape of luxury products by means of foreign trade, etc.

Our pamphleteer overlooks two things:

As a result of the introduction of machinery, a mass of workers is constantly being thrown out of employment, [a section of] the POPULATION is thus MADE REDUNDANT; the SURPLUS PRODUCE therefore finds fresh labour for which it can be exchanged without any increase in population and without any need to extend the absolute labour time. Let us assume that 500 workers were employed previously, whereas now there are 300 workers, who perform relatively more surplus labour. The 200 can be employed by the surplus PRODUCE as soon as it has increased sufficiently. One portion of the old [variable] capital is converted into fixed capital, the other gives employment to fewer workers but extracts from them more SURPLUS

---

[a] In the manuscript, Marx wrote "Malthus" in the margin.— *Ed.*
[b] See this volume, pp. 177-208.— *Ed.*

VALUE in relation to their number and in particular also more SURPLUS PRODUCE. The remaining 200 are material created for the purpose of capitalising additional SURPLUS PRODUCE.

[XIV-853a] The transformation of NECESSARIES into LUXURIES by means of foreign trade, as interpreted in the pamphlet, is correct in itself:

1) because it puts an end to the nonsensical idea that wages depend on the amount of NECESSARIES produced, as if these NECESSARIES had to be consumed in this form by the producers or even by the whole body of people engaged in production, in other words as if they must be turned back into variable capital or "circulating capital", as it is termed by Barton and Ricardo;

2) because it determines the whole social pattern of backward nations—for example, the SLAVE-HOLDING STATES in the United States of North America (see *Cairnes*[a]) or *Poland*, etc. (as was already understood by old *Büsch*,[b] unless he stole the idea from Steuart)—which are associated with a world market based on capitalist production. No matter how large the SURPLUS PRODUCE they extract from the SURPLUS LABOUR of their SLAVES in the simple form of COTTON or CORN, they can adhere to this simple, undifferentiated LABOUR because foreign trade enables them [to convert] these simple products into any kind of use value.

The assertion that the portion of the annual product which MUST BE EXPENDED as WAGES depends on the size of the "CIRCULATING CAPITAL", would be *al pari*[c] to the assertion that, when a large part of the product consists of "buildings", and houses for workers are built in large numbers relative to the size of the working population, the workers must consequently live in cheap and well-built houses because the supply of houses increases more quickly than the demand for them.

It is correct, on the other hand, that, if the SURPLUS PRODUCE is large and the large part of it is to be employed as capital, then there must be an increase in the demand for labour and therefore also in that part of the SURPLUS PRODUCE which is exchanged for WAGES (provided large numbers of workers did not have to be thrown out of work in order to obtain a SURPLUS PRODUCE of this size). At all events, it is not the *absolute size* of the SURPLUS PRODUCE (in whatever

---

[a] J. E. Cairnes, *The Slave Power: Its Character, Career, & Probable Designs...*, London, 1862.— *Ed.*

[b] J. G. Büsch, *Theoretisch-praktische Darstellung der Handlung in ihren mannichfaltigen Geschäften*, Hamburg, 1808, Book 5, Ch. 2.— *Ed.*

[c] Equal.— *Ed.*

form it may exist, even that OF NECESSARIES) which necessarily requires it TO be EXPENDED as variable capital and which consequently causes an increase in wages, but it is the desire to capitalise which results in a large part of the surplus PRODUCE being laid out in variable capital, and this would *consequently* make wages grow with the accumulation of capital if machinery did not constantly make [a section of] the population REDUNDANT and if an ever greater portion of capital (in particular as a result of foreign trade) were not exchanged for capital, not for labour. The portion of SURPLUS PRODUCE which is already produced directly in a form in which it can only serve as capital, and that portion of it which acquires this form as a result of foreign trade, grow more rapidly than the portion which must be exchanged against IMMEDIATE LABOUR.

The proposition that wages depend on EXISTING CAPITAL and that therefore a rapid accumulation of capital is the sole means by which wages are made to rise, amounts to this:

On the one hand, to a *tautology,* if we disregard the form in which the conditions of labour exist as capital. How rapidly the number of workers can be increased without worsening their living conditions depends on the *productivity of labour* which a given number of workers perform. The more raw materials, tools and means of subsistence they produce, the greater the means at their disposal not only to bring up their children so long as these cannot work themselves, but to realise the labour of the new, growing generation, and consequently to make the growth of population keep up with, and even OUTDO, the growth of production, since with the growth of the population, the [workers'] skill increases, division of labour grows, the possibility [for using] machinery grows, constant capital grows, in short, the productivity of labour grows.

While the growth of population depends on the productivity of labour, the productivity of labour depends on the growth of population. It is a case of reciprocity. But this, expressed in capitalist terms, signifies that the means of subsistence of the working population depend on the productivity of capital, on the largest possible portion of their product confronting them as a force which commands their labour. Ricardo himself expresses the matter *correctly* — I mean the tautology—when he makes WAGES depend on the productivity of capital, and the latter dependent on the productivity of labour.[a] That labour depends on the growth of capital signifies nothing more than, on the one hand, the tautology

---

[XIV-854] that the increase in the means of subsistence and the means of employment of the population depends on the productivity of the population's own labour and, secondly, expressed in capitalist terms, that it *depends on the fact* that the population's own product confronts them as *alien property* and that as a consequence, their own productivity confronts them as the *productivity* of the things which they create.

In practice this means that the worker must appropriate the smallest possible part of his product in order that the largest possible part of it may confront him as *capital*; he must surrender as much as possible to the capitalist *gratis,* in order that the latter's means for purchasing his labour anew—with what has been taken away from the worker without compensation—may increase as much as possible. In this case it can happen that, if the capitalist has made the worker work a great deal for nothing, he may then, in exchange for what he has received for nothing, allow the worker to do a little less work for nothing. However, since this prevents the achievement of what is aimed at, namely, *accumulation of capital as rapidly as possible,* the worker must live in such CIRCUMSTANCES that this reduction in the amount of labour he performs for nothing is in turn counteracted by a growth of the working population, either relatively as a result of the use of machinery, or absolutely as a result of early marriage. (It is the same relationship which is derided by the RICARDIANS when the MALTHUSIANS preach it between LANDLORDS and capitalists.) The workers must relinquish the largest possible part of their product to capital without receiving anything in return, so as, when conditions are *more favourable,* to buy back with new labour a part of the product so relinquished. However, since the conditions for the favourable change are at the same time counteracted by this favourable change, it can only be temporary and must turn again into its own opposite.

3) What applies to the transformation of NECESSARIES into LUXURIES by means of foreign trade, applies in general to luxury production, whose unlimited diversification and expansion depends, however, on foreign trade. Although the workers engaged in luxury production produce capital for their EMPLOYERS, their product, *in natura,* cannot be turned back into capital, either constant or variable capital.

Luxury products, apart from those which are sent abroad to be exchanged for NECESSARIES which enter into variable capital either in whole or in part, simply constitute *surplus labour* and moreover surplus labour which is immediately IN THAT SHAPE OF SURPLUS PRODUCE which the rich consume as REVENUE. But they do not represent only the surplus labour of the workers who produce them. On the average, these perform the same surplus labour as the workers in other branches of industry. But in the same way as $^1/_3$ of the product, which contains $^1/_3$ of the surplus labour, can be considered as the embodiment of this surplus labour, and the remaining $^2/_3$ as reproduction of the capital advanced, so the surplus labour of the producers of the NECESSARIES which constitutes the WAGES of the producers of LUXURIES can also be considered as the necessary labour of the working class as a whole. Their surplus labour consists 1) of that part of the NECESSARIES which is consumed by the capitalists and their RETAINERS; and 2) of the total amount of LUXURIES. With regard to the individual capitalist or DIFFERENT TRADES the matter appears quite different. For the capitalist, one part of the LUXURIES CREATED by him represents merely an equivalent for the capital laid out.

If too large a part of surplus labour is embodied directly in LUXURIES, then clearly, accumulation and the DEGREE OF reproduction will stagnate, because too small a part is reconverted into capital. If too small a part is embodied in luxuries, then the accumulation of capital (that is, of that part of the SURPLUS PRODUCE which can *in natura* serve as capital again) will proceed more rapidly than increase in population, and the rate of profit will fall, unless a foreign market for NECESSARIES exists.

In the exchange between capital and REVENUE [a] I have regarded wages, too, as REVENUE and in general have merely examined the relationship of constant capital to REVENUE. The fact that the REVENUE of the worker appears at the same time as variable capital is important only in so far as in the accumulation of capital—the formation of new capital—the surplus consisting of means of subsistence (NECESSARIES) in the possession of the capitalist producing them can be exchanged directly for the surplus consisting of raw materials or machinery in the possession of the capitalist producing constant capital. Here one form of REVENUE is exchanged for the other, [XIV-855] and, once the exchange is EFFECTED, the REVENUE of A is converted into the constant capital of B and the REVENUE of B into the variable capital of A.

In considering this circulation, reproduction and manner of replacement of the different capitals, etc., one must *d'abord* [b] disregard foreign trade.

---

[a] See present edition, Vol. 31, pp. 130-51.— *Ed.*

[b] First of all.— *Ed.*

Secondly, it is necessary to distinguish between the two aspects of the phenomenon:

1) Reproduction on the existing scale,

2) reproduction on an extended scale, or accumulation; transformation of REVENUE into capital.

Ad 1) I have shown:

That what the *producers of the means of subsistence* have to replace is 1) their constant capital, 2) their variable capital. The part of the value of their product in excess of these two constitutes the SURPLUS PRODUCE, the MATERIAL EXISTENCE OF SURPLUS VALUE, WHICH IN ITS TURN IS ONLY THE REPRESENTATIVE OF SURPLUS LABOUR.

Variable capital, that part of their product which represents it, is made up of WAGES, the REVENUE of the worker. This part already exists here in the *natural form* in which it serves as variable capital once again. With this part, the equivalent reproduced by the worker, the labour of the worker is bought once again. This is the exchange of capital for IMMEDIATE LABOUR. The worker receives this part in the form of money with which he buys back his own product, or other products of the same category. This is the exchange of the *different portions of the variable part of capital for one another* after the worker has in the form of money received an assignment to his quota. This is exchange of one part of newly added labour for another part within the same category (means of subsistence).

The part of the SURPLUS PRODUCE (newly added labour) consumed by the capitalists (who produce means of subsistence) themselves, is either consumed by them *in natura* or they exchange one type of SURPLUS PRODUCE existing in consumable form against another type. This is the exchange of REVENUE for REVENUE, both of them consisting of newly added labour.

We cannot really speak of exchange between REVENUE and capital in the above transaction. Capital (NECESSARIES) is exchanged against labour (labour capacity). This is therefore not an exchange of REVENUE for capital. It is true that as soon as the worker receives his WAGES, he consumes them. But what he exchanges for capital is not his REVENUE, but his labour.

The 3rd part, constant capital, is exchanged for a part of the product of those manufacturers who produce constant capital; namely, for that part which represents newly added labour. This consists of an equivalent for the WAGES (that is, of variable capital) and of the SURPLUS PRODUCE, the SURPLUS VALUE, the REVENUE of the capitalists which exists in a form in which it can only be consumed industrially and not individually. On the one hand, this is therefore exchange of the *variable capital of these producers* for a part of the means of subsistence which constitute constant capital. In fact they exchange a part of their product which constitutes variable capital but exists in the form of constant capital, for a part of the product of those manufacturers who produce the means of subsistence, a part which constitutes constant capital but exists in the form of variable capital. Here newly added labour is exchanged for constant capital.

On the other hand, that part of the product which represents SURPLUS PRODUCE but exists in the form of constant capital is exchanged for a portion of the means of subsistence which represents constant capital for its producers. Here REVENUE is exchanged for capital. The REVENUE of the capitalists who produce constant capital is exchanged for the means of subsistence and replaces the constant capital of the capitalists who produce the means of subsistence.

Finally, a part of the product of the capitalists who produce constant capital, namely, that part which itself represents constant capital, is replaced partly *in natura,* partly through barter (concealed by money) between the producers of constant capital.

It is assumed in all this that the scale of reproduction=the original scale of production.

If we enquire now what part of the total annual product is made up of newly added labour, then the calculation is quite simple.

A) *Consumable articles,* which consist of 3 parts. [Firstly,] the REVENUE of the capitalists=the SURPLUS LABOUR added during the year.

Secondly, wages, i.e. variable capital which is equal to the newly added labour by which the workers have reproduced their WAGES.

Finally, the third part, raw materials, machinery, etc. This is constant capital, that part of the value of the product which is only retained, not produced. That is, it is not labour newly added during the course of the year.

[XIV-856] If we call constant capital c, variable capital v, and SURPLUS PRODUCE, the REVENUE r, then this category consists of:

c (which constitutes a part of the product) is merely retained value and does not consist of newly added labour; on the other hand, $v+r$ consist of labour newly added during the course of the year.

The total product (or its value) P^a after deduction of c, therefore, consists of newly added labour.

Thus the product of category A,

$P^a - c^1$ =the labour newly added during the course of the year.

B) *Articles for industrial consumption.*

Here also $v^{II} + r^{II}$ are made up of newly added labour. But not c^{II}, the constant capital which operates in this sphere. But $v^{II} + r^{II} = c^{I}$ for which they are exchanged. c^{I} is transformed into variable capital and REVENUE for B. On the other hand, v^{II} and r^{II} are transformed into c^{I}, into constant capital for A.

The product of category P^b,

$P^b - c^{II}$ =the labour newly added during the course of the year.

But $P^b - c^{II} = c^{I}$, for the whole product of P^b after deduction of c^{II}, the constant capital employed in this category, is exchanged for c^{I}.

After $v^{II} + r^{II}$ have been exchanged for c^{I}, the matter can be presented as follows:

P^a consists solely of newly added labour, the product of which is divided between profits and WAGES, that is, it constitutes the EQUIVALENT OF NECESSARY LABOUR and the EQUIVALENT OF SURPLUS LABOUR. For the $v^{II} + r^{II}$ which now replace c^{I} are equal to the newly added labour in category B.

Thus the whole product of P^a—not only its SURPLUS PRODUCE, but also its variable capital and its constant capital—consists of the products of labour newly added during the course of the year.

On the other hand, P^b can be regarded in such a way that it does not represent any part of the newly added labour, but merely old labour which is retained. For its part c^{II} does not represent newly added labour. Neither does the part c^{I} which it has received in exchange for $v^{II} + r^{II}$, for this c^{I} represents the constant capital laid out in A, and not newly added labour.

The whole part of the annual product which, as variable capital, constitutes the REVENUE of the workers and as SURPLUS PRODUCE constitutes the consumption fund of the capitalists, therefore can be resolved into newly added labour, whereas the remaining part of the product, which represents constant capital, can be resolved into nothing but old labour which has been retained and simply replaces constant capital.

Consequently, just as it is correct to say that the whole portion of the annual product which is consumed as REVENUE WAGES and PROFITS (together with the BRANCHES OF PROFIT, RENT, INTEREST, etc., as well as the WAGES of the UNPRODUCTIVE LABOURERS) consists of newly added labour, so it is false to assert that the total annual product can be resolved into REVENUE, WAGES and PROFITS and thus merely into portions of newly added labour. A part of the annual product can be resolved into constant capital, which regarded as value does *not* constitute newly added labour and, as regards USE, does not form part of either WAGES or PROFITS. Regarded as value it represents ACCUMULATED LABOUR in the real sense of the word, and its use value is the USE of this ACCUMULATED PREVIOUS LABOUR. On the other hand, it is equally correct that the *labour added during the year* is not represented entirely by that part of the product which can be resolved into WAGES and PROFITS. For these WAGES and PROFITS buy SERVICES, that is, labour which does not enter into the product of which WAGES and PROFITS form [a part]. These SERVICES are labour which is used up in the consumption of the product and does not enter into its immediate production.

[XIV-857] *Ad* 2). It is a different matter with regard to accumulation, transformation of REVENUE into capital, *reproduction on an extended scale*, in so far as this latter does not simply result from *more productive employment* of the old capital. Here the whole new capital consists of newly added labour, that is, of SURPLUS labour in the form of profit, etc. But although it is correct that here the entire element in new production arises from and consists of newly added labour—which is a part of the SURPLUS LABOUR of the LABOURERS—it is wrong to assume, as the economists do, that, when it is converted into capital, it can be resolved into variable capital alone, that is, WAGES. Let us suppose for example that a part of the SURPLUS PRODUCE of the FARMER is exchanged for a part of the SURPLUS PRODUCE of the machine manufacturer. It is then possible that the latter will convert the corn into variable capital and employ more workers, directly or indirectly. On the other hand, the FARMER has converted a part of his SURPLUS PRODUCE into constant capital, and it is possible that, as a result of this conversion, he will discharge some of his old workers instead of taking on new ones. The FARMER may cultivate more land. In this case, a part of his corn will be converted not into WAGES, but into constant capital, etc.

It is precisely accumulation which reveals clearly that everything—i.e. REVENUE, variable capital and constant capital—is nothing but *appropriated alien* labour; and that both the conditions of labour with which the worker works, and the equivalent he receives for his labour, consist of labour performed by the worker and appropriated by the capitalist, who has *not given any equivalent for it.*

[The same applies] even to original accumulation. Let us assume that I have saved £500 from my WAGES. In fact, therefore, this sum represents not only *accumulated labour* but, in contrast to the "accumulated labour" of the capitalist, *my* own labour accumulated by me and for me. I convert the £500 into capital, buy raw material, etc., and take on workers. Profit is, say, 20%, that is, £100 a year. In 5 years I shall have "eaten up" my capital in the form of REVENUE (provided new accumulation does not continuously take place and the £100 is consumed). In the 6th year, my capital of £500 itself consists of other people's labour appropriated without any equivalent. If, on the other hand, I had always accumulated ¹/₂ of the profit made, the process would have been slower, for I would not have consumed so much and would have accumulated more rapidly.

	Capital	Profit	Consumed
First year	500	100	50
Second year	550	110	55
Third year	605	121	60
Fourth year	665	133	66
Fifth year	731	146	73
Sixth year	804	160	80
			384
Seventh year	884	176	88
			472
Eighth year	972	194	97
			569

My capital will have been almost doubled by the 8th year although I have consumed more than my original capital. The capital of 972 does not contain a single FARTHING of paid labour or of labour for which I have returned any kind of equivalent. I have consumed my entire original capital in the form of REVENUE, that is, I have received an equivalent for it, which I have consumed. The new capital consists solely of the appropriated labour of other people.

In considering surplus value as such, the original form of the product, HENCE of the SURPLUS PRODUCE, is of no consequence. It becomes important when considering the actual process of reproduction, partly in order to understand its forms, and partly in order to grasp the influence of luxury production, etc., on reproduction. Here is another example of how *use value* as such acquires economic significance.

[XIV-858] Now to return to our pamphlet.

* "Suppose the whole labour of the country to raise just sufficient for the support of the whole population; it is evident there is no surplus labour, consequently, nothing that can be allowed to accumulate as capital. Suppose the whole labour of the country to raise as much in *one* year as could maintain it two years, it is evident one year's consumption must perish, or for one year men must

cease from productive labour. But the *possessors of the surplus produce, or capital,* will neither maintain the population the following year in idleness, nor allow the produce to perish; they will employ them upon something not directly and immediately productive, for instance, in the erection of machinery, etc. But the third year, the whole population may again return to productive labour, and the machinery erected in the last year coming now into operation,* it is evident the produce will be greater than the first year's produce for the PRODUCE of the MACHINERY IN ADDITION. This SURPLUS PRODUCE,[a] that is an even larger amount, MUST PERISH OR BE PUT TO USE AS BEFORE; and this USANCE again adds to the PRODUCTIVE POWER of the society till MEN *MUST* CEASE FROM PRODUCTIVE LABOUR FOR A TIME, OR THE PRODUCE OF THEIR LABOUR MUST PERISH. This is the PALPABLE CONSEQUENCE IN THE SIMPLEST STATE OF SOCIETY" ([pp.] 4-5).[b]

  * "The demand of other countries is limited, not only by *our* power to produce, but by *their* power to produce,"*

// This is the answer to Say's assertion that we do not produce too much, but they produce too little.[44] THEIR POWER TO PRODUCE IS NOT NECESSARILY EQUAL TO OUR POWER TO PRODUCE. //

  * "for do what you will, in a series of years the whole world can take little more of us, than we take of the world, so that all your foreign trade, of which there is so much talking, never did, never could, nor ever can, add one shilling, or one doit to the wealth of the country, as for every bale of silk, chest of tea, pipe of wine that ever was imported, something of equal value was exported; and even the profits made by our merchants in their foreign trade are paid by the consumer of the return goods here" ([pp.] 17-18).

"Foreign trade is mere barter and exchange for the convenience and enjoyment of the capitalist: he has not a hundred bodies, nor a hundred legs: he cannot consume, in cloth and cotton stockings, all the cloth and cotton stockings that are manufactured; therefore they are exchanged for wines and silks; but those *wines and silks represent the surplus labour of our own population,* as much as the cloths and cottons, and in this way the *destructive power of the capitalist is increased beyond all bounds*: by foreign trade the capitalists contrive to outwit nature, who had put a 1,000 natural limits to their exactions, and to their wishes to exact; there is no limit now, either to their power, or desires" * (l.c., [p.] 18).

One sees that he accepts Ricardo's teaching on FOREIGN TRADE. In Ricardo's work its only purpose is to support his *theory of value* or to demonstrate that his views on foreign trade are not at variance with it. But the pamphlet stresses that it is not only NATIONAL LABOUR, but also NATIONAL SURPLUS LABOUR which is embodied in the outcome of FOREIGN TRADE.

If SURPLUS LABOUR or surplus VALUE were represented only in the national SURPLUS PRODUCE, then the increase of value for the sake of value and therefore the EXACTION OF SURPLUS LABOUR would be restricted by the limited, narrow circle of use values in which the value of labour would be represented. But it is foreign TRADE which develops its [the surplus value's] real nature as value by

---

  [a] In the pamphlet: "surplus labour".— *Ed.*
  [b] Marx quotes with some abridgements.— *Ed.*

developing the labour embodied in it as social labour which manifests itself in an unlimited range of different use values, and this in fact gives meaning to abstract wealth.

* "It is *the infinite variety of wants*, and of the *kinds* of commodities" * // and therefore also the *infinite variety of real labour, which produces those different kinds of commodities// "*necessary to their gratification*, which alone renders the passion for wealth" //and hence the passion for appropriating other people's labour// "indefinite and insatiable" (*Wakefield*'s edition* of Adam Smith, [*An Inquiry into the Nature and Causes of the Wealth of Nations*,] Vol. I, London, 1835,[13] p. 64, note).

But it is only FOREIGN TRADE, the development of the market to a world market, which causes money to develop into world money and *abstract labour* into social labour. Abstract wealth, value, money, HENCE *abstract labour*, develop in the measure that concrete labour becomes a totality of different modes of labour embracing the world market. Capitalist production rests on the *value* or the development of the labour embodied in the product as social labour. But this is only [possible] on the basis of FOREIGN TRADE and of the world market. This is at once the precondition and the result of capitalist production.

[XIV-859] The pamphlet is no theoretical treatise. [It is a] protest against the false reasons given by the economists for the DISTRESS and the "NATIONAL DIFFICULTIES" of the times. It does not, consequently, make the claim that its conception of SURPLUS VALUE as *SURPLUS LABOUR* carries with it a general criticism of the entire system of economic categories, nor can this be expected of it. The author stands rather on Ricardian ground and is only consistent in stating one of the consequences inherent in the system itself and he advances it in the interests of the working class against capital.

For the rest, the author remains a captive of the economic categories as he finds them. Just as in the case of Ricardo the confusion of SURPLUS VALUE with profit leads to undesirable contradictions, so in his case the fact that he christens SURPLUS VALUE the *INTEREST OF CAPITAL*.

To be sure, he is in advance of Ricardo in that he first of all reduces all SURPLUS VALUE to SURPLUS LABOUR, and when he calls SURPLUS VALUE *INTEREST OF CAPITAL*, he at the same time emphasises that by this he understands the general form of SURPLUS LABOUR in contrast to its particular forms—rent, interest of money and industrial profit.

* "*Interest* paid to the capitalists, whether in the *nature*" * (it should be *shape, form) "*of rents, interests of money*, or *profits of trade*" * ([*The Source and Remedy*..., p.] 23).

He thus distinguishes the general form of SURPLUS LABOUR or SURPLUS VALUE from their particular forms, something which neither Ricardo nor Adam Smith [does], at least not consciously or consistently. But on the other hand, he applies the name of one of these particular forms—INTEREST—to the general form. And this suffices to make him relapse into economic SLANG.

* "The progress of increasing capital would, in established societies, be marked by the decreasing interest of money, or, what comes to the same, the decreasing quantity of the labour of others that would be given for its use" * ([p.] 6).

This passage reminds one of Carey.[a] But with him it is not THE LABOURER WHO USES CAPITAL, BUT CAPITAL WHICH USES LABOUR. Since by INTEREST he understands SURPLUS LABOUR IN ANY FORM, the matter of the REMEDY OF OUR "NATIONAL DIFFICULTIES" amounts to an increase in *wages*; for the reduction OF INTEREST means a reduction of SURPLUS LABOUR. However, what he really means is that in the exchange of capital for labour the appropriation of alien labour should be reduced or that the worker should appropriate more of his own labour and capital less.

Reduction of SURPLUS LABOUR can mean two things:

Less work should be performed over and above the time which is necessary to reproduce the labour capacity, that is, to create an equivalent for WAGES;

or, less *of the total quantity of labour* should assume the *form of* SURPLUS LABOUR, that is, the form of time worked gratis for the capitalist; therefore less of the product in which labour manifests itself should take the form of SURPLUS PRODUCE; in other words, the worker should receive more of his own product and less of it should go to the capitalist.

The author is not quite clear about this himself, as can be seen from the following passage which is really the last word in this matter as far as the pamphlet is concerned:

A nation is really rich only if no interest is paid for the use of capital; if the working day is only 6 hours rather than twelve.[b] WEALTH IS *DISPOSABLE TIME* AND NOTHING MORE ([p.] 6).

Since what is understood by interest here is profit, rent, interest on money—in short, all the forms of surplus value—and since, according to the author himself, capital is nothing but the PRODUCE OF LABOUR, ACCUMULATED LABOUR WHICH IS ABLE TO EXACT IN EXCHANGE FOR ITSELF NOT ONLY AN EQUAL QUANTITY OF LABOUR, BUT SURPLUS LABOUR, according to

[a] See K. Marx, *Outlines of the Critique of Political Economy...* (present edition, Vol. 28, pp. 499-502).—*Ed.*

[b] This is a summary of the ideas set forth in the pamphlet. Cf. present edition, Vol. 30, p. 204.—*Ed.*

him the phrase: capital bears no interest, therefore means that capital [XIV-860] does not exist. The product is not transformed into capital. No SURPLUS PRODUCE and no SURPLUS LABOUR exist. Only then is a nation really rich.

This can mean however: There is no PRODUCE and no LABOUR *over and above* the product and the LABOUR required for the reproduction of the workers. Or, they [the workers] *themselves* appropriate this surplus either of the product or of the LABOUR.

That the author does *not simply* mean the latter is, however, clear from the fact that the words "no interest [is paid] for the use of capital" are juxtaposed to [the proposition that] "A nation is really rich if the working day is 6 hours rather than twelve"; "*WEALTH IS DISPOSABLE TIME, AND NOTHING MORE*".

This can now mean:
If everybody has to work, if the contradiction between those who have to work too much and those who are idlers disappears— and this would in any case be the result of capital ceasing to exist, of the product ceasing to provide a title to alien SURPLUS LABOUR—and if, in addition, the development of the productive forces brought about by capital is taken into account, society will produce the necessary ABUNDANCE in 6 hours, [producing] more than it does now in 12, and, moreover, all will have 6 hours of "DISPOSABLE TIME", that is, real wealth; time which will not be absorbed in direct productive labour, but will be available for ENJOYMENT, for leisure, thus giving scope for free activity and development. Time is *scope* for the development of man's FACULTIES, etc. It will be recalled that the economists themselves justify the SLAVE LABOUR of the WAGE LABOURERS by saying that it creates leisure, free time for *others*, for another section of society—and thereby also for the society of WAGE LABOURERS.

Or it can also mean: The workers now work 6 hours more than the time (*now*) required for their own reproduction. (This can hardly be the author's view, since he describes what they use *now* as an inhuman minimum.) If capital ceases to exist, then the workers will work for 6 hours only and the idlers will have to work the same amount of time. The material wealth of all would thus be depressed to the level of the workers. But all would have DISPOSABLE TIME, that is, free time for their development.

The author himself is obviously not clear about this. NEVERTHE-LESS, there remains the fine statement:

A nation is really rich if the working day is 6 hours rather than twelve. WEALTH IS DISPOSABLE TIME, AND NOTHING MORE.

Ricardo himself, in the CHAPTER entitled "Value and Riches, Their Distinctive Properties",[a] also says that real wealth consists in producing the greatest possible amount of VALUES IN USE having the least possible VALUE. This means, in other words, that the greatest possible ABUNDANCE OF MATERIAL WEALTH is created in the shortest possible labour time. Here also, the "DISPOSABLE TIME" and the enjoyment of that which is produced in the labour time of others, [appear] as the true WEALTH, but like everything in capitalist production—and consequently in its interpreters—[it appears] in the form of a contradiction. In Ricardo's work the contradiction between RICHES and VALUE later [appears] in the form that the net product should be as large as possible in relation to the gross product, which again, in this contradictory form, amounts to saying that those classes in society whose time is only partly or not at all absorbed in material production although they enjoy its fruits, should be as numerous as possible in comparison with those classes whose time is totally absorbed in material production and whose consumption is, as a consequence, a mere ITEM in production costs, a mere condition for their existence as beasts of burden. There is always the wish that the smallest possible portion of society should be doomed to the slavery of labour, to forced labour. This is the utmost that can be accomplished from the capitalist standpoint.

The author puts an end to this. TIME OF LABOUR, even if exchange value is eliminated, always remains the creative substance of wealth and the measure of the *cost* of its production. But FREE TIME, DISPOSABLE TIME, is wealth itself, partly for the enjoyment of the product, partly for FREE ACTIVITY which—unlike LABOUR—is not determined by a compelling extraneous purpose which must be fulfilled, and the fulfilment of which is regarded as a natural necessity or a social duty, according to one's inclination.

It is self-evident that if TIME OF LABOUR is reduced to a normal length and, furthermore, labour is no longer performed for someone else, but for myself, and, at the same time, the social contradictions between MASTER AND MEN, etc., being abolished, it acquires a quite different, a free character, it becomes real social labour, and finally the basis of DISPOSABLE TIME—the TIME OF LABOUR of a MAN who has also DISPOSABLE TIME, must be of a much higher quality than that of the beast of burden.

---

[a] D. Ricardo, *On the Principles of Political Economy, and Taxation*, 3rd ed., London, 1821, Ch. XX.—*Ed.*

[XIV-861] 2) PIERCY RAVENSTONE, M.A.,
THOUGHTS ON THE FUNDING SYSTEM, AND ITS EFFECTS,
LONDON, 1824

A most remarkable work.

The author of the pamphlet discussed above understands SURPLUS VALUE in its original form, i.e. that of *SURPLUS LABOUR.* Consequently his attention is mainly centred on the extent of labour time. In particular, the conception of *SURPLUS LABOUR* or VALUE in its absolute form; the extension of labour time beyond that required for the reproduction of the labourer himself, not the reduction of NECESSARY LABOUR as a result of the development of the productive powers of labour.

The reduction of this NECESSARY LABOUR is the principal aspect examined by Ricardo, but in the way it is carried out in capitalist production, namely, as a means for extending the amount of labour time accruing to capital. This pamphlet, on the contrary, declares that the final aim is the *reduction of* the producers' *labour time* and the cessation of labour for the *POSSESSOR OF SURPLUS PRODUCE.*

Ravenstone seems to assume the working day as given. Hence, what he is particularly interested in—just as was also the author of the pamphlet previously discussed, so that the theoretical questions only crop up incidentally—is RELATIVE SURPLUS VALUE or the SURPLUS PRODUCE (which accrues to capital) as a result of the development of the productive power of labour. As is usual with those who adopt this standpoint, SURPLUS LABOUR is conceived here more in the form of SURPLUS PRODUCE, whereas in the previous pamphlet, SURPLUS PRODUCE is conceived more in the form of SURPLUS LABOUR.

* "To teach that the wealth and power of a nation depend on its *capital,* is to make industry ancillary to riches, to make men subservient to property" * ([p.] 7).

The opposition evoked by the Ricardian theory—on [the basis of] its own assumptions—has the following characteristic feature.

To the same extent as political economy developed—and this development finds its most trenchant expression in Ricardo, as far as fundamental principles are concerned—it presented labour as the sole element of value and the only creator of use value, and the development of the productive forces as the only real means for increasing wealth; the greatest possible development of the productive powers of labour as the economic basis of society. This is, in fact, the foundation of *capitalist production.* Ricardo's work,[a] in particular, since it demonstrates that the law of value is not

---

[a] *On the Principles of Political Economy, and Taxation.—Ed.*

invalidated either by landed property or by capitalist accumulation, etc., is, in reality, only concerned with eliminating all contradictions or phenomena which appear to run counter to this conception. But in the same measure as it is understood that labour is the *sole* source of exchange value and the active source of use value, "*capital*" is likewise conceived by the same economists, in particular by Ricardo (and even more by Torrens, Malthus, Bailey, and others after him), as the regulator of production, the source of wealth and the aim of production, whereas labour is regarded as wage labour, whose representative and real instrument is inevitably a pauper (to which Malthus' theory of population contributed), a mere production cost and instrument of production dependent on a minimum wage and forced to drop even below this minimum as soon as the existing quantity of labour is "superfluous" for capital. In this contradiction, political economy merely expressed the essence of capitalist production or, if you like, of wage labour, of labour alienated from itself, which stands confronted by the wealth it has created as alien wealth, by its own productive power as the productive power of its product, by its enrichment as its own impoverishment and by its social power as the power of society. But this definite, *specific,* historical form of social labour, as it appears in capitalist production, is proclaimed by these economists as the general, eternal form, as something determined by nature and *these* relations of production as the absolutely (not historically) necessary, natural and reasonable relations of social labour. Their thoughts being entirely confined within the bounds of capitalist production, they assert that the *contradictory* form in which social labour manifests itself there, is just as necessary as the form itself freed from this contradiction. Since in the selfsame breath they proclaim, on the one hand, *labour* as such (for them, labour is synonymous with wage labour) and on the other, *capital* as such—that is, the poverty of the workers and the wealth of the non-workers—to be the sole source of wealth, they are perpetually involved in absolute contradictions without being in the slightest degree aware of them. (*Sismondi* was epoch-making in political economy because he had an inkling of this contradiction.[a]) Ricardo's phrase "LABOUR OR CAPITAL"[b] reveals in a most striking fashion both the contradiction inherent in the terms and the naïvety with which they are stated to be identical.

---

    [a] See this volume, pp. 247-48.— *Ed.*
    [b] See present edition, Vol. 31, pp. 407-11, and this volume, pp. 247-48.— *Ed.*

Since the same real development which provided bourgeois political economy with this striking theoretical expression, unfolded the real contradictions contained in it, especially the contradiction between the growing wealth of the English "nation" and the growing misery of the workers, and since moreover these contradictions are given a *theoretically* compelling if unconscious expression in the Ricardian theory, etc., it was natural for those [XV-862] thinkers who rallied to the side of the proletariat to seize on this contradiction, for which they found the theoretical ground already prepared. Labour is the sole source of exchange value and the only active creator of use value. This is what you say. On the other hand, you say that *capital* is everything, and the worker is nothing or a mere production cost of capital. You have refuted yourselves. Capital is *nothing* but defrauding of the worker. *Labour* is *everything*.

This, in fact, is the ultimate meaning of all the writings which defend the interests of the proletariat from the Ricardian standpoint basing themselves on his assumptions. Just as little as he [Ricardo] understands the identity of *capital* and *labour* in his own system, do they *understand* the contradiction they describe. That is why the most important among them—Hodgskin, for example—accept all the economic preconditions of capitalist production as eternal forms and only desire to eliminate capital, which is both the basis and necessary consequence [of these preconditions].[a]

Ravenstone's main idea is as follows: The development of the productive powers of labour creates *capital* or property, in other words a surplus produce for "idlers",[b] non-workers[c]; and indeed the more the productive power of labour develops, the more it produces this, its parasitical excrescence which sucks it dry. Whether the title to this surplus produce accrues to the non-worker because he already possesses wealth, or because he possesses land, landed property, does not affect the case. Both are *capital,* that is, mastery over the product of other people's labour. For Ravenstone property[c] is merely *appropriation* of the products of other people's labour and this is only possible in so far as and in the degree that *productive industry* develops. By productive industry Ravenstone understands industry which produces necessaries. Unproductive industry, the industry of consumption,[111] is a consequence of the development of capital, or property. Ravenstone appears ascetic like the author of

---

a See this volume, pp. 401-10, 445-46.— *Ed.*

b In the manuscript, this word is followed by its German equivalent.— *Ed.*

c See this volume, p. 396.— *Ed.*

the pamphlet discussed above.[a] In this respect he himself remains a captive of the notions set forth by the economists. Without *capital,* without PROPERTY, the NECESSARIES of the workers would be produced in abundance, but there would be no luxury industry. Or it can also be said that Ravenstone, like the author of the pamphlet discussed above, understands or at least in fact admits the *historical necessity* of capital; since capital, according to the author of the pamphlet, produces *surplus labour* over and above the labour strictly necessary for the maintenance [of the worker] and at the same time leads to the creation of machinery (what he calls fixed capital) and gives rise to foreign trade, the world market, in order to utilise the SURPLUS PRODUCE filched from the workers partly to increase productive power, partly to give this SURPLUS PRODUCE the most diverse forms of use value far removed from those required by necessity. Similarly, according to Ravenstone, no "CONVENIENCES", no machinery, no luxury products would be produced without CAPITAL and PROPERTY, neither would the development of the natural sciences have taken place, nor the literary and artistic productions which owe their existence to leisure or the urge of the wealthy to receive an equivalent for their "SURPLUS PRODUCE" from the non-workers.

Ravenstone and the pamphleteer do not say this in justification of capital, but simply seize on it as a point of attack because all this is done in *opposition* to the workers and not *for* them. But in fact they thus admit that this is a result of capitalist production, which is therefore a historical form of social development, even though it stands in contradiction to that part of the population which constitutes the basis of that whole development. In this respect they share the narrow-mindedness of the economists (although from a diametrically opposite position) for they confuse the *contradictory form* of this development with its content. The latter wish to perpetuate the contradiction on account of its results. The former are determined to sacrifice the fruits which have developed within this antagonistic form, in order to get rid of the contradiction. This distinguishes their opposition to political economy from that of contemporary people like Owen[b]; likewise from that of Sismondi, who harks back to antiquated forms of the contradiction in order to be rid of it in its acute form.[c]

---

[a] *The Source and Remedy of the National Difficulties...—Ed.*

[b] See R. Owen, *The Book of the New Moral World...,* London, 1836.—*Ed.*

[c] See this volume, pp. 247-48, and also K. Marx, *The Poverty of Philosophy. Answer to the "Philosophy of Poverty" by M. Proudhon* (present edition, Vol. 6, p. 137).—*Ed.*

It is the "WANTS" of the poor which "CONSTITUTE HIS" (the rich man's) "WEALTH.... When all were equal, none would labour for another. * The necessaries of life would be overabundant whilst its comforts were entirely wanting" ([p.] 10).

"The industry which produces is the parent of property; that which aids consumption is its child" ([p.] 12).

"The growth of property, this greater ability to maintain idle men, and unproductive industry, that in political economy is called capital" ([p.] 13).

"As the destination of property is expense, as without that it is wholly useless to its owner, its existence is intimately connected with that [XV-863] of the industry of consumption" (l.c.).

"If each man's *labour were but enough to procure his own* food, there *could be no property,* and no part of a people's industry could be turned away to work for the wants of the imagination" ([pp.] 14-15).

"In every stage of society, as increased numbers and better contrivances add to each man's power of production, the *number of those who labour is gradually diminished....* Property grows from the improvement of the means of production; its sole business is [the] encouragement of idleness. When each man's labour is barely sufficient for his own subsistence, as there can be no property, there will be no idle men. When one man's labour can maintain five, there will be four idle men for one employed in production: in no other way can the produce be consumed. ...the object of society is to magnify the idle at the expense of the industrious, to create power out of plenty" * ([p.] 11).

(With regard to RENT he says (not quite correctly, for it is precisely here that it is necessary to explain why [rent] accrues TO THE LANDLORD and not TO THE FARMER, THE INDUSTRIAL CAPITALIST) what applies to SURPLUS VALUE in general, in so far as it develops as a result of the increase in the productive power of labour.

* "In the early stages of society, when men have no artificial assistance to their powers of industry, the proportion of their earnings which can be afforded to rent is exceedingly small; for land has no natural value, it owes all its produce to industry. But every increase of skill adds to the proportion which can be reserved for rent.* Where the labour of 9 is required for the maintenance of 10, only $1/10$ of the GROSS PRODUCE can go TO RENT. Where one man's labour is sufficient for 5, $4/5$ WILL GO TO RENT, or the other CHARGES of the STATE, WHICH CAN ONLY BE PROVIDED FOR OUT OF THE SURPLUS PRODUCE OF INDUSTRY. The first proportion seems to have prevailed in England at the time of the CONQUEST,[112] the last is that which actually takes place now since only $1/5$ part of the people are [...] employed in the cultivation of the land" ([pp.] 45-]46).

* "So true it is that society turns every improvement but to the increase of idleness" * ([p.] 48).)

Note. An original piece of work. Its real subject is the modern system of national debt, as its title indicates.

Amongst other things he says:

"The entire war against the French Revolution * has achieved no higher adventure than the turning of a few Jews into gentlemen, and a few blockheads into political economists" * ([pp.] 66[-67]).

"The funding system has one beneficial consequence although * the ancient gentry of the land * are robbed * of a large portion of their property to transfer it to these new fangled hidalgos as a reward for their skill in the arts of fraud and peculation ... if it encourage fraud and meanness; if it clothe quackery and pretension in the garb of wisdom; if it turn a whole people in[to] a nation of jobbers ... if it break down all the prejudices of rank and birth to render money the only distinction among men ... it destroys the perpetuity of property"* ([pp.] 51-52).

3) *LABOUR DEFENDED AGAINST THE CLAIMS OF CAPITAL;*
OR, THE UNPRODUCTIVENESS OF CAPITAL PROVED.
BY A LABOURER, LONDON, 1825.
(WITH REFERENCE TO THE PRESENT COMBINATIONS AMONGST JOURNEYMEN)

4) THOMAS HODGSKIN, *POPULAR POLITICAL ECONOMY.*
FOUR LECTURES DELIVERED AT THE LONDON MECHANICS' INSTITUTION,
LONDON, 1827

The anonymous first work is also by Hodgskin. Whereas the PAMPHLETS mentioned previously and a series of similar ones have disappeared without trace, these writings, especially the first one, made a considerable stir and are still regarded as belonging to the major works of English political economy (cf. John Lalor, *Money and Morals,* London, 1852 [pp. XXIV and 319-22]). We shall consider each of these works in turn.

Labour Defended etc. As the title indicates, the author wishes to prove the *"UNPRODUCTIVENESS OF CAPITAL"*. Ricardo does not assert that capital is PRODUCTIVE OF VALUE. It only adds its own value to the product, and its own value depends on the labour time required for its reproduction. It only has value as ACCUMULATED LABOUR (or rather [XV-864], REALISED LABOUR) and it only adds this—its value—to the product in which it is embodied. It is true that he is inconsistent when discussing the general rate of profit. But this is precisely the contradiction which his opponents attacked.

As far as the productivity of capital in relation to *use value* is concerned, this is construed by Smith, Ricardo and others, and by political economists in general, as meaning nothing else than that products of previous useful work serve anew as means of production, as objects of labour, instruments of labour and means of subsistence for the worker. The objective conditions of labour do not face the worker, as in the primitive stages, as mere natural objects (as such, they are never capital), but as natural objects already transformed by human activity. But in this sense the word "capital" is quite superfluous and meaningless. Wheat is nourishing not because it is capital but because it is wheat. The use value of wool derives from the fact that it is wool, not capital. In the same way, the action of the steam engine has nothing in common with its existence as capital. It would do exactly the same work if it were not "capital" and if it belonged, not to the factory owner, but to the workers. All these things serve in the real labour process because of the relationship which exists between them as *use values*—not as exchange values and still less as capital—and the labour which is embodied in them. Their productivity in the real labour process, or rather the productivity of the labour material-ised in them, is due to their nature as objective conditions of real labour and not to their *social existence* as *alienated, independent conditions* which *confront* the worker and are embodied in the capitalist, the MASTER over living labour. It is as WEALTH, as *Hopkins* (not our Hodgskin) rightly says,[a] and not as "*NET*" WEALTH, as PRODUCE and not as "NET" PRODUCE, that they are here consumed and used. It is true that the particular social form of these things in relation to labour and their real determinateness as factors of the labour process are as confused and inseparably interwoven with one another in the minds of the economists as they are in the mind of the capitalist. Nevertheless, as soon as they analyse the labour process, they are compelled to abandon the term capital completely and to speak of *material of labour, means of labour, and means of subsistence.*[113] But the determinate form of the product as material, instrument and means of subsistence of the worker expresses nothing but the relationship of these *objective* conditions to labour; labour itself appears as the activity which dominates them. It says however nothing at all about [the relationship of] labour and capital, only about the relationship of the purposeful activity of men to their own products in the process of reproduction. They neither cease to be products of labour nor mere objects which are at the disposal of labour. They merely express the relationship in which labour appropriates the objective world which it has created itself, at any rate in this form; but they do not by any means express *any other domination of these things over labour,* apart from the fact that activity must be appropriate to the material, OTHERWISE IT WOULD NOT BE purposeful activity, labour.

One can only speak of the *productivity* of capital if one regards capital as the embodiment of definite social relations of produc-tion. But if it is conceived in this way, then the historically transitory character of these relations becomes at once evident, and the general recognition of this fact is incompatible with the continued existence of this relationship, which itself creates the means for its abolition.

---

[a] See Th. Hopkins, *On Rent of Land...*, London, 1828, p. 126, and also present edition, Vol. 31, p. 366.—*Ed.*

But the economists do not regard capital as such a relationship because they cannot admit its *relative* character, and do not understand it either. They simply express in theoretical terms the notions of the practical men who are engrossed in capitalist production, dominated by it and interested in it.

In his polemic, Hodgskin himself starts out from a standpoint which is economically narrow-minded.[a] In so far as they [the economists] define capital as an eternal production relation, they reduce it to the general relations of labour, to its material conditions, relations which are common to all modes of production and do not express the specific nature of capital. In so far as they hold that capital produces "value", the best of them and Ricardo included, admit that it does not produce any value which it has not previously received and constantly continues to receive from labour, since the value of a product is determined by the labour time necessary to reproduce it, that is, its value is the result of living, present labour and not of past labour. And as Ricardo emphasises, increase in the productivity of labour is marked by the continuous devaluation of the products of past labour. On the other hand, the economists continually mix up the definite, specific form in which these things constitute capital with their nature as things and as simple elements of every labour process. The mystification contained in capital—as EMPLOYER OF LABOUR[b]—is not explained by them, but it is constantly expressed by them unconsciously, for it is inseparable from the material aspect of capital.

[XV-867][114] The first pamphlet[c] draws the correct conclusions from Ricardo and reduces SURPLUS VALUE to SURPLUS LABOUR. This is in contrast to Ricardo's opponents and followers who continue to adhere to his confusion of SURPLUS VALUE with profit.

In opposition to them, the second pamphlet[d] defines relative SURPLUS VALUE more exactly as being dependent on the level of development of the productive power of labour. Ricardo says the same thing, but he avoids the conclusion drawn by the second pamphlet, namely, that the increase in the productive power of labour only increases capital, the wealth of others which dominates labour.

---

a See this volume, p. 394.—*Ed.*

b See p. XXI—1317 of Marx's manuscript (present edition, Vol. 34); cf. also this volume, pp. 302-03.—*Ed.*

c *The Source and Remedy of the National Difficulties...*—*Ed.*

d P. Ravenstone, *Thoughts on the Funding System, and Its Effects.*—*Ed.*

Finally, the third pamphlet[a] bursts forth with the general statement, which is the inevitable consequence of Ricardo's presentation—that *capital is unproductive.* This is in contrast to Torrens, Malthus and others who, taking one aspect of the Ricardian theory as their point of departure, turn Ricardo's statement that labour is the creator of value into the opposite— that capital is the creator of value. The pamphlet, moreover, disputes [the statement]—which recurs in all of them, from Smith to Malthus, especially in the latter where it is elevated into an absolute dogma (ditto in the case of James Mill)—that labour is absolutely dependent on the *amount of capital available,* as this is the condition of its existence.

Pamphlet No. 1 ends with the statement:

* "Wealth is nothing but disposable time." *[b]

According to Hodgskin, CIRCULATING CAPITAL is nothing but the *juxtaposition* of the different kinds of social labour (COEXISTING LABOUR) and accumulation is nothing but the amassing of the productive powers of social labour, so that the accumulation of the skill and knowledge (SCIENTIFIC POWER) of the workers themselves is the chief [form of] accumulation, and infinitely more important than the accumulation—which goes hand in hand with it and merely represents it—of the *existing objective* conditions of this accumulated activity. These objective conditions are only nominally accumulated and must be constantly produced anew and consumed anew.

* "Productive capital and skilled labour are one." "Capital and a labouring population are precisely synonymous" * [*Labour Defended against the Claims of Capital..,* p. 33].

These are simply further elaborations of Galiani's [thesis]:

"The real wealth ... is man" (*Della Moneta,* Custodi, Parte Moderna, t. III, [p.] 229).[c]

The whole objective world, the "world of commodities", vanishes here as a mere aspect, as the merely passing activity, constantly performed anew, of socially producing men. Compare this "idealism" with the crude, material fetishism into which the Ricardian theory develops "IN [the writings of] THIS INCREDIBLE COBBLER",[109] McCulloch, where not only the difference between man

---

a [Th. Hodgskin,] *Labour Defended against the Claims of Capital; or, the Unproductiveness of Capital Proved...,* London, 1825.— *Ed.*

b See this volume, pp. 389-90.— *Ed.*

c Marx quotes in Italian.— *Ed.*

and animal disappears but even the difference between a living organism and an inanimate object. And then let them say that as against the lofty idealism of bourgeois political economy, the proletarian opposition has been preaching a crude materialism directed exclusively towards the satisfaction of coarse appetites.

In his investigations into the productivity of capital, Hodgskin is remiss in that he does not distinguish between how far it is a question of producing use values or exchange values.

Further—but this has historical justification—he takes capital as it is defined by the economists. On the one hand (in so far as it operates in the real process of labour) as a merely physical condition of labour, and therefore of importance only as a material element of labour, and (in the process of valorisation) nothing more than the quantity of labour measured by time, that is, nothing different from this quantity of labour itself. On the other hand, although in fact, in so far as it appears in the real process of production, it is a mere *name* for, and *rechristening* of, labour itself, it is represented as the power dominating and engendering labour, as the basis of the productivity of labour and as wealth alien to labour. And this without any intermediate links. This is how he found it. And he counterposes the real aspect of economic development to its bourgeois humbug.

*"Capital is a sort of *cabalistic word,* like church or state, or any other of those *general terms* which are invented by those who fleece the rest of mankind to conceal the hand that shears them"* (*Labour Defended...,* [p.] 17).

In accordance with the tradition he found prevailing among the economists, he distinguishes between circulating and fixed capital; circulating capital moreover is described as mainly that part which consists of, or is used as, means of subsistence for the workers.

It is maintained that "*division of labour* is impossible without *previous accumulation of capital*" [p. 8].[a] But *"the effects attributed to *a stock of commodities,* under the *name of circulating capital,* are caused by *co-existing labour*"* ([p.] 9).

Faced with the crude conception of the economists, it is quite correct to say that "CIRCULATING CAPITAL" is only THE "NAME" for a "STOCK OF" PECULIAR "COMMODITIES". Since the economists have not analysed the specific social relationship which is represented in the *metamorphosis of commodities,* they can understand *only* the material aspect of "CIRCULATING" capital. All the differentiations in capital arising from the circulation process [XV-868]—in fact the

---

[a] Hodgskin quotes McCulloch here.— *Ed.*

circulation process itself—are actually nothing but the metamorphosis of commodities[a] (determined by their relationship to wage
labour as capital) as an aspect of the reproduction process.

DIVISION OF LABOUR is, in one sense, nothing but CO-EXISTING LABOUR,
that is, the CO-EXISTENCE of *different* kinds of labour which are
represented in DIFFERENT KINDS OF PRODUCE OR RATHER COMMODITIES. The
DIVISION OF LABOUR in the capitalist sense, as the breaking down of the
particular labour which produces a definite commodity into a
series of simple and co-ordinated operations divided up amongst
different workers, presupposes the division of labour within
society outside the workshop, as SEPARATION OF OCCUPATIONS. On the
other hand, it [division of labour] increases it [separation of
occupations]. The product is increasingly produced as a commodity in the strict sense of the word, its exchange value becomes the
more independent of its immediate existence as use value, and its
production becomes more and more independent of its consumption by the producers and of its existence as use value for the
producers, the more one-sided it itself becomes, and the greater
the variety of commodities for which it is exchanged, the greater
the kinds of use values in which its exchange value is expressed,
and the larger the market for it becomes. The more this happens,
the more the product can be produced as a commodity; therefore
also on an increasingly *large scale.* The producer's indifference to
the use value of his product is expressed *quantitatively* in the
amounts in which he produces it, which bear no relation to his
own consumption needs, even when he is at the same time a
consumer of his own product. The *division of labour* within the
workshop is one of the methods used in this *production en masse*
and consequently in the production of the product. Thus the
division of labour within the workshop is based on the division of
OCCUPATIONS in society.

The size of the market has two aspects. First, the mass of
consumers, their numbers. But secondly, also, the number of
OCCUPATIONS which are independent of one another. The latter is
possible without the former. For example, when spinning and
weaving become divorced from domestic industry and agriculture,
all those engaged in agriculture become a market for spinners and
weavers. They likewise [form markets] for one another as a
consequence of the separation of their occupations. What the
division of labour in society presupposes above all, is that the

---

[a] See K. Marx, *A Contribution to the Critique of Political Economy.* Part One
(present edition, Vol. 29, pp. 324-34).— *Ed.*

different kinds of labour have become independent of one another in such a way that their products confront one another as commodities and must be EXCHANGED, that is, undergo the metamorphosis of commodities and stand in relation to one another as *commodities*. (This is why in the Middle Ages, the towns prohibited the spread of as many professions as possible to the countryside, not merely for the purpose of preventing competition—the only aspect seen by Adam Smith[a]—but in order to create markets for themselves.) On the other hand, the proper development of the division of labour presupposes a certain density of population. The development of the DIVISION OF LABOUR in the workshop depends even more on this density of population. This latter DIVISION is, to a certain extent, a precondition for the former and in turn intensifies it still further. It does this by splitting formerly correlated occupations into separate and independent ones, also by increasing and differentiating the indirect preliminary work they require; and as a result of the increase in both production and the population and the freeing of capital and labour it creates NEW WANTS and NEW MODES OF THEIR SATISFACTION.

Therefore when Hodgskin says "DIVISION OF LABOUR" is the effect not OF A STOCK OF COMMODITIES CALLED CIRCULATING CAPITAL but OF "CO-EXISTING LABOUR", it would be tautologous if in this context he understood by DIVISION OF LABOUR the SEPARATION OF TRADES. It would only mean that DIVISION OF LABOUR is the cause or the EFFECT of the DIVISION OF LABOUR. He can therefore only mean that DIVISION OF LABOUR within the workshop depends on the SEPARATION OF OCCUPATIONS, the SOCIAL DIVISION OF LABOUR, and is, IN A CERTAIN SENSE, ITS EFFECT.

It is not A "STOCK OF COMMODITIES" which gives rise to this SEPARATION OF OCCUPATIONS and with it the DIVISION OF LABOUR in the workshop, but it is the SEPARATION OF OCCUPATIONS (and DIVISION OF LABOUR) that is manifested in the STOCK OF COMMODITIES, or rather in the fact that A STOCK OF PRODUCTS becomes a STOCK OF COMMODITIES. // The PROPERTY, the characteristic feature of the *capitalist mode of production* and therefore of capital itself in so far as it expresses a definite relation of the producers to one another and to their product, is inevitably always described by the economists as the PROPERTY of the THING. //

[XV-869] If, however, "*PREVIOUS ACCUMULATION OF CAPITAL*" is being discussed from an economic standpoint (see Turgot, Smith,[b] etc.)

---

[a] A. Smith, *An Inquiry into the Nature and Causes of the Wealth of Nations...*, Book I, Ch. X, Part 2.—*Ed.*

[b] A. Smith, *An Inquiry into the Nature and Causes of the Wealth of Nations...*, Vol. II, London, 1843, pp. 250-51; see also present edition, Vol. 30, pp. 366-67.—*Ed.*

as a condition for the DIVISION OF LABOUR, then what is understood by
this is the previous CONCENTRATION OF A *STOCK OF COMMODITIES* as *capital*
in the possession of the buyer of labour, since the kind of
cooperation characteristic of the division of labour presupposes a
CONGLOMERATION of workers—consequently, accumulation of the
means of subsistence necessary for them while they are working—
increased productivity of labour—consequently, increase in the
amount of raw materials, instruments and *matières instrumentales*
which must be available in order that labour proceeds continuously, since it constantly requires large amounts of these things—
in short, the objective conditions of production on a large
scale.

Here, *accumulation of capital* cannot mean increase in the
amount of means of subsistence, raw materials and instruments of
labour as a *condition for the division of labour*, for in so far as the
accumulation of capital is taken to mean this, it is a consequence
of the division of labour, not its precondition.

Similarly, *accumulation of capital* cannot here mean that means of
subsistence for the workers must be available in general before
new necessaries are reproduced, or that products of their labour
must constitute the raw material and means of labour for the new
production which they carry out. For this is the condition of
labour in general and was just as true *before the development* of the
division of labour as it is after it.

On the one hand: if we consider the material element of
accumulation, it means nothing more than that the division of
labour requires the concentration of means of subsistence and
means of labour at particular points, whereas formerly these were
scattered and dispersed as long as the workers in individual
TRADES—which could not have been very numerous under these
conditions—themselves carried out all the manifold and consecu-
tive operations required for the production of one or more
products. Not an increase in *absolute* terms is presupposed, but
CONCENTRATION, the gathering together of more at a given point, and
of *relatively* more [means of labour] compared with the numbers
of workers brought together there. More flax, for example, [is
used] by the workers in manufacture (in proportion to their
numbers) than the relative amount of flax required in proportion
to all the peasants—both men and women—who used to spin flax
as a sideline. Hence, CONGLOMERATION of workers, CONCENTRATION of
raw materials, instruments, and means of subsistence.

On the other hand: if we consider the historical foundation on
which this process develops, from which manufacture arises, the

industrial mode of production whose characteristic feature is the division of labour, then this CONCENTRATION can only take place in the form that these workers are assembled together as wage workers, that is, as workers who must sell their labour capacity because their conditions of labour confront them as alien property, as an independent, alien force. This implies that these conditions of labour confront them as *capital*; in other words, these means of subsistence and means of labour (or, what amounts to the same thing, the disposal of them through the intermediary of money) are in the hands of individual owners of money or of commodities, who, as a result, become *capitalists.* The loss of the conditions of labour by the workers is expressed in the fact that these conditions become independent as capital or as things at the disposal of the capitalists.

Thus primitive accumulation, as I have already shown,[a] means nothing but the separation of labour and the worker from the conditions of labour, which confront him as independent forces. The course of history shows that this separation is a factor in social development. Once capital exists, the capitalist mode of production itself evolves in such a way that it maintains and reproduces this separation on a constantly increasing scale until the historical reversal takes place.

It is not the ownership of money which makes the capitalist a capitalist. For money to be transformed into capital, the prerequisites for capitalist production must exist, whose first historical presupposition is that separation. The separation, and therefore the existence of the conditions of labour as capital, is given in capitalist production; this separation which constantly reproduces itself and expands, is the foundation of production.

Accumulation by means of the reconversion of profit, or SURPLUS PRODUCE, into capital now becomes a continuous process as a result of which the increased products of labour which are at the same time its objective conditions, conditions of reproduction, continuously confront labour as *capital,* i.e. as forces—personified in the capitalist—which are alienated from labour and dominate it. Consequently, it becomes a specific function of the capitalist to accumulate, that is, to reconvert a part of the SURPLUS PRODUCE into conditions of labour. And the stupid economist concludes from this that if this operation did not proceed in this contradictory, specific way, it could not take place at all. Reproduction on an

---

[a] See K. Marx, *Outlines of the Critique of Political Economy...* (present edition, Vol. 28, pp. 387-99).— *Ed.*

extended scale is inseparably connected in his mind with *accumulation,* the capitalist form of this reproduction.

[XV-870] Accumulation merely presents as a *continuous process* what in *primitive accumulation* appears as a distinct historical process, as the process of the emergence of capital and as a transition from one mode of production to another.

The economists, caught as they are in the toils of the notions proper to the agents of the capitalist mode of production, advance a double *quid pro quo,* each side of which depends on the other.

On the one hand, they transform capital from a relationship into a thing, A STOCK OF COMMODITIES (already forgetting that commodities themselves are *not* things) which, in so far as they serve as conditions of production for new labour, are called capital and, with regard to their mode of reproduction, are called circulating capital.

On the other hand, they transform things into capital, that is, they consider the social relationship which is represented in them and through them as an attribute which belongs to the thing as such as soon as it enters as an element into the labour process or the technological process.

The concentration in the hands of non-workers *of raw materials and of the disposition over the means of subsistence* as powers dominating labour, the *preliminary* condition for the division of labour (later on, the division of labour increases not only concentration, but also the amount [available for] concentration by increasing the productive power of labour), in other words the *preliminary accumulation of capital* as the condition for the division of labour therefore means for them the augmentation or concentration (they do not differentiate between the two) of means of subsistence and means of labour.

On the other hand, these necessaries and means of labour would not operate as objective conditions of production if these things did not possess the attribute of being capital, if the product of labour, the condition of labour, did not absorb labour itself, if past labour did not absorb living labour, and if these things did not belong to themselves or *per procurationem*[a] to the capitalist instead of to the worker.

As if the division of labour was not just as possible if its conditions belonged to the associated workers (although historically it could not AT FIRST appear in this form, but can only achieve it as a result of capitalist production) and were regarded by the

---

[a] By proxy.— *Ed.*

latter as their own products and the material elements of their own activity, which they are by their very nature.

Furthermore, because in capitalist production capital appropriates the SURPLUS PRODUCE of the worker, consequently, because it has *appropriated* the products of labour and these now confront the worker in the form of capital, it is clear that the conversion of the SURPLUS PRODUCE into conditions of labour can only be initiated by the capitalist and only in the form that he turns the product of labour—which he has appropriated without any equivalent—into a means of production of new labour performed without receiving an equivalent. Consequently, the extension of reproduction appears as the transformation of profit into capital and as a *saving* by the capitalist who, instead of consuming the SURPLUS PRODUCE which he has acquired gratis, converts it anew into a means of exploitation of labour but is able to do this only in so far as he converts it again into productive capital; this entails the conversion of SURPLUS PRODUCE into means of labour. As a result, the economists conclude that the SURPLUS PRODUCE cannot serve as an element of new production if it has not been transformed previously from the product of the worker into the property of his EMPLOYER in order to serve as capital once again and to repeat the old process of exploitation. The more inferior economists add to this the idea of HOARDING and the accumulation of treasure. Even the better ones—Ricardo, for example—transfer the notion of renunciation from the hoarder to the capitalist.

The economists do not conceive capital as a relation. They cannot do so without at the same time conceiving it as a historically transitory, i.e. a relative—not an absolute—form of production. Hodgskin himself does not share this concept. In so far as it justifies capital it does not justify its justification by the economists, but on the contrary refutes it. Thus Hodgskin is not concerned in all this.

As far as matters stood between him and the economists, the kind of polemic he had to wage seemed to be mapped out beforehand and quite simple. To put it simply, he had to vindicate the one aspect which the economists elaborate "scientifically" against the fetishistic conception they accept *sans raison*,[a] naïvely and unconsciously from the capitalist way of looking at things. The utilisation of the products of previous labour, of labour in general, as materials, tools and means of subsistence, is necessary if the worker wants to use his products for new production. This

---

[a] Without thinking.— *Ed.*

particular mode of consumption of his product is productive. But what on earth has this kind of utilisation, this mode of consumption of his product, to do with the domination of this product over him, with its existence as capital, with the concentration [XV-870a] in the hands of individual capitalists of the right to dispose of raw materials and means of subsistence and the exclusion of the workers from ownership of their product? What has it to do with the fact that first of all they have to hand over their product gratis to a third party in order to buy it back again with their own labour and, what is more, they have to give him more labour in exchange than is contained in the product and thus have to create more SURPLUS PRODUCE for him?

Past labour exists here in two forms. As *product, use value.* The process of production requires that the workers consume one portion of this product [and use] another portion as raw materials and instruments of labour. This applies to the technological process and merely demonstrates the relations that have to exist in *industrial production* between the workers and the products of their own labour, their own products, in order to turn them into means of production.

Or, [as] *value.* This only shows that the value of their new product represents not only their present, but also their past labour, and that by increasing it they retain the old value, because they increase it.

The claim put forward by the capitalist has nothing to do with this process as such. It is true that he has appropriated the products of labour, of past labour, and that he therefore possesses a means for appropriating new products and living labour. This, however, is precisely the kind of procedure against which protests are made. The preliminary concentration and accumulation necessary for the "division of labour" must not take the form of *accumulation of capital.* It does not follow that because they are necessary, the capitalist must inevitably have the disposal of the conditions of labour of today created by the labour of yesterday. If accumulation of capital is supposed to be nothing but ACCUMULATED LABOUR, it by no means implies that accumulation OF OTHER PEOPLE'S LABOUR has to take place.

Hodgskin however does not follow this simple path, and at first this seems strange. In his polemic against the productivity of capital, to begin with, against circulating and then even more, against fixed capital, he seems to oppose or to reject the importance of *past labour,* or of its *product* for reproduction as a condition of new labour. From this follows the importance of past labour embodied in products for labour as present ἐνέργεια.[a] Why this change?

Since the economists identify past labour with *capital*—past labour being understood in this case not only in the sense of concrete labour embodied in the product, but also in the sense of social labour, materialised labour time—it is understandable that they, the Pindars of capital, emphasise the *objective* elements of production and overestimate their importance as against the *subjective element*, living, immediate labour. For them, labour only becomes efficacious when it becomes *capital* and confronts itself, the passive element confronting its active counterpart. The producer is therefore controlled by the product, the subject by the object, labour which is being embodied by labour embodied in an object, etc. In all these conceptions, past labour appears not merely as an objective factor of living labour, subsumed by it, but vice versa; not as an element of the power of living labour, but as a power over this labour. The economists ascribe a false importance to the objective factor of labour compared with labour itself in order to have also a *technological* justification for the *specific social form,* i.e. the *capitalist form,* in which the relationship of labour to the conditions of labour is turned upside-down, so that it is not the worker who makes use of the conditions of labour, but the conditions of labour which make use of the worker. It is *for this reason* that Hodgskin asserts on the contrary that this objective factor, that is, the entire material wealth, is quite unimportant compared with the living process of production and that, in fact, this wealth has no value in itself, but only in so far as it is a factor in the living production process. In doing so, he underestimates somewhat the value which the labour of the past has for the labour of the present, but in opposing economic fetishism this is quite all right. If in capitalist production—HENCE in political economy, ITS THEORETICAL EXPRESSION—past labour were met with only as a pedestal, etc., created for labour by labour itself, then such a controversial issue would not have arisen. It only exists because in the real life of capitalist production, as well as in its theory, *materialised labour* appears as a contradiction to itself, to *living labour.* In exactly the same way in religiously constrained reasoning, the product of thought not only claims but exercises domination over thought itself.

---

[a] Activity.—*Ed.*

27*

[XV-865] [114] The proposition

* "The effects attributed to a *stock of commodities*, under the name of circulating capital, are caused by *co-existing labour*" * ([p.] 9),[a]

means first of all:

The simultaneous co-existence of living labour brings about a large part of the effects which are attributed to the product of previous labour UNDER THE NAME OF CIRCULATING CAPITAL.

For example, a part of CIRCULATING CAPITAL consists of the stock of means of subsistence WHICH THE CAPITALIST IS SAID TO HAVE STORED UP TO SUPPORT THE LABOURER WHILE WORKING.

The *formation of a reserve stock* is by no means a feature peculiar to capitalist production although, since under it production and consumption are greater than ever before, the amount of commodities on the market—the amount of commodities in the sphere of circulation—is likewise greater than ever before. Here memories of HOARDING, of *accumulation of treasure* by *hoarders* are still discernible.

The consumption fund must be disregarded first of all because we are speaking here of capital and of industrial production. What has reached the sphere of individual consumption, whether it is consumed more quickly or more slowly, has ceased to be capital. // Although it can be partly reconverted into capital, for instance, houses, parks, crockery, etc. //

* "Do all the capitalists of Europe possess at this moment one week's food and clothing for all the labourers they employ? Let us first examine the question as to food. One portion of the food of the people is *Bread*, which is never prepared till within a few hours of the time when it is eaten... The produce of the baker cannot be stored up. In no case can the material of bread, whether it exist as corn or flour, be *preserved without continual labour*.* The CONVICTION of the worker employed by the *cotton spinner, that he will obtain bread when he requires it, and his master's conviction that the money he pays him will enable him to obtain it, arise simply from the fact that the bread has always been obtained when required" (l.c., [p.] 10).

"Another article of the labourer's food is milk, and milk is manufactured ... twice a day. If it be said that the cattle to supply it are already there, why, the answer is, they require *constant attention and constant labour, and their food, through the greater part of the year, is of daily growth.* The fields in which they pasture, require the hand of man.* The same applies to *meat; it cannot be stored up, for it begins instantly to deteriorate after it is brought to market" * ([p.] 10).

Because of moths, even of clothing * "only a *very small stock is ever prepared*, compared to the general consumption" * ([p.] 11).

"Mill says, and says justly, * what is annually produced is annually consumed,[b] so

---

[a] Cf. this volume, p. 401.— *Ed.*

[b] J. Mill, *Elements of Political Economy*, 2nd ed., London, 1824, p. 220.— *Ed.*

that, in fact, *to enable men to carry on all those operations which extend beyond a year,* there cannot be *any stock of commodities stored up.* Those who undertake them must rely, therefore, not *on any commodities already created,* but that other men will labour and produce what they are to subsist on till their own products are completed. Thus, should the labourer admit that some accumulation of circulating capital is necessary for operations terminated within the year ... it is plain, that in all operations which extend beyond a year, the labourer does not, and cannot, rely on *accumulated* capital" ([p.] 12).

"If we duly consider the number and importance of those wealth producing operations which are not completed within the year, and the numberless products of daily labour, necessary to subsistence, which are consumed as soon as produced, we shall be sensible that *the success and productive power of every different species of labour is at all times* m o r e *dependent on the co-existing productive labour of other men than on any* accumulation of circulating capital" ([p.] 13).

"It is by the *command* the capitalist possesses *over the labour of some men,* not by his possessing *a stock of commodities,* that he is *enabled* to support and consequently employ *other labourers*" ([p.] 14).

"The only thing which can be said to be stored up or previously prepared, is the *skill of the labourer*" ([p.] 12).

"All the effects usually attributed to accumulation of circulating capital are derived from *the accumulation and storing up of skilled labour,* and this most important operation is performed, as far as the great mass of the labourers is concerned, without *any circulating capital* whatever" ([p.] 13).

"The number of labourers must at all times depend on the *quantity of circulating capital,* or, as I should say, on the quantity of the *products of co-existing labour,* which labourers are allowed to consume" ([p.] 20).

[XV-866] "Circulating capital ... is created only for consumption; while fixed capital ... is made, not to be consumed, but to aid the labourer in producing those things which are to be consumed" * ([p.] 19).

Thus first of all:

"The success and productive power of every different species of labour is at all times more dependent on the *co-existing* productive labour of other men than on any accumulation of circulating capital",[a] that is, of "COMMODITIES ALREADY CREATED". These "ALREADY CREATED COMMODITIES" confront "THE PRODUCTS OF CO-EXISTING LABOUR".

// The part of capital which consists of instruments and materials of labour is as "COMMODITIES ALREADY CREATED" always a precondition in each *particular* TRADE. It is impossible to spin cotton which has not yet been "CREATED", to operate spindles which have yet to be manufactured, or to burn coal which has not yet been brought up from the mine. These always enter the process as forms of existence of PREVIOUS LABOUR. EXISTING LABOUR thus DEPENDS ON ANTECEDENT LABOUR and not ONLY ON CO-EXISTING LABOUR, although this ANTECEDENT LABOUR, whether in the form of means of labour or materials of labour, can only be OF ANY USE (PRODUCTIVE USE) when it is in contact

---

[a] Cf. above on this page.— *Ed.*

with living labour as a material element of it. Only as an element of industrial consumption, i.e. consumption by labour.

But when considering circulation and the reproduction process, we have seen that it is only possible to reproduce the commodity after it is finished and converted into money, because *simultaneously* all its elements have been produced and reproduced by means of CO-EXISTING LABOUR.[a]

A twofold progression takes place in production. Cotton, for example, advances from one phase of production to another. It is produced first of all as raw material, then it is subjected to a number of operations until it is fit to be exported or, if it is further worked up in the same country, it is handed over to a spinner. It then goes on from the spinner to the weaver and from the weaver to the bleacher, dyer, FINISHER, and thence to various workshops where it is worked up for definite USES, i.e. articles of clothing, bed-linen, etc. Finally it leaves the last producer for the consumer and enters into individual consumption if it does not enter into industrial consumption as means (not material) of labour. But whether it is to be consumed industrially or individually, it has acquired its final form as use value. What emerges from one sphere of production as a product enters another as a condition of production, and in this way, goes through many SUCCESSIVE phases until it receives its last FINISH as use value. Here PREVIOUS LABOUR appears continually as the condition for CO-EXISTING LABOUR.

Simultaneously, however, while the product is advancing in this way from one phase to another, while it is undergoing this real metamorphosis, production is being carried on in every phase. While the weaver spins the yarn, the spinner is simultaneously spinning cotton, and fresh quantities of [raw] cotton are in the process of production.

Since the continuous, constantly repeated process of production is, at the same time, a process of reproduction, it is therefore equally dependent on the *CO-EXISTING LABOUR* which produces the various phases of the product simultaneously, while the product is passing through metamorphoses from one phase to another. Cotton, yarn, fabric, are not only produced one after the other and from one another, but they are produced and reproduced *simultaneously,* alongside one another. What appears as the EFFECT of ANTECEDENT LABOUR, if one considers the production process of the

---

[a] See present edition, Vol. 30, pp. 449-51 and this volume, pp. 104-05, and 116-17.— *Ed.*

individual commodity, presents itself at the same time as the effect of CO-EXISTING LABOUR, if one considers the *reproduction process* of the commodity, that is, if one considers this production process in its continuous motion and in the entirety of its conditions, and not merely an isolated action or limited in its scope. There exists not only a cycle comprising various phases, but all the phases of the commodity are simultaneously produced in the various spheres and branches of production. If the same peasant first plants flax, then spins it, then weaves it, these operations are performed in SUCCESSION, but not simultaneously as the mode of production based on the division of labour within society presupposes.

No matter what phase of the production process of an individual commodity is considered, the ANTECEDENT LABOUR only acquires significance as a result of the LIVING LABOUR which it provides with the necessary conditions of production. On the other hand, however, these conditions of production without which LIVING LABOUR cannot realise itself always appear in the process as the result of ANTECEDENT LABOUR. Thus the COOPERATING LABOUR of the contributing branches of labour always appears as a passive factor and, as such a passive factor, it is a precondition. The economists emphasise this aspect. In reproduction and circulation, on the other hand, the mediating social labour on which the [production] process of the commodity in each particular phase depends and by which it is determined, appears as present, CO-EXISTING, CONTEMPORANEOUS LABOUR. The INCIPIENT FORMS of the commodity and its SUCCESSIVE or completed forms are produced simultaneously. Unless this happened it would not be possible, after it has undergone its real metamorphosis, to reconvert it from money into its conditions of existence. [XV-870b] A commodity is thus the product of ANTECEDENT LABOUR only in so far as it is the product of CONTEMPORANEOUS LIVING LABOUR. From the capitalist point of view, therefore, all material wealth appears only as a fleeting aspect of the flow of production as a whole, which includes the process of circulation. //

Hodgskin examines only one of the constituent parts of circulating capital. One part of circulating capital is however continuously converted into fixed capital and *matière instrumentale* and only the other part is converted into articles of consumption. Moreover, even that part of circulating capital which is ultimately transformed into commodities intended for individual consumption always exists, alongside the final form in which it emerges from the FINISHING PHASE as end product, simultaneously in the earlier phases in its INCIPIENT FORMS—[as] raw material or semi-manufactured goods, removed in various degrees from the final form of the product—in which it cannot as yet enter into consumption.[a]

The problem Hodgskin is concerned with is: what is the relation of the present labour performed by the worker for the capitalist to the labour contained in those articles on which his WAGES are spent, which, in actual fact, are the use values of which variable capital consists? It is admitted that the worker cannot work without finding these articles ready for consumption. And that is why the economists say that circulating capital—the PREVIOUS LABOUR, COMMODITIES ALREADY CREATED which the capitalist has stored up—is the condition for labour and, amongst other things, also the condition for the division of labour.

When the conditions of production, and especially circulating capital are being discussed in the sense Hodgskin views them, it is usual to declare that the capitalist must have accumulated the means of subsistence which the worker has to consume before HIS NEW COMMODITY IS FINISHED, that is, while he works, while the commodity he produces is only *in statu nascendi*.[b] This is shot through with the notion that the capitalist either gathers things like a hoarder or that *he* stores up a supply of means of subsistence like the bees their honey.

This however is merely a *modus loquendi*.[c]

First of all, we are not speaking here of the SHOPKEEPERS who sell means of subsistence. These must naturally always have a full STOCK IN TRADE. Their stores, SHOPS, etc., are simply reservoirs in which the various commodities are stored once they are ready for circulation. This kind of storing is merely an *interim period* in which the commodity remains until it leaves the sphere of circulation and enters that of consumption. It is its mode of existence as a *commodity* on the market. Strictly speaking, as a commodity it exists only in this form. It does not affect the matter whether, instead of being in the possession of the first seller (the producer), the commodity is in the possession of the 3rd or 4th and finally passes into the possession of the seller who sells it to the real consumer. (It merely means that, in the intermediate stages, exchange of capital (really of capital+profit, for the producer sells not only the capital in the commodity but also the profit made on the capital), for capital is taking place, and in the last stage

---

[a] In the manuscript, Marx wrote "Circulating capital" in the margin near the paragraph.— *Ed.*

[b] In the nascent state.— *Ed.*

[c] A mode of expression, a figure of speech.— *Ed.*

exchange of capital for REVENUE (provided the commodity is intended not for industrial but for individual consumption, as is assumed here). The commodity which is a finished use value and marketable, enters the market as a commodity, in the phase of circulation; all commodities enter this phase when they undergo their first metamorphosis, the transformation into money. If this is called "storing up" then it means nothing more than "circulation" or the existence of commodities as commodities.) This kind of "storing" is exactly the opposite of treasure-hoarding, the aim of which is to retain commodities permanently in the form in which they are capable of entering into circulation, and it achieves this only by withdrawing commodities in the form of money from circulation. If production, and therefore also consumption, is varied and on a mass scale, then a great quantity of the most diverse commodities will be found continually at this *stopping place*, at this *intermediate station*, in a word, in circulation or on the market. Regarded from the standpoint of *quantity*, storing on a large scale in this context means nothing more than production and consumption on a large scale.

The STOP *made by the commodities,* their sojourn at this stage of the process, their presence on the market instead of in the MILL or in a private house (as articles of consumption) or in the SHOP or the store of the SHOPKEEPER, is only a [XV-871] tiny fraction of time in their life-process. The immobile, independent existence of this "world of commodities", "of things", is only illusory. The station is always full, but always full of different travellers. The same commodities (commodities of the same kind) are constantly produced anew in the sphere of production, available on the market and absorbed in consumption. Not the identical commodities, but commodities of the same type, can always be found in these 3 stages *simultaneously.* If the INTERVAL is prolonged so that the commodities which emerge anew from the sphere of production find the market still occupied by the old ones, then it becomes overcrowded, a STOPPAGE occurs, the market is SURCHARGED, the commodities decline in value, there is *overproduction.* Where, therefore, the intermediate stage of circulation acquires independent existence so that the flow of the stream is not merely held up, where the existence of the commodities in the circulation phase appears as *storing up,* then this is not brought about by a free act on the part of the producer, it is not an aim or an immanent aspect of production, any more than the flow of blood to the head leading to apoplexy is an immanent aspect of the circulation of the blood. Capital as *commodity capital* (and this is the form in which it appears in the circulation phase, on the market) must not become stationary, it must only constitute a pause in the movement. Otherwise the reproduction process is interrupted and the whole mechanism is thrown into confusion. This objectified wealth which is concentrated at a few points is—and can only be—very small in comparison to the continuous stream of production and consumption. Wealth, therefore, according to Smith, is "the *annual*" reproduction.[a] It is not, that is to say, something out of the dim past. It is always something which emerges from yesterday. If, on the other hand, reproduction were to stagnate due to some disturbances or others, then the stores, etc., would soon empty, there would be shortages and it would soon be evident that the permanency which the existing wealth appears to possess, is only the permanency of its being replaced, of its reproduction, that it is a continuous objectification of social labour.

The movement $C—M—C$ also takes place in the transactions of the SHOPKEEPER. In so far as he makes a "profit", it is a matter which does not concern us here. He sells a commodity and buys the same commodity (the same type of commodities) over again. He sells them to the consumer and buys them again from the producer. Here the same (type of) commodity is converted perpetually into money and money back again continuously into the same commodity. This movement, however, simply represents continuous reproduction, continuous production and consumption, for reproduction includes consumption. (The commodity must be sold, must reach the sphere of consumption in order that it can be reproduced.) It must be accepted as a use value. (For $C—M$ for the seller is $M—C$ for the buyer, that is, the conversion of money into a commodity as a use value.) The reproduction process, since it is a unity of circulation and production, includes consumption, which is itself an aspect of circulation. Consumption is itself both an aspect and a condition of the reproduction process. If one considers the process in its entirety, the SHOPKEEPER, in fact, pays the producer of the commodities with the same sum of money as the consumer pays him when he buys from him. He represents the consumer in his dealings with the producer and the producer in his dealings with the consumer. He is both seller and buyer of the same commodity. The money with which he buys is, in fact, considered from a purely formal standpoint, the final metamor-

---

[a] A. Smith, *An Inquiry into the Nature and Causes of the Wealth of Nations...*, Vol. II, London, 1843, pp. 250-52 and 355 ff.— *Ed.*

phosis of the consumer's commodity. The latter transforms his money into the commodity as a use value. The passing of the money into the SHOPKEEPER's hands thus signifies the consumption of the commodity or, considered formally, the transition of the commodity from circulation into consumption. In so far as he buys again from the producer with the money, this constitutes the first metamorphosis of the producer's commodity and signifies the transition of the commodity into the *INTERVAL*, where it remains as a *commodity* in the sphere of circulation. *C—M—C*, in so far as it represents the transformation of the commodity into the consumer's money and the transformation back again of the money, whose owner is now the SHOPKEEPER, into the same commodity (a commodity of the same kind), expresses merely the *constant* passing over of commodities into consumption, for the vacuum left by the commodity reaching the sphere of consumption must be filled by the commodity emerging from the production process and now entering this stage.

[XV-872] The *period during which the commodity stays* in circulation and is replaced by a new commodity naturally depends also on the length of time in which the commodities remain in the production sphere, that is, on the duration of their reproduction time, and varies in accordance with their different length. For example, the reproduction of corn requires a year. The corn harvested in the autumn, for example, of 1862 (in so far as it is not used again for seed) must suffice for the whole coming year—until autumn 1863. It is thrown all at once into circulation (it is already in circulation when it is placed in the farmers' granaries) and absorbed in the various reservoirs of circulation— storehouses, corn merchants, millers, etc. These reservoirs serve as channels both for the commodities issuing from production and those going to the consumer. As long as the commodities remain in them, they are *commodities* and are therefore on the market, in circulation. They are withdrawn only piecemeal, in small quantities, by the annual consumption. The replacement, the stream of new commodities which are to displace them, arrives only in the following year. Thus these reservoirs are only depleted gradually, in the measure that their replacements move forward. If there is a surplus and if the new harvest is above the AVERAGE, then a STOPPAGE takes place. The space which these particular commodities were to have occupied in the market is overstocked. In order to permit the whole quantity to find a place on the market, the price of the commodities is reduced, and this causes them to move again. If the total quantity of use values is too large, they accommodate themselves to the space they occupy by a CONTRACTION of their *prices.* If the quantity is too small, it is expanded by an increase of their *prices.*

On the other hand, commodities which quickly deteriorate as use values remain only for a very short time in the reservoirs of circulation. The period of time during which they have to be converted into money and reproduced, is prescribed by the nature of their use value which, if it is not consumed daily or almost daily, is spoilt and consequently ceases to be a commodity. For exchange value along with its basis, use value, disappears provided the disappearance of use value is not itself an act of production.

In general, it is clear that although in *absolute* terms the *quantity* of the commodities which have been stored up in the reservoirs of circulation increases as a result of the development of industry, because production and consumption increase, this same quantity represents a decrease in comparison with the total annual production and consumption. The *transition* of commodities from circulation to consumption takes place more rapidly. And for the following reasons. The speed of reproduction increases:

1) When the commodity passes rapidly through its various production phases, that is, when each production phase of the production process is reduced in length; this is due to the fact that the labour time necessary to produce the commodity in each one of its forms is reduced; this is a result, therefore, of the development of the division of labour, use of machinery, application of chemical processes, etc. (The development of chemistry makes it possible to artificially speed up the transition of commodities from one state of aggregation to another, their combination with other material which, for instance, occurs in dyeing, their separation from [other] substances as in bleaching; in short, both [modifications in] the form of the same substance (its state of aggregation) as well as changes to be brought about in the substance, are artificially accelerated quite apart from the fact, that for vegetative and organic reproduction, plants, animals, etc., are supplied with cheaper substances, that is, substances which cost less labour time.)

2) Partly as a result of the combination of various branches of industry, that is, the establishment of centres of production for particular industrial branches, [partly] through the *development of means of communication,* the commodity proceeds rapidly from one phase to another; in other words, the interim period, the interval during which the commodity remains in the intermediate station between one production phase and another is reduced, that is, the

transition from one phase of production to another is shortened.

3) This whole development—the shortening both of production phases and of the transition from one phase to another—presupposes production on a large scale, mass production and, at the same time, production based on a large amount of constant capital, especially fixed capital; [it requires] therefore a continuous flow of production. But not in the sense in which we have earlier considered the flow, that is, not as the closing and overlapping of the separate production phases, but in the sense that there are no *deliberate* breaks in production. These occur as long as work is done to order, as in [XV-873] the handicrafts, and continue even in manufacture properly so called (in so far as this has not been reshaped by large-scale industry). But now, however, work is carried out on the scale allowed by the capital. This process does not wait on demand, but is a function of capital. Capital works on the same scale continuously (if one disregards accumulation or expansion) and constantly develops and extends the productive forces. Production is therefore not only *rapid,* so that the commodity quickly acquires the form in which it is suitable for circulation, but it is continuous. Production here appears only as constant reproduction and at the same time it takes place on a mass scale.

Thus if the commodities remain in the circulation reservoirs for a long time—if they accumulate there—then they will soon glut them as a result of the speed with which the waves of production follow one another and the huge amount of goods which they deposit continuously in the reservoirs. It is in this sense that *Corbet,* for example, says THE MARKET IS *ALWAYS* overstocked.[a] But the same circumstances which produce this speed and mass scale of reproduction likewise reduce the necessity for the accumulation of commodities in these reservoirs. In part—in so far as it is concerned with *industrial consumption*—this is already implied by the close succession of the production phases which the commodity itself or its ingredients have to undergo. If coal is produced daily on a mass scale and brought to the manufacturer's door by railways, steamships, etc., he does not need to keep a STOCK of coal, or at most only a very small one; or, what amounts to the same thing, if a SHOPKEEPER acts as an intermediary, he only needs to keep a small amount of stock over and above the amount he sells daily

---

[a] Th. Corbet, *An Inquiry into the Causes and Modes of the Wealth of Individuals; or the Principles of Trade and Speculation Explained,* Part I, London, 1841, pp. 115-17; cf. also this volume, p. 130.— *Ed.*

and which is daily delivered to him. The same applies to yarn, iron, etc. But apart from *industrial consumption*, in which the stock of commodities (that is, the stock of the ingredients of commodities) must decline in this way, the SHOPKEEPER likewise enjoys the benefits of the speed of communications first of all, and secondly, the certainty of a continuous and rapid renewal and delivery. Although his STOCK of commodities may grow in size, each element of it will remain in his reservoir, in a state of transition, for a shorter period of time. In relation to the total amount of commodities which he sells, that is, in relation to the scale of both production and consumption, the STOCK of commodities which he *accumulates* and *keeps* in store, will be small. It is different in the less developed stages of production where reproduction proceeds slowly—where therefore more commodities must remain in the circulation reservoirs—, the means of transport are slow, the communications difficult and, as a consequence, the *renewal of STOCK* can be interrupted and a great deal of time elapses as a result between the emptying and the refilling of the reservoir— that is, the *renewal* of the STOCK IN hand. The position is then similar to that of products whose reproduction takes place yearly or half-yearly, that is, in more or less prolonged periods of time, owing to the nature of their use values.

(For example, cotton is an illustration of how transport and communications affect the emptying of the reservoirs. Since ships continually ply between Liverpool and the UNITED STATES—speed of communications is one factor, continuity another—all the cotton supply is not shipped at once. It comes on to the market gradually (the producer likewise does not want to flood the market all AT ONCE). It lies at the docks in Liverpool, that is, already in a kind of circulation reservoir, but not in such quantities—in relation to the total consumption of the article—as would be required if the ship from America arrived only once or twice [a year,] after a journey of six months. The cotton manufacturer in Manchester and other places stocks his warehouse roughly in accordance with his immediate consumption needs, since the electric telegraph and the railway make the TRANSFER from Liverpool to Manchester possible at a moment's notice.)

Special filling of the reservoirs—in so far as this is not due to the overstocking OF THE MARKET, which can happen much more easily in these circumstances than under archaically slow conditions— occurs only for speculative reasons and merely in exceptional cases because of A REAL or SUSPECTED FALL OR RISE OF PRICES. Regarding this *relative decline* in stock, that is, the commodities which are in circulation, compared with the amount of production and consumption, see *Lalor*,[a] [*The*] *Economist, Corbet*[b] (give the corresponding quotations [XV-874] after Hodgskin). *Sismondi* wrongly saw something lamentable in all this (his writings to be looked up as well).[c]

(On the other hand, there is indeed a continuous *extension of the market* and in the degree that the *interval of time* decreases in which the commodity remains on the market, its *flow in space* increases, that is, the market expands spatially, and the periphery in relation to the centre, the production sphere of the commodity, is circumscribed by a constantly extending radius.)

The fact that consumption lives from hand to mouth, changes its linen and its coat as rapidly as it does its opinions, and does not wear the same coat ten years running, etc., is connected with the speed of reproduction, or is another expression of it. To an increasing extent consumption—even of articles where this is not demanded by the nature of their use value—takes place almost simultaneously with production and becomes therefore more and more dependent on the PRESENT, CO-EXISTING LABOUR (since it is, IN FACT, exchange of CO-EXISTING LABOUR). This takes place in the same degree in which past labour becomes an ever more important factor of production, even though this past itself is after all a very recent and only relative one.

(The following example demonstrates how closely the keeping of a stock is linked with deficiencies of production. As long as it is difficult to keep cattle throughout the winter, there is no fresh meat in winter. As soon as stock-farming is able to overcome this difficulty, the *stock* previously made up of substitutes for fresh meat—pickled or smoked varieties—ceases of itself.)

(The product only becomes a commodity where it enters into circulation. The production of goods as commodities, hence circulation, expands enormously as a result of capitalist production for the following reasons:

1. *Production* takes place on a large scale; the *quantity*, the *huge amounts produced*, therefore, do not stand in any kind of quantitative relationship to the producer's needs; IN FACT it is *pure chance* whether he consumes any, even a small part of his own

---

[a] J. Lalor, *Money and Morals: a Book for the Times*, London, 1852, pp. 43-44.— *Ed.*

[b] Th. Corbet, *An Inquiry into the Causes and Modes of the Wealth of Individuals...*— *Ed.*

[c] J. Ch. L. Simonde de Sismondi, *Études sur l'économie politique*, Vol. 1, Brussels, 1837, p. 49 ff.— *Ed.*

product. He only consumes his own product on a mass scale where he produces PART OF THE INGREDIENTS OF HIS OWN CAPITAL. On the other hand, in the earlier stages only those products which exceed the amount required by the producer himself become commodities or, at any rate, this is mainly the case.

2. The *narrow range* of goods produced [stands] in inverse ratio to the increased variety of needs. This leads to previously combined branches of production becoming increasingly separated and independent—in short, to increasing division of labour within society—a contributing factor is the establishment of new branches of production and the multiplication of KINDS OF COMMODITIES produced. ([To be inserted] at the end, after Hodgskin, also *Wakefield* about this.) This VARIEGATION and DIFFERENTIATION OF COMMODITIES arises in two ways. The different *phases of one and the same product,* as well as the auxiliary operations (that is, the labour connected with various constituent parts, etc.) are separated and become different branches of labour, independent of one another; or various phases *of one* product become DIFFERENT KINDS OF COMMODITIES. But secondly, owing to labour and capital (or labour and SURPLUS PRODUCT) becoming free; on the other hand, to the discovery of new practical applications of the same use value, either because new needs arise as a result of the modification of No. 1 (for example, the need for more rapid and universal means of transport and communication arising with the application of steam in industry) and therefore new means of satisfying them, or new possibilities of utilising the same use value are discovered, or new substances or new methods (plastic-galvanisation, for instance) for treating well-known substance in different ways, etc. All this amounts to the following: *One produce in its successive phases or conditions converted into different commodities.* Creation of *new products* or new *values in use* as commodities.*

3. *Transformation of the majority of the population* who formerly consumed a mass of products *in naturalibus*[a] into *wage workers.*

4. *Transformation of the tenant farmer into an industrial capitalist* (and with it the conversion of rent into money rent) and generally of all payments in kind (taxes, etc., rent) into money payments). In general—industrial exploitation of the land with the result that it is no longer confined to its own muck-heap as previously, but that both its chemical and mechanical conditions of production—even seeds, fertilisers, cattle, etc.—are subjected to the process of exchange of matter.

---

[a] In kind, in this context it means: within the framework of a natural economy.— *Ed.*

5. *Mobilisation of a mass of previously "inalienable" possessions* [*by conversion*] *into commodities* and the creation of forms of property which only exist in negotiable papers. On the one hand, alienation of landed property. //The lack of property of the masses causes them, for example, to regard the dwelling in which they live as a commodity.// [On the other hand,] railway shares, in short, all kinds of shares.

[XV-875] Back again to Hodgskin now.

It is obvious that by *"storing up"* [means of subsistence] *for* the workers by the capitalists one cannot understand that commodities which are passing from production into consumption are in the circulation reservoirs, in the circulation system, on the market. This would mean that the products circulate for the benefit of the worker and become *commodities* for his sake; and that in general, the production of products as commodities is undertaken for his sake. The worker shares with every other [commodity owner] the need to transform the commodity he sells—which in actual fact, though not in form, is his labour—at first into money in order to convert the money back again into commodities which he can consume. It is perfectly obvious that [no] division of labour (in so far as it is based on commodity production), [no] wage labour and, in general, no capitalist production can take place without *commodities*—whether they be means of consumption or means of production—being available on the market; that this kind of production is impossible *without* commodity circulation, [without] the commodities spending a period of time in the circulation reservoirs. For the product is a commodity κατ' ἐξοχήν [a] only within the framework of circulation. It is as true for the worker as for anybody else that he must find his means of subsistence in the form of *commodities.*

The worker, moreover, does not confront the SHOPKEEPER as a worker confronts a capitalist, but as money confronts the commodity, as a buyer faces the seller. There is no relationship of wage labour to capital here, except, of course, where the SHOPKEEPER is dealing with his *own* workers. But even they, in so far as they buy things from him, do not confront him as workers. They confront him as workers only in so far as he buys from them. Let us therefore leave this *circulation agent.*

But as far as the industrial capitalist is concerned, his *stock,* his accumulation, consists of:

---

[a] In the strict sense of the word.— *Ed.*

[First,] his fixed capital, i.e. buildings, machinery, etc., which the worker does not consume or, in so far as he does consume them, does so through labour, and thus consumes them industrially *for* the capitalist, and although they are means of labour they are not means of subsistence for him.

Secondly, his raw materials and *matières instrumentales,*[a] the STOCK of which, in so far as it does not enter directly into production, declines, as we have seen. This likewise does not consist of means of subsistence for the workers. This "*accumulation*" by the capitalist for the worker means nothing more than that he does the worker the favour of depriving the latter of his conditions of labour as property and converting the means of his labour (which are themselves merely the transformed product of his labour) into means for the exploitation of labour. In any case, the worker, while he uses the machines and the raw materials as means of labour, does not live on them.

Thirdly, the commodities, which he keeps in the storehouse or warehouse before they enter into circulation. These are products of labour, not means of subsistence stored in order to maintain it, labour, during the course of production.

Thus the "accumulation" of means of subsistence by the capitalist for the worker means merely that he must possess enough money in order to pay wages with which the worker withdraws the articles of consumption he needs from the circulation reservoirs (and, if we consider the class as a whole, with which he buys back part of his own product). This money, however, is simply the transformed form of the commodity which the worker has sold and handed over. In this sense, the means of subsistence are "stored up" for him in the same way as they are stored up for his capitalist, who likewise buys consumption goods, etc., with money (the transformed form of the same commodity). This money may be a mere token of value, it therefore does not have to be a representation "OF PREVIOUS LABOUR" but, in the hands of whoever possesses it, simply expresses the realised price not of past labour (or previously [sold] commodities) but of the CONTEMPORANEOUS LABOUR or commodities which he sells. [Money has] merely a formal existence.[b] Or—since in previous modes of production the worker also had to eat and consume during the course of production irrespective of the period of time required for the

---

a Instrumental materials.— *Ed.*
b See K. Marx, *A Contribution to the Critique of Political Economy.* Part One (present edition, Vol. 29, p. 289).— *Ed.*

production of his product—"storing up" may mean that the worker must first of all transform the product of his labour into the product of the capitalist, into capital, [XV-876] in order to receive back a portion of it in the form of money, in lieu of payment.

What interests Hodgskin about this whole process (with regard to the process as such it is indeed a matter of indifference whether the worker receives the product of CONTEMPORANEOUS OR PREVIOUS LABOUR, just as it does not matter whether he receives the product of his own previous labour or the product of labour performed simultaneously in a different branch) is this:

A great part, [or] the greatest part of the products consumed daily by the worker—which he must consume whether his own product is finished or not—represents by no means STORED UP LABOUR OF BYGONE TIMES. On the contrary they are TO A GREAT DEGREE products of labour performed the same day or during the same week in which the worker produces his own commodity. For example, bread, meat, beer, milk, newspapers, etc. Hodgskin could also have added that they are partly the products of *future* labour, for the worker who buys an overcoat with what he has saved out of 6 months' WAGES buys one which has only been made at the end of the 6 months, etc. (We have seen that the whole of production presupposes *simultaneous* reproduction of the required constituent parts and products in their different forms as raw materials, semi-manufactured goods, etc. But all fixed capital presupposes *future* labour for its reproduction and for the reproduction of its equivalent, without which it cannot be reproduced.) Hodgskin says that during the course of the year the worker must RELY TO SOME DEGREE ON PREVIOUS LABOUR (because of the nature of the production of corn, vegetable raw materials, etc.). (This does not apply to a house, for example. As regards use values which, by their nature, only wear out slowly, are not consumed at once, but gradually used up, it is not due to any action specially devised for the benefit of the workers that these products of previous labour are available on the "market". The worker also used to have a "dwelling" before the capitalist "piled up" deadly stinkholes for him. (See *Laing* on this.[a])) (Apart from the enormous mass of day-to-day needs which are of decisive importance especially to the *worker,* who, at best, can only satisfy his everyday needs, we have seen that, in general, *consumption* becomes more and more

---

[a] S. Laing, *National Distress; its Causes and Remedies,* London, 1844, pp. 149-54.— *Ed.*

CONTEMPORANEOUS with *production,* and therefore, if one considers society as a whole, consumption depends more and more on *simultaneous* production, or rather on the products of *simultaneous* production.) But when operations extend over several years, the worker must "depend" on his own production, on the simultaneous and future producers of other commodities.

The worker always has to find his means of subsistence in the form of *commodities* on the market (the "SERVICES" he buys are *eo ipso*[a] only brought into being at the moment they are bought); they are relative, the PRODUCE OF ANTECEDENT LABOUR, that is of LABOUR which is ANTECEDENT to their existence as produce but which is by no means ANTECEDENT TO HIS OWN LABOUR WITH WHOSE PRICE HE BUYS THIS PRODUCE. They can be CONTEMPORANEOUS PRODUCTS, and are so most of all for those who live from hand to mouth.

TAKING IT ALL IN ALL the "storing up" of means of subsistence for the worker by the capitalist comes to this:

1) Commodity production presupposes that articles of consumption which one does not produce oneself are available on the market as commodities, or that *in general, commodities* are produced *as commodities.*

2) The majority of the commodities consumed by the worker in the final form in which they confront him as commodities, are IN FACT products of *simultaneous* labour (they are therefore by no means stored up by the capitalist).

3) In capitalist production, the means of labour and the means of subsistence produced by the worker himself confront him as capital, the one as constant, the other as variable capital; these, the worker's conditions of production, appear as the property of the capitalist; their transfer from the worker to the capitalist and the partial return of the worker's product to the worker, or of the value of his product to the worker, is called the "storing up" of circulating capital for the worker. These means of subsistence which the worker must always consume before his product is finished, become "circulating capital" because he, instead of *buying* them direct or *paying* for them with the value either of his past or of his future [XV-877] product, must first of all receive a *draft* (money) on it; a draft moreover which the capitalist is entitled to issue only thanks to the worker's past, present or future product.

Hodgskin is concerned here with demonstrating the dependence of the worker on the CO-EXISTING LABOUR of other workers as against his dependence on PREVIOUS LABOUR,

---

[a] By that fact.— *Ed.*

1) in order to do away with the phrase about "storing up";

2) because "PRESENT LABOUR" confronts capital, whereas the economists always consider "PREVIOUS LABOUR" to be capital *eo ipso,* that is, an *alienated* and independent form of labour which is hostile to labour itself.

To grasp the all-round significance of CONTEMPORANEOUS LABOUR as against PREVIOUS labour is however in itself a very important achievement.

Hodgskin thus arrives at the following:

Capital is either a mere name and pretext or it does not express a *thing,* the social relation of the labour of one person to the CO-EXISTING LABOUR of another, and the consequences, the EFFECTS of this relationship, are ascribed to the things which make up so-called circulating capital. Despite the fact that the commodity exists as money, its realisation in use values depends on CONTEMPORANEOUS LABOUR. ([The labour performed in] the course of a year is itself CONTEMPORANEOUS.) Only a small portion of the commodities entering into direct consumption are the product of more than one year's labour and when they are—such as cattle, etc., they require renewed labour every year. All operations requiring more than a year depend on continuous annual production.

* "It is by the command the capitalist possesses over *the labour of some men,* not by his possessing a stock of commodities, that he is enabled to *support* and consequently employ *other* labourers" * ([p.] 14).

Money however gives everyone "COMMAND" over "THE LABOUR OF SOME MEN", over the labour embodied in their commodities as well as over the reproduction of this labour, and to that extent therefore over labour itself.

What is really "stored up", not however as a dead mass but as something living, is the *skill* of the worker, the level of development of labour. (It is true, however, that the stage of the development of the productive power of labour which exists at any particular time and serves as the starting-point, comprises not only the skill and capacity of the worker, but likewise the material means which this labour has created for itself and which it daily renews. (Hodgskin does not emphasise this because, in opposing the crude views of the economists, it is important for him to lay the stress on the *subject*—so to speak, on the subjective in the subject—in contrast to the object.)) This is really the primary factor, the point of departure and it is the result of a process of development. *Accumulation* in this context means *assimilation,* continual preservation and at the same time transformation of what has already been handed over and realised. In this way Darwin makes "accumulation" through inheritance the driving principle in the formation of all organic things, of plants and animals; thus the various organisms themselves are formed as a result of "accumulation" and are only "inventions", gradually accumulated inventions of living beings.[a] But this is not the only prerequisite of production. Such a prerequisite in the case of animals and plants is external nature, that is both inorganic nature and their relationship with other animals and plants. Man, who produces in society, likewise faces an already modified nature (and in particular natural factors which have been transformed into means of his own activity) and definite relations existing between the producers. This accumulation is in part the result of the historical process, in part, as far as the individual worker is concerned, TRANSMISSION OF SKILL. Hodgskin says that as far as the majority of the workers are concerned, circulating capital plays no part in this accumulation.

He has demonstrated that "THE STOCK OF COMMODITIES" (means of subsistence) "PREPARED" is always small in comparison with the total amount of consumption and production. On the other hand, the DEGREE OF SKILL of the existing population is always the precondition of production as a whole; it is therefore the principal accumulation of wealth and the most important result of ANTECEDENT LABOUR; its form of existence, however, is living labour itself.

[XV-878] *"All the effects usually attributed to accumulation of circulating capital are derived from the *accumulation and storing up of skilled labour,* and this most important operation is performed, as far as the great mass of the labourers is concerned, without any circulating capital whatever"* ([p.] 13).

With regard to the assertion of the economists that the number of workers (and therefore the well-being or poverty of the existing working population) depends on the amount of circulating capital available, Hodgskin comments correctly, as follows:

*"The number of labourers must at all times depend on the *quantity* of *circulating capital,* o r, as I should say, on the *quantity of the products of co-existing labour,* which labourers are *allowed* to consume"* ([p.] 20).

What is attributed to CIRCULATING CAPITAL, to a STOCK OF COMMODITIES, is the effect of "CO-EXISTING LABOUR". In other words, Hodgskin says that the effects of a certain social form of labour are ascribed to objects, to the products of this labour; the relationship itself is imagined to exist in *material* form. We have already seen that this is a characteristic of labour based on commodity production, on

---

[a] See Ch. Darwin, *On the Origin of Species by Means of Natural Selection, or the Preservation of Favoured Races in the Struggle for Life.—Ed.*

exchange value, and this *quid pro quo* is revealed in the commodity, in money (Hodgskin does not see this), and to a still higher degree in capital.[a] The effects of things as materialised aspects of the labour process are attributed to them in capital, in their personification, their independence in respect of labour. They would cease to have these effects if they were to cease to confront labour in this *alienated form.* The *capitalist,* as capitalist, is simply the personification of capital, that creation of labour endowed with its own will and personality which stands in opposition to labour. Hodgskin regards this as a pure subjective illusion which conceals the deceit and the interests of the exploiting classes. He does not see that the way of looking at things arises out of the actual relationship itself; the latter is not an expression of the former, but vice versa. In the same way, English socialists say: "We need capital, but not the capitalist."[b] But if one eliminates the capitalist, the means of production cease to be *capital.*

//The "VERBAL OBSERVER", Bailey, and others remark[c] that "VALUE", "valeur" express a property of things. In fact the terms originally express nothing but the use value of things for people, those qualities which make them useful or agreeable, etc., to people. It is in the nature of things that "VALUE", "valeur", "Werth" can have no other etymological origin. Use value expresses the natural relationship between things and men, in fact the existence of things for men. *Exchange value,* as the result of the social development which created it, was later superimposed on the word value=use value. It [exchange-value] is the *social* existence of things.

> *Sanskrit Wer* [means] cover, protect, consequently respect, honour and love, cherish. From these the adjective *Wertas* (EXCELLENT, RESPECTABLE) is derived; *Gothic,* wairths; *Teutonic,* wert; ANGLO-SAXON, weorth, vordh, wurth; *English,* WORTH, WORTHY; *Dutch,* waard, waardig; *Alemannic,* werth; *Lithuanian,* werthas (respectable, precious, dear, estimable). *Sanskrit,* Wertis; *Latin,* virtus; *Gothic,* wairthi; *Teutonic,* Werth.[d]

The value of a thing is, in fact, its own *virtus,*[e] while its exchange value is quite independent of its material QUALITIES.

---

[a] K. Marx, *A Contribution to the Critique of Political Economy.* Part One (see present edition, Vol. 29, pp. 275-78, 289 and 387).— *Ed.*

[b] See J. F. Bray, *Labour's Wrongs and Labour's Remedy; or, the Age of Might and the Age of Right,* Leeds, 1839, p. 59; also present edition, Vol. 31, p. 247.— *Ed.*

[c] See this volume, pp. 316 and 347.— *Ed.*

[d] See [H. J.] Chavée, *Essai d'étymologie philosophique ou recherches...,* Brussels, 1844, p. 176. Here and below, Marx quotes from Chavée partly in French.— *Ed.*

[e] Virtue.— *Ed.*

Sanskrit Wal [means] cover, fortify; [*Latin*] *vallo*,[a] *valeo*,[b] *vallus*[c]: *valor* is the power itself. HENCE *valeur, VALUE.* Compare Wal with the Teutonic *walle, walte*[d] and English WALL, WIELD.[e] [115]//

Hodgskin now turns to *fixed capital.* It is productive power which has been produced and, in its development in large-scale industry, it is an instrument which *social* labour has created for itself.

As far as fixed capital is concerned:

*"... all instruments and machines are the produce of labour" ([p.] 14).[f] "As long as they are merely the result of *previous* labour, and are not applied to their respective uses by labourers, they do not repay the expense of making them. ... most of them diminish in value from being kept... *Fixed capital does not derive its utility from previous, but present labour;* and does not *bring its owner a profit* because it has been stored up, but because it is a *means of obtaining command over labour"* * ([pp.] 14-]15).

Here at last, the nature of capital is understood correctly.

[XV-879] *"After any instruments have been made, what do *they* effect? Nothing. On the contrary they begin to rust or decay unless used or applied by labour" ([p.] 15). "Whether an instrument shall be regarded as productive capital or not, depends entirely on its *being used,* or not, by some productive labourer" ([pp.] 15-16).

"One easily comprehends why ... the road-maker should receive some of the benefits, accruing only to the road-user; but I do not comprehend *why all these benefits should go to the road itself,* and be *appropriated* by a set of persons who neither make nor use it, under the name of profit for their capital" ([p.] 16).

"The vast utility of the steam-engine does not depend on stored up iron and wood, but on that *practical and living knowledge of the powers of nature* which enables some men to construct it, and others to guide it" ([p.] 17).

"Without knowledge they" (the machines) "could not be invented; without manual skill and dexterity they could not be made, and without skill and labour they could not be productively used. But there is nothing more than the knowledge, skill, and labour required, on which the capitalist can found a claim to any share of the produce" ([p.] 18).

"After he" (man) "has *inherited the knowledge of several generations,* and *when he lives congregated into great masses,* he is enabled by his mental faculties to complete the work of nature" (l.c.).

"It is not the *quantity* but the *quality* of the fixed capital on which the productive industry of a country depends. ... fixed capital as a means of nourishing and supporting men, depends for its efficiency, altogether on the skill of the labourer, and consequently the productive industry of a country, as far as fixed capital is concerned, is in *proportion* to *the knowledge and skill of the people"* ([pp.] 19-20).

---

[a] To surround with a wall, to fortify, to defend.— *Ed.*
[b] To be strong, vigorous.— *Ed.*
[c] Wall.— *Ed.*
[d] Rule, govern, control.— *Ed.*
[e] See [H. J.] Chavée, op. cit., p. 70.— *Ed.*
[f] Here and below, Marx quotes from [Th. Hodgskin,] *Labour Defended..*— *Ed.*

Compound interest.

"A mere glance must satisfy every mind that *simple profit* does not decrease but increase in the progress of society, i.e. the same quantity of labour which at any former period produced 100 qrs of wheat, and 100 steam-engines, will now produce somewhat more.... In fact, also, we find that a much greater number of persons now live in opulence on profit in this country than formerly. It is clear, however, that *no labour, no productive power*, no ingenuity, and no art, *can answer the overwhelming demands of compound interest.* But all saving *is made from the revenue of the capitalist*" * (that is from * simple profit), so that actually these demands are constantly made, and as constantly the productive power of labour refuses to satisfy them. A sort of balance is, therefore, constantly struck" * [116] ([p.] 23).

For example, if the profit were always accumulated, a capital of 100 at 10% would amount to something like 673, or—since a little *plus ou moins*[a] makes no difference here—say 700, in 20 years. Thus the capital will have multiplied itself sevenfold over a period of 20 years. According to this yardstick, if only simple interest were paid, it would have to be 30% per annum instead of 10, that is, three times as much profit, and the more we increase the number of years that elapse, the more the rate of interest or the rate of profit calculated at simple interest per annum will increase, and this increase is the more rapid, the larger the capital becomes.

In fact, however, capitalist accumulation is nothing but the reconversion of interest into capital (since interest and profit for our purpose, i.e. for the purpose of our calculation, are identical). Thus it is compound interest. First there is a capital of 100; it yields 10[%] profit (or interest). This is added to the capital which is now 110. This now becomes the capital. The interest on this amount is therefore not simply interest on a capital of 100 but interest on $100C+10I$. That is compound interest. Thus, at the end of the 2nd year, we have $(100C+10I)+10I+1I=(100+10I)+11I=121$. This is the *capital* at the beginning of the 3rd year. In the 3rd year we get $(100C+10I)+11I+12^{1}/_{10}I$, so that at the end of it the capital is $133^{1}/_{10}$.

[XV-880] We have:

Capital	Interest	Total
First year 100	10	110
Second year $(100+10)$	$10+1'$*	121
Third year $(100+20I+1I')=121$	$10+2'+^{1}/_{10'}$	$133^{1}/_{10}$
Fourth year $(100+30I+1I'+$ $+[2]I'+^{1}/_{10''})=133^{1}/_{10}$	$(10+3'+^{1}/_{10''}+^{2}/_{10''}+$ $+^{1}/_{100'''})=$	$146^{41}/_{100}$

---

[a] More or less.— *Ed.*

[Capital]	[Interest]	[Total]
Fifth year $(100+40I+1I'+2I'+ +1/_{10}I''+3I'+1/_{10}I''+2/_{10}I''+ +1/_{100}I''')=146^{41}/_{100}$ etc.	$[10+4^{641}/_{1,000'}=$	$161^{51}/_{1,000}]$

In the 2nd *year* the capital	comprises	*10 interest* (simple)
In *the 3rd year* the capital	comprises	21 interest
In *the 4th year* the capital	comprises	$33^1/_{10}$ interest
In *the 5th year* the capital	comprises	$46^{41}/_{100}$ interest
In *the 6th year* the capital	=	$161^{51}/_{1,000}$, consequently $61^{51}/_{1,000}$ [interest]
In *the 7th year* the capital	=	$177^{1,561}/_{10,000}$ $[77^{1,561}/_{10,000}$ interest]
In *the 8th year* [the capital]	=	$194^{87,171}/_{100,000}$ $[94^{87,171}/_{100,000}$ interest]
[In the 9th year the capital	=	$214^{358,881}/_{1,000,000}$, which comprises $114^{358,881}/_{1,000,000}$ interest]

* The sign ′ indicates interest on interest.

In other words, more than half the capital is made up of interest in the 9th year and the portion of capital consisting of interest thus increases in geometrical progression.

We have seen that over 20 years, capital increased sevenfold, whereas, even according to the "most extreme" assumption of Malthus, the population can only double itself every 25 years. But let us assume that it doubles itself in 20 years, and therefore the working population as well. Taking one year with another, the interest would have to be 30%—three times greater than it is. If one assumes, however, that the rate of exploitation remained unchanged, in 20 years the doubled population (and it would be unfit for work during a considerable part of these 20 years, scarcely during half this period would it be able to work, in spite of the employment of children) would only be able to produce twice as much labour as it did previously, and therefore only twice as much surplus labour, but not three times as much.

The rate of profit (and consequently the rate of interest) is determined:

1) If the rate of exploitation is assumed to be constant—by the number of workers in employment, by the absolute mass of workers employed, that is, by the growth of the population. Although this number increases, its ratio to the total amount of capital employed declines with the accumulation of capital and with industrial development (consequently the rate of profit [declines] if the rate of exploitation remains the same). Likewise

the population does not by any means [increase] in the same geometrical progression as the computed compound interest. The growth of the population at a given stage of industrial development is the explanation for the increase in the amount of surplus value and of profit, but also for the fall in the rate of profit.

2) [By] the absolute length of the normal working day, that is, by increasing the rate of surplus value. Thus the rate of profit can increase as a result of the extension of labour time beyond the normal working day. However, this has its *physical* and—BY AND LARGE—its social LIMITS. That in the same measure as workers set more capital in motion, the same capital commands more absolute labour time [XV-881] IS OUT OF THE QUESTION.

3) If the normal working day remains the same, SURPLUS LABOUR can be increased relatively by reducing the necessary labour time and reducing the prices of the necessaries which the worker consumes, in comparison with the development of the productive power of labour. But this very development of productive power reduces variable capital relative to constant. It is physically impossible that the surplus labour time of, say, 2 men who displace 20, can, by any conceivable increase of the absolute or relative labour time, equal that of the 20. If each of the 20 men only work 2 hours of surplus labour a day, the total will be 40 hours of surplus labour, whereas the total life span of the 2 men amounts only to 48 hours in one day.

The value of labour capacity does not fall in the same degree as the productive power of the workers or of capital increases. This increase in productive power likewise increases the ratio between constant and variable capital in all branches of industry which do not produce NECESSARIES (either directly or indirectly) without giving rise to any kind of alteration in the VALUE OF LABOUR. The development of productive power is not even. It is in the nature of capitalist production that it develops industry more rapidly than agriculture. This is not due to the nature of the land, but to the fact that, in order to be exploited really in accordance with its nature, land requires different social relations. Capitalist production turns towards the land only after its influence has exhausted it and after it has devastated its natural qualities. An additional factor is that, as a consequence of landownership, agricultural products are more expensive compared with other commodities, because they are sold at *their* value and are not reduced to their cost price. They form, however, the principal constituent of the NECESSARIES. Furthermore, if $^1/_{10}$ of the land is dearer to exploit than the other $^9/_{10}$, these latter are likewise hit "artificially" by this relative infertility, as a result of the law of competition.[a]

The rate of profit would in fact have to grow if it is to remain constant while accumulation of capital is taking place. As long as capital yields 10% of surplus labour, the same worker must, as soon as interest accumulates on interest and thus increases the capital employed, produce threefold, fourfold, fivefold IN PROGRESSION OF COMPOUND INTEREST, WHICH IS NONSENSE.

The *amount of capital* which the worker sets in motion, and whose value is maintained and reproduced by his labour, is something quite different from the *value* which he adds, and therefore from the surplus value. If the amount of capital=1,000 and the labour added=100, then the capital reproduced=1,100. If the amount=100 and the labour added=20, then the capital reproduced=120. The rate of profit in the first case=10% and in the second=20%. Nevertheless, more can be accumulated from 100 than from 20. Thus the flow of capital or its "accumulation" continues // apart from depreciation as a result of the increase in productive power // in proportion to the force it already possesses, but not in proportion to the size of the rate of profit. This explains that accumulation—its amount—may increase in spite of a falling rate of profit, apart from the fact that, while productivity rises, a larger portion of the REVENUE can be accumulated, even when the rate of profit declines, than when there is a high rate of profit together with lower productivity. A high rate of profit—in so far as it is based on a high rate of surplus value—is possible if very long hours are worked, although the labour is unproductive. It is possible because the workers' needs, and *therefore* the minimum wage, are very small, although the labour is unproductive. The lack of energy with which the labour is performed will correspond to the low level of the minimum [wage]. Capital is accumulated slowly in both cases despite the high rate of profit. The population is STAGNANT and the labour time which the product costs is high, although the wages received by the workers are small.

[XV-882] I have explained the decline in the rate of profit in spite of the fact that the rate of surplus value remains the same or even rises, by the decrease of the variable capital in relation to the constant, that is, of the living PRESENT LABOUR in relation to the PAST LABOUR which is EMPLOYED AND REPRODUCED.[b] Hodgskin and the man who

---

[a] See present edition, Vol. 31, pp. 427-32, 484-87, 519-21.— *Ed.*
[b] See this volume, pp. 73-74, 543.— *Ed.*

wrote *The Causes and Remedy of Distress*[a] explain it by the fact that it is impossible for the worker to fulfil the demands of CAPITAL which ACCUMULATES like *COMPOUND INTEREST*.

* "No labour, no productive power, no ingenuity, and no art, can answer the overwhelming demands of compound interest. But all saving is made from the revenue of the capitalist" * (that is from * simple profit) "so that actually these demands are constantly made, and as constantly the productive power of labour refuses to satisfy them. A sort of balance is, therefore, constantly struck" * [116] (l.c., [p.] 23).[b]

In its general sense, this amounts to the same thing. If I say that, as capital accumulates, the rate of profit declines because constant capital increases in relation to variable capital, it means that, disregarding the specific form of the different portions of capital, the capital employed increases in relation to the LABOUR EMPLOYED. The profit falls not because the worker is exploited less, but because altogether less labour is employed in relation to the capital employed. For example, let us assume that the ratio of variable to constant capital$=1:1$. Then, if the total capital$=1,000$, $c=500$ and $v=500$. If the rate of surplus value$=50\%$, then 50% of $500=50\times5=250$. Thus the rate of profit on $1,000$ yields a profit of $250,=^{250}/_{1,000}=^{25}/_{100}=^1/_4=25\%$.

If the total capital$=1,000$ and if $c=750$ and $v=250$, then at 50% [the rate of surplus value] 250 will yield 125. But $^{125}/_{1,000}=^{25}/_{200}=^5/_{40}=^1/_8=12^1/_2\%$.

But in comparison with the first case [less] living labour is employed in the second case. If we assume that the annual wage of the worker$=£25$, then in the first case $£500$ employed$=20$ workers; in the second case wages$=£250=10$ workers. The same capital employs 20 workers in one case and only 10 in the other. In the first case, the ratio of total capital to the number of working days$=1,000:20$; in the second, $1,000:10$. In the first case, for each of the 20 workers $£50$ capital (constant and variable) is used (for $20\times50=500\times2=1,000$). In the second case, the capital employed per individual worker is $£100$ (for $100\times10=1,000$). Consequently, in both cases, the capital which is allocated to WAGES is, *pro rata,* the same.

The formula I have given provides a new ground for explaining why, with accumulation, less workers are employed by the same amount of capital or, what amounts to the same thing, why a greater amount of capital has to be used for *the same amount* of

a A reference to *The Source and Remedy of the National Difficulties...—Ed.*
b [Th. Hodgskin,] *Labour Defended...*; cf. also this volume, p. 431.—*Ed.*

labour. It comes to the same thing if I say that 1 worker is employed for a capital outlay of 50 in one case, and 1 worker for a capital outlay of 100 in the other, that therefore only half a worker is employed by a capital of 50; in other words, if I say that in one case there is 1 worker for 50 capital and only half a worker for 50 capital in the other, or if I say that in one case 50 capital is used by 1 worker and in the other case 50×2 capital is used by 1 worker.

This latter formula is the one used by Hodgskin and others. According to them, accumulation means in general the demand for compound interest; in other words, that more capital is expended on *one* worker and that he has therefore to produce more surplus labour proportionally to the amount of capital expended on him. Since the capital expended on him increases at the same rate as COMPOUND INTEREST, but on the other hand, his labour time has very definite limits which even relatively "NO PRODUCTIVE POWERS" can reduce in accordance with the DEMANDS of this COMPOUND INTEREST, "A SORT OF BALANCE IS CONSTANTLY STRUCK".[116] "SIMPLE profit" remains the same, or rather it grows. (This is IN FACT the SURPLUS LABOUR or SURPLUS VALUE.) But as the result of the accumulation of capital it is COMPOUND INTEREST which is disguised in the form of SIMPLE INTEREST.

[XV-883] It is clear furthermore that if COMPOUND INTEREST=accumulation, then, apart from the absolute limits of accumulation, the growth of this interest depends on the extent, the intensity, etc., of the accumulation process itself, that is, on the *mode of production.* OTHERWISE compound interest is nothing but appropriation of the *capital* (property) of *others* in the form of interest as was the case in Rome and in general with usurers.

Hodgskin's view is as follows: Originally £50 capital, for example, falls *pro rata* to one worker, on which he produces, let us say, a profit of [£]25.[117] Later, as a result of the conversion of a part of the interest into capital and of the fact that this process repeats itself again and again, a capital of £200 is allocated to the worker. If the entire interest of 50% received per annum were always capitalised, the process would be complete in less than 4 years. Just as the worker produced [a profit of] 25 on [a capital of] 50, he is now expected to produce 100 on a capital of 200, or 4 times as much. But that is impossible. To do that either the worker would have to work 4 times as long, that is, 48 hours a day if he worked 12 hours previously, or the VALUE OF LABOUR would have to fall by 75 per cent as a result of increased productive power of labour.

If the working day=12 hours, £25 the [annual] wage, and the worker produces £25 profit [per annum], then he has to work as much for the capitalist as he does for himself. That is for 6 hours or half the working day. In order to produce 100, he would have to work 4×6 hours for the capitalist in a 12-hour working day—which is NONSENSE. Let us assume that the working day is lengthened to 15 hours, then the worker still cannot produce 24 hours work in 15 hours. And still less can he work for 30 hours, which is what would be necessary, since [he would have to work] 24 hours for the capitalist and 6 for himself. If he worked the whole of his labour time for the capitalist, he would be able to produce only 50; he would only double the amount of interest, that is, he would produce 50 [profit] on a capital of 200, whereas he produced 25 for 50 capital. The rate of profit=50% in the second case and 25% in the first. But even this is impossible, since the worker must live. No matter how much productive power increases, if, as in the above example, the value of 12 hours=75, then that of 24 hours=2×75=150. And since the worker must live, he can never produce 150 profit, still less 200. His surplus labour is always a *part* of his working day, from which it does not at all follow, as Mr. Rodbertus thinks,[a] that profit can never=100%. It can never=100% if it is calculated on the working day as a whole (for it is *itself* included in it). But it can most certainly be 100% in relation to that part of the working day which is paid for.

Let us take the above example of 50%.

Capital		Surplus value	Rate of surplus value	Rate of profit
Constant	Variable			
25	25	25	100%	50%

Here the profit, half a working day=$^1/_3$ of the whole [product]. [XV-884] Then the surplus value=100%.

If the worker worked $^3/_4$ of the working day for the capitalist, then:

Capital		Surplus value	[Rate of] profit	Rate of surplus value
Constant	Variable			
25	$12^1/_2$	$37^1/_2$		300%
Total capital				
$37^1/_2$		$37^1/_2$	100%	

---

a See present edition, Vol. 31, pp. 319-21.—*Ed.*

For 100:

Capital		Surplus value	Rate of surplus value
Constant	Variable		
$66^2/_3$	$33^1/_3$	100	300%
[Total capital] 100			

Rate of profit
100%

Let us examine this a little more closely and see what is implied by the view that [the rate of] *profit falls* because, in consequence of progressive accumulation, it does not constitute SIMPLE *profit* (consequently the rate of exploitation of the worker does not decline but, as Hodgskin says, increases [a]) but COMPOUND *profit* and it is impossible for labour to keep pace with the demands of COMPOUND INTEREST.

It has to be noted first of all that this has to be defined in more detail if it is to make any sense at all. Regarded as a product of accumulation (that is, of the appropriation of surplus labour)— and this approach is necessary if one considers reproduction as a whole—all capital is made up of profit (or of interest, if this word is considered to be synonymous with profit and not with INTEREST in the strict sense). If the rate of profit=10%, then this is "compound interest", compound profit. And it would be impossible to see how 10 to 100 could—in economic terms—differ from 11 to 110. So what emerges is that "SIMPLE PROFIT" too is impossible, or at least that SIMPLE PROFIT must also decline, because, in fact, SIMPLE PROFIT is made up in exactly the same way as compound profit. If one narrows the problem, that is, considers solely interest-bearing capital, then compound interest would swallow up profit and more than profit; and the fact that the producer (capitalist or not) has to pay the lender compound interest means that sooner or later, in addition to profit, he has to pay him part of his capital as well.

Thus it should be noted first of all that Hodgskin's view only has meaning if it is assumed that capital grows more rapidly than population, that is, than the working population. (Even this latter is a relative growth. It is in the nature of capital to overwork one section of the working population while it turns another into paupers.) If the population grows at the same rate as capital, then there is no reason whatsoever why I should [not] be able to extract from 8 x workers with £800 the same surplus labour that I can extract from x workers with £100. [XV-885] Eight times 100

[a] See this volume, pp. 431-32.— *Ed.*

capital makes no greater demand on 8 times *x* workers than 100 capital on *x* workers. Thus "Hodgskin's" *argument* becomes groundless. (In reality, things turn out differently. Even if the population grows at the same rate as capital, capitalist development nevertheless results in one part of the population being made REDUNDANT, because constant capital develops at the expense of variable capital.)

//* "It is very material, with reference to *labour*, whether you distribute them" (*goods*[a]) "so as to induce a *greater supply of labour* or a less: whether you distribute them where they will be conditions for labour, or where they will be opportunities for idleness" (*An Inquiry into those Principles respecting the Nature of Demand etc.*, London, 1821, [p.] 57).

"That increased supply (of labour) is promoted by the increased *numbers* of mankind" (l.c., [p.] 58).

"The not being able to *command so much labour* as before, too, is only important where the labour would produce no more than before. If labour has been rendered more productive, production will not be checked, though the *existing mass of commodities should command less labour than before*" * (l.c., [p.] 60).

This is directed against Malthus. TRUE, PRODUCTION WOULD NOT BE CHECKED, BUT THE RATE OF PROFIT WOULD. These cynical propositions stating that A "MASS OF COMMODITIES *COMMANDS* LABOUR", reflect the same cynicism which finds expression in Malthus' explanation of value [b]; *command of the commodity over labour* is very good and is absolutely characteristic of the nature of capital.

The same author makes the following correct observation directed against West:

* "The author of *An Essay on the Application of Capital to Land* says [p. 24] that more will be given for labour when there is most increase of stock, and *that* ... will be when the profits on stock are highest. 'The greater the profits of stock,' he adds, 'the higher will be the wages of labour.' The fault of this is, that a word or two is left out: 'The greater *have been* the profits of stock, ... The higher *will be* the wages of labour'... The high profits and the high wages are not *simultaneous*; they do not occur in the same *bargain*; the one counteracts the other, and reduces it to a level. It might as well be argued, 'the supply of a commodity is most rapid when the price is highest; therefore, large supply and high price go together.' It is a mixing up of cause and effect" * (l.c., [pp.] 100-01).//

Hodgskin's proposition, therefore, has meaning only if, as a result of the process of accumulation, more *capital* is set in motion by the same worker, or if the capital grows *pro rata* to labour. That is, if, for example, the capital was 100 and becomes 110 by accumulation, and if the same worker who produced a surplus

---

a In the manuscript, this word is followed by its German equivalent.— *Ed.*
b See this volume, pp. 211-12 and 225.— *Ed.*

value of 10, is to produce a surplus value of 11, corresponding to the growth of capital, i.e. compound interest. So that it is not simply the same capital he set in motion previously which, after its reproduction, is to yield the same profit (SIMPLE PROFIT) but this capital has been increased by his surplus labour [so that] he has to provide surplus labour for the original capital (or its value)+his own accumulated (i.e. capitalised) surplus labour. And since this capital increases every year, the same worker would constantly have to furnish more labour.

It is however only possible for more capital to be applied per worker:

First. If the productive power of labour remains the same, then this is only possible if the worker prolongs his labour time absolutely, i.e., for example, if he works 15 hours instead of 12 hours, or if he works more intensively and performs 15 hours' labour in 12 hours, does 5 hours' labour in 4 hours or $^5/_5$ hour's labour in $^4/_5$ of an hour. Since he reproduces his means of subsistence in a definite number of hours, then, in this case, 3 hours of labour are won for the capitalist in the same way as if the productive power of labour had been increased, while, in fact, it is labour which has been increased, not its productive power. If the intensification of labour were to become general, then the value of commodities would fall in proportion to the reduced labour time which they cost. The degree of intensity would become the average intensity of labour, its natural quality. If, however [XV-886], this only occurs in particular spheres, then it amounts to more complex labour, simple labour raised to a higher power. [Less than] an hour of more intensive labour then counts as much—and creates as much value—as an hour of the more extensive labour. For example, in the above case, $^4/_5$ of an hour [produces] as much as $^5/_5$, or an hour.

Both the extension of labour time and the increase of labour through its greater intensification by means of the compression of the pores of labour as it were, have their limits (although the London bakers, for example, regularly work 17 hours [a day] if not more), very definite, physical, limitations, and it is when encountering these that compound interest—COMPOSITE profit—ceases.

Within these limitations the following applies:

If the capitalist pays nothing for the extension or INTENSIFICATION of labour, then his SURPLUS VALUE (his profit as well, provided there is no CHANGE in the VALUE of the constant capital, for we assume that the mode of production remains the same)—and, in accordance with the proviso, his profit—increases more rapidly than his capital. He pays NO NECESSARY LABOUR for the capital which has been added.

If he pays for the surplus labour at the same rate as previously, then the growth of the SURPLUS VALUE is proportionate to the increase in capital. The profit grows more rapidly. For there is a more rapid turnover of fixed capital, while the more intensive use of the machinery does not cause the wear and tear to increase at the same rate. There is a reduction of expenditure on fixed capital, for less machinery, workshops, etc., are required for 100 workers who work longer hours than for 200 workers employed simultaneously. Likewise fewer OVERLOOKERS, etc. (This gives rise to a most satisfactory situation for the capitalist, who is able to expand or contract his production without hindrance, in accordance with the market conditions. In addition, his power grows, since that portion of labour which is over-employed, has its counterpart in an unemployed or semi-employed reserve army, so that competition amongst the workers increases.)

Although there is in this case no change in the purely numerical ratio between NECESSARY LABOUR and SURPLUS LABOUR—this is however the only case where both can simultaneously increase in the same proportion—the exploitation of labour has NEVERTHELESS grown, both by means of an extension of the working day and by its INTENSIFICATION (condensation) provided the working day is not shortened at the same time (as with the Ten Hours Bill[118]). The period for which the worker is fit to work is reduced and his labour capacity is exhausted in a much greater measure than his wages increase and he becomes even more of a work machine. But disregarding the latter aspect, if he lives for 20 years working a normal working day and only 15 years when his working day is extended or intensified, then he sells the value of his labour capacity in 15 years in the latter case and in 20 years in the former. In one case it has to be replaced in 15 years, in the other, in 20 years. A value of 100 which lasts for 20 years is replaced if 5% is paid on it annually, for $5 \times 20 = 100$. A value of 100 which lasts 15 years is replaced if $6^{10}/_{15}$ or $6^{2}/_{3}\%$ is paid on it annually. But in the given case, the worker receives for 3 hours of additional labour only an amount equivalent to the daily value of his labour capacity calculated over 20 years. Assuming that he works 8 hours NECESSARY LABOUR and 4 hours SURPLUS LABOUR, then he receives $^{2}/_{3}$ of each hour, for $\dfrac{12 \times 2}{3} = 8$. And in the same way he receives 2 out of the 3 hours OVERTIME that he works. Or $^{2}/_{3}$ of each hour. But this is only the value of his hourly labour capacity on the assumption that it will last for 20 years. If he uses it up in 15 years, its value [per hour] increases.

ANTICIPATION of the future—real ANTICIPATION—occurs in the production of wealth only in relation to the worker and to the land. The future can indeed be anticipated and ruined in both cases by premature over-exertion and exhaustion, and by the disturbance of the balance between expenditure and income. In capitalist production this happens to both the worker and the land. As far as so-called ANTICIPATION is concerned, in relation to the national debt, for example, Ravenstone remarks with justice:

[XV-887] * "In pretending to stave off the expenses of the present hour to a future day, in contending that you can burthen posterity to supply the wants of the existing generation,* they assert the absurd proposition *that you can consume what does not yet exist, that you can feed on provisions before their seeds have been sown in the earth" (Ravenstone, l.c., [*Thoughts on the Funding System, and Its Effects,* p.] 8).

"All the wisdom of our statesmen will have ended in a great transfer of property from one class of persons to another, in creating an enormous fund for the reward of jobs and peculation"* (l.c., [p.] 9).

It is different in the case of the worker and the land. What is EXPENDED here EXISTS as δύναμις[a] and the life span of this δύναμις is shortened as a result of accelerated EXPENDITURE.

Finally, if the capitalist is forced to pay more for OVER-TIME than for normal labour time, then, according to the facts outlined above, this is by no means an increase in wages, but only compensation for the increased value of OVERTIME—and in reality overtime pay is rarely sufficient to cover this. In fact, in order to pay for the increased wear and tear of the labour capacity, when OVERTIME is worked, a higher rate ought to be paid for every working hour not merely for OVERTIME. Thus there is UNDER ALL CIRCUMSTANCES an increased exploitation of labour. At the same time, as a result of the accumulation of capital, a [relative] reduction in SURPLUS VALUE takes place at all events and also a decline in the rate of profit, in so far as this is not counteracted by saving on constant capital.[119]

This is therefore a situation where, in consequence of the accumulation of capital—of the appearance of COMPOSITE profit—the rate of profit must decline. If on a capital of 300 (the original amount) the rate of profit was 10[%] (that is [profit came to] 30), and if for an additional 100 it is 6[%], then profit is 36 for 400.

---

[a] Power, capacity.— *Ed.*

Thus on the whole it is 9 for 100. And the rate of profit has fallen from 10[%] to 9.

But, as has been stated, on this basis (if the productivity of labour remains the same) not only must the profit on ADDITIONAL CAPITAL fall, but at a certain point it must cease altogether, thus the whole accumulation based on this COMPOSITE PROFIT would BE STOPPED. In this case, the decline in profit is linked with increased exploitation of labour and the STOPPAGE of profit AT A CERTAIN POINT is not due to the worker or SOMEBODY ELSE receiving the whole product of his labour, but to the fact that it is physically impossible to work over and above a certain amount of labour time or to increase the intensity of labour beyond a certain degree.

Second. The only other case, where, with the number of workers remaining constant, more capital is applied per worker, and therefore the surplus capital can be laid out and used for the increased exploitation of the same number [XV-888] [of workers] occurs when *the productivity of labour increases, i.e. the method of production is changed.* This presupposes a CHANGE in the organic ratio between constant and variable capital. In other words, the increase in the capital in relation to labour is here identical with the increase of constant capital as compared with variable capital and, in general, with the amount of living labour employed.

This is where Hodgskin's view merges with the general law which I have outlined. The SURPLUS VALUE, i.e. the exploitation of the worker, increases, but, at the same time, the rate of profit falls because the variable capital declines as against the constant capital, because in general, the amount of living labour falls relatively in comparison with the amount of capital which sets it in motion. A larger portion of the annual product of labour is appropriated by the capitalist under the signboard of capital, and a smaller portion under the signboard of profit.

(Hence the phantasy of the *Rev. Thomas Chalmers* to the effect that the smaller the amount of the annual product laid out by the capitalists as capital, the larger the profit they pocket.[a] The ESTABLISHED CHURCH[69] then comes to their assistance and sees to it that a large part of the SURPLUS PRODUCE is consumed instead of being capitalised. The miserable priest confuses cause with effect. Moreover, with a smaller rate the amount of profit increases as the size of the capital laid out grows. In addition, the quantity of use values which this smaller proportion represents,

---

[a] See Th. Chalmers, *On Political Economy in Connexion with the Moral Prospects of Society,* 2nd ed., Glasgow, 1832, pp. 88-89.— *Ed.*

increases. At the same time, however, this leads to the centralisation of capital, since the conditions of production now demand the application of capital on a mass scale. It brings about the swallowing up of the smaller capitalists by the bigger ones and the "decapitalisation" of the former. This is once again, only in a different form, the separation of the conditions of labour from labour // for there is still a great deal of self-employment amongst the smaller capitalists; in general the labour done by the capitalist stands in inverse proportion to the size of his capital, that is, to the degree in which he is a capitalist. This process would soon bring capitalist production to a head if it were not for the fact that, alongside the centripetal forces, counteracting tendencies exist, which continuously exert a decentralising influence; this need not be described here, for it belongs to the chapter dealing with the competition of capitals //.[30] It is this separation which constitutes the concept of capital and of *primitive* accumulation, which then appears as a continual process in the accumulation of capital and here finally takes the form of the centralisation of already existing capitals in a few hands and of many being divested of capital.)

The fact that the (proportionally) declining quantity of labour is not fully offset by increased productivity, or that the ratio of surplus labour to the capital expended does not increase at *the same* rate as the *amount of labour employed* declines, is due partly to the fact that the development of the productivity of labour reduces the VALUE OF LABOUR, the NECESSARY LABOUR, only in certain capital investment spheres, and that, even in these spheres, it does not develop uniformly, and that factors exist which nullify this effect; for example, the workers themselves, although they cannot prevent reductions in (the value of) wages, will not permit them to be reduced to the absolute minimum; on the contrary, they can compel a certain quantitative participation in the general growth of wealth.

But this growth of surplus labour too is relative, [and is only possible] within certain limits. In order to make this growth correspond to the demands of COMPOSITE INTEREST, the necessary labour time in this case would have to be reduced to zero in the same way as [the surplus labour time] had to be extended endlessly in the case considered previously.

The rise and fall in the rate of profit—in so far as it is determined by the rise or fall of wages resulting from the conditions of demand and supply [in the labour market], or caused by the temporary rise or fall in the prices of NECESSARIES compared with those of LUXURIES, as a result of the changes in demand and supply and the rise or fall in wages to which this leads—has as little to do with the general law of [XV-889] the rise or fall in the profit rate as the rise or fall in the market prices of commodities has to do with the determination of value in general. This has to be analysed in the chapter on the real movement of wages.[120] If the balance of demand and supply is favourable to the workers, then wages rise, then it is *possible* (but by no means certain) that the prices of certain NECESSARIES, especially food, will rise correspondingly for a time. The author of the *Inquiry into Those Principles etc.* rightly remarks in this connection:

> In this case * there will be "an increase of demand for necessaries, in proportion to that for superfluities, as compared with what would have been the proportion between those two sorts of demand, if he had exerted that command" * (i.e. the capitalist, his COMMAND over commodities) * "to procure things for his own consumption. Necessaries will thereby exchange for more of things in general... And, in part, at least, these necessaries will be food" * (l.c., [pp. 21-]22).

He then correctly expresses the Ricardian view as follows:

> * "At all events, then, the increased price of corn was not the *original* cause of that rise of wages which made profits fall, but, on the contrary, the rise of wages was the cause of the increased price of corn at first, and the nature of land, yielding less and less proportional returns to increased tillage, made part of that increase of price *permanent,* prevented a complete *reaction* from taking place through the principle of population" * (l.c., [p.] 23).

Hodgskin and the author of *The Cause and Remedy,*[a] since they explain the fall OF PROFITS by the impossibility of LIVING LABOUR TO COME UP TO THE DEMANDS OF "COMPOUND INTEREST", and although they do not go into detail, are much nearer the truth than Smith and Ricardo, who explain the FALL OF PROFITS by the RISE in WAGES, one of them, in REAL and NOMINAL WAGES, the other, in NOMINAL WAGES, WITH RATHER A DECREASE OF REAL WAGES. Hodgskin and all the other proletarian opponents have enough common sense to emphasise the FACT that the proportional number of those who live on profit has increased with the development of capital.

Now a few concluding passages from Hodgskin's *Labour Defended etc.*

The treatment of the exchange value of the product, HENCE of the labour embodied in the commodity, as social labour:

> * "Almost every product of art and skill is the *result of joint and combined labour.*" *

(This is the result of capitalist production.)

_____

a *The Source and Remedy of the National Difficulties...*—Ed.

*"So dependent is man on man, and so much does this dependence *increase* as society advances, that hardly any labour of any single individual ... is of the least value but as forming a part of the great social task."*

// This passage has to be quoted, and in doing so [it is necessary to emphasise] that it is only on the basis of capital that *commodity* production or the production of products as commodities becomes all-embracing and affects the nature of the products themselves. //

*"... Wherever the division of labour is introduced, the judgement of other men intervenes before the labourer can realise his earnings, and there is no longer any thing which we can call the material[a] reward of individual labour. Each labourer produces only some part of a whole, and each part, having no value or utility of itself, there is nothing on which the labourer can seize and say: 'this is my product, this I will keep to myself'. Between the commencement of any joint operation, such as that of making cloth, and the division of its product among the different persons whose combined exertions have produced it, the judgement of men must intervene several times, and the question is how much of this joint product should go to each of the individuals whose united labour produced it?" ([p.] 25).

"I know no way of deciding this [XV-890] but by leaving it to be settled by the unfettered judgements of the labourers themselves" (l.c.).

"I must add that it is doubtful whether one species of labour is more valuable than another; certainly it is not more necessary"* ([p.] 26).

Finally Hodgskin writes about the *relation of capital* [and labour]:

*"Masters are *labourers* as well as their journeymen. In this character their interest is precisely the same as that of their men. But they are also either capitalists or the agents of the capitalist, and in this respect their interest is decidedly opposed to the interest of the workmen" (l.c., [p.] 27).

"The wide spread of education among the journeyman mechanics of this country, diminishes daily the value of the labour and skill of almost all masters and employers, by increasing the numbers of persons who possess their peculiar knowledge" ([p.] 30).

"The *capitalist* is the *oppressive middleman*" between the different labourers.* If he is put out of view, *"it is plain that *capital* or the *power to employ labour* and *co-existing labour* are one; and *productive capital* and *skilled labour* are also *one*; consequently capital and a labouring population are precisely synonymous. In the system of nature, mouths are united with hands and with intelligence"* ([p.] 33).

The capitalist mode of production disappears with the form of alienation which the various aspects of social labour bear to one another and which is represented in *capital.* This is the conclusion arrived at by Hodgskin.

The primitive accumulation of capital.[b] Includes the CENTRALISATION

---

[a] Hodgskin has "the natural".— *Ed.*

[b] See this volume, pp. 385-86, 405-06 and pp. XXII—1395-97, 1402-07, 1438-40, 1461-63 of the manuscript (present edition, Vol. 34), and also Marx's *Outlines of the Critique of Political Economy...* (present edition, Vol. 28, pp. 387-99).— *Ed.*

Page 890 of Notebook XV of the Economic Manuscript
of 1861-1863

of the conditions of labour. It means that the conditions of labour acquire an independent existence in relation to the worker and to labour itself. This historical act is the historical genesis of capital, the *historical* process of separation which transforms the conditions of labour into capital and labour into wage labour. This provides the basis for capitalist production.

Accumulation of capital on the basis of capital itself, and therefore also on the basis of the relationship of capital and wage labour, reproduces the separation and the independent existence of material wealth as against labour on an ever increasing scale.

CONCENTRATION *of capital.* Accumulation of large amounts of capital by the destruction of the smaller capitals. Attraction. Decapitalisation of the intermediate links between capital and labour. This is only the last degree and the final form of the process which transforms the conditions of labour into capital, then reproduces capital and the separate capitals on a larger scale and finally separates from their owners the various capitals which have come into existence at many points of society, and centralises them in the hands of big capitalists. It is in this extreme form of the contradiction and conflict that production—even though in alienated form—is transformed into social production. There is social labour, and in the real labour process the instruments of production are used in common. As *functionaries* of the process which at the same time accelerates this *social* production and thereby also the development of the productive forces, the capitalists become superfluous in the measure that they, on behalf of society, enjoy the usufruct and that they become overbearing as *owners* of this social wealth and *commanders* of social labour. Their position is similar to that of the feudal lords whose exactions in the measure that their *services* became superfluous with the rise of bourgeois society, became mere outdated and inappropriate privileges and who therefore rushed headlong to destruction.

[* *REVENUE AND ITS SOURCES**][121]

[XV-891] The form of REVENUE and the sources of REVENUE are the *most fetishistic* expression of the relations of capitalist production. It is their form of existence as it appears on the surface, divorced from the hidden connections and the intermediate connecting links. Thus the *land* becomes the source of *rent, capital* the source of *profit,* and labour the source of *wages.* The distorted form in which the real inversion is expressed is naturally reproduced in the views of the agents of this mode of production. It is a kind of fiction without fantasy, a religion of the vulgar. In fact, the vulgar economists—by no means to be confused with the economic investigators we have been criticising—translate the concepts, motives, etc., of the representatives of capitalist production who are held in thrall to this system of production and in whose consciousness only its superficial appearance is reflected. They translate them into a doctrinaire language, but they do so from the standpoint of the ruling section, i.e. the capitalists, and their treatment is therefore not naïve and objective, but apologetic. The narrow and pedantic expression of vulgar conceptions which are bound to arise among the representatives of this mode of production is very different from the urge of political economists like the Physiocrats, Adam Smith and Ricardo to grasp the inner connection of the phenomena.

However, of all these forms, the most complete fetish is *interest-bearing capital*.[a] This is the original starting-point of capital—money—and the formula $M—C—M$ is reduced to its two extremes—$M—M$—money which creates more money. It is the original and general formula of capital reduced to a meaningless résumé.

The *land* or *nature* as the source of *rent,* i.e. of landed property, is fetishistic enough. But as a result of a convenient confusion of use value with exchange value, the common imagination is still able to have recourse to the productive power of nature itself, which, by some kind of hocus-pocus, is personified in the LANDLORD.

Labour as the source of *wages,* that is, of the worker's share in his product, which is determined by the specific social form of labour; labour as the cause of the fact that the worker by means of his labour buys the permission to produce from the product (i.e. from capital considered in its material aspect) and has in labour the source by which a part of his product is returned to him in the form of payment made by this product as his employer—this is pretty enough. But the common conception is in so far in accord with the facts that, even though labour is confused with wage labour and, consequently, wages, the product of wage labour, with the product of labour, it is nevertheless obvious to anybody who has common sense that labour itself produces its own wages.

Capital, in so far as it is considered in the *production process,* still continues to a certain extent to be regarded as an instrument for

---

a See also this volume, pp. 456-58, 488-90 and 494-95.—*Ed.*

acquiring the labour of others. This may be treated as "right" or "wrong", as justified or not justified, but here the relation of the capitalist to the worker is always presupposed and assumed.

Capital, in so far as it appears in the *circulation process,* confronts the ordinary observer mainly in the form of *merchant capital,* that is, a kind of capital which is engaged only in this operation, hence profit in this field is in part linked with a vague notion of general swindling, or more specifically, with the idea that the merchant swindles the industrial capitalist or the consumer in the same way as the industrial capitalist swindles the worker, or as the producers swindle one another. In any case, profit here is explained as a result of EXCHANGE, that is, as arising from a social relation and not from a thing.

On the other hand, *interest-bearing capital* is the perfect fetish. It is capital in its finished form—as such representing the unity of the production process and the circulation process—and therefore yields a definite profit in a definite period of time. In the form of interest-bearing capital only this function remains, without the mediation of either production process or circulation process. Memories of the past still remain in capital and profit, although because of the divergence of profit from surplus value and the uniform profit yielded by all capitals—that is, the general rate of profit—capital becomes [XV-892] very much obscured, something dark and mysterious.

Interest-bearing capital is the consummate *automatic fetish,* the self-valorising value the money-making money, and in this form it no longer bears any trace of its origin. The social relation is consummated as a relation of things (money, commodities) to themselves.

This is not the place for a more detailed examination of interest and its relation to profit; nor is it the place for an examination of the ratio in which profit is divided into industrial profit and interest. It is clear that capital, as the mysterious and self-generating source of interest, that is, source of its [own] increase, finds its consummation in capital and interest. It is therefore especially in this form that capital is imagined. It is capital *par excellence.*

Since, on the basis of capitalist production, a certain sum of values represented in money or commodities—actually in money, the converted form of the commodity—makes it possible to extract a certain amount of labour gratis from the workers and to appropriate a certain amount of SURPLUS VALUE, SURPLUS LABOUR, SURPLUS PRODUCE, it is obvious that money itself can be sold as capital, that is, as a commodity *sui generis*, or that capital can be bought in the form of commodities or of money.

It can be sold as the source of profit. I enable someone else by means of money, etc., to appropriate SURPLUS VALUE. Thus it is quite in order for me to receive part of this SURPLUS VALUE. Just as land has value because it enables me to intercept a portion of SURPLUS VALUE, and I therefore pay for this land only the SURPLUS VALUE which can be intercepted thanks to it, so I pay for capital the SURPLUS VALUE which is created by means of it. Since, in the capitalist production process, the value of capital is perpetuated and reproduced in addition to its surplus value, it is therefore quite in order that, when money or commodities are sold as capital, they return to the seller after a period of time and he does not alienate it [money] in the same way as he would a commodity but retains ownership of it. In this way, money or commodities are not sold as money or commodities, but in their second power, as *capital*, as self-increasing money, or commodity value. Money is not only increased, but is preserved in the total process of production. It therefore remains capital for the seller, and comes back to him. The sale consists in the fact that another person, who uses it as productive capital, has to pay its owner a certain part of his profit, which he only makes through this capital. Like land, it is rented out as a value-creating thing which in this process of generating value is preserved and continually returned, and therefore can also be returned to the original seller. It is only capital in virtue of its RETURN to him. Otherwise he would sell it as a commodity or buy with it as money.

In any case, the form considered in itself (in fact, it [money] is alienated periodically as a means for exploiting labour, for making surplus value) is this, that the thing now appears as capital and capital appears as a mere thing; the whole result of the capitalist production and circulation process appears as a property inherent in a thing, and it depends on the owner of money, i.e. of the commodity in its constantly exchangeable form, whether he expends it as money or rents it out as capital.

We have here the relation of capital as PRINCIPAL to itself as *fructus*,[a] and the profit which it yields is measured against its own value, which (in accordance with the nature of capital) is not diminished in this process. It is thus clear why superficial criticism—in exactly the same way as it wants [to maintain] commodities and combats money—now turns its wisdom and

---

[a] Yield.— *Ed.*

reforming zeal against interest-bearing capital without touching upon real capitalist production, but merely attacking one of its consequences. This polemic against interest-bearing capital, undertaken from the standpoint of capitalist production, a polemic which today parades as "socialism", occurs, incidentally, as a phase in the development of capital itself, for example, in the 17th century, when the industrial capitalist had to assert himself against the old-fashioned usurer who, at that time, still [confronted] him as a superior power.[a]

[XV-893] The complete *objectification, inversion* and *derangement* of capital as interest-bearing capital—in which, however, the inner nature of capitalist production, [its] derangement, merely appears in its most palpable form—is capital which yields "COMPOUND INTEREST". It appears as a Moloch demanding the whole world as a sacrifice belonging to it of right, whose legitimate demands, arising from its very nature, are however never met and are always frustrated by a mysterious fate.

The characteristic movement of capital, both in the production and in the circulation processes, is the return of the money or commodity to its starting-point—to the capitalist. This expresses, on the one hand, the real metamorphosis, the conversion of the commodity into its conditions of production, and the conversion of the conditions of production back into the form of the commodity—i.e. reproduction, and, on the other hand, the formal metamorphosis, the conversion of the commodity into money and of the money back into the commodity. Finally, the multiplication of value: $M—C—M'$. The original value, which is however increased during the process, always remains in the possession of the same capitalist. Only the forms change in which he possesses it: money, commodity, or the form of the production process itself. In the case of interest-bearing capital, this *return* of capital to its starting-point acquires a quite *external* aspect, divorced from the real movement whose form it is. *A* spends his money not as money but as capital. No CHANGE takes place here in the money. It only changes hands. Its real conversion into capital takes place only while it is in the hands of *B*. But it has become capital for *A* as a result of the transfer of the money from *A*'s hands into those of *B*. The real RETURN of capital from the production and circulation process takes place for *B*. But for *A*, the return takes place in the same way as the alienation did. The money passes

---

[a] See K. Marx, *Outlines of the Critique of Political Economy...* (present edition, Vol. 28, pp. 244-45 and Vol. 29, pp. 218-21).—*Ed.*

from *B* back again to *A*. He *lends* the money instead of spending it.

In the real production process of capital, each particular movement of money expresses an aspect of reproduction, whether it be the conversion of money into labour, the conversion of the finished commodity into money (the end of the act of production) or the reconversion of the money into commodities (renewal of the production process, recommencement of reproduction). The movement of money when it is *lent* as *capital*, that is, when it is not converted into capital but enters into circulation as capital, expresses nothing more than the TRANSFER of the same money from one person to another. The property rights remain with the lender, but the possession is transferred to the industrial capitalist. For the lender, however, the conversion of the money into capital begins at the moment when he spends it as capital instead of spending it as money, i.e. when he hands it over to the industrial capitalist. (It remains capital for him even if he does not lend it to the industrial capitalist but to a spendthrift, or to a worker who cannot pay his rent. The whole pawnshop business [is based on this].[a]) True, the other person converts it into capital, but this is an operation beyond that in which the lender and the borrower are involved. *This mediation is effaced,* is not visible, is not directly included in it. Instead of the real conversion of money into capital, there appears only the empty form of this process. Just as in the case of labour capacity, *the use value of money here becomes that* of creating exchange value, more *exchange value than it itself contains.* It is *lent as self-valorising value,* as a commodity, but a commodity which, precisely because of this quality, differs from commodities as such and therefore also *possesses a specific form of alienation.*

The starting-point of capital is the commodity owner, the owner of money, in short, the capitalist. Since in the case of capital both starting-point and point of return coincide, it returns to the capitalist. But the capitalist exists here in a dual form, as the owner of capital and as the industrial capitalist who really converts money into capital. The capital actually issues [XV-894] from him [the industrial capitalist] and returns again to him. But only as possessor. The capitalist exists in a dual form—juridically and economically. The capital as property consequently returns to the juridical capitalist, the LEFT-HANDED SAM. But the return of the

---

[a] See J. D. Tuckett, *History of the Past and Present State of the Labouring Population...,* Vol. I, London, 1846, Ch. IX, especially p. 114; see also K. Marx, *Outlines of the Critique of Political Economy...* (present edition, Vol. 29, p. 230).—*Ed.*

capital, which includes the maintenance of its value and posits it as a self-maintaining and self-perpetuating value, is indeed brought about by intermediate steps for capitalist II but not for capitalist I. In this case therefore, the return is not the consequence and result of a series of economic processes but is effected by a particular juridical transaction between buyer and seller, by the fact that it is *lent instead of being sold, and therefore it is posited only temporarily*. What *is sold is*, in fact, *its use value*, whose *function in this case* is to produce *exchange value*, to yield profit, to produce more value than it itself contains. As money it does not change through being used. It is however expended as money and it flows back as money.

The form in which it returns depends on the mode of reproduction of the capital. If it is loaned as money, then it comes back in the form of circulating capital, that is, its whole value is returned+surplus value, in this case, that part of surplus value or of profit which consists of interest; the sum of money loaned+the additional amount which has arisen from it.

If it is loaned out in the form of machinery, buildings, etc., in short, in a material form in which it functions as fixed capital in the process of production, then it returns in the form of fixed capital, as an annuity, that is, for example, as an annual amount=to the replacement of the wear and tear=to that part of the value which has entered the circulation process+that part of the SURPLUS VALUE which is calculated as profit (in this case a part of the profit), interest on the fixed capital (not in so far as it is fixed capital, but in so far as in general it is capital of a definite amount).

In profit as such, SURPLUS VALUE, and consequently its real source, is already obscured and mystified:

1) Because, considered from the formal standpoint, profit is SURPLUS VALUE calculated on the whole of the capital advanced, so that each part of capital—fixed and circulating—laid out on raw materials, machinery or labour, yields an equal amount of profit.

2) Because, just as in the case of a single given capital of 500, for example, every fifth part yields 10%, if the SURPLUS VALUE=50, *so* now, as a result of the establishment of the *general rate of profit*, every capital of 500 or 100, no matter which sphere it operates in, irrespective of the relative proportions of variable and constant capital, no matter how varied the periods of turnover, etc., will yield the same average profit—say 10%—in the same period of time as any other capital under quite different organic conditions. Because, therefore, the *profit* of individual capitals regarded in

isolation and the *surplus value* which is produced by them in their own sphere of production become in fact different magnitudes.

It is true that point 2 merely develops further what has already been implied in point 1.

The basis of interest however is this already externalised form of surplus value, i.e. its existence as *profit*. This form differs from its first simple appearance, in which it still reveals the umbilical cord of its birth, and is, at first sight, by no means recognisable as a form of surplus value. Interest directly presupposes not surplus value, but *profit*, of which it is merely a part placed in a special category or division. It is therefore much more difficult to recognise surplus value in interest than in profit, since interest is directly connected with surplus value only in the form of profit.

The time needed for the RETURN [of capital] depends on the real production process; in the case of interest-bearing capital, its return as capital *appears* to depend merely on the agreement between lender and borrower. So that the RETURN of the capital in this transaction no longer appears to be a result determined by the production process, but it seems that the capital never loses the form of money for a single instant. These transactions are nevertheless determined by the REAL RETURNS. But this is not *evident* in the transaction itself.

[XV-895] Interest, as distinct from profit, represents the *value* of *mere ownership* of *capital*—i.e. it transforms the ownership of *money* (of a sum of values, commodities, whatever the form may be) in itself, into ownership of capital, and consequently commodities or money as such into self-valorising value. The conditions of labour are of course capital only in so far as they confront the worker as his non-property and consequently function as someone else's property. But they can function in this way only in contradiction to labour. The *antagonistic existence of these conditions in relation to labour makes their owners capitalists,* and turns these conditions owned by them into capital. But capital in the hands of MONEYED capitalist A does not have this contradictory character which turns it into capital and which therefore makes ownership of money appear as ownership of capital. *The actual formal determinant by means of which money or a commodity is converted into capital is obliterated.* MONEYED capitalist A does not confront the worker at all, but only another capitalist—capitalist B. What he sells him is actually the "use" of the money, the results it will produce WHEN CONVERTED INTO PRODUCTIVE CAPITAL. But in fact it is not the use which he sells directly. If I sell a commodity, then I sell a specific use value. If I buy money with commodities, then I buy the functional use value which money, as the converted form of commodities, possesses. I do not sell the use value of the commodity along with its exchange value, nor do I buy the particular use value of the money along with the money itself. But money as money—before its conversion into and its function as capital, a function which it does not perform while it is in the hands of the MONEY-LENDER—has no other use value than that which it possesses as a commodity (gold, silver, its material substance) or as money which is the converted form of a commodity. What the MONEY-LENDER sells in actual fact to the industrial capitalist, what really happens in the transaction, is simply this: he transfers the ownership of the money to the industrial capitalist for a certain period of time. He disposes of his ownership title for A CERTAIN TERM, and as a result the industrial capitalist has bought the ownership for A CERTAIN TERM. Thus his money appears to be capital before it is alienated and the mere ownership of money or a commodity—separated from the capitalist production process—[is regarded] as capital.

The fact that it becomes capital only after it has been alienated makes no difference, any more than the use value of cotton is altered by the fact that its use value only emerges after it has been alienated to the spinner or that the use value of meat only becomes apparent after it has been transferred from the butcher's shop to the consumer's table. Hence money, once it is not spent on consumption, and commodities, once they are not used as means of consumption by their owners, transform those who possess them into capitalists and are in themselves—separated from the capitalist production process and even *before* their conversion into "productive" capital—capital, that is, they are self-valorising, self-preserving and self-increasing value. It is their immanent attribute to create value, to yield interest, just as the attribute of the pear tree is to produce pears. And it is as such an interest-bearing thing that the MONEY-LENDER sells his money to the industrial capitalist. Because money preserves itself, i.e. is value which preserves itself, the industrial capitalist can return it at any time fixed by contract. Since it produces a definite amount of surplus value, interest, annually, or rather since value accrues to it over any period of time, he can also pay back this surplus value to the lender annually or in any other conventionally established period of time. Money as capital yields surplus value daily in exactly the same way as wage labour. While interest is simply a *part* of the profit *established under a special name,* it *appears here* as [the surplus value specifically created by] capital as such, separated from the production process, and consequently deriving only from the mere ownership of capital, the ownership of money and commodities, separated from the relations which give rise to the contradiction between this property and labour, thus turning it into capitalist property. [Interest seems to be] a specific kind of *surplus value* the *generation* of which is due to the mere ownership of capital and therefore to an intrinsic characteristic of capital; whereas on the contrary, *industrial profit* appears to be a mere addition which the borrower obtains by employing capital productively, that is, by exploiting the workers with the help of the capital borrowed (or, as people also say, by his work as a capitalist, the function of the capitalist being equated here with labour, and even identified with wage labour, since the [XV-896] industrial capitalist, by really taking part in the production process, appears in fact as an active agent in production, as a worker, in contrast to the idle, inactive money-lender whose function of property owner is separate from and outside the production process).

Thus it is *interest,* not *profit,* which appears to be the *creation of value* arising from capital as such and therefore from the mere ownership of capital; consequently it is regarded as the specific REVENUE created by capital. This is also the form in which it is conceived by the vulgar economists. In this form all intermediate links are obliterated, and the *fetishistic face* of capital, as also the concept of the *capital-fetish,* is complete. This form arises necessarily, because the juridical aspect of property is separated from its economic aspect and one part of the profit under the name of interest accrues to *capital in itself*[122] which is completely separated from the production process, or to the *owner of this capital.*

To the vulgar economist who desires to represent capital as an independent source of value, a source which creates value, this form is of course a godsend, a form in which the source of profit is no longer recognisable and the result of the capitalist process—separated from the process itself—acquires an independent existence. In $M—C—M'$ an intermediate link is still retained. In $M—M'$ we have the incomprehensible form of capital, the most extreme inversion and materialisation of production relations.

A general *rate of interest* corresponds naturally to the *general rate of profit.* It is not our intention to discuss this further here, since the analysis of interest-bearing capital does not belong to this general section but to that dealing with *credit.*[123] However, the observation that the general rate of profit appears much less as a palpable, solid fact than does the *rate of interest* is important to fully work out these manifestations of capital. True, the rate of interest fluctuates continuously. [It may be] 2% today (on the money market for the industrial capitalist—and this is all we are discussing), 3% tomorrow, and 5% the day after. But it is 2 per cent, 3 per cent, 5 per cent for all borrowers. It is a general condition that every sum of money of £100 yields 2%, 3% or 5%, while the same value in its real function as capital yields very different amounts of real profit in the different spheres of production. The real profit deviates from the ideal average level, which is established only by a continuous process, a reaction, and this only takes place during long periods of circulation of capital. The rate of profit is in certain spheres higher for some years, while it is lower in succeeding years. Taking the years together, or taking a SERIES of such EVOLUTIONS, one will *in general* obtain the AVERAGE PROFIT. Thus it never appears as something directly given, but only as the average result of contradictory oscillations. It is different with the rate of interest. In its *generality,* it is a fact which is established daily, a fact which the industrial capitalist even regards as a precondition and an ITEM of calculation in his operations. The general rate of profit exists indeed only as an ideal *average figure,* in so far as it serves to estimate the real profit; it exists only as an average figure, as an abstraction, in so far as it is established as something which is in itself complete, definite, given. In reality, however, it exists only as the determining tendency in the movement of equalisation of the real different rates of profit, whether of individual capitals in the same sphere or of different capitals in the different spheres of production.[a]

[XV-897] What the lender demands of the capitalist is calculated on the *general* (AVERAGE) *rate of profit,* not on individual deviations from it. Here the AVERAGE becomes the *precondition.* The rate of interest itself *varies,* but does so for all *borrowers.*

A definite, equal rate of interest, on the other hand, exists not only on the average but in actual fact (even though it is accompanied by variations between minimum and maximum rates according to whether or not the borrower is FIRST-RATE) and the deviations appear rather as exceptions brought about by special circumstances. The meteorological bulletins do not indicate the state of the barometer more exactly than stock-exchange bulletins do the state of interest rates, not for this or that capital, but for

---

[a] See present edition, Vol. 31, pp. 260-65, 274-76, 280-81, 302-04, 407-10, 423, 430-33, and this volume, pp. 258, 261 and 273-74.—*Ed.*

the *capital available on the money market, that is, capital available for lending.*

This is not the place to go into the reasons for this greater stability and equality of the rate of interest on loan capital in contradistinction to the less tangible form of the general rate of profit. Such a discussion belongs to the section on credit.[30] But this much is obvious: the fluctuations in the *rate of profit* in every sphere—quite apart from the special advantages which individual capitalists in the same sphere of production may enjoy—depend on the existing level of market prices and their fluctuations around cost prices. The difference in the *rates of profit* in the *various* spheres can only be discerned by comparison of the market prices in the different spheres, that is, the market prices of the *different* commodities, with the cost prices of these different commodities. A decline in the rate of profit below the ideal average in any particular sphere, if prolonged, suffices to bring about a withdrawal of capital from this sphere, or to prevent the entry of the AVERAGE amount of new capital into it. For it is the inflow of new, ADDITIONAL capital, even more than the redistribution of capital already invested, that equalises the distribution of capital in the different spheres. The SURPLUS PROFIT in the different spheres, on the other hand, is discernible only by comparison of the market prices with cost prices. As soon as any difference becomes apparent in one way or another, then an outflow or inflow of capital from or to the particular spheres [begins]. Apart from the fact that this act of equalisation requires time, the average profit in each sphere becomes evident only in the average profit rates obtained, for example, over a cycle of 7 years, etc., according to the nature of the capital. Mere fluctuations—*below* and *above*—if they do not exceed the average extent and do not assume extraordinary forms, are therefore not sufficient to bring about a TRANSFER OF CAPITAL, and in addition the TRANSFER of fixed capital presents certain difficulties. Momentary booms can only have a limited effect, and are more likely to attract or repel ADDITIONAL CAPITAL than to bring about a REDISTRIBUTION of the capital invested in the different spheres. One can see that all this involves a very complex movement in which, on the one hand, the market prices in each particular sphere, the relative cost prices of the different commodities, the position with regard to demand and supply within each individual sphere, and, on the other hand, competition among the capitalists in the different spheres, play a part, and, in addition, the speed of the equalisation process, whether it is quicker or slower, depends on the particular organic composition of the different capitals (more fixed or circulating capital, for example) and on the particular nature of their commodities, that is, whether their nature as use values facilitates rapid withdrawal from the market and the diminution or increase of supply, in accordance with the level of the market prices.

In the case of money capital on the other hand, only two sorts of buyers and sellers, only two types of demand and supply, confront each other on the money market. On the one side, the borrowing class of capitalists—on the other, the money-lenders. The commodity has only one form—money. All the different forms assumed by capital according to the different spheres of production or circulation in which it is invested, are obliterated here. It exists here in the undifferentiated, always identical form, that of independent exchange value, i.e. of money. Here competition between the different spheres ceases; they are all lumped together as borrowers of money, and capital too confronts them all in a form in which it is still indifferent to the way it is utilised. Whereas productive capital [XV-898] *emerges only in movement and competition between the different spheres as the joint capital of the whole class, capital here actually—as regards the pressure exerted—acts as such in the demand for capital.* On the other hand, money capital (the capital on the money market) really possesses the form which enables it as a common element, irrespective of its particular employment, to be distributed amongst the different spheres, amongst the capitalist class, according to the production needs of each separate sphere. With the development of large-scale industry, moreover, money capital, in so far as it appears on the market, is represented less and less by the individual capitalist, the owner of this or that parcel of capital available on the market, but is concentrated, organised and is [subject] in quite a different way from real production to the control of the bankers who represent the capital. So that in so far as the form of the demand is concerned, the weight of a class confronts it [this capital]; and as far as supply is concerned, it appears as loan capital *en masse,* the loan capital of society, concentrated in a few reservoirs.

These are some of the reasons why the *general rate of profit* appears as a hazy mirage in contrast to the *fixed rate of interest* which, although it fluctuates in magnitude, nevertheless fluctuates in the same measure for all borrowers and therefore always confronts them as something fixed, given; just as money despite the changes in its value has the same value for all commodities. Just as the market prices of commodities fluctuate daily, which does not prevent them from being *quoted* daily, so it is with the rate of interest, which is likewise quoted regularly as the *price* of money. This is the established price of capital, for capital is here offered as a special kind of commodity—*money*—and consequently its *market price* is established in the same way as that of all other commodities. The rate of interest is therefore always expressed as the *general rate of interest*, as a fixed amount [to be paid] for a certain amount of money; whereas the rate of profit within a *particular* sphere may vary although the market prices of commodities are the same (depending on the conditions under which individual capitals produce the same commodities; since the individual rate of profit does not depend on the market price of the commodity but on the difference between the market price and the cost price [6]) and it is equalised in the different spheres in the course of operations only as a result of constant fluctuations. In short, only in MONEYED CAPITAL, the money capital which can be lent, does capital become a *commodity*, whose quality of self-valorisation has a *fixed price*, which is quoted as the prevailing rate of interest.

Thus capital acquires its pure fetish form in *interest-bearing* capital, and indeed in its direct form of *interest-bearing money capital* (the other forms of interest-bearing capital, which do not concern us here, are in turn derived from this form and presuppose it). Firstly, as a result of its continuous existence as *money*, a form in which all its determining features are obliterated and its real elements invisible; in this form it represents merely independent exchange value, value which has become independent. The money form is a transient form in the real process of capital. On the money market capital always exists in this form. *Secondly*, the surplus value it produces, which again assumes the form of money, seems to accrue to capital as such, consequently to the mere owner of money capital, i.e. of capital separated from its process. Here *M—C—M* becomes *M—M*, and just as its form here is the undifferentiated money form (for money is precisely the form in which the differences between commodities as use values are obliterated, consequently also the *differences between productive capitals, which are made up of the conditions of existence of these commodities, the particular forms of the productive capitals themselves are obliterated*) so the surplus value it produces, the surplus money which it is or which it becomes, appears as a definite rate measured by the amount of the money. If the rate of interest is 5%, then 100 used as capital becomes 105. This is the quite tangible form of self-valorising value or of money-making money, and at the same time the quite irrational form, the incomprehensible, mystified form. In the discussion of capital we started from $M—C—M$, of which $M—M'$ was only the result.[a] We now find $M—M'$ *as the subject.* Just as growth is characteristic of trees, so money-bearing (τόχος[b]) is characteristic of capital in this, its pure form as money. The incomprehensible superficial form we encounter and which has therefore constituted the starting-point of our analysis, is found again as the result of the process in which the form of capital is gradually more and more alienated and rendered independent of its inner substance.

[XV-899] We started with money as the converted form of the commodity. What we arrive at is *money as the converted form of capital,* just as we have perceived that the commodity is the precondition and the result of the production process of capital.

This aspect of capital, which is the most fantastic and at the same time comes nearest to the popular notion of it, is both regarded as the "basic form" by the vulgar economists and made the first point of attack by superficial critics; the former, partly because the inner connections are least apparent here and capital emerges in a form in which it *appears* to be an independent source of value, partly because its *contradictory* character is totally concealed and effaced in this form and no contradiction to labour [is evident]. On the other hand, [capital is subjected to] attack because it is the form in which it is at its most irrational and provides the easiest point of attack for the vulgar socialists.[124]

The polemic waged by the bourgeois economists of the 17th century (Child, Culpeper[c 125] and others) against interest as an independent form of surplus value merely reflects the struggle of the rising industrial bourgeoisie against the old-fashioned usurers, who monopolised the pecuniary resources at that time. Interest-bearing capital in this case is still AN ANTEDILUVIAN FORM OF capital which has yet to be subordinated to industrial capital and to acquire the dependent position which it must assume— theoretically and practically—on the basis of capitalist production. The bourgeoisie did not hesitate to accept State aid in this as in other cases, where it was a question of making the traditional production relations which it found, adequate to its own.

---

[a] See present edition, Vol. 30, pp. 9-20.— *Ed.*

[b] *Tokos*—to bear, produce, the product; figuratively: interest on money lent.— *Ed.*

[c] See J. Child, *Traités sur le commerce et sur les avantages qui résultent de la réduction de l'interest de l'argent; avec un petit traité contre l'usure;* par Thomas Culpeper. Amsterdam and Berlin, 1754. See also this volume, p. 540, and Marx's *Outlines of the Critique of Political Economy...* (present edition, Vol. 29, pp. 225 and 230).— *Ed.*

It is clear that any other kind of division of profit between various kinds of capitalists, that is, increasing the industrial profit by reducing the rate of interest and vice versa, does not affect the essence of capitalist production in any way. The kind of socialism which attacks interest-bearing capital as the "basic form" of capital not only remains completely within the bounds of the bourgeois horizon. In so far as its polemic is not a misconceived attack and criticism prompted by a vague notion and directed against capital itself, though identifying it with one of its derived forms, it is nothing but a drive, disguised as socialism, for the development of bourgeois credit and consequently only expresses the low level of development of the existing conditions in a country where such a polemic can masquerade as socialist, and is itself only a theoretical symptom of capitalist development although this bourgeois striving can assume quite startling forms such as that of "*crédit gratuit*"[a] for example. The same applies to Saint-Simonism with its glorification of banking[126] (*Crédit mobilier*[127] later).

The commercial and interest-bearing forms of capital are older than industrial capital,[b] which, in capitalist production, is the *basic form* of the capital relation, as it dominates bourgeois society— and all other forms are only derived from it or secondary: derived as is the case with interest-bearing capital; secondary means that the capital fulfils a special function (which belongs to the circulation process) as for instance commercial capital. In the course of its evolution, industrial capital must therefore subjugate these forms and transform them into derived or special functions of itself. It encounters these older forms in the epoch of its formation and development. It encounters them as *antecedents,* but not as antecedents established by itself, not as forms of its own life-process. In the same way as it originally finds the commodity already in existence, but not as its own product, and likewise finds money circulation, but not as an element in its own reproduction. Where capitalist production has developed all its manifold forms and has become the dominant mode of production, interest-bearing capital is dominated by industrial capital, and commercial capital becomes merely a form of industrial capital, derived from the circulation process. But both of them must first be destroyed as independent forms [XV-900] and subordinated to industrial

---

[a] Free credit. A reference to P. J. Proudhon, *Gratuité du crédit. Discussion entre M. Fr. Bastiat et M. Proudhon,* Paris, 1850. See this volume, pp. 518-30.— *Ed*

[b] See K. Marx, *Outlines of the Critique of Political Economy...* (present edition, Vol. 29, pp. 226-30).— *Ed.*

capital. Violence (the State) is used against interest-bearing capital by means of compulsory reduction of interest rates, so that it is no longer able to dictate TERMS to industrial capital. But this is a method characteristic of the least developed stages of capitalist production. The real way in which industrial capital subjugates interest-bearing capital is the creation of a procedure specific to itself—the *credit system*. The compulsory reduction of interest rates is a measure which industrial capital itself borrows from the methods of an earlier mode of production and which it rejects as useless and inexpedient as soon as it becomes strong and conquers its territory. The *credit system* is its own creation, and is itself a form of industrial capital which begins with manufacture and develops further with large-scale industry. The credit system originally is a *polemical form* directed against the old-fashioned usurers (GOLDSMITHS in England, Jews, Lombards, and others). The 17th-century writings in which its first mysteries are discussed are all produced in this polemical form.[a]

Commercial capital is subordinated to industrial capital in various ways or, what amounts to the same thing, it becomes a function of the latter, it is industrial capital engaged in a special function.[b] The *merchant,* instead of buying commodities, buys wage labour with which he produces the commodities which he intends to sell on the market. But commercial capital thereby loses the fixed form which it previously possessed in contrast to production. This was the way the medieval guilds were undermined by manufacture and the handicrafts confined to a narrower sphere. The *merchant* in the Middle Ages was simply a *dealer in commodities* produced either by the town guilds or by the peasants (apart from sporadic areas where manufacture developed, for instance in Italy and Spain).[c]

This transformation of the merchant into an industrial capitalist is at the same time the transformation of commercial capital into a mere form of industrial capital. The *producer,* conversely, becomes a merchant. For example, the CLOTHIER himself buys material in accordance with the size of his capital, etc., instead of gradually obtaining his material in small amounts from the merchant and

---

[a] See, for instance, J. Child, *Traités sur le commerce et sur les avantages...*, and also this volume, p. 537 and pp. XV—950a-950b of the manuscript (present edition, Vol. 33).— *Ed.*

[b] In the manuscript, this sentence is crossed out with a pencil.— *Ed.*

[c] See J. H. M. Poppe, *Geschichte der Technologie seit der Wiederherstellung der Wissenschaften bis an Ende des achtzehnten Jahrhunderts,* Vol. I, Göttingen, 1807, p. 70.— *Ed.*

working for him. The conditions of production enter into the process [of production] as commodities which he himself has bought. And instead of producing for individual merchants or for particular customers, he now produces for the world of commerce.

In the first form, the merchant dominates production and commercial capital dominates the handicrafts or rural domestic industry which it sets in motion. The crafts are subordinated to him. In the second form, production becomes capitalist production. The producer is himself a merchant, merchant capital now acts as an intermediary only in the circulation process, thus fulfilling a definite function in the reproduction process of capital. These are the 2 forms. The merchant as such becomes a producer, an industrialist. The industrialist, the producer, becomes a merchant. Industrial capital only emerges with commodity circulation as its precondition, and moreover the commodity circulation that has developed into trade.[a] Originally, *trade* is the precondition for the transformation of guild, rural domestic and feudal agricultural production into capitalist production. It develops the product into a commodity, partly by creating a market for it, partly by giving rise to new commodity equivalents and partly by supplying production with new materials and thereby initiating new kinds of production which are based on trade from the very beginning because they depend both on production for the market and on elements of production derived from the world market. In the 16th century, it was the discoveries and MERCANTILE ADVENTURERS that called forth manufacture.[b] As soon as it gains strength (and this applies to an even greater extent to large-scale industry), it in turn creates the market, conquers it, opens up, partly by force, markets which it conquers, however, by means of its *commodities*. From now on, trade is merely a servant of industrial production for which a constantly expanding market has become a very condition of existence, since constantly expanding mass production, circumscribed not by the existing limits of trade (in so far as trade is only an expression of the existing level of demand), but solely by the amount of capital available and the level of productive power of labour, always floods the existing market and consequently seeks constantly to expand and remove its boundaries. Trade is now the servant of industrial capital, and carries out one of the functions emanating from the conditions of production of industrial capital.

---

[a] In the manuscript, this sentence is crossed out with a pencil.— *Ed.*

[b] In the manuscript, this sentence is crossed out with a pencil. "It" in the next sentence is replaced with "manufacture".— *Ed.*

During its first stages of development, industrial capital seeks to secure a market and markets by force, by the *colonial system* (together with the prohibition system). The industrial capitalist faces the world market; [he] therefore compares [XV-901] and must constantly compare his own cost prices with market prices not only AT HOME, but also ON THE WHOLE MARKET OF THE WORLD. He always produces taking this into account. In the earlier period this comparison is carried out only by the merchant estate, thus enabling merchant capital to dominate over productive capital.

// DIFFERENT FORMS OF CAPITAL[128]

I) *The Abstract Form.* $M-C-M$. And $M-M'$. But the latter only as the result. This abstract form corresponds to *all* the forms of capital, including the pre-industrial ones. Directly, $M-C-M$ even appears only as the expression of *commercial capital,* and $M-M'$, in so far as it is not perceived as a result of the latter, appears as *interest-bearing capital.* As an independent form of capital, commercial capital does not presuppose the capitalist mode of production and contradicts the production of products as *commodities,* determined in view of this by their value, by labour time, not only in the sale but also in the production itself.[a] It conditions *modes of production* other than the capitalist one if it is the dominant form of capital. Still more so $M-M'$ as *interest-bearing capital.* It presupposes commodity production, money, money and commodity circulation; as the dominant form of capital, it completely excludes capital from production itself.

II) *The Principal Form of Modern Capital,* or of *Capital Dominating the Mode of Production.* As such, this can only be a form of capital dominating the production process itself, and thus is "*productive capital*". (It must be a form which, while it presupposes circulation as a premiss, manifests its specificity, or the conditions of the production process, in the production process itself.) *The conditions of labour as capital become independent* over against labour as *wage labour.* The conditions of labour as master of labour itself, but a mastery mediated through simple commodity exchange, circulation, sale and purchase. *Increase of exchange value*—the goal of production.

---

[a] In the manuscript, this sentence is crossed out with a pencil. "It" in the next sentence is replaced with "Commercial capital".— *Ed.*

III) *Special Forms of Capital in the Production Process Itself*: Constant capital and variable capital; the part of capital which is exchanged for *commodities as its elements* and the part which *is exchanged* for *living labour as a commodity*.

IV) 1) *Productive Capital* or *Circulating Capital*. First Form: Capital in the production process; *Second Form*: Capital in the process of circulation.

2) From the *form of circulation* of productive capital follow the differences: *Fixed capital, circulating capital*. Or, in relation to the *reproduction process* of capital, one part appears only as circulating, the other as fixed.

V) *Circulating Capital. Capital in the Circulation Process.*

First distinction: According to the forms which it assumes in the circulation process. *Commodity capital, money capital* and *productive capital*. In this last form, it is again dissolved into its production elements and constantly appears here as commodity and labour. But with the transformation into productive capital it again returns from the sphere of circulation into the sphere of production, appearing now as reproduction.

Second distinction: The return to the sphere of production becomes real only when labour is bought and the commodity is posited as raw material, etc., in short, as elements of the labour process.

There are, however, intervals in the circulation process. 1) Commodity capital in the interval before it is converted into money. Thus, it is a process. *Conversion of commodity into money* or the sale of commodity. 2) Conversion *of money into commodity*. Second interval. Second process: *purchase. Thus selling in order to buy, and to that extent in order to sell*—for money is only converted into conditions of production in order to convert the latter again into commodity and this again into money—appears here as [XV-902] capital in the circulation process and the *reproduction process*; the production process itself as a moment of the circulation process, and the circulation process as a moment of the production process, contains—as a function of capital—capital determined by this particular function.

In the movement of capital, the transition of commodity capital into money capital and vice versa appears only as *transition,* as forms through which it constantly runs but which merely constitute a moment of its reproduction process. There is always, constantly, a part of capital (though not of *the same* capital) which is present in the market as commodity, in order to become money, and present in the market as money in order to become commodity. And this part is constantly in the *movement* of conversion from commodity to money, from money to commodity, from commodity to money. In so far as this function of circulating capital becomes the *distinct function* of a particular capital, establishes itself as a distinct function, this capital is COMMERCIAL CAPITAL, *merchant capital,* etc. //

Interest is therefore nothing but a part of the profit (which, in its turn, is itself nothing but SURPLUS VALUE, unpaid labour), which the industrial capitalist pays to the owner of the borrowed capital with which he "works", either exclusively or partially. Interest is a part of profit—of SURPLUS VALUE—which, established as a special category, is separated from the total profit under its own name, a separation which is by no means based on its origin, but only on the manner in which it is *paid out* or appropriated. Instead of being appropriated by the industrial capitalist himself—although he is the person who at first holds the whole surplus value in his hands no matter how it may be distributed between himself and other people under the names of rent, industrial profit and interest—this part of the profit is deducted by the industrial capitalist from his own REVENUE and paid to the owner of capital.

If the rate of profit is given, then the relative level of the rate of interest depends on the ratio in which profit is divided between interest and industrial profit. If the ratio of this division is given, then the absolute level of the rate of interest (that is, the ratio of interest to capital) depends on the rate of profit. It is not intended to investigate here how this ratio is determined. This belongs to the analysis of the real movement of capital, i.e. of capitals, while we are concerned here with the general forms of capital.

The formation of interest-bearing capital, its separation from industrial capital, is a *necessary* product of the development of industrial capital, of the capitalist mode of production itself. Money (a sum of value, which is always convertible into the conditions of production) or the conditions of production into which it can be converted at any time and of which it is only the converted form—money employed as capital, commands a definite quantity of other people's labour, more labour than it itself contains. It not only preserves its value in exchange with labour, but increases it, posits SURPLUS VALUE. The value of money or of commodities as *capital* is not determined by the value they possess as money or as commodities, but by the amount of surplus value which they "produce" for their owners. The product of capital is profit. On the basis of capitalist production, whether money is spent as money or as capital depends only on the different ways in which money is *employed.* Money (a commodity) *in itself* is capital on the basis of capitalist production (just as *labour capacity in itself* is labour) since, 1) it can be converted into the conditions of production and is, as it exists, only an abstract expression of them, their existence as *value*; and 2) the material elements of wealth in themselves possess the property of being capital because their opposite—wage labour, which turns them into capital—is present as the basis for social production.

Rent is likewise simply a name for a part of the surplus value which the industrialist has to pay out, in the same way as *interest* is another part of surplus value which, although it accrues to him (like rent), has to be handed over to someone else. But the great difference here is the following: through landed property, the landowner *prevents* capital from making the value of agricultural products equal to their cost prices. Monopoly of landed property enables the landowner to do this. It enables him to pocket the difference between value and cost price. On the other hand—as far as differential rent is concerned—this monopoly enables the landowner to pocket the excess of the market value over the individual value of the product of a particular piece of land, in contrast to the other TRADES, where this difference in the form of SURPLUS PROFIT flows into the pockets of the capitalists who operate under more favourable conditions than the AVERAGE conditions which satisfy the greater part of demand, thus determining the bulk of production and consequently regulating the market value of each particular sphere of production. Landed property is a *means* for grabbing a part of the surplus value produced by industrial capital. On the other hand, loan *capital—pro tanto*[a] that the capitalist operates with borrowed capital—is a *means* for producing the *whole* of the [XV-903] surplus value. That money (commodities) can be loaned out as capital means nothing more than that it is *in itself* capital. The abolition of landed property in the Ricardian sense, that is, its conversion into State property so that rent is paid to the State instead of to the landowner,[b] is the ideal, the heart's desire, which springs from the deepest, inmost essence of capital. Capital cannot abolish landed property. But by converting it into rent the capitalists as a *class* appropriate it and use it to defray their State expenses, thus appropriating in a roundabout way what cannot be retained directly. Abolition of

---

[a] To the extent.— *Ed.*
[b] In the manuscript: "FARMER".— *Ed.*

interest and of interest-bearing capital, on the other hand, means the abolition of capital and of capitalist production itself. As long as money (commodities) can serve as capital, it can be sold as capital. It is therefore quite in keeping with the views of the petty-bourgeois Utopians that they want to keep commodities but not money, industrial capital but not interest-bearing capital, profit but not interest.

There are not two different kinds of capital—interest-bearing and profit-yielding—but *the selfsame* capital which operates in the process as capital, produces a profit which is divided between two different capitalists—one standing outside the process, and, as owner, representing capital *in itself* //but it is an essential condition of this capital that it is represented by a *private owner*; without this it does not become capital as opposed to wage labour//, and the other representing operating capital, capital which takes part in the process.[129]

The further "ossification" or transformation of the *division* of profit into something independent appears in such a way that the *profit on* e v e r y s i n g l e capital—and therefore also the *average profit* based on the equalisation of capitals—is split or divided into two component parts separated from, or independent of, each other, namely, interest and industrial profit, which is now sometimes called simply *profit* or acquires new names such as WAGES OF LABOUR OF SUPERINTENDENCE, etc. If the rate of profit (average profit)=15% and the *rate of interest* (which, as we have seen, is always established in the *general* form)=5% (the general rate being always quoted in the money market as the "value" or "price" of money), then the capitalist—even when he is the owner of the capital and has not *borrowed* any part of it, so that the profit does not have to be divided between two capitalists—considers that 5% of these 15% represents *interest* on his capital, and only 10% represents the profit he makes by the productive employment of the capital. This 5 per cent interest, which he as an "industrial capitalist" owes to himself as "owner" of the capital, is due to his *capital in itself,* and consequently it is due to him as owner of the *capital in itself* (which is at one and the same time the existence of capital for itself, or the existence of capital as the capitalist, as property which debars other people from [owning] it), capital abstracted from the production process as opposed to operating capital, capital involved in the production process, and to the "industrial capitalist" as representative of this operating, "working" capital. "Interest" is the fruit of capital in so far as it does not "work" or operate, and profit is the fruit of "working", operating capital. This is similar to the way in which the FARMING capitalist—who is at the same time also a landowner, the owner of the soil which he exploits in capitalist fashion—assigns that part of his profit which constitutes *rent*, this surplus profit, to himself not as capitalist but as landowner, attributing it not to capital but to landed property so that he, the capitalist, owes himself "rent" as a landowner. Thus one aspect of capital confronts another aspect of the same capital just as rigidly as do landed property and capital which, in fact, constitute the separate claims to appropriation of other people's labour which are based on two essentially different means of production.

If, on the one hand, 5 PARTNERS own a COTTON MILL which represents a capital of £100,000 and yields a profit of 10%, that is, £10,000, then each of them gets $^1/_5$ of the profit=£2,000. On the other hand, if a single capitalist invested the same amount of capital in a MILL and made the same amount of profit—£10,000— he would not consider that he received £2,000 profit as a PARTNER and the other £8,000 *compagnie* PROFIT for the non-existent 4 PARTNERS. Consequently, in itself the *mere division of profit* between different [XV-904] capitalists who have different legal claims on the same capital and who are in one way or another joint owners of *the same* capital, does not by any means establish different categories for the separate portions. Why then [should] the accidental division between lender and borrower of capital [do so]?

Prima facie it is simply a question of the division of profit when there are two owners of the capital with different titles—a *prima facie* legal, but not economic aspect. In itself it makes no difference at all whether a capitalist produces with his own or with other people's capital or in what proportion he uses his own capital to that of other people. How does it happen that this division of profit into [industrial] profit and interest does not appear as an accidental division, dependent on the accident whether or not the capitalist really has a share with *someone else*, or on whether he by chance is operating with his own or with someone else's capital, but that, on the contrary, even when he operates exclusively with his own capital, he in any case splits himself into two—into a mere owner of capital and into a user of capital, into capital which is outside the production process and capital which takes part in the production process, into capital which *in itself* yields interest and capital which yields profit because it is *used in the production process*?

There is a real reason at the root of this. Money (as an expression of the value of commodities in general) in the [production] process appropriates surplus value, no matter what name it bears or whatever parts it is split into, only because it is already presupposed as *capital before* the production process. It maintains, produces and reproduces itself as capital *in* the process and moreover on a continually expanding scale. Once the capitalist mode of production is given and work is undertaken on this basis and within the social relations which correspond to it, that is, when it is not a question of the process of formation of capital, then even *before* the [production] process begins money as such is *capital* by its very nature, which, however, is only realised in the process and indeed only becomes a reality in the process itself. If it did not enter into the process as capital it would not emerge from it as capital, that is, as profit-yielding money, as self-valorising value, as value which produces surplus value. It is the same as with money. For example, this coin is nothing but a piece of metal. It is only money in virtue of its function in the circulation process. But if the existence of the circulation process of commodities is presupposed, the coin not only functions as money, but as such it is in every single case a precondition for the circulation process before it enters into it.

Capital is not only the result of, but the precondition for, capitalist production. Money and commodities as such are therefore latent capital, potential capital; this applies to all commodities in so far as they are convertible into money, and to money in so far as it is convertible into those commodities which constitute the elements of the capitalist process of production. Thus money—as the pure expression of the value of commodities and of the conditions of labour—is in itself as capital preposited to capitalist production. What is capital regarded not as the result of, but as the prerequisite for, the process [of production]? What makes it capital before it enters the process so that the latter merely develops its immanent character? The social framework in which it exists. The fact that living labour is confronted by past labour, activity is confronted by the product, man is confronted by things, labour is confronted by its own materialised conditions as alien, independent, self-contained subjects, personifications, in short, as *someone else's property* and, in this form, as "EMPLOYERS" and "COMMANDERS" of labour itself, which they appropriate instead of being appropriated by it. The fact that value—whether it exists as money or as commodities—and in the further development the conditions of labour confront the worker as the *property of other people*, as independent properties, means simply that they confront him as the *property* of the non-worker or, at any rate, that, as a capitalist, he confronts them not as a worker but as the *owner* of value, etc., as the *subject* in which these things possess their own will, belong to themselves and are personified as independent forces. *Capital* as the prerequisite of production, capital, not in the form in which it emerges from the production process, but as it is before it enters it, is the contradiction in which it is confronted by labour as the labour of other people and in which capital itself, as the property of other people, confronts labour. It is the contradictory social framework which is expressed in it and which, separated from the process itself, [XV-905] expresses itself in *capitalist property as such.*

This aspect—separated from the capitalist production process itself of which it is the constant result, and as its constant result it is also its constant prerequisite—manifests itself in the fact that money, commodities are as such, *latently,* capital, that they can be *sold as capital,* and that in this form they represent the *mere ownership of capital,* and the *capitalist as the mere owner,* apart from his capitalist functions. Money and commodities considered as such constitute command over other people's labour and therefore self-valorising value and a claim to the appropriation of other people's labour.

It is thus quite obvious that the title to and the means for the appropriation of other people's labour is this *relationship* and not some kind of labour or equivalent supplied by the capitalist.

Interest therefore appears as the *surplus value* due to capital as capital, to the mere ownership of capital, as the surplus value derived by capital from the production process because it enters it as capital, and therefore due to capital *as such* independently of the production process, although it is only realised *in* the production process; capital thus already contains the surplus value in a latent form. On the other hand, *industrial profit* [appears] as the portion of surplus value accruing to the capitalist not as the owner of capital, but as the operating owner representing the operating capital. In the same way as everything in this mode of production appears to be upside down, so ultimately does the final reversal in the relation of interest to profit, so that the portion of profit separated under a special heading appears as the product intrinsically belonging to capital, and industrial profit appears as a mere addition appended to it.

Since the MONEYED CAPITALIST in fact receives his part of the surplus value only as *owner of capital,* while he himself remains outside the

production process; since the price of capital—that is, of the mere
title to ownership of capital—is quoted on the money market as
the rate of interest in the same way as the market price of any
other commodity; since the share of surplus value which *capital in
itself,* the *mere ownership* of capital, secures is thus of a *stable*
magnitude, whereas the rate of profit fluctuates, at any given
moment it varies in the different spheres and within each sphere it
is different for the individual capitalists, partly because the
conditions under which they produce are more or less favourable,
partly because they exploit labour in capitalist fashion with
different degrees of circumspection and energy, and partly
because they cheat buyers or sellers of commodities with different
degrees of luck and cunning (PROFIT UPON EXPROPRIATION, ALIENATION)—it
therefore appears natural to them, whether they are or are not
owners of the capital involved in the production process, that
interest is something due to capital as such, to the ownership of
capital, to the owner of capital, whether they themselves own the
capital or someone else; industrial profit, on the other hand,
appears to be the result of *their* labour. As operating capitalists—
as real agents of capitalist production—they therefore confront
themselves or others representing merely idle capital, as *workers*
they consequently confront themselves or others as *property owners.*
And since they are, as matters stand, workers, they are in fact
wage workers, and because of their superiority they are simply
better-paid wage workers, which they owe partly also to the fact
that they pay themselves their wages. Whereas, therefore, *interest*
and *interest-bearing capital* merely express the contradiction of
materialised wealth as against labour, and thereby its existence as
capital, this position is turned upside down in the consciousness of
men because, *prima facie,* the MONEYED CAPITALIST does not appear to
have any relations with the wage worker, but only with other
capitalists, while these other capitalists, instead of appearing to be
in opposition to wage labour, appear rather as *workers,* in
opposition to themselves or to other capitalists considered as mere
owners of capital, representing the mere existence of capital. The
individual capitalist, moreover, can either lend his money *as capital*
or employ it *himself* as capital. In so far as he obtains *interest* on it,
he only receives for it the price which he would receive if he did
not "operate" as a capitalist, if he did not "work". It is clear,
therefore, that what he really gets from the production process—
in so far as it is only interest—is due to capital alone, not to the
production process itself and [XV-906] not to himself as a
representative of operating capital.

Hence also the pretty phrases used by some vulgar economists to the effect that, if the industrial capitalist did not get any profit in addition to interest, he would lend his capital out for interest and become a rentier, so that all capitalists would stop producing and all capital would cease operating as capital, but nevertheless it would still be possible to live *on the interest.* In similar vein, Turgot has already said that if the capitalist received no interest, he would buy land (capitalised rent) and live off rent.[a] But in this case the interest would still be derived from surplus value, since for the Physiocrats rent represents the real surplus value. Whereas in that vulgarised concept things are turned upside down.

Another fact should be noted. Interest is part of the *costs* for the industrial capitalist who has borrowed money, the term costs is here used in the sense that it represents the value advanced. For example, a capital of £1,000 does not enter the capitalist production process as a commodity worth £1,000 but as *capital*; this means that if a capital of £1,000 yields 10% interest per annum, then it enters into the annual product as a value of 1,100. This shows clearly that the *sum of values* (and the commodities in which it is embodied) becomes capital not only in the production process but that, as capital, it is preposited to the production process and therefore already contains within itself the surplus value due to it as mere capital. For the industrial capitalist who operates with borrowed capital, interest, in other words capital as capital—and it is this only in so far as it yields surplus value (so that if it is worth 1,000 as a commodity, for example, it is worth

$$1,100 \text{ as capital, i.e.} = 1,000 + \frac{1,000}{10}, \quad C + \frac{C}{x})\text{—enters into his costs.}$$

If the product only yielded interest, this, though it would be a surplus over and above the *value* of the capital advanced, regarded as a mere commodity, would not be a surplus over and above the value of the commodity considered as capital, for the industrialist has to pay out this surplus value; it is part of his outlay, part of the expenses he has incurred in order to produce the commodities.

As far as the industrialist who operates with his own capital is concerned, he pays the interest on his capital to himself and regards the interest as [part of] his outlay. In fact, what he has advanced is not simply a capital of £1,000 for example, but the value of £1,000 as capital, and this value would be £1,050 if the

---

[a] [A. R. J.] Turgot, "Réflexions sur la formation...", in: *Oeuvres...*, new ed., Vol. 1, Paris, 1844. §§ 73, 85. Cf. also present edition, Vol. 30, pp. 356 and 367.— *Ed.*

rate of interest=5%. This is moreover no idle consideration as far as he is concerned. For the £1,000 used as *capital* would yield him £1,050 if he lent it out instead of employing it productively. Thus, in so far as he advances the £1,000 to himself as capital, he is advancing himself £1,050. *Il faut bien se rattraper sur quelqu'un et fusse-t-il sur lui méme!*[a]

The value of commodities worth £1,000 is £1,050 as capital. This means that capital is not a simple quantity. It is not a simple commodity, but a commodity raised to a higher power; not a simple magnitude, but a proportion. It is a proportion of the principal sum, a given value, to itself as surplus value. The value of C is $C(1+\frac{1}{n})^1$ (for one year) or $C+\frac{C}{x}$. It is no more possible by means of the elementary rules of calculation to understand capital, that is, the commodity raised to a higher power, or money raised to a higher power, than it is to understand or to calculate the value of x in the equation $a^x=n$.

Just as in the case of *interest*, part of the profit, of the surplus value produced by capital, appears to have been *advanced* by the capitalist, so also in AGRICULTURAL PRODUCTION another part—*rent* [appears to have been advanced]. This seems to be less obviously irrational because in this case rent appears to be the annual price of the land which thus enters into production as a commodity. A "price of land" is indeed even more irrational than a price of capital, but this is not apparent in the form as such. Because in this case the land appears to be the use value of a commodity and the rent its price. (The irrationality consists in this, that land, i.e. something which is not the product of human labour, has a price, that is, a value expressed in money and consequently a value, and is therefore to be regarded as objectified social labour.) Considered purely formally, land, just as any other commodity, is expressed in two ways, as use value and as exchange value, and the exchange value is expressed nominally as price, that is, as something which the commodity as use value is absolutely not. On the other hand, in the statement: [a capital of] £1,000 equals £1,050, or £50 is the annual price of £1,000, something is compared with itself, exchange value with exchange value, and the exchange value as something different from itself is supposed to be its own price, that is, the exchange value expressed in money.

[XV-907] Thus two forms of surplus value—interest and rent,

---

[a] One must, after all, recover what is due to oneself, even if one takes it out of one's own pocket!— *Ed.*

the results of capitalist production—enter into it as prerequisites, as *advances* which the capitalist himself makes; for him, therefore, they do not represent any surplus value, i.e. any surplus over and above the advances made. As far as these forms of surplus value are concerned, it *appears* to the individual capitalist that the production of surplus value is a part of the *production costs* of capitalist production, and that the appropriation of other people's labour and of the surplus over and above the value of the commodities consumed in the process (whether these enter into the constant or into the variable capital) is a dominating condition of this mode of production. To a certain extent this applies also to average profit, in so far as it constitutes an element of cost price, and *hence a condition of supply, of the very creation of the commodity*. Nevertheless, the industrial capitalist rightly regards this surplus, this part of surplus value—although it constitutes an element of production—as a surplus over *his* costs; he does not regard it as belonging to *his* advances in the same way as interest and rent. In critical moments, profit too confronts the capitalist in fact as a condition of production, since he curtails or stops production when profit disappears or is reduced to a marked degree as a result of a fall in prices. Hence the nonsensical pronouncements of those who consider the different forms of surplus value to be merely forms of distribution; they are just as much forms of production.[a][130]

We have seen that capital in the circulation process establishes itself as commodity capital and as money capital, according to the stages of the circulation process in which it happens to be; we could also speak of phases of the reproduction process.[b] If I start from M, from money, the value with which the process opens, this money must *d'abord*[c] be thrown into circulation in order to be converted into capital. The money buys material for labour, means of labour and labour capacity. This is merely transformation of money into commodity, an act of circulation. In fact, the act of circulation which constitutes the final stage in the circulation of the simple commodity is the first phase in the circulation of capital, $M—C$, precisely because it begins with money, the converted image of the commodity, a mere form of it which is itself a product of the circulation of commodities. This first act is followed by the production process proper, in which the means of

---

a See this volume, p. 531.— *Ed.*
b Ibid., pp. 468-69.— *Ed.*
c To begin with.— *Ed.*

labour, the material of labour and the active labour capacity, thrown together in one crucible, disappear. It is in fact a *process of the consumption* of the commodities bought; but, in accordance with its specific character, this consumption is *industrial consumption,* in so far as it produces anything at all; *capitalist production* by virtue of the special manner in which labour capacity is consumed. As a result of this production process, which constitutes a pause in the circulation, and which takes up consumption itself into the economic process, the *commodity* or, since the separate commodity is here nothing, the totality of commodities appears as equal to the original value+the absorbed surplus value, to the *mass of commodities* of which capital now consists. Next follows the second act of circulation interrupted by the production process or industrial consumption, namely the throwing of the commodity on the market, into circulation, and its conversion into money, i.e. its sale. This money No. 2 is different from money No. 1. It was a premiss, it is now a result. It was money that had to be converted into capital; it is capital converted into money. It was the starting-point, it is now a return to itself. It is value that has not only been preserved but has increased itself. It was 100. And it is 110; that is, 100+10. Its value and an aliquot part of the original sum as SURPLUS. Here the two circulation acts appear as separated by the production process and both of them as standing outside it. The process lies between them. The one starts it, the other follows it. But reproduction also occurs. The value contained in the commodity that served as the means is preserved and increased in the commodity that is the result of the production process. On the other hand, the money that forms the starting-point is preserved and increased in the money that forms the end point. In this way the entire process appears as the unity of the production process and the circulation process and to this extent as the reproduction process. However, this unity of a *single* process is in fact production, not reproduction.

Let us consider the pure form first; let us designate the commodities into which money is converted—that is to say, the *ingredients* of the commodity which is to be produced—as C' as distinct from the commodity which emerges from the production process.

[XV-908] (I) *Single Cycle of Production*

1)	2)	3)
$M—C'$ ------------------	C' *in process.* Result, C -------------------------	$C—M'$
1st *act of circulation* ---	*consumption of C', process of production of C*	2nd *act of circulation*

What is called reproduction here is merely *maintenance* of the preposited value. The value of M is maintained in C', in C and in the second M', where it reappears. What is produced is surplus value, and this takes place in the production process, WHENCE THE VALUE OF $C>C'$. That the greater value of C is expressed in more money than C' in M or M in C' signifies nothing but that realised in M' is the value of M and C', which has not only been maintained but also increased in the production process. M' instead of M is in fact the *product* of the whole process; but it is merely the altered form of C instead of C'. The same C' does not appear again as reproduced, and M' appears merely as a result of the process of which it was the starting-point. It does not appear itself as a moment in the flow of the process but only as a crystal of it.

On the other hand, the continuity of production and circulation—a continuity conditioned by the nature of capitalist production—shows the two circulation acts in a different sense and in a different position than in the single production process, in which $M—C'$ is only a circulation act which expresses the *beginning* (not the repetition) of the production process, and $C—M,$ only a circulation process which expresses its *end* and thus in no way its resumption. Viewing the process in its continuity, and thus as a flowing unity of the circulation and production process, we can start from each of the points, whether they seem to be intermediate or end points, as from our point of departure. Thus, first, from *money* as the starting-point of a single production process; *second,* from the *commodity* (product) as the immediate result of the production process; finally from the production process itself, C' as process.

(II) *Continuity of the Production Process. Reproduction*

1)	2)	3)	4)	5)	6)
(a) $M—C'$ ----	C' in process	$C—M'$ --------	$M'—C'$ -------	C' in process---	$C—M''$ etc.
1st act of circulation	process of production of C	2nd act of circulation	3rd act of circulation	process of production of C	4th and last act of circulation, etc.

1)	2)	3)	4)
(b) $C—M$ ------	$M—C'$ ---------	C' in process---	C
1st act of circulation	Second act of circulation	process of production of C	(Result of process, reproduction of C)

1)	2)	3)
(c) C' in process -------------- (process of production of C)	$C—M$ --------- First act of circulation	$M—C'$ --------- C' in process (resumption of the production process, which thus appears as a Second act of circulation reproduction process)

Only when one starts from money as in (a) does the reproduction process appear *prima facie* as mere repetition. It can always begin again with *M*, but it can also end with it.

When, however, one starts out from *C* or the process of production itself, and also ends with it—since the movement is circular—it is clear that at some moment the reproduction process, which must continue, is interrupted. The result of the production process must enter into circulation in (c) and the *commodity* must be converted into money in (b). What distinguishes all 3 forms of II from form I is this: In I), in the single production process, the real production process lies in the middle, and at the two separated extremes, *M—C'* lies before it and *C—M* after.

[XV-910] [131] By contrast, in all the 3 forms of the reproduction process the mutually opposed phases of the commodity metamorphosis or the total circulation *C—M—C'* (*C—M* and *M—C'*) appear as a movement preceding the renewal of the production process. *C—M—C'* appears as the circulation phase proper of the reproduction process, or else the metamorphosis of the commodity appears as a moment of the reproduction process. True, (b) and (c) show—the one, that the commodity *C* has renewed itself, that it has been reproduced; the other, that the production process itself is renewed, but both indicate that their end is only a link of a further process. By contrast, in (a), where one begins with *M*, the reflux of money, the reappearance of the commodity in the form of money, is the only form which can both constitute the beginning of reproduction and end the production process. In the simple metamorphosis *C—M—C'*, which we considered in money circulation,[a] the consumption of the commodity falls outside the economic form. As industrial consumption, as a production process, it constitutes a link in the real metamorphosis of commodities. Leaving out money, we have (1) *C—C'*. A commodity is exchanged for the elements of its being. (2) *C' in process.* Consumption of these elements through labour. The production process. Finally, the third *C*. Thus *C—C'—C'* (in process)— *C*. Each act of circulation, just as the total metamorphosis, the unity of the reversed phases *C—M—C'*, appear as mere moments of the reproduction process. On the other hand, the production process itself appears as a moment in the whole of the cycle, is itself incorporated in circulation.

---

[a] See K. Marx, *A Contribution to the Critique of Political Economy.* Part One (present edition, Vol. 29, pp. 324-34).— *Ed.*

The 3rd figure of (II) shows only the production process as distinct from the entire circulation process. In order that it may resume itself, $C—M—C'$ must be gone through, and the rate of its renewal depends on the rate of this metamorphosis.

In the 2nd figure of (II) we start from the commodity. The rate at which it is renewed essentially depends on the rate at which it goes through the production process.

Finally in figure 1' of (II) the conditions are presented together. The rate at which M is produced as M' depends, first, on the rate of the conversion of M into C', $M^{(1)}—C'$, second, on the duration of the production process, $C'^{(2)}$ in process, third, on the speed of the metamorphosis $C—M—C'$.[132]

Let us consider the road travelled by capital before it appears in the form of interest-bearing capital.

In the immediate process of production, the matter is fairly simple. SURPLUS VALUE has not as yet assumed a *separate* form, apart from the fact that it is SURPLUS VALUE as distinct from the VALUE which is equivalent to the VALUE reproduced in the product. In the same way as VALUE in general resolves into LABOUR, so SURPLUS VALUE consists of SURPLUS LABOUR, unpaid labour. Hence SURPLUS VALUE is only measured by that part of capital which really changes its value—the variable capital, i.e. the capital which is laid out in wages. Constant capital appears only as the condition enabling the variable part of capital to operate. It is quite simple: if with £100, i.e. the labour of 10 [men], one buys the labour of 20 [men] (that is, commodities in which the labour of 20 [men] is embodied), the value of the product will be £200 and the surplus value will amount to £100, equal to the unpaid labour of 10 [men]. Or, supposing 20 men worked half a day each for themselves and half for capital—20 half-days equal 10 whole ones—the result would be the same as if only 10 men were paid and the others worked for the capitalist gratis.

Here, in this embryonic state, the relationship is still very obvious, or rather it cannot be misunderstood. The difficulty is simply to discover how this appropriation of labour without any equivalent arises from the law of commodity exchange—out of the fact that commodities exchange for one another in proportion to the amount of labour time embodied in them—and, to start with, does not contradict this law.

[XV-911] The circulation process obliterates and obscures the connection. Since here the mass of surplus value is also determined by the *circulation time of capital,* an element foreign to labour time seems to have entered.

Finally, in capital as the finished phenomenon, as it appears as a whole, [as] the unity of the circulation and the production processes, as the expression of the reproduction process—as a definite sum of values which produces a definite amount of profit (surplus value) in a definite time, a definite period of circulation—in capital in this form the production and circulation processes exist only as a reminiscence and as aspects which determine the surplus value *equally,* thereby disguising its simple nature. Surplus value now appears as profit. This profit is, first, received for a definite period of circulation of capital, and this period is distinct from the labour time; it is, secondly, surplus value calculated and drawn not on that part of capital from which it originates directly, but quite indiscriminately on the total capital. In this way its source is completely concealed. Thirdly, although the mass of profit is still quantitatively identical in this first form of profit with the mass of surplus value produced by the individual capital, the rate of profit is, from the very beginning, different from the rate of surplus value; since the rate of surplus value is $\frac{s}{v}$ and the rate of profit is $\frac{s}{c+v}$. Fourthly, if the rate of surplus value is presumed given, it is possible for the rate of profit to rise or to fall and even to move in the opposite direction to the rate of surplus value.

Thus, surplus value in the first form of profit already assumes a form which not only makes it difficult to perceive that it is identical with surplus value, i.e. surplus labour, but appears directly to contradict this view.

Furthermore, as a result of the conversion of profit into *average profit,* the establishment of the general rate of profit and, in connection with it or posited by it, the conversion of values into cost prices, the profit of the individual capital becomes *different* from the actual surplus value produced by the individual capital in its particular sphere of production, and different, moreover, not only in the way it is expressed—i.e. rate of profit as distinct from rate of surplus value—but it becomes substantially different, that is, in this context, quantitatively different. Profit does not merely *seem* to be different, but *is* now in fact different from surplus value not only with regard to the individual capital but also with regard to the total capital in a particular sphere of production. Capitals of equal magnitude yield equal profits; in other words, profit is proportional to the size of the capital. Or profit is determined by the value of capital advanced. The relation of profit to the organic composition of capital is completely obliterated and no longer recognisable in all these formulae. On the other hand, it is quite obvious that capitals of the same magnitude which set in motion very different amounts of labour, thus commanding very different amounts of surplus labour and consequently producing very different amounts of SURPLUS VALUE, yield the same amount of profit. Indeed, the basis itself—the determination of the value of commodities by the labour time embodied in them—appears to be invalidated as a result of the conversion of values into cost prices.

In this quite alienated form of profit and in the same measure as the form of profit hides its inner core, capital more and more acquires a material form, is transformed more and more from a relationship into a thing, but a thing which embodies, which has absorbed, the social relationship, a thing which has acquired a fictitious life and independent existence in relation to itself, a natural-supernatural entity; in this form of *capital and profit* it appears superficially as a ready-made precondition. It is the form of its reality, or rather its real form of existence. And it is the form in which it exists in the consciousness and is reflected in the imagination of its representatives, the capitalists.

This fixed and ossified (metamorphosed) form of profit (and thereby of capital as its producer, for capital is the cause and profit is the result; capital is the reason, profit is the effect; capital is the substance, profit is the adjunct; capital is capital only in so far as it yields profit, only in so far as it is a value which produces profit, an additional value)—and therefore also of capital as its cause, capital which maintains itself and expands by means of profit—the external aspect of this ossified form is strengthened even more by the fact that the same process of the equalisation of capital, which gives profit the form of average profit, separates part of it in the form of *rent* as something independent of it and arising from a different foundation, the land. It is true that rent originally emerges as a part of profit which the FARMER pays to the LANDLORD. But since this SURPLUS PROFIT is not pocketed by the FARMER, and the capital he employs does not differ in any way as capital from other capitals (it is precisely because SURPLUS PROFIT is not derived from capital as such that the farmer pays it to the LANDLORD), the land itself appears to be the source of this part of the value of the commodity (its surplus value) and the LANDLORD [appears to represent] the land only [XV-912] as a juridical person.

If the rent is calculated on the capital advanced, then a thread still remains which indicates its origin as a distinct part of profit, that is, of surplus value in general. (The position is, of course, quite different in a social order where landed property exploits labour directly. In that case, it is not difficult to recognise the origin of SURPLUS WEALTH.) But the rent is paid on a definite area of land; it is capitalised in the value of the land; this value rises and falls in accordance with the rise or fall of rent. The rise or fall of rent is calculated with regard to a piece of land which remains unchanged (whereas the amount of capital operating on it changes); the difference in the types of land is reflected in the amount of rent which has to be paid for a given yardage, the total RENTAL is calculated on the total area of the land in order to determine the average RENTAL, for example, of a square yard. Rent, like every phenomenon created by capitalist production, appears at the same time as a stable, given precondition existing at any particular moment, and thus, it is for each individual an independently existing magnitude. The FARMER has to pay rent, so much per acre of land, according to the quality of the land. If its quality improves or deteriorates, then the rent he has to pay on so many ACRES rises or falls. He has to pay rent for the land quite irrespective of the capital he employs on it, just as he has to pay interest irrespective of the profit he makes.

The calculation of rent on industrial capital is another critical formula of political economy which demonstrates the inner connection between rent and profit, its basis. But this connection does not *appear* in reality; rather the calculation of rent is based on the real area of land, the intermediate links are thereby eliminated and rent acquires its externalised independent aspect. It is an independent form only in this externalisation, in its complete separation from its antecedents. So many square yards of land bring in so much rent. In this formula, in which rent, a part of surplus value, *is represented in relation to a particular natural element, independent of human labour,* not only the nature of surplus value is completely obliterated, because the nature of value itself is obliterated; but, just as the source of rent appears to be land, so now *profit* itself appears to be due to *capital as a particular material instrument of production.* Land is part of nature and brings in rent. Capital consists of products and these bring in profit. That one use value which is produced brings in profit, while another which is not produced brings in rent are simply two different forms in which things *produce value,* and the one form is just as comprehensible and as incomprehensible as the other.

It is clear that, as soon as surplus value [is split up] into different, *separate* parts, related to various production elements—such as nature, products, labour—which only differ *physically,* that is, as soon as in general surplus value acquires *special* forms, separate from one another, independent of one another and regulated by different laws, the common unit—surplus value—and consequently the nature of this common unit, becomes more and more unrecognisable and does not manifest itself in the *appearance* but has to be discovered as a hidden mystery. This assumption of independent forms by the various parts—and their confrontation as independent forms—is completed as a result of each of these parts being reduced to a particular element as its measure and its special source; in other words, each part of surplus value is conceived as the effect of a special cause, as an adjunct of a particular substance. Thus profit is related to capital, rent to land, wages to labour. These ready-made relations and forms, which appear as preconditions in real production because the capitalist mode of production moves within the forms it has created itself and which are its results, confront it equally as ready-made preconditions in the process of reproduction. As such, they in fact determine the actions of individual capitalists, etc., and provide the motives, which are reflected in their consciousness. Vulgar political economy does nothing more than express in doctrinaire fashion this consciousness, which, in respect of its motives and notions, remains in thrall to the appearance of the capitalist mode of production. And the more it clings to the shallow, superficial appearance, only bringing it into some sort of order, the more it considers that it is acting "naturally" and avoiding all abstract subtleties.

[XV-913] In connection with the circulation process dealt with above[a] it has to be added that the categories arising out of the circulation process crystallise as attributes of particular sorts of capital, fixed, circulating and so on, and thus appear as definite material attributes of certain commodities.

In the final state in which profit, assumed as something given, appears in capitalist production, the innumerable transformations and intervening stages through which it passes are obliterated and unrecognisable, and consequently the nature of capital is also obliterated and unrecognisable. This state becomes even more rigid owing to the fact that the same process which gives it its final FINISH causes part of the profit to confront it as *rent,* thus

---

[a] See this volume, p. 482.— *Ed.*

transforming profit into a *particular* aspect of surplus value, an aspect based on capital as a special material instrument of production, in exactly the same way as rent is based on land; thus this state, separated from its inner essence by a mass of invisible intermediate links, reaches an even more *externalised* form, or rather the form of absolute *externalisation*, in interest-bearing capital, in the separation of interest from profit,in interest-bearing capital as the simple form of capital, the form in which capital is antecedent to its own reproduction process. On the one hand, this expresses the absolute form of capital $M—M'$, self-valorising value. On the other hand, the intermediate link C, which still exists in genuine merchant capital whose formula is $M—C—M'$, has disappeared. Only the relation of M to itself and measured by itself remains. It is capital expressly removed, separated from the process, as an antecedent it stands outside the process whose result it is and through which alone it is capital.

//[Here] the fact is disregarded that interest may be a mere TRANSFER and need not represent real surplus value, as, for example, when money is lent to a "spendthrift", i.e. for consumption. The position may be similar when money is borrowed in order to make *payments*. In both cases it is loaned as money, not as·capital, but it becomes *capital* to its owner through the mere act of lending it out. In the second case, [if it is used to] DISCOUNT [bills] or as a LOAN ON temporarily NOT VENDIBLE COMMODITIES, it can be associated with the circulation process of capital, the necessary conversion of commodity capital into money capital. In so far as the acceleration of this conversion process—such acceleration is a general feature of credit—speeds up reproduction, and therefore the production of surplus value, the money lent is capital. On the other hand, in so far as it only serves to pay *debts* without accelerating the reproduction process, perhaps even limiting it or making it impossible, it is a mere *means of payment,* only money for the borrower, and for the *lender it is, in fact, capital independent of the process of capital.* In this case interest, like PROFIT UPON EXPROPRIATION, is a FACT independent of capitalist production— the production of surplus value. It is in these two forms of money—money as means of purchase of commodities intended for consumption and as means of payment of debts—that interest, like PROFIT UPON EXPROPRIATION, constitutes a form which, although it is reproduced in capitalist production, is nevertheless independent of it and [represents] a form of interest which belongs to earlier modes of production. It is in the nature of capitalist production, however, that money (or commodities) can exist as capital and can be sold as capital outside the production process, and that this can also be the case with the older forms, in which it is not converted into capital but only serves as money. The third of the older forms of interest-bearing capital is based on the fact that capitalist production does *not as yet* exist, but that profit is still acquired in the form of interest and the capitalist appears as a mere usurer. This implies: 1) that the producer still works independently with his own means of production, and that the means of production do not yet work with him (even if slaves form a part of these means of production, for in these circumstances slaves do not constitute a separate economic category any more than draught animals do; there is at best a physical difference between them, i.e. dumb instruments, and speaking and feeling instruments[133]); 2) that the means of production belong only nominally to the producer; in other words, that because of some incidental circumstances he is unable to reproduce them from [the proceeds of] the sale of his commodities. These forms of interest-bearing capital occur, consequently, in all forms of society which include commodity and money circulation, whether slave labour, serf labour or free labour is predominant in them. In the last-mentioned form, the producer pays the capitalist his surplus labour in the form of interest, which therefore includes profit. We have here the whole of [XV-914] capitalist production without its advantages, the development of the social forms of labour and of the productive powers of labour to which they give rise. This form is very prevalent among peasant nations who already have to buy a portion of the necessaries of life and instruments of production as commodities (alongside whom, therefore, separate urban industries already exist) and who, in addition, have to pay taxes, rent, etc., in money. //

Interest-bearing capital functions as such only in so far as the money lent is really converted into capital and produces a SURPLUS of which interest constitutes a part. This does not however invalidate the fact that interest and interest-bearing have become attributes of it independently of the process. Any more than the use value of cotton as cotton is nullified by the fact that it has to be spun or used in some other way, in order to demonstrate its useful properties. And thus capital [demonstrates] its capacity to yield interest only by becoming part of the production process. But labour capacity likewise demonstrates its ability to produce value only when it functions as labour, is realised as labour in this process. This does not rule out that, in itself, as an ability, it is a value-creating activity and does not merely become such as a result of the process, but rather is antecedent to the process. It is bought as such. A person can buy it without setting it to work (as, for example, when a theatre manager hires an actor not in order to give him a role in a play, but to prevent him from performing in a rival theatre). Whether or not a man who buys labour capacity uses its faculty for which he pays, i.e. its faculty to create value, is of no concern to the man who sells it, and makes no difference to the commodity sold, just as it makes no difference whether the man who buys capital uses it as such, that is, employs the quality of creating value which is inherent in it, in the process. What he pays for in these two cases is the surplus value and the capacity of maintaining its own value *in itself*—potentially, by the nature of the commodity which has been bought—contained in the capital in the one case and in the labour capacity in the other. This is why the capitalist who operates with his own capital regards part of the surplus value as interest, that is, as surplus value which is yielded by the production process, because it has been brought into the production process by the capital independently of the process.

Rent and the relationship land—rent may appear as a much more mysterious form than that of interest [and the relationship] capital—interest. But the irrational element in rent is not formulated or shaped in such a way that it expresses a *relation of capital itself.* Since land itself is productive (of use value) and is itself a living productive force (of use value or for the creation of use values), it is possible either SUPERSTITIOUSLY to confuse use value with exchange value, i.e. to confuse it with a specific social form of the labour contained in the product. In this case, the reason for the irrationality lies in itself, since rent as a category *sui generis* is independent of the capitalist process as such. Or "enlightened" political economy may deny altogether that rent is a form of SURPLUS VALUE, because it is not connected with either labour or capital, and declare that it is merely a SURCHARGE which the landowner is able to make as a result of his monopoly of landownership.

The position is different in the case of interest-bearing capital. Here it is a question not of a relation which is alien to capital, but of the capital relation itself; of a relation which arises out of capitalist production, is specific to it, and expresses the essence of capital itself; of an aspect of capital in which it appears *as capital.* Profit is still related to operating capital, to the process in which surplus value (and profit itself) is produced. Whereas in *profit* the form of surplus value has become alienated, strange, so that its simple form and therefore its substance and source of origin are not immediately discernible, this is not the case in *interest-bearing capital*; on the contrary it is *precisely* this alienated form which is presupposed and declared to be the *essential* feature of *interest.* The alienated form has assumed an independent and rigid existence as something *antagonistic* to the real nature of surplus value. The relationship of capital to labour is obliterated in interest-bearing capital. In fact, interest presupposes profit, of which it is only a part. The way in which surplus value [XV-915] is divided into interest and profit and distributed between different sorts of capitalists is actually a matter of complete indifference to the wage worker. *Interest* is definitely regarded as the OFFSPRING OF CAPITAL, separate, independent and outside the capitalist process. It is due to *capital as capital.* It enters into the production process and therefore proceeds from it. Capital is impregnated with interest. It does not derive interest from the production process, but brings it into it. The surplus of profit over interest, the amount of surplus value which capital derives solely from the production process, i.e. the surplus value it produces as operating capital, acquires a separate form, namely, that of *industrial profit* (employer's profit, industrial or commercial, depending on whether the stress is laid on the production process or the circulation process), in contrast to interest, a value created by *capital as such, capital for itself,* and *capital as capital.* Thus even the last form of surplus value, which to some extent recalls its origin, is separated and conceived not only as an alienated form, but as one which is in direct contradiction to its origin; consequently the nature of capital and of surplus value as well as that of capitalist production in general is, finally, completely mystified.

Industrial profit, in contradistinction to *interest,* represents capital in the process in contradistinction to capital outside the process, capital as a process in contradistinction to capital as property; it therefore represents the capitalist as functioning capitalist, as representative of *working capital* as opposed to the capitalist as mere personification of capital, as mere owner of capital. He thus appears as *working capitalist* in contrast to himself as *capitalist,* and further, as *worker* in contrast to himself as mere *owner.* Consequently, in so far as any relation between surplus value and the process is still preserved, or apparent, this is done precisely in the form in which THE VERY NOTION OF SURPLUS VALUE IS NEGATED. *Industrial profit* is resolved into labour, not into *unpaid* labour of other people but into *wage labour,* into wages for the capitalist, who in this case is placed into the same category as the wage worker and is merely a more highly paid worker, just as in general wages vary greatly.

Money is indeed not converted into capital as a result of the fact that it is exchanged against the material conditions required for the production of the commodity, and that in the labour process these conditions—materials of labour, means of labour and labour—begin to ferment, act on one another, combine with one another, undergo a chemical process and form the commodity like a crystal as a result of this process. The outcome of this would be no capital, no surplus value. This abstract form of the labour process is common to all modes of production whatever their social form or their particular historical character. The process only becomes a capitalist process, and money is converted into capital only: 1) if *commodity production,* i.e. the production of products in the form of commodities, becomes the general form of production; 2) if the commodity (money) is exchanged against labour capacity (that is, actually against labour) as a commodity, and consequently if labour is wage labour; 3) this is the case however only when the objective conditions, that is (considering the production process as a whole), the products, confront labour as independent forces, not as the property of labour but as the property of someone else, and thus in the form of *capital.* Labour as wage labour and the conditions of labour as capital (that is, consequently, as the property of the capitalist; they are themselves properties personified in the capitalist and whose property in them, their property in themselves, they represent as against labour) are expressions of the same relationship, only seen from opposite poles. This condition of capitalist production is its invariable result. It is its *antecedent* posited by itself. Capitalist production is antecedent to itself and is therefore posited with its conditions as soon as it has evolved and functions in circumstances appropriate to it. However, the *capitalist production process* is not just a production process pure and simple. The contradictory, socially determined feature of its elements evolves, becomes reality only in the process itself, and this feature is the predominant characteristic of the process, which it turns precisely into that socially determined mode of production, the *capitalist process of production.*

[XV-916] The *formation process* of capital—when capital, i.e. not any particular capital, but capital in general, only evolves—is the *dissolution process,* the *parting product* of the social mode of production preceding it. It is thus an *historical process,* a process which belongs to a definite historical period. This is the period of its *historical genesis.* (In the same way the existence of the human race is the result of an earlier process which organic life passed through. Man comes into existence only when a certain point is reached. But once man has emerged, he becomes the permanent presupposition of human history, likewise its permanent product and result, and he is *presupposition* only as his own product and result.) It is here that labour must separate itself from the conditions of labour in their previous form, in which it was identical with them. It becomes *free* labour only in this way and only thus are its conditions converted into *capital* and confront it as such. The process of capital becoming capital or its development *before* the capitalist production process exists, and its realisation in this process itself belong to two historically different periods. In the second, capital is *taken for granted,* and its existence and automatic functioning is presupposed. In the first period, capital is the sediment resulting from the process of dissolution of a different form of society. It is the *product* of a different [form of society], not the product of its own reproduction, as is the case later. The existing basis on which capitalist production works is wage labour, which is however at the same time reproduced continuously by it. It is therefore based also on *capital,* the form assumed by the conditions of labour, as its given presupposition, a presupposition however which, like wage labour, is its continuous presupposition and its continuous product.

On this basis, *money,* for example, is, as such, capital because the conditions of production in themselves confront labour in an alienated form, they confront it as someone else's property and thus dominate it. Then capital can also be sold as a *commodity* which has this attribute, that is, it can be sold as capital, as is the case when capital is loaned at interest.

But while thus the aspect of the specific social determination of capital and of capitalist production—a specific social determination which is expressed juridically in capital as property, in capital property as a special form of property— *is established,* and *interest,* therefore, appears as that *part of surplus value* which is produced by capital in this determinate form, independent of this determination considered as the determination of the process as a whole, then the other part of surplus value, the SURPLUS of profit over interest, *industrial profit,* must obviously represent value which does not arise from capital as such, but from the production process separated from its social determination, which has indeed already found its special mode of existence in the formula, capital—interest. Separated from capital, however, the production process becomes *labour process* in general. Consequently, the industrial capitalist as distinct from himself as capitalist, that is, the industrialist in contradistinction to himself as capitalist, i.e. owner of capital, is merely a simple functionary in the labour process; he does not represent functioning capital, but is a functionary irrespective of capital, and therefore a particular representative of the labour process in general, a *worker*. In this way, industrial profit is happily converted into *wages* and is equated with ordinary wages, differing from them only quantitatively and in the special form in which they are paid, i.e. that the capitalist pays wages to himself instead of someone else paying them to him.

The nature of surplus value (and therefore of capital) is not only obliterated in this final division of profit into *interest* and *industrial profit*, but it is definitely presented as something quite different.

Interest represents part of surplus value; it is merely a portion of profit which is separated and classified under a special name, the portion which accrues to the person who merely owns the capital, the portion he intercepts. But this merely *quantitative* division is turned into a *qualitative division* which transforms both parts in such a way that not even a trace of their original essence seems to remain. [XV-917] This is first of all confirmed by the fact that *interest* does not appear as a division which makes no difference to production, and takes place only "occasionally" when the industrialist operates with someone else's capital. Even when he operates with his own capital his profit is split into *interest* and *industrial profit*, thereby transforming the mere quantitative division into a *qualitative* one which does not depend on the accidental circumstance whether the industrialist owns or does not own his capital; the *qualitative* division arises out of the nature of capital and of capitalist production itself. There exist not simply two portions of profit distributed to two different persons, but two separate *categories* of profit which are related in different ways to capital and consequently to different determinate aspects of capital. Apart from the reasons mentioned earlier, this assumption of an independent existence is established all the more easily since *interest-bearing capital* appears on the scene as a historic form before industrial capital and continues to exist alongside it in its old form and it is only in the course of the development of industrial capital that the latter subordinates it to capitalist production by turning it into a *special form* of industrial capital.

The mere quantitative division thus becomes a qualitative one. Capital is itself divided. In so far as it is a *prerequisite* of capitalist production, in so far, therefore, as it *expresses* a *specific social relation,* the *alienated form of the conditions of labour,* it is realised in *interest.* It realises its character as capital in interest. On the other hand, in so far as it operates in the process, this process appears as something separate from its specific capitalist character, from its specific social determination—as mere *labour process* in general. Therefore, in so far as the capitalist plays any part in it, he does so not as a capitalist—for this aspect of his character is allowed for in interest—but as a functionary of the labour process in general, as a *worker,* and his wages take the form of *industrial profit.* It is a special type of labour—LABOUR OF DIRECTION—but after all types of labour in general differ from one another.

Thus the nature of surplus value, the essence of capital and the character of capitalist production are not only completely obliterated in these two forms of surplus value, they are turned into their opposites. But even in so far as the character and form of capital are complete [it is] nonsensical [if] presented without any intermediate links and expressed as the subjectification of objects, the objectification of subjects, as the reversal of cause and effect, the religious *quid pro quo,* the pure form of capital expressed in the formula $M—M'$. The ossification of relations, their presentation as the relation of men to things having a definite social character is here likewise brought out in quite a different manner from that of the simple mystification of commodities and the more complicated mystification of money. The transubstantiation, the fetishism, is complete.

Thus *interest* in itself expresses precisely the existence of the conditions of labour as *capital* in their social contradiction and in their transformation into personal forces which confront labour and dominate labour. It sums up the *alienated* character of the conditions of labour in relation to the activity of the subject. It represents the ownership of capital or mere capital property as the means for appropriating the products of other people's labour, as the control over other people's labour. But it presents this character of capital as something belonging to it [capital] apart from the production process itself and by no means as resulting from the specific determinate form of the production process itself. Interest presents capital not in opposition to labour, but, on the contrary, as having no relation to labour, and merely as a relation of one capitalist to another; consequently, as a category which is quite extrinsic to, and independent of, the relation of capital to labour. The division of the profit amongst the capitalists does not affect the worker. Thus *interest,* the form of profit which is the special expression of the *contradictory character* of capital, is an expression in which this contradiction is completely obliterated and explicitly left out of account. Apart from expressing the capacity of money, commodities, etc., to valorise their own value, interest, in so far as it presents surplus value as something deriving from money, commodities, etc., as their natural fruit, is therefore merely a manifestation of the mystification of capital in its most extreme form; in so far as it at all represents a social relation *as such*, it expresses [XV-918] merely relations between capitalists, and by no means relations between capital and labour.

On the other hand, the existence of this form of *interest* gives the other part of profit the *qualitative form* of *industrial profit*, of wages for the labour of the industrial capitalist not in his capacity as capitalist, but as a *worker* (industrialist). The particular functions which the capitalist as such has to perform in the labour process and which are incumbent precisely on him as distinct from the workers, are represented as mere labour functions. He produces surplus value not because he works *as a capitalist*, but because he, the capitalist, also *works*. It is just as if a king, who, as king, has nominal command of the army, were to be assumed to command the army not because he, as the owner of the kingship, *commands*, plays the role of commander-in-chief, but on the contrary that he is king because he *commands*, exercises the function of commander-in-chief. If thus one part of surplus value, i.e. interest, is completely separated from the process of exploitation, then the other part, that is, industrial profit, emerges as its direct opposite, not as appropriation of other people's labour, but as the creation of value by one's own labour. This part of surplus value is therefore no longer surplus value, but its opposite, an equivalent given for labour performed. Since the *alienated character* of capital, its opposition to labour, is displayed outside the exploitation process, that is, outside the sphere where the *real action of this alienation* takes place, all the contradictory features are eliminated from this process itself. Consequently, *real* exploitation, the sphere where these contradictory features are put into practice and where they manifest themselves in reality, appears as its exact opposite, as a substantially different kind of labour, which belongs however to the same socially determined form of labour—wage labour—to the same *category* of labour. The work of the exploiter is identified here with the labour which is exploited.

This conversion of one part of profit into *industrial profit* arises, as we have seen, from the conversion of the other part into *interest.* The social form of capital—that it is property—devolves on the latter part; on the former part devolves the economic function of capital, its function in the labour process, but detached, abstracted from the social form, the contradictory form in which it exercises this function. How this is further justified by learned reasoning is to be examined in greater detail in connection with the apologetic interpretation of profit as [remuneration for] LABOUR OF SUPERINTENDENCE.[a] Here the capitalist is equated with his MANAGER, as Adam Smith already noted.[b] Industrial profit does indeed include some part of WAGES—in those cases where the MANAGER does not draw them. Capital appears in the production process as the director of labour, as its commander (CAPTAIN OF INDUSTRY) and thus plays an active role in the actual labour process. But in so far as these functions arise out of the specific form of capitalist production—that is, out of the domination of capital over labour as *its* labour and, therefore, over the workers as its instruments, out of the nature of capital, which appears as the *social entity,* the subject of the social form of labour personified in it [capital] as power over labour—this work (it may be entrusted to a MANAGER) which is linked with exploitation is, of course, labour which, in the same way as that of the wage worker, enters into the value of the product; just *as in the case of slavery, the labour of the overseer* has to be paid for like that of a worker. If man attributes an independent existence, clothed in a *religious form,* to his relationship to his own nature, to external nature and to other men so that he is dominated by these notions, then he requires *priests* and *their* labour. With the disappearance of the religious form of consciousness and of these relationships, the labour of the priests will likewise cease to enter into the social process of production. The labour of priests will end with the existence of the *priests* themselves and, in the same way, the labour which the capitalist performs *qua* capitalist, or causes to be performed by someone else, will end together with the existence of the capitalists. (The example of slavery has to be amplified by quotations.)[134]

Incidentally, these apologetics aimed at reducing profit to wages, i.e. the WAGES OF LABOUR OF SUPERINTENDENCE, boomerang on the apologists themselves, for English [XV-919] socialists have rightly declared: Well, in future, you shall only draw the WAGES usually paid to MANAGERS. Your INDUSTRIAL PROFIT should be reduced to WAGES

---

a See pp. XVIII—1100-01 of the manuscript (present edition, Vol. 33).— *Ed.*
b A. Smith, *An Inquiry into the Nature and Causes of the Wealth of Nations,* Book I, Ch. VI.— *Ed.*

OF SUPERINTENDENCE or DIRECTION OF LABOUR not merely in words, but in practice.

(It is of course impossible to examine in detail this nonsense and twaddle with all its contradictions. For example, INDUSTRIAL PROFIT rises and falls in inverse [proportion] to interest or rent. The SUPERINTENDENCE OF LABOUR, the particular amount of labour really performed by the capitalist, has however nothing whatever to do with it, any more than with the *decline in wages.* This kind of wages has the peculiarity that it falls and rises in inverse proportion to real wages (in so far as the rate of profit is determined by the rate of surplus value, and in so far as all the *conditions of production* remain unchanged, it is determined *exclusively* by this). But "little contradictions" of this kind do not prevent the apologetic VULGARIAN from regarding them as identical. The labour performed by the capitalist remains absolutely the same whether he pays low or high wages, whether the worker receives high or low wages. Just as the wages paid for a working day do not affect the amount of labour involved. Moreover, the worker works more intensively when he gets better wages. The labour of the capitalist, on the other hand, is something strictly determined, it is determined both qualitatively and quantitatively by the amount of labour he has to direct, not by the wages paid for this labour. He can no more intensify his labour than the cotton operative can work up more cotton than is available in the mill.)

And they [the English socialists] add: the office of manager, the LABOUR OF SUPERINTENDENCE, can now be bought on the market in the same way as any other kind of labour capacity, and is relatively just as cheap to produce and therefore to buy. Capitalist production itself has brought about that the LABOUR OF DIRECTION walks the streets, separated completely from the ownership of capital, whether one's own or other people's. It has become quite unnecessary for *capitalists* to perform this LABOUR OF DIRECTION. It is actually available, separate from capital, not in the SHAM SEPARATION which exists between the INDUSTRIAL CAPITALIST and the MONEYED CAPITALIST, but that between INDUSTRIAL MANAGERS, etc., and capitalists of every sort. The best demonstration of this are the cooperative factories built by the workers themselves.[135] They are proof that the capitalist as functionary of production has become just as superfluous to the workers as the LANDLORD appears to the capitalist with regard to bourgeois production. *Secondly:* In so far as the labour of the capitalist does not arise from the process as a capitalist [production] process, and therefore disappears automatically with the disappearance of capital, i.e. in so far as it is not simply a name for the function of exploiting other people's labour, but in so far as it arises from the social form of labour—cooperation, division of labour, etc.—it is just as independent of capital as is this form itself once it has stripped off its capitalist integument. To assert that this labour, as *capitalist labour*, as the function of the capitalist, is necessary, only shows that the VULGARIAN cannot *conceive* the social productive power and the social character of labour developed within the framework of capital as something separate from the capitalist form, from the form of alienation, from the antagonism and contradiction of its aspects, from its inversion and *quid pro quo. Et c'est justement ce que nous affirmons.*[a]

It is in *interest-bearing capital*—in the division of profit into interest and profit—that capital finds its most objectified form, its pure fetish form, and the nature of surplus value is presented as something which has altogether lost its identity. Capital—as an entity—appears here as an independent source of value; as something which creates value in the same way as land [produces] rent, and labour wages (partly wages in the proper sense, and partly industrial profit). Although it is still the price of the commodity which has to pay for wages, interest and rent, it pays for them because the land which enters into the commodity produces the rent, the capital which enters into it produces the interest, and the labour which enters into it produces the wages, [in other words these elements] produce the portions of value which accrue to their respective owners or representatives—[XV-920] the landowner, the capitalist, and the worker (wage worker and industrialist). From this standpoint therefore, the fact that, on the one hand, the price of commodities determines wages, rent and interest and, on the other hand, the price of interest, rent and wages determines the price of commodities, is by no means a contradiction contained in the theory, or if it is, it is a contradiction, a *cercle vicieux*, which exists in the real movement.

True, the rate of interest fluctuates, but only like the market price of any other commodity in accordance with the ratio of demand and supply. This by no means invalidates the notion of interest being inherent in capital just as the fluctuations in the prices of commodities do not invalidate prices as designations appropriate to commodities.

Thus land, capital and labour on the one hand—in so far as they are the sources of rent, interest and wages and these are the

---

[a] And it is precisely what we say.— *Ed.*

constituent elements of commodity prices—appear as the elements which create value, and on the other hand, in so far as they accrue to the owner of each of these means for the production of value, i.e. in so far as he derives the portion of the value created by them, they appear as sources of REVENUE, and rent, interest and wages appear as forms of *distribution.* (As we shall see later, it is the result of stupidity that the VULGARIANS, as opposed to critical economy, in fact regard forms of distribution simply as forms of production *sub alia specie*[a] whereas the critical economists separate them and fail to recognise their identity.)

In interest-bearing capital, capital appears to be the *independent source of value* or surplus value it possesses as money or as commodities. And it is indeed this source in itself, in its material aspect. It must of course enter into the production process in order to realise this faculty; but so must land and labour.

One can therefore understand why the vulgar economists prefer [the formula]: land—rent; capital—interest; labour—wages, to that used by Smith[b] and others for the elements of price (or RATHER for its *decomposita*[c]) and where [the relation] *capital—profit* figures, just as on the whole the capital relation as such is expressed in this form by all the classical economists. The concept of profit still contains the inconvenient connection with the process, and the real nature of surplus value and of capitalist production, in contradistinction to their *appearance,* is still more or less recognisable. This connection is severed when interest is presented as the intrinsic product of capital and the other part of surplus value, industrial profit, consequently disappears entirely and is relegated to the category of wages.

Classical political economy seeks to reduce the various fixed and mutually alien forms of wealth to their inner unity by means of analysis and to strip away the form in which they exist independently alongside one another. It seeks to grasp the inner connection in contrast to the multiplicity of outward forms. It therefore reduces rent to surplus profit, so that it ceases to be a specific, *separate* form and is divorced from its apparent source, the land. It likewise divests interest of its independent form and shows that it is a part of profit. In this way it reduces all types of REVENUE and all independent forms and titles under cover of which the non-workers receive a portion of the value of commodities, to

---

[a] Under a different aspect.— *Ed.*

[b] See present edition, Vol. 30, pp. 400-04, and Vol. 31, pp. 439-42, 456-57.— *Ed.*

[c] Here: the parts into which it can be broken down.— *Ed.*

the single form of profit. Profit, however, is reduced to surplus value since the value of the whole commodity is reduced to labour; the amount of paid labour embodied in the commodity constitutes wages, consequently the surplus over and above it constitutes unpaid labour, surplus labour called forth by capital and appropriated gratis under various titles. Classical political economy occasionally contradicts itself in this analysis. It often attempts directly, leaving out the intermediate links, to carry through the reduction and to prove that the various forms are derived from one and the same source. This is however a necessary consequence of its analytical method, [XV-921] with which criticism and understanding must begin. Classical economy is not interested in elaborating how the various forms come into being, but seeks to reduce them to their unity by means of analysis, because it starts from them as given premises. But analysis is the necessary prerequisite of genetical presentation, and of the understanding of the real, formative process in its different phases. Finally a failure, a deficiency of classical political economy is the fact that it does not conceive the *basic form of capital,* i.e. production designed to appropriate other people's labour, as an *historical* form but as a *natural form* of social production; the analysis carried out by the classical economists themselves nevertheless paves the way for the refutation of this conception.

The position is quite different as regards *vulgar political economy,* which only becomes widespread when political economy itself has, as a result of its analysis, undermined and impaired its own premises and consequently the opposition to political economy has come into being in more or less economic, utopian, critical and revolutionary forms. For the development of political economy and of the opposition to which it gives rise keeps pace with the *real* development of the social contradictions and class conflicts inherent in capitalist production. Only when political economy has reached a certain stage of development and has assumed well-established forms—that is, after Adam Smith—does the separation of the element whose notion of the phenomena consists of a mere reflection of them take place, i.e. its vulgar element becomes a special aspect of political economy. Thus *Say* separates the vulgar notions occurring in *Adam Smith's* work and puts them forward in a distinct crystallised form. *Ricardo* and the further advance of political economy caused by him provide new nourishment for the vulgar economist (who does not produce anything himself): the more economic theory is perfected, that is, the deeper it penetrates its subject-matter and the more it develops as a contradictory system, the more is it confronted by its own, increasingly independent, vulgar element, enriched with material which it dresses up in its own way until finally it finds its most apt expression in academically syncretic and unprincipled eclectic compilations.

To the degree that economic analysis becomes more profound it not only describes contradictions, but it is confronted by its own contradiction simultaneously with the development of the actual contradictions in the economic life of society. Accordingly, vulgar political economy deliberately becomes increasingly *apologetic* and makes strenuous attempts to talk out of existence the ideas which contain the contradictions. Because he finds the contradictions in Smith relatively undeveloped, *Say's* attitude still seems to be critical and impartial compared, for example, with that of *Bastiat*, the professional conciliator and apologist, who, however, found the contradictions existing in the economic life worked out in Ricardian economics and in the process of being worked out in socialism and in the struggles of the time. Moreover, vulgar economy in its early stages does not find the material fully elaborated and therefore assists to a certain extent in solving economic problems from the standpoint of political economy, as, for example, *Say*, whereas a Bastiat needs merely to busy himself with plagiarism and attempts to argue away the *unpleasant* side of classical political economy.

But Bastiat does not represent the last stage. He is still marked by a lack of erudition and a quite superficial acquaintance with the branch of learning which he prettifies in the interests of the ruling class. His apologetics are still written with enthusiasm and constitute his real work, for he borrows the economic content from others just as it suits his purpose. The last form is the *academic form*, which proceeds "historically"[136] and, with wise moderation, collects the "best" from all sources, and in doing this contradictions do not matter; on the contrary, what matters is comprehensiveness. All systems are thus made insipid, [XV-922] their edge is taken off and they are peacefully gathered together in a miscellany. The heat of apologetics is moderated here by erudition, which looks down benignly on the exaggerations of economic thinkers, and merely allows them to float as oddities in its mediocre pap. (That they look down in an equally superior manner on the phantasies of the socialists need hardly be stressed.) Since such works only appear when political economy has reached the end of its scope as a science, they are at the same time the *graveyard* of this science. Even the genuine thought of a

Smith or a Ricardo, and others—the vulgar elements not just peculiar to them—is made to appear insipid in these works and becomes a VULGARISM. Professor *Roscher* is a master of this sort of thing and has modestly proclaimed himself to be the Thucydides of political economy.[105] His identification of himself with Thucydides may perhaps be based on his conception of Thucydides as a man who constantly confuses cause with effect.

In the form of *interest-bearing capital* it becomes quite obvious that capital *without* expending any labour appropriates the fruits of other people's labour. For it appears here in a form in which it is separated from the production process as such. But it can do this only because, in this form, it indeed enters by itself, *without* labour, into the labour process, as an element which in itself creates *value*, i.e. is a source of value. While it appropriates part of the value of the product without labour, it has also created it without labour, *ex proprio sinu*, out of itself.

Whereas the classical, and consequently the critical, economists are exercised by the form of alienation and seek to eliminate it by analysis, the vulgar economists, on the other hand, feel completely at home precisely with the *alienated form* in which the different parts of value confront one another; just as a scholastic is familiar with God the Father, God the Son, and God the Holy Ghost, so are the vulgar economists with land—rent, capital—interest, and labour—wages. For this is the form in which these relationships appear to be directly connected with one another in the world of phenomena, and therefore they exist in this form in the thoughts and the consciousness of those agents of capitalist production who remain captive to it. The more the vulgar economists in fact content themselves with translating common notions into doctrinaire language, the more they imagine that their writings are plain, *in accordance with nature* and the public interest, and free from all theoretical hair-splitting. Therefore, the more alienated the way in which they conceive the formations of capitalist production, the closer they approach the nature of common notions, and the more they are, as a consequence, in their natural element.

This, moreover, renders a substantial service to apologetics. For [in the formula:] land—rent, capital—interest, labour—wages, for example, the different forms of surplus value and configurations of capitalist production do not confront one another as alienated forms, but as extraneous and independent forms, merely different from one another but *not antagonistic*. The different REVENUES are derived from quite different sources, one from land, the second from capital and the third from labour. Thus they do not stand in any hostile connection to one another because they have no inner connection whatsoever. If they nevertheless work together in production, then it is a harmonious action, an expression of harmony, as, for example, the peasant, the ox, the plough and the land in agriculture, in the real labour process, work together *harmoniously* despite their dissimilarities. In so far as there is any contradiction between them, it arises merely from compⁱtition as to which of the agents shall get more of the product, of the value they have jointly created. Even if this occasionally brings them to blows, nevertheless the outcome of this competition between land, capital and labour finally shows that, although they [XV-923] quarrel with one another over the division, their rivalry tends to increase the value of the product to such an extent that each receives a larger piece, so that their competition, which spurs them on, is merely the expression of their harmony.

Mr. Arnd, for example, says in criticism of *Rau*:

"Similarly, the author allows himself to be led by some of his predecessors to adding to the three elements of national wealth (wages, capital rent, land rent) a fourth, that of employers' profit.[a] This entirely destroys the basis—constructed with such circumspection by Adam Smith—for any further development of *our science*" (!); "such a development is consequently quite out of the question in the work under consideration" (Karl Arnd, *Die naturgemässe Volkswirthschaft, gegenüber dem Monopoliengeiste und dem Communismus, mit einem Rückblicke auf die einschlagende Literatur*, Hanau, 1845, p. 477).

By "capital rent" Mr. Arnd means *interest* (l.c., p. 123). According to this one might think that Adam Smith reduces national wealth to *interest on capital*, rent and wages, whereas on the contrary he quite expressly declares that *profit* results from the valorisation of capital and repeatedly and expressly states that *interest*—in so far as it constitutes surplus value at all—is only a form *derived* from profit. Thus the vulgar economist reads into his sources the direct opposite of what they contain. Where Smith writes "PROFIT" Arnd reads "INTEREST". It would be interesting to know what he supposes Adam Smith's "INTEREST" to mean.

This same "circumspect" developer of "*our science*" makes the following interesting discovery:

"In the natural course of goods production there is just *one* phenomenon which, in countries where all available land is under cultivation, seems in some measure to regulate the rate of interest; this is the proportion in which the timber in European forests is augmented through their annual growth. This new growth occurs quite *independently of the exchange value of the timber*" (how strange that the

---

a K. H. Rau, *Lehrbuch der politischen Oeconomie*, Heidelberg, 1837, pp. 139-40.— Ed.

33–733

trees arrange their new growth "independently of exchange value"!) "at the rate of 3 or 4 to 100. Accordingly *therefore*" //since this additional increase in the number of trees is "independent of their exchange value", no matter how much their exchange value may depend on their new growth//, "a decline" (in the rate of interest) "below the level at present prevailing in the richest countries is not likely" (l.c., [pp.] 124-25).

This deserves to be called the "forest-grown rate of interest", and in the same work its inventor has rendered another service to "our science" as the philosopher of the "dog tax".[137]

// Profit (including INDUSTRIAL profit) is proportionate to the amount of the capital advanced; on the other hand, the WAGES drawn by the industrial capitalist [stand] in inverse ratio to the amount of capital. [They are] considerable where the capital is small (because, in this case, the capitalist is something between an exploiter of other people's labour and a person who lives off his own labour), and insignificant where the capital is large, or they are quite independent of it in the case where a MANAGER [is employed]. One part of the LABOUR of direction merely arises from the antagonistic contradiction between capital and labour, from the antagonistic character of capitalist production, and belongs to the *faux frais de production*[a] in the same way as $^9/_{10}$ of the "labour" occasioned by the circulation process. A conductor does not have to be the owner of the instruments used by the orchestra, nor is it one of his functions as a conductor to speculate on the subsistence costs of the members of the orchestra, or, in general, to have ANYTHING to do with their "wages". It is very remarkable that economists like John Stuart Mill, who cling to the forms of "INTEREST" and "INDUSTRIAL PROFIT"[b] in order to convert "INDUSTRIAL PROFIT" into WAGES FOR SUPERINTENDENCE OF LABOUR, admit along with Smith, Ricardo and all other economists worth mentioning, that the AVERAGE RATE OF INTEREST[c] is determined by the AVERAGE RATE OF PROFIT, which according to Mill stands in inverse ratio to the RATE OF WAGES, and it is therefore nothing but unpaid labour, surplus labour.

Two FACTS provide the best proof that the WAGES OF SUPERINTENDENCE do not enter into the AVERAGE RATE OF PROFIT at all.

[XV-924] 1) That in cooperative factories,[135] where the GENERAL MANAGER receives a salary as in all other factories, and is responsible for the whole LABOUR OF DIRECTION—the overseers themselves are simply workers—the rate of profit is not below, but above, the AVERAGE RATE OF PROFIT.

---

[a] Overhead costs of production.— *Ed.*

[b] See present edition, Vol. 31, pp. 35-37.— *Ed.*

[c] In the manuscript, this expression is preceded by its German equivalent.— *Ed.*

2) That where profit is continuously substantially above the AVERAGE RATE, as in individual, non-monopolised branches of business such as those of small SHOPKEEPERS, FARMERS, etc., this is correctly explained by the economists as being due to the fact that these people pay themselves their own WAGES. Where only the proprietor himself works, his profit consists of—1) the interest on his small capital; 2) his WAGES; 3) that part of the surplus time which, because of his capital, he is able to work for himself instead of for someone else; i.e. the part not already represented by interest. If, however, he employs workers, then their surplus time has to be added.

Of course the worthy *Senior* (Nassau) also converts INDUSTRIAL PROFIT into WAGES OF SUPERINTENDENCE.[a] But he forgets this humbug as soon as it is a question, not of doctrinaire phrases, but of practical struggles between workers and factory owners. Thus, he opposes the *shortening of the working day*, because in a working day of say $11\frac{1}{2}$ hours, the workers allegedly work only 1 hour for the capitalist, and the product of this 1 hour constitutes the capitalist's profit[b] (apart from the *interest* for which they also work 1 hour according to his own calculation). Suddenly here industrial profit is equal to the value added by the unpaid labour time of the worker and not to the value added by the labour which the capitalist performs in the production process of commodities. If industrial profit were the product of the capitalist's own labour, then Senior should not have deplored that the workers work only 1 hour for the capitalist for nothing instead of two, and even less should he have said that, if the workers worked only $10\frac{1}{2}$ hours instead of $11\frac{1}{2}$, there [would be] *no* profit *at all.* He should have said that if the workers worked only $10\frac{1}{2}$ hours instead of $11\frac{1}{2}$, the capitalist would not receive WAGES OF SUPERINTENDENCE for $11\frac{1}{2}$ hours but only for $10\frac{1}{2}$ hours, he would thus lose 1 hour's WAGES OF SUPERINTENDENCE. In which case the workers would answer that if ordinary WAGES for $10\frac{1}{2}$ hours have to suffice for them, then the HIGHER WAGES the capitalist receives for $10\frac{1}{2}$ hours should suffice for him.

It is incomprehensible how economists like John Stuart Mill, who are RICARDIANS and even express the principle that profit

---

[a] See N. W. Senior, *An Outline of the Science of Political Economy*, London, 1836, Ch. IV, and also p. XVIII—1130 of the manuscript (present edition, Vol. 33).— *Ed.*

[b] See K. Marx, *Outlines of the Critique of Political Economy...* (present edition, Vol., 29, pp. 203-04).— *Ed.*

merely=SURPLUS VALUE, SURPLUS LABOUR, in the form that the rate of profit and wages stand in inverse ratio to one another and that the rate of wages determines the rate of profit (which is incorrect when put in this form), suddenly convert INDUSTRIAL PROFIT into the individual LABOUR of the capitalist instead of into the SURPLUS LABOUR of the worker, unless the function of exploitation OF FOREIGN LABOUR is called LABOUR by them, the result of this is indeed that the WAGES of this LABOUR are exactly equal to the amount OF FOREIGN LABOUR APPROPRIATED, in other words, they depend directly on the DEGREE OF EXPLOITATION, not on the DEGREE OF EXERTION THAT THIS EXPLOITATION COSTS THE CAPITALIST. (In so far as this function of exploitation OF LABOUR really requires labour in the process of capitalist production, it is represented by the WAGES of GENERAL MANAGERS.) I say that it is incomprehensible that, after they as RICARDIANS have reduced profit to its real element, they allow themselves to be misled by the antithesis of INTEREST and INDUSTRIAL PROFIT which is simply a *disguised form* of profit and is regarded as this independent form due to ignorance of the nature of profit. Only because one part of profit, *interest*, appears to be due to capital as a thing, an automatically functioning, automatically creating thing, apart from the process, the other part appears as INDUSTRIAL PROFIT, as arising from the activity taking place in the process (really the active process, this however also includes the activity of the operating capitalist) and *therefore* as due to the labour of the capitalist. Consequently, because capital and the surplus value which arises from it and is called interest are considered *mysteries.* This view, which arises entirely from notions reflecting the most superficial aspects of the external form of capital, is the exact opposite of Ricardo's view and ALTOGETHER inconsistent with his conception of value. In so far as capital is value, its value is determined by the labour contained in it before it enters into the process. In so far as it enters the process as a thing, it does so as use value, and as such, it can never create exchange value, WHATEVER ITS USE. One can see how splendidly the RICARDIANS understand their own master. In relation to the MONEYED CAPITALIST, the INDUSTRIAL [capitalist], who embodies functioning capital and therefore actually squeezes out surplus labour, is of course quite justified in pocketing a part of this surplus. In relation to the MONEYED CAPITALIST, he is a worker, but a *worker who is a capitalist, in other words, an exploiter of other people's labour.* [XV-925] But in relation to the workers it is *strange* to plead that the exploitation of their labour costs the capitalist labour and that, therefore, they have to pay him for this exploitation; it is the PLEA of the SLAVE-DRIVER addressed to the SLAVE.//

Every precondition of the social production process is at the same time its result, and every one of its results appears simultaneously as its precondition. All the *production relations* within which the process moves are therefore just as much its products as they are its conditions. The more one examines its nature as it really is, [the more one sees that] in the last form it becomes increasingly consolidated, so that independently of the process these conditions appear to determine it, and their own relations appear to those competing in the process as objective conditions, objective forces, forms of things, the more so as, in the capitalist process, every element, even the simplest, the commodity for example, is already an inversion and causes relations between people to appear as attributes of things and as relations of people to the social attributes of these things.

//* "Profit [a] = remuneration for the productive employment of savings; profit properly so called is the remuneration for the *agency for superintendence during this productive employment*" * ([*The*] *Westminster Review*, January 1826, p. 107 et seq.).[b]

Thus interest here is declared to be remuneration for the fact that money, etc., is employed as capital; it therefore arises from capital as such, which is remunerated for its QUALITY *qua* capital. INDUSTRIAL PROFIT, on the other hand, [is remuneration] for the function of the capital or capitalist "DURING THIS PRODUCTIVE EMPLOYMENT", i.e. in the production process itself.//

// Even a blind sow sometimes finds an acorn and so does McCulloch in the following passages. But even this, as he presents it, is only an inconsistency, since he does not distinguish SURPLUS VALUE from profit. Secondly, it is again one of his thoughtless, eclectic acts of plagiarism. According to fellows like Torrens, etc., for whom VALUE is determined by capital—and the same applies to Bailey—profit is proportionate to the capital (advanced). Unlike Ricardo, they do not consider that profit and surplus value are identical concepts, but only because they have no need whatsoever to explain profit on the basis of value, since they regard the visible form of surplus value—*profit* as the relation of SURPLUS VALUE to the capital advanced—as the original form and, in fact, they merely translate the apparent form into words. The passages in Mac's work, who (1) is a RICARDIAN and (2) plagiarises Ricardo's opponents—without attempting to reconcile [the conflicting ideas]—read:

---

[a] In *The Westminster Review*: "Interest".— *Ed.*

[b] Marx gives a free rendering of the passage. Cf. present edition, Vol. 29, p. 170.— *Ed.*

Ricardo's law [138] is true only "IN THOSE CASES IN WHICH THE *PRODUCTIVENESS OF INDUSTRY REMAINS CONSTANT*" ([J.R.] McCulloch, [*The*] *Principles of Political Economy*, London, 1825,[100] p. 373), that is, the productiveness of the industry which produces constant capital.

"PROFITS DEPEND ON THE PROPORTION which they bear to the capital by which they are produced, and not on the PROPORTION TO WAGES. If the productiveness of industry is *universally* doubled and the additional product thus obtained is divided between capitalists and workers, then the proportion of the share of the capitalists to that of the workers remains unchanged, although the *rate of profit* calculated on the capital advanced has risen" (l.c., [pp.] 373-74).[a]

Even in this case, as Mac also notes, one can say that WAGES have fallen relatively as compared with the product, because *profits* have risen. (But in this case it is the rise in PROFITS which is the cause of the fall in WAGES.) This calculation, however, rests on the incorrect method of calculating WAGES as a share in the product, and, as we saw previously, Mr. John Stuart Mill seeks to generalise the Ricardian law in this sophistical manner.[b]/[139]

Interest is only a part of profit, the part which is paid to the owner of capital by the industrial, operating capitalist. Since he can appropriate surplus labour only by means of capital (money, commodities), etc., he has to hand over a portion of it to the man who makes capital available to him. And the lender, who wants to enjoy the advantages of money as capital without letting it function as capital, can do this only by being content with a part of the profit. They are IN FACT CO-PARTNERS, one of them being the juridical owner of the capital, and the other, while he employs it, the economic owner. But since the profit only arises from the production process, is only its result and has first to be produced, *interest* is in fact merely a claim on part of the surplus labour which has yet to be performed, a title to future labour, a claim on a *portion of the value* of commodities which do not as yet exist, it is therefore only the result of a production process which takes place during the period at the end of which the interest only falls due.

[XV-926] Capital is bought (that is, it is lent at interest) before it is paid for. Money functions here as means of payment as it does in relation to labour capacity, etc. The price of capital—i.e. interest—enters therefore just as much into the advances made by the industrialist (and into the advances made to himself where a man is operating with his own capital) as the price of COTTON which, for example, is bought today, but for which he has to pay perhaps in 6 weeks' time. This fact is in no way altered either by the

---

[a] Marx quotes McCulloch with some alterations.— *Ed.*
[b] See present edition, Vol. 31, pp. 65-68.— *Ed.*

fluctuations in the rate of interest—the market price of money—
or the fluctuations in the market prices of other commodities. On
the contrary. The market price of money—the name for
interest-bearing capital as money capital—is fixed on the money
market by competition between buyer and seller, by demand and
supply, like the price of any other commodity. The struggle
between the MONEYED and INDUSTRIAL capitalists is simply a struggle
over the division of the profit, over the share which is to accrue to
each of the two sections when the division is made. The
relationship (demand and supply), like each of its two extremes, is
itself a result of the production process or, in common parlance,
[is determined] by the business situation existing at the time, the
actual position in which the reproduction process and its elements
find themselves. But, formally and apparently, it is this struggle
which determines the *price* of capital (i.e. interest) before capital
enters into the reproduction process. This determination, moreover,
occurs outside the real production process, and depends on factors
independent of the process; this price determination appears
rather as one of the conditions within which the process has to
take place. Thus the struggle appears not only to establish the
property title to a definite part of the future profit, but to cause
this part not to emerge as a result of the production process, but
on the contrary to enter into it as a precondition, as the price of
capital, just as the prices of commodities or wages enter into it as
preconditions, although in the course of the reproduction process
they in fact continuously emerge from it. Each component of the
price of a commodity, in so far as it appears as an advance—as an
already existing commodity price which enters into the production
price—ceases to represent SURPLUS VALUE [a] as far as the industrial
capitalist is concerned. That part of the profit which thus enters
into the process as the price of capital is reckoned as part of the
cost of the outlay; it therefore no longer appears to be SURPLUS and
is converted from a *product* of the process into one of its given
presuppositions—a *condition of production*—which as such enters
into the process in an independent form and determines its
result.

(If, for example, the rate of interest falls, and the situation
obtaining on the market requires a reduction in the price of
commodities below cost price, the industrialist can lower the
commodity price without reducing the rate of industrial profit; he

---

[a] In the manuscript, this English term is given after its German equivalent.—
Ed.

can indeed lower the price and secure a higher INDUSTRIAL profit, which, however, will be regarded by the man operating only with his own capital as a fall in the rate of profit, a reduction in the GROSS PROFIT. Everything which appears as a *given condition of production*, such as the prices of commodities, wages, capital—the market prices of these elements—affects the determination of the *market price* of the commodity at any particular time; the real *cost price* of a particular commodity is established only within the fluctuations of the market prices, and is only the self-equalisation of these market prices, just as the *value* of commodities is only established as a result of the equalisation of the cost prices of all the different commodities. Thus, the *cercle vicieux* of the VULGARIAN, whether he is a theoretician regarding matters from the capitalist standpoint or is in fact a capitalist—namely, that the prices of commodities determine wages, interest, profit and rent [and] that, on the other hand, the prices of labour, interest, profit and rent determine the prices of commodities—[is] merely an *expression of the circular movement* in which the general laws assert themselves in contradictory fashion in the real movement and in appearance.)

A part of the surplus value—*interest*—thus appears as the *market price* of capital, which enters into the process, and is therefore regarded not as surplus value but as a condition of production. Thus, the fact that two sets of capitalists share the surplus value, one set remaining outside the process and the other participating in it, is presented in such a way that one part of surplus value is due to capital outside the process and the other part to capital within the process. The fact that the division is established beforehand is presented as the independence of one part from the other, as the independence of one part from the process itself; and finally as the immanent attribute of things, *money, commodities*, but of these things as *capital*; this again appears not as the expression of a relationship, but in such a way that this money, these commodities are *technologically* intended for the labour process and because of this they become capital. Defined in this way, they are the simple elements of the labour process itself [XV-927] and *as such* they are *capital*.

There is nothing mysterious at all in the fact that the value of the commodity is made up partly of the value of the commodities contained in it, partly of the value of the labour—that is to say, the paid labour—partly of the unpaid but nonetheless salable labour, and that the part of its value which consists of unpaid labour—i.e. its surplus value—is in turn divided into interest, INDUSTRIAL profit and rent; in other words, the immediate *accapa-*

reur[a] and "producer" of the whole of this surplus value has to hand over portions of it to others, one portion to the LANDLORD, another to the owner of the capital, and he keeps the third for himself; he does so however under a name—INDUSTRIAL profit—which distinguishes it from interest and rent, and from surplus value and profit. The breakdown of surplus value, that is, of part of the value of commodities, into these special headings or categories, is very understandable and does not conflict in the least with the law of value. But the whole matter is mystified because these different parts of surplus value acquire an independent form, because they accrue to different people, because the titles to them are based on different elements, and finally because of the autonomy with which certain of these parts [of surplus value] confront the process as its conditions. From parts into which value can be divided, they become independent elements which *constitute* value, they become *constituent elements.* This is what they are as far as market prices are concerned. They really become the constituent elements of the market price. How their apparent independence as conditions of the process is regulated by the inherent law so that they are only *apparently* independent, does not become evident at any moment in the course of the production process, nor does it operate as a determining conscious motive. Exactly the opposite. The highest consistency which can be assumed by this semblance of results taking the form of independent conditions becomes firmly established when *parts of surplus value*—in the form of prices of the conditions of production—are included in the price.

And this is the case with regard to both interest and rent. They are part of the outlay of the INDUSTRIAL capitalist and the FARMER. They seem here no longer to represent unpaid surplus labour, but paid surplus labour, that is, surplus labour for which an equivalent is paid during the production process, although not to the worker whose surplus labour it is, but to other people, i.e. the owners of capital and of land. They constitute surplus labour *quoad* the worker, but they are equivalents *quoad* the capitalist and the landowner to whom they have to be paid. Interest and rent therefore appear not as SURPLUS, and still less as surplus labour, but as *prices* of the commodities "capital" and "land", for they are paid to the capitalist and the landowner only in their capacities as owners of commodities, only as owners and sellers of these commodities. That part of the value of the commodity which represents interest, therefore, appears as *reproduction* of the *price*

---

[a] Monopoliser.— *Ed.*

paid for capital, and that part which represents rent appears as *reproduction* of the price paid for the land. These prices therefore become *constituent* parts of the total price. This does not merely *appear* to be the case to the industrial capitalist; for him interest and rent really constitute part of his outlay, and whereas, on the one hand, they are determined by the *market price* of his commodity—as the market price it is a determination of a commodity in which a social process or the result of a social process appears as a particular aspect belonging to the commodity, and the UP AND DOWN of this process, its movement, appears as the fluctuations of the commodity price—on the other hand, the *market price* is determined by them, in just the same way as the market price of COTTON determines the market price of yarn and, on the other hand, the market price of yarn determines the demand for COTTON, hence the market price of COTTON. Since parts of surplus value, i.e. interest and rent, enter into the production process as the *prices* of commodities—of the commodity land and the commodity capital—they exist in forms which not only conceal, but which disavow their real origin.

That surplus labour, *unpaid* labour, constitutes just as essential an element of the capitalist production process as *paid* labour, is expressed here by the fact that factors of production—land and capital—distinct from labour have to be paid for, in other words, that *costs* besides the price of the commodities advanced and wages enter into the price. Parts of surplus value—interest and rent—appear here as costs, as advances made by the exploiting capitalist.

Average profit enters into the production price of commodities as a determining factor and thus already here surplus value [appears to be] not a result, but a condition, not one of the parts into which the value of the commodity is divided, but a constituent part of its *price*. But AVERAGE *profit*, like the *production price* itself, acts rather as a determining IDEAL and at the same time appears as *surplus* over and above the advances made [XV-928] and as a price which is different from the cost price properly speaking. Whether or not [average profit is obtained] and whether it is higher or lower than the profit corresponding *to the market price*—that is, corresponding to the direct result of the process—determines the reproduction process, or RATHER the scale of reproduction; it determines whether more or less of the capital existing in this or that sphere [of production] is withdrawn or invested; it also determines the ratio in which newly accumulated capitals flow into these particular spheres, and finally, to what extent these particular spheres act as buyers in the money market. On the other hand, as *interest* and *rent*, the separate portions of surplus value in a quite definite form become preconditions for the individual production prices and are anticipated in the form of advances.

//*Advances*, that is, what is paid out by the capitalist, may be defined as *costs*. Profit accordingly appears as a surplus over these costs. This applies to the individual prices of production. And consequently, one can call the prices determined by the advances cost prices.[6]

Production costs can be defined as prices determined by the AVERAGE PROFIT—that is, the price of the capital advanced+the AVERAGE PROFIT—since this profit is the condition for reproduction, a condition which regulates the SUPPLY and the distribution of capital amongst the various spheres [of production]. These prices are *production prices*.

Finally, the real amount of labour (objectified and immediate labour) it costs to produce a commodity, is its *value*. It constitutes the real production cost of the commodity itself. The price which corresponds to it is simply the value expressed in money. The term "production costs" is used alternately in all 3 senses. //

If no surplus value were produced, then of course together with surplus value the part of it which is called interest would also cease to exist, and so would the part which is called rent; the *anticipation* of surplus value would likewise come to an end, in other words, it would no longer constitute a part of the production costs in the shape of the *price* of commodities. The existing value entering into production would not emerge from it as *capital* at all, and accordingly, could not enter into the reproduction process as *capital*, nor be lent out as *capital*. It is thus the continuous reproduction of the same relations—the relations which postulate capitalist production—that causes them to appear not only as the social forms and results of this process, but at the same time as its continual *prerequisites*. But they are these only as prerequisites continually *posited*, created, *produced* by the process itself. This reproduction is, however, not conscious reproduction; on the contrary, it only manifests itself in the continuous existence of these relations as *prerequisites* and as *conditions* dominating the production process. The parts, for example, into which the commodity value can be resolved are turned into its *constituent* parts which confront one another as independent parts, and they are consequently also independent in relation to their *unity*, which on the contrary appears to be a *compound* of these parts. The bourgeois sees that the product continually becomes the condition of production. But he does not perceive that the production relations themselves, the social forms in which he produces and which he regards as given, natural relations, are the continuous product—and only for that reason the continuous prerequisite—of this specific social mode of production. The different relations and aspects not only become independent and assume a strange mode of existence, apparently independent of one another, but they seem to be the direct properties of things; they assume a material shape.

Thus the participants in capitalist production live in a bewitched world and their own relationships appear to them as properties of things, as properties of the material elements of production. It is however in the last, most derivative forms—forms in which the intermediate stage has not only become invisible but has been turned into its direct opposite—that the various aspects of capital appear as the real agencies and direct representatives of production. Interest-bearing capital is personified in the MONEYED CAPITALIST, industrial capital in the INDUSTRIAL CAPITALIST, rent-bearing capital in the LANDLORD as the owner of the land, and lastly, labour in the wage worker. They enter into the competitive struggle and into the real process of production as these rigid forms, personified in independent personalities that appear at the same time to be mere representatives of personified things. Competition presupposes this externalisation. These forms conform to its nature and have come into being in the natural evolution of competition, and on the surface competition appears to be [XV-929] simply the movement of this inverted world. In so far as the inner connection asserts itself in this movement, it appears as a mysterious law. The best proof is political economy itself, a science which seeks to rediscover the hidden connection. Everything enters into competition in this last, most externalised form. The market price, for example, appears to be the dominant factor here, just as the rate of interest, rent, wages, industrial profit appear to be the constituents of value, and the price of land and the price of capital appear as given ITEMS with which one operates.

We have seen how Adam Smith first reduces value to wages, profit (interest) and rent, and then, conversely, presents these as independent constituent elements of commodity prices.[a] He expresses the secret connection in the first version and the outward appearance in the second.

If one comes still closer to the surface of the phenomenon, then,

---

[a] See present edition, Vol. 30, pp. 399-403.— Ed.

in addition to the AVERAGE rate of profit, interest and even rent can be represented as constituent parts of commodity prices (that is, of *market prices*). Interest [can be so represented] quite directly, since it enters into the cost price. Rent—as the price of land—may not determine the price of the product directly, but it determines the mode of production, whether a large amount of capital is concentrated on a small area of land, or a small amount of capital is spread over a large area of land, and whether this or that type of product is produced—e.g., cattle or corn—the market price of which covers the rent most effectively, for the rent must be paid before the TERM stipulated by contract expires. In order that rent should not bring about a reduction in INDUSTRIAL profit, pasture is turned into arable land and arable land into pasture, etc. Rent therefore determines the market prices of individual commodities not directly, but only indirectly, by influencing the proportions in which the various types of commodities are produced in such a way that demand and supply will secure the best price for each so that rent can be paid. Even though rent does not directly determine the market price of corn, for example, it determines directly the market price of cattle, etc., in short, of commodities produced in the spheres where rent is not regulated by the market prices of their products but where the market prices of products are regulated by the rate of rent borne by the grain-producing land. The price of meat, for example, is always too high in industrially developed countries, that is, it is not only far above its production price, but above its value. For the price must cover not only the cost of production, but also the rent which the land would carry if corn were grown on it. Otherwise, meat produced by large-scale stock-breeding—where the organic composition of capital approximates far more closely [to the composition of capital in industry] or may have an even greater preponderance of constant capital over variable capital—could only pay a very small amount of *absolute rent,* or even none at all. The rent which it pays, and which enters directly into its price, is, however, determined by the absolute+the differential rent which the land would pay as arable land. This differential rent, moreover, does not exist here in most cases. The best proof is that meat pays rent on the kind of land where corn does not.

If, therefore, *profit* enters into the production price as a determining factor, it can be said that wages, interest and, TO A CERTAIN DEGREE, rent constitute determining elements of the market price and CERTAINLY of the production price. Of course, ultimately everything can be reduced to value which is determined by labour time, for on the whole the movement of interest is determined by profit, while corn rent on the other hand is determined partly by the rate of profit, partly by the value of the product and the equalisation of the different values produced on different kinds of land to the market value; the rate of profit, however, is determined partly by wages, partly by the productivity of labour in those spheres of production which produce constant capital—in the last analysis therefore by the level of wages and the productivity of labour; wages, however, are the equivalent of a part of the commodity (that is, [they are] equal to the paid portion of labour contained in the commodity, and profit is equal to the unpaid portion of labour contained in the commodity). Finally, the productivity of labour can affect the price of commodities only in two ways, either it affects their value, i.e. reduces it, or it affects their surplus value, that is, increases it. Cost price is nothing but the value of the capitals advanced+the surplus value they produce distributed amongst the different spheres according to the quota of the total capital which each sphere represents. Thus, cost price resolves into value if one considers the total capital and not the individual spheres. On the other hand, the market prices in each sphere are continually reduced to the cost price as a result of the competition between the capitals of the different spheres. Competition amongst the capitalists in each individual sphere seeks to reduce the market price of commodities to their market value. Competition between capitalists of different spheres reduces market values to common cost prices.[a]

Ricardo opposes Smith's establishment of value out of the parts of value which are determined by itself.[b] But he is not consistent. Otherwise it would have been impossible for him to argue with Smith whether profit, wages and rent or, as he says, merely profit and wages, enter into price, that is, enter as *constituent* parts.[c] Regarded analytically, they enter into it as soon as they are paid. He ought to have put it in this way: The price of every commodity is reducible to profit and wages, the prices of some commodities (and of very many, *indirectly*) are reducible to profit, rent and wages. But *no* commodity price is constituted by them [XV-930] for they are not independent factors acting *de propriis fontibus*,[d] having a definite magnitude, and *making up* the value of

---

[a] See present edition, Vol. 31, pp. 427-33.— *Ed.*
[b] See D. Ricardo, *On the Principles of Political Economy, and Taxation*, Ch. 1.— *Ed.*
[c] See present edition, Vol. 31, pp. 545-46.— *Ed.*
[d] Of their own accord.— *Ed.*

commodities; on the contrary, when the value is given, it can be divided into those parts in many different proportions. The magnitude of *value* is not determined by the addition or combination of given factors—i.e. profit, wages and rent—but one and the same *magnitude of value,* a given *amount of value,* is broken down into wages, profit and rent, and according to different circumstances it is distributed between these 3 categories in very different ways.

Assuming that the production process repeats itself continuously under the same conditions, in other words, that reproduction takes place under the same conditions as production, which presupposes that productivity of labour remains unchanged, or at least that variations in productivity do not alter the relationships of the different agents of production; thus, even if the value of commodities were to rise or fall as a result of changes in productive power, the distribution of the value of commodities amongst the different factors of production would remain the same. In that case, although it would not be theoretically accurate to say that the different parts of value determine the value or price of the whole, it would be useful and correct to say that they constitute it in so far as one understands by constituting the formation of the whole by adding up the parts. The value would be divided at a steady and constant rate into value and surplus value, and the value would be resolved at a constant rate into wages and profit, the profit again being broken down at a constant rate into interest, INDUSTRIAL PROFIT and RENT. It can therefore be said that P—the price of the commodity—is resolved into wages, profit (interest) and rent, and, on the other hand, wages, profit (interest) and rent are the constituents of the value or rather of the price. This uniformity or similarity of reproduction—the repetition of production under the same conditions—does not exist. Productivity itself changes and changes the conditions. The conditions, on their part, change productivity. But the divergences are reflected partly in superficial oscillations which even themselves out in a short time, partly in a gradual accumulation of DIVERGENCES [a] which either lead to a crisis, to a violent, seeming restoration of the old relationships, or very gradually assert themselves and are recognised as a change in the conditions. Interest and rent, which anticipate surplus value, presuppose that the g e n e r a l character of reproduction will remain the same. And this is the case as long

---

[a] In the manuscript, the English term is given in brackets after its German equivalent.— *Ed.*

as the capitalist mode of production continues. Secondly, it is presupposed moreover that the *specific relations* of this mode of production remain the same during a certain period, and this is in fact also *plus ou moins*[a] the case. Thus the result of production *crystallises* into a *permanent and therefore prerequisite condition of production,* that is, it becomes a permanent *attribute of the material conditions of production.* It is *crises* that put an end to this apparent *independence* of the various elements of which the production process continually consists and which it continually reproduces.

// What *value* is for the genuine economist the *market price* is for the practical capitalist, that is, in each case the primary factor of the whole movement. //

The form of interest-bearing capital characteristic of and in accordance with capitalist production is *credit.* It is a form created by the capitalist mode of production itself. (The subordination of *commercial capital* does not IN FACT require such a new creation since commodity and money, and the circulation of commodities and money, remain the elementary prerequisites of capitalist production and are only turned into absolute prerequisites; commercial capital, on the one hand, is therefore the general form of capital and, on the other hand, in so far as it represents capital in a specific function—capital which operates exclusively in the circulation process—its determination by productive capital does not in any way alter its form.) The equalisation of values to cost prices occurs only because the individual capital functions as an aliquot part of the total capital of the whole class and, on the other hand, because the total capital of the class is distributed amongst the various individual spheres according to the needs of production. This is brought about by means of credit. Credit not only makes this equalisation possible and facilitates it, but one part of capital—in the form of MONEYED capital—appears in fact to be the material common to the whole class and employed by it. This is one purport of credit. The other is the continual attempt made by capital to shorten the metamorphoses which it has to undergo in the circulation process, to anticipate the circulation time, its transformation into money, etc., and in this way to counteract its own [XV-931] limitations. Finally, the function of *accumulating,* in so far as it is not conversion into capital but the supply of surplus value in the form of capital, becomes, in part, the responsibility of a special class, in part everything *accumulated* by society in this

---

[a] More or less.— *Ed.*

sense becomes accumulation of capital and is placed at the disposal of the industrial capitalists. Operations of this kind take place at a very large number of isolated points in society, [their results] are concentrated and collected in certain reservoirs. Money which lies idle due to freezing of the commodities in the metamorphosis, is thus converted into capital.

Land—rent and capital—interest are irrational expressions in so far as rent is defined as the *price* of land and interest as the *price* of capital. The common origin is still recognisable in the forms of interest-bearing capital, rent-bearing capital, profit-bearing capital, since, in general, *capital* involves appropriation of surplus labour; so that these different forms merely express the fact that the surplus labour produced by capital is, as concerns capital in general, divided between two types of capitalists, and in the case of AGRICULTURAL CAPITAL, it is divided between CAPITALIST and LANDLORD.

Rent as the (annual) *price* of land and interest as the *price* of capital are just as irrational as $\sqrt{-3}$. The latter form contradicts the number in its simple, elementary forms just as those do in the case of capital in its simple form of commodities and money. They [rent and interest] are in the converse sense irrational. Land—rent, i.e. rent as the price of land, defines land as a commodity, a use value which has a value WHOSE MONETARY EXPRESSION=ITS PRICE. But a use value which is not the product of labour cannot have a value; in other words, it cannot be defined as the objectification of a definite quantity of social labour, as the social expression of a certain quantity of labour. It is nothing of the kind. Only if it is the product of concrete labour can use value take the form of exchange value—become a commodity. Only under this condition can this concrete labour, for its part, be expressed as *social labour,* value. Land and price are INCOMMENSURABLE magnitudes, nevertheless they are supposed to bear a certain relation to each other. Here a thing which has no value has a price.

Interest as the price of capital, on the other hand, expresses the converse irrationality. Here a commodity which has no *use value* has a dual value, it has a value in the first place and in addition a price, which is different from this value. For capital *is,* to begin with, nothing but a *sum of money* or a *quantity of commodities*=a certain sum of money. If the commodity is lent out as capital, then it is nothing but a *sum of money* in camouflaged form. For what is lent *as capital* is not so many pounds of cotton, but so much *money* whose value exists in the form of cotton. The *price* of the capital is therefore related to it only as the existence of a *sum of money*, i.e., a certain amount of value expressed in money and existing in the form of exchange value. How is it possible for an amount of value to have a price apart from the price which is expressed in its own money form? Price after all is the value of the commodity as *distinct* from its use value. Price in contradistinction to the value of the commodity, price as the value of a sum of money (for price is simply the expression of value in money) is therefore a *contradictio in terminis.*[a]

This irrationality of expression (the irrationality of the thing itself arises from the fact that, as regards interest, capital as the prerequisite appears divorced from its own process, in which it becomes capital and consequently self-valorising value, and that, on the other hand, rent-bearing capital exists only as AGRICULTURAL capital, as capital which only yields rent in a particular sphere, and this form in which it appears is *transmitted to the element that differentiates it in general from* INDUSTRIAL CAPITAL)—this irrationality of expression is so much felt by the VULGARIAN that he falsifies both expressions in order to make them appear rational. He asserts that interest is paid on capital in so far as it is use value, and therefore talks about the utility which the products or means of production have for reproduction and of the utility which capital has as a material element of the labour process. But, after all, its utility, its use value, already exists in its form as a commodity and without this it would not be a commodity and would have no value. As money, it is the expression of the value of commodities and is [XV-932] convertible into them in proportion to their own value. But if I convert money into a machine, into cotton, etc., then I convert it into use values of *the same* value. The conversion is concerned only with the *value form.* As money, it has the use value of being convertible into any other commodity, a commodity, however, of the same value. As a result of this transformation, the value of money changes no more than that of the commodity when it is converted into money. The use value of the commodities into which I can convert money does not give the money, in addition to its value, a price which is different from its value. If, however, I presuppose the conversion and assert that the price is paid for the use value of the commodities, then the use value of the commodities is not paid for at all or is only paid in so far as their exchange value is paid for. How the use value of any commodity is utilised, whether it enters into individual or

---

[a] Contradiction in terms.— *Ed.*

industrial consumption, has absolutely no bearing on its exchange value. It only determines who will buy it—the industrial capitalist or the immediate consumer. The productive usefulness of a commodity can therefore account for the fact that the commodity has exchange value at all, for the labour embodied in the commodity is paid for only if it has use value. Otherwise it is not a commodity—it is a commodity only as the unity of use value and exchange value. But this use value can by no means account for the fact that as exchange value or as price, it has in addition another and different price as well.

One can see how the VULGARIAN wants to get over the difficulty here by seeking to convert *capital*—that is, the money or the commodity in so far as these have a *specifically different* determinateness from themselves as money or commodity—into a mere *commodity*, in other words, by disregarding precisely the specific difference which has to be explained. He does not wish to say that this means for the exploitation of surplus labour and therefore of more value than the value contained in it. Instead he says: It has more value than its own value because it is an ordinary commodity like any other, that is, it possesses a use value. Here capital is identified with commodity, whereas the point to be explained is how the commodity can function as capital.

The VULGARIAN, in so far as he does not echo the Physiocrats, deals with land in the opposite way. In the previous case, he converted capital into a commodity in order to explain the *difference* between capital and commodity and the conversion of the commodity into capital. Now he converts land into capital because the capital-relation as such is more in tune with his ideas than the price of land. Rent can be regarded as interest on capital. For example, if the rent is 20 and the rate of interest is 5, then it can be said that this 20 is interest on a capital of 400. And in fact the land then sells at 400, which simply amounts to the sale of the rent for a period of 20 years. This payment of the anticipated 20 years' rent is thus the price of the land. The land is thereby converted into capital. The annual payment of 20 merely represents 5% interest on the capital which was paid for the land. And in this way, the formula land—rent is converted into capital—interest, which, for its part, is transmogrified into payment for the use value of commodities, that is, into the relationship of use value to exchange value.

The more analytical VULGARIANS understand that the price of land is nothing more than an expression for the capitalisation of rent; [that] in fact [it is] the purchase price of rent for a number of years and that it is determined by the prevailing rate of interest. They understand that rent presupposes this capitalisation of rent and that, on the other hand, it is therefore impossible to explain rent by its own capitalisation. They therefore deny the existence of rent itself by asserting that it is interest on the capital invested in the land.[a] This does not prevent them from admitting that land in which no capital is invested yields rent, any more than it prevents them from admitting that *equal amounts* of capital invested in land of different fertility yield *different* amounts of rent, or that *unequal amounts* of capital invested in land of unequal fertility may yield *the same* amounts of rent. [They admit] that likewise the capital invested in land—if indeed it is TO ACCOUNT FOR THE RENT PAID for the land—may yield perhaps five times as much interest, that is, five times as much rent, as is yielded by the same amount of capital invested as fixed capital in industry.

One perceives that here the difficulty is always eliminated by *disregarding* it and substituting a relationship expressing the opposite of the *specific difference* which has to be explained, and therefore, in any case, *not* expressing the difference at all.

[XV-933] Since the commodity (money) is lent as *capital*, it can be lent as *circulating* or *fixed capital*. Money can be lent in both forms, for instance as fixed capital, when it is paid back in the form of an annuity, so that, along with the interest, part of the capital is always returned. Other commodities, such as houses, machines, etc., can often be lent only as fixed capital, by nature of their use value. But all loan capital, whatever its form, and however the form of its *repayment* may be modified by the specific nature of the use value in which it exists, is always only a particular form of money capital. For what is lent here is a definite sum of money, in whatever use value it might exist, and interest is computed with reference to this sum. If that which is lent is not money or circulating capital but fixed capital, it is paid back also in the manner of fixed capital. The lender periodically gets interest and a part of the consumed value of the fixed capital itself, an equivalent for the periodic wear and tear. In the end, the unconsumed part of the loan fixed capital comes back *in natura*.

The form in which loan capital circulates is as follows:

1) Money functions as a *means of payment*, that is to say, capital is alienated or sold, but paid back only after a certain period. The function of money as a means of payment originates, as we have

---

[a] See also present edition, Vol. 31, pp. 268, 367-68, 371, 388-89.—*Ed.*

seen,[a] in the simple exchange of commodities. Therefore there is nothing characteristic of money capital here.

2) After a certain period capital returns to the lender, whether piecemeal along with interest, or as a whole with interest, or during a part of the period only interest is paid, and only at the end of different periods capital returns along with the interest of the last period.

Clearly, these modes of *repayment* or RETURN *of capital to the lender* are nothing but the movement which capital generally follows in its circuit, a return to its starting-point. If, for instance, capital is repaid annually piecemeal along with interest, then this is the manner in which fixed capital returns, coming back to its starting-point in the circulation. If, on the other hand, it is returned as a whole at the end of the year or some other period along with the interest, then this is the manner in which circulating capital flows back. Loan capital returns twice; in the actual process it returns to the INDUSTRIAL CAPITAL, and then the RETURN is repeated once again as a TRANSFER to the MONEYED CAPITALIST, as *repayment* of the same to its real owner, its legal starting-point.

In the actual process of circulation capital always appears as commodity or money. It is converted, through sale and purchase, from one form to the other. What is exchanged here are always equivalents. For a commodity to become money, the capitalist must sell the commodity; for money to become a commodity, he must buy that commodity. In the first case he gives away the commodity and receives money for it, in the second, he gives away money and receives a commodity for it. In short, the circulation process resolves itself into the metamorphosis of the commodity and thus into a series of EXCHANGES. This is so if we regard each phase of circulation as a moment of the whole process; in general, if we regard capital in so far as it functions as commodity or money, and its movement must therefore present itself as selling or buying. It is different if we consider the whole of the process. If we start with money, a certain sum of money is laid out and returns after a certain period—both this sum and a surplus of money over and above the originally expended sum of money. An increased sum of money returns. If we start with the commodity, it appears as the starting-point—before the production process, in the form of conditions of production which are themselves a commodity and whose sum therefore represents, as a sum of

---

[a] See K. Marx, *A Contribution to the Critique of Political Economy.* Part One (present edition, Vol. 29, pp. 370-80, especially p. 374).— *Ed.*

values, in its total price, a certain sum of money. If we consider the commodity as it re-emerges, having gone through the production process, we see that the form of its use value has changed. But that is beside the point here. The commodity represents now a mass of commodities of a higher price than before, a greater sum of money, THE REPLACEMENT OF THE ORIGINAL VALUE+A SURPLUS VALUE. It is preserved and multiplied after it has gone through a certain cycle.

But money, in so far as it is lent as capital, is lent precisely as this self-preserving and self-increasing sum of money which returns after a certain period with a profit, and which can go through the same process over and over again. It is not laid out either as money or as commodity, and thus is neither exchanged for a commodity nor sold (as a commodity) for money. It is not laid out as a commodity or as money, *but as capital*. The relation to itself, as it appears in the context of the whole of the process, is here incorporated in it simply as its character, its determinateness, without the mediating intermediate movement. And in this determinateness it is sold. This determinateness itself, though, is only the result of the process and the conditions in which the capitalist production process [XV-934] moves. Therefore, to join battle against this result, this mere crystallisation of the process, while leaving it be at its very core—and its core is wage labour; to want to leave alone the process and to babble away the result of this process, that is really Proudhonic wisdom.[a]

// The *price of the production* of a commodity can only change for two reasons: the *profit rate changes,* the AVERAGE RATE OF PROFIT. This is only made possible by the fact that the AVERAGE *rate of surplus value* itself changes or the AVERAGE *relation* of this rate to the capital outlay does. In so far as the rate of surplus value does not rest on wages being pressed below their minimum or rising above their minimum, and movements of this kind are to be regarded as merely oscillatory, this can only occur either because the value of labour capacity goes down or up, the former when the means of subsistence are reproduced at less expense, and the latter when they are reproduced at more. Both impossible without a change in the productivity of the labour which produces the means of subsistence, i.e. without a change in the *value* of the commodities forming part of the worker's consumption. Or the *relation* of this AVERAGE rate of SURPLUS VALUE to society's constant capital changes.

---

[a] Cf. K. Marx, *Outlines of the Critique of Political Economy...* (present edition, Vol. 28, p. 61).—*Ed.*

Since the change here does not originate in the rate, it must originate in a change in constant capital. Its mass, technologically considered, grows or decreases in relation to variable capital, and the mass of its value goes up or down with the growth or decrease of its mass itself. In this case, therefore, a change occurs in the mode of production. If the same labour is required to set more constant capital in motion, then labour has become more productive. If contrariwise, contrariwise. A change has thus occurred in labour productivity, and a change must have taken place in the value of certain commodities. If the *price of the production* of a commodity changes in the wake of a CHANGE IN THE GENERAL RATE OF PROFIT, its own value may remain unchanged. But there must have been a change in the value of other commodities.

Second: The overall profit rate remains *unchanged*. Then the price of the production of a commodity can only change because its own value has changed. Because less or more labour is required to produce the commodity itself, whether through a change in the productivity of labour which produces it in its ultimate form (for instance, the less the labour expended on 1 lb. of yarn, the less the necessary labour and the less the wages, and thus the costs decrease) or in that which produces the commodities that go into it as its ingredients. If one considers as the price of production not a fixed sum but the value of the advanced capital, the costs+the AVERAGE profit, thus $C+A.P.$,[140] it is clear that the price of production may remain the same however great the changes in the value of the commodity. No matter how the value of C changes, A.P. retains the same rate. If C equals 100, then, if profit=10%, $C+A.P.=110,=C+{}^1/_{10}C$. If the value of C falls to 50, then the production price$=50+A.P.=55=C+{}^1/_{10}C$.

All changes in the production price of commodities are reducible to changes in value; but not all changes in the value of commodities necessarily express themselves in the CHANGE of the production price, for the latter is determined not only by the value of the particular commodity but also by the value of all commodities, so that a change in commodity A can be levelled out by an opposite one in commodity B, the overall relation therefore remaining the same. Assume that with a capital of 100 I can produce 2,000 lbs of yarn instead of the previous 1,000 lbs only. If profit=10%, 1,000 lbs of yarn cost £110 in the first case; in the second case, 2,000 lbs of yarn cost £110. In the first case, 1 lb. of yarn costs $2^1/_5$ s. In the second case, 1 lb. of yarn costs only $1^1/_{10}$ s. In both cases the production price is the same. For in the first case the production price for 1 lb. of yarn=2s. (costs)$+{}^1/_5$ s.,=10%=${}^1/_{10}$

of the costs. Production price therefore=C (2s.)+10% ($^1/_5$s.). In the second case C=1s.+$^1/_{10}$s., or 10%. Production price therefore, ditto,=C+10%. Here, the value of the commodity has changed, but not the production price. True, the change in value is expressed in the change of the price of the commodity, $1^1/_{10}$s. instead of $2^2/_5$, but these different prices contain the same relation of costs and profit and therefore the same production price.//

In interest-bearing capital, the movement of capital is made shorter; the mediating process is omitted, and so for instance the capital of 1,000 is fixed as a thing that is in itself 1,000 and, after a certain period, transforms itself into 1,100, in the same way as wine in the cellar improves its use value after a certain period of time. Capital is now a thing, but as a thing it is capital. It can for this reason be sold as a particular commodity along with other commodities, or RATHER money, commodity can now be sold as *capital.* That is the manifestation of capital in its [XV-935] most independent form. Money now has love in its body.[a] Once it is lent—or present in the production process (in so far as it yields industrial interest as separate from profit), it may sleep or be awake, by day and by night, interest grows on it.

Directly after this, Luther's naive polemic against interest's ingrown being in capital.[b]

The general profit rate in *Ricardo.*

* "The *remaining value* or *overplus* will in each trade be in proportion to the *value of the capital employed.*" * (Ricardo, [*On the Principles of Political Economy, and Taxation,* 3rd ed., London, 1821, p. 84]).

Realised in interest-bearing money capital is the devout wish of the hoarder.

Proudhon's polemic against Bastiat on the question of interest[c] is characteristic both of the manner in which the VULGARIAN defends the categories of political economy and of the way in which superficial socialism (Proudhon's polemic hardly deserves the name) attacks them. We shall return to this in the section on the VULGARIANS.[141] Here only a few preliminary remarks.

The return movement [of money] should not have shocked Proudhon as being something peculiar if he understood anything at all about the movement of capital. Neither should the SURPLUS VALUE contained in the returning amount. This is a characteristic

---

[a] Allusion to a passage in Goethe's *Faust,* Part I, "Auerbach's Cellar in Leipzig". Cf. present edition, Vol. 29, p. 90 and Vol. 30, p. 112.— *Ed.*

[b] See this volume, pp. 531-40.— *Ed.*

[c] Fr. Bastiat, [P. J.] Proudhon, *Gratuité du crédit. Discussion entre M. Fr. Bastiat et M. Proudhon,* Paris, 1850.— *Ed.*

feature of capitalist production. (For Proudhon however, as we shall see, the SURPLUS is a SURCHARGE. Altogether his criticism is that of a novice, he has not mastered the first elements of the science he intends to criticise. Thus, he has never understood that money is a necessary form of the commodity. (See Part One.[a]) Here he even confuses money and capital because loan capital appears as money capital in the form of money.) What might have struck him was not the SURPLUS for which no equivalent was paid, since SURPLUS VALUE—and capitalist production is based on it—is VALUE which has cost no equivalent. This is not a specific feature of interest-bearing capital. The specific feature—in so far as we are considering the form of the movement—is only the first phase, that is, precisely the opposite of what Proudhon has in mind, namely, that the lender hands over the money without receiving an equivalent for it *de prime abord*[b] and that, therefore, the RETURN of the capital with interest, as regards the transaction between borrower and lender, [is not related to] the metamorphoses which capital undergoes and which, in so far as they are mere metamorphoses of economic form, consist of a series of EXCHANGES, conversion of commodities into money and conversion of money into commodities; in so far as they are real metamorphoses, that is, [elements of] the production process, they coincide with industrial consumption. Here consumption itself constitutes a phase of the movement of economic forms.

But what money in the hands of the lender does not do, it does in the hands of the borrower who really employs it as capital. It performs its real movement as capital in the hands of the borrower. It returns to him as money+profit, money+$\frac{1}{x}$money.

The movement between lender and borrower only expresses the source and the starting-point of capital. It is money when it passes from the hands of A into those of B. It becomes capital in B's hands, and as such, AFTER undergoing A CERTAIN REVOLUTION, IT RETURNS WITH PROFIT. This interlude, the real process, which comprises both the circulation process and the production process, is not connected with the transaction between borrower and lender. It [the transaction] recommences only after the money *has been* realised as capital. The money now passes back into the hands of the lender along with a SURPLUS, which, however, comprises only

---

[a] K. Marx, *A Contribution to the Critique of Political Economy.* Part One (present edition, Vol. 29, pp. 294-95).— *Ed.*

[b] At the outset.— *Ed.*

part of the surplus realised by the borrower. The equivalent which the borrower receives is industrial profit, that is, the part of the SURPLUS which he retains and which he appropriates only by means of the money borrowed. All this is not visible in the transaction between him and the lender. This is limited to two acts. Transfer from A's hands into those of B. Interval during which the money remains in B's hands. After this interval the money along with interest returns into A's hands. If one examines merely this form—the transaction between A and B—then one regards the mere form of capital without the intervening stage: a certain amount of money a is handed over and after A CERTAIN PERIOD returns as $a + \frac{1}{x}a$ without the assistance of any intermediate link apart from the period of time which elapses between the departure of the sum of money a and its return as $a + \frac{1}{x}a$.

And it is in this abstract form, which, indeed, exists as an independent movement alongside the real movement of capital, opens it and closes it, that Mr. Proudhon considers the matter in hand, so that everything inevitably remains incomprehensible to him. If instead of buying and selling, lending in this form were to be abolished, then, according to Proudhon, the SURPLUS would disappear. In fact only the division of the SURPLUS between two sets of capitalists would disappear. But this division can and must be constantly generated anew whenever it is possible to convert commodities or money into capital, and, on the basis of wage labour, this is always possible. Should it be impossible for commodities and money to become capital and therefore be lent as capital *in posse*, they must not confront wage labour. If they are thus not to confront it as *commodities* and *money* and consequently labour itself is not to become a commodity, then that amounts [XV-936] to a return to pre-capitalist modes of production in which it [labour] does not become a commodity, and for the greater part still exists in the form of serf or slave labour. On the basis of free labour, this is only possible where the workers are the owners of their conditions of production. Free labour develops within the framework of capitalist production as *social* labour. To say that they are the owners of the conditions of production amounts to saying that these belong to the united workers and that they produce as such, and that their own output is controlled jointly by them. But wanting to preserve wage labour and thus the basis of capital, as Proudhon does, and at the same time to eliminate the "drawbacks" by abolishing a secondary form of capital, reveals the novice.

Gratuité du crédit. Discussion entre M. Fr. Bastiat et M. Proudhon, Paris, 1850.[142]

He regards lending as something evil because it is not a sale.

The lending of money at interest "is the ability of *selling* the same *object* over and over again, and receiving the *price* of it, over and over again, without ever giving up the ownership of what is sold" ([*Gratuité du crédit*, p.] 9, *First Letter* of Chevé, one of the editors of *La Voix du Peuple*).[a]

He is led astray by the fact that the "object" (money or a house, for example) does not change owners, as in purchase and sale. But he does not see that when money is handed over, no equivalent is received in return; that, on the contrary, in the real process, in the form and on the basis of exchange, not only an equivalent, but a SURPLUS which is not paid for, is received; in so far as exchange of objects takes place, no CHANGE OF VALUES occurs, the same person remains the "owner" of the same VALUE, and in so far as there is a SURPLUS, there is no exchange. When the exchange of commodity and money begins again, the SURPLUS is already absorbed in the commodity. Proudhon does not understand how profit, and therefore interest as well, originates from the law of exchange of values. Hence he argues that "house", "money", etc., should not be exchanged as "capital" but as "commodities ... at cost price" ([pp. 43-]44).

"Actually, the hatter who sells hats ... obtains the value of them, neither more nor less. But the capitalist who loans out his capital ... not merely gets his capital back in full; he gets back more than his capital, more than he brought to the exchange; over and above his capital, he gets an interest" ([p.] 69).[b]

Mr. Proudhon's hatters do not appear to be *capitalists* but louts journeymen.

"It is impossible, with *interest on capital* being added in commerce to the worker's *wages* to *make up the price of the commodity,* for the worker to be able to buy back what he himself has produced. Living by working is a principle which, under the rule of interest, is implicitly self-contradictory" ([p.] 105).[c]

In letter IX (pp. 144-52), the worthy Proudhon confuses money as means of circulation with money as capital, and on this basis concludes that the "capital" existing in France yields 160% (viz. 1,600 million in annual interest on the national debt, mortgages, etc., for a capital of 1,000 million ... "the sum of money ... circulating in France").

---

[a] Marx quotes in French. Below, in analysing Proudhon's views, he uses quite a few French expressions.— *Ed.*

[b] Marx quotes partly in French and partly in German.— *Ed.*

[c] Here and below, Marx quotes Proudhon in French.— *Ed.*

Further:

"As, by the accumulation of interest, *capital-money,* from exchange to exchange, always returns to its source, it follows that the re-lending, always done by the same hand, always profits the same person" ([p.] 154).

Because capital is lent out in the form of money, Proudhon believes that capital-money, that is, *currency,* possesses this specific attribute. Everything should be *sold* but nothing *lent.* In other words: In the same way as he wanted commodities to exist but did not want them to become "money", so here he wants commodities, money, to exist but they must not develop into capital. When all phantastic forms have been stripped away, this means nothing more than that there should be no advance from small, petty-bourgeois peasant and artisan production to large-scale industry.

"Since value is *only a proportion,* and all products necessarily bear a certain *proportion to one another,* it follows that from the social point of view products are always values and realised values; for society, the distinction between capital and product does not exist. The distinction is completely subjective to the individuals" (l.c., [p.] 250).

What mischief is caused when such philosophical German terms as "subjective" fall into the hands of a Proudhon. The bourgeois social forms are "subjective" for him. And the subjective, and moreover erroneous, abstraction that, because the exchange value of commodities expresses a *proportion,* it expresses every possible proportion between commodities and does not express a third thing to which the commodities are proportional—this false "subjective" abstraction is the social point of view [XV-937] according to which not only commodity and money, but commodity, money and capital are identical. Thus, from this "social point of view", all cats are indeed grey. Finally there is also the SURPLUS in the form of morality:

"All labour *must* yield a *surplus*" ([p.] 200).

With which moral precept the SURPLUS is naturally defined very nicely.

It might appear that in the trinity land—rent, capital—profit (interest), labour—wages, the last group is the most rational. At least it states the SOURCE from which wages flow. But it is on the contrary the most irrational of them all, and the basis for the other two, in the same way as *wage labour* in general presupposes land in the form of *landed property* and the product in the form of *capital.* Only when labour confronts its conditions in this form, is it wage labour. As wage labour it is defined by the formula labour—wages. Since wages here appear to be the specific product of labour, its sole product (and they are indeed the sole product of labour *for* the wage worker), the other parts of value—*rent* and *profit* (*interest*)—appear to flow just as necessarily from other specific sources. And just as that part of the value of the product which resolves in wages [is conceived] as the *specific* product of labour, so those parts of value which are made up of rent and profit must be regarded as specific results of agencies *for* which they exist and to which they accrue, that is, as OFFSPRING OF THE EARTH AND OF CAPITAL, RESPECTIVELY.[143]

Luther, who lived in the period of the dissolution of medieval civil society into the elements of modern society—a process which was accelerated by world trade and the discovery of new gold deposits—naturally knew capital only in its 2 antediluvian [forms] of interest-bearing capital and merchant capital. Whereas in its early phase capitalist production, having gained strength, seeks to subordinate interest-bearing capital to industrial capital by force—this was in fact done first of all in Holland, where capitalist production in the form of manufacture and large-scale trade first blossomed, and in England in the 17th century it was, partly in very naïve terms, declared to be the primary requisite of capitalist production—on the other hand, during the transition to capitalist production, the first step is the recognition that "usury", the old-fashioned form of interest-bearing capital, is a condition of production, a necessary production relation; in the same way as later on its justification is recognised by industrial capital, which regards it as flesh of its own flesh, as soon as industrial capital subordinates interest-bearing capital to itself (18th century, *Bentham*[a]). Luther is *superior* to Proudhon. The difference between *lending* and *buying* does not confuse him, for he perceives that usury exists equally in both. The most striking feature of his polemic is that he makes his main point of attack the fact that *interest is an innate element of capital.*

I) Books *Vom Kaufhandel und Wucher*[b] written in 1524. Part VI of Luther's *Works*, Wittenberg, 1589. (This was written on the eve of the Peasant War.)

Trade (*merchant capital*):

"There is now great outcry against the nobles or robbers amongst the merchants" //one can see why the merchants are for the princes and against the

---

[a] J. Bentham, *Defence of Usury*, London, 1787.—*Ed.*

[b] M. Luther, *Von Kauffshandlung und Wucher.*—*Ed.*

peasants and knights//, "that they have to conduct their trade in great danger and that they are arrested, beaten, despoiled and robbed, etc., in consequence of trading. But if they suffered these things for the sake of righteousness, then, in truth, all merchants would be holy men.... But since such great unrighteousness and un-Christian thieving and robbery is rife throughout the whole world because of the merchants, and often enough amongst them themselves, why should we wonder if God wills it that such great wealth, gained by unrighteous means, is lost or stolen in its turn, and that because of it, the merchants are knocked on the head or arrested?... And it is the duty of the princes to punish such unrighteous commerce with due force and to see to it that their subjects are not fleeced so shamefully by the merchants. But because they do not do this, God uses the knights and the robbers and punishes the wickedness of the merchants through them; they must be His devils. Just as He plagues with devils or destroys with enemies the Land of Egypt and the whole world. Thus He causes one scoundrel to be flogged by another, but He does not indicate thereby that knights are lesser robbers than merchants, since the merchants rob the whole world every day while a knight only robs one or two people once or twice a year" ([p.] 296).

"...Follow the words of Isaiah: Thy princes have become the companions of thieves.[a] While they hang thieves who have stolen a guilder or half a guilder, they consort with those who rob the whole world and who steal more safely than any others; truly, the proverb—big thieves hang [XV-938] little thieves—still holds good, and, as Cato, the Roman senator, said: Little thieves are put into dungeons and in the stocks, but great thieves parade in gold and silk. But what will God have to say in the end? He will do as He said when He spoke through the mouth of Ezekiel: He will crush and melt prince and merchant, one thief and another, into one another like lead and brass,[b] just as happens when a town is burned down, so that there will be princes and merchants no longer, and I fear that this is not so far off" ([p.] 296a).

Usury. Interest-bearing capital:

"I am told that nowadays 10 guilders, i.e. 30 [per cent], are charged annually in any Leipzig market[144]; some add also the Neunburg market so that it comes to 40 [per cent]. I don't know whether it is even higher. Shame on you, where the devil will it end?... Whoever in Leipzig now has 100 florins, takes 40 in a year, this means that he has eaten up a peasant or a burgher in a year. If he has 1,000 florins, then he takes 400 in a year, that is, he eats up a squire or a rich gentleman in a year. If he has 10,000, he takes 4,000 in a year, that is, he eats up a rich count in a year. If he has 100,000, as must happen in the case of the great merchants, then he takes 40,000 in a year, that is, he eats up a great, rich prince in a year. If he has 1,000,000 then he takes 400,000 in a year, that is, he eats up some great king in a year. And he suffers not any danger in so doing, neither to his body nor to his treasure, labours not, sits by the fire and roasts apples; thus a chair thief may sit at home and eat up a whole world in 10 years" ([pp.] 312-13).[c]

//II) *Eyn Sermon auf das Evangelion von dem reichen Mann und armen Lazaro etc.*, Wittenberg, 1555.

"We must not regard the rich man according to his outer bearing, for he wears sheep's clothing and his life shines and seems pretty and covers up the wolf most

---

[a] Isaiah 1:23.— *Ed.*
[b] Ezekiel 22:18-22.— *Ed.*
[c] This quotation is taken from Luther's *An die Pfarrherrn wider den Wucher zu predigen*, Wittenberg, 1540.— *Ed.*

perfectly. For the Gospel does not charge him that he committed adultery, murder, robbery, sacrilege or anything that the world or reason would censure. Indeed he is as honest in his life as that Pharisee who fasts twice a week and is not as other men." [a]//

Here Luther tells us how usurer's capital arises, [through] the ruination of the citizens (petty bourgeois and peasants), the knights, the nobility and the princes. On the one hand, the usurer comes into possession of the surplus labour and, *in addition, the conditions of labour* of bourgeois, peasants, members of craft guilds, in short, of the small commodity producers who need money in order, for example, to make payments before they convert their commodities into money, and who have to buy certain of their conditions of labour, etc. On the other hand, the usurer appropriates rent from the owners of rent, that is, from the prodigal, pleasure-seeking *richesse.* Usury is a powerful means for establishing the preconditions for industrial capital—a mighty agency for separating the conditions of production from the producers, in so far as it has the twofold result, firstly, of establishing independent fortunes in the form of money, secondly, of appropriating the conditions of labour to itself, that is, ruining the owners of the old conditions of labour, just like the merchant. And both have the common feature that they acquire an independent fortune, that is, they accumulate in their hands in the form of money claims part of the annual surplus labour, part of the conditions of labour and also part of the accumulated annual labour. The money actually in their hands constitutes only a small portion of both the annual and the annually accumulated wealth and circulating capital. That they acquire *fortunes* means that a significant portion of both the annual production and the annual revenue accrues to them, and this is payable not *in natura,* but in the converted form, in money. Consequently, in so far as money does not circulate actively as currency, is not in movement, it is accumulated in their hands. They also hold some of the reservoirs of circulating money and to an even larger extent they hold and accumulate titles to production, but in the form of money titles, titles to commodities converted into money. [XV-939] On the one hand, usury leads to the ruin of feudal wealth and property; on the other hand, it brings about the ruin of petty-bourgeois, small-peasant production, in short, of all forms in which the producer still appears as the owner of his means of production.

The worker in capitalist production *does not own* the conditions of production, [he owns] neither the land he cultivates nor the

---

[a] Luke 18:11-12.—*Ed.*

tools with which he works. This alienation of the conditions of production corresponds here, however, to a REAL CHANGE in the mode of production itself. The tool becomes a machine, and the worker works in the workshop, etc. The mode of production no longer tolerates the dispersal of the instruments of production connected with small property, just as it does not tolerate the dispersal of the workers themselves. In capitalist production, usury can no longer *separate* the conditions of production from the workers, from the producers, because they have already been separated from them.

Usury *centralises* property, especially in the form of money, only where the means of production are scattered, that is, where the worker produces more or less independently as a small peasant, a member of a craft guild (small trader), etc. As peasant or artisan, whether the peasant is or is not a serf, or the artisan is or is not a member of a craft guild. The usurer here not only appropriates the part of the SURPLUS LABOUR belonging to the bondsman himself, or in the case of the free peasant, etc., the whole SURPLUS LABOUR, but he also appropriates the instruments of production, though the peasant, etc., remains their nominal owner and treats them as his property in the process of production. This kind of usury rests on this particular basis, on this *mode of production,* which it does not change, to which it attaches itself as a parasite and which it impoverishes. It sucks it dry, enervates it and compels reproduction to be undertaken under constantly more atrocious conditions. Thus the popular hatred of usury, especially under the conditions prevailing in antiquity, where this determination of production— in which the conditions of production are the property of the pro- ducer—was at the same time the basis of the political relationships, of the independence of the *citoyen.* This comes to an end as soon as the worker no longer possesses any conditions of production. And with it the power of the usurer likewise comes to an end. On the other hand, in so far as slavery predominates or the surplus labour is consumed by the feudal LORD and his RETAINERS and they fall prey to the usurer, the mode of production also remains the same, only it becomes more oppressive. The debt-ridden SLAVE- HOLDER or feudal LORD squeezes more out because he himself is being squeezed dry. Or, finally, he makes way for the usurer, who becomes a landowner, etc., like the *eques,*[a][145] etc., in Ancient Rome. In place of the old exploiter, whose exploitation was to some extent a means of political power, there appears A COARSE,

---

[a] Knight.— *Ed.*

MONEY-HUNTING PARVENU. But the mode of production itself remains unchanged.

The usurer in all pre-capitalist modes of production has a revolutionary impact only in the *political* sense, in that he destroys and wrecks the forms of property whose constant reproduction in the same form constitutes the stable basis of the political structure. [Usury] has a centralising effect as well, but only on the basis of the old mode of production, thus leading to the disintegration of society—apart from the slaves, serfs, etc., and their new masters—into a mob. Usury can continue to exist for a long time in Asiatic forms [of society] without bringing about real disintegration, but merely giving rise to economic decay and political corruption. It is only in an epoch where the other conditions for capitalist production exist—free labour, a world market, dissolution of the old social connections, a certain level of the development of labour, development of science, etc.—that usury appears as one of the factors contributing to the establishment of the new mode of production; and at the same time causing the ruin of the feudal LORDS, the pillars of the anti-bourgeois elements, and the ruin of small-scale industry and agriculture, etc., in short, as a factor leading to the centralisation of the conditions of labour in the form of capital.

The fact that the usurers, merchants, etc., possess "fortunes" simply means that the wealth of the nation, in so far as it takes the form of commodities or money, is concentrated in their hands.

At the outset capitalist production has to fight against usury to the extent that the usurer himself does not become a producer. With the establishment of capitalist production the domination of the usurer over surplus labour, a domination which depends on the continued existence of the old mode of production, ceases. The industrial capitalist collects the surplus directly in the form of profit; he has also already seized part of the conditions of production and he appropriates part of the annual accumulation directly. From this moment, and especially as soon as industrial and commercial wealth develops, the usurer—that is, the lender at interest—is merely a person who is differentiated from the industrial capitalist in result of the division of labour, but is subordinated to industrial capital.

[XV-940] III) *An die Pfarrherrn wider den Wucher zu predigen, etc.* Wittenberg, 1540 (*without* PAGINATION).

Trading (buying, selling) and lending. (Unlike Proudhon, Luther is not deceived by these differences of form!)

"Fifteen years ago I wrote against usury since it had already become so widespread that I could hope for no improvement. Since that time, it has exalted itself to such a degree that *it no longer wishes to be a vice, sin or infamy but* extols itself as downright virtue and honour as if it conferred a great favour on and did a Christian service to the people. What will help and counsel us now that infamy has become honour and vice virtue? Seneca says with good reason: *Deest remedii locus, ubi, quae vitia fuerunt, mores fiunt.*[a] Germany has become what it had to become, accursed avarice and usury have corrupted it completely....

"First concerning *lending* and *borrowing*: Where money is lent and more or better is demanded and taken in return, that is usury, anathemised in all laws. Therefore all those who take five, six or more on a hundred on money lent are usurers, and they know they are acting as such and are called the idolatrous servants of covetousness and of Mammon.... And one should say the same in respect of corn, barley and other goods, where more or better is demanded in return, that it is usury, goods stolen and extorted. For lending means my handing over my money, goods or chattels to somebody for as long as he needs them, or for as long as I can and wish to, and he returns the same things to me in his own good time, in as good a condition as that in which I lent him them.

"Thus they *also* make *a usury out of buying and selling*. But this is too much to deal with in one single bite. We must deal with one thing now, with usury as regards loans; when we have put a stop to this (as on the Day of Judgment), then we will surely read the lesson with regard to *usurious trade*.

"Thus Squire Usurer says: Friend, as things are at present, I do my neighbour a great *service* in that I lend him a hundred at five, six, ten. And he thanks me for such a loan as a very special favour. He does, in truth, entreat me for it and pledges himself freely and willingly to give me five, six, ten guilders in a hundred. Should I not be able without extortion to take this interest with a good conscience?...

"Extol thyself, put on finery and adorn thyself ... but whoever takes more or better than he gives, that is usury, and is *not service, but wrong* done to his neighbour, as when one steals and robs. All is not service and benefit to a neighbour that is called service and benefit. For an adulteress and adulterer do one another great service and pleasure. A horseman does an incendiary a great service, by helping him to rob on the highway, and attack the people and the land. The papists do ours a great service, in that they don't drown, burn, murder all of them, or let them all rot in prison; but let some live, and only drive them out, or take from them what they have. The devil himself does his servants a great, inestimable service.... To sum up, the world is full of great, excellent, and daily service and benefit.... The poets write about the Cyclops Polyphemus, who said he would do Ulysses an act of friendship, namely, that he would eat his companions first and then Ulysses last.[b] In sooth, this would have been a service and a fine favour. Such services and good deeds are performed nowadays most diligently by the high-born and the low-born, by peasants and burgesses, who buy goods up, pile up stocks, bring dear times, [XV-941] increase the price of corn, barley and of everything people need; they then wipe their mouths and say: Yes—one must have what one must have; I let my things out to help people although I might—and could—keep them for myself; and God is thus fooled and deceived.... The sons of men have become very holy.... So that now nobody can profiteer, be covetous or wicked; the

---

[a] There is no remedy where that which was regarded as unvirtuous becomes the habit.— *Ed.*

[b] Homer, *Odyssey*, IX, 369-370.— *Ed.*

world has really become holy, *everyone serves his fellows,* nobody harms anybody else...

"But if this is the kind of service he does, then he does it for Satan himself; although a poor needy man requires such service and must accept it as a service or favour that he is not eaten up completely...

"He does and must do thee such a favour" //pay interest to the usurer// "if he wants to get *money.*"

//One can see from the above that usury increased greatly in Luther's time and was already justified as a "*service*" (Say, Bastiat[a]). Even the formulation of competition or harmony existed: "Everyone serves his fellows."

In the world of *antiquity,* during the better period, usury was forbidden (i.e. interest was not allowed). Later it was lawful, and very prevalent. Theoretically the view always [predominated] that interest is actually wicked (as was stated by *Aristotle*[b]).

In the *Christian Middle Ages,* it was a "sin" and prohibited by "the canon".

Modern times. Luther. The Catholic-pagan view still prevailed. [Usury] became very widespread (as a result partly of the monetary needs of the government, [partly] of the development of trade and manufacture, and the necessity to convert the products into money). But its civic justification is already asserted.

Holland. The first apologia for usury. It is also here that it is first modernised and subordinated to industrial or commercial capital.

England. 17th century. The polemics are no longer directed against usury as such, but against the amount of interest, and the fact that it dominates credit. The desire to establish the form of credit. Regulations are imposed.

18th century. Bentham.[c] Unrestricted usury is recognised as an element of capitalist production.//

Interest as compensation for loss[d]:

"Well then, speaking in worldly and juridical fashion (we shall have to wait until later to speak about it theologically), you, Baltzer, are due to give me the hundred guilders along with all the losses and charges which have been added." //By charges, he means legal charges, etc., which the lender has incurred because he himself could not pay his debts.// "...It is therefore right and proper and likewise according to reason and natural law that you make restitution to me of

---

[a] See p. XXI—1326 of the manuscript (present edition, Vol. 34).— *Ed.*

[b] Aristoteles, *De republica libri VIII et oeconomica,* Book I, Ch. 10, in: *Aristotelis opera,* Vol. X, Oxford, 1837, p. 17. See also K. Marx, *Capital,* Vol. I, Ch. IV (present edition, Vol. 35).— *Ed.*

[c] J. Bentham, *Defence of Usury.—Ed.*

[d] Below, Marx quotes from Luther's *An die Pfarrherrn...—Ed.*

everything—both the *capital sum and the loss...* In legal books, the Latin word for this indemnification is *interesse...*[a]

"Something else can happen in the way of loss. If you, Baltzer, do not give me back my hundred guilders by Michaelmas and I have to make a purchase, say to buy a garden, a plot of land or a house, or anything from which I and my children could derive great use or sustenance, then I must forego it and you do me damage and are a hindrance to me so that I can never get such a bargain again because of your delay and inactivity, etc. But since I lent you the hundred guilders, you have caused me to suffer twofold damage because *I cannot pay on the one hand and cannot buy on the other* and thus must suffer loss on both sides. This is called *duplex interesse, damni emergentis et lucri cessantis....*[b]

"Having heard that Hans has suffered loss on the hundred guilders which he lent and demands just recompense for this loss, they rush in and charge *such double compensation on every 100 guilders,* namely, for expenses incurred and for the inability to buy the garden, *just as though every hundred guilders could grow double interest naturally, so that whenever they have a hundred guilders, they loan them out and charge for two such losses which however they have not incurred at all....*

"Therefore thou art a usurer, *who makes good thine own imagined losses with your neighbour's money,* losses which no one has caused thee and which thou canst neither prove nor *calculate.* The lawyers call such losses *non verum, sed phantasticum interesse.*[c] *A loss which each man dreams up for himself....*

"It will not do [XV-942] to say I might incur a loss because I might not have been able to *pay or buy.* That would mean *ex contingente necessarium,*[d] making something that must be out of something which is not, to turn a thing which is uncertain into a thing which is absolutely sure. Would such usury not eat up the world in a few years?...

"If the lender *accidentally* incurs a loss through no fault of his own, he must be recompensed, but it is different in such deals and just the reverse. There he seeks and *invents* losses to the detriment of his needy neighbours; thus he wants to maintain himself and get rich, to be lazy and idle and to live in *luxury and splendour on other people's labour* and worry, danger and loss. So that I sit behind the stove and let *my hundred guilders gather wealth for me throughout the land,* and, because they *are only loaned, I keep them safely in my purse* without any risk or worry; my friend, who would not like that?

"And what has been said about money which is loaned applies also to corn, wine and such like goods which are lent, for they also may occasion such double damage. But *such double damage is not something naturally accruing to the goods,* but may arise *by accident* only and cannot therefore be reckoned as damage unless it has actually occurred and been proved, etc....

"Usury there must be, but woe to the usurers....

"All wise, reasonable heathen have also inveighed against usury as something exceedingly evil. Thus Aristotle, in his *Politics,* says that usury is against nature and for this reason: it always takes more than it gives.[e] Thereby it abolishes the means and measure of all virtue, which we call like for like, *aequalitas arithmetica,*[f] etc....

---

[a] Literally: to be between, to make difference (in the property status of a person before he suffered a loss and after it).—*Ed.*

[b] Twofold compensation, for the loss incurred and for the gain missed.—*Ed.*

[c] Not real but imagined losses.—*Ed.*

[d] Making a necessity out of accident.—*Ed.*

[e] Cf. this volume, p. 537.—*Ed.*

[f] Arithmetical equality.—*Ed.*

"But taking from other people, stealing or robbing, is called a shameful way of maintaining oneself, and those who do so are called, by your leave, thieves and robbers, whom we are accustomed to hang on the gallows; a usurer however is a nice thief and robber and sits on a chair, therefore we call him a *chair thief*.... ·

."The heathen were able, by the light of reason, to conclude that a usurer is a double-dyed thief and murderer. We Christians, however, hold them in such honour, that we fairly worship them for the sake of their money.... Whoever eats up, robs, and steals the nourishment of another, that man commits as great a murder (so far as in him lies) as he who starves a man or utterly undoes him. Such does a usurer, and sits the while safe on his chair, when he ought rather to be hanging on the gallows, and be eaten by as many ravens as he has stolen guilders, if only there were so much flesh on him, that so many ravens could stick their beaks in and share it....

"But the dealers and usurers will cry out that what is written under hand and seal must be honoured. To this the jurists have given a prompt and sufficient answer. *In malis promissis.*[a] Thus the theologians say that some people give the devil something under hand and seal signifies nothing, even if it is written and sealed in blood. For what is against God, Right and Nature is null and void. Therefore let a Prince who can do so, take action, tear up bond and seal, take no notice of it, etc....

"Therefore is there, on this earth, no greater *enemy of man* (after the devil) than a gripe-money, and usurer, for *he wants to be God over all men.* Turks, soldiers, and tyrants are also bad men, yet must they let the people live, and confess that they are bad, and enemies, and do, nay, must, now and then show pity to some. But a usurer and money-glutton, such a one would have the whole world perish of hunger and thirst, misery and want, so far as in him lies, so that he may have all to himself, and every one *may receive from him as from a God and* [XV-943] *be his serf for ever.* This is what gladdens his heart, refreshes his blood. And, at the same time, he can wear sable cloaks, golden chains, rings, gowns, wipe his mouth, be deemed and taken for a worthy, pious man, who is more merciful than God Himself, more loving than the Mother of God, and all the holy Saints....

"And they write of the great deeds of Heracles, how he overcame so many monsters and frightful horrors in order to save his country and his people. For usury is a great huge monster, like a werewolf, who lays waste all, more than any Cacus, Geryon or Antaeus, etc. And yet decks himself out, and would be thought pious, so that people may not see where the oxen have gone (that he *drags backwards into his den*)."[b]

//ˑAn excellent picture, it fits the capitalist in general, who pretends that what he has taken from others and brought into his den, *emanates from him*, and by causing it to go *backwards* he gives it the semblance of having *come from his den*.//

"But Heracles shall hear the cry of the oxen and of the prisoners and shall seek Cacus even in cliffs and among rocks, and shall set the oxen loose again from the villain. For Cacus means the villain that is a *pious usurer*, and steals, robs, eats everything. And will not own that he has done it, and thinks no one will find him out, because the oxen, drawn backwards into his den, make it seem, from their foot-prints, that they have been *let out.* So the usurer would deceive the world, as though he were of use and *gave the world oxen, which he, however, rends, and eats all alone....*

a In evil promises.— *Ed.*

b Here and below see Virgil, *Aeneid,* VIII, 185 et seq.— *Ed.*

"Therefore, a usurer and miser is, indeed, not truly a human being, sins not in a human way and must be looked upon as a werewolf, more than all the tyrants, murderers and robbers, nearly as evil as the devil himself, but one who sits in peace and safety, not like an enemy, but like a friend and citizen, yet robs and murders more horribly than any enemy or incendiary. And since we break on the wheel, and behead highwaymen, murderers and house-breakers, how much more ought we to break on the wheel and kill all usurers, and hunt down, curse and behead all misers...."

A highly picturesque and striking description of both the character of old-fashioned usury, on the one hand, and of capital in general, on the other, with the "*interesse phantasticum*",[a] the "indemnification which naturally accrues" to money and commodities, the general phrases about usefulness, the "pious" air of the usurer who is not "as other men", the appearance of giving when one is taking, and of letting out when one is pulling in, etc.

* "The great premium attached to the possession of Gold and Silver, by the power it gives of selecting advantageous moments of purchasing, gradually gave rise to the trade of the *Banker*.... [The banker] differs from the old *Usurer* ... that he lends to the rich and *seldom or never to the poor*. Hence he lends with less risk, and can afford to do it on cheaper terms, and for both reasons, he avoids the popular odium which attended the Usurer" * (F. W. Newman, *Lectures on Political Economy*, London, 1851, [p.] 44).

The INVOLUNTARY ALIENATION of feudal landed property develops with usury and money.

"THE INTRODUCTION OF MONEY WHICH BUYS ALL THINGS, and hence the FAVOUR for the CREDITOR who loans MONEY to the landowner, BRINGS IN THE NECESSITY OF LEGAL ALIENATION for the advance" (John Dalrymple, *An Essay towards a General History of Feudal Property in Great Britain*, 4th ed., London, 1759, [p.] 124).

[XV-944] "According to Thomas Culpeper (1641), Josiah Child (1670) and Paterson (1694), wealth depends upon the reduction, even if a forced one, of the interest rate of gold and silver. Abided by in England for almost 2 centuries" (Ganilh [*Des systèmes d'économie politique...*, 2nd ed., Vol. I, Paris, 1821, pp. 58-59]).[b]

When *Hume*—in opposition to Locke—declared that the rate of interest is regulated by the rate of profit,[c] he had a much higher development of capital in mind. This was even more true of Bentham when he wrote his defence of usury[d] towards the end of the 18th century. A reduction in the rate of interest [was imposed] by law from the time of Henry VIII to that of Queen Anne.

---

a Imagined loss.— *Ed.*

b Marx gives a free rendering of Ganilh's text (in German). See also this volume, p. 463.— *Ed.*

c See pp. XX—1293a-1294a and XXII—1397 of the manuscript (present edition, Vol. 34).— *Ed.*

d J. Bentham, *Defence of Usury.—Ed.*

"In the Middle Ages, no country had *a general rate of interest*. First, the strictness of the clergy. Insecurity of the legal provisions for protecting loans. The interest rate was so much the higher in individual cases. The limited *circulation of money*, the *need to make most payments in cash*, for the bill business was not yet developed. Therefore wide divergences in interest rates and in the concept of usury. In Charlemagne's time, it was considered usurious to charge 100%. In Lindau on Lake Constance, in 1348,[a] local burghers took $216^2/_3\%$. In Zurich, the City Council fixed the legal interest rate at $43^1/_2\%$.[b] In Italy, 40% had sometimes to be paid, although the usual rate from the 12th to the 14th century did not exceed 20%. Verona decreed that $12^1/_2\%$ should be the legal rate. Frederick II fixed the rate at 10%, but only for Jews. He did not wish to speak for Christians. In Rhenish Germany, 10% was the usual rate as early as the 13th century" (Hüllmann, *Geschichte des Städtewesens etc.*, Part II, [Bonn, 1827, pp.] 55-57).[c]

The enormous rates of interest in the Middle Ages (in so far as they were not paid by the feudal aristocracy, etc.) were based in the towns, in very large measure, on the gigantic profits UPON ALIENATION which the merchants and urban craftsmen made out of country people, whom they cheated.

In Rome, as in the entire ancient world—apart from merchant cities, like Athens and others, which were particularly developed industrially and commercially—[high interest was] a means used by the big landowners not only for expropriating the small proprietors, the plebeians, but for appropriating their persons.

"Usury was initially free in Rome. The law of the Twelve Tables [146] (303 A.U.C.[d]) fixed interest on money at 1% per annum (Niebuhr says 10%[e]). These laws were promptly violated. Duilius (398 A.U.C.) once again reduced the interest on money to 1%, *unciarium foenus*.[f] Reduced to $^1/_2\%$ in 408; in 413, lending at interest was absolutely forbidden by a referendum'held by the tribune Genucius. It is not surprising that in a republic in which industry and wholesale and retail trade were forbidden to citizens, *trading in money* was *likewise forbidden*" (Dureau de la Malle, l.c., [*Economie politique des Romains*,] Vol. II, [Paris, 1840, pp.] 259-61). "This state of affairs lasted for 300 years, till the capture of Carthage. Then [the maximum chargeable] 12%; the usual rate 6% per annum (l.c., p. 261). Justinian fixed the interest rate at 4%. In Trajan's time, the *usura quincunx*[g] was the legal interest of 5%. In Egypt in 146 B.C., the commercial rate of interest was 12%" ([pp. 262-]63).[h] [147]

---

a Hüllmann has "1344".— *Ed.*

b Hüllmann has "$45^1/_3\%$".— *Ed.*

c The quotation is slightly abridged and modified.— *Ed.*

d A.U.C.— *anno urbis conditae*—in the year of the founding of the city (Rome),753 B.C.— *Ed.*

e B. Niebuhr, *Römische Geschichte*, Part 3, Berlin, 1832, pp. 66-67.— *Ed.*

f An increase of one ounce.— *Ed.*

g An interest of 5 ounces.— *Ed.*

h Marx quotes partly in French, partly in German, and slightly abridges the quotation.— *Ed.*

[ADDENDA]

[XIII-front cover] [148] *Hopkins* (passage to be looked up) [149] naïvely (describes) RENT OF LAND as the original form of SURPLUS VALUE, and profit as derived from this.

He writes:

*"When the ... producers were both agriculturists and manufacturers, the landowner received, as *rent of land,* a value of £10. Suppose this rent to have been paid $1/2$ in raw produce, and the other $1/2$ in manufactures;—on the *division* of the producers into the two classes of agriculturists and manufacturers* this could be continued. *In practice, however, it would be found more convenient for the cultivators of the land, *to pay the rent,* and to charge it on their produce, when exchanging it against the produce of the labour of the manufacturers; so as to divide the payment into two equitable proportions between the two classes, and to leave wages and profits equal in each department"* (Th. Hopkins, [*Economical*] *Enquiries relative to the Laws which Regulate Rent, Profit, etc.,* London, 1822, [p.] 26).

[XIII-670a] [150] *Decrease in the Rate of Profit.*

Calculated on the total capital the [rate of] profit of the larger capital, which employs more constant capital (machinery, raw material) and relatively less living labour, will be lower than that of the smaller [amount of] profit yielded by the smaller capital employing more living labour in proportion to the total capital. The [relative] decrease in variable capital and the relative increase in constant capital, although both parts are growing, is only another *expression for the increased productivity of labour.*

*"*The landed* and *trading interests* are eternally jarring and jealous of each other's advantages" ([N. Forster,] *An Enquiry into the Causes of the Present* [*High*] *Price of Provisions etc.,* London, 1767, [p.] 22, note).

"...whether it were not wrong to suppose *Land itself* to be *Wealth?* And whether the Industry of the people is not first to be considered, as that which constitutes Wealth, which makes even Land and silver to be Wealth, neither of which would have any value, but as *means and motives* to Industry?" (*The Querist. By Dr. George Berkeley*, London, 1750, Query 38).

"A diminishing surface suffices to supply man with food as population multiplies" (*The Natural and Artificial Right of Property Contrasted etc.* By Hodgskin, anonymously. London, 1832, [p.] 69).*

(Similar ideas were expressed by *Anderson* even earlier).[a]

* "At present, all the wealth of society goes first into the possession of the *capitalist,* and even most of the land has been purchased by him; *he pays* the landowner his rent, the labourer his wages, the tax and the tithe gatherer their claims, and *keeps a large, indeed the largest* and *a continually increasing share of the annual produce of labour for himself.* The capitalist may now be said to be the *first owner* of all the wealth of the community; though no law has conferred on him the right to this property" * (l.c., [p.] 98).

* "This change has been effected *by the taking of interest on capital,* and by the process of compound interest; and it is not a little curious, that all the lawgivers of Europe endeavoured *to prevent this by statutes,* viz., statutes against usury" * (l.c., [p.] 98, note).

* "The power of the capitalist over all the wealth of the country, *is a complete change in the right of property,* and by what law, or series of laws, was it effected?" * (l.c., [p.] 99).

[XV-862a] [151] Because SURPLUS VALUE and surplus labour are identical, a *qualitative* limit is set to the accumulation of capital, the *total working day* (the period in the 24 hours during which labour capacity can be active), the given stage of development of the productive forces and the *population,* which limits the *number* of working days that can be utilised simultaneously. If, on the contrary, surplus profit is understood in the abstract form of *interest,* that is, as the proportion in which capital increases by means of a mystical SLEIGHT OF HAND, then the limit is purely *quantitative* and there is absolutely no reason why capital cannot add to itself interest as capital every morning, thus creating interest on interest in infinite progression.

---

[a] See present edition, Vol. 31, pp. 371-73.— *Ed.*

NOTES
AND
INDEXES

NOTES

1 The *Theories of Surplus Value* on which Marx began work in March 1862 constitutes the fifth and final section of the first chapter of his study of capital, "The Production Process of Capital". His original intention was to examine absolute and relative surplus value in their combination. The *Theories of Surplus Value* was to form an historical survey pursuant to the chapter on surplus value, similar to that introducing the chapters on commodity and on money in *A Contribution to the Critique of Political Economy*.

However, substantial changes occurred in the character of the *Theories of Surplus Value* during the course of Marx's work on the manuscript. It considerably exceeded the scope of the tasks set by the author, both in terms of volume (approx. 100 printed sheets) and content. The manuscript not only examined the views of bourgeois economists but also elaborated a number of important theoretical propositions of Marx's economic doctrine.

The *Theories of Surplus Value* were first published in English in 1951 in an abridged form as: K. Marx, *Theories of Surplus Value*. A selection from the volumes published between 1905 and 1910 as *Theorien über den Mehrwert*, edited by K. Kautsky, taken from Marx's preliminary manuscript for the projected fourth volume of *Capital*. Translated from the German by G. A. Bonner and Emile Burns, Lawrence & Wishart, London, 1951.

The work was published in full in 1963-71 as: K. Marx, *Theories of Surplus Value* (Vol. IV of *Capital*). Part I, Foreign Languages Publishing House, Moscow, 1963; Part II, Progress Publishers, Moscow, 1968; Part III, Progress Publishers, Moscow, 1971.

The present volume contains the concluding part of Marx's *Theories of Surplus Value*. Volume 30 is given over to the first five notebooks of the Economic Manuscripts of 1861-63 and the beginning of the *Theories of Surplus Value* (notebook VI and part of notebook VII), whilst Volume 31 contains the continuation of the *Theories of Surplus Value* (the remainder of notebook VII, notebooks VIII to XI and part of notebook XII).—7

2 At the side of this line in the manuscript there is written in pencil, without any indication as to where it should be inserted: "(circulating and fixed capital, p. 643) in Ricardo".—7

[3] The two final points were subsequently crossed out in pencil and instead of them Marx inserted the point "Theory of Cost Price".—7

[4] The actual location of the materials in notebooks XIV and XV does not always accord with that given by Marx in the table of contents. Notebook XIV, for example, contains only the beginning of the section on the adversaries of the economists. The continuation of this section is to be found in the first half of notebook XV.

The section on Bray is located in notebook X of the manuscript (see present edition, Vol. 31, pp. 245-50). This section was not completed.

The sections on Ramsay, Cherbuliez and Richard Jones are to be found on pp. XVIII—1086-1157 (present edition, Vol. 33). Marx did not follow up his original intention to complete the fifth section in notebook XIV.

The survey of revenue and its sources is located in the second half of notebook XV (this volume, pp. 449-541).

The section on Ravenstone begins on p. XIV—861 (this volume, p. 392). This section is preceded by that numbered 1) and devoted to the anonymous pamphlet *The Source and Remedy of the National Difficulties*.

The end of the section on Hodgskin is contained on pp. XVIII—1084-1086 (see present edition, Vol. 33).

Marx did not write any section specifically devoted to vulgar political economy. He dealt with this subject in the section entitled "Revenue and Its Sources".—8

[5] This excerpt enclosed in brackets is a supplement to the Marxian analysis of Ricardo's theory of cost price and, in terms of content, belongs to p. XI—549 of the manuscript (see present edition, Vol. 31, p. 439).—9

[6] The term "*cost price*" (*Kostpreis, Kostenpreis*) was used by Marx in three different senses: 1) in the sense of the costs of production for the capitalist ($c+v$), 2) in the sense of the "immanent costs of production" of a commodity ($c+v+s$) which coincide with the value of the commodity, and 3) in the sense of the price of production ($c+v+$average profit). Here the term is used in the third sense.

In notebooks X-XIII of the manuscript Marx used the term "cost price" to mean the price of production, or the average price. He thus treats the two terms as identical (see present edition, Vol. 31, pp. 402-03, 559).

In notebooks XIV-XV of the manuscript this term is used now in the sense of the price of production, and now in that of the costs of production for the capitalist (see this volume, pp. 261, 271, 462).

The use of the term "Kostenpreis" in three different senses is due to the fact that "Kosten" has three different meanings in political economy, as specifically pointed out by Marx (see this volume, pp. 269-73, 513): 1) in the sense of what is advanced by the capitalist, 2) in the sense of the price of the capital advanced plus average profit, 3) in the sense of the actual (or immanent) production costs of the commodity itself.

Apart from these three meanings which we encounter in the classics of bourgeois political economy, there exists a fourth, vulgar meaning of the term "costs of production" as used by J. B. Say. He defined the "costs of production" as something paid for the "productive services" performed by labour, capital or land (J. B. Say, *Traité d'économie politique*. Seconde édition, Tome II, Paris, 1814, p. 453). Marx resolutely rejects this vulgar interpretation of "costs of production" (see, for example, present edition, Vol. 31, pp. 361, 439 and this volume, p. 102).—9, 102, 210

7 Here and below Marx quotes Adam Smith as cited by David Ricardo in *On the Principles of Political Economy, and Taxation*, third edition, London, 1821, pp. 227, 229 and 230.—18

8 This definition of monopoly price is given by Ricardo in Chapter XVII of *On the Principles of Political Economy, and Taxation*, third edition, London, 1821, pp. 289-90. A similar definition of monopoly price given by Adam Smith is quoted by Marx on p. XII—623 of the manuscript (present edition, Vol. 31, p. 558).—22

9 In the original: "More exactly, £16 $12^1/_2$s. disregarding a few fractions not even=2d."

The total profit equals £64 $\frac{211016}{346731}$, and the average profit on capital £16 $\frac{52754}{346731}$,

or £16.1521. $16^1/_7 = 16.1429$.—27

10 Marx is referring to sections IV and V of the first chapter of Ricardo's book *On the Principles of Political Economy, and Taxation* in which the author analyses the impact of a rise or fall of wages on the "relative value" of commodities produced by capitals of different organic composition. In his manuscript Marx gave a detailed critique of these two sections (see present edition, Vol. 31, pp. 400-25).—27

11 Here Marx illustrates by way of an example one of the ways in which the organic composition of agricultural capital can come closer to that of industrial capital. As the starting point he takes

$60c + 40v$—for agricultural capital,
$80c + 20v$—for non-agricultural capital.

Marx assumes that, with increased productivity of agricultural labour, the number of workers employed in this sector falls by a quarter. There is a corresponding change in the organic composition of agricultural capital: the same product as previously called for the expenditure of 100 units of capital $(60c + 40v)$ now only calls for 90 units of capital $(60c + 30v)$ which, in percentage terms, represents $66^2/_3c + 33^1/_3v$. The organic composition of capital in agriculture has thus drawn closer to the organic composition of capital in industry.

Marx further assumes that the fall in the number of agricultural workers is accompanied by a fall in wages by one quarter as a result of the decline in the price of corn. In this case, it must be assumed that wages in industry will fall by the same proportion. However, since agricultural capital has a lower composition, a fall in wages will be reflected to a greater extent here than in the case of non-agricultural capital. This would lead to a further reduction of the difference in the composition of capital in agriculture and that in industry.

Given a fall in wages of one quarter, agricultural capital of $66^2/_3c + 33^1/_3v$ will be transformed into capital of $66^2/_3c + 25v$ or, in percentage terms, $72^8/_{11}c + 27^3/_{11}v$.

Given a fall in wages of one quarter, non-agricultural capital composed of $80c + 20v$ will be transformed into capital composed of $80c + 15v$ or, in percentage terms, $84^4/_{19}c + 15^{15}/_{19}v$.

In the case of further reduction in the number of agricultural workers and further falls in wages, the organic composition of agricultural capital would grow increasingly close to the organic composition of non-agricultural capital.

In examining this hypothetical case, and in order to illustrate the influence a rise in the productivity of agricultural labour has on the organic composition of agricultural capital, Marx refrains from considering the effect of a simultaneous, and frequently more rapid, increase in the productivity of industrial labour, which would be expressed in a further rise of the organic composition of industrial capital as compared with agricultural. On the correlation between the organic composition of capital in industry and in agriculture, see present edition, Vol. 31, pp. 254-56, 325-26, 334-35, 337, 341-43, 464-65.—29

[12] When numbering the pages, Marx left out "649".—31

[13] Marx has 1836. It is still not known whether an 1836 edition actually existed. The quotation has been checked with the 1835 edition. Cf. this volume, p. 371.—35, 371, 388

[14] Marx is referring to the book: D. Ricardo, *Des principes de l'économie politique et de l'impôt*. Traduit de l'anglais par F. S. Constancio, avec des notes explicatives et critiques par J. B. Say. Seconde édition, Tome II, Paris, 1835, pp. 206-07. Marx is not quite correct here. In his notes on Ricardo's text Say "gloats" over the fact that Ricardo uses supply and demand to determine the value of *money* and not the "value of labour". Marx quotes the relevant passage from Say's notes in *The Poverty of Philosophy* (see present edition, Vol. 6, p. 151).—36, 285

[15] The reference is to the pamphlet by James Deacon Hume *Thoughts on the Corn-Laws...*, London, 1815. Commenting on Adam Smith's proposition "that the price of labour is governed by the price of corn", Hume writes: "Dr. Smith in speaking of corn must be understood to be speaking of food, because the value of all agricultural produce ... has a natural tendency to equalize itself" (p. 59).—38

[16] *Fluxion*—a term in an early system of differential and integral calculus worked out by Isaac Newton. Newton gave the name *fluents* (from the Latin *fluens*—flowing) to denote magnitudes of a system which (the magnitudes) change simultaneously and incessantly depending on time, and *fluxions* (from the Latin *fluxio*—flow) to the speed at which the fluents change. Thus fluxions are time derivatives of fluents.—43

[17] Marx is referring to the value newly created by twenty workers: each hour of work by these twenty labourers creates a value of £2, and a working day of 14 hours creates a value of £28.—47

[18] The value of the total product is made up of the value transferred to the product (c) and the newly created value ($v+s$). Since Marx ignores fixed capital in this case, the value transferred amounts to that of the raw materials. In the example given, the value of the raw materials is £93$1/3$ (the amount of cotton turned into yarn in one hour equals 133$1/3$ pounds, and in 14 hours 1,866$2/3$ pounds; each pound of cotton costs one shilling). Together with the newly created value (£28) this makes £121$1/3$.—47

[19] Here and on pp. XIII—690 and XIV—774 of his manuscript (this volume, pp. 97, 247) Marx points out the place in Ricardo's *Principles...* where the word "producer" is used in the sense of "labourer". Elsewhere in the book Ricardo uses the word "producer" in the sense of "industrial capitalist" (see, for example, the quotations from Ricardo given on pp. 57, 62 and 176 of this volume).—55, 97, 247

[20] See Thomas de Quincey, *The Logic of Political Economy*, Edinburgh, London, 1844, p. 158: "Now, then, is rent a disturbance of value simply in the sense of

being a modification, (as here explained,) or does it suspend and defeat the law? Ricardo has not pushed the question to that formal issue; but, generally, he has endeavoured to bring the question of rent into immediate relation with value, by putting the question upon it in this shape—'Whether the appropriation of land, and the consequent creation of rent, will occasion any variation in the relative value of commodities, independently of the quantity of labour necessary to production?' Whether, in short, the proportions between the two labours producing A and B will continue, in spite of rent, to determine the prices of A and B; or whether this law will be limited by the law of rent; or whether, in any case, this law will be actually set aside by rent?"—59, 92

21 Marx is referring here to such critics of Ricardo as Say who reproached Ricardo that he "sometimes reasons on abstract principles to which he gives too general validity" and thus allegedly arrives at conclusions which do not accord with reality (J. B. Say, *Traité d'économie politique...*, 5 éd., Paris, 1826, p. LXXXI).—72

22 Marx has "13$^1/_2$ tons", which is the amount of the rent calculated for the individual value of a ton. However, since previous calculations were based on the market value of a ton, an appropriate correction has been made here.—81

23 The figure 51$^{11}/_{39}$ tons results from the following calculation: if 16$^2/_3$ workers in III) of Table E) produce 62$^1/_2$ tons, then, provided labour productivity remains the same, 13$^{79}/_{117}$ workers will produce $\frac{13^{79}/_{117} \times 62^1/_2}{16^2/_3} = 51^{11}/_{39}$ tons. (See table on pp. 84-85).—89

24 Marx is referring to the book: W. Blake. *Observations on the Effects Produced by the Expenditure of Government during the Restriction of Cash Payments*, London, 1823. Excerpts from this book on the question dealt with in the text are to be found together with Marx's remarks in the *Outlines of the Critique of Political Economy* (see present edition, Vol. 29, pp. 168-70).—94

25 The reference is to the world exhibition, opened in London on May 1, 1862, displaying the latest achievements of science, agricultural and industrial products and works of art.
   The source of this quotation is unknown.—94, 199

26 In Volume Three of *Capital* (Chapter XXII) Marx shows that it is possible for the rate of profit and the rate of interest to move in opposite directions at various phases in the capitalist cycle (see present edition, Vol. 37).—102

27 Here Marx returns to the question as to what is the influence on the average rate of profit, and thus on cost prices, of profits obtained from colonial and foreign trade in general which exceed those in the metropolis. Marx shows that Smith's views on this question accorded more closely with the truth than those of Ricardo (see this volume, pp. 11-12, 70-72). Cf. also *Capital*, Volume Three, Chapter XIV (present edition, Vol. 37).—103

28 This example is based on the supposition that, given higher labour productivity, 20 quarters of wheat expended as seed will yield a harvest 50 per cent greater than before. If the previous harvest, for example, amounted to 100 quarters, it will now amount to 150 quarters given the expenditure of the same amount of labour, but these 150 quarters will cost the same as 100 quarters did previously, i.e. £300. Whilst the seed previously constituted 20 per cent of the harvest (in terms of volume and value alike), it now represents just 13$^1/_3$ per cent.—107

[29] The words "See MacCulloch" in brackets were later inserted by Marx in pencil. Marx first expressed the idea of using the sinking fund as a means of accumulation in his letter to Engels of August 20, 1862 (see present edition, Vol. 41, pp. 411-12). Marx returned to this problem when he was already working on Book II of *Capital*. He dealt with it in the letter to Engels of August 24, 1867, referring to letters dating back to 1862. He stated that he had found some clues in MacCulloch (see present edition, Vol. 42, p. 408). What he meant was J. R. MacCulloch, *The Principles of Political Economy...*, Edinburgh, London, 1825, pp. 181-82. Marx returns to this subject on pages XIV—777 and 781 of his manuscript (see this volume, pp. 251-52, 257).—112

[30] Working on his manuscript of 1861-63 devoted to the study of capital, Marx based himself on the plan he had drawn up when preparing to compile the manuscript of 1857-58. He had intended to include in the book on capital special sections devoted to competition and credit (see Marx's letter to Engels of April 2, 1858, present edition, Vol. 40, p. 298).

When subsequently preparing the manuscript of Volume Three of *Capital*, Marx considered it expedient to deal here with a number of questions related to competition and credit (see present edition, Vol. 37).—116, 162, 444, 460

[31] Marx is referring to James Mill's idea that there will always and necessarily be an equilibrium between production and consumption, supply and demand, the sum of purchases and the sum of sales. See J. Mill, *Elements of Political Economy*, London, 1821, pp. 186-95. Marx deals in greater detail with this view of Mill's (which he first expressed in the pamphlet *Commerce Defended...*, London, 1808) in *A Contribution to the Critique of Political Economy*, Part One (see present edition, Vol. 29, p. 333).—125, 134

[32] The *continental blockade* announced by Napoleon I in November 1806 prohibited the continental European countries from trading with England, greatly hindering the import of some commodities, including sugar and coffee, to Europe. Following Napoleon's defeat in Russia in 1812, the continental blockade was virtually ignored, and in 1814 it was removed altogether.—128

[33] The passage from p. XIII—718 of the manuscript has been placed here in accordance with its substance.—135

[34] On p. X—426 of the manuscript Marx specifies this as follows: "sold *under* its price, i.e., for less than the sum of money which represents its [the commodity's] value" (see present edition, Vol. 31, p. 215).—135

[35] Marx is referring to that part of his study which subsequently grew to become Volume Three of *Capital*. Cf. also present edition, Vol. 31, pp. 282 and 397.—143

[36] The pages have been rearranged according to Marx's direct instructions. Pages 770a, 771a and 861a of the manuscript are the outside back cover of notebook XIII, the inside front cover and inside back cover of notebook XIV respectively.—144

[37] This page of the manuscript is damaged, and for this reason it was impossible to decipher the word "crisis" with certainty.—145

[38] This page of the manuscript, which is the inside front cover of notebook XIV, carries the table of contents of the notebook (see this volume, pp. 7-8) and the remark "Continuation of cover page (last) of notebook XIII". See also Note 36.—145

39 The top left-hand corner of this page has been torn off in the manuscript so that only the right-hand side of the first seven lines has been preserved, making it impossible to reproduce the text in full. From what has survived it can be assumed that this passage deals with crises occurring as a result of changes in the value of variable capital. The passage in question has been omitted from the present volume.— 146

40 Marx made short remarks on the forms of crisis on the covers of notebook XIII (page 770a of the manuscript) and notebook XIV (pp. 771a and 861a). In accordance with Marx's remark "To page 716", these pages have been inserted above.
    The insertion in brackets was made by Marx at a later date and it is here that he describes these new forms.— 147

41 The manuscript continues with a brief insertion in brackets on Ricardo's views of money and exchange value. In line with its substance, this insertion has been placed on p. 135 of this volume as a note at the bottom of the page.— 149

42 This insertion, which opens p. 720 of the manuscript, has been placed here in accordance with its substance.— 150

43 Marx is referring to notebooks I-V of his manuscript, and in particular to the sections on the production of absolute and relative surplus value (see present edition, Vol. 30, pp. 172-346).— 151

44 Marx is referring to Say's argument stated in *Lettres à M. Malthus...*, Paris, Londres, 1820, p. 15, that the cause of the flooding of the Italian market with English goods was the underproduction of Italian goods which might be exchanged for English ones. This argument by Say is quoted in the anonymous discourse *An Inquiry into Those Principles...*, London, 1821, p. 15, from which Marx made excerpts. Cf. also present edition, Vol. 31, pp. 133, 166.— 160, 311

45 Compare with the critique by Marx of James Mill's and Say's theses on the impossibility of general overproduction which he presented in his economic manuscript of 1857-58 (see present edition, Vol. 28, pp. 338-39, 351-52).— 161

46 Sismondi's explanation for crises was "the growing disproportion between production and consumption" (J. C. L. Simonde de Sismondi, *Nouveaux principes d'économie politique, ou de la richesse dans ses rapports avec la population.* Seconde édition, T. 1, Paris, 1827, p. 371). Cf. also this volume, pp. 247-48.— 163

47 The top left-hand corner of this page in the manuscript is missing. The words reinstated are given in square brackets.— 178

48 Marx apparently believed that here Ricardo was referring to the speech he had made in the House of Commons on December 16, 1819 with regard to William de Crespigny's proposal that a commission be set up to discuss Robert Owen's plan for the elimination of unemployment and an improvement in the situation of the lower classes.
    In this speech Ricardo stated that "machinery did not lessen the demand for labour" (*The Times*, No. 10804, December 17, 1819).— 181

49 The reference is to the revolution of 1688 (the overthrow of the Stuart dynasty and the enthronement of William III of Orange), after which the constitutional

monarchy was consolidated in England on the basis of a compromise between the landed aristocracy and the bourgeoisie.

The *enclosures*—the forced eviction of peasants from their land by the feudal lords (the land was then surrounded with fences, ditches, etc.). This practice took its classical form in England between the late 15th and early 19th centuries. It led to the abolition of communal land and the demise of the class of small landowners.—208

[50] According to the *Poor Laws* which existed in England from the 16th century, a special tax was levied in each parish to benefit the poor. Those parishioners who were unable to provide for themselves and their families received assistance through the poor relief fund.—208

[51] In this section, Marx analyses works written by Malthus following the appearance of Ricardo's *On the Principles of Political Economy, and Taxation* (1817). In his works, Malthus attempted to oppose Ricardo's labour theory of value and his call for the all-out development of the productive forces to the detriment of individuals and even whole classes (see this volume, pp. 243-44) with a vulgar apologetic theory aimed at defending the interests of the most reactionary strata of the dominant classes.

Malthus as an exponent of the "theory of population" is mentioned only in passing in this chapter. Marx provides a general description of Malthus' work *An Essay on the Principle of Population* in the section "Notes on the History of the Discovery of the So-Called Ricardian Law" (see present edition, Vol. 31, pp. 344-51).—209

[52] The quotation given here is not from *Inquiry into the Nature and Progress of Rent...* but from *Observations on the Effects of the Corn Laws...*, London, 1815. Marx had evidently confused the two.—209

[53] Above, on p. 4 of his book, Malthus comments on Smith's views as follows: "The substance of his argument is, that corn is of so peculiar a nature, that its real price cannot be raised by an increase of its money-price", and so Smith supposes that "the real price of corn is unchangeable".—209

[54] A critique of Smith's view of the value of labour as the "standard measure of value" and proof that this view contradicts other, more profound views of value on Smith's part, was presented by Marx on pp. VI—248-249 and XII—653-655 of the manuscript (see present edition, Vol. 30, pp. 382-83 and this volume, pp. 38-40).—209

[55] Ricardo's failure to analyse the origin of surplus value and his inability to solve the exchange of labour for capital were shown by Marx on pp. XII—650-652 and XII—655-656 of the manuscript (see this volume, pp. 32-36, 40-43).—210

[56] "*Profit upon expropriation*", or "*profit upon alienation*" is a concept formulated by James Steuart which Marx cites and analyses at the beginning of his *Theories of Surplus Value* (see present edition, Vol. 30, pp. 351-52).—211, 371

[57] Marx describes Malthus as such since, in a number of his works, the latter claimed that the destitution of the working masses resulted from the population's ability to multiply at a far greater rate than the ability of the soil to produce foodstuffs for human consumption; the population grows in geometrical progression whilst the volume of means of subsistence increases only in arithmetical terms.—217

⁵⁸ Marx is quoting from the French translation of Smith's book made by Garnier: A. Smith, *Recherches sur la nature et les causes de la richesse des nations*, Paris, 1802. Marx made excerpts from this book whilst in Paris in the spring of 1844. In the present edition, all quotations from the French edition of Smith's book are reproduced in English in accordance with: A. Smith, *An Inquiry into the Nature and Causes of the Wealth of Nations*. With a Life of the Author, an Introductory Discourse, Notes, and Supplemental Dissertations. By J. C. McCulloch. In four volumes. Edinburgh, London, 1828. The page references are given in square brackets. Marx made extensive use of the 1828 edition when working on the manuscript of 1861-63.—221

⁵⁹ This definition of value was drawn up by Cazenove on the basis of statements by Malthus and Adam Smith, Malthus having borrowed from the latter the determination of a commodity value by the amount of living labour purchased in exchange for this commodity.—225

⁶⁰ This quotation from Malthus reproduces Adam Smith's reasoning as illustrated on p. VII—302 of the manuscript (see present edition, Vol. 31, p. 11): "...The labour of a manufacturer *adds,* generally, to the value of the materials which he works upon, *that of his own maintenance, and of his master's profit.* The labour of a menial servant, on the contrary, adds to the value of nothing. ... A man *grows rich* by employing a multitude of manufacturers: he grows poor by maintaining a multitude of menial servants" (A. Smith, *An Inquiry into the Nature and Causes of the Wealth of Nations*. With a Life of the Author, an Introductory Discourse, Notes, and Supplemental Dissertations. By McCulloch. Vol. II, Edinburgh, London, 1828, pp. 93-94). By giving the title to the relevant section ("The Distinction Between Productive and Unproductive Labour") in terms typical of Smith, Marx is hinting that this view of Malthus' was borrowed from Smith. Marx gives a detailed analysis of Smith's interpretation of productive labour as labour objectified in a commodity on pp. VII—316-316 of the manuscript (present edition, Vol. 31, pp. 16-31).—228

⁶¹ *Lord Dundrearyism* (or *Dundrearyism*)—pompous foppishness. Lord Dundreary is a character from the comedy *Our American Cousin* by the English writer Tom Taylor which was first performed in 1858.—230, 240

⁶² The calculations given here disprove the arguments of Malthus which Marx cited above (see p. 229). In one of his notebooks of excerpts, Marx called this reasoning "ridiculous".—231

⁶³ Here, and in some places below, Marx uses the term "*cost price*" ("*Kostpreis*", "*Kostenpreis*") to mean the costs of production for the capitalist ($c + v$). See Note 6.—234

⁶⁴ Since p. XIII—770 of the manuscript is damaged, the text reinstated in substance by the editors has been given in square brackets.—237

⁶⁵ The last page of notebook XIII, numbered 770a, has been transferred to p. 716 of the manuscript as indicated by Marx (see this volume, pp. 144-45).
The text on the inside front cover of notebook XIV, p. 771a, is the continuation of p. 770a (see this volume, pp. 145-46).
Above the text on the first page of notebook XIV, p. 771, Marx wrote: "A Contribution to the Critique of Political Economy. XIV."—239

⁶⁶ Here, this term is used in the special sense illustrated by Marx on p. 703 of his manuscript: "their surplus produce (which means here, the excess of their

product over that part of it which=their constant capital" (see this volume, p. 122), i.e., (v+s).

In the example under consideration, Marx assumes constant capital to be zero, so that the "surplus produce" coincides with the value of the product.—240

[67] See Note 30.

In his plan for the third section of *Capital* written at a later date, in January 1863, Marx remarks: "Query: whether Sismondi and Malthus should also be included in the *Theories of Surplus Value*" (see p. XVIII—1139 of the manuscript, present edition, Vol. 33), though there he makes only isolated comments on the views of Sismondi.—245

[68] When developing his utopian plan for social transformations, Owen proved that, both economically and from the viewpoint of everyday domestic life, the most expedient structure for a settlement of a community is a parallelogram or a square.—247

[69] The *Established Church* is the name given in England to the Anglican Church, or Church of England.—248, 443

[70] Marx failed to write the section "The Relationship Between Capital and Wage Labour Presented from an Apologetic Standpoint".—251

[71] The reference is to the plan for the nationalisation of land as advocated from 1775 by the English Utopian Socialist Thomas Spence. He called for the abolition of private property in land, its transfer to the parishes and the distribution of land rent (following the payment of all taxes and communal expenses on the part of the parish) among the parishioners in equal portions for all (cf. Th. Spence, *The Meridian Sun of Liberty...*, London, 1793).—252

[72] Marx considered it a peculiar characteristic of Smith's economic theory that he combined two lines of study—esoteric, i.e., the study of economic relations in their internal, concealed nexus, and exoteric, i.e., the investigation of these relations in the forms in which they manifest themselves on the surface. This brought with it contradictory interpretations of the self-same categories. See present edition, Vol. 31, pp. 390-91, 394.—258

[73] On the difference between *production time* and *labour time* which occurs particularly in agriculture, and on the peculiarities in the development of capitalism in agriculture connected with it, see K. Marx, *Outlines of the Critique of Political Economy* (present edition, Vol. 28, pp. 521-22, Vol. 29, pp. 58-60).—262

[74] See J. Mill, *Elements of Political Economy*, London, 1821, p. 74. Here, Marx is probably quoting this passage from the book by Samuel Bailey, *A Critical Dissertation on the Nature, Measures, and Causes of Value*, London, 1825, p. 202 where it is likewise regarded as being directed against Torrens. Cf. this volume, p. 287.—266

[75] Malthus rejected the labour theory of value, reducing the value of commodities to the costs of production and regarding profit as a nominal increase in the value of a commodity and circulation as the sphere where this surplus came into being. Malthus was thus returning to the mercantilists' ideas on profit obtained as a result of the alienation of commodities. See present edition, Vol. 30, pp. 348, 351-52, 374 and this volume, pp. 214-16, 220-22, 225-28.—267, 280

76 Here, Marx assumes that all costs of corn production which occur in Torrens for a volume of 100 quarters amount to expenditure on seed. In fact, a considerably smaller volume of seed is required to produce 120 quarters of corn, say, 20 or 30 quarters. The remaining 70 or 80 quarters go to pay for the instruments of labour, fertiliser, wages for the workers, etc. However, this fact is of no significance to Marx's argument.—268

77 Marx describes capitalists as competitors—"hostile brothers"—at the end of Chapter X of Volume Three of *Capital* (present edition, Vol. 37). Cf. also present edition, Vol. 31, p. 264.—272

78 The piece from the words "Mill's passage..." to "p. 99" was written by Marx on the left margin of p. XIV—792 of the manuscript and placed here in accordance with the insertion mark.—276

79 In 1882 the German mathematician Ferdinand Lindemann proved that the value of π is transcendental and that it is therefore impossible to square the circle algebraically.—277

80 A detailed critique of the practice of bourgeois economists of splitting up the object under study into production, distribution, exchange and consumption is given by Marx in the "Introduction" to the Economic Manuscripts of 1857-58 (see present edition, Vol. 28, pp. 17-48).—278

81 The treatment of these problems begins on p. 290 of this volume.—287

82 In the list of printer's errors appended to MacCulloch's book *Discours sur l'origine...*, "élever (to raise)" is corrected to "eluder", so that the phrase should be translated as: "the farmer who rents this last acre, cannot evade paying the corresponding rent".—293

83 Marx is referring to Say's note on Chapter 7 "On Foreign Trade" of Ricardo's book *Des principes de l'économie politique, et de l'impôt*. Traduit de l'anglais par F. S. Constancio, avec des notes explicatives et critiques, par Jean-Baptiste Say, T. 1, Paris, 1819, p. 209, in which Say gives the example of sugar imported by France from the Antilles and costing less than would sugar produced in France itself.—294

84 In the first of his *Essays on Some Unsettled Questions of Political Economy* (London, 1844), "Of the Laws of Interchange between Nations; and the Distribution of the Gains of Commerce among the Countries of the Commercial World", John Stuart Mill remarks: "We may often, by trading with foreigners, obtain their commodities at a smaller expense of labour and capital than they cost to the foreigners themselves. The bargain is still advantageous to the foreigner, because the commodity which he receives in exchange, though it has cost us less, would have cost him more" (pp. 2-3).—294

85 What Marx means here by *fictitious capital* is the capital of the debt owed by the state, since the state (be it bourgeois or bourgeois-landowner) spends the loans it has received not as capital and pays interest on them from the taxes it has collected from the population. See K. Marx, *Capital*, Vol. III, Ch. XXIX (present edition, Vol. 37).—299

86 In his manuscript of 1861-63 Marx repeatedly returns to the proposition of the English bourgeois economists that "capital employs labour" (see this volume and present edition, Vol. 34).—303

87 The anonymous author is mistaken. The statement in question by Say is to be found in his *Traité d'économie politique...*, 4 éd. T. 2, Paris, 1819, p. 60.—309

[88] Chapter 19 in Ricardo's *Principles...* is called "On Sudden Changes in the Channels of Trade", with trade being taken to mean not only trade as such but also productive activity in a given country. Cf. this volume, p. 129.—309

[89] Marx is referring to one of the notebooks in which he made notes on political economy. The first 63 pages of notebook VII, which Marx mentions here, contain the end of the economic manuscript of 1857-58 (see present edition, Vol. 29, pp. 85-253). Starting from page 63a (on which Marx wrote "Begun on February 28, 1859") notebook VII contains excerpts from works by Luther, Linguet, Galiani, Verri, Paoletti, Malthus, Richard Jones and others. On page 134 of notebook VII, Marx copied from *An Inquiry into Those Principles...* (pages 110 and 112) a number of passages in which an anonymous author criticises and makes fun of Say.—310

[90] Marx is referring to notebook XII of his excerpts on the cover of which he wrote "London, 1851, July". Page 13 of this notebook carries excerpts from pages 97, 99, 103-04, 106-08 and 111 of the anonymous *Inquiry into Those Principles...*

A reference to landowners whose rent lowers capitalist profit is to be found in the excerpt from pp. 54-55 of *An Inquiry...*, which is located on p. 12 of Marx's notebook XII.—310

[91] Prior to this, on p. 110, the anonymous author gave a quotation from Say's book *Lettres à M. Malthus*, Paris, 1820 (p. 46) containing the proposition that "products are bought only for products". This proposition had previously figured in Say's book *Traité d'économie politique*, 2 éd., T. 2, Paris, 1814 (p. 382). See also this volume, pp. 124-25, 132, 307.—311

[92] The first edition of this book appeared in 1844. The pages indicated by Marx for the quotations in this volume accord with this edition.—311

[93] *Posited* (Marx has "*Gesetztes*")—a term in Hegelian philosophy used to describe something which is caused as opposed to something without cause, original or primary—something having its foundation not in itself but in something else.—316

[94] Here Marx continues the analysis of Bailey's views which he began earlier (see this volume, p. 312).—320

[95] This is the way in which Marx ironically refers to the anonymous author of *Observations on Certain Verbal Disputes in Political Economy...*—324

[96] In the example discussed by Marx, the area of a parallelogram and that of a triangle will be equal if the height of the parallelogram equals $\frac{h}{2}$ or if its base equals $\frac{b}{2}$.—330

[97] The "*portion*" of a product accruing to the workers (and, consequently, to the capitalist) means the number of natural units of the product in which the newly added labour is objectified, whilst "*proportion*" refers to the percentage of this product accruing to one or other of the parties.—335, 339

[98] If, instead of the random figures "50, 60 or 70 qrs per man", we take the figures which correspond to Bailey's example given above (this volume, p. 338) we will obtain $12\frac{1}{2}$, 25 or $37\frac{1}{2}$ qrs per man.—342

[99] When numbering the pages, Marx missed out "838".—351

[100] Marx has "1830", i.e. the year when the second edition of MacCulloch's book appeared. Since the pages given accord with the first edition, an appropriate correction has been made here.—353, 369, 508

[101] A hint at the words of one of Wallenstein's soldiers in Schiller's drama of the same name (Part I, Scene VI).—356

[102] From 1824 on MacCulloch gave lectures on political economy dedicated to the memory of Ricardo. When the University of London was founded, MacCulloch took the chair of political economy (1828-32).—356

[103] The reference is to the policy of the *Whigs*—an English political party in the 17-19th centuries which represented the interests of the gentry who had become bourgeois and the big trading and financial bourgeoisie. Following the parliamentary reform of 1832, the Whigs held office alternately with the Tories, pursuing an anti-working class policy and attempting to suppress the Chartist movement. In the mid-19th century, they merged with other political groupings to form the Liberal Party.—356

[104] Marx is evidently referring to the second edition of MacCulloch's book *The Principles of Political Economy,* which appeared in 1830, since the first edition of the book which Marx usually cites was published in 1825, i.e. before Smith's *Wealth of Nations* with "notes and dissertations" by MacCulloch.—357

[105] Marx ironically gives Roscher the name of the great Ancient Greek historian Thucydides because "Professor Roscher ... has modestly proclaimed himself to be the Thucydides of political economy" (see this volume, p. 502). Roscher's immodest reference to Thucydides can be found in the preface to the first edition of his *Die Grundlagen der Nationalökonomie* (1854).

At a number of points Marx shows that Roscher grossly distorted both the history of economic relations and the history of economic theories. Cf. present edition, Vol. 31, pp. 352-54.—369, 502

[106] In October 1862, when notebook XIV of the manuscript was written, the section on the "Conversion of Surplus Value into Capital" had not yet materialised.

On Wakefield's merits, see present edition, Vol. 30, pp. 256-57.—371

[107] By "*surplus produce*" Wakefield means that part of the produce which exceeds what is necessary to "replace capital with ordinary profits" (Wakefield's commentary to Volume II of his edition of *An Inquiry into the Nature and Causes of the Wealth of Nations* by Adam Smith, London, 1835, pp. 215 and 217).—371

[108] Among the opponents of the economists Marx also included J. F. Bray whose statements he examined in notebook X of his manuscript (see present edition, Vol. 31, pp. 245-50).—373

[109] "*This most incredible cobbler*" was the way the author of the pamphlet *Some Illustrations of Mr. M'Culloch's Principles of Political Economy* described MacCulloch. See p. 370 above.—374, 400

[110] The section "*Revenue and Its Sources*" features as an "episode" on the cover of notebook XIV (see this volume, p. 8). But Marx deals with this issue in notebook XV of the manuscript, in connection with his critique of vulgar political economy (see this volume, p. 499 et seq.). Marx wrote about "Price's fantasy" at a later stage, on p. XVIII—1066 of the manuscript (present edition, Vol. 33).—376

111 By "*industry of consumption*" Ravenstone means the production of luxury goods and the performance of all kinds of services for the owners of capital or property. See this volume, p. 396.—394

112 The reference is to the conquest of England in 1066 by William, Duke of Normandy, who became known as William the Conqueror and was enthroned as William I of England, thus founding a new Norman dynasty. Although the process of feudalisation had made considerable progress in England by this time, a major part of the peasantry remained free and the feudally dependent landholders had not yet merged to form a single stratum of serfs, and the feudal estate did not yet exist everywhere, nor had it taken on its classic form. The Norman Conquest played a crucial role in completing this process.—396

113 A critique of bourgeois economists who as apologists of bourgeois society confused capital with material elements of the labour process was given by Marx in his economic manuscript of 1857-58 (see present edition, Vol. 28, pp. 188-89, 235-36). In his manuscript of 1861-63, Marx returns to this question in the section "Unity of the Labour Process and the Valorisation Process" (see present edition, Vol. 30, pp. 95, 98-99).—398

114 When writing notebook XV, Marx skipped over pages 865 and 866. Having filled in p. 870a, he continued writing on the empty pages. Following p. 870a, the text continues on pp. 865 and 866, and then on p. 870b. The progression from one non-adjacent page to another was indicated by Marx himself.—399, 410

115 Later, in a letter to Engels of June 16, 1864, Marx gave these quotations which he had found in Chavée (see present edition, Vol. 41, pp. 540-41).—430

116 The passage immediately following this in Hodgskin's pamphlet·makes it clear that what the author means by "striking a sort of balance" is: "The capitalists permit the labourers to have the means of subsistence, because they cannot do without labour, contenting themselves very generously with taking every particle of produce not necessary to this purpose".—431, 435, 436

117 The figures indicate that they refer to a period of one year.—436

118 A reference to the *Ten Hours Bill*, passed by the British Parliament on June 8, 1847, which applied only to adolescents and women and was ignored by many manufacturers.—441

119 The manuscript continues with a passage in square brackets which, in accordance with its content, has been placed on p. 330 of this volume as a note at the bottom of the page.—442

120 The chapter on the real movement of wages was not written by Marx. He deals with this question in Volume One of *Capital* (see present edition, Vol. 35).—445

121 On p. XV—890 of the manuscript, Marx interrupts his analysis of Hodgskin's views and embarks on a survey of revenue and its sources and of vulgar political economy. A considerable part of notebook XV of the manuscript is devoted to these two subjects which are analysed in close interconnection. Judging by the plan for notebooks XIV and XV, he originally intended to write two separate sections, "Episode: Revenue and Its Sources" and "Vulgar Political Economy", respectively (see this volume, p. 8). Subsequently, Marx intended to incorporate this survey into the third part of *Capital*, as can be seen from the plan for this part which he drew up in January 1863 and according to which Chapter IX was to be headed "Revenue and Its Sources" (see p. XVIII—1139 of the

manuscript, present edition, Vol. 33). Later some of the material contained in this section was used almost word for word by Marx when preparing the manuscript of Volume Three of *Capital*. Marx returned to his interrupted section on Hodgskin on p. XVIII—1084 of the manuscript (see present edition, Vol. 33).—449

122 Here Marx uses the term "capital in itself" ("*Capital an sich*") for the first time. However, he had already examined questions related to this concept in the *Outlines of the Critique of Political Economy* (see present edition, Vol. 28, pp. 171-204).—458

123 By "*this general section*" Marx means the section on "capital in general" which, according to the plan Marx had worked out when preparing the economic manuscript of 1857-58, was to begin the book on capital. See also Note 30.—458

124 Marx is referring here to Proudhon and his supporters.—463

125 The first edition of Child's book appeared in London in 1668 as a small pamphlet. In 1669-70 ten additional chapters were written following which the book was republished on several occasions. The first edition of Culpeper's discourse appeared in London in 1621; from 1668 it was printed as an appendix to Child's book.—463

126 Marx is referring to such followers of Saint-Simon as S. A. Bazard and B. P. Enfantin who accorded a special role to the banking system in the future organisation of the economy, the so-called industrial system.—464

127 The reference is to the *Société générale du Crédit mobilier,* a big French joint-stock bank founded by the Péreire brothers in 1852. The bank was closely associated with the government of Napoleon III and under its protection engaged in large-scale speculation. It went bankrupt in 1867 and was liquidated in 1871.

In 1856-57 Marx wrote five articles on the speculative activities of this bank for *The People's Paper* and the *New-York Daily Tribune* (see present edition, Vol. 15, pp. 8-24, 270-77, 357-60).—464

128 Marx digresses here to the analysis of different forms of capital. He dealt with this subject in more detail in *Capital*, Volume Three.

The interrupted passage is continued on p. XV—902 of the manuscript (see this volume, p. 469).—467

129 Below Marx examines the separation of certain parts of surplus value into different forms of revenue.—471

130 Here Marx interrupts his discussion of the separation of certain parts of surplus value and turns to various issues concerning the process of reproduction. He examined this question in greater detail at a later stage, on pp. XXII—1371-1394 of his manuscript in the section "Reproduction", which he wrote in the framework of his discussion of "The Production Process of Capital" (see present edition, Vol. 34).—478

131 When numbering the pages, Marx missed out "909".—481

132 Below Marx continues his interrupted discussion on the separation of certain parts of surplus value (see this volume, p. 478).—482

133 Marx devoted his attention to "dumb instruments, and speaking and feeling

instruments" at a later stage, in Volume One of *Capital* (Part III, Ch. VII, Sect. 2, Note, present edition, Vol. 35).—488

[134] The quotations on the "labour of the overseer" were given by Marx in Chapter XXIII of Volume Three of *Capital* which he wrote two to three years later (see present edition, Vol. 37).—496

[135] In 1844, workers in the town of Rochdale (Manchester industrial region) who had been influenced by Owen's ideas took the initiative in organising a consumers' cooperative, the Rochdale Equitable Pioneers' Society, which became the prototype for workers' cooperatives in England and other countries. Workers' cooperatives often combined productive functions with their activities as consumers' societies. See also p. XVIII—1100 of the manuscript (present edition, Vol. 33) and *Capital*, Volume Three, Part V, chapters XXIII and XXVII (ibid., Vol. 37).—497, 504

[136] Marx is referring to the so-called old *historical school,* a trend which emerged in German vulgar political economy in the mid-19th century and owed its origins to W. Roscher.—501

[137] Arnd devoted a separate paragraph in his book to justifying and describing the expedience of a dog tax. See K. Arnd, *Die naturgemässe Volkswirtschaft...,* S. 420-21. See also present edition, Vol. 29, p. 226.—504

[138] The reference is to Ricardo's proposition that a rise of profits can never be brought about otherwise than by a fall of wages, nor a fall of profits otherwise than by a rise of wages.—508

[139] In terms of substance, the passage enclosed by Marx in oblique lines belongs to p. XIV—850a of the manuscript (this volume, p. 370).—508

[140] In the formula for the price of production, the letters C and A.P. are used to denote costs and average profit respectively.—525

[141] When drawing up the table of contents for notebook XV, Marx intended to devote a section to "*Vulgar Political Economy*" (see this volume, p. 8). In the plan for the third section, "Capital and Profit", which he compiled in January 1863, the penultimate, eleventh point is headed "*Vulgar Economy*" (see p. XVIII—1139 of the manuscript, present edition, Vol. 33). This plan was compiled about two months after he had written the section "Revenue and Its Sources" (November 1862), but Marx did not write a chapter specifically devoted to vulgar political economy.—526

[142] The text which follows below (pp. 529-30) is a reproduction in parts almost verbatim, of a fragment of the economic manuscript of 1857-58 (see present edition, Vol. 29, pp. 219-21). Marx used this passage when writing Volume Three of *Capital*, Part V, Ch. XXI (present edition, Vol. 37).—529

[143] In terms of substance, this paragraph belongs to p. XV—907 of the manuscript (this volume, p. 478).—531

[144] The reference is to the 100-guilder bond which paid interest three times a year at the Leipzig Fair. Three trade fairs were held annually in Leipzig at the New Year, Easter (spring) and Michaelmas (September 29, Harvest Festival).—532

[145] *Knights*—in early Roman history—equites, or rich citizens constituting a privileged class liable for service in the cavalry. Subsequently this name was given to Roman slave-owning merchants and usurers belonging to the class of equites.—534

146 *Laws of the Twelve Tables*—an ancient memorandum on Roman law. They were compiled in the mid-5th century B.C. as the result of the battle between the plebs and the patricians and were a record of the common law valid in Rome; these laws reflected the social relations in Roman society during the period when the slave-owning system was being consolidated. On the one hand, they protected private property and, on the other, they retained vestiges of the gentile system. The laws set out the stipulations on debts in great detail.— 541

147 In this same notebook XV, Marx first gives an analysis of loan capital and a critique of vulgar political economy, which bases its apologetics on making a fetish of revenue and its sources as they appear on the surface; and then he goes on to analyse commercial capital.

Marx does not return to the critical historical part of his work until pp. XVIII—1086-1157 of the manuscript (present edition, Vol. 33).— 541

148 The outside front cover (unnumbered) of the notebook is labelled "XIII" and carries the inscription "*A Contribution to the Critique of Political Economy*" together with a remark on Hopkins which was written at a later date and appears below.— 542

149 Marx is referring to notebook XII of his excerpts which he compiled in London in 1851. The excerpt from T. Hopkins' book which Marx gives below is to be found on p. 14 of this notebook. See also present edition, Vol. 31, p. 289.—542

150 The page numbered by Marx as 670a is the inside front cover of notebook XIII which was written in the autumn of 1862. This page carries the heading "5) *Theories of Surplus Value etc.*", beside it the note "*Roscher: Interest, Profit. p. 693*" and the table of contents of notebook XIII (see this volume, p. 7). The passage headed "Decrease in the Rate of Profit" was written later. The quotations given on this page were written down not earlier than May 1863 since they are taken from the additional notebooks of excerpts A and B which were not compiled until this time.— 542

151 Page 862a is the inside front cover of notebook XV and was numbered by Marx after he had filled in the notebook in question. This page carries the table of contents of notebook XV (see this volume, p. 8). The passage given below is separated from the table of contents by a line.— 543

NAME INDEX

S

T

INDEX OF LITERARY AND MYTHOLOGICAL NAMES

INDEX OF QUOTED
AND MENTIONED LITERATURE

WORKS BY KARL MARX

A Contribution to the Critique of Political Economy. Part One (present edition, Vol. 29)
— Zur Kritik der politischen Oekonomie, Erstes Heft. Berlin, 1859.— 124, 138, 232, 264, 278, 302, 317, 320, 429, 481, 523, 527

Outlines of the Critique of Political Economy (Economic Manuscripts of 1857-58) (present edition, Vols. 28-29)
— Grundrisse der Kritik der politischen Ökonomie [manuscript].— 310, 405

WORKS BY DIFFERENT AUTHORS

Aristoteles. *De republica libri VIII et oeconomica.* (Politica.) In: *Aristotelis opera ex recensione Immanuelis Bekkeri. Accedunt indices Sylburgiani.* Tomus X. Oxonii, 1837.— 537, 538

Arnd, K. *Die naturgemässe Volkswirthschaft, gegenüber dem Monopoliengeiste und dem Communismus, mit einem Rückblicke auf die einschlagende Literatur.* Hanau, 1845.— 503

[Bailey, S.] *A Critical Dissertation on the Nature, Measures, and Causes of Value; Chiefly in Reference to the Writings of Mr. Ricardo and His Followers.* By the Author of *Essays on the Formation and Publication of Opinions.* London, 1825.— 37, 126, 222, 276-77, 299, 312, 320, 324, 327-34, 336-40, 344-48, 350-51
— *A Letter to a Political Economist; Occasioned by an Article in the Westminster Review on the Subject of Value.* By the Author of the *Critical Dissertation on Value* therein reviewed. London, 1826.— 312

Barton, J. *Observations on the Circumstances which Influence the Condition of the Labouring Classes of Society.* London, 1817.— 187, 201-08

Bastiat, Fr. *Gratuité du crédit. Discussion entre M. Fr. Bastiat et M. Proudhon.* Paris, 1850.— 464, 526, 529-30

Bentham, J. *Defence of Usury; Shewing the Impolicy of the Present Legal Restraints on the Terms of Pecuniary Bargains.* In a series of letters to a friend. To which is added, A Letter to Adam Smith. On the Discouragements opposed by the above Restraints to the Progress of Inventive Industry. London, 1787.— 531, 537, 540

Berkeley, G. *The Querist, Containing Several Queries, Proposed to the Consideration of the Public.* London, 1750.—543

Bible
   The Old Testament
      Ezekiel.—532
      Isaiah.—532
   The New Testament
      Luke.—533
      Matthew.—252

Blake, W. *Observations on the Effects Produced by the Expenditure of Government during the Restriction of Cash Payments.* London, 1823.—93

Bray, J. F. *Labour's Wrongs and Labour's Remedy; or, the Age of Might and the Age of Right.* Leeds, 1839.—429

Buchanan, D. *Observations on the Subjects Treated of in Dr Smith's Inquiry into the Nature and Causes of the Wealth of Nations.* Edinburgh, 1814.—22

Büsch, J. G. *Theoretisch-praktische Darstellung der Handlung in ihren mannichfaltigen Geschäften.* Dritte, vermehrte und verbesserte Ausgabe mit Einschaltungen und Nachträgen von G. P. H. Norrmann. Erster Band. Hamburg, 1808.—378

Cairnes, J. E. *The Slave Power: Its Character, Career, & Probable Designs: Being an Attempt to Explain the Real Issues Involved in the American Contest.* London, 1862.—378

Carey, H. C. *Principles of Political Economy.* Part the first: *Of the Laws of the Production and Distribution of Wealth.* Philadelphia, 1837.—367

[Cazenove, J.] *Outlines of Political Economy; Being a Plain and Short View of the Laws Relating to the Production, Distribution, and Consumption of Wealth; to which is added, A Brief Explanation of the Nature and Effects of Taxation, Suited to the Capacity of Every One.* London, 1832.—209, 253-57, 353-54

Cazenove, J. Preface, notes, and supplementary remarks. In: Malthus, T. R. *Definitions in Political Economy, Preceded by an Inquiry into the Rules which Ought to Guide Political Economists in the Definition and Use of Their Terms; with Remarks on the Deviation from These Rules in Their Writings.* A new edition... London, 1853.—209, 210, 212, 218-19, 224-29

Chalmers, Th. *On Political Economy in Connexion with the Moral State and Moral Prospects of Society.* Second edition. Glasgow, 1832.—93, 248, 443

Chavée, [H. J.] *Essai d'étymologie philosophique ou Recherches sur l'origine et les variations des mots qui expriment les actes intellectuels et moraux.* Bruxelles, 1844.—429-30

Child, J. *Traités sur le commerce et sur les avantages qui résultent de la réduction de l'intérest de l'argent; avec un petit traité contre l'usure; par Thomas Culpeper. Traduits de l'anglois.* Amsterdam et Berlin, 1754.—463, 465

Corbet, Th. *An Inquiry into the Causes and Modes of the Wealth of Individuals; or the Principles of Trade and Speculation Explained.* In two parts. London, 1841.—419, 421

Dalrymple, J. *An Essay towards a General History of Feudal Property in Great Britain...* The fourth edition corrected and enlarged. London, 1759.—540

Darwin, Ch. *On the Origin of Species by Means of Natural Selection, or the Preservation of Favoured Races in the Struggle for Life.* The first edition came out in London in 1859.— 428

[De Quincey, Th.] *Dialogues of Three Templars on Political Economy, chiefly in relation to the Principles of Mr. Ricardo.* In: *The London Magazine,* April-May, 1824.— 58, 59, 311

De Quincey, Th. *The Logic of Political Economy.* Edinburgh, London, 1844.— 59, 92, 311

Destutt-Tracy, A. L. C. *Élémens d'idéologie.* Première partie. *Idéologie proprement dite.* Seconde édition. Paris, 1804.— 325

Destutt de Tracy, [A. L. C.] *Élémens d'idéologie. IVe et Ve parties. Traité de la volonté et de ses effets.* Paris, 1815.— 366

Dureau de la Malle, [A. J. C. A.] *Économie politique des Romains.* Tome second. Paris, 1840.— 541

Encyclopaedia Britannica, or Dictionary of Arts, Sciences, and General Literature. Eighth edition in 21 volumes. Edinburgh, 1853-1860.— 370

[Forster, N.] *An Enquiry into the Causes of the Present High Price of Provisions.* In two parts. London, 1767.— 542

Fullarton, J. *On the Regulation of Currencies; Being an Examination of the Principles, on Which It Is Proposed to Restrict, within Certain Fixed Limits, the Future Issues on Credit of the Bank of England, and of the Other Banking Establishments Throughout the Country.* London, 1844.— 129

Galiani, F. *Della moneta. Libro I e II.* In: *Scrittori classici italiani di economia politica.* Parte moderna. Tomo III. Milano, 1803.— 400

Ganilh, Ch. *Des systèmes d'économie politique, de la valeur comparative de leurs doctrines, et de celle qui paraît la plus favorable aux progrès de la richesse.* Seconde édition, avec de nombreuses additions relatives aux controverses récentes de MM. Malthus, Buchanan, Ricardo, sur les points les plus importans de l'économie politique. Tome premier. Paris, 1821.— 540

[Garnier, G.] *Notes du traducteur.* In: Smith, A. *Recherches sur la nature et les causes de la richesse des nations.* Tome premier. Paris, 1802.— 221

Godwin, W. *An Enquiry Concerning Political Justice, and Its Influence on General Virtue and Happiness.* Vols. I-II. London, 1793.— 253

Goethe, J. W. von. *Faust. Der Tragödie erster Teil.*— 284, 362, 526

[Hodgskin, Th.] *Labour Defended against the Claims of Capital; or, the Unproductiveness of Capital Proved with Reference to the Present Combinations amongst Journeymen.* By a Labourer. London, 1825.— 397, 400-03, 410-11, 427-31, 434-35, 445-46
— *The Natural and Artificial Right of Property Contrasted.* A Series of Letters, Addressed without Permission, to H. Brougham... By the Author of "Labour Defended against the Claims of Capital". London, 1832.— 543

Hodgskin, Th. *Popular Political Economy. Four Lectures Delivered at the London Mechanics' Institution.* London, Edinburgh, 1827.— 397

Homer. *Odyssey.*— 536

Hopkins, Th. *Economical Enquiries Relative to the Laws Which Regulate Rent, Profit, Wages, and the Value of Money.* London, 1822.—542
— *On Rent of Land, and Its Influence on Subsistence and Population: with Observations on the Operating Causes of the Condition of the Labouring Classes in Various Countries.* London, 1828.—398

Horace (Quintus Horatius Flaccus). *Ars poetica.*—248
— *Epistolae.* Liber I.—248

Hüllmann, K. D. *Staedtewesen des Mittelalters.* Zweiter Theil. *Grundverfassung.* Bonn, 1827.—541

An Inquiry into Those Principles, Respecting the Nature of Demand and the Necessity of Consumption, Lately Advocated by Mr. Malthus, from Which It Is Concluded, that Taxation and the Maintenance of Unproductive Consumers Can Be Conducive to the Progress of Wealth. London, 1821.—116, 250-52, 305-11, 439, 445

King, G. *Natural and Political Observations and Conclusions upon the State and Condition of England.* 1696. In: Chalmers, G. *An Estimate of the Comparative Strength of Great Britain; and of the Losses of Her Trade, from Every War since the Revolution; with an Introduction of Previous History.* A new edition. London, 1804.—208

Laing, S. *National Distress; Its Causes and Remedies.* London, 1844.—425

Lalor, J. *Money and Morals. A Book for the Times.* London, 1852.—397, 421

Luther, M. *An die Pfarrherrn wider den Wucher zu predigen.* Vermanung. Wittemberg, 1540.—532, 535-40
— *Eyn Sermon auff das Evangelion von dem reychen man und armen Lasaro.* Wittemberg, 1555.—532
— *Von Kauffshandlung und Wucher.* In: Der Sechste Teil der Bücher des Ehrnwirdigen Herrn Doctoris Martini Lutheri... Wittembergk, 1589.—531-32

[MacCulloch, J. R. Review of] *Considerations on the Accumulation of Capital, and Its Effects on Exchangeable Value.* London, 1822. In: *The Edinburgh Review, or Critical Journal.* Vol. XL, No. 79, March 1824.—370

MacCulloch, J. R. *A Descriptive and Statistical Account of the British Empire: Exhibiting Its Extent, Physical Capacities, Population, Industry, and Civil and Religious Institutions.* Fourth edition, revised. With an appendix of tables. Vols. I-II. London, 1854.—357
— *A Dictionary, Practical, Theoretical, and Historical, of Commerce and Commercial Navigation.* Illustrated with maps and plans. A new edition, corrected, enlarged, and improved; with a supplement. London, 1847.—357
— *Discours sur l'origine, les progrès, les objets particuliers, et l'importance de l'économie politique. Contenant l'esquisse d'un cours sur les principes et la théorie de cette science.* Traduit de l'anglois par G.^me Prevost. Et suivi de quelques observations du traducteur sur le système de Ricardo. Genève, Paris, 1825.—293-97
— *The Principles of Political Economy: with a Sketch of the Rise and Progress of the Science.* Edinburgh, London, 1825.—257, 353-54, 357, 369
— *The Principles of Political Economy...* Second edition, corrected and greatly enlarged. London, 1830.—357-59
— Supplemental notes and dissertations. In: Smith, A. *An Inquiry into the Nature and Causes of the Wealth of Nations.* In four volumes. Vol. IV. Edinburgh, London, 1828.—357-59, 364, 367-69

Owen, R. *The Book of the New Moral World, Containing the Rational System of Society, Founded on Demonstrable Facts, Developing the Constitution and Laws of Human Nature and of Society*. London, 1836.— 395

Poppe, J. H. M. *Geschichte der Technologie seit der Wiederherstellung der Wissenschaften bis an das Ende des achtzehnten Jahrhunderts*. Erster Band. Göttingen, 1807.— 465

Prevost, G. *Réflexions du traducteur sur le système de Ricardo*. In: MacCulloch, J. R. *Discours sur l'origine, les progrès, les objets particuliers, et l'importance de l'économie politique*... Genève, Paris, 1825.— 293-97, 370

Price, R. *An Appeal to the Public, On the Subject of the National Debt*. London, 1772.— 375

Proudhon, [P. J.] *Gratuité du crédit*— see Bastiat, Fr. *Gratuité du crédit. Discussion entre M. Fr. Bastiat et M. Proudhon*.

Rau, K. H. *Lehrbuch der politischen Oekonomie*. Erster Band. *Volkswirthschaftslehre*. Dritte vermehrte und verbesserte Ausgabe. Heidelberg, 1837.— 503

Ravenstone, P. *Thoughts on the Funding System, and Its Effects*. London, 1824.— 392-93, 395-97, 399, 442

Ricardo, D. *Des principes de l'économie politique et de l'impôt*; traduit de l'anglais par F. S. Constancio; avec des notes explicatives et critiques, par M. Jean-Baptiste Say. T. 1-2; Paris, 1819.— 294
— *Des principes de l'économie politique et de l'impôt*. Seconde édition, revue, corrigée et augmentée d'une notice sur la vie et les écrits de Ricardo, publiée par sa famille. T. 1-2. Paris, 1835.— 36
— *On the Principles of Political Economy, and Taxation*. London, 1817.— 209, 245, 258, 275, 392, 516
— *On the Principles of Political Economy, and Taxation*. Second edition. London, 1819.— 307
— *On the Principles of Political Economy, and Taxation*. Third edition. London, 1821.— 9-15, 18-19, 21-22, 29, 32-37, 39, 49, 52-58, 60-64, 67-69, 71-72, 95-103, 106, 125, 128-34, 136, 149, 152, 154-56, 164-65, 167-70, 172-82, 191-201, 246, 299-300, 302-04, 309, 313, 325, 338-39, 350-51, 355, 364-68, 391, 526
— *On Protection to Agriculture*. London, 1822.— 247

Roscher, W. *Die Grundlagen der Nationalökonomie. Ein Hand- und Lesebuch für Geschäftsmänner und Studierende*. Dritte, vermehrte und verbesserte Auflage. Stuttgart und Augsburg, 1858. In: Roscher, W. *System der Volkswirthschaft*. Erster Band. Stuttgart und Augsburg, 1858.— 129, 366, 369

Say, J.-B. *Lettres à M. Malthus, sur différens sujets d'économie politique, notamment sur les causes de la stagnation générale du commerce*. Paris, Londres, 1820.— 309
— Notes explicatives et critiques. In: Ricardo, D. *Des principes de l'économie politique et de l'impôt; traduit de l'anglais par F. S. Constancio*... T. 1-2. Paris, 1819.— 294
— *Traité d'économie politique, ou simple exposition de la manière dont se forment, se distribuent et se consomment les richesses*. Deuxième édition. Tome premier. Paris, 1814.— 179, 365; Tome second. Paris, 1814.— 13, 124-25, 307
— *Traité d'économie politique*... Quatrième édition, corrigée et augmentée, à laquelle se trouve joint un épitome des principes fondamentaux de l'économie politique. Tome second. Paris, 1819.— 294

Operation of the Act 7 & 8 Vict. c. 32. Being a Continuation of the History of Prices from 1793 to 1839. London, 1848.—162

Torrens, R. *An Essay on the Production of Wealth; with an Appendix, in Which the Principles of Political Economy Are Applied to the Actual Circumstances of This Country.* London, 1821.—218, 258, 262-68

Tuckett, J. D. *A History of the Past and Present State of the Labouring Population, Including the Progress of Agriculture, Manufactures, and Commerce, Shewing the Extremes of Opulence and Destitution among the Operative Classes. With Practical Means for Their Employment and Future Prosperity.* In two volumes, Vol. I. London, 1846.—454

Turgot, [A. R. J.] *Réflexions sur la formation et la distribution des richesses.* In: Turgot, [A. R. J.] *Oeuvres.* Nouvelle édition classée par ordre de matières avec les notes de Dupont de Nemours augmentée de lettres inédites, des questions sur le commerce, et d'observations et de notes nouvelles par MM. Eugène Daire et Hippolyte Dussard et précédée d'une notice sur la vie et les ouvrages de Turgot par M. Eugène Daire. Tome premier. Paris, 1844.—476

Virgil (Publius Vergilius Maro). *Aeneid.*—539

[Wakefield, E. G. A Commentary to Adam Smith's *Wealth of Nations.*] In: Smith, A. *An Inquiry into the Nature and Causes of the Wealth of Nations.* Vols. I, II. London, 1835.—35, 387-88

[West, E.] *Essay on the Application of Capital to Land, with Observations Shewing the Impolicy of Any Great Restriction of the Importation of Corn, and That the Bounty of 1688 Did Not Lower the Price of It.* By a Fellow of University College, Oxford. London, 1815.—439

Wilson, J. *Capital, Currency, and Banking; Being a Collection of a Series of Articles Published in the "Economist" in 1845, on the Principles of the Bank Act of 1844, and in 1847, on the Recent Monetarial and Commercial Crisis; Concluding with a Plan for a Secure and Economical Currency.* London, 1847.—129

ANONYMOUS ARTICLES
PUBLISHED IN PERIODIC EDITIONS

The Standard, No. 11889, September 19, 1862: *America in the Exhibition* (in the column "The International Exhibition").—200

The Westminster Review, Vol. V, January-April, 1826: *Effect of the Employment of Machinery &c. upon the Happiness of the Working Classes.* London, 1824.—507

INDEX OF PERIODICALS